Patterns in Prehistory

Patterns

MANKIND'S FIRST THREE

NEW YORK   OXFORD

in Prehistory

MILLION YEARS

Robert J. Wenke

OXFORD UNIVERSITY PRESS   1980

Copyright © 1980 by Oxford University Press, Inc.

Library of Congress Cataloging in Publication Data

Wenke, Robert J
Patterns in prehistory.

Bibliography: p.
Includes index.
1. Man, prehistoric.   I.   Title.
I.   Title.
GN740.W46   573′.3   78-25942
ISBN 0-19-502556-3
ISBN 0-19-502557-1 pbk.

Printed in the United States of America

For Chris and Ann Wenke

Preface

Patterns in Prehistory is about the great transformations of the human past, beginning with the appearance of the first culture-bearing animals some several million years ago and dealing successively with the physical and cultural development of our Paleolithic ancestors, the appearance of the first domesticated plants and animals and their associated agricultural economies, and the rise of the first states and great empires.

Writing a survey of such a vast and eventful time span involves many difficulties, perhaps the most important of which is the selection and construction of a theoretical framework that presents the archaeological evidence as a coherent whole and "explains" it in some sense, yet still manages to reflect the divergent, often contradictory theoretical and methodological perspectives of modern archaeology. Unlike chemistry, physics, or biology, the discipline of archaeology includes little agreement on theoretical and methodological matters, and the archaeological evidence does not "speak for itself." Over the last century archaeologists have excavated thousands of sites, from medieval English market towns to Australopithecine camps on the African veldt, but few archaeologists agree on what we can or should do with all this information. Most do agree that a primary goal should be the use of archaeological methods and data to describe, or in a sense reconstruct, what happened in prehistory, and much of this book is devoted to precisely this goal: the description of the physical characteristics, diet, technology, residence patterns, social arrangements, and other lifeways of our ancestors. But some archaeologists—particularly a vocal group in the United States

—argue that archaeology can be made into a formal science that "explains" what happened in the past in terms of general principles or laws that rival the laws of the natural sciences in their power, elegance, and testability.

In writing *Patterns in Prehistory* I have tried to evaluate in a preliminary way some specific attempts to analyze archaeological data from this "scientific" perspective, and throughout the book I have adopted the evolutionary, deterministic, theoretical perspective that I think best represents the future of archaeology. I have made an effort to avoid most of the polemical and programmatic disputes about archaeological method and theory that currently grace the professional literature, as I am convinced that a book such as this is not the appropriate place for their discussion. Nonetheless, some familiarity with these matters is indispensable to an understanding of what many contemporary archaeologists are doing and why, and thus I have tried to reflect in outline these methodological and theoretical concerns.

Few of the people who read this book will ever do field archaeology in a professional capacity, and for this reason more emphasis has been given here to the great problems of prehistory than to the techniques and methods of archaeology. Similarly, while mastery of a considerable amount of material is necessary before one can think creatively about the major problems of prehistory, I have tried to avoid assaulting the reader with an undigestible amount of specific, technical data. Archaeology yields to no discipline in the utter boredom its subject matter can convey—if the data are not placed within the context of larger problems.

A detailed account of world prehistory is now far beyond the scope of a single volume, a circumstance requiring difficult, frustrating decisions about which geographical areas and time periods to consider and to what extent. Because this book focuses on *origins,* specifically, the origins of culture, agriculture, and complex societies, I have had to concentrate on the archaeological record most directly related to these concerns. Thus, for example, the early agricultural societies of the Near East and the Mediterranean area are treated in much greater detail than those in temperate Europe, because the evidence suggests that the formation of the first European agricultural societies was influenced by the older, more complex civilizations in the Near East and the Mediterranean world.

Another difficult problem in writing a book of this nature is the highly variable quality and extent of research in different areas. The rise of the first Chinese states, for example, is a complex, fascinating archaeological problem, but compared to early states in Mesopotamia or Mesoamerica, we know very little about Chinese developments. For this reason, Chinese prehistory and that of other areas are treated somewhat superficially and inconclusively here.

Also, the pace of archaeological research is such today that one person cannot hope to do justice to the record for the entire world, particularly if one's linguistic competency is limited—as mine is—to English and laborious French and German. Consequently, I was forced to ignore important sources in other languages, and I regret the parochial perspective that must necessarily result from this obstructed view of the archaeological record.

I have quoted from primary sources rather more extensively than is the fashion in books of this type, principally because I think it important that the reader have some direct contact with the diverse, often contrasting views of contemporary archaeologists, and also because a book such as this requires one to loot and plunder the works of thousands of people, and I think it only fair that occasionally they be given a chance to speak for themselves.

Ideally, a survey of world prehistory should be written by someone with many years of diverse archaeological field experience, a person not only multilingual and well read in the discipline but also with a knowledge of and a sympathy for the latest theoretical matters. If this Renaissance person is somewhere writing such a work I am unaware of it, but I welcome his or her efforts. Like many others I was driven to write my own account of world prehistory by my personal dissatisfaction with existing works; and like most other authors, having written my own book, I am filled with a new-found appreciation of my predecessors' efforts. Truly it has been said that "writing books is easy: all you have to do is put a piece of paper in a typewriter and stare at it until drops of blood appear on your forehead."

Indeed, a book like this would not be possible were it not for the assistance of many people, and I have been particularly fortunate in this regard. My wife, Nanette M. Pyne, edited every page of three drafts of the manuscript, making many valuable suggestions about logic, content, and style in the process, particularly in regards to Mesoamerican prehistory, where her expertise far exceeds my own. She also prepared many of the illustrations and organized the bibliography. I suppose I might eventually have finished the book without her help, but I suspect I would still be trying to write chapter 1 and dangling scores of participles in the process.

I also wish to thank Robert C. Dunnell, chairman of the Department of Anthropology at the University of Washington, who despite his demanding schedule spent many hours discussing the entire manuscript with me and making invaluable suggestions about content, logic, and organization. Gerald Eck, Donald Grayson, and Steven Harrell, my colleagues at the University of Washington, gave much-needed advice in matters relating to their specialities and I am very grateful for their time and attention. George Quimby, director of the Burke Museum, the University of Washington, supplied many photographs and other illustrations, as well as countless anecdotes about the history of American archaeology.

Henry Wright, of the University of Michigan, read the manuscript and offered innumerable useful comments and suggestions, and contributed many of the ideas on which the book is based. Jeffrey Parsons, also of the University of Michigan, gave me crucial advice on the chapter on ancient Peru. The several anonymous persons selected by Oxford University Press to read early drafts of the manuscript also merit high marks for diligence and constructive criticisms. None of these people, of course, bears responsibilities for errors I have made in interpreting their contributions.

I owe a particular debt to Robert J. Tilley of Oxford University Press who first proposed this book to me and then oversaw the whole project with patience and solicitude. Joyce Berry, also of Oxford University Press, efficiently organized the illustrations, and Abby Levine, the text editor, did an excellent job of polishing the last draft of the manuscript.

Finally, I would like to acknowledge the thousands of scholars whose work formed the basis for this book. I have tried to cite their contributions frequently and fairly, and I hope I have not distorted their intentions and contributions.

Seattle R.J.W.
April 1979

Contents

Patterns in Prehistory

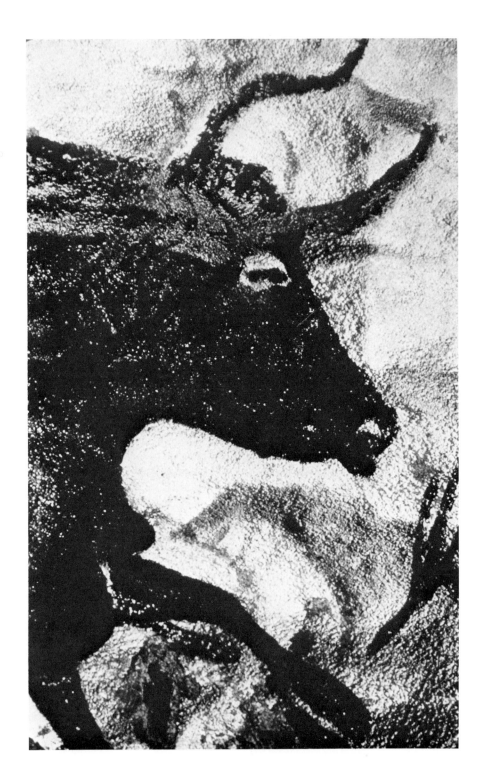

1

Prehistory, History, and Archaeology

History is philosophy teaching by examples.

Dionysius of Halicarnassus (40 B.C.)

Archaeologists and prehistorians have been studying the physical and cultural remains of ancient peoples in every part of the world for centuries, and the general outlines of world prehistory are well known. The broken skulls and crude stone tools of some of our earliest hominid ancestors have been excavated, and archaeologists have reconstructed the diet, technology, and even some of the social life of people who lived hundreds of thousands of years ago. We have found the remains of some of the earliest domesticated plants and animals and agricultural communities, and we know much about their successors, the great civilizations that flowered thousands of years ago in the Near East, China, Peru, Mexico, Egypt, and elsewhere.

Yet, despite this vast store of information and the perspective we now have on the first several million years of our physical and cultural development, many fundamental questions about the meaning and significance of our knowledge remain largely unresolved.

What, for example, can we hope to learn when we study prehistory? Should our objective be a detailed description of the events and cultures of the past, or can we hope to explain the past in terms of general principles? Are there patterns or regularities in prehistory and history that suggest our physical and cultural development can be accounted for in terms of laws? Does prehistory have any relevance to the world of today? In short, why should we study the past?

Many people spend an obligatory few years—often as college undergraduates—in earnest debate about questions concerning the nature of history and human existence, but eventually most go on to more immediate and resolvable concerns. Archaeologists, however, have never given up on these issues—in fact, they have developed them into something of an art form. Debates about the proper goals of archaeology and the significance of prehistory have been particularly spirited during the last two decades, and while there are still many contending views about what the goals of archaeology should be, there is at least general agreement about what most archaeologists have been doing in the past. Specifically, these traditional objectives of archaeology have been: (1) the compilation of culture histories; (2) the reconstruction of the lifeways of ancient peoples; and (3) the description and analysis of cultural processes (L. Binford 1968; Willey and Phillips 1958).

Because these specific goals form the structure of all that follows in this book, as well as the foundation of modern archaeology, it is important that we consider each in some detail.

CULTURE HISTORY

Until the nineteenth century most Western people accepted the biblical premise that the world was little more than 6,000 years old and that almost from the very beginning our ancestors had lived in towns and villages, engaged in agriculture, commerce, war, and crafts, and organized themselves in complex political and social forms. Indeed, in the 1850s the eminent Dr. Lightfoot of Cambridge University, on the basis of his study of the Book of Genesis, proclaimed that the world had been created on October 23, 4004 B.C., at the civilized hour of 9:00 A.M.

However, with the gradual acceptance of Darwinian evolutionary thought and the archaeological demonstration that our ancestors had lived for millions of years as hunters and gatherers, interest grew in finding out exactly when, where, and how the great transformations of prehistory had occurred. When, for example, had our ancestors achieved "fully human" form, and when did they first take up farming and village life? What were the interrelationships between the countless societies that had flourished in the many millennia before historical records were kept? Eventually, these culture historical questions crystallized into the recognized goal of locating every prehistoric culture in time and space and arranging them "in a way which accurately reveals their generic affinities" (L. Binford 1968: 8).

Culture history in this sense was usually based on several kinds of dating methods (discussed in chapter 2) and on extensive comparisons of the stone tools, pottery, jewelry, and other artifacts recovered in the course of archaeological fieldwork. Comparative lists were made tabulating different kinds of artifacts found at each site and, based on the similarity of these artifacts, inferences were made about the cultural relationships between the peoples who had once lived in these communities.

Thus, if two sites located only a few miles apart are found to have very similar types and amounts of pottery, tools, houses, plant and animal remains, and burials, many archaeologists would infer that these people probably lived at about the same time, spoke the same or a related language, and generally participated in the same cultural traditions. Sites having very different lists of artifacts are considered to reflect different cultural traditions. If a sharp "break" occurs in the archaeological record, and artifacts of different styles seem to have replaced traditional forms very abruptly at many sites, archaeologists often conclude there was an invasion by a different cultural group. Archaeologists have always been very fond of invasions as "explanations" of these kinds of changes in the archaeological record, preferring them even to that other old standby, climatic change. But we shall see that many such "explanations" are often overly simplistic and inaccurate.

Culture historians have made impressive contributions to the study of the past, and much of this book is simply a summary of their achievements. Most of the major cultural transformations of prehistory have been located in time and space, and the cultural affinities of thousands of extinct societies have been established. But culture historians generally have been more successful at *describing* what happened in prehistory than in *explaining* prehistory. For example, over the last century they have located and dated many of the first agricultural communities in the world, those established in the Near East shortly after 9000 B.C. But they have not yet devised a compelling explanation of why people lived in the Near East for hundreds of thousands of years before 9000 B.C. without ever once taking up agriculture, or why, at about the same time people in the Near East were beginning to cultivate plants and

raise animals, people in China, India, Egypt, Mexico, Peru, and elsewhere were also, for the first time, beginning to take up agriculture as a
way of life.

In addition, some culture historians have shown a pronounced
Western bias: since American and Western European cultures are technologically and in other ways the most "advanced" cultures in the
world, the archaeological record has often been viewed in terms of the
way in which modern Western man evolved from the first culture-
bearing animals (Dunnell 1977a: 8–9). Thus, cultural historical "explanations" of, for example, the appearance of agriculture and urban
communities have tended to assume that these developments were the
"natural" and inevitable products of prehistoric peoples who, like most
Westerners, were constantly trying to improve their standard of living.
As a consequence, such explanations have often involved only unveri-
fied inferences about the factors that might have been involved.

RECONSTRUCTING PAST LIFEWAYS

Much of the last century of archaeology has been devoted to trying to
reconstruct as completely as possible the diet, technology, residences,
burial practices, seasonal movements—in short, the lifeways—of ancient
peoples.

Archaeologists have usually done this by excavating sites and interpreting their discoveries with the help of analogy, inference, and liberal amounts of imagination. If an archaeologist excavated a 20,000-
year-old site in a cave in southern France and uncovered a concentration
of ash, charcoal, burned bones, and cracked, blackened stones, he would
no doubt infer that he had found a hearth where ancient people had
roasted meat and congregated for warmth. The archaeologist might
then look for sites near the cave where these ancient peoples had hunted
game and made tools, and, based on what he found, he might try to describe the kinds of animals these people hunted, how they killed and
butchered them, how many people lived in the cave at any one time,
and what season of the year they had lived there.

Thus, these archaeologists often see themselves as ethnographers of
ancient peoples, and just as an ethnographer describes the daily life of
the people he is studying, a cultural reconstructionist, substituting
analogy and inference for direct observation, tries to describe daily

1.1
This sixteenth-century engraving of Florida Indians exemplifies ethnocentrism, or interpreting other cultures and early cultures in one's own terms. The four women on the right are highly reminiscent of Italian Renaissance renderings of Venus and the Three Muses. Many European scholars of the last three centuries were ethnocentric in their analyses of ancient and non-European cultures—most of which they assumed had incompletely evolved to the high level of European civilization.

life in extinct cultures. Many anthropological museums illustrate such cultural reconstructions by displaying *dioramas,* small scenes from daily life in ancient societies, represented with clay figures, painted backgrounds, and miniature artifacts.

The last twenty years have seen remarkable advances in the strategy and tactics of cultural reconstruction. Techniques have been devised to recover and identify minute plant and animal fragments so that ancient diets can be precisely defined. Microscopic analyses of artifacts provide new insights into ancient technologies, and advances in soil chemistry and infrared photography have contributed greatly to the accuracy of archaeological inferences about ancient lifeways. Elaborate mathematical models and sophisticated computers are now routinely used to analyze archaeological data, as researchers try to sort through the tens of thousands of artifacts that may be relevant to reconstructing a particular group's activities.

Attempts at cultural reconstruction have also been strengthened in recent years by changes in the *logic* of archaeological research. Many early expeditions were conducted with few explicit research objectives beyond finding specimens for museums, and as a result excavation and analytical techniques were not as productive as they might have been. There is now a growing recognition that the archaeological record is finite and that to use it most effectively we must specify the objectives of each project and then try to formulate precise hypotheses that can be "tested" by data gathered in the course of the fieldwork. These issues are discussed more fully below.

Despite these many improvements in the ways and means of reconstructing ancient cultures, cultural reconstructions often include a large measure of speculation, particularly when dealing with extremely ancient societies, whose artifacts and lifeways may have no historical analogues.

In any event, cultural reconstructions, like culture histories, are *descriptions,* not *explanations,* and should time travel ever be invented—to take a somewhat improbable illustration—these two goals of archaeology would be entirely fulfilled. Still, many archaeologists continue to do both culture history and cultural reconstruction, regarding them as indispensable preliminary steps to the third major goal of archaeology, the explanation of cultural processes.

THE EXPLANATION OF CULTURAL PROCESSES

Archaeologists long ago recognized that there may be more to the study of prehistory than just writing culture histories and reconstructing ancient lifeways.

> Some day world culture history will be known as far as archaeological materials and human intelligence permit. Every possible element of culture will have been placed in time and space. The invention, diffusion, mutation and association of elements will have been determined. When taxonomy and history are thus complete, shall we cease our labors and hope that the future Darwin of Anthropology will interpret the great historical scheme that will have been erected? . . . Candor would seem to compel the admission that archaeology could be made much more pertinent to general cultural studies if we paused to take stock of its possibilities. Surely we can shed some light not only on the chronologi-

cal and spatial arrangements and associations of elements, but on conditions underlying their origin, development, diffusion, acceptance and interaction with one another. These are problems of cultural process. (Steward and Setzler 1938; 5–7)

The analysis of cultural process, then, involves trying to explain why prehistory and history have turned out as they have. The difference between *explaining* and *describing* can be illustrated by an analogy with the relationship of the Linnaean system of biological classification and Darwinian evolutionary theory. In the eighteenth century, Linnaeus developed a descriptive classification of biological species that later scholars used to interpret the ancestry of various genera, families, and orders, but not until Darwin's theory of natural selection and, later, the development of population genetics, were scientists able to explain to some extent *why* and *how* the biological world had evolved (L. Binford 1968: 15). Similarly, attempts to reconstruct extinct cultures and to write culture histories have provided us with descriptive classifications and have located many prehistoric cultures in time and space, but they have not explained the mechanisms and principles that determine why these cultures developed as they did.

Not all scholars are agreed, however, that it will ever be possible to explain human prehistory and history in a way analogous to the explanations of biological and other "natural" phenomena. People have for centuries taken contrasting positions on this issue. Some argue that there is a regular pattern to the developments of history, but that this plan is known only to God, and we as yet can see only "through a glass darkly." Others, particularly in our own age, see prehistory and history as ultimately unintelligible, as the chaotic combination of personalities, events, accidents, and the conscious acts of billions of people. It may be possible, they suggest, to "explain" the causes of a particular war or economic development, but so many uncontrolled and unknown variables influence human affairs and are so complexly intertwined that it is difficult, if not impossible, to reduce this complexity to meaningful "laws of history." As the authors of one popular college history textbook expressed it:

Search as we may, there seems to be little hope of ever discovering any plan or law of historical development. Human destiny appears to be determined by countless, varied factors working in multifarious combinations, to say nothing of the element of chance, which cannot be discounted entirely. There is still something alluring in the venerable proposition that if Cleopatra's nose had been a little smaller, Marc Antony might not have fallen in love with her and the whole history of Rome might have taken a different turn. (Langer 1968: 20–21)

In sharp contrast to this view are the views of those who believe our past and future are governed by inflexible laws, and that it is possible to discover these laws. As early as the first century B.C., Dionysius of Halicarnassus argued that "history is philosophy teaching by examples." This remark suggests there is a purpose and direction in history that can be read if we use the principles of philosophy to strip away the complexity of individuals and events. And in our own age the Marxian view of prehistory and history as governed by known, unyielding laws of economics is among the most widely accepted and profoundly influential theoretical perspectives.

Given this fundamental disagreement about the nature of prehistory and history, how should we study and understand the past? In what sense can we hope to explain it?

This book is based on the premise that we can indeed do more than simply classify and describe the characteristics and histories of extinct cultures: It assumes that cultural processes can be analyzed, explained, and to some extent predicted. Because the issues here are complex and controversial, before we begin our review of world prehistory we must examine in more detail what archaeologists are trying to do when they study world prehistory with the objective of explaining cultural processes.

Culture and Explanation

Many anthropologists define *culture* in terms very similar to those of E. B. Tylor: "Culture . . . is that complex whole which includes knowledge, belief, art, morals, law, custom, and any other capabilities and habits acquired by man as a member of society" (1913: 5–6).

From an archaeological viewpoint, a somewhat more useful conception of culture is that it is the uniquely human capacity for reasoning and using symbols in the course of adapting to our physical and social environments (White 1959). The implication here is that while other animals have evolved instincts and physical characteristics such as migration, flight, and gills to adapt to their environments, people have evolved imagination, creativity, and intelligence. This does not mean we have not evolved physically—we have; but the greatest change has been in our ability to use clothing, fire, religion, and other cultural things to adapt to our environments, rather than developing fur, feathers, or claws. Put more succinctly: "Culture is all those means whose forms are not under direct genetic control . . . which serve to adjust individuals and groups within their ecological communities" (L. Binford 1968: 323).

Given this definition, several aspects of culture become particularly important to the study of world prehistory. First, culture can be considered a uniquely human thing. Chimpanzees use and modify sticks and occasionally employ stones as tools, and some have even been taught to "talk" using plastic symbols and hand signs. But the differences between the average person's ability to make and use tools, to use language, and, generally, to use symbols and the ability of chimps (and other animals) are quantitatively great enough to be considered qualitatively different. As Leslie White points out, casting a vote or sprinkling holy water is far removed from the abilities of other animals (1959: 230). Moreover, for millions of years, one generation of chimpanzees has been very much like the next in the amount of knowledge it accumulates and passes on, but humans can share in the arts and sciences of the billions of people who lived and died before us.

Second, all life exists only because it is able to divert free energy to its own purposes. Almost all energy captured by plants and animals is in the form of direct sunlight and food, but people have devised stone and metal tools, nets, baskets, dams, engines, and myriad other ways of converting energy to their own purposes. "Culture thus becomes primarily a mechanism for harnessing energy and of putting it to work in the service of man, and, secondarily, of chanelling and regulating his behavior not directly concerned with subsistence and offense and defense" (White 1949: 390–91). An important element in this view of culture as an energy-conversion mechanism is that throughout prehistory there has been a general *evolution* in the ability of cultures to harness energy. Most people today individually consume more goods and energy than did a thousand people of a century or two ago.

There is an obvious parallel in the way cultures and biological species have changed over time. In both cases there has been an increase in complexity accompanied by greater diversity of forms. Just as biological life began as unicellular organisms and has evolved into multi-cellular beings of amazing variety, the first cultures were made up of hunters and gatherers whose descendants have produced nation-states and empires.

We might extend our analogy here to the means by which in-creased complexity and diversity appear. In the biological world, mu-tations and other factors produce genetic innovations, which are then shaped by natural selection and random chance. In the cultural sphere, innovations of technology, social organization, and ideology are con-stantly appearing, but only some are "selected," in the sense that they become fixed in particular systems.

This analogy must not be pushed too far, however. Cultural trans-mission is through learning processes, whereas genetic change is through the comparatively slow and inflexible mechanisms of mutation, selec-tion, and drift. The most "primitive" band of Australian hunters and gatherers can profit directly from the development of antibiotics and other advances of industrial nations, but there is no way mammals can transmit their body-temperature regulation systems to reptiles. It took humans millions of years to progress from stone to metal tools, but only a few thousand years to develop atomic power and the gaudy tech-nology of our age. By comparison, biological evolution has been slow and gradual.

But are there any general principles pertaining to the evolution of culture that are as productive as the concepts of natural selection and population genetics have been in biological evolution? A number of people have tried to formulate such principles, and the results, while very interesting, are somewhat less powerful than in the case of biologi-cal concepts. Leslie White, for example, suggests that "other factors re-maining constant, culture evolves as the amount of energy harnessed per capita per year is increased, or the efficiency of the instrumental means of putting the energy to work is increased (1949: 368–69). But this, of course, is a truism: White *defines* evolved societies as those that have harnessed relatively great amounts of energy and have put this en-ergy to work efficiently. On the other hand, this truism has the same vir-tue as the idea of natural selection: it directs our attention to deter-mining the mechanisms and forces that have produced evolved cultures.

Similarly, Marshall Sahlins has proposed the *Law of Evolutionary Potential:* "The more specialized and adapted a form in a given evolu-tionary stage, the smaller is its potential for passing to the next stage"

1.2
Sculpture of an Aztec deity reflected in an obsidian mirror with carved wood frame.
Religion played an important evolutionary role in all ancient civilizations.

(Sahlins and Service 1960: 97). The major cultural transformations in prehistoric Mesoamerica, for example, frequently came from less-developed, "uncivilized" peoples. "The Toltecs, Chichimecs, and Aztecs were each a primitive, helpless group of newcomers at first, compared to the established occupants of the region. But this was an evolutionary privilege, and they in turn rapidly rose to dominate their locality and beyond by combining in their own development the most effective aspects of the culture around them. And the last shall be first" (Sahlins and Service 1960: 106).

Similar examples are available in the modern world. The destruction of Japan and Germany during the First and Second World Wars "freed" these countries from commitment to traditional methods of industry and social organization, and the last twenty years have seen Japan and Germany economically outstrip England—the nominal victor in the war—which was and still is in many ways locked into an antiquated technology.

There is, of course, nothing inevitable about cultural—or biological—evolution in terms of long range prospects: an atomic war could reduce the fauna of the earth to nothing more complicated than a cockroach—our computers, the United Nations, and Beethoven notwithstanding.

Evolutionary potential and many other ideas about cultural evolution have frequently been criticized for being tautological and vacuous, and it is at least true that these concepts have failed to explain what happened in prehistory to the satisfaction of most prehistorians.

Yet another important aspect of culture from an archaeological point of view concerns the terms in which archaeologists hope to explain cultural processes and cultural evolution. Currently, while most archaeologists agree that we can profitably study cultural processes, there is heated disagreement about the form explanations of cultural processes will eventually take. Traditionally, *scientific* explanations have had two aspects: (1) *prediction,* in the sense that one can make an absolute statement about, or a statistical estimate of, the probability of something happening, on the basis of knowing the sequence of prior events; and (2) *control,* in the sense that one is able to state the relationships among a set of events in such a way that, theoretically, one can modify the outcome of a sequence of events by altering one or more of the related factors (Meehan 1968). Thus, the laws of gravity, thermodynamics, and atomic structure allow scientists to predict and control to some extent the operations of the "natural" world.

Some archaeologists believe that if we are able to develop the correct theories and methods, we shall be in a good position to be able to "postdict" and predict and control the operations of cultural systems in a manner analogous to that of chemistry and physics.

> One distinctive feature of scientific archeology is a self-conscious concern with the formulation and testing of . . . laws. General laws in archeology that concern cultural processes can be used to describe, explain, and predict cultural differences and similarities represented in the archeological record, and thus to further the ultimate goal of anthropology, which is the description, explanation, and prediction of cultural differences and similarities. . . . Emphasis on formulation and testing of general laws means that archeology is conceived as a formal

scientific discipline with the same logical structure as all other scientific disciplines. (Watson, LeBlanc, and Redman 1971: 3)

The idea of eventually explaining and predicting human cultural development in these terms is difficult for many people to accept, and even some anthropologists view such aspirations as similar to, to paraphrase an earlier authority, a blind man in a dark room looking for a black hat—that isn't there. But there are some reasons why many scholars have confidence in our eventual success in explaining cultural processes in general terms. If one examines the course of cultural development around the world over the last several million years, it is apparent that major cultural transformations did not occur randomly in time and space. For example, during the first 3 million years of our careers as tool-using animals not one of our ancestors ever domesticated a single plant or animal species or engaged in agriculture. For at least 2 million years everyone was essentially a simple hunter and gatherer, yet within the last 10,000 years people in widely different parts of both the Old and New Worlds *independently* domesticated a wide range of plants and animals and developed agricultural systems similar in every important characteristic. Moreover, in the centuries following this achievement, societies in both the Old and New Worlds independently developed the same complex organizational structures involving cities, occupational specializations, elaborate arts and crafts, and other characteristics we associate with civilization.

It just does not seem likely that the close correspondence between peoples in the Old and New Worlds—who were not even aware of each other's existence—in the timing and manner in which they domesticated plants and animals, took up farming, and established civilizations is simply a coincidence. With all the millions of years of our past and all the world's environments that have been exploited, this close developmental correspondence could not possibly have occurred because people in these different areas just happened to think of the same new ideas at about the same time. Clearly, the implication of this evidence is that a limited number of real, measurable factors determined when and where such major cultural changes would occur, and it is not unduly optimistic to expect that such factors will eventually be understandable within a general theory of cultural change.

Nor should it be thought that the archaeological record is so fragmentary that we cannot hope to use it to analyze cultural processes. As Albert Spaulding notes:

1.3
When Cortez and his men landed at Tabasco, Mexico, they were at first treated as
gods and given presents of women and goods. The Spanish were amazed to find
that the Americans had vast cities, great pyramids, and other elements of civilization. Since the sixteenth century, many scholars have attempted to explain how and
why such cultures in the Old and New Worlds independently followed such similar
cultural developmental trajectories.

> The new archaeologists do not accept limitations on our ability to
> generalize on past human behavior based on (1) a conviction that the be-
> havior was (and is) inherently idiosyncratic because of the special char-
> acter of human nature and (2) a conviction that the archaeological rec-
> ord is so deficient and capricious that we cannot hope to proceed far in
> our understanding of past societies. Instead, they argue that we must
> assume the operation of general laws and processes at all levels of hu-
> man cultural development and that the archaeological record reflects
> this lawfulness, thus providing the logical justification for the applica-
> tion of scientific method. (1973: 337–38)

In fact, if it is at all possible to analyze cultural processes, it would
seem that archaeologists would be in a better position than other social
scientists to do so, for archaeologists have access to a body of evidence
that covers millions of years and derives from countless cultural forms,
from African hunting and gathering societies of a million years ago to
contemporary complex industrial nation-states. Most anthropologists

studying living societies are limited in their observation of cultural change to developments occurring over a relatively short time and in few places; but archaeologists can look at the record of human behavior over long periods of time and in all parts of the world. Moreover, the historian is often limited in his analysis of cultural changes because most historical documents are written by and about the most powerful and influential members of societies, often ignoring fundamental economic and social changes as they affect the great mass of the populace. The archaeological record, however, "reveals in the static patterning of directly observable material what the people actually did in the past, not what they thought they did or what they said they thought they did" (Watson, LeBlanc, and Redman 1971: 25).

This is not to say, of course, that studies of contemporary peoples or of historical evidence are not important to the study of cultural processes. Nonetheless, the enormous and diversified body of archaeological evidence would seem to offer the best chance of analyzing these processes.

In conclusion, it is important to note that while the study of prehistory has been practiced for centuries, this discipline is still in its infancy, especially in the matter of the analysis of cultural processes. Many scholars (e.g., L. Johnson 1972; Bergman 1975) question whether anthropology and archaeology, despite the "scientific approach," computers, and other aids, can realistically hope to reduce our 3-million-year cultural heritage to a complex body of laws and principles possessing validity and predictive power, and certainly few or no such laws or principles currently enjoy widespread acceptance. Nonetheless, some limited progress has been made, and the rest of this book is in essence an attempt to review the archaeological record and to find in this evidence any significant patterns and processes that might indicate that the great problems of culture and the past can eventually be resolved.

While some archaeologists are searching for a body of laws with which to explain the operation of cultures, both past and present, others believe there is little hope of finding any "cultural laws" that resemble the laws of physics and chemistry. Instead, they argue, we should attempt to study cultural processes with the objective of finding the universal principles that apply to all *living systems,* including cultural systems. Thus, they draw a sharp distinction between the analysis of the living world and that of the nonliving world. According to archaeologist Kent Flannery, an influential proponent of this view (widely known as the *systems-theory approach*):

[Systems-theory] archeologists are not for chaos and against law. They recognize the existence of universal or nearly universal principles that govern a system's operation (principles such as positive and negative feedback, and the increase of information-processing institutions with systems of a higher order of complexity). But these archeologists are skeptical about the existence of an undiscovered set of "covering laws" that are specific to human behavior. Hence they are less concerned with a search for "laws of human behavior" than with a search for the ways human populations (in their own way) do the things that other living systems do. They tend to avoid "if A, then B" assertions because their systems orientation makes them skeptical of linear causality; they prefer feedback models in which causality is multivariate and mutual. In terms of scientific ethic, these archeologists are not particularly preoccupied with "making archeology relevant" because they feel we are still in a poor position to know what will be "relevant" in the year 2000. They are unconvinced that the new archeology will clean up our slums although, admittedly, it keeps a lot of young archeologists off the streets. (1973: 52)

In subsequent chapters we shall consider various attempts to analyze archaeological data in terms of this systems-theory approach.

Before leaving the topic of *how* we might analyze cultural processes, we might note *why* we concern ourselves with these analyses. Whether or not we can ever devise laws of culture or history, the long perspective of prehistory may be able to give us at least a few hints about how we might manage our societies and the consequences of various courses of action. In many countries, particularly the United States, decisions about political, social, and economic matters are usually made as if the past had little relevance to the present, as if the ways we use our natural resources and organize ourselves socially were, somehow, appearing in the world for the first time. But as I shall attempt to demonstrate, many of our most fundamental institutions and cherished ideals go back thousands of years, and it is not inconceivable that we could learn something useful by examining what happened over the millennia to societies very like our own.

In any case it is not necessary to justify the study of the past entirely in pragmatic terms. There is much to be said for the view that a knowledge of the major aspects of human prehistory and history is a necessary part of a liberal education in the best sense of that term, and that only with a perspective on our millions of years of development is it possible to appreciate one's own situation. As Søren Kirkegaard expressed it, "life must be lived forward, but can only be understood backward," and such a perspective on the past needs no utilitarian justification. Like the study of art or music, the contemplation of world prehistory can evoke insights and comprehensions that need not be reduced to trying to learn something from the past in order to improve in some way our prospects, or to formulate laws of history.

Finally, we might note the response of Albert Einstein, who, when considering a similar question, said: "What, then, impels us to devise theory after theory? Why do we devise theories at all? The answer to the latter question is simply: because we enjoy 'comprehending,' i.e., reducing phenomena by the process of logic to something already known or (apparently) evident" (1950).

We have no illusions, however, about explaining prehistory and history in any ultimate sense: neither the law of gravity, the laws of thermodynamics, nor any conceivable laws of history or culture possess any ultimate purpose that humanity can comprehend.

Major Trends in the History
of Prehistoric Studies

The great antiquity of the human genus and the major cultural transformations that shaped our past have only been appreciated for less than a century, but the ways in which we think about culture and prehistory are shaped by intellectual traditions going back many centuries. Thus, we must preface our review of our past with some discussion of the "great ideas" or theories that have influenced the study of prehistory.

THE ANCIENT NEAR EASTERN AND GREEK PERSPECTIVES

We find ideas about the nature of history and culture in the oldest documents known, the clay cuneiform texts that appeared in the Near East shortly before 3000 B.C. The few historical and cosmological texts that exist from this period describe an essentially unchanging world. Ancient Near Eastern peoples believed the gods had directly shown them how to grow crops, build cities, work metals, and conduct other arts and crafts, and the course of history and the nature of human existence were generally seen as under the gods' direct control. The early scribes were not ignorant of the major events preceding their own age, but their view was essentially not an explanatory one. They felt no compulsion to try to explain why they lived in cities, for example, because they believed people had always lived in cities and had been taught to do so by the gods. A similar view appears frequently in the Old Testament and in other religious traditions.

A major break with this static perspective is first found in the literature of Greece during the last several centuries before the birth of Christ. Many Western intellectual traditions, including the discipline of history and the foundations of anthropology, owe much to the "Golden Age" of classical Greek culture. Men like Thucydides and Herodotus were the first, as far as we know, to travel widely and compile extensive descriptions of the people, cultures, and places of their world. They were also the first to give somewhat explanatory accounts of major historical events. In his history of the Peloponnesian War—the decades of hostilities between Athens, Sparta, and other Greek cities in the fifth century B.C.—Thucydides tried to explain how the struggle began. He described the personalities involved, the strategies of the various warring powers, and the economic realities of the time. In short, by arranging the events and circumstances preceding the war in what he thought was a causal chain, he wrote what we now recognize as a modern historiography. Most modern historians still do essentially the same thing.

Another aspect of classical Greek thought that has profoundly influenced anthropology, archaeology, and history is the concept of the "Great Chain of Being," or, in Latin, the *Scala Naturae* (Lovejoy 1960), which is founded on Greek ideas about the nature of God and "perfection." Greek philosophers found it inconceivable that the world they knew could have arisen by chance, because there seemed to be such a precise design in its every part. The migrations of birds, the intricate interdependences between plants and animals, the regularity of the seasons, the beauty of the world—all argued to them the existence of a Supreme Intelligence, and therefore they defined God as the perfect being who created and controls the world. The Greeks' conception of perfection, however, had a somewhat different connotation than it does for us, for they understood it to be in essence wholeness, or completeness—

1.4
Detail of a bronze figure from a Greek shipwreck, ca 460 B.C. Greek art reflected Greek philosophical ideas of wholeness, perfection, and symmetry.

a concept vividly evident in classical Greek statuary and literature, with its emphasis on symmetry and unity.

Aristotle assumed that the natural world would be rationally ordered according to what he charmingly called "powers of soul," representing different levels within the perfectly whole universe. Thus, a horse is higher than a sunflower because a horse can think, after a fashion, and a man is higher than a horse because he can reason and apprehend God. It is impossible that there should be any "missing links" in the chain, or that any parts of the chain should cease to exist. God, being perfect, could not create an imperfect, that is, incomplete, universe; nor could his sustaining powers allow a whole level of this perfection to vanish:

> Vast chain of being! which from God began,
> Natures aethereal, human, angel, man,
> Beast, bird, fish, insect, what no eye can see,
> No glass can reach; from Infinite to thee,
> From thee to nothing.—On superior pow'rs

Were we to press, inferior might on ours;
Or in the full creation leave a void,
Where, one step broken, the great scale's destroy'd;
From Nature's chain whatever link you strike,
Tenth, or ten thousandth, breaks the chain alike.

                                                    Alexander Pope

The idea of this Great Chain of Being pervades literature and science well into the nineteenth century, and, obviously, there were grave difficulties in reconciling this concept with the evolutionary theories of Darwin and the discoveries of modern archaeology. For if God had created and sustained every bacterium, every sparrow, every Neanderthal, how could it happen that thousands of species had come into existence, flourished, and vanished? How could humans possibly have evolved from lower primate species and lived for millions of years as "subhuman" races and species now long since extinct?

Yet it is easy to understand the attractiveness of such a philosophy. It placed humanity, the masterwork of the Great Creator, "but little lower than the angels" in the scheme of things. Furthermore, it explained why we were here and why the world seems so marvelously intricate and designed: God put us here to glorify Him and He designed the world in every detail for this purpose.

Another element of Greek philosophy deeply embedded in Western thought, one that parallels the idea of the Great Chain of Being, is the notion of free will. The Greeks for their time and place in history had a remarkably exalted idea of human potential. Although they usually held the gods responsible for many of their fortunes and misfortunes, and although they invented many gods, the Greeks stressed the responsibility and free choice of individuals; they saw each man as responsible for his own actions, with the capacity to choose rightly and wrongly, and capable of influencing the outcome of events (Kitto 1951).

As long as people's activities were thought of as freely arrived-at choices, it was possible to use vague psychological terms to explain why some people lived in tribes, states, or empires, or why there were wars or poverty. It could be said that the Persians "preferred" dictatorships or the Greeks had a "natural tendency" toward democracy. Given these assumptions about why people behave as they do, it was difficult to "explain" cultures in terms of more basic factors of environment and economy.

Some Greek philosophers, however, departed from this intellectual tradition and advanced explanations of history and culture based at least partly on determining factors of environment, technology, and economy; and the basic outlines of this dispute between "free will" and "determinism" endure as a controversy in contemporary philosophy. As we shall see, the guiding spirit of contemporary archaeology is that cultural forms are determined, are explainable in terms of real, measurable factors of environment, subsistence, technology, and religion, and that humans at a given time can be considered constants, with every population having essentially the same mental abilities and inherent characteristics.

CHRISTIANITY

Because anthropology and archaeology have been almost exclusively Western pursuits until the last few decades, it is not surprising that Christianity has had a strong influence on the way archaeology has been conceived of and practiced. Early Christian theologians drew heavily on classical Greek philosophy, transferring almost intact the Aristotelian idea of the Great Chain of Being and the fixity of the species; in addition, they emphasized the doctrine of free will. The Christian idea of time also affected the development of scientific theory. The early Church fathers, working from the Genesis account, believed that the earth was only about 6,000 years old, far too short a time for the biological evolution of humans and all other animals.

But Christianity was not an entirely negative factor in the history of anthropology and archaeology. Later Christianity stressed the importance of studying the universe through logical and scientific analysis in order to demonstrate the majesty of God, and much of the scientific progress of the last centuries has come directly out of Christian intellectual traditions.

THE ENLIGHTENMENT

The "Enlightenment" was that great period of intellectual ferment in the eighteenth century when many of our contemporary ideas about the nature of culture and history began to emerge. Although scholars of

1.5
Sir Charles Lyell (1797–1875), a British geologist, demonstrated that the earth's surface had been formed through the action of geological forces which are still operating today.

this era retained the basic structure of Greek thought, there was a renewed interest in the use of science and logic. Galileo, Kepler, Newton, Descartes, Bacon, and many others had shown that the natural world was understandable in terms of the elegant (i.e., comprehensive, yet reduced to the simplest possible terms) ideas of mathematics and physics, and as a result scholars everywhere began to apply what came to be called the *scientific method* to the understanding of human history and the problem of cultural origins. For example, the Marquis de Condorcet (1743–1794), a French philosopher, proposed a series of universal laws he thought governed the history of human social organizations, and he went so far as to use his analysis to try to predict the future of the world.

This interest in an evolutionary and systematic account of human history was widespread, as exemplified by Voltaire's 1745 essay on the customs and spirits of nations and Edward Gibbon's sweeping *Decline and Fall of the Roman Empire* (1776), both of which were attempts to formulate and use general principles of historical explanation. Influential evolutionary accounts of prehistory and history were also published by John Millar (in 1771) and G. A. Ferguson (in 1819). These writers tried to explain the diversity of political and social forms around the world in terms of the economies, technologies, and environments in which they were found. We shall see a later expression of this "materialism" in Karl Marx's work.

Even before Millar and Ferguson were writing, advances in the sciences of geology and zoology were becoming very important in determining views of prehistory and history. When a construction project in London in 1715 revealed many worked stones lying amid the remains of varieties of elephants, saber-toothed cats, and other animals no longer existing as species, it was difficult to account for these finds within the concepts of the fixity of the species and the age of the earth as described in the Bible.

In France, Georges Cuvier (1769–1832) undertook an extensive analysis of fossilized bones and concluded that hundreds of animal species had become extinct and that there seemed to be an evolutionary trajectory to the biological world. In the early 1800s French naturalist Jean Lamarck (1744–1829) published his reasons for believing the world to be much older than the 6,000 years described in the Bible, and he arranged the biological world in a sequence, from human beings to the smallest invertebrates, in a way similar to later evolutionary schemes. He even noted that the structure of organs and the faculties of animals are "entirely the result of the circumstances in which the race of each species has been placed by nature" (quoted in A. B. Adams 1969: 132), an idea very similar to Darwin's later conception.

In England in the 1830s William "Strata" Smith and Charles Lyell, among others, attempted to show that the earth was formed through the action of slow geological processes—processes still in effect. Lyell's contributions were particularly important because the dawning realization of the earth's great age had led some scientists and clergy to a belief in a series of "catastrophes," the last of which was Noah's flood. Adherents of this position saw the fossil animal bones deep in the earth's strata as evidence that God had "destroyed" the world at various times with floods. Although contemporary scientists suspect that the geological processes forming the earth may have been more abrupt than Lyell thought, his *Principles of Geology* (1832), which went through eleven editions in his lifetime, still stands as a remarkably accurate work.

In 1848 John Stuart Mill published his *Principles of Political Economy,* in which he set forth the same basic evolutionary account of prehistory and history his eighteenth-century predecessors had designed, but Mill elaborated it into a series of six stages: (1) hunting; (2) pastoralism; (3) Asiatic (by which he meant the great irrigation civiliza-

tions of China and the Near East); (4) Greco-Roman; (5) feudal; and
(6) capitalist. He complemented this classification with an extensive
analysis of the economic factors determining these stages, and his materialist orientation was similar in many respects to the dominant theoretical perspective of contemporary American archaeology.

At about the same time Mill was writing, another Englishman,
Herbert Spencer, published several books that proved to be a watershed
of theory for scholars in many fields during the next century. Spencer's
primary contribution was that he applied the concepts of "natural selection" to human societies some years before Darwin applied them to
the biological world. Indeed, as Marvin Harris has argued, the term
Social Darwinism, which was used to describe Spencer's ideas, is a mis-
nomer, since Darwin applied the ideas of Spencer and other students of
social evolution to the biological world, not the reverse (Harris 1968:
128–29).

Spencer was much influenced by Thomas Malthus, who in 1798
had noted that human societies—and indeed all biological species—
tended to reproduce in numbers far faster than they increased the available food supply. For human groups this meant a life of struggle in
which many were on the edge of starvation and more "primitive" societies lost out in the struggle for survival to the more "advanced" cultures. Unlike Malthus, Spencer believed that eventually natural selection would produce a perfect human society.

> Progress, therefore, is not an accident, but a necessity. Instead of civili-
> zation being artifact, it is part of nature; all of a piece with the develop-
> ment of the embryo or the unfolding of a flower. The modifications
> mankind have undergone, and are still undergoing, result from a law
> underlying the whole organic creation; and provided the human race
> continues, and the constitution of things remains the same, those modi-
> fications must end in completeness. . . . So surely must the things we
> call evil and immorality disappear; so surely must man become perfect.
> (1883: 80)

BIOLOGICAL AND CULTURAL EVOLUTION

On a warm Saturday afternoon in June 1860, about a thousand people
gathered in Oxford, England, to witness a debate on Charles Darwin's
theory of biological evolution. For many years Darwin had traveled the

1.6
Charles Darwin (1809–1882)
altered forever our conception
of our place in nature and
the universe.

globe, and he had come back to England convinced the biological sciences had been in total error for centuries concerning not only the origins and nature of biological species but also the very nature of mankind and history. Before Darwin, most people, including many influential scientists, had assumed that the Bible accurately described the creation and operation of the natural world. The varieties of plants and animals were thought to be the direct product of God's creative might, while mankind itself was viewed as a special act of creation.

But Darwin's years of research convinced him that the natural world and its workings could be explained in more straightforward and scientific terms. While collecting biological and geological specimens in South America, he had been struck by the great diversity of plant and animal life, particularly in the Galapagos Archipelago off the coast of Ecuador, where he found islands geologically similar and within sight of one another, but nevertheless inhabited by significantly different species of plants and animals. Why should there be such diversity in such a small area, especially since geological evidence indicated these islands were quite young and of about the same age?

It was evident (after some reflection) that such facts as these could only be explained on the supposition that species gradually became modified; and the subject haunted me. But it was equally evident that neither the action of the surrounding conditions, nor the will of the organism . . . could account for the innumerable cases in which organisms of every kind are beautifully adapted to their habits of life—for instance, a woodpecker or a tree-frog to climb trees, or a seed for dispersal by hooks or plumes. I had always been much struck by such adaptations, and until these could be explained it seemed to me almost useless to endeavor to prove by indirect evidence that species had been modified. (Darwin, quoted in A. B. Adams 1969: 334)

Darwin knew of course that for millennia farmers had used selective breeding to improve their animals in specific ways, such as increased milk production in cows, draught power in horses, and sheep-tending abilities in dogs. But these changes were the result of purposeful intervention in these animals' breeding patterns. How could such *selection* come about in the natural world?

With Darwin as with Spencer, the reading of Thomas Malthus's essay on population growth stimulated a momentous conclusion. "Being well prepared to appreciate the struggle for existence which everywhere goes on from long-continued observation of the habits of animals and plants, it at once struck me that under these circumstances favorable variations would tend to be preserved and unfavorable ones to be destroyed" (quoted in A. B. Adams 1969: 335).

With these observations and deductions, then, Darwin provided the world with answers to a whole range of perplexing questions. Why did animals and plants change over time? Because their environments had changed and those best adapted to these new environments survived to pass on their personal characteristics. Why was there such variety in the biological world? Because many different environments could be inhabited, and natural selection was constantly shaping biological populations to fit into any newly created environments. Why do plants and animals seem to work together in such an integrated, symmetrical, self-sustaining whole? Because that is the *only* way it could work: natural selection mercilessly dispatches individuals and populations that do not fit the structured whole, and what might "fit" in one generation does not necessarily "fit" in the next.

Darwin knew nothing about the genetic mechanisms we recognize today as the agencies through which natural selection operates, and he believed that characteristics acquired by an organism in its lifetime could be passed on to its offspring. We now know this to be a misconception, but it does not detract from Darwin's basic contribution.

Darwin never really lost his belief in Christianity, and he tried to minimize the relevance of his theories to questions of culture and religion; but he had put in motion an intellectual revolution that has continued to the present and has battered the very foundations of Western ideas about the nature of God, mankind, and history. Through logic and evidence, Darwin and his proponents showed there had been hundreds of millions of years in which the world had been dominated by reptiles, years in which there were no people. The implications were inescapable. How could God be glorified by countless generations of snakes and lizards and dinosaurs breeding, fighting, and dying in primeval swamps? Why should we consider mankind a special act of creation

1.7
Darwinian ideas were widely ridiculed in the popular press when first announced, and Darwin himself was greatly distressed by the use some people made of his ideas to attack Victorian social and religious conventions.

Man Found only in a Fossil State—Reappearance of Ichthyosauri

A LECTURE: "You will at once perceive," continued Professor Ichthyosaurus, "that the skull before us belonged to some of the lower order of animals; the teeth are very insignificant, the power of the jaws trifling, and altogether it seems wonderful how the creature could have procured food."

if man, too, developed from earlier, simpler forms, from ancestors who were no more imaginative, intelligent, creative, or religious than any other animal?

It is difficult for us today to appreciate the profound shock generated by the ideas of Darwin and his proponents. Evolutionary biology is now as accepted a part of modern biological science as the atomic theory in chemistry, or the Theory of Relativity, and few professionals in the sciences doubt the essential validity of evolutionary theory. But in that room at Oxford in 1860, Darwin and his advocate, Thomas Huxley, were reviled and ridiculed. This hostility characterized reaction to Darwinian ideas well into our own times, and it is not at all surprising that this should be so. For the logical extension of Darwin's ideas to the origins of humanity could be seen from the beginning to strip away comforting illusions about man's purpose and place in a world that "made sense."

> Until Darwin, what was stressed . . . was precisely the harmonious co-operative working of organic nature, how the plant kingdom supplies animals with nourishment and oxygen, and the animals supply plants with manure, ammonia, and carbonic acid. Hardly was Darwin recognized before these same people saw everywhere nothing but *struggle*. (Friedrich Engels, quoted in Meek 1953: 186)

In the poem "Dover Beach," Matthew Arnold likened the Christian faith and view of the world to a comforting tide that surrounded the world as a shining sea, but which was withdrawing under the onslaught of revolutionary ideas of the nineteenth century including Darwinism:

> The Sea of Faith
> Was once, too, at the full, and round earth's shore
> Lay like the folds of a bright girdle furl'd.
> But now I only hear
> Its melancholy, long, withdrawing roar,
> Retreating, to the breadth
> Of the night-wind, down the vast edges drear
> And naked shingles of the world.
>
> Ah, love, let us be true
> To one another! for the world, which seems
> To lie before us like a land of dreams,

So various, so beautiful, so new,
Hath really neither joy, nor love, nor light,
Nor certitude, nor peace, nor help for pain;
And we are here as on a darkling plain
Swept with confused alarms of struggle and flight,
Where ignorant armies clash by night.

In this way, Darwin and other evolutionists posed the essential problems archaeologists must deal with. They showed that the institutions of man—the cities, arts, crafts, agriculture, domestic animals, religion, governments—all evolved out of earlier, simpler forms; they implied that we have no special claim to exemption from the processes of the universe. And, perhaps most important of all, Darwin's ideas made it reasonable to ask whether or not there were any laws that described our cultural as well as our physical evolution.

MODERN ARCHAEOLOGY

Even before Darwin and Lyell, many Europeans were particularly interested in antiquity and their own national origins. All over Europe there were and still are projects to study the remains of the "first Germans," the "first Dutch," and so on—all usually well supported by their national governments.

Out of this context one of the cornerstones of modern archaeology, the so-called *three-age system,* was devised. In 1776 P. F. Suhm wrote a history of Denmark, Norway, and Holstein, postulating that the ancient tools found in these areas were first made of stone, then of bronze, and finally of iron. In the early nineteenth century Christian Thomsen used this concept to arrange the exhibits in the newly founded National Museum of Denmark and wrote a guidebook to the museum that included a careful analysis of the succession of stone, bronze, and iron tools in Europe in general.

Thomsen's successor at the museum, Jens Jacob Worsaae, has been called the first professional archaeologist. In the 1850s he wrote a history of the antiquities of Denmark in which he set forth the three-age system in very clear terms, described the basic principles of archaeological excavation, and stressed the importance of the preservation of archaeological materials. But his most significant achievement was to prove the accuracy of the three-age system through excavations: in

European sites containing all three types of tools, the iron tools were closest to the surface, followed by the copper and bronze implements, with stone tools invariably occurring in the deepest levels. He correctly interpreted this as a means of inferring relative chronology.

These advances in Scandinavian archaeology came at a time when evolutionary theories were also very influential in the United States and Europe. For example, in 1877, Lewis Henry Morgan, an American, published an account of the "progress" of human societies through the millennia to a nineteenth-century industrialism, and four years later the English anthropologist E. B. Tylor promulgated a particularly influential materialistic evolutionary determinism.

> Human life may be roughly classified into three great stages, Savage, Barbaric, Civilized, which may be defined as follows. The lowest or *savage* state is that in which man subsists on wild plants and animals, neither tilling the soil nor domesticating creatures for his food. . . . Men may be considered to have risen into the next or *barbaric* state

1.8
The excavation of sites like Pompeii during the eighteenth century stimulated great interest in archaeology. Here, Sir William Hamilton shows British visitors the initial excavations at the Temple of Isis in 1765.

1.9
J.J.A. Worsaae (1821–1885), a Danish archaeologist, published in 1843 an analysis of archaeological excavation techniques and classification that greatly influenced modern archaeology. Worsaae's excavations and studies confirmed that all over Europe cultures had gone through successive "stone, bronze, and iron ages."

when they take to agriculture. . . . Lastly, *civilized* life may be taken as beginning with the art of writing, which, by recording history, law, knowledge, and religion for the service of ages to come, binds together the past and the future in an unbroken chain of intellectual and moral progress. (1960: 18–19)

Other scholars long before Tylor had proposed similar evolutionary schemes, but Tylor grounded his ideas firmly on archaeological data that indicated the parallel but independent evolution of cultural complexity in both the Old and New Worlds.

Cultural Materialism

The materialist bent of eighteenth- and nineteenth-century philosophy was given great impetus by Karl Marx (1818–1883) and Friedrich Engels (1820–1895), and through their and their students' writings the materialist perspective has come to be one of the most important of all anthropological viewpoints. This perspective is complex, fluid, and difficult to summarize, but in general terms, what was new and important about Marxism for anthropology and archaeology was its stress on material factors as the causes of cultural change. Marx's position as the "Darwin" of the social sciences is tied to this concept. In Marx's own words:

> In the social production which men carry on they enter into definite relations that are indispensable and independent of their will; these relations of production correspond to a definite stage of development of their material powers of production. The sum total of these relations of production constitutes the economic structure of society—the real foundation, on which rise legal and political superstructures and to which correspond definite forms of social consciousness. The mode of production in material life determines the general character of the social, po-

1.10
Karl Marx (1818–1883) showed that many aspects of religion, politics, and society could be better understood by analyzing a society's economic and technological bases.

litical and spiritual processes of life. *It is not the consciousness of men that determines their existence, but, on the contrary, their social existence determines their consciousness.* (1904: 11–12; emphasis added)

Marx and Engels were not the first to propose that economic matters influence other parts of culture, but as Marvin Harris notes:

> Marx and Engels were the first to show how the problem of consciousness and the subjective experience of the importance of ideas for behavior could be reconciled with causation on the physicalist model. If there had been an orderliness in human history, it cannot, as the Enlightenment philosophers supposed, have originated from the orderliness of men's thoughts. Men do not think their way into matrilineality, the couvade, or Iroquois cousin terminology. In the abstract, can a good reason be found why anyone should bother to think such apparently improbable thoughts? And if one man had thought of them, whence arose the compulsion and the power to convince others of their propriety? For surely it could not be that these improbable ideas construed as mere spontaneous products of fancy occur simultaneously to dozens of people at a time. Obviously, therefore, thoughts must be subject to constraints; that is, they have causes and are made more or less probable in individuals and groups of individuals by prior conditions. (1968: 230–31)

And what were these prior conditions? To Marx and Engels the environmental, economic, and technological spheres of society were the causal factors. Each society, they felt, could be divided into three parts: (1) the economic base; (2) the legal and political structures and organizations; and (3) the social consciousness, or ideology. Marx and Engels referred to the legal, political, and ideological spheres as *superstructure* and maintained they could be explained largely in terms of their economic bases. We shall later consider in more detail some of the attempts by Marxians and other materialists to explain the cultural changes of prehistory and early history in these terms.

Historical Particularism

The impact of Marx, Morgan, Tylor, and the other evolutionists and materialists on anthropology was profound, but their influence on archaeology was not nearly as marked. While many early archaeologists tried to document the succession of stone, bronze, and iron ages in various parts of the world and most had an explicitly evolutionary view of the past, there were few specific attempts to test the materialist view of history. Instead, during the first half of the twentieth century, archaeology, in the United States at least, fell under the influence of a school of thought called *historical particularism,* whose dominant figure was Franz Boas.

As Harris (1968) has pointed out, to understand Boas's contributions it is essential to realize that American and European anthropology and archaeology of this period were rife with bizarrely incorrect evolutionary ideas. Many of the most prominent anthropologists sincerely believed that the Anglo-Saxon race and English-speaking peoples were morally, culturally, physically, and spiritually superior to all others and that the course of prehistory and history had been a long evolutionary climb to this pinnacle. These abuses of the evolutionary perspective had disillusioned many scholars with the whole idea of trying to explain cultural differences in evolutionary and materialist ways, and as a consequence they were very receptive to Boas's stress on scientific objectivity.

True to his natural science training, Boas believed that the cultures of the world were composed of natural analytical units that, like atoms or molecules, could be examined, described, and ultimately understood within a system of explanatory principles. He insisted on fieldwork and the patient, exhaustive collection of data, on the assumption that at some point generalizations could be derived from these data. This would be, then, an anthropology stripped of its speculative, evolutionary content, an anthropology based on the collection of solid, documented evidence (Harris 1968: 257).

The influence of Boas's antievolutionary and antimaterialist perspective was particularly strong among American archaeologists of the early twentieth century, and under Boas's influence American anthropologists described primitive societies in painfully complete detail. Similarly, this period was also the "Golden Age" of cultural reconstruction and culture history. It was widely assumed that progress in explaining prehistoric cultural developments would be made only when much more archaeological evidence had been accumulated and the "facts were allowed to speak for themselves." Many archaeologists of this era also thought that the New World cultures had been heavily influenced by migrations and contacts from Old World cultures prior to the fifteenth century, and that any parallels between Old and New World cultures were either the result of these contacts or were unpatterned, independent inventions.

CONTEMPORARY ARCHAEOLOGY

In the late 1950s and the 1960s American archaeology began a return to the evolutionary perspective, scientific objectives, and materialist approach anticipated by Spencer, Marx, and Morgan. Although major shifts in theory and method are never the result of a single individual, Lewis Binford has played a particularly important role in shaping contemporary archaeology. While a student of Leslie White at the University of Michigan, Binford was greatly impressed with White's evolutionary, materialistic vision of anthropology, and in an influential and programmatic series of papers Binford argued that archaeologists should turn their attention away from endless excavations and attempts to reconstruct ancient cultures and culture histories, and concentrate instead on the study of cultural processes and the formulation of cultural laws. Binford particularly stresses the importance of problem orientation and the testing of hypotheses. He, and many like-minded contemporary archaeologists, assert that archaeological research should be conducted by: (1) selecting a general problem, for example, the origins

1.11
Archaeology in the early years of this century was often more like looting than scientific research. Here, workmen at a site near Les Eyzies, France, destroy a Paleolithic site while looking for nicely fashioned stone tools.

of agriculture; (2) formulating a series of testable statements, or hypotheses, about the causal relationships involved; (3) designing and executing the field research necessary to evaluate the hypotheses; (4) accepting, rejecting, or modifying the hypotheses on the basis of the fieldwork; and (5) modifying the general model of cultural process in the light of the reworked hypotheses, and formulating new testable hypotheses.

Many virtues are claimed for this "deductive" approach, particularly (1) that it requires the archaeologist to stipulate in advance and in detail what he is looking for and why, thus providing a necessary link between problems of cultural process and the archaeological data; and (2) that hypothesis testing provides the only efficient means for evaluating the correctness of our inferences (Hill 1972: 79). In addition, many contemporary archaeologists believe the problem-oriented, hypothesis-testing approach to be more "scientific" because they think the great advances in the physical and natural sciences were made principally by adopting this approach. Many complex questions about the philosophy of science are at issue here, most of which are beyond the scope of this book, but it is important to recognize that many of the most influential contemporary American archaeologists—and many archaeologists of other nationalities as well—are committed to the hypothesis-testing, problem-oriented approach.

The contemporary emphasis on the problems of cultural process and the hypothesis-testing approach has directly stimulated an interest in *cultural ecology*. In order to test hypotheses about such complex processes as the origins of agriculture, it became necessary to study in great detail the relationships between ancient peoples and their physical environments. Many new methods and techniques were developed to retrieve and analyze pollen, small seeds, animal bones, and other biological materials, and archaeologists became interested in models of population growth, predator-prey relationships, carrying capacity, and other constructs of the biological sciences. In effect, by becoming more interested in problems of cultural process, archaeologists have had to turn their attention to kinds of data previous generations of archaeolo-

---

1.12
Julian Steward's scheme of cultural evolution (1949) is a recent attempt at the kinds of categorization of cultural evolution that were begun by Mill, Spencer, Condorcet, and other eighteenth- and nineteenth-century scholars.

ABSOLUTE CHRONOLOGY OF THE MAJOR ERAS

	MESOPO-TAMIA	EGYPT	INDIA	CHINA	N. ANDES	MESO-AMERICA
2000 A.D.					Spanish Conquest	
					Cyclical conquests	Cyclical conquests
1000 A.D.				Cyclical conquests	Regional florescence	Regional florescence
B.C.	Cyclical conquests	Cyclical conquests	Cyclical conquests	Dark Ages	Formative	Formative
1000 B.C.				Initial conquests		Incipient agriculture
		Dark Ages	Dark Ages	Regional florescence	Incipient agriculture	Hunting and gathering
2000 B.C.	Dark Ages	Initital conquests	Initial conquests			
	Initital conquests			Formative	Hunting and gathering	
3000 B.C.	Regional florescence	Regional florescence	Regional florescence	Incipient agriculture		
4000 B.C.	Formative	Formative	Formative			
5000 B.C.			Incipient agriculture	Hunting and gathering		
6000 B.C.	Incipient agriculture	Incipient agriculture				
7000 B.C.		Hunting and gathering	Hunting and gathering			
8000 B.C.						
9000 B.C.	Hunting and gathering					

gists were either unaware of or unconcerned with. This has led to the development of interdisciplinary research, in which archaeological expeditions include experts in ancient climates, paleobotany and paleozoology, geology, and various other specialties.

Another correlate of the growing interest in problems of cultural process and the hypothesis-testing approach has been an emphasis on computerized statistical analyses. In a sense, the analysis of cultural processes and rigorous hypothesis testing were possible only after computer technology and statistical techniques had reached a fairly sophisticated level, because most archaeological hypotheses have been formulated in ways that require the screening and analysis of massive data sets. Many sophisticated forms of mathematical simulation modeling, sampling, and statistical seriation procedures are currently being applied to archaeological data sets, and it appears that archaeology will become increasingly dependent on computers and mathematics. Whereas only a decade ago archaeology was a refuge for the humanistically inclined student who was not interested in (or not very good at) mathematics, most graduate programs in archaeology now require some competence in this area.

Bibliography

Adams, Alexander B., 1969. *Eternal Quest*. New York: Putnam's.

Bergman, F. 1975. "On the Inadequacies of Functionalism and Structuralism." *Michigan Discussions in Anthropology*. 1: 3–23.

Binford, Lewis R. 1968. "Archeological Perspectives." In *New Perspectives in Archeology*, eds. Sally R. Binford and Lewis R. Binford. Chicago: Aldine.

Birdsell, J. B. 1972. *Human Evolution*. Chicago: Rand McNally.

Boas, Franz. 1948. *Race, Language and Culture*. New York: Macmillan.

Buck, R. C. 1956. "On the Logic of General Behavior Systems Theory." In *The Foundations of Science and the Concept of Psychology and Psychoanalysis*, eds. Herbert Feigl and Michael Scriven. Minnesota Studies in the Philosophy of Science. 1: 223–28. Minneapolis: University of Minnesota Press.

Dunnell, Robert C. 1977. "Anthropological Potential of Archaeological Models of Function." Seattle. Mimeographed.

Einstein, Albert. 1950. "On the Generalized Theory of Gravitation." *Scientific American*. 182(4): 13–17.

Eisely, Loren. 1946. *The Immense Journey*. New York: Time, Inc.

Flannery, Kent V. 1973. "Archeology with a Capital 'S'." In *Research and Theory in Current Archeology*, ed. Charles L. Redman. New York: Wiley.

Harris, Marvin. 1968. *The Rise of Anthropological Theory*. New York: T. Y. Crowell.

Hill, J. N. 1972. "The Methodological Debate in Contemporary Archaeology: A Model." In *Models in Archaeology*, ed. David L. Clarke. London: Methuen.

Johnson, Leroy. 1972. "Problems in 'Avant-Garde' Archaeology." *American Anthropologist*. 74: 366–77.

Kitto, H. D. F. 1951. *The Greeks*. Baltimore: Penguin.

Langer, William L. 1968. "How History Is Written." Introduction to *Western Civilization*, eds. Paul Mackendrick et al. New York: American Heritage Publishing Co.

LeBlanc, Steven. 1974. "Two Points of Logic Concerning Data, Hypotheses, General Laws, and Systems." In *Research and Theory in Current Archeology*, ed. Charles L. Redman. New York: Wiley.

Lovejoy, Arthur O. 1960. *The Great Chain of Being: A Study of the History of an Idea*. New York: Harper & Row.

Marx, Karl. 1904. *The Critique of Political Economy*, trans. I. N. Stone. Chicago: International Library Publication Co.

Meehan, Eugene J. 1968. *Explanation in Social Sciences: A System Paradigm*. Homewood, Ill.: Dorsey.

Meek, R. L. 1953. *Marx and Engels on Malthus*. London: Lawrence and Wishart.

Morrison, Philip. 1973. "Review of *The Domination Nature*, by William Leiss." *Scientific American*. 228(6): 117–18.

Plog, Fred T. 1975. "Systems Theory in Archaeological Research." In *Annual Review of Anthropology*. 4: 207–24.

Sahlins, Marshall D. and Elman R. Service, eds. 1960. *Evolution and Culture*. Ann Arbor: University of Michigan Press.

Salmon, Merrilee H. 1975. "Confirmation and Explanation in Archaeology." *American Antiquity*. 40(4): 459–64.

Spaulding, Albert C. 1973. "Archeology in the Active Voice: The New Anthropology." In *Research and Theory in Current Archeology*, ed. Charles L. Redman. New York: Wiley.

Spencer, H. 1883. *Social Statics*. New York: Appleton.

Steward, Julian H. and Frank M. Setzler. 1938. "Function and Configuration in Archaeology." *American Antiquity*. 4(1): 4–10.

Tylor, Edward B. 1913. *Primitive Culture*. 5th ed. London: J. Murray.

———. 1960. *Anthropology*. Ann Arbor: The University of Michigan Press. Original publication 1881.

Watson, Patty Jo, Steven A. LeBlanc, and Charles L. Redman. 1971. *Explanation in Archeology*. New York: Columbia University Press.

White, Leslie A. 1949. *The Science of Culture*. New York: Grove Press.

———. 1959. "The Concept of Culture." *American Anthropologist*. 61: 227–51.

Willey, Gordon R. and Phillip Phillips. 1958. *Method and Theory in American Archaeology*. Chicago: University of Chicago Press.

2

Fundamentals of Archaeology

·To be ignorant of what happened before you
were born is to be ever a child. For what is a
man's lifetime unless the memory of past events
is woven with those of earlier times?

Cicero

People are messy animals. Perhaps 3 million years ago our ancestors began littering the African landscape with stone tools and gnawed bones,
and ever since we have been sinking deeper and deeper into our own
garbage. Strictly speaking, all this junk, from the first stone tools to today's indestructible plastic bottles, is the *archaeological record*. And
the major premise of archaeology is that we can look at selected segments of this 3-million-year accumulation of debris and see reflections
of the factors that have shaped human physical and cultural evolution.

Archaeologists tend to look at the archaeological record largely in
terms of *artifacts, features,* and *sites.* Artifacts are things that owe any
of their physical characteristics or their place in space to human activity
(Dunnell 1971: 201). Thus, a carefully shaped stone arrowhead is an
artifact, but so is a stone that has simply been pushed aside so that a
Pleistocene hunter could sleep more comfortably. Bones, pollen, and
other organic remains can also be considered artifacts, sometimes called
ecofacts (Binford 1964), if they owe characteristics of form (as do domesticated plants) or placement to human activity. Archaeologists usually
analyze artifacts not simply as objects but as constellations of *attributes*
such as size, shape, color, and wear patterns.

2.1
A cemetery site in western Iran. More than 1000 graves were looted of bronze artifacts.

Hearths, ovens, wells, pits, tombs, and other clusters of artifacts representing specific activities are usually referred to as *features*.

The concept of an archaeological *site* is less precise than the concept of an artifact, but typically it means a particularly dense concentration of artifacts and features. Thus, the ancient city of Babylon in Mesopotamia is a site, but so is DK 1 at Olduvai Gorge, East Africa, where just a few score stone tools lie amid broken animal bones. Ancient villages and towns are easily identifiable, since they are marked by walls, collapsed buildings, and massive quantities of pottery and other debris, and it is convenient to think of the archaeological record in this case as composed of many discrete sites representing different settlements. But the areas between these sites are often littered with artifacts representing small work parties, "picnic lunches," temporary labor camps, and a host of other activities, and if we concentrated only on the settlement sites, we would miss much of the archaeological record. The concept of an archaeological site is particularly imprecise when applied to the archaeological record left by the countless bands of hunters and gatherers who roamed the world for millions of years before the first settlements appeared, and whose tools and other debris are scattered in a multitude of tiny hunting camps, tool-manufacturing sites, kill sites, and base camps. In general, therefore, sites are regarded simply as high points in plots of artifact densities.

PRESERVATION

A depressing number of things can destroy archaeological remains. Floods wash them away, glacial ice sheets grind them to fragments, rodents go out of their way to burrow through them, and rivers and winds bury them under blankets of soil. The greatest destruction, however, is caused by people. Thousands of sites have been buried beneath parking lots or destroyed by the construction of roads, bridges, buildings, and dams. But it is not only modern civilization that is to blame; people of all ages have knowingly and unknowingly destroyed the record of the past.

In recent years the worst destruction has occurred through looting. In many countries it has become a flourishing industry; peasants rob sites and sell their finds to antiquities dealers (Figure 2.1), who ship items mainly to the Americas and Europe. Even the amateur who is just trying to find a few arrowheads or nice "Indian pots" probably does not realize that he or she is destroying invaluable and irreplaceable information and objects. Archaeologists are usually not interested in artifacts for their own sake; artifacts are most useful when they are recovered in the context in which they were used and deposited. Thus, once a looter removes artifacts from a site, the most valuable characteristics of the artifacts are forever lost.

Even those sites relatively untouched by environmental and human disturbances are greatly altered by the natural processes of decay. Stone tools are almost indestructible, but bones, hides, wood, plants, and people rot. Even pottery, which normally can withstand tens of thousands of years of exposure, will break down if the soil is highly saline, or if immersed in water long enough.

Certain artifacts do preserve well under such conditions as extreme aridity, cold, or—for some things—complete immersion in water. Entire mammoths have been retrieved from frozen pits in Siberia, and well-preserved human corpses thousands of years old have been recovered from peat bogs in Europe (Figure 2.2). Dry caves provide excellent preservation conditions, where corpses, feces, leather, and other things can be found in near-perfect condition.

2.2
Tollund Man, a well-
preserved 2000-year-old corpse
from the peat bogs of Denmark. Note the rope with
which he was hanged.

LOCATING ARCHAEOLOGICAL REMAINS

It does not take a trained archaeologist to locate the pyramids of Egypt
or the huge Mayan temple complexes of Central America, but many
other archaeological remains are less evident, such as those covered by
drifting sand or alluvial soils, buried beneath contemporary settlements,
or located in remote, unsurveyed areas.

Until very recently, most archaeological sites were found by accident or unsystematic exploration. The highly significant 300,000-year-
old human bones and tools found at Choukoutien, China, in the 1920s
were discovered by peasants digging up animal bones to be ground into
an aphrodisiac preparation. The construction of a subway system in
Mexico City in the 1960s turned up many previously unknown but
highly important archaeological remains.

In modern archaeology, however, one no longer sets out on expeditions to remote places on the simple assumption that something interesting will turn up; instead, archaeologists usually work within the context of a specific problem and design their research to locate remains
directly relevant to this problem. If one were interested in the origins
of maize agriculture in ancient Mexico, one would read the many reports written on this subject, define a geographical region where maize

is likely to have been first cultivated, and then conduct archaeological surveys to locate relevant sites within this region.

Actually locating such sites might involve walking surveys, where five or ten archaeologists, working from maps or aerial photographs, simply line up and walk over a selected area, recording sites as they are found. Aerial, infra-red, and regular photographs and other special photogrammetric techniques can often be used to reveal ancient agricultural fields, roads, and other features not visible from the ground (Figure 2.3). Archaeologists also use geological indications to search for cultural remains. In East Africa, for example, erosion has revealed large expanses of what a million years ago was the surface of the Serengeti Plain, and artifacts are frequently found protruding from these exposures.

Some rather exotic methods have lately been developed to assist archaeologists in finding sites. Underwater archaeological surveys have been conducted by divers, although the cost of such surveys is high and the area covered usually very small. A device called a *magnetometer* has also been used with some success to locate buried archaeological re-

2.3
Aerial view of modern town and adjacent ancient settlement near Qasr-i Abu Nasr, Iran. The lines of circular pits are ancient *qanats,* or underground canals.

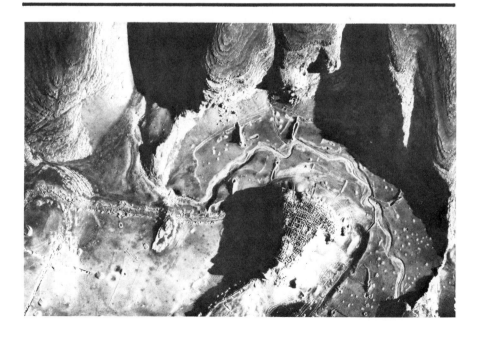

mains. It works on the principle that the earth's magnetic field is minutely affected by buried features, such as buildings, roads, and kilns, so that if one measures magnetic intensity at a large number of points within an area, one can locate these buried features (Figure 2.4).

But one of the most productive ways of finding sites is still to ask local people if they know of any in their neighborhood. However they are located, archaeological sites can either be simply mapped and recorded, or they can be excavated—depending on the resources and objectives of the project. Because of the tremendous cost and time requirements of excavation, only a tiny fraction of archaeological sites found are ever excavated (Figure 2.5), and the decision as to which are excavated must be made very carefully to get the most information possible. A recent survey in western Iran (Wenke 1975–76), for example, located more than 1,000 archaeological sites within only 1,200 square kilometers, and excavating only 10 percent of those would require decades of work and millions of dollars.

2.4
Sample results from a proton magnetometer survey. The figures show deviations of each reading from what would be expected over undisturbed ground. Large positive and negative deviations (circled) suggest a buried pottery kiln.

Anomalies in 1 gamma units

Ditch   50 feet   N

1	−2	3	10	4	−3	6	2	6	5	8	4	−1	−2	−8	−6	−7
1	−2	2	9	3	1	7	11	19	18	17	7	2	3	−5	−4	−4
2	0	7	7	2	8	16	24	35	45	34	15	1	−4	−4	−8	−5
2	3	11	4	6	16	32	50	74	91	69	20	−2	−4	−6	−10	−7
4	6	12	4	10	21	33	47	74	95	67	22	−2	−5	−5	−5	−5
2	7	7	7	13	23	28	36	45	36	15	−3	−5	−6	−6	−5	−4
2	13	4	6	10	19	18	21	2	−9	−15	−8	−9	−3	−3	−5	−5
6	10	2	1	4	4	3	−8	−18	−21	−16	−12	−9	−3	−4	−4	−3
7	6	0	−2	−5	−6	−11	−16	−18	−15	−14	−11	−4	−1	0	−2	−2
11	2	1	0	−1	−4	−7	−9	−7	−7	−4	−2	1	1	2	−2	0
5	−1	1	2	0	−3	−6	−6	−6	−5	−4	−1	−1	1	2	−1	1
2	3	2	1	0	−1	−5	−7	−8	−7	−6	10	−32	15	0	1	1

Iron

2.5
A recent view of the remains of Nineveh, a large Mesopotamian settlement first established in the fifth millennium B.C. Like all Near Eastern "tell" sites, it is composed of collapsed buildings and walls, pottery frgaments, stone tools, and other debris.

EXCAVATION

The methods used to excavate archaeological sites depend on the kind of remains involved and the objectives of the archaeologists. Normally, the first step is to make a careful map of the site so that objects and features found can be given precise three-dimensional coordinates. Then the site is gridded into, say, five-by-five-meter blocks, and a sample of these blocks is selected for excavation. Actual digging is done with dental tools, paintbrushes, trowels, shovels, bulldozers, or dynamite—depending, again, on the objectives and context. At a million-year-old site in Olduvai Gorge, the placement of each stone, tool, and bone may be mapped, each artifact drawn, and any human skeletal material removed with great care. In a 3,000-year-old mud-brick building in the Near East, however, there are often hundreds of thousands of fragments of pottery and it is not possible or considered useful to make a three-dimensional plan indicating the location of each. Nonetheless, precise plans are made of all buildings, kilns, and other features.

Whatever kind of site is being excavated, a great deal of time and care is required. One usually tries to excavate according to the *cultural stratigraphy* (Figure 2.6) of the site, so that the different layers of debris are removed as depositional units—as opposed to simply digging the site by arbitrary levels. Most of the dirt removed from a site should be passed through fine mesh screens so that very small bones, beads, and other remains are retrieved. Samples of organic materials for carbon-14 dating or other chemical analysis must be removed carefully. Agriculture and human habitation often change soil chemistry, so soil samples are frequently taken for chemical analysis. Burials have to be cleaned, drawn, photographed, and removed.

Every archaeological site is unique and nonrenewable, and once excavated, the remains can never be replaced. Thus, the greatest care must be taken to recover and record as much information as possible.

Most contemporary archaeological research projects involve geologists, botanists, palynologists (experts on plant pollen), architects, faunal experts, and other specialists. No one archaeologist can hope to know about the most recent research in all these fields, and successful projects require the organization and integration of torrents of highly technical information.

2.6

Profile drawing from Tepe Sabz, near Deh Luran, Iran. Occupations range from ca 6500 B.C. to ca 4000 B.C.

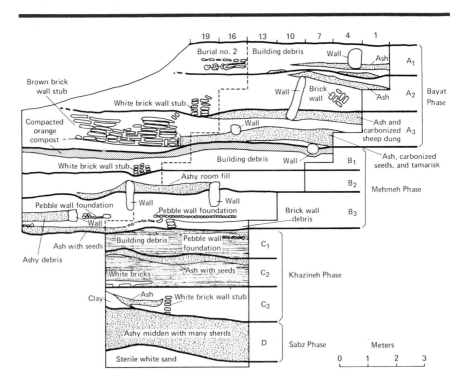

SAMPLING

The scale of the archaeological record and the slow pace of archaeological field research pose major problems for the study of major cultural processes. We know, for example, that the development of agriculture in the Near East, Mesoamerica, and elsewhere was the product of factors operating over large regions for many centuries and involving hundreds of thousands of people. Can we ever hope to understand developments as complex as this if time and money so limit the number of sites we can excavate?

To deal with this problem, archaeologists have turned to the technique of *statistical sampling,* the essentials of which are familiar to most people. American polling organizations regularly ask a few thousand people how they are going to vote in an election and use this information to make very reliable predictions about the voting behavior of the larger *population* (all individuals who actually vote). One of the reasons sampling works in elections is that pollsters *stratify* their samples: they know from previous elections that people in the North vote differently as a group from those in the South, that older voters tend to be more conservative than younger people, and that certain occupational groups are far more likely to vote than others. Thus, they break up, or stratify, their samples so that these and other subpopulations are proportionately represented. Then by using complex procedures of statistical inference they are often able to estimate election results quite precisely.

Archaeologists also use sampling theory and procedures. If they wish to know something relatively straightforward, such as the number and kinds of sites in a large region, they can divide the area up into subareas—perhaps stratifying it according to ecological zones—and then go out and record the number of sites in perhaps 10 percent of all the *sample units.* Excellent results are usually obtained from such procedures, if the objective is simply an estimate of site numbers. But more complex questions about, for example, the importance of long-distance trade or the changing patterns of animal exploitation might require the excavation of thirty or forty sites before archaeologists can make valid statistical inferences, and such samples are usually beyond the resources of contemporary archaeology.

In the face of such difficulties, archaeologists have opted for the only realistic strategy: they use statistical sampling techniques, knowing

that they often don't meet the theoretical requirements for optimal statistical inference, but feeling that useful—if not perfect results—can be
obtained. Fortunately, most statistical sampling techniques are very
"robust" in that one can strain their assumptions badly and still get
quite reasonable results.

The most basic *sampling design* is a *simple random sample*. Typically one grids an area, assigns each square a number, and then, using a
random number table, selects for examination some fraction of the total number of squares. There is nothing magical about a square shape
for the sampling unit: circles, rectangles, or any other shape may be
used, depending on statistical and archaeological considerations. Simple
random sampling is useful if one knows little about the site or area being sampled, but it is often more productive to stratify one's sample. On
a Near Eastern mound site it may be possible to spot the location of
buried temples by the shape of the mound and the type of artifacts on
the surface. In such a case one might want to stratify the sampling procedure by dividing the site up into two subareas (Figure 2.7), one of
which includes the temple area, and then taking random samples from
within these two areas. This ensures that an important feature such as
a temple will not be missed by the vagaries of simple random sampling.

There are a number of important sampling strategies in archaeology, and it is important to remember that there is no single "right" way
to sample—all decisions about sampling design must be made on the
basis of specific archaeological problems and objectives.

Dating Methods in Archaeology

A large proportion of early archaeological research was devoted to estimating the dates of important "firsts," such as the arrival of the first
people in the New World or the domestication of the first plants and
animals. But even with the recent increased interest in more general archaeological problems, it has still been very important to estimate the
age of archaeological finds. For example, in a later chapter we shall consider the hypothesis that wars brought on by expanding human population densities were the primary cause of the rise of state societies in ancient Peru. To evaluate this possibility it is necessary to be able to
estimate changes in ancient population densities, and this must be done

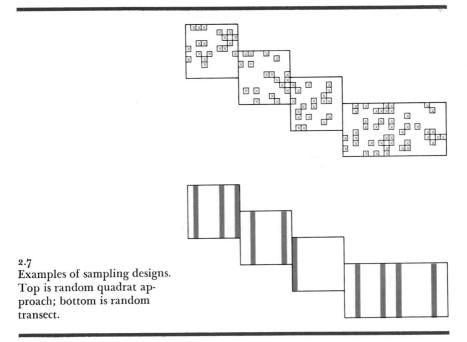

2.7
Examples of sampling designs.
Top is random quadrat ap-
proach; bottom is random
transect.

archaeologically by estimating the ages of hundreds of sites, so that we can determine which were occupied concurrently.

To solve these and other problems of chronology, archaeologists rely on two different kinds of dating methods. In some situations the objective is to obtain a *chronometric* date: that is, an age expressed in years, such as "that house was built 7,200 years ago." Chronometric estimates are often referred to as *absolute* dates.

In many situations chronometric dates may be difficult to obtain or simply unnecessary for the problem at issue, and for these situations archaeologists have devised several methods of *relative seriation,* in which the objective is to arrange sites or artifacts in a sequence that reflects the order in which they were created—even though we may not know for certain the actual age of any of them.

CHRONOMETRIC DATING TECHNIQUES

Dendrochronology is an elegant and reliable method of dating based on the analysis of the cross-sections of tree trunks. Most trees add a single "ring" each year to their circumference, and the width of this band is

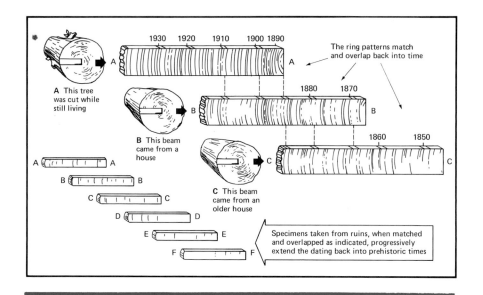

2.8
Deriving dates through dendrochronology.

determined mainly by water availability. Thus, if we count the number
of rings, the age of a tree can be established with great precision. Normally the tree grows faster in wet years than in dry ones; therefore, over
the centuries there is a unique series of changes in ring widths, and a
record of these changes can be established by comparing cross-sections
of trees that overlapped in time (Figure 2.8). By comparing beams,
posts, and other archaeological artifacts to cross-sections taken from
trees that live for thousands of years (like the bristlecone pine), it is
often possible to determine the exact year in which the tree used to
make the artifact was cut.

Since local climates vary, dendrochronological records must be
built up for each region, and at present detailed records are available
only for the American West and a few other places.

The most widely used chronometric technique is *carbon-14 dating,*
the theory of which was first outlined in the 1940s by Willard Libby
and others. It is based on the fact that solar radiation striking the upper atmosphere converts a small amount of atmospheric nitrogen into
the radioactive isotope C^{14}. Wind and other factors mix this C^{14} throughout the atmosphere, and because all living organisms exchange gases
with the atmosphere, the ratio of C^{14} in their cells is equal to that in
the atmosphere. When the organism dies, the C^{14} trapped in its cells be-

gins to revert to nitrogen. Because we know that approximately half of any given quantity of C¹⁴ will disintegrate in about 5,730 years (i.e., its *half-life* is 5,730 years), we can estimate the time an organism has been dead by measuring the amount of C¹⁴ remaining in its cells (Figure 2.9). After about 50,000 years, too little persists to be measurable with current laboratory methods, and thus only specimens of this age or younger can be dated with the C¹⁴ method. Radiocarbon dates are often given in years "B.P." (Before Present), and a recent conference has established 1950 as the standard for computing dates B.P.

Carbon-14 dating works best on wood and charcoal, but paper, leather, bone, skin, peat, and many other organic materials can also be dated by this method. Grains and grasses make excellent archaeological samples when charred by fire, because they preserve well and are short-lived compared to trees (where the sample being dated may come from the core and thus be centuries older than its use by humans).

The ratio of C¹⁴ in the atmosphere has not been entirely constant over the last 50,000 years, and thus carbon-14 dates have had to be "corrected" by measuring the ratio of C¹⁴ in tree rings dated through dendrochronology (Figure 2.10). Samples used for C¹⁴ dating must be

2.9
Relationship between the radiocarbon age (years B.P. calculated using half-life of 5,730 yrs.) of tree-ring dated wood and true calendar tree-ring age (yrs. B.C.) as determined from bristlecone pines and other long-lived trees. The straight diagonal line represents the coincidence of radiocarbon and true calendar ages. The calibration curve is shown as a dashed line for the periods for which there is a scarcity of data.

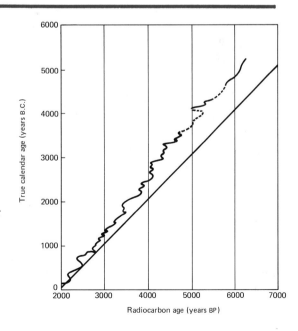

collected very carefully to ensure that they are not contaminated with younger or older carbon sources, such as ground water or petroleum deposits.

Potassium-argon dating is based on the fact that a radioactive isotope of potassium (K^{40}), present in minute quantities in rocks and volcanic ash, decays into the gas argon (Ar^{40}) at a known rate (half of a given amount of K^{40} will change into Ar^{40} in about 1.3 billion years). Because Ar^{40} is a gas, it escapes when rock is molten (as in lava), but when the rock cools, the Ar^{40} is trapped inside. By using sensitive instruments to measure the ratio of K^{40} to Ar^{40}, it is possible to estimate the time since the rock or ash cooled and solidified.

Because of the long half-life of K^{40} (1.3 billion years), potassium-argon dating can be used to estimate dates of materials many millions of years old. Presently, techniques have been developed to date accurately materials as young as 50,000 years old, but potassium-argon dating works best with samples between 100,000 and 5 million years old. Contamination from atmospheric argon, as well as "leakage" of Ar^{40} from some of the more permeable kinds of rocks, restricts accurate potassium-argon dating to stone that is relatively hard and contains at least 1 percent potassium (Aitken 1974: 7–9).

The most successful archaeological applications of potassium-argon dating have been in East Africa, where volcanic formations of solidified lava and compressed ash overlaying archaeological sites in Olduvai Gorge and nearby areas have yielded dates in excess of 2 million years. Unfortunately, many very interesting early sites in southern Africa, Europe, and elsewhere do not occur in volcanic areas and thus cannot be dated with this method.

Recent variations on the potassium-argon method, including the Ar^{40}-Ar^{39} method (Aitken 1974: 9), have improved the reliability of radiometric estimates.

If clay is heated to about 700°C. and then allowed to cool, iron-oxide particles in the clay will align themselves with the earth's magnetic field—the same magnetic field that makes an ordinary compass point north. If the direction of the earth's magnetic field had remained constant, the iron-oxide particles in ancient kilns, ovens, and hearths would all be aligned toward magnetic north. But the magnetic field has often varied in direction, as expressed in terms of the angle of declination between magnetic north and true north and the angle of dip. At various times there have been complete reversals, during which the

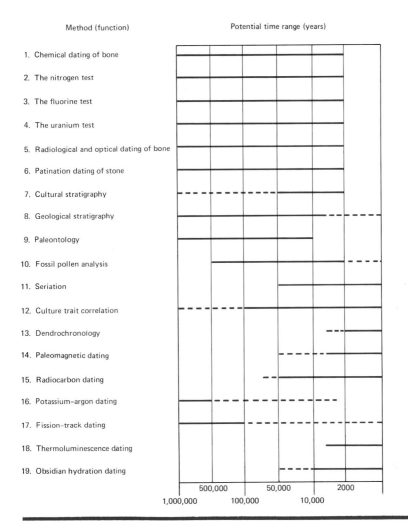

Method (function)   Potential time range (years)

1. Chemical dating of bone
2. The nitrogen test
3. The fluorine test
4. The uranium test
5. Radiological and optical dating of bone
6. Patination dating of stone
7. Cultural stratigraphy
8. Geological stratigraphy
9. Paleontology
10. Fossil pollen analysis
11. Seriation
12. Culture trait correlation
13. Dendrochronology
14. Paleomagnetic dating
15. Radiocarbon dating
16. Potassium–argon dating
17. Fission–track dating
18. Thermoluminescence dating
19. Obsidian hydration dating

500,000   50,000   2000
1,000,000   100,000   10,000

2.10
Summary of dating methods. Effective time ranges are estimates, and the accuracy of some methods has not been demonstrated. The broken line indicates the relatively less reliable range of these methods.

magnetic "North Pole" has become the magnetic "South Pole" and vice versa, and by compiling a record of these magnetic variations it is possible to date hearths and other features made of heated clay by measuring the alignment of their iron-oxide particles.

Although a promising dating technique, *paleomagnetism* has important limitations. The hearth or oven being dated must be in exactly the same position as when it was last fired, and thus any artifact likely to have been moved since firing, such as pottery vessels, cannot be dated with this approach. Another problem is that changes in the earth's magnetic field do not follow any predictable pattern. Thus, a record of these changes has to be constructed, and C^{14} or some other dating method applied to the record to calibrate the sequence of magnetic field changes. And because variations in magnetic field are expressed differently in different parts of the world, it is necessary to build up local records of magnetic changes. Individual sequences appear to be valid for areas no more than 800 to 1,600 kilometers across, and variations between, for example, Rome, Paris, London, and New York at any given time can be considerable (Aitken 1974: 6).

In recent years several other techniques have been devised to provide chronological information in cases where radiocarbon, potassium-argon, or dendrochronological methods are not appropriate, but most remain experimental.

An indirect method of dating is available if artifacts are found in association with well-preserved plant, pollen, or animal remains. Thoughout the history of our genus, the plants and animals we have exploited have changed considerably, as natural evolutionary forces have continually caused some species to become extinct and replaced them with new varieties. Scientists have worked out detailed records of when and where many of these extinct species lived, and thus archaeological remains found in association with them can be given relative dates. Dating by floral and faunal associations was especially important before the discovery of physical-chemical dating methods.

RELATIVE DATING

Many archaeological sites contain no floral or faunal material suitable for carbon-14 dating, do not occur in volcanic contexts where potassium-argon dating is possible, or for some other reason cannot be dated with absolute dating techniques. In such situations, or in cases where the problem under consideration does not require absolute dates, archaeologists often turn to a relative dating technique called the *seriation method*.

The seriation method is based on the observation that the styles and fashions of the things we make change over time. New styles follow predictable patterns: they appear first in a small area and are used by only a few people; they then become popular over much larger regions;

and eventually they become "unfashionable" and disappear. Shades of lipstick, styles of furniture, automobiles, and clothing, and millions of other things, including styles of ancient artifacts, are known to follow this pattern.

Archaeologists use these popularity curves of stylistic elements to arrange—or "seriate"—a group of sites in a sequence that expresses their relationship in time. If samples of pottery from two different sites share many stylistic elements in about the same frequencies, we might assume that these sites—if they are relatively close together—were occupied at about the same time; if they share few or no designs, or have the same designs in very different frequencies, we might conclude that they were not occupied contemporaneously. A large number of sites or pottery types can be seriated in this manner by manipulating their sequence in a frequency graph (Figure 2.11).

The seriation method is most reliable when there are large samples of artifacts that are both durable and expressive stylistically—typical characteristics of pottery. Even moderately fired pottery can survive thousands of years of being buried with rubbish, and almost every pottery-making culture appears to have invested considerable aesthetic talents in painting, burnishing, incising, scraping, or otherwise decorating their pottery. Stone artifacts, on the other hand, although also frequently highly stylized, are less easily decorated, and their form is usually more directly related to use.

While the seriation method has been the mainstay of archaeology for decades, it cannot be applied to every situation. Stylistic elements change as a function of both time and space, so that differences in the types of pottery used by two groups living 100 kilometers apart may indicate the time it took a particular style to reach the most distant community, rather than whether or not they were both occupied at the same time. In the same manner, clothing fashions from Paris and New York often reach rural parts of the United States only after they are already outmoded at their places of origin. To correct for distortions introduced by distances archaeologists use the seriation method on samples from a very restricted geographical area. Another problem is that, as in the case of stone tools, style and function sometimes tend to overlap, and it is difficult for the archaeologist to disentangle them. Tools and technologies also have a popularity curve in time.

Despite its limitations, the seriation method has been shown to work extremely well in many cases, particularly when coupled with so-

Cochuma
incised

Cochuma
black–on–white

Cochuma
white–on–red

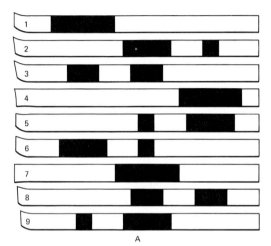

A

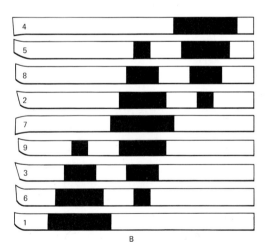

B

2.11
Relative seriation of nine archaeological sites on the basis of three pottery styles. The percentage of each pottery style at each site is indicated by the length of the colored area on a paper strip. Paper slips are then rearranged to form unimodal curves, or "battleship shapes." This indicates a sequence through time because styles generally follow a unimodal curve through time: they are invented, achieve more and more popularity, and then die out.

phisticated statistical techniques (Drennan 1976) and with chronometric dating techniques. Since relative dating does not indicate direction of change in time, these absolute or chronometric techniques are necessary to establish reference points within relative seriations.

Also important in this context is the *principle of stratification,* which simply means that in any archaeological site, those layers of soil or other deposits laid down first will be at the bottom, so that layers are successively older as we dig deeper. In practice, however, this general principle does not always hold true, because mudslides, earlier excavations, and other factors can redeposit layers in an inverted or confused fashion. In these cases an experienced archaeologist may be able to unravel the stratigraphic problems.

Interpreting the Archaeological Record

A fundamental procedure of science, or any form of analysis, is classification. To understand how the world operates we have to break it up into groups of similar things and then discover the relationships between these groups. Modern chemistry or physics, for example, would be inconceivable were it not for classes such as electrons, atoms, and molecules and the laws of thermodynamics. In the same way, evolutionary biology is possible only because of concepts of chromosomes, cells, and species and the principles of population genetics. Similarly, psychology and sociology deal in basic units like individuals, families, and economic classes. It is obvious that it would be impossible even to meet the requirements of everyday life if we could not classify and generalize from traffic lights, hot stoves, and so forth.

These notions about classification and analysis are quite straightforward and simple, but when we consider the kinds of data that archaeologists work with, we find that archaeological classifications and analyses have differed somewhat from those of other disciplines. Archaeologists have bits of broken pottery, house foundations, and stone tools, but these have not been organized in classifications in the same ways the atom and the cell have. A potassium atom is exactly the same thing to a Japanese chemist and an American chemist; but when a French archaeologist describes stone tools from southern France as "handaxes," the artifacts he is describing differ in many respects from North Chinese "handaxes" as described by a Chinese archaeologist.

Part of the difference between atoms and handaxes in this respect is of course a matter of perspectives: every potassium atom, like every artifact, is unique in its location in time and space, and only by the mental process of classification can we find their common structure and consider them all representatives of a single class. But as we shall see, archaeological classifications have generally been constructed with much more limited purposes in mind than have the units of the natural sciences.

One of the most common classifications in archaeology has been in terms of *functional types*. An example of this is Mary Leakey's categorization of the 1.75-million-year-old tools from Olduvai Gorge as "cleavers," "scrapers," and "handaxes." Such a classificatory system is based in part on ideas about how our earliest ancestors actually *used* these tools. Archaeologists who use functional types as part of their classification system usually do so on the basis of analogy with objects of known function: if they find a small, triangular piece of stone that looks like a modern arrowhead, they assume that the stone tool was used as an arrowhead. Obviously, imagination plays a role in creating functional types, particularly when archaeologists are dealing with very old remains left by people very unlike known or existing cultures in terms of their technology and economy.

Another widely used archaeological classificatory approach employs *chronological types*. Chronological (or "historical") types are artifacts whose combination of attributes are known to be limited to particular time periods. We have already noted that stylistic elements such as pottery styles and house architecture have limited distribution in time, and by sorting artifacts into groups based on their similarity of stylistic elements we can often devise relative chronologies of archaeological remains. Most of the pottery types devised by archaeologists to describe the pottery of the Indians of the American Southwest, for example, are chronological types, and if one knows these well, it is possible to date precisely the occupation of small sites without excavating them.

Some archaeologists also make use of *cognitive types*. According to this approach, the maker of every artifact had in his or her mind a "mental template" or idealized pattern of what the artifact should look like, based on that person's cultural heritage, and each artifact is seen as an approximation to this ideal. No one doubts that most artifacts are in fact made this way. There is great stylistic similarity in the pottery, basketry, houses, and even stone tools of most prehistoric peoples. And we ourselves have a developed sense of the way things "ought to be" in styles of clothing, music, and art. Thus, archaeologists who work with cognitive types think artifacts should be classified into types that reflect these mental templates, a procedure that would involve getting back into the "mind" of the "person behind the artifact."

A growing number of archaeologists, however, have concluded that while cognitive types often correspond to the stylistic ideas of the artifact makers, there is no way to verify what these were and how they were used (Thomas 1974: 13). As Lewis Binford notes, most archaeologists are poorly equipped to do the "paleopsychology" required in working with mental templates.

Many other kinds of classifications have been used by archaeologists in addition to functional, chronological, and cognitive types, but all of them are similar in the sense that they produce groups of artifacts that are specific to time and place. A chronological type for the American Southwest is not at all like a chronological type for prehistoric Turkey, and the functional types from Olduvai Gorge are different from those of Siberia. Thus, archaeological classifications are in essence very unlike the atoms, cells, and other units that form the foundations for other sciences, and they are created and used for a very different purpose: atoms and cells were created as classificatory units so that natural processes could be understood, but archaeological units have been created to reconstruct the lifeways and histories of extinct peoples.

Archaeologists are currently debating the whole notion of classification in archaeology, and some feel it is time we establish classificatory systems more like those of the natural sciences, in the sense of units that are not rigidly bound to specific places and specific times. There is no agreement yet about what these units would be, although they certainly will not be "pottery bowls," "arrowheads," or the other common categories.

Bibliography

Aitken, M. J. 1974. *Physics and Archaeology.* 2nd ed. Oxford: Clarendon Press.

Allibone, T. E. et al. 1970. *The Impact of the Natural Sciences on Archaeology.* New York: Oxford University Press.

Binford, Lewis R. 1964. "A Consideration of Archaeological Research Design." *American Antiquity*. 29: 425–41.

Brill, R., ed. 1971. *Science and Archaeology*. Cambridge, Mass.: MIT Press.

Brothwell, Don and Eric Higgs. 1969. *Science in Archaeology*. 2nd ed. New York: Praeger.

Chaplin, Raymond E. 1971. *The Study of Animal Bones from Archaeological Sites*. New York: Seminar Press.

Cornwall, I. W. 1958. *Soils for the Archaeologist*. London: Phoenix House.

Crabtree, D. 1972. *An Introduction to Flintworking*. Occasional Papers of the Idaho State University Museum, no. 28. Pocatello.

Deetz, J. 1967. *Invitation to Archaeology*. Garden City, N.Y.: Natural History Press.

Doran, J. and F. Hodson. 1975. *Mathematics and Computers in Archaeology*. Cambridge, Mass.: Harvard University Press.

Drennan, Robert D. 1976. "A Refinement of Chronological Seriation Using Non-metric Multidimensional Scaling." *American Antiquity*. 41(3): 290–302.

Dunnell, Robert. 1970. "Seriation Method and Its Evaluation." *American Antiquity*. 35(3): 305–19.
———. 1971. *Systematics in Prehistory*. New York: Free Press.

Goodyear, F. 1971. *Archaeological Site Science*. New York: American Elsevier.

Hester, T. R., R. F. Heizer, and J. A. Graham. 1975. *Field Methods in Archaeology*. 6th ed. Palo Alto: Mayfield Pub. Co.

Hole, Frank and R. F. Heizer. 1973. *An Introduction to Prehistoric Archaeology*. 3rd ed. New York: Holt.

Jarman, H., A. Legge, and J. Charles. 1972. "Retrieval of Plant Remains from Archaeological Sites by Froth Flotation." In *Papers in Economic Prehistory*, ed. E. Higgs. Cambridge: Cambridge University Press.

Michael, H. N. and E. K. Ralph, eds. 1971. *Dating Techniques for the Archaeologist*. Cambridge, Mass. and London: MIT Press.

Michels, J. W. 1973. *Dating Methods in Archaeology*. New York: Seminar Press.

Mueller, James, ed. 1975. *Sampling in Archaeology*. Tucson: University of Arizona Press.

Renfrew, Jane M. 1973. *Palaeoethnobotany*. New York: Columbia University Press.

Semenov, S. 1964. *Prehistoric Technology*, trans. M. W. Thompson. London: Cory, Adams & Mackay.

Strong, D. E., ed. 1973. *Archaeological Theory and Practice*. London: Seminar Press.

Thomas, David H. 1974. *Predicting the Past: An Introduction to Anthropological Archaeology*. New York: Holt.

Tite, M. S. 1972. *Methods of Physical Examination in Archaeology*. London and New York: Seminar Press.

Wenke, Robert J. 1975–76. "Imperial Investments and Agricultural Developments in Parthian and Sasanian Khuzestan: 150 B.C. to A.D. 640." *Mesopotamia.* 10–11: 31–217.

Wheeler, Mortimer. 1954. *Archaeology from the Earth.* Baltimore: Penguin.

3

The Pleistocene

> In the bleak mid-winter
>   Frosty wind made moan
> Earth stood hard as iron,
>   Water like a stone.
> Snow has fallen, snow on snow,
>   Snow on snow,
> In the bleak mid-winter
>   Long ago.
>
> Christina Rossetti

One of the central facts of human physical and cultural evolution is that the appearance and first 3 million years of our genus coincides with the *Pleistocene* ("most recent") geological period, when much of the world was, on the average, cooler and wetter than it is today. And before attempting to analyze the factors that shaped our evolution, we must have some understanding of the Pleistocene environments in which this evolution occurred.

The existence of vastly different climates and environments in the ancient past was suggested to European scholars of the eighteenth century by the observation that Europe was littered with huge boulders composed of kinds of stone very different from the bedrock on which these boulders were found. Analysis revealed that many such boulders came from sources hundreds of miles away, and to explain this some scholars hypothesized that these stones had been frozen in icebergs that had drifted south during the "Great Flood" and had subsequently been deposited as the icebergs melted.

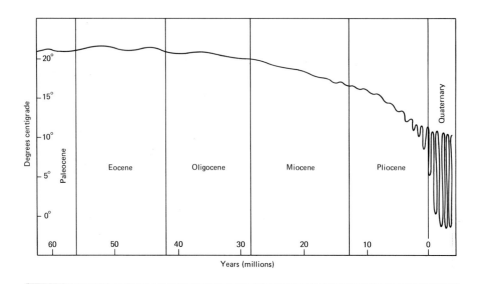

3.1
Estimated curve of mean annual temperature in central Europe over the last 60 million years. The time scale of the last million years is greatly exaggerated.

In 1837, however, the great Swiss naturalist Louis Agassiz published his view that these boulders had been transported by huge sheets of ice that had at one time covered much of Europe, and when English geologist Charles Lyell visited Agassiz's research station in the Swiss Alps, Agassiz quickly convinced him of the validity of his "ice age" by showing him huge gravel ridges (called *moraines*) left by the retreating glaciers and other evidence of glacial activity (Adams 1969: 289).

Soon many scholars were mapping the extent of these glacial movements in Europe and North America, and in 1874 Scottish geologist James Geikie published *The Great Ice Age,* in which he proposed that the Ice Age, or Pleistocene, as it came to be called, be subdivided into six glacial periods of intense cold, each separated by a warmer "interglacial period."

During the last century we have learned a great deal more about the Pleistocene and the earlier geological and climatological history of our planet. We know that the earth has existed for about 4.5 billion years and that for all but the last few million years worldwide climates were warmer than they are today (Figure 3.1). Then, about 13 to 10 million years ago, during the late Miocene period, the first glaciers appeared in the Arctic and Antarctic. During this same period, movements of the earth's crust and volcanic activity formed the Alps, Himalayas, and other great mountain chains, and snow and ice began to appear in these newly elevated regions. Worldwide temperatures at this time, although fluctuating considerably, slowly fell.

Between about 3 million and 10,000 years ago, the approximate dates of the Pleistocene period, glaciers appeared in mid-latitude regions on several occasions, covering large areas of the world. Glaciation was most extensive in far-northern latitudes (Figure 3.2), but glaciers also covered higher elevations in South America, Tasmania, and even some equatorial zones. Average worldwide temperatures may have fallen as much as 15°C during the coldest periods. Between these periods of glacial advance were interglacial periods, when average temperatures increased (perhaps 2 to 3°C warmer than today) and the glaciers retreated.

3.2
Barnard Glacier, Alaska.

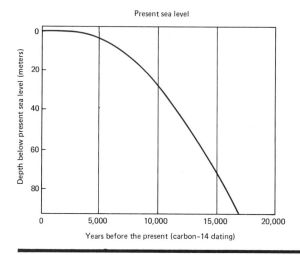

3·3
Graph showing position of sea level relative to land since the peak of the last glaciation.

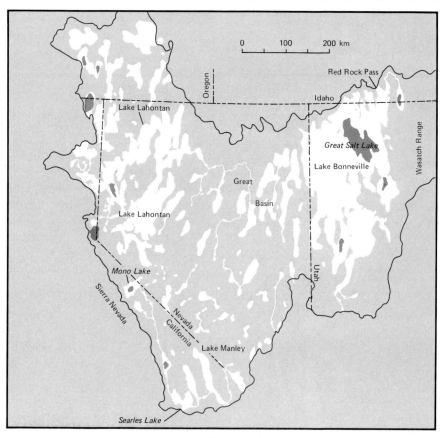

3·4
Distribution of Pleistocene pluvial lakes in the Great Basin of the western United States.

During the height of glacial expansion (about 20,000 years ago), 29 percent of the earth's surface was covered with ice, compared to only about 10 percent today. The movements of these glaciers—the result of gravity acting on the relatively plastic structure of glacial ice and the melting of ice at a glacier's bottom—were relatively rapid. It is estimated that the ice sheet that 75,000 years ago crossed the area now occupied by the city of Seattle moved at a rate of about 100 to 150 meters a year (Flint 1971).

Ice sheets were an astounding 3 kilometers thick in some areas and their tremendous weight deeply depressed parts of the earth's crust. As the glaciers melted and retreated, these depressed areas slowly rose toward their original elevations—a process still going on in some areas. It is predicted, for example, that both the Baltic Sea and Hudson's Bay will eventually almost disappear as the crust underlying them slowly recovers its preglacial elevation (Flint 1971: 563–64).

Although the formation of large glaciers was the most conspicuous result of temperature fluctuations during the Pleistocene, there were many other important related developments. So much of the oceans' water was bound up in ice that sea level fell as much as 140 meters during the coldest periods, exposing large areas of continental shelves and forming land bridges linking Alaska and Siberia, England and Europe, and most of the Indonesian archipelago with the Asian mainland (Figure 3.3). As atmospheric and oceanic temperatures fluctuated, profound changes took place in the distribution of plant and animal species, and cold- and warmth-preferring species alternately expanded at each other's expense.

Near the glaciers, meltwater enlarged existing lakes, while in drier areas farther removed, increased precipitation and lowered evaporation rates allowed many lakes (called *pluvial lakes*) to increase greatly in size (Figure 3.4). Searles Lake in southeastern California, now just a dry, salt-encrusted flat, was once 230 meters deep (Flint 1971: 565). Evidence suggests, however, that average worldwide precipitation rates did not increase substantially in the Pleistocene: rainfall patterns were simply shifted from one area to another. Nor is increased precipitation required to account for the spread of the glaciers; calculations show that at present precipitation rates glaciers equaling those of the Pleistocene could be built up in only a few thousand years—if worldwide temperature averages fell just a few degrees (ibid.: 1971).

The effect of the glacial periods on tropical and subtropical regions is not well documented. The Sahara Desert appears to have been somewhat wetter and cooler during glacial periods, as do other presently arid zones.

THE CAUSES OF CLIMATIC AND GLACIAL CHANGE

We still do not have a complete explanation of Pleistocene climate changes, but there are some interesting hypotheses. Climatic change and glacial change, while highly interrelated, are really two different phenomena: glacial change is only one of the major effects of climatic change. And it appears unlikely that either phenomenon has a single explanation. Instead, at least six factors may have been important: (1) variations in solar radiation, particularly in the "sunspots" that occasionally flare out from the solar surface; (2) veils of cosmic dust that may in the past have shielded the earth from solar radiation and lowered temperatures; (3) variations in the earth's orbit; (4) variations in the transmissivity and absorptivity of the earth's atmosphere; (5) lateral and vertical movements of the earth's crust; and (6) changes in the system of atmosphere and ocean circulation (Flint 1971: 805).

Evidence is not yet available to test all these factors, but it appears that the two most important for climatic changes may have been variations in solar radiation and the great mountain-building activity of the late Miocene period. These mountains, besides forming areas where glaciers could occur, may also have disrupted air flow, lowering temperatures in areas sheltered from southerly winds. Obviously, since there were several long, warm, interglacial periods—including the present one—after the earth's major mountain chains had been formed, we cannot explain the colder Pleistocene temperatures only in terms of these mountains. But it has recently been shown that a strong correlation exists between solar radiation fluctuations and temperatures on earth, and this factor, in combination with late Miocene mountain-building activity, may explain much of the temperature fluctuations of the last 3 million years.

CALIBRATING THE PLEISTOCENE

From an archaeological perspective, the most interesting thing about the Pleistocene is that its climatic variations correlate rather neatly with some of the most significant stages of hominid cultural and physical evolution. For example, the first tool-using animals appeared shortly after large glaciers formed for the first time in mid-latitude regions; hominid brain size and technological sophistication seem to correlate to some degree with the hominid invasions of cold northern Pleistocene environments; and the appearance of domesticated plants and agricultural systems closely follows the end of the last glacial period, some 10,000 years ago. Many scholars tried to explain these developments as direct results of Pleistocene environmental changes, but we now recognize such explanations as being drastically oversimplified. Nonetheless, environmental conditions have obviously been important factors in human physical and cultural evolution.

Existing glaciers have been studied intensively, and much information about their rates of movement and ecological effects has been gathered. One of the most precise records of Pleistocene climatic changes, however, comes from the ocean floor. Throughout the oceans live microscopic planktonic organisms called *Foraminifera,* some species of which prefer warmer temperatures, while others prefer cooler waters. By drilling into the ocean floor, scientists can obtain cores that contain the remains of millions of *Foraminifera,* and by analyzing these as to warmth- or cold-preferring species, it is possible to build up a sequence of water-temperature changes over long periods.

On land surfaces, the glaciers left numerous traces. In some areas the bedrock has been broken and scoured and shows long parallel grooves cut by ice-borne rocks. These glaciers carried within their kilometer-high walls of ice considerable debris, including sand, gravel, rocks, trees, animal bones, and huge boulders, and when the glaciers melted and retreated, they deposited this debris in formations called *glacial drift.* In the interglacial periods the surfaces of these glacial drift formations weathered and became capable of supporting plant life, and eventually they were converted into soils. Plant and animal remains from glacial drift indicate local climatic conditions during these interglacial periods. Subsequent glacial advances covered over or displaced these earlier soil layers, leaving a stratigraphic record of periods of glacial advance and retreat.

Through these various analyses, a record of Pleistocene climate changes and their correlations with cultural changes has been established. It is summarized in Figure 3.5. We shall have occasion to refer to these various changes in later chapters as we try to explain the major developments of human prehistory.

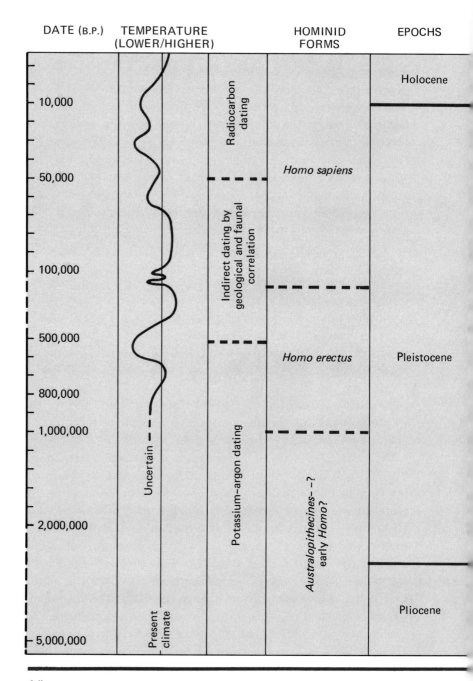

3.5
Simplified correlation of climatic, glacial, and cultural periods. Charts such as these are constantly being refined and reorganized as new data become available; terminology is not standard.

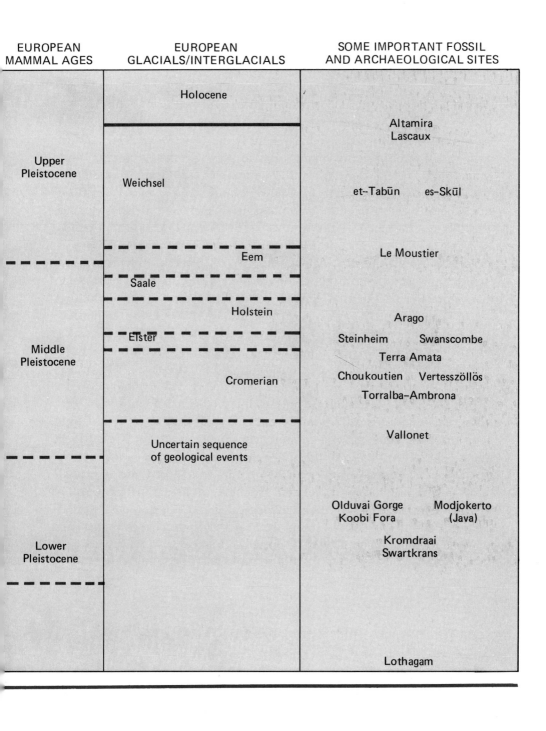

EUROPEAN MAMMAL AGES	EUROPEAN GLACIALS/INTERGLACIALS	SOME IMPORTANT FOSSIL AND ARCHAEOLOGICAL SITES
	Holocene	
Upper Pleistocene	Weichsel	Altamira Lascaux
		et–Tabūn es–Skūl
	Eem	Le Moustier
	Saale	
	Holstein	Arago
Middle Pleistocene	Elster	Steinheim Swanscombe
		Terra Amata
	Cromerian	Choukoutien Vertesszöllös
		Torralba–Ambrona
		Vallonet
	Uncertain sequence of geological events	
		Olduvai Gorge Modjokerto Koobi Fora (Java)
Lower Pleistocene		Kromdraai Swartkrans
		Lothagam

Finally, we must note that the terminology of the Pleistocene period subdivisions and the correlated cultural stages such as the "Paleolithic" is quite imprecise and has been frequently revised. The *Paleolithic* is generally taken to mean simply the "Old Stone Age," and as such is still applicable to some groups in New Guinea, Australia, and other places where stone tools are commonly used and metal implements are unknown. The terms *Lower, Middle,* and *Upper* Paleolithic are generally thought of as corresponding to successive periods during the Pleistocene when techniques of stone-tool manufacture were increasing in efficiency, but it is difficult to attach exact dates to these periods because these technological changes took place in different places at different times. Subdivisions of the Paleolithic in France are relatively precisely defined, and these are indicated in chapter 5 (Figure 5.10). The term *Mesolithic* ("Middle Stone Age") is also somewhat sloppily used, but generally is taken to mean the period between the end of the last glacial period (ca. 8000 B.C.) and the beginnings of agriculture, which occurred at different times in different places. The Mesolithic in northern Europe, for example, extends from about 8000 to about 4000 B.C., but many groups in marginal areas in northern Europe remained essentially hunters and gatherers well into the last millennium B.C., and hence are properly considered as at the "Mesolithic" stage. The term *Neolithic* (or "New Stone Age") refers to the period from the beginnings of agriculture to the widespread use of metal tools—again a time span that varied from area to area. The term *Holocene* is defined geologically and climatically and refers to the period from the end of the last glaciation to the present. Other terminology associated with the Pleistocene is presented in Figure 3.5.

Bibliography

Adams, Alexander B. 1969. *Eternal Quest.* New York: Putnam's.

Agassiz, Louis. 1840. *Études sur les glaciers.* Neuchâtel, Switzerland: By the Author.

Bishop, W. W. 1976. "Pliocene Problems Relating to Human Evolution." In *Human Origins,* eds. Glenn Issac and E. R. McCown. Menlo Park, Calif.: W. A. Benjamin.

Butzer, Karl W. 1971. *Environment and Archaeology: An Introduction to Pleistocene Geography.* 2nd ed. Chicago: Aldine-Atherton.

Cornwall, I. W. 1970. *Ice Ages: Their Nature and Effect.* New York: Humanities Press.

Flint, Richard F. 1965. "The Pliocene-Pleistocene Boundary." In *International Studies on the Quaternary*, eds. H. E. Wright and D. G. Frey. Geological Society of America, Special Paper no. 84.

―――. 1971. *Glacial and Quaternary Geology.* New York: Wiley.

―――. 1974. "Pleistocene Epoch." *Encyclopaedia Britannica.* 14: 558–69.

Kurtén, Björn. 1968. *Pleistocene Mammals of Europe.* Chicago: Aldine.

Martin, Paul and H. E. Wright, eds. 1967. *Pleistocene Extinctions: The Search for a Cause.* New Haven: Yale University Press.

Porter, S. C. and G. H. Denton. 1967. "Neoglaciation." *Scientific American.* 222: 100–111.

Zeuner, F. E. 1959. *The Pleistocene Period.* London: Hutchinson.

4

The Origins of Culture

Man is an exception, whatever else he is. If it is
not true that a divine being fell, then we can only
say that one of the animals went entirely off its
head.

G. K. Chesterton

The outlines of the origins of culture can be described with deceptive
simplicity. Primates with physical characteristics tending faintly in the
direction of mankind first appeared in Africa and perhaps other warm
regions of the Old World 10 million or more years ago. These primates
may well have had some of the mental and social capacities we associate
with human behavior, but our first direct evidence of cultural behavior
comes from Africa at about 2 million years ago in the form of crudely
worked stone tools. By 2 million years ago our ancestors were making
stone tools in ways and with a frequency not found among any other
primates and in forms indicating considerable planning and symbolic
thinking. Over the first 2 million years in which these primates used
stone tools, their brains increased dramatically in size, and by about a
million years ago they had developed systematic food sharing, cooperative work groups, complex social relationships, and other characteristics that distinguish humans from all other primates. No one knows
when the subtleties of human language, mathematical logic, mysticism,
and aesthetic sense were added to the human repertoire, but they too
are part of the problem of the origins of culture.

How did it happen that after hundreds of millions of years of cultureless animal life on this planet, our primate ancestors managed to break so radically with the past? What was the relationship between tool use, brain enlargement, and the evolution of human social systems?

In chapter 1 we reviewed some of the early attempts to come to grips with these questions, and we noted that Darwin's ideas about the biological evolution of the human species and the discovery of stone tools in association with the bones of extinct animals in extremely ancient geological strata had convinced many people of the great antiquity of the human race. But as long as no bones were found that could be attributed to a human ancestor intermediate between ourselves and other primates in physical form, it was still possible for many to cling to the idea that humans were an exception: that we were an extremely old species, older than had previously been suspected, but that we had not evolved as other species had.

Those who had studied Darwin and Lyell, however, and who were aware of the archaeological evidence of early humans in Europe knew it was just a matter of time before the first fossil "missing link" was found. The great French scholar Boucher de Perthes, grown old and tired of waiting, offered a 200-franc reward to the discoverer of the first "antediluvian" man in France. His enterprising workers were soon

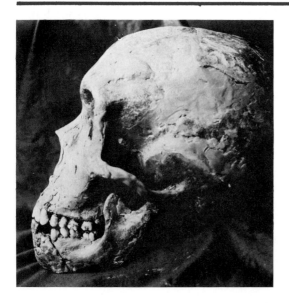

4.1
A reconstruction of a Neanderthal cranium—an early, disputed clue about our ancestry.

"finding" human remains in many places—all put there, of course, by the workmen themselves in hopes of collecting the money.

Ironically, the first premodern hominids had already been discovered some years before, although they were not found in association with stone tools and extinct animals as de Perthes had hoped. In 1848 work at a quarry on Gibraltar had revealed a skull whose receding chin, heavy brow ridges, and thick bones indicated a being who, if not a "missing link," was certainly not a type of human still living anywhere. The importance of this skull was not recognized for many years, even though a paper on it was delivered to a prestigious London scientific conference. But eight years after this find, another discovery was made that ultimately was to corroborate the significance of the Gibraltar fossil.

This discovery was a skullcap (Figure 4.1) and some limb bones found in 1856 in a cave in the Neander Valley near Dusseldorf, Germany, and although these remains were dismissed by the great German anatomist Rudolf Virchow as those of a deformed human, Johann Karl Fuhlrott, the discoverer of this first "Neanderthal," argued from the beginning that the remains were of an early form of human. Virchow's opinion, however, and those of others who variously labeled it an ancient Celt, a victim of rickets, an idiot, or a Cossack, conspired to deny these bones their proper significance for many years.

In 1886 two partial skeletons similar to the Neanderthal specimen were recovered in a cave in Spy, Belgium, in direct association with stone tools and the bones of rhinoceroses, mammoths, and other animal species known to have been long extinct. Although Virchow also refused to accept these as ancient men, the tide of opinion had turned and scientists everywhere were soon looking eagerly for additional specimens of early hominids.

One such individual was a young Dutch physician, Eugene Dubois, who was so convinced the ancestral homeland of our species was Southeast Asia that he arranged to have himself transferred to an army post in the Dutch East Indies so that he could search for fossil remains. It might seem that Dubois was incredibly optimistic about finding these materials, and we now know that the odds against his finding early fossil humans were overwhelming. But Dubois was working at a time when very little was known about the distribution of fossils, and for all he or anyone else knew, there might have been millions of fossil men waiting to be discovered. Actually, his search was not unerring. He spent several

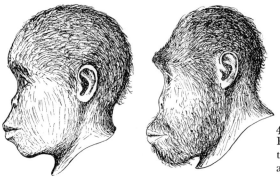

4.2
Robert Broom's conception of the Taung fossil, as a child and as an adult.

years wandering the wilds of Sumatra without finding much of interest, and only when he arranged a transfer to Java did he make his great discovery. In 1890 he unearthed a fragment of a lower jaw, and over the next few years he recovered a skullcap and—about fifteen meters away, but in the same geological stratum—a femur (thighbone). Comparative studies and measurements soon demonstrated that on the basis of cranial capacity, tooth size, and other criteria, his finds represented an individual at an evolutionary stage somewhere between nonhuman primates and modern humans, and he eagerly accepted his find as the "missing link."

For the next thirty years controversy raged over Dubois's find, some authorities again claiming it to be a deformed freak, others identifying it as a gigantic form of chimpanzee with no relation to human ancestry, and still others recognizing it as an early form of our genus and a direct ancestor of modern humans. There is some evidence that toward the end of his life Dubois himself lost confidence in his interpretation, and he apparently died thinking his find may have been only a gigantic form of erect-walking ape. Dubois's fossil had an approximate brain volume of 1,040 cc, about a third less than modern people, which suggested to its discoverer that if this animal were in fact a human ancestor, it was an ancestor considerably different from ourselves and from "Neanderthal man." Because no tools of any kind were found with the bones from Java, few inferences could be made about the animal's capacities.

Nonetheless, in 1906 the German anatomist Gustav Schwalbe published his comprehensive *Studien zur vorgeschichte des Menschen* in which he proposed three successive stages of hominid evolution: *Pithecanthropine* (represented by Dubois's fossils), *Neanderthal,* and *modern.* It was apparent, however, that if this were the correct succession of hominid forms, there would have to be many intermediate types not yet found.

The addition of a presumed fourth and earliest stage of hominid evolution did not come until the 1920s, when Raymond Dart, a South African anatomist, discovered a nearly complete skull of a very strange-looking child encased in stone quarried from a mine some 300 kilometers from Johannesburg, at the Taung site. Darwin had suggested the earliest hominids would be found in southern Africa, and Dart was soon convinced he had fulfilled this prediction. The skull indicated a brain volume much less than that of an individual of similar age of either Pithecanthropine, Neanderthal, or modern type, and the teeth and other physical characteristics convinced Dart he had found mankind's earliest, most primitive ancestor, which he labeled *Australopithecus africanus* ("Southern ape of Africa") (Figure 4.2). Dart's conclusions were discounted by some of the most influential scientists in Europe, mainly because it is generally difficult to interpret crania from extremely young primates and also, perhaps, because Dart had little standing in the rigidly hierarchical academic communities at Oxford and Cambridge. But while Dart's claims were being challenged, another important find was made, this time in northeastern China, 60 kilometers from Peking at a mining installation called Choukoutien.

Fossilized bones from the area had been used for centuries as aphrodisiacs, but a somewhat more scientific interest was stimulated in 1921 when a single human-looking tooth was given to an English anatomist teaching at a Peking medical college. The anatomist, Henry Black, recognized the tooth as belonging to an ancient form of hominid, and as a consequence the first of many years of excavations at Choukoutien were begun. Altogether, the remains of about forty individuals were found, including many skull fragments, and it was obvious upon complete study that these individuals were similar in brain size, facial structure, and other characteristics to the hominid found by Dubois on Java. This supported Schwalbe's proposed Pithecanthropine stage, and fossils of this type were accorded the name *Sinanthropus* or *Homo erectus* ("erect man"). The Chinese fossils were associated with thousands of stone tools, which also supported Schwalbe's inclusion of them in the human line.

A few years after the Choukoutien finds, interest shifted back to South Africa where, in 1936, paleontologist Robert Broom had found fragments from about six hominids in stones blasted out of a quarry at

Sterkfontein, some kilometers west of Johannesburg. Two years later he found more remains on a farm only a few kilometers from Sterkfontein, and his comparative studies established that all of these finds were similar to the Australopithecine baby recovered by Raymond Dart.

The effect of these finds from South Africa was twofold: they established Africa as the most likely location where culture-bearing animals first appeared, and they finally and widely established the idea that we had evolved from animals very different from ourselves. Neanderthal man, while seen as a brutish savage, was at least recognizably human, but the South African fossils established the idea that our ancestors were little different from other, nonhuman primates.

Thus, by about 1940 the outlines of our physical evolution were well known, at least insofar as the major fossil types are concerned, and most of the fossil discoveries since 1930 have simply added to our collections of *Australopithecus, Homo erectus,* and *Homo sapiens neanderthalensis.* Predictably, however, the simple accumulation of fossil evidence has not told us how and why cultural behavior first appeared and developed. Moreover, several very old fossils have recently been found that do not fit comfortably into the *Australopithecus—Homo erectus—Homo sapiens* framework.

The Evidence of the Evolution of Culture

There are several lines of evidence we can follow in tracing our ancestors' cultural and physical evolution, including: (1) paleontology, the study of ancient forms of animal life, including the ancestors of mankind; (2) the study of contemporary nonhuman primates, whose behavior patterns may give us clues to the behavior of our own ancestors; (3) the study of contemporary or recent hunting and gathering peoples, whom we assume to be living in environments and patterns similar to those of our Paleolithic ancestors; and (4) the analysis of the archaeological record, the stones and bones and other tools used by our ancestors.

PALEONTOLOGY AND THE ORIGINS OF CULTURE

Using fossilized animal bones and other evidence, paleontologists have been able to describe in some detail the course of biological evolution since the formation of the earth some 4.5 billion years ago, including the evolution of many of the animal types that are part of our own ancestry.

As Table 4.1 indicates, animal and plant life on this planet go back many billions of years before the first humans appeared. Vertebrates—animals with internal skeletons—appeared only about 600 million years ago, marking a major evolutionary advance. By 400 million years ago, the first amphibians appeared and the conquest of the earth's land surfaces had begun. Dinosaurs appeared perhaps as early as 200 million years ago and were widespread until the age of mammals, which began perhaps 100 million years ago. Since that time mammals, including ourselves, have radiated into most parts of the world.

But, taken as an overall sequence, is there any trend in the evolution of animal life on this planet that would help us understand the appearance of culture and our own physical type?

One possible answer to this question is suggested by the comparison of the ratio of brain size to body size in successive animal forms during the many millions of years before the first culture-bearing animals appeared. Anatomist Harry Jerison has done this using plaster casts of representatives of the major animal orders that have appeared during the last several hundred million years. He devised an *encephalization index* by dividing the total brain volume of each animal by the two-thirds power of its body size (the exponent was used because of the geometric relationship between surface area and volume in three-dimensional objects). This simple index thus represents a scaled ratio of brain volume to overall size.

Jerison's results (Figure 4.3) give us an answer of a sort to one of our questions. The evolution of the size of the human brain does *not* represent some unexpected and novel step off the general evolutionary trajectory of life on this planet. We are clearly a continuation of a process that began at least 600 million years ago, a process involving long-term natural selection in some animal forms for increased brain-to-body ratios and, presumably, mental capacity. We should note that this process has not been continuous and that many major changes were made in physical form and structure without significant changes in brain-to-body ratios.

In many fictional treatments of the future, people are portrayed with enormous heads and correspondingly impoverished physiques. Is this likely, given Jerison's data? Human brain size in fact seems to have

TABLE 4.1   Geologic Time Scale and Life History of the Earth

Era	Period	Epoch	Began millions of years ago	Duration in millions of years	Some important events in life of the times
Cenozoic	Quaternary	Recent	.01	.01	Modern genera of animals with man dominant.
		Pleistocene	3(2.5–3.0)	3	Early men and many giant mammals now extinct.
	Tertiary	Pliocene	10	7	Anthropoid radiation and culmination of mammalian specialization.
		Miocene	25	15	
		Oligocene	40	15	Expansion and modernization of mammals.
		Eocene	60	20	
		Paleocene	70(±2)	10	
Mesozoic	Cretaceous		135	65	Dinosaurs dominant to end; both marsupial and placental mammals appear; first flowering plants appear and radiate rapidly.
	Jurassic		180	45	Dominance of dinosaurs; first mammals and birds; insects abundant, including social forms.
	Triassic		225	45	First dinosaurs and mammal-like reptiles with culmination of laborinthodont amphibians.

decreased slightly since a high point of about 1,550 cc in the average Neanderthal living in western Europe 60,000 years ago, but 60,000 years is insignificant in the span of animal life on our planet, and encephalization ratios may well continue to increase—or decrease—during the next millions of years. We too, no doubt, are in a sense "missing links" in the ancient evolutionary experiment that is the history of animal life on this planet.

Jerison's data do not mean that we can equate simple brain volume with intelligence. Certainly a gross correlation exists between the two, but in the human species at least, increases in what we may vaguely label "intelligence" were probably achieved by internal restructuring of the brain as well as by overall size increases. Obviously, there is a biological limit to the amount of body energy that can be invested in gross

Era	Period	Epoch	Began millions of years ago	Duration in millions of years	Some important events in life of the times
Paleozoic	Permian		270	45	Radiating primitive reptiles displace amphibians as dominant group; glaciation widespread.
	Carboniferous		350	80	Amphibians dominant in luxurious coal forests; first reptiles and trees.
	Devonian		400	50	Dominance of fishes; first amphibians.
	Silurian		440	40	Sea scorpions and primitive fish; invasion of land by plants and arthropods.
	Ordovician		500	60	First vertebrates, the jawless fish; invertebrates dominate the seas.
	Cambrian		600(±20)	100	All invertebrate phyla appear and algae diversify.
Pre-cambrian	Not well established		Back to earth origins 4.5+ billion years ago?		First known fossils as early as 3.3 billion years ago. A few soft multicellular invertebrates in latest phases.

SOURCE   J. B. Birdsell. 1972. Human Evolution. Chicago: Rand McNally.

amount of brain tissue while still allowing successful live birth and normal functioning in the other biological requisites of animal life.

Finally, the general trend of increasing brain volumes throws into relief the general principle of natural selection. If we ask why increasing encephalization continued over so many hundreds of millions of years, we can find an answer, at this point, only in a tautology: encephalization ratios increased because this development conferred survival advantages on countless generations of animal life—and our reason for assuming increasing brain size was selectively advantageous is that encephalization ratios increased over time.

Yet this circular reasoning is not necessarily unproductive because it directs us to ask why and to demonstrate how such things as encephalization changes could have contributed to the survival of a species in

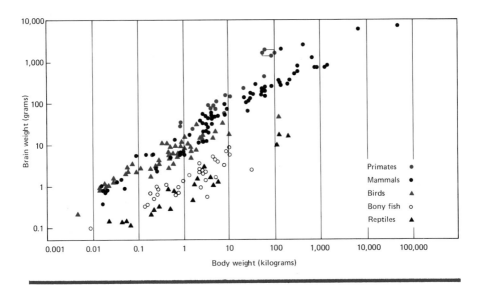

4·3
Brain size plotted against body size for some 200 species of living vertebrates that represent an evolutionary sequence through time. The points connected by lines represent the extreme variations of measurements reported for *Homo sapiens sapiens*.

particular environments and time periods. In other words, it provides us with a research strategy. We are still left, however, with the problem of documenting how, when, and where the transition to cultural behavior took place.

The Evolution of the Primates

The evolution of primates, the biological order to which we belong, is a complicated and only partly understood story, but one directly relevant to the origins of culture.

One of the most difficult things for the people of the nineteenth century to accept was the idea that as a species we are the progeny of nonhuman and extinct primates, and thus it is perhaps fortunate that the study of our evolution had not progressed to the point where our ultimate primate ancestor, a kind of tree shrew, was recognized. Imagine how difficult it would have been for even the educated public of the 1860s to accept the idea that we are the descendants of a small, pink-nosed, libidinous, insect-eating animal, whose modern form, the shrew, is on a pound-for-pound basis among the most ferociously effective predators known (Figure 4.4).

Our evolution from this "tree shrew" apparently began about 150
million years ago. The first primates probably appeared about 70 million years ago in the Paleocene, during which mammals moved into
many niches vacated by reptiles. The fossil record for the subsequent
65 million years is extremely fragmentary, but it appears that among
our earliest ancestors was a gibbon-like creature named *Aegyptopithecus
zeuxis,* which lived in the Middle Oligocene (ca. 30 million years ago).

The next stage of primate development, during the Miocene (about
28 to 10 million years ago) saw the evolution of what paleontologist
Elwyn Simons has collectively called the *Dryopithecines* (Simons and
Pilbeam 1965), the remains of which have been found at various points
along a great arc from central Africa through Turkey, the Indian subcontinent, and into China (Figure 4.5). Although the evidence is once
again sketchy, Dryopithecines seem to have adapted to a diversity of
environments along this arc, including perhaps the semitemperate latitudes of Eurasia. Very little postcranial fossil material has been found,
but evidence indicates a largely herbivorous animal ranging in size from
that of a modern gibbon to some that appear to have been larger than
modern gorillas.

For our own evolution, the most interesting aspect of the Dryo-
pithecine radiation is that at some point in the metamorphosis of

4.4
This species of Southeast Asia
tree shrew resembles closely
the small insectivorous ratlike
animals believed to be ancestral to all primates, including ourselves.

Aegyptopithecus to *Dryopithecus* a separate genus evolved that seems to have led eventually to ourselves. This genus was probably *Ramapithecus,* an apelike creature whose remains have been found in Africa, Germany, India, China, and possibly Spain. About twenty individuals have been found, the first in 1932 in the Siwalik Hills, 300 kilometers north of New Delhi. *Ramapithecus* remains are limited to small fragments of cranial material and teeth, but these are highly interesting.

Most physical anthropologists were surprised to find the dental arch of *Ramapithecus* so similar to that of modern humans (Figure 4.6). It has always been assumed our own dentition is the result of millions of years of tool use, in which the burden of food processing has been progressively shifted from the teeth to tools. It is an axiom of evolutionary theory that physical organs and structures that lose their functions tend to decrease in size over time. An example is the blind fish living in the complete darkness of caves in Kentucky where sight is of no advantage. Similarly, the spread of agriculture during the last 9,000

4.5
Distribution of some fossil finds of great apes of the Oligocene, Miocene, and later periods. The dots represent Dryopithecines, which flourished for more than 25 million years and gave rise to the great ape *Gigantopithecus* (circles) and to *Ramapithecus* (crosses), a probable hominid and human ancestor.

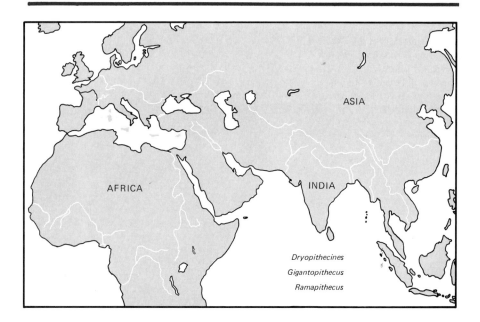

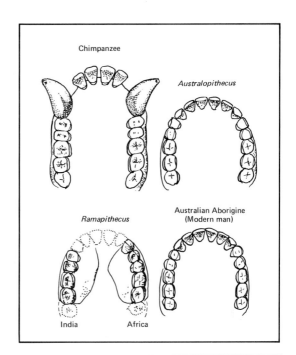

4.6
Comparative primate
dentition.

years has reduced the demands on human dentition in many areas to
the extent that in populations in, for example, the Near East or Europe,
where agriculture has been practical for many millennia, average tooth
size is much less than among, for example, Australian aborigines, who
have never been farmers. It seems that there is a basic economy to nature such that it is not advantageous to invest energy in structures with
no purpose or function, and animals using this energy most effectively
are likely to have greater reproductive success—which is, after all, the
main criterion of evolutionary success.

This suggests there was something about the adaptation of *Ramapithecus* that allowed the development of relatively small teeth. In chimpanzees and other primates the incisors and canines are the primary defensive weapons and the only means of ripping and tearing prey or
food, and a chimpanzee or baboon without large canines would have
difficulty protecting himself, getting food, or eating. How then did
Ramapithecus come to have a dental pattern similar to our own if he
was, as we assume, an apelike animal very similar in mentality and diet
to chimpanzees and other apes?

Obviously, we must consider the possibility that he was a tool user. He probably would not have been using complex tools like worked stone or net baskets; more likely he employed only unworked rocks or perhaps a rock with a single flake knocked off one edge. But even simple tools would have shifted the selective process on dentition to the point that, over the extremely long time *Ramapithecus* seems to have existed (perhaps 10 million years), dentition would have been reduced. We know that in the evolution of *Homo sapiens sapiens* (modern man) from Neanderthal and Pithecanthropine forms, for example, the size of teeth was drastically reduced and that this reduction correlated with an impressive improvement in stone-tool technology. But these changes may also have been accomplished by dietary and other changes. At least some animals, including a lemur-type mammal (*Hadropithecus*), had substantially reduced canines but no exceptional tool-using ability.

The few fragmentary remains of *Ramapithecus* do not allow us to resolve these questions, although there are a few interesting bits of evidence: near a Ramapithecine jaw fragment at Fort Ternan in East Africa was an angular piece of basalt that must have been carried into the area, because it is of a type of stone not naturally found there, and associated with the basalt piece were animal bones that had been cracked and smashed and an animal skull that had had its top battered off.

Little can be inferred from such sketchy data, but they offer grounds for speculation (Kranz 1975). Some anthropologists (e.g., Buettner-Janusch 1966) have suggested that perhaps *Ramapithecus,* or some other early Miocene or late Oligocene hominoid, was faced with a major environmental change in Africa and other tropical areas, with grasslands and savannas spreading and replacing forests as the climate became drier and warmer. Under these conditions, it is suggested, the selective advantage might have shifted from a quadrupedal gait to an upright posture and bipedalism, as hunting small animals, scavenging, and collecting seeds and other grassland vegetable products became increasingly important. The shift from more or less random food gathering to hunting and systematic food collection would have encouraged the development of social cooperation and groupings, as well as the development of tools and the mental abilities required to plan hunts and other group activities.

Others (e.g., Conroy and Pilbeam 1975: 80) dispute this interpretation, suggesting that tooth reduction began too early to be associated with tool or weapon use and was more likely a result of shifting diets and attendant changes in chewing functions.

People, Apes, and Monkeys

Recently, biochemist Vincent Sarich (1971) and others have used the techniques of molecular biology to study the chemical composition of the blood of many primate species in an attempt to resolve the problem of the relationship of ourselves to *Ramapithecus* and other extinct and contemporary primates. These scholars assume that evolutionary change in certain albumin protein substances found in all primate blood has proceeded at a constant or predictable rate, and that therefore the evolutionary distance—and time since separation—between any two primate species can be calculated by comparing these blood substances. On this basis Sarich argues that apes and Old World monkeys diverged about 23 million years ago, the gibbon and mankind about 12 million years ago, and that gorillas, chimpanzees, and humans had a common ancestor only 4 to 5 million years ago (Figure 4.7). This reconstruction conflicts in some ways with the paleontological and archaeological evidence. As we shall see, some very early forms of the genus *Homo,* which differ sharply from gorillas and chimpanzees, are thought to date to as early as 3.8 million years ago—which would be very close to the point of divergence determined by blood protein studies.

Because of technical questions about the reliability of blood chemistry studies (Uzzell and Pilbeam 1971), most scholars today still put the separation of humans from the apes at about 20 to 30 million years ago, but additional blood chemistry studies and new fossil finds may eventually alter this view.

Our ability to determine the validity of these ideas about human origins are particularly restricted by the fact that very few fossils have been found that can be placed in the period between the Ramapithecine radiation at about 14 to 10 million years ago and the appearance of the Australopithecines at about 5 million years ago. Evidence indicates that this was a period of awesome geological and climatic change, during which Africa may have been somewhat isolated from other continents as deserts spread across large parts of Southwest Asia (that is, Asia west of India and south of the Caucasus). Fossil-bearing land surfaces that date to the period between 14 and 5 million years ago

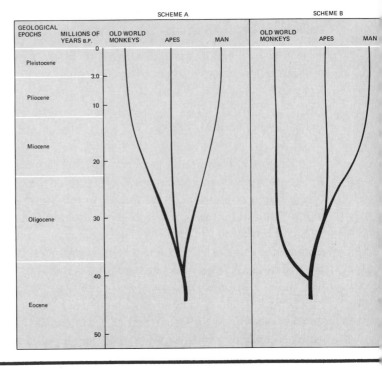

4·7
Four simplified versions of primate evolution. Present evidence

are rare and not extensively researched, and it may be some time before we are able to fill in this frustrating gap in the fossil record.

Australopithecus and Early *Homo*

The crucial period in the evolution of culture was between 5 million years ago, when the first Australopithecines appeared, and a million years ago, by which time all (or almost all) the world's hominids belonged to a single general type, *Homo erectus,* a hominid who on the basis of physical form, tool use, and patterns of social organization must be classed as our own direct ancestor.

Fragments of several hundred hominids have been found and dated to before a million years ago, and while much progress has been made in interpreting them, severe problems remain. It has been well and truly said that human paleontology shares with theology and extraterrestrial biology the peculiar trait that there are many more practi-

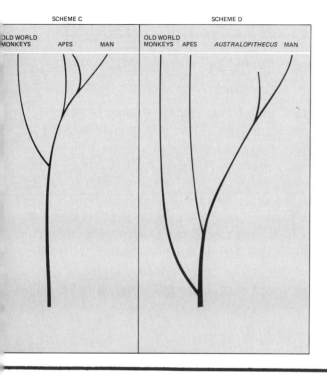

SCHEME C

OLD WORLD
MONKEYS   APES   MAN

SCHEME D

OLD WORLD
MONKEYS APES   *AUSTRALOPITHECUS* MAN

does not conclusively reject or support any of these schemes.

tioners than objects of study (Pilbeam and Gould 1974), and this situation has given rise to many, often conflicting, hypotheses.

Let us begin with the Australopithecines. The earliest *Australopithecus* yet discovered, a jaw fragment from the Lake Turkana (formerly Lake Rudolph) region near Lothagam in East Africa (Figure 4.8), has been dated to about 5.5 million years ago. Not a single identifiable stone or bone tool was found with this fossil, but this does not preclude the possibility that the Australopithecines were tool users at this early date. Most Australopithecine material, however, comes from the period between about 3 to 1 million years ago, and almost all authenticated finds come from the Great Central African Plateau and cluster in two areas: equatorial Africa, mainly Tanzania, Kenya, and Ethiopia, and South Africa. Tentatively identified Australopithecines have come from Java, China, and Israel, but most of these are very fragmentary and of dubious taxonomic status.

In physical form the Australopithecines seem clearly intermediate between ourselves and our cousins, the pongids (apes), in dental morphology, but their brain size, averaging about 450 cc, is within the limits of modern apes (Table 4.2). Cranial fragments and teeth are more plentiful than postcranial skeletal material, but there seems little doubt that the Australopithecines were erect, bipedal animals with a walking ability not much inferior to that of modern people. The backbone was curved so that weight was suspended over the pelvis, which was shaped so as to permit upright posture and walking.

Measurements of the size and shape of Australopithecine bones suggests two groups: individuals averaging about 107 to 127 centimeters in height and about 18 to 27 kilograms weight, and those that on the average were taller and heavier—sometimes by as much as 150 percent. Other morphological characteristics distinguish these two groups, such as the larger teeth and brain of the larger form of Australopithecine. Some argue these differences represent simply the size differences between males and females of the same species, but a more popular view

TABLE 4.2   Some Early Hominid Cranial Volumes

Hominid	Volume (cm³)	Range (cm³)
Australopithecines		
Taung	494	
Makapansgat	600*	
Sterkfontein	435	
Sterkfontein	480	
Kromdraai	650*	
Swartkrans		550–700†
Olduvai		
Zinjanthropus	600‡	
Homo habilis	673§	
Homo erectus		900–1225
Neanderthal		1300–1640
Modern man		850–1700

SOURCE   John Buettner-Janusch. 1973. *Physical Anthropology: A Perspective*. New York: Wiley.

* **Rough** estimates from fragmentary remains.
† **Upper** and lower estimates based on differing opinions of reconstruction of cranium.
‡ **Lower** limit as postulated by Leakey.
§ **Based** on reconstruction of cranium.

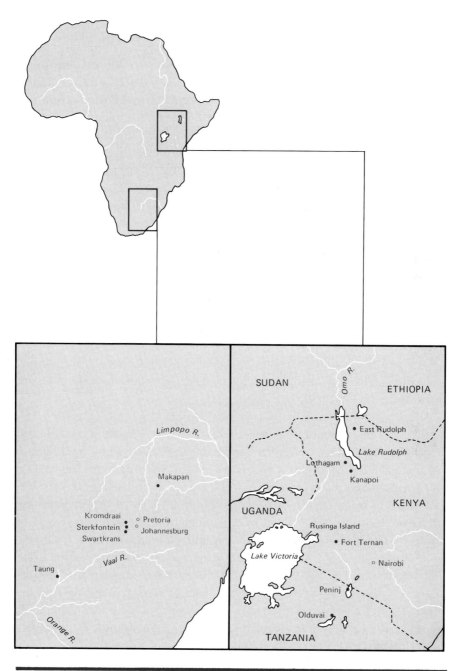

4.8
Distribution of some important early hominid sites in East and southern Africa.

is that these two groups represent different species of the same genus, and accordingly the smaller form has been labeled *Australopithecus africanus* and the larger form *Australopithecus robustus*. Others, following the suggestion of John Robinson (1954), prefer to categorize the larger, more robust Australopithecines as a separate genus, which they call *Paranthropus*. Robinson argues that *Paranthropus* was a cultureless, non-tool-using herbivore that still climbed trees to get much of its food, but was also capable of upright posture and a "waddling" gait and was able to exploit open savanna environments. *Australopithecus*, the smaller variant of early hominid, was in his opinion a culture-bearing, tool-using omnivore, more efficiently adapted to a life as an upright, bipedal hunter, scavenger, and collector in a savanna environment.

For most of the last thirty years there has been a widespread conviction that at least some of the Australopithecines were tool-using, culture-bearing animals directly ancestral to *Homo erectus,* and therefore to ourselves. Recently, however, several fossils have been recovered that raise the possibility that our own lineage split off from that of the Australopithecines more than 3 million years ago, with most of the Australopithecine forms becoming extinct without issue.

These taxonomic issues are complex, and before we consider possible phylogenetic relationships, let us consider some important recent fossil finds.

OMO AND EAST TURKANA   Since the late 1960s important fossil and archaeological finds have been made in the Koobi Fora region, also around Lake Turkana. Most fossils are crania, jaw fragments, and teeth, all of which have been classified as belonging to both *Australopithecus* and an early form of our own genus, *Homo*. Much of the original excitement about these finds was stimulated by the dates first assigned to them (on the basis of potassium-argon and paleomagnetic techniques), which range from 2.9 to 2.6 million years ago. In addition, sixty stone tools were found at the site of Koobi Fora on the lake shore in a geological context that initially also was given an approximate date of between 2.9 and 2.6 million years ago. If these dates are correct, these tools would be the earliest concentration of artifacts ever found. But recent—and controversial—reanalysis strongly suggests a date of "only" 1.8 to 1.6 million years ago (Curtis et al. 1975). Other bones and stones continue to be unearthed in the Omo–East Turkana area (Howell and Isaac 1976: 475), however.

American and French scientists have been exploring the Omo River Valley in Ethiopia since about 1966 and have found there some of the oldest artifacts and hominid fossils known. Over 100 hominid fossil fragments have been found, mainly isolated teeth, but also significant fragments of skulls, jaws, and even several postcranial bones. These fossils come from two areas, the Usno Formation, estimated at between 2.6 and 2.5 million years old, and the Shungura Formation, which dates to about 2.5 to 1.7 million years ago. A few fragments in the Shungura Formation—mainly teeth—may date to 3.5 million years ago. The majority of the fragments seem to belong to a hominid of the Australopithecine type, although there is considerable size variation, and recently some finds have been classified as early members of our own genus, *Homo*. A French-American expedition to the Awash River area of northern Ethiopia has recovered a number of interesting fossils over the last several years (Arambourg and Coppens 1969), including "Lucy," a primate between three and four feet tall and about twenty years of age. Lucy may have lived more than 3.5 million years ago, but there are complex problems in dating this fossil. She appears to be too small and primitive in some morphological characteristics to be considered a *Homo,* but there have been some (largely unpublished) suggestions that she represents an erect, bipedal, but perhaps non-tool-using primate of a previously undefined Australopithecine species. If so, Lucy may lend support to the view that other, later Australopithecines were not on the direct line of human evolution. The discovery of other primate remains in the Awash region since 1975 may resolve some of the chronological and taxonomic problems (Isaac and McCown 1976). To date no tools of any sort can be associated with these early primates in the Awash River area.

Artifacts have been reported at several points in the Omo area, from levels dating to about 3 million years ago, which would make these tools the oldest known in the world (Tobias 1973: 314). The artifacts—crudely worked stones for the most part—are not completely analyzed, but here, too, as at Koobi Fora, at least some of them appear in association with fragmentary animal bones (Harris and Isaac 1976).

THE LAETOLIL BEDS The Laetolil Beds are a series of fossil-bearing deposits on the southern Serengeti Plain in Tanzania, some fifty kilometers south of the base camp at Olduvai Gorge. Thirteen hominid fossil specimens were found there during 1974 and 1975, and radio-

4.9
Louis, Mary, and Richard Leakey excavating a site in Bed I at Olduvai Gorge.

metric dates for the fossils—mainly teeth and mandible fragments—average between 3.77 and 3.59 million years ago. Some scholars consider these fossils early members of the genus *Homo*. Not a single stone or bone artifact was found with these hominid remains, although over 6,000 animal bones were recovered, representing the usual cross-section of savanna species, including antelopes, cows, rabbits, hares, giraffes, pigs, elephants, rhinoceroses, and rodents—the species range one might expect from flood deposits, nonhuman hunting, *or* human hunting.

OLDUVAI GORGE   Olduvai Gorge, perhaps the most famous archaeological area in the world, includes many discrete concentrations of bones and worked stones scattered throughout a twenty-kilometer-long erosional gully in the Serengeti Plain. A German entymologist "discovered" Olduvai in 1911, but the search for early hominids was not begun until 1931, when paleontologist Louis B. Leakey visited the site (Figure 4.9). Leakey, born in Kenya the son of British missionary parents, died in 1972 after decades of almost continuous work in Olduvai Gorge. Like many prominent scientists, he has been criticized both for unfaltering

confidence in his own hypotheses and for his theatrical flair for pub-
licizing himself and his findings, but the fact remains that much of what
we know about early hominid evolution is a result of his and his wife's
work. Through years of little money, demanding manual labor, and the
privations of East Africa, he and his wife Mary kept working at Olduvai,
providing generations of scholars with data that even today are still being analyzed and debated.

In the years after their first visit the Leakeys found many stone
artifacts and animal bones, but no identifiable early hominid remains.
Finally, in 1959 when their research money was nearly exhausted, Mary
Leakey found the skull of an *Australopithecus*—an adolescent individual resembling Dart's finds in South Africa. For nineteen days the
Leakeys worked to free the skull and bones from the enclosing rock,
and eventually they reconstructed the skull almost completely. This
find convinced the National Geographic Society to fund further work
at Olduvai, and in succeeding years the Leakeys and their children have
recovered fragments of many other hominids ranging in age from about
1.75 million to 500,000 years ago. Significant as these fossils are, from an
archaeological perspective the major importance of Olduvai Gorge lies
in its concentrations of stone tools, for it is the only site in the world
where reasonably large samples of tools (Figures 4.10A and 4.10B) and
animal bones dating to between 2 and 1 million years ago have been
found. We shall consider these sites in detail below (pp. 128–134).

By 1973 fragments from about forty-eight individuals had been recovered from Olduvai Gorge. Most appear to be Australopithecines, but
in 1961 Louis Leakey announced the discovery in Bed I of a more
"modern"-appearing hominid, which he called *Homo habilis* ("handy
man")—suggesting that *H. habilis,* not the Australopithecines, was the
direct ancestor of *H. erectus* and ourselves. Leakey estimated the cranial
capacity of *H. habilis* at about 680 cc, somewhat larger than that of
most Australopithecines, and his reconstruction of this fossil implied
that it had a smoother skull and more modern-looking teeth, feet, and
other features than the Australopithecines. Since 1961 other supposed
H. habilis remains have been found at Olduvai, but their classification
and dating remain matters of controversy. Many anthropologists believe
that *H. habilis* is really *Australopithecus africanus,* others that it may
even be *Homo erectus* (Brace 1967: 78). Those who accept the designation of *H. habilis* feel that recent finds of apparently early forms of
Homo in the Omo and East Turkana regions support their view of the

Olduvai *H. habilis* as a contemporary of Australopithecines and that *H. habilis,* and not the Australopithecines, gave rise to our own lineage. They thus regard *H. habilis* as a form (*Australopithecus habilis*) distinct from *Australopithecus africanus,* suggesting that these are two different species (Pilbeam and Vaišnys 1975: 12).

On the important question of who made the tools at Olduvai Gorge, Mary Leakey has recently concluded it was *Homo habilis.* She reports that *Homo habilis* remains were found in six different localities in Bed I and Lower Bed II in direct association with what she calls *Oldowan* tools. On the other hand, Australopithecine remains have been found throughout Beds I and II, and none of the associations for either hominid is so convincing that we can come to any final conclusion.

4.10
(A) Sharp-edged tools can be produced by striking fine-grained stones with a hammerstone. As indicated, the blow sends percussion "waves" through the stone in a cone shape, and the stone fractures along the edges of the cone. Tools can be "retouched," or more finely finished, by detaching flakes along the tool edge.

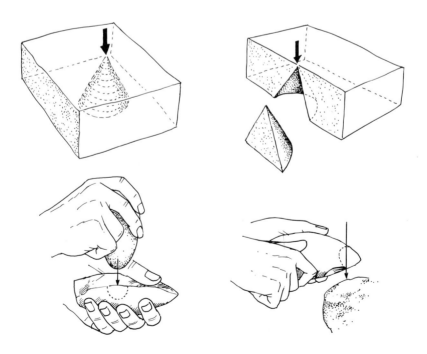

SOUTH AFRICA The archaeology of early South Africa is complicated by the lack of volcanic activity in this area during the last several million years, rendering it impossible to date materials from this area radiometrically. Consequently, it is difficult to correlate the material from Olduvai, Laetolil, and other northern sites with the South African data. Most South African dates are based on faunal comparisons with radiometrically dated East African sites and on paleomagnetic dating.

As noted previously, early in this century Raymond Dart, Robert Broom, and others had found in South Africa hominid fossils they classified as *Australopithecus*. Most of these specimens were found in naturally cemented limestone formations so thick and hard that the remains had to be blasted out with explosives, and not a single tool, hearth, or other evidence of cultural activity was initially found with these early specimens. Subsequent research, however, has produced additional fossils and some associated tools.

(B) Choppers made from lava cobbles at DK I, Olduvai Gorge.

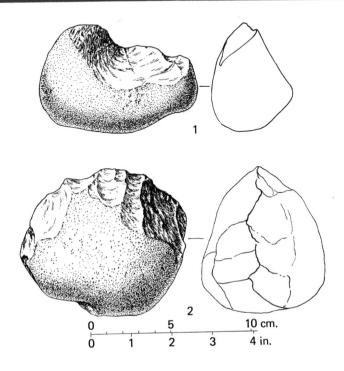

Sterkfontein   Recently a skull with numerous *Homo* features was discovered at the cave site of Sterkfontein in association with stone tools and animal bones that suggest a date of 2 to 1.5 million years ago. Directly beneath these deposits were the fragments of a hominid classified as *Australopithecus africanus* occurring in association with animal bones consistent with a date of about 3 to 2.5 million years ago, but without any associated stone tools. This has been interpreted to mean that the maker of the tools at Sterkfontein was a member of the genus *Homo,* not an Australopithecine, and further, that these findings are "in keeping with the widely-held and strongly supported view that *A. africanus* is still the most likely claimant to have been ancestral to *H. habilis* and to later species of man" (Hughes and Tobias 1977: 312).

Makapansgat and Swartkrans   These two cave sites contained several important hominid fossils, most of which can be classified as Australopithecines, but only a few artifacts. It has not been possible either to link the artifacts from Makapansgat with the artifacts from other African sites, in terms of style or techniques of manufacture, or to perform statistical analyses of any scope. Mary Leakey concluded that the artifacts from Swartkrans are similar to the Oldowan B (Bed II) examples, but here too the sample is extremely small. Estimates of dates for the faunal remains and artifacts at Makapansgat are between 3 and 2.5 million years ago, while Swartkrans appears to be somewhat younger, perhaps from 2.5 to 1.7 million years ago (Tobias 1973: 323).

There are various other hominid fossils and tools in South Africa that collectively pose several interesting interpretive problems. For example, Australopithecine bones have never been found south of the famous Taung site, where Dart found the first Australopithecine, and it is unclear whether this is because of insurmountable ecological barriers or some other obstacle. Also, between about 3 million and a million years ago, the number of carnivore species inhabiting the areas south of Taung declined drastically, from about twenty to twelve, and Richard Klein notes the possibility that this "was at least in part due to the arrival and subsequent evolutionary success of meat-eating hominids" (1977: 197).

Almost all the South African fossils have been found in what were once deep subterranean caverns, usually in association with many other animal species. If the Australopithecines were killing animals and living in these caverns, such a location for these remains might be ex-

TABLE 4.3 Roster of Some Australopithecine Fossil Discoveries

Region	Site	Kind	Number of individual fossils*
South Africa	Taung	Gracile	1
	Kromdraai	Robust	6
	Makapansgat	Gracile	30
	Sterkfontein	Gracile	40
	Swartkrans	Robust	60
East Africa	Olduvai Gorge	Robust	3
	Olduvai Gorge	Gracile	6
	Garusi	Gracile	1
	Peninj (Lake Natron)	Robust	1
	Lake Baringo (Ngorora Formation)	Gracile ?	1†
	Lake Baringo (Ngorora Formation)	Robust	1
	Lothagam Hill	?	1‡
	Kanapoi	?	1§
	East Rudolf, Kenya (Kobbi Fora, Ileret)	Gracile and robust	30
	Chesowonja	Robust	1
	Kanam	?	1
Ethiopia	Omo	Gracile	10
	Omo	Robust	3
West Africa	Chad (Yayo, Koro Toro)	Gracile	1
Java	Djetis	Robust	2
China	Drugstore	?	1?

SOURCE John Buettner-Janusch. 1973. *Physical Anthropology: A Perspective.* New York: Wiley.

* The exact numbers of different individuals are difficult to determine for finds at several of the sites. The numbers reported here are based upon summaries in the literature.
† Molar tooth crown only.
‡ Single mandible.
§ Distal end of humerus (elbow).

pected, but most of the tool associations in South Africa appear to be with members of the genus *Homo,* not with the Australopithecines (Klein 1977). Thus, some archaeologists have suggested that the Australopithecine bones here are the result of these hominids being preyed upon by leopards, who dropped the bones near holes where floods could wash them into these caverns (ibid.). There are some problems with this rather intricate reconstruction, but few other likely explanations have been proposed.

Raymond Dart has argued that the South African Australopithecines were working bone and other materials into tools, but recent reanalysis of the artifacts on which he bases his interpretation has convinced many that Dart's "artifacts" are really just bones broken and warped by natural forces (Klein 1977: 117).

Early Hominid Taxonomy

The early hominid fossils from Africa pose many important interpretative problems, most of which are primarily in the province of physical anthropology and thus beyond the scope of this book. Physical anthropologists are a naturally contentious lot, and they disagree heatedly about the interpretation and taxonomic status of almost every early hominid. Some issues in these debates relate directly to our hypotheses about the origins of culture, such as: (1) what are the phylogenetic (evolutionary) relationships of the early hominid fossils to each other and to *Homo sapiens sapiens,* and (2) which of these hominids made the tools at Olduvai Gorge, Koobi Fora, and the other very early sites? This first question arises because of the great variation in size and shape of some physical features of these early hominids. There is marked diversity among living humans too, of course, particularly in height, cranial volume, skin color, musculature, and other features. But if we consider the hominids of between about 5 and 1 million years ago, there seems to be more relative variation in tooth size and shape, cranial volume and shape, overall height, and other factors than is present among ourselves. And, significantly, these types of variation involve physical structures that seem intimately tied to the diet and activities of these animals, indicating perhaps very real differences and changes in their basic ecological adaptations.

How can we classify and interpret these fossils in a way that accurately reflects their interrelationships? First we should note that biological classifications have traditionally been attempts to arrange organisms in categories that reflect phylogeny, that is, their evolutionary ancestry. Thus, physical anthropologists have approached these fossils with the intention of establishing a classification that describes the evolutionary relationships among the various early hominids and their relationship to us, *Homo sapiens*. It must be remembered that biological diversity represents a long series of fine gradations worked out over billions of years of evolution, and therefore in our classifications of organic things we are constantly faced with the problem of deciding how much of a difference and what kinds of differences are required to place any two organisms in different classes. Such decisions should depend on the problems under consideration, of course.

A major point of controversy in classifying early hominids involves the criteria for making distinctions at the species and genus levels, specifically, to how many different genera and species do the early hominid fossils belong? One definition of a genus and a species is:

> The species within a genus form a phylogenetic unit, descended from a common ancestor and functionally adapted to a similar mode of life. The genus . . . is a group of one or more closely related phyletic lineages along which discontinuous segments or "species lineages" are recognized. All members of the genus share a fundamental adaptive zone different in some particular way from that of other such groups. This adaptive zone may or may not be precisely definable, but it is inferred by the common possession of a particular suite of functionally integrated characters. (Maglio 1973: 14)

To illustrate, the genus *Canis* includes the common domesticated dog (*Canis familiaris*), the wolf (*Canis lupus*), the jackal (*Canis aureus*), and a variety of other very similar animals that differ in specific ways but look very much alike and "make their living" in fundamentally similar ways. Even though the Arctic wolf lives in a very different environment from the African jackal, both are social predators who eat the same types of animals and live in similar social units.

The classic definition of species also commonly carried the idea of reproductive isolation: that for any of several reasons different species do not mate or biologically cannot produce viable and fertile offspring. A frequent barrier to the mating of different species is simply the great geographical distances that separate them, but even contiguous populations may be prevented from fertile matings by evolutionary changes in their biological and genetic characteristics.

The application of these and other ideas about classification to the hominid fossil record has often been a matter of trying to apply to the hominid bones the same kinds of distinctions used to define modern species, but in the case of the ancient hominids we lack precise control over the range of intraspecies variation in physical features, and we also lack information about the ecological relationships among early hominids. For example, when examining two specimens of *Australopithecus africanus,* we may be dealing with individuals who lived a million and a half years apart, were of different sexes, and may have lived as part of populations adapted to different environmental zones. Given these taxonomic considerations, the division of early hominids into different genera and species involves great difficulties.

The simplest taxonomic approach is to lump all Australopithecines and supposed early *Homo* into one category, *Homo africanus,* which is assumed to be the direct lineal ancestor of *H. erectus* and ourselves (Brace 1967; 1973; Wolpoff 1973). From this perspective, the variation in brain size, skull shape, and other features observed in early hominids can be viewed in the same way as the size differences between males and females and the subspecies variation one finds in every animal population. No species distinctions are made between modern-day "races" of mankind, even between pygmies and other larger populations, and thus it can be argued that, in view of our poor chronological information, the size and other differences observed among the early fossils are insufficient to warrant their division into different genera.

Regarding this view, anthropologist C. Loring Brace maintains that the evidence for the tool-using abilities of the Australopithecines is overwhelming. He notes that the Australopithecines were upright bipedal animals with, compared to other primates, reduced jaw and teeth size. How else, Brace asks, could such a slow, diurnal creature, lacking any dental or other defenses, survive in the competitive world of the African savannas? In this same context Brace has also argued that the use of tools and the cultural behaviors associated with this facility represent an *ecological niche* (1967: 56). Biologists have noted that every species of animal has its own particular kinds of food sources, although similar species tend to overlap somewhat, and "the likelihood of stable coexistence between species varies inversely with their degree of ecological similarity" (Swedlund 1974: 520). If two very similar animals exploit essentially the same food resources in the same way (occupy the same ecological niche), we would expect that eventually one of the species will become extinct. This principle of *competitive exclusion* has been demonstrated in the laboratory by placing two very similar species of flour beetles in the same vessel of flour: inevitably, the extinction of one of the species results.

If we consider the use of stone tools and the mental capacities such tools imply to constitute an ecological niche, then we might not expect that there would be more than one genus of tool users at any single time during the evolution of the hominids. In fact, Brace argues there would not even be two different species of tool users at one time (1967: 56–57).

There is some support for Brace's position, in that tool use and cultural behavior seem quickly and dramatically to have suppressed the rate of speciation in hominids. Today *Homo sapiens sapiens* from the Arctic to the deserts of Australia exhibit no differences approaching those required to classify us into different species, and it is now generally accepted that there has been only one species of hominid since about 120,000 years ago, when *Homo sapiens neanderthalensis* first appeared. No other animal, except those domesticated by humans, has occupied anything like an equivalent range of environments over an equivalent length of time without undergoing speciation. Obviously then, tool use and cultural behavior effectively change the natural selective pressures that induce speciation; but the question is, how much was this also a factor in the period of initial tool use some several millions of years ago?

Some anthropologists dispute the appropriateness of the competitive exclusion principle as applied to the first tool-using hominids, and many in this camp argue that there were probably two or more species of Australopithecines living contemporaneously, and that one or more of these species had the capacity to make stone tools. Regarding the possibility that the physical variation between *A. africanus* and *A. robustus* may be simply the difference between males and females, they note that some South African sites contain as many as eight individual Australopithecines that seem to belong to just one of these types—an unlikely sorting if these are really all males or females. Further, they note that *A. robustus* apparently lived long after *A. africanus* disappeared, an impossibility if these are two different sexes. Sexing and dating these fossils is difficult and the matter of the sexual dimorphism is not entirely resolved, but in view of this evidence many anthropologists now believe that there were two species of Australopithecines, and that *A. robustus* may have become extinct without issue, while *A. africanus* gave rise to early *Homo* and thus ourselves. Several variants of this scheme have been proposed, differing in the date of separation of the various groups and other details (Figure 4.11).

An alternative scheme is that none of the Australopithecines were ancestral to the human line, that they in fact were contemporaries of early representatives of the genus *Homo*. This position is based on the discovery by Richard Leakey of the 1470 Skull in the East Turkana area, on Mary Leakey's discovery in 1975 at Laetolil of a possible *Homo* provisionally dated to between 3.3 and 3.7 million years ago, and on other recent finds in East Africa. In each of these cases, however, controversies have arisen about the dates of the fossils, their physical reconstruction, and the importance of their morphological differences from other fossils. In the case of Skull 1470, Richard Leakey's original age estimate of about 3 million years is now widely considered to be erroneous, with a figure of about 2 million years being much more likely (Figure 4.12).

It is apparent that resolution of these controversies will require many additional fossils and, more importantly, better models and hypotheses. As Swedland has demonstrated (1974), many earlier ideas about, for example, one form of Australopithecine "driving" other forms into extinction by direct competition and about the supposed re-

4.11
Graphical representation of various hypothetical reconstructions of human evolution. The multiplication of branches in later reconstructions may be a misinterpretation of natural population variability, but samples are at present too small to determine this.

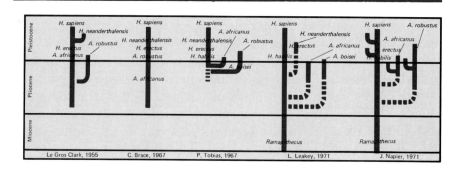

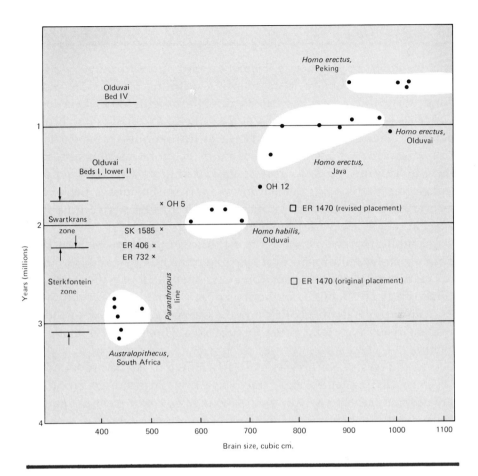

4.12

The increase in hominid cranial capacity over time. Estimates of dates and cranial volumes are subject to considerable error. The small "x"s mark fossils assigned by some to the genus *Paranthropus*.

lationships of these early hominids simply do not seem to square with ecological relationships evident among contemporary animal species.

AUSTRALOPITHECINES OUTSIDE AFRICA   In 1941 a single hominid mandible fragment was found in Java just above a geological level provisionally dated to about 1.8 million years ago. In thickness of bone this fossil is indistinguishable from a robust Australopithecine, but in tooth size and shape it seems to be very close to the *Homo erectus* remains from Choukoutien, China (Robinson 1953). Some have called this fossil an *Australopithecus*, others a *Homo erectus,* and still others a *Meganthropus paleojavanicus*. Other fossils exhibiting some of the same characteristics were later discovered near the original find. One fossil might be a freak, but when two show the same characteristics one begins to suspect that a creature with a mixture of *Australopithecus* and *Homo erectus* features was already in Java—and therefore, presumably, elsewhere in Southeast Asia—by at least 2 to 1.8 million years ago, and perhaps earlier (Sartono 1975). Lending support to this idea is the recent discovery of several teeth in various sites in central eastern China that some have classified as Australopithecine.

Complicating the picture is the discovery in the Djetis beds on Java of an incomplete adult male skull, a complete skull of a child (less than two years old), plus three mandibular fragments, all of which date radiometrically to about 1.9 million years ago (Von Koenigswald 1975: 306). Their general morphology and the estimated volume of the adult cranium (900 cc.) would seem to suggest a *Homo erectus* grade of hominid.

All the Australopithecines and early *Homo* in Africa are found in a savanna environment, yet to reach Java from Africa, even given the very different climates of millions of years ago, would seem to require that successive generations of these early hominids adapted to tropical rainforests or coastal areas. Adapting to a tropical rainforest would appear to be extremely difficult for Australopithecines or even for *Homo erectus,* because there are very few food resources on the forest floor. Possibly the intertidal zones were more productive; unfortunately, any trace of human occupation here would have been erased by the fluctuating sea levels of the last hundred thousand years.

What does this all mean in terms of the probable course of hominid evolution? Again, it is simply too early to say. It might mean that the transition from *Australopithecus* to *Homo erectus* was made earlier in Java than in Africa—if the transition took place at all. Since the "Australopithecine" jaw fragment at Djetis comes from a level beneath that of the so-called *Homo erectus* specimens, this is at least a possibility. It might also mean that by about 2 million years ago Australopithecines had radiated out into most of the warmer latitudes of the Old World; and if we are to accept the schemes that have them becoming extinct without issue, we must explain how this extinction could have taken place over such an enormous range. We would assume this range would have been possible in the first place only through the use of tools, and thus we come back to the problem of culture as an ecological niche and the competitive exclusion principle. If, on the other hand, the Australopithecines were not tool users, and were specifically adapted to savanna environments, how could they have made it through all these contrasting environments into China and perhaps Java? Another possibility is that there were two or more independent centers of evolution of *Homo erectus,* one in Africa and one in Southeast Asia. There may even have been independent centers of evolution of an Australopithecine-type hominid, given the similarities between the two Javanese mandible fragments and *Paranthropus* (or, *Australopithecus robustus*) material from Africa, but this is not likely.

Clarification of the relationship of the Javanese and African materials will require many more fossil finds and additional years of research, as will the more general problem of the reconstruction of hominid phylogeny. At this point it is not useful to argue too vehemently or in too much detail all the possible routes by which we might have evolved, and our presentation of the problem here is intended mainly as background for the more general problems of human ecology.

THE EVOLUTION OF HUMAN BEHAVIOR

Whatever the exact phylogenetic relationship of the various early hominids, we are still faced with the problem of identifying the forces and mechanisms that produced the first culture-bearing animals and, ultimately, were responsible for the special abilities of *Homo sapiens sapiens.* Our evidence on this problem comes from several sources.

Comparative Primatology

Because chimpanzees, baboons, and other primates inhabit physical environments similar to those in which our first culture-bearing ancestors appeared, a study of the physical and behavioral characteristics that distinguish us from other primates may enable us to construct some testable ideas about the origins of culture. Given our assumptions about the nature of biological evolution, we must assume that we share a distant ancestor with other primates and that the differences between the contemporary descendants of this ancestor are a compressed and detailed record of the environments our respective ancestors have inhabited since our divergence.

One obvious point of comparison is that, scaled according to body size, we have a much larger brain volume than any other animal. In fact, even in absolute terms, human brains average about 1,000 cc more than the largest primates, the central African gorillas.

A second point of comparison involves *sexual dimorphisms,* the physical differences between the males and females of each species. Among some primate species, one of the most evident sexual dimorphisms is simple physical size, although a survey of numerous primate species (Napier and Napier 1967) indicates that a pronounced size difference between the sexes is relatively infrequent, being largely confined to the Old World apes. In fact, in about 25 percent of all mammal species the females are larger than the males, even in such diverse types of animals as certain species of whales, antelopes, and rabbits. We must assume then that "marked morphological and behavioral dimorphism is not a primitive characteristic of primates but has evolved in certain genera in relation to particular patterns of living" (Crook 1972: 235).

One clue as to what patterns of living these might have been can be seen in the size differences of the sexes in living nonhuman primates. Male and female gibbons, who spend most of their lives in trees, are almost identical in size; among chimpanzees, who spend some of their time on the ground, males are usually larger than females; and among gorillas, who are almost completely terrestrial, males average almost twice the size of females. Why should the physical size of the sexes show this association with terrain?

One probable factor in the evolution of both sexual dimorphisms and the overall increase in size of *Homo sapiens sapiens* of both sexes is the need for defense against predators. Our ancestors apparently evolved in open savanna-type environments where competition and predation by large cats and other carnivores would have been significant, and thus it is not at all surprising that part of our evolution in these environments would have been in the direction of greater physical size. A human with a rifle, or even a crude spear, would have some reasonable defenses, but until tool use reached this point there would no doubt have been strong direct selection for increasing physical size. It must be remembered that our earliest tool-using ancestors were only about three or four feet tall, weighing perhaps sixty or seventy pounds— not too formidable compared with their competitors. Today, on the savannas of Africa, baboon populations are able to survive, despite occasional predation by leopards and lions, partly because they have retained impressive canine and incisor teeth (Figure 4.13). By Ramapithecine times, however, our ancestors had probably lost these dental defenses.

Another possible explanation of primate sexual dimorphism concerns "sexual selection." Charles Darwin was among the earliest modern naturalists to argue that these size differences arose in some species because reproductive success was to a great extent determined by the physical size of the males: males competed with other males for sexually receptive females, and the largest, strongest ones won and passed on their own genetic components. The larger males would transmit their genes to both males and females, of course, and thus we might expect an increase in overall size. But size is under hormonal control too, and for reasons not entirely understood the environment can activate growth

4.13
Baboon eating small antelope.

potential differently in males and females. Size differences may also be the result of female choice, if females consistently choose mates larger or smaller than average size.

In some animal species sexual dimorphisms seem to be linked to differences in feeding strategies of males and females, and while this may have been of some importance to our early primate ancestors, the kinds of food eaten by males and females probably overlapped considerably soon after tool use and embryonic human social organizations formed (Pianka 1974). Nonetheless, early hominid males and females would probably have been under increasingly different selective pressures as soon as males began specializing in hunting and females in gathering—specializations that may have appeared only comparatively late and sporadically.

Crook (1972) points out one sexual dimorphism in humans that may be tied to subsistence specializations, namely that for every 100 female children conceived, 120 males are conceived, although of these only 105 survive to birth (also, mortality is 25 percent higher for males in the first year of life). This gender imbalance may be a compensation for the greater male mortality resulting from the greater rigors of hunting and other activities males might have specialized in early on in hominid evolution, although a 1 : 1 sex ratio is certainly not a necessary element for human survival.

Subsistence specializations may also have changed selective pressures to produce in males somewhat greater physical strength, on the average. This extends to more than simple gross musculature: males have a stronger heart than females and have more red blood cells per unit volume of blood. Again, one interpretation of this would seem to be that through our evolutionary history there has been a greater positive selection for these characteristics in males than in females as a result of the requirements of having to defend the group against predators, of having to be effective predators themselves, and, perhaps, of competition among males for females.

One other aspect of sexual dimorphism among humans is particularly intriguing when seen in comparison with nonhuman primates: namely, the secondary sexual characteristics that differentiate human males and females. Among human females, breasts are significantly larger than among males—in fact, the size, shape, and other differences distinguishing male and female breasts are much more pronounced than in any other mammal species. This difference cannot be explained in terms of function, since breast size seems to have almost no relationship to effective functioning in human beings. Similarly, the human penis is far larger, relatively and absolutely, than that of any other primate, including the gorilla. In addition, human females have softer skin and higher voices than males and have lost more of their body hair—although compared to the other species of primates, males also have remarkably little body hair.

Another major difference between humans and other animals is that human females do not exhibit *estrus;* that is, women's receptivity to sexual intercourse does not seem to increase in any large degree with the rise in estrogen levels that precedes ovulation. This contrasts with other nonhuman primates, where female sexual receptivity often varies considerably during periods determined by estrogen levels. Again, this is a matter of degree, and it is perhaps unnecessary to point out that human females are not constantly sexually receptive; but as a statistical generalization, they are much more so than other female primates. How can we account for this puzzling evolutionary development?

One interesting possibility is that

> in all probability the evolutionary development of hair reduction, increased skin sensitivity and tactile changes involving skin tension were [sic] all associated with increasing the tactile sensations of coital body contact especially in the frontal presentation. Likewise the breasts of young women taken together with other features (limb contour, complexion, and the like) seem to represent the main visual sexual releasers for the male. While the latter features may have been due to straightforward intersexual selection by ancient males the former features have probably been selected in both sexes for their effect in improving sexual rewards, in inducing sexual love and in maintaining pair bonds. The same is also likely to be true for the presence of orgasm in women and the absence of the more typical mammalian estrus. The functional significance of all these correlated changes is most plausibly seen within the context of the adaptations of seed-eating and of later partially carnivorous protohominids to open country life with associated shifts in social organization. (Crook 1972: 254)

Crook's suggested link between adaptations to savanna environments and the evolution of human sexual dimorphisms bears directly on our major problem here, the determinants of the evolution of culture, and it suggests that we might be able to learn something about this by examining behavior patterns in nonhuman primates.

Comparative Primate Ethology

One approach has been to specify exactly what differentiates humans from nonhuman primates in terms of behavior patterns, and then to hypothesize ways in which these different patterns might have been a selective advantage under the conditions thought to have existed when culture-bearing animals first evolved.

Although studies of this kind have been going on for some years, many earlier researchers concentrated on zoo populations. The behavioral effects produced by these artificial environments in such decidedly untropical settings as Detroit, St. Louis, and Washington were not fully appreciated by some early researchers, and the phenomenal levels of homosexuality, parental rejection of young, aggressiveness, withdrawal, and other apparently dysfunctional behaviors led many early researchers to some bizarre speculations about hominid origins.

However, once investigators in the late 1950s and early 1960s began to observe these animals in their natural habitats, a very different picture of primate behavior began to emerge.

BABOONS   Baboons inhabit a diversity of environments, but our most reliable and complete information comes from savanna-adapted populations in central and East Africa. Savannas are relatively flat, arid expanses with scattered trees and occasional water holes, and their mixed grasses, shrubs, and other plants usually support very high densities of grazing animals such as zebras, buffalos, and other ungulates.

Unlike the humans who inhabit this area, baboons, although having complex and efficient communication systems, do not possess "language." Efforts to teach nonhuman primates to use colored discs, light switches, or other implements notwithstanding, it is apparent that neither baboons nor any other primate can use symbols at anything like the level any normal human can. Similarly, while baboons have been observed using sticks and stones for minor manipulations of the environment, this behavior is sporadic, largely unplanned, and does not seem to increase in range or efficiency from generation to generation, as does human tool use.

Consider also the matter of what zoologists call a *dominance hierarchy*. The strong dominance hierarchy of baboons is expressed in many ways, but most obviously in access to food and sex. Within the baboon troop the eldest males have almost unimpeded access to food and sex,

4.14
Baboon troop moving in defensive formation across open country, with older males and juveniles guarding females and dependent young.

and they protect their privileges with aggressive behavior. Younger males are allowed access to females only on the sufferance of more dominant males, although they are constantly testing this dominance by attempting to strike up meaningful relationships with concupiscent females. Often this will incite a dominant male to charge and make threatening gestures and rude remarks. Similarly, when desirable but limited food is available, such as fruit or a clutch of eggs, the dominant males and females take what they want first. A mother and child may share some foods, but there is no systematic food sharing between adult members of the group.

Thus, in trying to explain how culture-bearing individuals developed from our primate ancestors, we must look for factors or conditions that would tend to break down these dominance hierarchies and promote the distinctive human family structure, with its food sharing, division of labor, and pair bonding.

When baboon troops move across savanna or open environments, they typically position members according to age and sex, as illustrated in Figure 4.14. Adolescent males are on the periphery, adult, dominant males are in the center, adult females are behind the adult males, and dependent young are stationed near the adult females. This is of course an excellent defensive formation, offering the best protection to the

4.15
Chimpanzees frequently hunt small and medium-size mammals. They are the only primates other than man whose adults regularly share food with each other.

young and females, upon whom the perpetuation of the group depends. There are many more adolescent males than necessary for reproduction, so although they would suffer the most losses to predators, the stability of the group would not suffer much. Significantly, when the baboon troop moves into more forested areas, the positioning becomes much more fluid and dispersed, indicating, not too surprisingly, that terrain is an important determinant of behavior for baboons, and that savanna environments seem to put a premium on group cohesiveness and dominance hierarchies.

Before we attempt to apply this observation to human origins, let us consider several contrasts between baboon behavior and that of chimpanzees, whom blood studies reveal to be our closest relatives.

CHIMPANZEES Chimpanzees also inhabit diverse environments, and generalizations about their behavior are as dangerous as in the case of baboons. But the most studied chimpanzees are those of the dense forests of Tanzania, and they form the basis for our discussion here.

The chimpanzees of this area behave very differently from the savanna-dwelling baboons. Access to food and sex is much less rigidly controlled, and the entire dominance hierarchy seems to be less in evidence. In one instance where a female was sexually receptive for a record twenty-one days, the males of the chimpanzee group, young and old alike, stood in line for her favors with only minor apparent bickering (von Lawick-Goodall 1971). Strictly speaking, chimpanzees do not have true estrus cycles, but they do have periods of greater and lesser sexual receptivity. This is not always typical behavior, and the adolescents were effectively barred from mating with some females in many cases, but in comparison with baboons, chimpanzees are absolute libertines in sexual matters.

Similarly, there is also a diminution of territoriality. Chimpanzees run for kilometers along trails through the forests, often alone or with one or two others, and individuals frequently leave one small group to go live with another. So relaxed are chimpanzees, in fact, about sex and territoriality, that they have aroused envious feelings in some human observers. "Chimpanzees, it seems, successfully achieve what *Homo sapiens* radicals only dream of: peaceful, non-competitive, non-coercive, non-possessive, egalitarian, jealousy-free, promiscuous, non-tyrannical communes" (Van den Berghe 1972: 772).

Many studies have shown that this may be a somewhat idealized picture. Chimpanzees have elaborate threat rituals and do menace each other according to a well-developed hierarchy. In addition, chimpanzees are the only animals besides ourselves who regularly use objects as weapons, usually wooden clubs or thrown rocks and debris (von Lawick-Goodall 1971). They fight over food and females, and sometimes over rank (von Lawick-Goodall 1968, 1971, 1973), and they are the only other primates known to practice cannibalism, having been observed on several occasions eating young chimps alive.

Books such as *African Genesis* by Robert Ardrey and *The Naked Ape* by Desmond Morris argue that much of our mentality, anatomy, and physiology is a result of millions of years of bloody, relentless hunting and killing. Indeed, if we look at chimpanzee predatory behavior we see that in its emotional content and its implications, hunting and meat eating may not be just another way of getting food. Primatologist G. Teleki (1973) has observed the hunting behavior of chimpanzees, and he found that hunting, loss of estrus, economic reciprocity, and human family structure may be intimately interrelated. He notes that adult males often cooperate in hunting small mammals and that there is a partial suspension of the dominance hierarchy during these times, as demonstrated by the fact that a low-dominance male sometimes leads the hunt. Significantly, although females and juveniles participate in hunting only rarely, they are often given meat by the males who make the kills, and females who are sexually receptive are more likely to get and eat meat (Symonds 1975: 46–47). Symonds describes how this might have contributed to the evolution of hominid social structure:

> Thus, there may have been a pattern in early human evolution in which the amount of meat a female received from males was directly proportional to the length of time she was in estrus, providing strong selective pressures for continued fertility and receptivity during lactation and an increasing segment of a female's cycle. Selection might then favor males who used surplus meat to increase their reproductive success at the expense of other males. (ibid.: 47–48)

If these speculations are correct they would at least demonstrate the accuracy of the epigram about the world's oldest profession. But we must be cautious about reading our whole evolutionary history in these few observations; a great deal more research must be done before we can assume these important links between loss of estrus, hunting, and food sharing (for a somewhat different perspective see Martin and Voorhies 1975).

CONTEMPORARY HUMAN HUNTERS AND GATHERERS

While the study of nonhuman primates offers many stimulating ideas about cultural origins, all tool-using, culture-bearing humans are very different from other animals in their potential and adaptations. For this reason, many anthropologists have tried to complement primatological studies with ethnographic studies of contemporary or recent "primitive peoples" who still live at an ecological and technological level similar to that of our earlier ancestors.

The expansion of industrialization has been such that although anthropologists do not really outnumber living hunters and gatherers, it is a certainty they soon will: people who get most of their resources from hunting and gathering undomesticated animals and plants persist only in the Arctic, Australia, South America, Africa, and a few other places, and even in these marginal areas hunters and gatherers have been much influenced by trade, disease, and other "disruptive" contacts with more complex societies.

Nonetheless, some aspects of contemporary or recent hunting and gathering societies may be relevant to the problem of the origins of culture, particularly in the case of the Kalahari Bushmen, a group that until recently inhabited many areas of the African savannas where we find evidence of our first culture-bearing ancestors.

The low level of productivity of the Bushmen's hot, arid environment, as manipulated by their simple technology (bows, arrows, digging sticks, etc.), requires that they spend most of the year in groups of twenty-five people or less, often on the move from one camp to another. Most of their diet is made up of vegetable products, tortoises, and other small game, but occasionally giraffes and other large animals are killed, usually through cooperative hunting by several males. There is no formal "leader" among the Bushmen, but a man may achieve some measure of prestige by being particularly good at hunting, tracking, or singing. No one, however, can claim more food or other resources simply because of his or her status. As in most if not all hunting and gathering societies, males have greater prestige than females, although females provide the bulk of the group's food by gathering and processing plants and eggs, nestlings, turtles, and other small animals. Bushman economic life is dominated by the principle of reciprocity: food and other resources are exchanged among kinsmen, balancing out the periodic shortages that may afflict any member or nuclear family in the band.

Like most hunting and gathering societies, the Bushmen are at least somewhat territorial. They move often but always within a relatively restricted region, usually twenty-five to thirty kilometers in all directions from a central water hole or home base.

Clearly, some degree of territoriality is an advantage if resources are not uniformly distributed; it is an advantage to know where reliable sources of flint, vegetables, game animals, and water are within one's territory, and the group forced out of its territory is faced with unpredictable supplies and, perhaps, the hostility of the group whose territory they are trespassing upon. Thus, any models or reconstructions we make regarding our early hominid ancestors should incorporate the assumption that they were probably at least loosely territorial.

The Kalahari Bushmen's culture also suggests that people living at this cultural level have devised highly efficient mechanisms for regulating their population densities according to the productivity of the environment. Through abortion, infanticide, and marriage rules the

Bushmen scale their numbers to a level far below that which could be supported in any average year, and studies of other animals suggest that this is a common strategy: there is a selective survival advantage to keeping densities below the absolute limits of the environment because this protects a population from the "boom or bust" cycles that eventually may put it on the edge of extinction.

MODELS OF CULTURAL ORIGINS

Our review of the paleontological, primatological, and ethnological background to the problem of the origins of culture has underscored the differences between humans and other primates and has alluded to some of the factors that may have been important in the evolution of culture. Let us consider at this point some of the ideas, or models, about how these differences were produced.

First, we should note that despite the models of early hominid behavior based on primate studies, and despite the seeming importance of savanna adaptations in cultural origins, it is still entirely possible that the fundamental steps in the origins of cultural behavior were taken long before stone-tool use and the relatively big-brained Australopithecines appeared on the African savannas. Changes in a predominantly vegetarian diet during Ramapithecine times may have begun inexorable changes in selective pressure on group structures, use of hands, and posture such that the appearance and forms of early cultural behavior were determined long before the radiation of the Australopithecines and early *Homo*.

On the other hand, although the first intimations of cultural behavior may have appeared among forest- or savanna-adapted Ramapithecine-type primates, adaptations to savanna environments by primates already using simple tools may have been an important part of later human evolution. Food sharing and group cooperation, for example, may have been shaped by our millions of years on the savanna. Baboons are savanna-adapted, yet they retain large canines and strict dominance hierarchies. We must explain how roughly similar savanna environments produced such different evolutionary trajectories in humans and baboons, and we must also consider the behavioral similarities between people and group-hunting canids, such as wolves, jackals, and dogs, all

of whom inhabit savanna and other open habitats and exhibit systematic food sharing between adults, sexual division of labor, relatively reduced dominance hierarchies, and relatively large home ranges. Thus,
savannas and other open environments appear to have selected for some
similarities and some differences in the behavior patterns of humans,
baboons, and canids, and we are unable at this point to untangle completely the evolutionary processes that produced these similarities and
differences. Obviously, the use of tools was a crucial element here.

The importance of tools to our ancestors can perhaps best be appreciated if one imagines oneself standing on the Serengeti Plain of 3
million years ago, trying to eat a small antelope one has just killed.
Half-starved and already harried by vultures and other scavengers, one
tries to rip into the body with one's teeth and nails. Even with the
relatively stout dentition of *Australopithecus,* or of our most distant
relative, *Ramapithecus,* it would have been almost a hopeless task. The
most nutritious parts, the liver, brain, and other internal organs, are
protected by thick layers of skin, flesh, and bone that resist the puny
tearing motions to which our ancestors would have been limited. But
with a single sharp piece of stone! Just a chip off one of the quartz pebbles abundantly scattered over this area would instantly have opened up
life-saving rations for several individuals.

With cooperative hunting and stone tools then, a vast new niche
would have opened to our ancestors. Even in our zoologically impoverished era a recent survey of Albert National Park, along the Ugandan
border, revealed hippopotami, antelopes, elephants, and other large
mammals in such numbers that there are an average of 130,000 pounds
of big game per square mile (Pfeiffer 1978: 128).

As zoologists George Schaller and Gordon Lowther note:

> The means by which scavenging and hunting hominids might fit into
> the ecological community without competing too extensively with other
> predators pose a number of questions. Their primate heritage suggests
> that they were diurnal, and selection pressure from their primate and
> carnivore way of life undoubtedly favored a social existence. The only
> other diurnal social carnivore is the wild dog, which hunts at dawn and
> dusk, and favors prey weighing 60 kilograms or less (about 130 pounds).
> An ecological opening exists for a social predator hunting large animals
> and scavenging during the day, an opening some early hominid may
> well have filled, assuming that none of the saber-toothed cats did so.
> (1969)

The sequence in which savanna adaptations, tool use, cooperative hunting, and cultural behavior appeared, and the possible interrelationships of these factors, constitute a complex problem. The first hominids probably developed out of a primate stock that had already adapted to savanna environments. It is significant that the oldest Australopithecine foot remains from Olduvai Gorge (1.8 million years ago) differ only in minor characteristics from our own (Poirier 1973: 87). Upright posture was not fully developed among the early Australopithecines, but the changes in hominid foot anatomy may mean that bipedalism and upright posture were initially unassociated with tools and resulted mainly from adapting to a savanna habitat. This development would free the hands, however, making tool use a considerable, but not really unexpected, accomplishment.

Chimpanzees frequently use small natural objects as tools. They have been observed stripping leaves off small twigs which they then insert in termite hives in order to "fish" for termites to eat, and they regularly use wadded up leaves to soak up drinking water from stumps and puddles. They also throw sticks and stones in aggression displays. Some anthropologists even consider chimpanzee tool use sufficient to qualify them as "protocultural" animals, and it is possible that semi-erect, increasingly bipedal primates in savanna environments were similarly making and using stick and unaltered stone artifacts long before the first chipped stone tools appeared several million years ago. If so, how can we mesh this developmental sequence with Schaller and Lowther's suggestion about an ecological niche being open for a social predator, hunting large animals and scavenging during the day? And how could this have been related to other aspects of cultural evolution?

Some have argued that systematic predation in savanna environments would have been the major factor in this developmental sequence; specifically, that group cooperation, food sharing, language, and other cultural behavior developed out of the selective forces that would come into play as hominids adapted to savanna environments and a reliance on big-game hunting (Cachel 1975). Already by 5 million years ago our ancestors had lost their dental defenses and were comparatively slow of foot, and big-game hunting would have been at least a possible way of surviving. We know climates in eastern and southern Africa were drier just prior to the periods when the first stone tools appeared, and possibly the increasing aridity forced some of our ancestors to expand their reliance on hunting. Some marginally habitable savanna environments, in particular, would have selected for increased hunting, for here meat may have been the difference between survival and starvation. Once meat eating became important, loss of estrus, stone-tool manufacture, social networks, and other cultural expressions might have been linked in sequence, similar to the sequence suggested by studies of chimpanzees (p. 121).

There are, however, a number of severe problems with this attractively simple scenario, particularly in the matter of big-game hunting. Early hominids, even those with crude stone tools, would have had a difficult time capturing and killing large game, even if they were alone on the savannas, simply because they were small and slow and faced ferocious competition from lions, canids, and other predators. Thus, other scholars suggest our ancestors combined scavenging and hunting small game with intensive foraging for eggs, plants, and other small resources. Even scavenging is not as easy as it might sound. Many animals die and are killed in savanna environments, but predators eat most of their kills within six or seven hours, and competition from canids and other scavengers is considerable. Washburn notes that if baboons in areas of Africa where there are still many lions tried to subsist on scavenging, they would have difficulty obtaining an ounce of meat a day per baboon (1968); it is noteworthy that no other primates appear to scavenge (Poirier 1973: 108).

Even if their scavenging was quite limited, early hominids could still significantly augment their vegetable foods by turning, not to big-game hunting, but to the hunting of sick and newborn animals. Competition would have been severe, but using group strategy and their evolving intelligence early hominids could have stalked these sick and young animals, causing them to "freeze," making them easy prey. Bushmen and other groups regularly engage in this sort of predation, and such kills can be supplemented by gathering eggs, invertebrates, tortoises, colonial nesting birds, and similar resources.

These forms of small-game hunting and scavenging would have rewarded group cooperation, reduced dominance hierarchies, improved communication systems, and encouraged the development of stone tools for processing meat and vegetable foods.

In summary, there are several conflicting ideas or models about the origins of culture, with some scholars stressing the importance of big-game hunting, others the importance of scavenging and other types of adaptations. Let us turn now to an examination of the archaeological evidence, in order to determine which, if any, of these models fits the evidence.

THE ARCHAEOLOGICAL RECORD AND
THE ORIGINS OF CULTURE

Archaeologists the world over have a recurrent fantasy in which it is early morning, about 2.8 million years ago, at a water hole on the East African savanna. Thousands of animals, including many of the first hominids, have come together, the hominids to scavenge, collect plant foods, and prey on the drinking animals. After hunting and killing animals and collecting other foods, the hominids make more tools, butcher the animals, eat them, and then disperse into their social units to sleep it off. Suddenly a nearby volcano becomes active, spewing out clouds of poison gas, dust, ash, and red-hot particles, killing all of the animals, including the hominids. The hominids and their tools and prey would thus be perfectly preserved under a thick blanket of protective ash, which would also facilitate radiometric dating. Although such sites have not been found, a catastrophe of this type is not impossible. In 1902 on Martinique about 28,000 people were killed within minutes when a volcanic eruption sent a landslide of ash, lava, and debris cascading over part of the island.

In the "real" world, however, our evidence of the initial period of the evolution of culture is extremely meager, and we are limited to just a few small sites, almost all of which are in southern and eastern Africa.

Olduvai Gorge

About 5 million years ago a large lake covered about 130 square kilometers of what today is the Serengeti Plain, in central East Africa. Countless generations of animals, including, no doubt, our hominid ancestors, lived near this lake and the streams that fed it, and today fossilized bones are thickly distributed through the black clay of the ancient shoreline and lake bed. About a half million years before the appearance of culture-bearing animals in this part of the world, the lake and the adjacent areas were the scene of dramatic geological activity. Volcanoes near the lake had been erupting for millions of years, and there was a particularly violent episode about a million and a half years ago, when a volcano to the south of the lake covered it and surrounding areas with a layer of ash and molten rock some 5 meters thick. Similar eruptions occurred in succeeding millennia, and today we can measure the intensity of each volcanic episode by gauging the thickness of each superimposed ash level. Sometime during and after these volcanic eruptions the climate of the area began a cycle of alternating dry and wet periods. For thousands of years it became drier, causing the lake to shrink in size, as millions of tons of windblown sand were deposited in the area. Other times rainfall increased and the lake regained its previous size, as demonstrated by the thousands of crocodile teeth found in these levels. These millions of years of volcanic activity and climatic change eventually covered the original lake and adjacent lands with a 100-meter-thick deposit of sand, ash, and lake sediments, the surface of which is the present Serengeti Plain. Ancient floods cut down through this plain at several points, revealing scores of archaeological sites.

DK I   Site DK I has been radiometrically dated to about 1.75 million years ago, making it one of the oldest in Olduvai Gorge. The site is composed of a layer several meters thick of bones, worked and unworked stone, and other debris. Because of the complex stratigraphy, it is difficult to separate this accumulation into different levels with any assurance that the divisions represent discrete hominid occupations.

The most prominent archaeological feature at DK I is a semicircle of stones (Figure 4.16) lying within a concentration of stone and animal bones. Measuring approximately 3 meters in diameter and made of chunks of vesicular basalt, this feature is interpreted by many as a foundation for a windbreak or some other temporary structure. Some stones are piled in small heaps; elsewhere they appear regularly spaced at intervals of about 60 centimeters.

The tools found here are similar to the other materials from Beds I and II at Olduvai: hundreds of crudely flaked stones, some of them showing evidence of use, others simply byproducts of the manufacturing process. The Leakeys labeled these stones as "cleavers," "hammerstones," "scrapers," and so forth, but we really don't know how they were used.

FLK I   This site is particularly important because several hominid bone fragments were found in its various levels, including the remains of an early hominid that Leakey named *Zinjanthropus*. This "Zinjanthropus floor" covers an area of more than 1,036 square meters and contains over 4,000 pieces of worked stone. Many stone artifacts and pieces of shattered bone are concentrated in a "working area" some 5 meters in diameter, and a relatively clear arc-shaped area in the midst of all this debris suggests that there may have been a temporary shelter here.

FLK N6   Level 6 of site FLK N, Upper Bed I, is interesting because it contained an almost complete elephant skeleton surrounded by about

4.16
DKI. Plan of the stone circle and the remains on the occupation surface. Stones, including artifacts, are shown in black. Fossil bones are shown in outline.

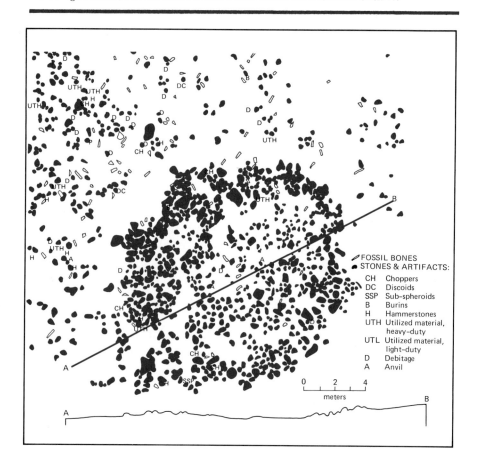

FOSSIL BONES
STONES & ARTIFACTS:

CH   Choppers
DC   Discoids
SSP   Sub-spheroids
B   Burins
H   Hammerstones
UTH   Utilized material,
          heavy-duty
UTL   Utilized material,
          light-duty
D   Debitage
A   Anvil

0   2   4
meters

thirty stone tools. The displacement of the bones, the types of stone tools found, and the absence of any other animal bones suggest that this was probably a "primary butchering" or "kill" site, that is, an area where an elephant was killed and butchered by early hominids. Possibly the animal was killed by some other predator and only scavenged by the humans, but there is little question the animal was consumed in some fashion by early hominids.

STATISTICAL ANALYSIS OF OLDUVAI SITES   There are scores of archaeological sites in Olduvai Gorge in addition to the three we have described here, all of the same approximate size, shape, and character; that is, small concentrations of bones and stones, probably representing the debris left by the foraging and scavenging activities of early hominids. Nowhere in these sites, however, is there evidence conclusively demonstrating that these hominids were systematically hunting as part of their normal subsistence system. Nor is there evidence they were aggregating into large groups—given that the largest sites yet excavated at Olduvai are only twenty to thirty meters in diameter.

On the other hand, the evidence from these sites certainly does not rule out the possibility, at least, that the individuals who made these tools and butchered these animals were systematic predators. What is needed is a somewhat more analytical approach, so that we can discern patterns not immediately evident from an impressionistic survey of the sites.

One example of a statistical analysis of the Olduwan material is presented in Table 4.4, where statistical coefficients have been calculated so as to express the spatial covariation of different kinds of artifacts: that is, what kinds of tools are found together and presumably used for the same tasks? As Table 4.4 indicates, the .83 coefficient between choppers and hammers at Olduvai suggests that they are found together in large numbers at some sites, but are both quite rare at others. In this way, four different *tool kits* have been defined: a chopper and hammer combination (.83 correlation); a lightly utilized flake (small stone fragments struck from a core) and polyhedron (worked, many-sided stones) combination (.79); discs and anvils (.91); and scrapers, which correlate with no other tools and therefore are presumed to have been used primarily by themselves or with all of the other tool kits. If we then look at these six sites and record which tool kits are most frequent at each, we begin to see some patterns. At DK I we find three of the tool kits represented in some numbers, while at FLK I only

TABLE 4.4   Statistical Analysis of Some Early Sites at Olduvai Gorge

1. Percentages* of tool types at six sites showing proportional variation from site to site:

	Site: DK I	FLK I	FLK N5	FLK NN3	FLK NN1	HWK II
Tool Type						
Choppers	12	8	37	27	23	44
Hammers	15	6	19	22	17	21
Light-utilized flakes	10	35	0	13	15	0
Polyhedrons	10	4	0	4	1	0
Discs	11	1	6	3	3	0
Anvils	6	2	8	5	3	0
Scrapers	2	20	5	1	7	3

* Columns do not sum to 100% because several tool types have been eliminated and others have been combined into a single type.

2. Calculation of a correlation coefficient* to express the strength of spatial relationships among tool types. Tool types that tend to occur together on the same sites tend to have high positive correlation coefficients and those that tend not to occur together have high negative correlations (the maximum range of the coefficient is $+1.00$ to -1.00). The coefficient used is Spearman's rank-order correlation coefficient. For statistical reasons, coefficients falling between about $+.40$ and $-.40$ are not considered "significant" because coefficients of this relatively low level are often a result of chance variation.

	Choppers	Hammers	L-U. flakes	Poly-hedrons	Discs	Anvils	Scrapers
Choppers	1.00						
Hammers	+.83	1.00					
L-U. flakes	−.78	+.50	1.00				
Polyhedrons	−.74	−.42	+.79	1.00			
Discs	−.47	−.15	−.14	+.43	1.00		
Anvils	−.20	+.03	−.21	+.20	+.91	1.00	
Scrapers	−.30	−.60	−.04	+.22	−.30	−.31	1.00

* For statistical reasons, correlation coefficients are not normally computed on percentages, in part because this procedure tends to exaggerate high positive and negative correlations.

3. Occurrences of tool kits at six early Olduvai sites:

Site:	DK I	FLK I	FLK N5	FLK NN3	FLK NN1	HWK II
Tool Kit						
Choppers & hammers heavy cutting*	+	−	+	+	+	+
L-U. flakes & polyhedrons	+	+	−	−	+	−
Discs & anvils	+	−	−	−	−	−
Scrapers scraping*	−	+	−	−	−	−

* Inferred function.
+ = present or frequent; − = rare or absent
After H. Wright. 1971.

the lightly utilized flake and polyhedron combination and scrapers are very numerous; and at the last four sites, only the chopper-hammer kit is at all frequent. There are, then, three different "types" of sites here, in terms of the tools found on them. How can we interpret this pattern?

First, DK I, where we have the most tool kits, is also the site with the semicircle of stones that may represent a windbreak or some other temporary structure. Similar constructions are used today by Kalahari Bushmen at their base camps, where they stay while not out foraging for food. To call DK I a base camp in this same sense requires a rather imaginative leap of faith, but there does seem to be a parallel here. In contrast to DK I, at FLK I we find two tool kits, one of which may have been a "light-cutting" or secondary butchering combination. Extremely small bone fragments, resulting from intensive fine butchering and marrow extraction, litter the surface of FLK I. Finally, the other four sites, FLK N5, NN3, and NN1 and HWK II, would seem to be "kill" sites or perhaps primary butchering locations. At HWK II, for example, an almost complete elephant skeleton was lying amidst stone tools, and another elephant skeleton was found in the upper levels of FLK N6. And the types of tools most common at these sites would seem most useful as killing and gross-butchering tools.

In summary, then, some of the sites in Olduvai Gorge fit into a pattern somewhat similar to that of contemporary hunters and gatherers. The patterning of tool distributions suggests that the hominids who made and used these tools lived in some ways, at least, in a manner reminiscent of the Kalahari Bushmen.

And, importantly, we can also find patterns in the animal bones at these sites. In Figure 4.17, the animal bones found at Olduvai have been classified into taxa and compared to the animal bones discarded by two groups of Kalahari Bushmen during a recent period (Speth and Davis 1976). The extremely close correspondence suggests that the Olduvai hominids in some cases ate very much the same foods as some contemporary Bushmen—at least in so far as the percentages of animal species they consumed. This close correspondence in some ways is really not so surprising because only certain types of resources are available to a relatively slow, bipedal, diurnal, tool-using primate on the East African savanna.

At present, Olduvai Gorge is the only area in the world where concentrations of tools and bones dating to before a million years ago have been found in sufficient numbers to warrant statistical analysis of the spatial distribution and internal composition of individual sites. Stone tools have been found, however, at many other sites, particularly in South and East Africa; generally these resemble the early Olduwan tools in size, shape, and style.

THE ORIGINS OF CULTURE:
SUMMARY AND CONCLUSIONS

The lack of known well-stratified sites (except in Olduvai Gorge) and the taxonomic problems of early hominids allow only very tentative conclusions about cultural origins. Our earliest culture-bearing ancestors probably appeared on the African savannas about 5 million years ago or earlier, and they seem to have evolved out of a semierect, savanna-adapted primate stock. The selective advantages of hunting and human-like social organization may have been emphasized by climatic changes that increased the amount of open, savanna-like environments in Africa, but there is no evidence that systematic "big-game" hunting was an important part of our early evolutionary stages.

Early *Homo* or *Australopithecus* probably lived in social groupings of about twenty-five individuals, and the "home base" of DK I at Olduvai suggests some territoriality and perhaps group stability. These hominids no doubt occasionally fell prey to lions, tigers, and various larger carnivores, but by keeping to open country, restricting their movements after dark, and developing aggressive display behavior, they probably were able to create a niche based on small-game hunting, scavenging, and extensive collecting. Hunting and other factors then probably contributed to the loss of estrus and the various other physical developments during our first several million years as a genus, as did the defensive and mobility requirements of life in open country. By about 2 million years ago our ancestors' tool-using repertoire had become quite complex: eleven different tools have been identified at one site in Olduvai Gorge, including choppers, chisels, and engravers (Poirier 1973: 103). Some division of labor probably existed, with females specializing in infant care and collecting activities, and males in defensive, hunting, and scavenging activities. Food sharing would have been a likely concomitant of these specializations, but its extent at this time is difficult to estimate.

The life span of hominids at the Australopithecine and early *Homo* stage was probably quite short; estimated age at death for *A. africanus* is 22.9 years and even earlier, 18.0 years, for *A. robustus* (McKinley 1971).

There has been considerable debate about whether or not the Australopithecines and/or early *Homo* had a spoken language resembling

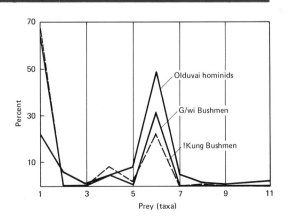

4.17
Frequency distribution of prey taken by Olduvai hominids compared to prey taken by modern Bushmen. Prey (taxa): (1) Chelonia; (2) Crocodylidae; (3) Primates; (4) Carnivora; (5) Suidae; (6) Bovidae; (7) Equidae (8) Giraffidae; (9) Rhinocerotidae; (10) Hippopotamidae; and (11) Proboscidae.

that of modern humans, some arguing that these early hominids had at least a limited spoken vocabulary, others suggesting that they were limited to chimpanzee-like grunts and cries. Human language capacities depend directly on certain structures of the vocal tract, and some anthropologists doubt that the early hominids had even the physical capacity to make many of the vowels widely used in contemporary language. The amount of brain tissue required for complex speech patterns is uncertain, although some of the later Australopithecines clearly had cranial volumes close to those of small-brained but entirely fluent and mentally normal modern individuals. Doubtless considerable "rewiring" of the human brain occurred over the last 2 million years, but we

4.18
Selected representative *Homo erectus* fossils.

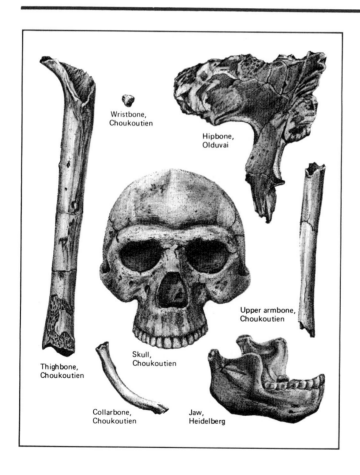

Wristbone,
Choukoutien

Hipbone,
Olduvai

Upper armbone,
Choukoutien

Thighbone,
Choukoutien

Skull,
Choukoutien

Collarbone,
Choukoutien

Jaw,
Heidelberg

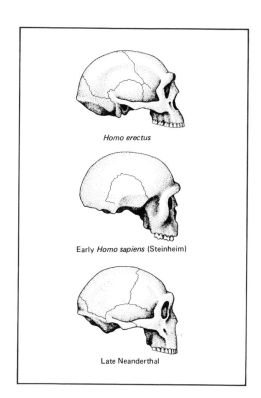

4.19
Typical skulls of highly variable late hominid populations

Homo erectus

Early *Homo sapiens* (Steinheim)

Late Neanderthal

are uncertain of the extent to which the evolution of language abilities was associated with these internal changes.

Clearly, language would have been a selective advantage for the co-ordination of hunting activities, for the social organization of primate groups, and for cementing the male-female and child-adult bonds that established human family structure, but none of these activities would seem to require the rich verbal facilities observed among all contemporary peoples. The archaeological record of a million years ago and earlier is fragmentary, but from the evidence we do have it appears that these early primates painted no pictures, carved no figurines, and made unrelievedly simple and "ugly" tools, and thus we might suspect that they also lacked the symbolic capacities required for complex language.

Homo Erectus and the Invasion of Temperate Climates

Every hominid fossil and artifact dating to more than a million years ago has been found in the warm regions of either Africa or Asia, but by about 900,000 years ago our hominid ancestors had spread out along the margins of the temperate latitudes and had begun to invade Pleistocene Europe and northern Asia (Figure 4.20). The intrepid individuals who made the first forays into temperate climates were probably either a transitional form between *Australopithecus* and *Homo erectus,* or full-fledged *Homo erectus.* Taxonomic issues pertaining to this period are complex, but whatever their designation, the hominids who first occupied Europe and northern Asia were likely a few inches short of five feet tall, walked fully erect, and had a cranial capacity of from 700 to 900 cc (Howells 1973: 61–64; Pilbeam 1975: 826–27).

These hominids (and all hominids, including ourselves) were tropical animals who could not possibly have survived Pleistocene European winters without clothing, fire, and tools. Fire was particularly important, not just for keeping warm, but for cooking food and, perhaps more importantly, for evicting bears and other carnivores from caves and rock shelters—the safest and warmest places to live in northern latitudes. There is also the somewhat romantic notion that fire may have been important in the evolution of the uniquely human sense of kinship and community, as for hundreds of thousands of years countless generations of hominids clustered around evening campfires, while outside storms raged and predators prowled (Pfeiffer 1978).

The problems of living in northern climates go beyond simply keeping warm. In winter most of the plants suitable for human consumption die, and many species of small game are no longer available. Under these conditions large mammals have only four ways to avoid starvation: they can hibernate, migrate, eat winter vegetation, or they can prey on animals that do one or more of these. The last was the only realistic alternative for our ancestors.

On the African savannas and in other warm environments women supply most of the food in hunting and gathering cultures, and even pregnant women, children, and the aged can gather much of their own food all year long. But such self-reliance would not have been possible in northern latitudes, where snow covered the ground for five or six months of the year. Already by a million years ago hominids living in southern environments may have developed systematic food sharing between adults, although we have no archaeological or other evidence for this.

That the men did the hunting, and not the women, incidentally, is only an inference, but it is an extremely likely one: in no known hunting and gathering society do women engage in big-game hunting, either with or instead of the men. Also, the size and strength differences between modern men and women may suggest that men were under very different selective pressures.

One of the most interesting aspects of the movement of hominids into temperate climates is that they changed significantly in physical form and cultural repertoire during the period they were moving north. Between about 1 million and 350,000 years ago, from the first occupation of northern areas until most of Europe and northern Asia were inhabited by humans, the versatility and efficiency of tools increased, and

4.20
Distribution of *Homo erectus* sites. *Homo erectus* was the first hominid to invade temperate climates and may have been more widely distributed than is represented here. Land bridges, now submerged, facilitated *H. erectus* movements.

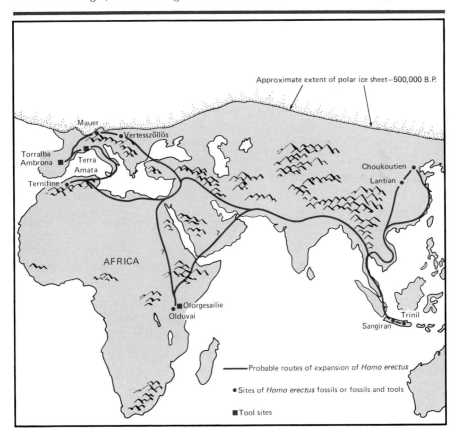

people became larger, bigger-brained, and more "modern" in facial structure. The hominid associated with these changes is *Homo erectus,* whose physical form was intermediate in many characteristics between ourselves and the Australopithecines, and who is almost certainly our direct ancestor. Like all biological, taxonomic labels, *"Homo erectus"* is a static category imposed on a continuum of biological change, and it is difficult to distinguish the first and last *H. erectus* from, respectively, their predecessors and successors. *H. erectus* is thought to have emerged between 2 million and a million years ago and to have evolved into *Homo sapiens* by about 300,000 to 200,000 years ago; but most of our fossil evidence for *H. erectus* dates to the relatively short period between 600,000 and 350,000 years ago.

Homo erectus remains have been found in most areas of the Old World, including Java, China, the Near East, Africa, and—in very fragmentary form—central and western Europe. Variation is considerable, but cranial volumes average between 750 and 1,200 cc, and, compared to us, these hominids had flat skulls, large brow ridges, thick cranial bones, and almost no chins (Howells 1973: 138). From the neck down, however, *Homo erectus* was very similar to modern human populations, although a bit shorter. Males averaged about 5′ 1″ in height, females a few inches less. It is interesting, incidentally, that as late as a few centuries ago most people were still, on the average, only a little taller than this—suggesting perhaps that there was little natural selection for increased height in the hundreds of thousands of years between *H. erectus* and the last several centuries. Alternatively, height is probably highly correlated with diet, and the "modern" size of *H. erectus* may mean that human nutrition has improved significantly only within the last one or two centuries.

Because the important physical and cultural changes associated with *Homo erectus* occurred at the same time these hominids were invading temperate latitudes, the possibility of a cause-and-effect relationship is raised. Only those groups that developed systematic food sharing and efficient hunting technologies and strategies would do well in these rigorous environments, and there would also probably have been some "natural selection" for larger body size (to conserve heat) and bigger brains.

If big-game hunting in northern climates was the stimulus to these varied cultural and physical developments, as some suggest (Pfeiffer 1978), we should find this relationship reflected in the archaeological record. For example, we would expect that the first sites showing more

efficient tools than the Olduwan styles would be found in northern latitudes, most likely in association with masses of bones of large animals.
We would also expect to find evidence of the first systematic and widespread use of fire in sites in northern latitudes.

The rigors of this adaptation may also have selected strongly for
food sharing, and out of this may have developed the complex kinship
networks and social relations we know to characterize all contemporary
human groups, even the most "primitive" hunters and gatherers. If so,
we might expect to find in northern latitudes the first sites reflecting
the coordinated activities of larger groups than are characteristic of
hominids in warmer latitudes. And if the rigors of life in cold climates
also selected for increased brain and body size, we might expect differences in these dimensions if we compare skeletal materials from northern and southern sites.

Except for these gross correlations, however, it is difficult to test the
hypothesis that adapting to cold climates and big-game hunting was a
primary evolutionary force. It is also difficult to delineate subtle patterns of cause and effect with the available fragmentary archaeological
evidence. Cultural innovations, such as the use of fire and more efficient
stone tools, must have spread quickly from area to area, and it is difficult to pin down their centers of origin. Most hunting and gathering
societies have exogamous marriage patterns, meaning they marry outside the group they spend most of the year with, and this produces a
constant mixture of genes and cultures.

Thus, it is possible that the use of fire, more efficient stone tools,
and bigger brains were stimulated by the selective environments along
the northern periphery of the Old World, but we would expect that
these and other innovations would soon spread to human populations
all over the Old World. And, given the gross dating techniques available to archaeologists, it is very difficult to determine precisely the exact
origins of these developments.

With these limitations in mind, let us survey some of the archaeological evidence from the period of 1 million to about 200,000 years
ago.

East Africa

Ironically, to consider the hypothesis that northern adaptations and
big-game hunting played important roles in hominid cultural and phys-

ical evolution, we must first turn our attention to the warm regions of East Africa, where recent finds raise serious—perhaps fatal—problems with this attractive and influential hypothesis.

The critical evidence comes principally from Olduvai Gorge, where at least one hominid has been found that suggests *Homo erectus* had evolved in this area about 1 million years ago. This is Olduvai Hominid 9, from Upper Bed II, radiometrically dated to between 1 million and 900,000 years ago (Isaac 1975: 509). The cranial fragments of this hominid have many characteristics in common with the *Homo erectus* of East Asia, including a cranial volume of about 1,000 cc. Equally important, as Glenn Isaac notes, the *Acheulian*-style (named after the French site at Acheul) stone tools associated with *Homo erectus* in Europe at a much later date (ca. 600,000 years ago at the earliest), were apparently already present in many East African sites more than a million years ago (1975: 504). Thus, Isaac concludes that the hypothesis of the importance of big-game hunting in human evolution is probably wrong and that the evidence from East Africa, in any case, "is not compatible with this view in its simplest form. The Lower Pleistocene does not emerge as a small-game hunting stage—nor is the contrast between the Lower and Middle Pleistocene that marked" (ibid.: 516). Given these various lines of evidence, Isaac contends that the original evolution of the distinctive physical and cultural characteristics of *Homo erectus* was limited to Africa and perhaps the warmer parts of Asia (ibid.: 495).

Other recent finds from Olduvai Gorge provide important evidence about the postcranial skeletal form of *Homo erectus*. In Bed IV, a left femoral shaft and a hipbone have been found in direct association with hundreds of stone tools and animal bones. Most of the tools are handaxes and cleavers with deep flaking scars and little "retouch" (secondary chipping to make the artifact more regular). Anatomically and metrically the hominid bones are most similar to the *H. erectus* individuals from Choukoutien (Poirier 1973: 150), and it is clear from their morphology that they belong to an erect-striding biped whose powers of locomotion were but little less than our own (ibid.).

The site of Olorgesailie, located about an hour's drive outside Nairobi, Kenya, is one of the few *Homo erectus* sites in Africa with a large concentration of undisturbed artifacts. The site area comprises many small concentrations of stone tools and bones spread out along a peninsula in an extinct lake. Most of the tools are cleavers and handaxes, and some show considerable chipping and blunting wear. Associated animal bones are from several species of large mammals, including a hippopotamus and, curiously, many individuals of an extinct species of baboon (but no hominids). The distribution of stones and bones suggests a hunting and scavenging hominid. There are no hearths or burned bones, but microscopic pieces of charcoal have been found all over the site. Whether these were the result of human or natural activity remains unclear. Potassium-argon dating of the Olorgesailie formation yields an age of about 480,000 years (Isaac 1975: 504).

Poirier interprets this site as evidence of relatively stable bands of twenty to thirty *Homo erectus* individuals, systematically hunting and scavenging in seasonal patterns, and thinks that the diversity of tool kits and site sizes indicates relatively cohesive social groups returning regularly to the same area and perhaps remaining in essentially the same place for several months (1973: 151–52).

South Africa

Having no volcanic formations, and few well-preserved and extensive sites, South Africa poses severe problems in dating early sites. Some archaeologists have proposed, however, that the world's first Acheulian stone tools appeared here, perhaps as early as a million years ago (Deacon 1975: 546–47).

In a recent review of the evidence, Deacon (1975) has suggested that the development of Acheulian-style tools in South Africa may have been largely an independent evolution, rather than an introduction from East Africa, and was perhaps associated with a general increase in *Homo erectus* population densities. Most South African sites associated with what are assumed to be *Homo erectus* populations are simple surface scatters of stone tools, but there are also some cave sites. There is no evidence of hearths or other uses of fire, and the few clues we have about South African *Homo erectus* diet suggest a scavenging, collecting, omnivorous routine, not obviously different from that of earlier hominids (Klein 1977: 120).

North Africa

Many apparently early sites have been found in Africa north of the Sahara, but most are small and difficult to date. One of the most important North African sites is Ternifine, in Algeria. Three hominid jaws and a cranial fragment found here are indistinguishable, in terms of their metrical characteristics, from some of the *Homo erectus* fossils found at Choukoutien in China (discussed below). More than 650 lithic (stone tool) artifacts were found at this site, most of them large choppers and chopping tools, bifaces (large stones that are worked on two sides to produce an edge), cleavers, flake tools, hammer stones, and waste flakes. Animal bones associated with the tools include elephants, gazelles, saber-toothed cats, and a giant baboon (Freeman 1975: 726–27).

Most of the tools from North African sites resemble those of equivalent age in Spain and Portugal (discussed below), but are quite distinct from those in France. Thus, "improbable though it may seem, this observation suggests that one route of expansion of Acheulian hunters from Africa to the Iberian Peninsula may have been direct, including passage of the Strait of Gibraltar" (Freeman 1975: 733).

Western Europe

The earliest well-documented archaeological site in Europe is Vallonet Cave, on the coast of southeastern France, where a small concentration of stone tools and broken animal bones has been dated to about 950,000 years ago (de Lumley 1975: 752). The tools from Vallonet look rather like the Olduwan implements, mainly crude choppers made from fist-sized pebbles and several flake tools. A number of apparently worked animal bones were also found, and the occupants of this small cave probably brought in antlers shed by deer (ibid.). The most abundant animal bones are from extinct forms of wild cow and bear, and there are also remains from antelopes, deer, boars, rhinoceroses, elephants, horses, hippopotami, seals, and, surprisingly, a monkey. Several bones appear to have been deliberately broken and a few flakes were struck off the end of a rhinoceros leg bone, but the large number of bear bones in the cave suggests that most of these animals were probably not brought back to the cave by hominids: cave bears no doubt carried their prey back to dens in these caves, and the presence of many of these bones is probably a result of their activities. Frost-cracked rocks and annual layers of ceiling-fall at Vallonet reflect at least some periods of cold, but there is no evidence of any hearths or fires. These would not have been necessary during the warmer parts of the year, of course, particularly since Vallonet is located on the coast, where the Mediterranean greatly moderates the climate. The presence in the cave of the bones of a monkey also suggests a fairly moderate climate.

Vallonet is the only well-documented site in Europe dating to about a million years ago, but there are many scatters of crude and perhaps equally old stone tools on the ancient river terraces of southern France. Most of these tools are very crude pebble-tool choppers and flakes that resemble closely the Vallonet artifacts, and in the few cases where animal bones are associated with the tools they are the same species found at Vallonet (de Lumley 1975).

Sites have been found in the Somme Valley, near Amiens, in the Seine and Rhone valleys, on the Roussillon Plain in southeastern France, and elsewhere in western Europe, but in every case reliable dating of the remains has been difficult.

TORRALBA-AMBRONA The sites of Torralba and Ambrona, located about 1.5 kilometers apart in a deep valley some 150 kilometers northeast of Madrid, provide convincing evidence that at least some groups in Middle Pleistocene Europe engaged in big-game hunting. Torralba was first discovered in 1888 when numerous animal bones and stone tools were found during construction of a railway. Excavations here in 1907 by a Spanish nobleman turned up many additional tools and bones, but unfortunately this dedicated amateur did not keep careful plans of his work, and his collections therefore are not particularly informative. Excavations at Torralba in the early 1960s by F. Clark Howell, however, exposed about 300 square meters of well-stratified archaeological deposits, from which were collected hundreds of pollen samples, several thousand stone tools, and countless animal bones. Analysis of the pollen samples has convinced most scholars that Torralba dates to about 400,000 years ago, but some think it is only about 200,000 years old. Pollen analysis indicates the area was a cool, swampy valley when the site was inhabited (Freeman 1975: 664). No hominid remains were found at the site, but presumably the occupants were *Homo erectus*.

The remains of at least thirty elephants were found at Torralba, as well as about twenty-five deer, twenty-five horses, ten wild oxen, and several rhinoceroses. Almost all the skeletons were disarticulated and many of the bones were smashed and split in an effort to get at the marrow. Nearly all the elephant skulls are missing, as are many of the other bones bearing the most edible cuts of meat—suggesting they were moved some distance to be butchered, and perhaps indicating the efforts of a large, cooperating work force (Freeman 1975: 676). The distribution of ages and sexes of the animals at this site is about what one would expect from a nonselective sample from local populations: that is, there is no evidence these hunters were concentrating on younger or older animals—they simply took what animals they could.

Thousands of bits of charcoal were found mixed with the bones and stones at Torralba, raising the possibility that these animals were driven into the bog with intentionally set fires. Scattered among the charcoal and other debris were preserved bits of wood, and some have speculated that wood may have been brought to the site to cook the butchered meat. Not a single hearth, ash concentration, or depression has been found, however.

The process of driving animals into the swamps and killing and butchering them must have been quite a spectacle, with great clouds of smoke, shrieking, demented animals, and running, shouting hominids. But we don't know how they actually slaughtered the animals. Not a single stone spearpoint was found at the site, and Freeman suggests that the animals were either stoned to death with the many fragments of rock found amid the bone or dispatched with wooden spears. It is a bit difficult to envisage stoning three or four large elephants to death, but however these animals were dispatched, it must have been a fantastic Hitchcockian nightmare played out in this Spanish valley hundreds of thousands of years ago.

The stratigraphy at Torralba is complex, and the site probably represents not one, but many different hunting episodes. Based on the distribution of tools and the number of animals killed, Freeman estimates that

> the total size of the cooperating social groups which provided the personnel responsible for the Torralba occupation residues was very large—perhaps on the order of a hundred individuals or more. Such large population aggregates might have been feasible only periodically or seasonally, but it is quite possible, given the undoubted natural wealth of the region in mid-Pleistocene times, that large human groups were a constant feature of the landscape. (1975: 682)

The site of Ambrona is similar to Torralba, and includes the remains of about forty elephants, as well as those of many other animals, mixed with numerous stone tools and clusters of carbon and ash. The

4.21
Reconstruction of a 300,000-year-old hut at Terra Amata, France.

only recognizable elephant cranium found had been smashed in what was almost certainly an attempt to get at the brains, and one of the elephant tusks had been whittled to a sharp point.

TERRA AMATA   In 1965 a bulldozer operation in an alley named Terra Amata in Nice, on the Mediterranean coast of France, uncovered a number of archaeological deposits dating to about 300,000 years ago. Twenty-one discrete living floors were found, six superimposed on a fossil beach, four on an ancient sandbar, and eleven on a dune island. The level of the Mediterranean 300,000 years ago was twenty-five meters higher than it is today, and the climate somewhat cooler and more humid.

The most interesting thing about Terra Amata is that the inhabitants of the site constructed large huts, ranging from eight to fifteen meters in length and from four to nearly six meters in width, most of them oval in shape (Figure 4.21) and estimated to have sheltered ten to twenty people. Nothing remains of the huts themselves, but their pattern is clearly evident in the long lines of postholes where supporting logs were driven into the sand, as well as in the rows of stones evidently used to brace the walls. Inside each hut was a hearth, and the floors of the huts were thickly covered with ash and the residue of organic debris, except for some areas close to the fire that were relatively free of debris, perhaps indicating places where people slept. Flat limestone blocks within the huts may have been seats or convenient places to prepare food (de Lumley 1969; Pfeiffer 1978: 141). The outlines of these various huts are so exactly superimposed and separated by such thin layers of sand that there is little doubt that the same or closely related groups were coming back each year to the same spot to build their huts and exploit local resources. Analysis of fossilized human feces revealed great quantities of pollen from plants that bloom in the spring and early summer, suggesting a temporary occupation each year at this time. Most of the animal bones found at the site were from stags, elephants, boars, ibex, and rhinoceroses but there were also bones of birds, turtles, rabbits, rodents, and a few fish and shellfish.

The stone tools from the site are mainly the large bifacially worked Acheulian tools found elsewhere in Africa and Europe at this time, and there are also a few bone tools and a worked piece of red ocher, a red mineral pigment widely used during the Paleolithic to color objects.

Unfortunately, not a single human remain has been found at Terra Amata, but based on the evidence from Europe and Asia during this period, it is likely that *Homo erectus* occupied this site. A single footprint was uncovered during excavations, and its modern shape and length indicate a fully bipedal hominid of about 5'1" in height.

Terra Amata's occupants were probably territorial hunters and gatherers who made regular seasonal rounds to exploit a diversity of resources, and who did considerable big-game hunting.

Central Europe

At Vertesszölös, a rock quarry west of Budapest, Hungary, about 400,000 years ago there were hot springs, and several layers of human occupational debris have been found near what would have been the banks of these springs. Excavations in the 1960s uncovered about 3,000 stone tools, many smashed and burned animal bones, and the occipital bone from one hominid and a few teeth from another (Vertes 1965). Initial measurements indicated that the teeth almost certainly came from a *Homo erectus,* but the estimated cranial capacity was about 1,400 cc—far larger than the *H. erectus* average. Since the animals associated with these human fossils date the hominid bones to about 400,000 to 350,000 years ago, such a large-brained individual would be very surprising. In fact, based on the estimated cranial capacity, many anthropologists concluded that the Vertesszölös hominid was a very early form of *Homo sapiens,* living at the same time as *H. erectus.* Recently, however, Milford Wolpoff has argued that the occipital bone almost certainly should be classified as *H. erectus,* because its physical characteristics are much more similar to known *H. erectus* fossils than to *H. sapiens* and because the initial estimates of cranial capacity were based on arguable reconstructions of certain morphological characteristics and on invalid statistical procedures (1971: 209–16).

The stone tools from Vertesszölös are about 20 percent choppers and chopping tools, most made from quartz pebbles. There are many scrapers, some denticulates (tools with a ragged, somewhat tooth-shaped edge) and borers, but bifacially worked cleavers and handaxes of the Acheulian type are completely absent. In form and type proportions the tools most closely resemble the Choukoutien and "evolved" Olduwan assemblages (discussed below), lending some tentative support to the idea that it was *H. erectus* whose activity we see reflected here.

No hearths have been found at the site, but there are burned bones, indicating the use of fire. Most of the animal remains found were from small rodents, particularly voles, dormice, and squirrels, but bears, deer, lions, canids, and rhinos were also represented.

A few fragments of teeth and bones found at Prezletice near Prague, Czechoslovakia, in 1960 may be the oldest human remains yet found in Europe. The animal remains from the site are of a species thought to have lived in glacial periods many thousands of years earlier than those found at Vertesszölös (Poirier 1973: 144). About fifty crude stone tools were found at the site, as well as an apparently worked deer bone.

The Near East

To date, few well-documented *H. erectus* fossils have been found in the Near East. An occipital bone and part of a frontal bone were found at Kibbutz Hazorea in Israel, in association with numerous Acheulian handaxes and heavy flakes (Anati and Haas 1967; Birdsell 1972: 279). However, analysis of this site is incomplete and the disturbed context of the find makes it difficult to date with any precision.

The site of 'Ubeidiya, three kilometers south of the Sea of Galilee in Israel, is somewhat better documented. About fourteen distinct archaeological assemblages have been uncovered at this site, all of them dating to no later than 640,000 years ago, and perhaps much earlier (Bar-Yosef 1975). The tools found here seem very similar to those from Middle and Upper Bed II at Olduvai Gorge, being mainly choppers, spheroids (rounded stones), handaxes, and used flakes. The faunal remains include large mammals, mollusks, and fish, but the remains have not been fully analyzed.

Many other Middle Pleistocene sites have been found in Palestine, most of them, unfortunately, small surface scatters very difficult to date and analyze. The majority are near springs or on lake shores, but others occur in mountain passes, plateaus, and the edges of mountain valleys (Bar-Yosef 1975). There are a few cave sites, but none have substantial depth.

It is difficult to reconstruct the diet and way of life of Near Eastern hominids during the Middle Pleistocene on the basis of the fragmentary data available, but there seems to have been some concentration on big-game hunting in semiforested and savanna areas. The more common animal remains include those from elephants, deer, hippopotami, and horses (Bar-Yosef 1975: 598). Other Middle Pleistocene sites occur in Syria, Iran, southeastern Anatolia, the Sinai Desert, Arabia, and many other places in the Near East (Clark 1975: 635), but few are very large or securely dated.

In an analysis of Middle Pleistocene sites in Africa and the Near East, J. Desmond Clark noted that, in contrast to sites in later periods, these sites do not seem to vary a great deal in the types of stone tools used, nor in the adaptation to different ecological zones. He concluded that most of these hominids probably ranged fairly widely, exploiting a diversity of plant and animal foods, making use of whatever happened to be available at any particular moment. Scavenging was probably still important; but selective hunting was supplying a significant portion of the diet (Clark 1975: 647).

East Asia

One of the most important *H. erectus* sites is Choukoutien (literally "Chicken Bone Hill"), a cave site located forty-three kilometers southwest of Peking in a range of limestone hills (Figure 4.22). Excavations in collapsed cave debris at the site between 1927 and 1937, and briefly in the late 1950s, revealed the remains of more than forty hominids, as well as over 100,000 stone tools, countless animal bones, and many hearths and ash layers, all well stratified in a deposit that is an astonishing fifty meters deep. Not all this was cultural debris—cave bears and other animals alternated with hominids in occupying the cave

4.22
Excavating at Choukoutien. The rope enclosures mark areas where the first and second hominid skulls were found.

and they probably brought in many of the animals. But Choukoutien has more superimposed occupational layers than any other known *Homo erectus* site. Analysis of the fauna and hominids and potassium-argon dating suggest a date of between 400,000 and 360,000 years ago for most of the cultural debris, although the basal layers may be somewhat older (Poirier 1973: 140).

The 14 skullcaps, 6 skull bones, 10 jaw fragments, 147 teeth, and assorted arm, leg, and hand bones found at Choukoutien all appear to have come from *Homo erectus*. Brain volumes average about 1,040 cc—somewhat larger than the *H. erectus* from Java—and teeth sizes fall between ourselves and Australopithecines (actually, they are only slightly larger than contemporary native Australian populations). Based on the few leg-bone fragments recovered, it is estimated that the Choukoutien hominids averaged about 5'1" in height—which may seem short, but it is significantly larger than Australopithecines and, as we have seen, only an inch or two less than the average height of most people of just a few hundred years ago.

The refuse at Choukoutien provides evidence for many insights into how these hominids lived. The winters of 360,000 years ago probably would have made fire a necessity, simply to avoid death from exposure, but the many cracked and burned animal bones indicate the inhabitants of these caves also cooked some of their food. Most of the meat was roasted venison (70 percent of the animal bones were from deer), but they also ate elephants, rhinoceroses, beavers, bison, boars, and horses. Some hackberry seeds from Choukoutien are the oldest known vegetable remains from an archaeological site, and they are probably found at Choukoutien only because the inhabitants of the site used fire, which chars and thus preserves organic material. This underscores the bias in the early hominid archaeological record toward animal bones, because all hominids ate considerable amounts of vegetable foods, but only when fire was used are these remains found.

Recent reanalysis of Choukoutien stratigraphy indicates that the winters during hominid occupations may have been more moderate than previously thought, but during the winters big-game hunting was probably still a necessary part of food gathering—as indicated by the massive concentrations of butchered animals. And here, too, we might wonder how these animals were killed, since not a single spear point or arrowhead was found among the more than 100,000 tools from this site. Traps and drives may have been used, but the diversity of species killed and the consistency with which they were dispatched suggest that much of the time people were hunting single animals without resorting to trapping them in bogs or driving them over cliffs. Possibly, sharpened wooden weapons were used, and if so the hunting prowess of *Homo erectus* was indeed remarkable.

Most of the tools at Choukoutien were made from quartz, which came from a formation a few kilometers away, and a green sandstone, available in a nearby stream. Crude flaked tools predominate, but a few tools might have been used as burins (for drilling and engraving) or chisels (Shapiro 1974: 80–81). The resemblance of the Choukoutien tools to the earliest European industries has often been noted, but most archaeologists place these tools within the "chopper-chopping tool tradition" that apparently developed independently in Southeast Asia and China, and they exclude the possibility of any significant contacts with European or African populations (Shapiro 1974: 82).

One other aspect of Choukoutien deserving comment is the evidence of cannibalism. Not a single skull from this site had an attached face, most of the cranial remains were mixed up with ashes, animal bones, and other refuse, and there is evidence that the base of each skull had been pried open to get at the brain. For the work involved in killing and butchering them, people don't yield much food, and this and the evidence of a preference for eating brains has led some to conclude that the cannibalism at Choukoutien was more a ritual than a regular subsistence practice (Poirier 1973: 140). Against this interpretation, however, we might note the careless discarding of hominid bone fragments with those of other animals in the garbage at Choukoutien, as well as the fact that no *H. erectus* site has ever yielded a single figurine, a wall painting, or even a careful burial—or any other evidence of ritual. In short, the hunters at Choukoutien may have invested their cannibalism with some emotion, but they were probably also grateful for the food.

All the Choukoutien hominid remains disappeared while being transferred from Peking to an American ship during the Japanese invasion of China prior to the Second World War. Recently, a woman in New York City, describing herself as the widow of one of the marines involved in this transfer, arranged a meeting with an American businessman who had been trying to locate these bones for some time. At the meeting, which at the woman's insistence took place on the observation deck of the Empire State Building, she showed him a photograph

TABLE 4.5   Roster of Some *Homo erectus* Fossil Finds

Region	Site	Name	Number of individual fossils
Java	Kedoeng Broeboes (Trinil)	*Pithecanthropus erectus*	1
	Trinil	*Pithecanthropus erectus*	4
	Sangiran (Trinil and Djetis)	*Pithecanthropus erectus*	2
	Modjokerto (Djetis)	*Homo modjokertensis*	1
	Ngangdong	*Homo soloensis**	10
	Sondé	*Pithecanthropus*	1
China	Choukoutien	*Sinanthropus pekinensis*	40
	Lantian	*Homo erectus*	2
North Africa	Ternifine	*Atlanthropus*	4
	Sidi Abderrahman	*Atlanthropus*	1
	Rabat	*Atlanthropus*	1
Israel	Lake Tiberias	*Australopithecus*	1
East Africa	Olduvai Gorge	*Homo erectus*	2–4
Zambia	Broken Hill	*Homo erectus**	2
South Africa	Swartkrans	*"Telanthropus capensis"*	8
	Saldanha Bay	*Homo erectus**	1
Europe	Heidelberg (Mauer)	*Homo neanderthalensis**	1
	Steinheim	*Homo neanderthalensis**	1
	Fontéchevade	*Homo neanderthalensis**	1
	Vertesszöllös	*Homo erectus**	1
	Swanscombe	*Homo sapiens*	1

SOURCE John Buettner-Janusch. 1973. *Physical Anthropology: A Perspective.* New York: Wiley.

* May also be considered Neanderthal.

of some bones but mysteriously fled when some tourists with cameras appeared. A copy of the photograph of the bones was eventually obtained from the still unidentified woman, and one skull looks very much like a true *H. erectus*—at least to Shapiro, Philip Tobias, and William Howells, all experts on the Choukoutien fossils (Shapiro 1974). To date, no progress has been made in locating any of the fossils, but fortunately, at the time of their discovery the great German anatomist Franz Widenreich made excellent plaster casts of them all and described them in superlative detail. It would be interesting to have the original bones, of course, but their metrical characteristics are already well established.

Other *H. erectus* fossils have been found at two places in Shensi Province, near Chenchiawo, and both of these very fragmentary finds closely resemble the fossils from the Djetis beds on Java. Cranial volume of the single skull found is estimated at about 780 cc, and the bones seem significantly thicker than those from Choukoutien. Consequently, most authorities date these Chinese fossils earlier than the Choukoutien remains. A single chipped-quartz tool was found about a kilometer from the fossils, but no tools were found in close association with them. The remains of many large mammals, however, were found in association with the hominid bones (Poirier 1973: 141).

We have already noted the major fossil finds from Java (p. 111), including the very important possibility that some of its *Homo erectus*-like fossils are up to 1.9 million years old. Although *Homo erectus*-like hominids seem to have lived in Java between 1.5 million and 500,000 years ago, they changed remarkably little during this period, except for a modest increase in brain volume and some dental reduction (Pilbeam 1975: 832).

SUMMARY AND CONCLUSIONS

Our brief summary of the artifacts and fossils of the Middle Pleistocene (Table 4.5) must conclude with that most familiar of all archaeological laments, "more research is needed." Nonetheless, given the evidence from East Africa, as well as the possibly early development of *Homo erectus* in Southeast Asia (p. 152), it would appear that the movement into northern latitudes and subsequent big-game hunting were not, by themselves, the major factors in the evolution of *Homo erectus* or his cultural repertoire. Generally, we have little positive evidence about exactly what factors were most powerful in producing the rapid increases in brain size and significantly more effective technologies of the Middle Pleistocene. Once the step to toolmaking and use and essentially human forms of social organization and communication had been made, subsequent cultural changes seem to have been shaped by strong competitive pressures, so that some innovations in material culture or behavior were strongly and directly "selected for." The circularity of this assessment can only be eliminated through evidence and analyses we do not yet possess.

4.23
Richard Leakey examining a possible human ancestor.

Bibliography

Anati, E. and N. Haas. 1967. "The Hazorea Pleistocene Site: A Preliminary Report." *Man.* 2(3): 454–56.

Arambourg, C. 1967. "Le deuxième mission scientifique de l'omo." *L'Anthropologie.* 71: 562–66.

Bar-Yosef, O. 1975. "Archeological Occurrences in the Middle Pleistocene of Israel." In *After the Australopithecines,* eds. K. W. Butzer and G. Isaac. The Hague: Mouton.

Birdsell, J. B. 1972. *Human Evolution.* Chicago: Rand McNally.

Bishop, W. W., A. Hill, and M. Pickford. 1975. "New Evidence Regarding the Quaternary Geology, Archaeology and Hominids of Chesowanja, Kenya." *Nature.* 258: 204–8.

Bishop, W. W. and J. A. Miller, eds. 1972. *Calibration of Hominid Evolution.* Published for the Wenner-Gren Foundation for Anthropological Research, New York, by Scottish Academic Press, U. of Toronto Press.

Brace, C. Loring. 1967. *The Stages of Human Evolution.* Englewood Cliffs, N.J.: Prentice-Hall.

———. 1973. "Sexual Dimorphism in Human Evolution." *Yearbook of Physical Anthropology,* vol. 16.

Brace, C. Loring and James Metress. 1973. *Man in Evolutionary Perspective.* New York: Wiley.

Buettner-Janusch, J. 1966. *Origins of Man.* New York: Wiley.

Butzer, K. W. 1975. "Geological and Ecological Perspectives on the Middle Pleistocene." In *After the Australopithecines,* eds. K. W. Butzer and G. Isaac. The Hague: Mouton.

Cachel, Susan. 1975. "A New View of Speciation." In *Australopithecus Paleoanthropology: Morphology and Paleoecology,* ed. R. H. Tuttle. The Hague: Mouton.

Campbell, Bernard, ed. 1976. *Humankind Emerging.* Boston: Little, Brown.

———, ed. 1972. *Sexual Selection and the Descent of Man 1871–1971.* Chicago: Aldine.

Clark, J. Desmond. 1975. "A Comparison of the Late Acheulian Industries of Africa and the Middle East." In *After the Australopithecines,* eds. K. W. Butzer and G. Isaac. The Hague: Mouton.

Conroy, Glenn C. and David Pilbeam. 1975. "Ramapithecus: A Review of Its Hominid Status." In *Australopithecus Paleoanthropology: Morphology and Paleoecology,* ed. R. H. Tuttle. The Hague: Mouton.

Coppens, Yves, F. Clark Howell, Glynn Ll. Isaac, and Richard E. F. Leakey, eds. 1976. *Earliest Man and Environments in the Lake Rudolf Basin.* Chicago: University of Chicago Press.

Crook, John H. 1972. "Sexual Selection, Dimorphism, and Social Organization in the

Primates." In *Sexual Selection and the Descent of Man 1871–1971*, ed. Bernard Campbell. Chicago: Aldine.

Curtis, G. H., T. Drake, T. Cerling, and X. Hampel. 1975. "Age of the KBS Tuff in Koobi Fora Formation, East Rudolf, Kenya." *Nature*. 258: 395–98.

Deacon, H. J. 1975. "Demography, Subsistence, and Culture During the Acheulian in Southern Africa." In *After the Australopithecines*, eds. K. W. Butzer and G. Isaac. The Hague: Mouton.

Falk, Dean. 1975. "Comparative Anatomy of the Larnyx in Man and the Chimpanzee: Implications for Language in Neanderthal." *American Journal of Physical Anthropology*. 43: 123–32.

Freeman, L. G. 1975. "Acheulian Sites and Stratigraphy in Iberia and the Maghreb." In *After the Australopithecines*, eds. K. W. Butzer and G. Isaac. The Hague: Mouton.

Harding, Robert and Shirley Strum. 1976. "The Predatory Baboons of Kekopey." *Natural History*. 85(3): 46–53.

Harris, J. and G. Isaac. 1976. "The Karari Industry: Early Pleistocene Archaeological Evidence from the Terrain East of Lake Turkana, Kenya." *Nature*. 262: 102–7.

Howell, F. C. and G. Ll. Isaac. 1976. "Introduction" to Part 3. In *Earliest Man and Environments in the Lake Rudolf Basin*, eds. Coppens et al. Chicago: University of Chicago Press.

Howells, William. 1973. *Evolution of the Genus Homo*. Reading, Mass.: Addison-Wesley.

Hughes, Alun R. and Phillip V. Tobias. 1977. "A Fossil Skull Probably of the Genus *Homo* from Sterkfontein, Transval." *Nature*. 265: 310–12.

Isaac, G. Ll. 1975. "Stratigraphy and Cultural Patterns in East Africa During the Middle Ranges of Pleistocene Time." In *After the Australopithecines*, eds. K. W. Butzer and G. Isaac. The Hague: Mouton.

——. 1975. "Sorting Out the Muddle in the Middle: An Anthropologist's Post-Conference Appraisal." In *After the Australopithecines*, eds. K. W. Butzer and G. Isaac. The Hague: Mouton.

Isaac, Glynn and Elizabeth R. McCown, eds. 1976. *Human Origins: Louis Leakey and the Early African Evidence*. Menlo Park, Calif.: W. A. Benjamin.

Jerison, Harry J. 1976. "Paleoneurology and the Evolution of the Mind." *Scientific American*. 234: 90–101.

Jolly, Clifford J. 1970. "The Seed-Eaters: A New Model of Hominid Differentiation Based on a Baboon Analogy." *Man*. 5: 1–26.

Klein, Richard G. 1977. "The Ecology of Early Man in Southern Africa." *Science*. 197(4299): 115–26.

Kranz, Grover. 1975. "The Double Descent of Man." In *Australopithecus Paleoanthropology: Morphology and Paleoecology*, ed. R. H. Tuttle. The Hague: Mouton.

Lawick-Goodall, J. van. 1968. "The Behavior of Free-living Chimpanzees in the Gombe Stream Area." *Animal Behavior Monographs*. 1(3): 161–311.

———. 1971. "Some Aspects of Aggressive Behavior in a Group of Free-living Chimpanzees." *International Social Science Journal.* 23: 89–97.

———. 1973. "The Behavior of Chimpanzees in Their Natural Habitat." *American Journal of Psychiatry.* 130: 1–12.

Leakey, L. S. B. 1965. *Olduvai Gorge 1951–1961.* Cambridge: Cambridge University Press.

Leakey, M. D. 1971. *Olduvai Gorge, Vol. 3, Excavations in Beds I and II, 1960–1963.* Cambridge: Cambridge University Press.

———. 1975. "Cultural Patterns in the Olduvai Sequence." In *After the Australopithecines,* eds. K. W. Butzer and G. Isaac. The Hague: Mouton.

Leakey, M. D., R. L. Hay, G. H. Curtis, R. E. Drake, and M. K. Jackes. With T. D. White. 1976. "Fossil Hominids from the Laetolil Beds." *Nature.* 262: 460–66.

Leakey, R. E. F. 1973. "Australopithecines and Hominines: A Summary on the Evidence for the Early Pleistocene of Eastern Africa." In *The Concepts of Human Evolution,* ed. S. Zuckerman. New York: Academic Press.

———. 1976. "An Overview of the Hominidae from East Rudolf, Kenya." In *Earliest Man and Environments in the Lake Rudolf Basin,* eds. Coppens et al. Chicago: University of Chicago Press.

Lumley, Henry de. 1969. "A Paleolithic Camp at Nice." *Scientific American.* 220: 42–59.

———. 1975. "Cultural Evolution in France in Its Paleoecological Setting During the Middle Pleistocene." In *After the Australopithecines,* eds. K. W. Butzer and G. Isaac. The Hague: Mouton.

McKinley, K. 1971. "Survivorship in Gracile and Robust Australopithecines: A Demographic Comparison and a Proposed Birth Model." *American Journal of Physical Anthropology.* 34(3): 417.

Maglio, V. J. 1973. "Origin and Evolution of the Elephantidae." *American Philosophical Society Transactions.* 63: 3.

———. 1975. "Pleistocene Faunal Evolution in Africa and Eurasia." In *After the Australopithecines,* eds. K. W. Butzer and G. Isaac. The Hague: Mouton.

Martin, Kay and Barbara Voorhies. 1975. *The Female of the Species.* New York: Columbia University Press.

Mettler, Lawrence and T. G. Gregg. 1969. *Population Genetics and Evolution.* Englewood Cliffs, N.J.: Prentice-Hall.

Napier, J. R. and P. H. Napier. 1967. *A Handbook of Living Primates.* London: Academic Press.

Pfeiffer, John E. 1978. *The Emergence of Man.* 3rd ed. New York: Harper & Row.

Pianka, Eric. 1974. *Evolutionary Ecology.* New York: Harper & Row.

Pilbeam, David R. 1975. "Middle Pleistocene Hominids." In *After the Australopithecines,* eds. K. W. Butzer and G. Isaac. The Hague: Mouton.

Pilbeam, David and Stephen Jay Gould. 1974. "Size and Scaling in Human Evolution." *Science.* 186: 892–901.

Pilbeam, David and J. Rimas Vaišnys. 1975. "Hypothesis Testing in Paleoanthropology." In *Australopithecus Paleoanthropology: Morphology and Paleoecology*, eds. R. H. Tuttle. The Hague: Mouton.

Poirier, Frank. 1973. *Fossil Man: An Evolutionary Journey*. St. Louis: C. V. Mosby.

Read-Martin, Catherine E. and Dwight W. Read. 1975. "Australopithecine Scavenging and Human Evolution: An Approach from Faunal Analysis. *Current Anthropology*. 16(3): 359–68.

Robinson, J. T. 1953. "Meganthropus, Australopithecines, and Hominids." *American Journal of Physical Anthropology*. 11(1): 1–38.

———. 1954. "The Genera and Species of the Australopithecinae." *American Journal of Physical Anthropology*. N.S. 12: 181–200.

———. 1972. "The Bearing of East Rudolf Fossils on Early Hominid Systematics." *Nature*. 240: 239–40.

Salzano, Francisco M. 1975. *The Role of Natural Selection in Human Evolution*. New York: American Elsevier.

Sarich, Vincent. 1971. "A Molecular Approach to the Question of Human Origins." In *Background for Man*, eds. P. Dolhinow and V. M. Sarich. Boston: Little, Brown.

Sartono, S. 1975. "Implications Arising from Pithecantropus VIII." In *Australopithecus Paleoanthropology: Morphology and Paleoecology*, ed. R. H. Tuttle. The Hague: Mouton.

Sauer, Norman J. and Terrill W. Phenice. 1977. *Hominid Fossils*. 2nd ed. Dubuque, Iowa: W. C. Brown.

Schaller, George B. and Gordon R. Lowther. 1969. "The Relevance of Carnivore Behavior to the Study of Early Hominids." *Southwestern Journal of Anthropology*. 25(4): 307–41.

Schwalbe, Gustav. 1906. *Studien zur Vorgeschichte des Menschen*. Stuttgart: E. Scheizerbart.

Shapiro, H. L. 1974. *Peking Man*. New York: Simon and Schuster.

Simons, Elwyn B. and D. R. Pilbeam. 1965. "Preliminary Revision of the Dryopithecinae (Pongidae, Anthropoidea)." *Folia Primatologica*. 3: 81–152.

Speth, John and D. Davis. 1976. "Seasonal Variability in Early Hominid Predation." *Science*. 192: 441–45.

Swedlund, A. 1974. "The Use of Ecological Hypotheses in Australopithecine Taxonomy." *American Anthropologist*. 76(3): 515–29.

Symonds, D. 1975. "The Origins of the Family." Santa Barbara: Mimeographed.

Teleki, Geza. 1973. "The Omniverous Chimpanzee." *Scientific American*. 228(1): 32–47.

Thompson, E. A. 1975. *Human Evolutionary Trees*. Cambridge: Cambridge University Press.

Tobias, P. 1973. "New Developments in Hominid Paleontology in South and East Africa." In *Annual Review of Anthropology*. 2: 311–34.

Uzzell, T. and D. Pilbeam. 1971. "Phyletic Divergence Dates of Hominoid Primates: A Comparison of Fossil and Molecular Data." *Evolution.* 25: 615.

Van den Berghe, P. L. 1972. "Sex Differentiation and Infant Care: A Rejoinder to Sharlotte Neely Williams." *American Anthropologist.* 74: 770–72.

Vertes, L. 1965. "Typology of the Buda Industry. A Pebble-tool Industry from the Hungarian Lower Paleolithic." *Quaternaria.* 7: 185–95.

Von Koenigswald, G. H. R. 1975. "Early Man in Java: Catalogue and Problems." In *Australopithecus Paleoanthropology: Morphology and Paleoecology,* ed. R. H. Tuttle. The Hague: Mouton.

Washburn, S. 1968. "Discussion." In *Man the Hunter,* eds. R. Lee and I. DeVore. Chicago: Aldine.

Washburn, S. L. and R. L. Ciochon. 1974. "Canine Teeth: Notes on Controversies in the Study of Human Evolution." *American Anthropologist.* 76(4): 765–84.

Wolpoff, Milford. 1971. Vertesszöllös and the Presapiens Theory." *American Journal of Physical Anthropology.* 35: 209–16.

———. 1973. "The Evidence for Two Australopithecine Lineages in South Africa." *Yearbook of Physical Anthropology,* vol. 17.

———. 1975. "Sexual Dimorphism in the Australopithecines." In *Australopithecus Paleoanthropology: Morphology and Paleoecology,* ed. R. H. Tuttle. The Hague: Mouton.

———. 1976. "Some Aspects of the Evolution of Early Hominid Sexual Dimorphism." *Current Anthropology.* 17(4): 579–606.

Wright, H. T. 1971. Unpublished statistical analysis of Olduvai Gorge stone tools.

Wymer, John. 1968. *Lower Paleolithic Archaeology in Britain.* Southhampton: Millbrook Press.

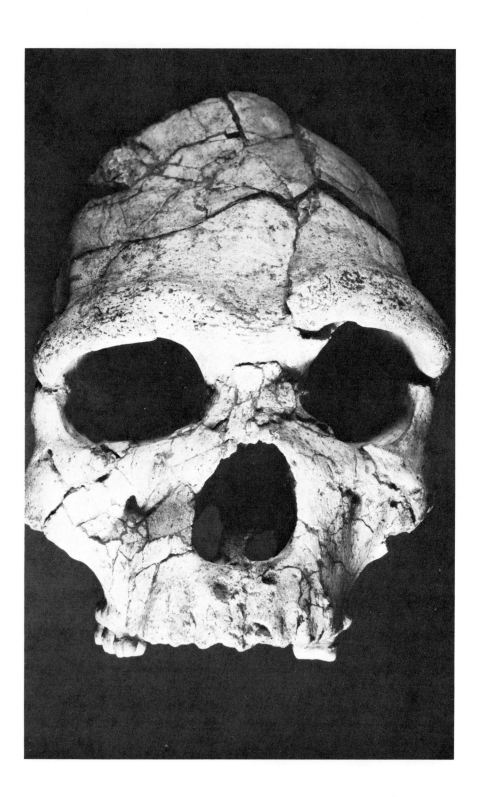

5

The Emergence
of *Homo sapiens sapiens*

Man is the missing link between anthropoid apes
and human beings.

Anonymous

By about 400,000 years ago our *Homo erectus* ancestors had become
skilled hunters and gatherers, exploiting environments from the temperate zones of Pleistocene Europe and North China to the tropics of
Africa and Java. In terms of brain size, technology, and numbers they
were much more like us than earlier hominids, and, if the evidence
from Torralba-Ambrona has been interpreted correctly (chapter 4), at
least some of them were living in complex webs of social relationships
involving a hundred or more individuals.

In basic patterns of subsistence and social organization, then,
Homo erectus appears to have been very similar to modern hunters and
gatherers; yet there is something alien about these creatures. We look
for artifacts expressing ritual or complex symbolism, but not a single
figurine, wall painting, or rock carving can be securely attributed to
Homo erectus. In some Upper Paleolithic sites (ca. 30,000 to 10,000
years ago) there are hundreds of beautifully crafted stone tools, some
so delicately worked that even moderate use would ruin them—tools
that must have been made in large part simply for the pleasure of creating something beautiful. But the tools of *Homo erectus* are, with few
exceptions, undeviatingly simple, efficient, utilitarian objects with little
evidence of stylistic expression.

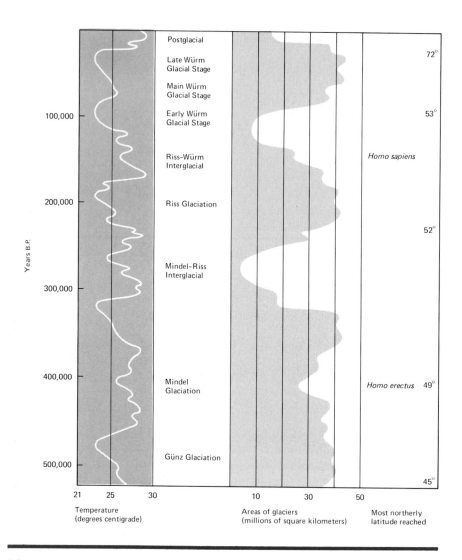

Years B.P.

Temperature (degrees centigrade)			Areas of glaciers (millions of square kilometers)			Most northerly latitude reached
21	25	30	10	30	50	

Postglacial

Late Würm Glacial Stage

Main Würm Glacial Stage

Early Würm Glacial Stage — 72°

Riss–Würm Interglacial — 53°

Homo sapiens

Riss Glaciation — 52°

Mindel–Riss Interglacial

Mindel Glaciation — 49°

Homo erectus

Günz Glaciation — 45°

100,000 / 200,000 / 300,000 / 400,000 / 500,000

5.1
Late Pleistocene chronology and correlation with species of *Homo* (using the old glacial and interglacial names).

Perhaps even more revealing, there are no known *Homo erectus* burials or ritual dispositions of corpses. Over the last 100,000 years, mortuary practices have almost everywhere been an occasion for the outpouring of human emotion, and even the simplest hunters and gatherers during this span usually disposed of their dead by digging a hole and placing a few stone tools or bits of shell in with the body; but not a single *Homo erectus* anywhere in the world appears to have been even intentionally buried, let alone sent off to the next world with a few provisions and expressions of goodwill.

These various absences of stylistic behavior among *Homo erectus* can be interpreted in several different ways. *Homo erectus,* with his brain about two thirds the size of our own, may simply have lacked the mental equipment to generalize and symbolize his experiences as we do. On the other hand, if the archaeological record is to be believed, many later, more "advanced" *Homo sapiens* cultures also neglected to bury their dead and to make figurines, wall paintings, and other aesthetic expressions. Some therefore suggest that *Homo erectus* had the potential for almost the same stylistic, religious, and social impulses that modern people feel, but lived in circumstances that did not elicit such expressions.

It is difficult to overstate the importance of the evolution of aesthetic, ritual, and social feelings, for it was precisely these kinds of mental characteristics that made possible the rise of great civilizations. Thus, we are particularly concerned in this chapter with the conditions under which these feelings first appeared (as reflected in the archaeological record) and with other concurrent important cultural developments.

Between 250,000 and 20,000 years ago the following major developments occurred in the Old World: (1) average human brain size increased to about 1,450 cc, although regional variation was still considerable; (2) the human chewing apparatus and associated facial architecture became smaller; (3) many technological innovations were made, including the bow and arrow, atlatl (throwing stick), bone and wood tools of diverse types, and techniques for extracting a relatively great amount of cutting edge from a given amount of stone; and (4) figurines, usually of bone or stone, began to be made, beautiful wall paintings and rock carvings were executed, and burials and arrangements of bones and tools appeared, all clearly reflecting a developed aesthetic consciousness.

How were our ancestors changed in these highly significant ways in the relatively short time between *Homo erectus,* at about 400,000 years ago, and ourselves, *Homo sapiens sapiens,* as we first emerged some 100,000 to 50,000 years ago?

Homo erectus to *Homo sapiens:*
The Archaeological and Fossil Record

There are several contrasting hypotheses about human evolution after *Homo erectus* (that is, after 400,000 years ago). An early view (Coon 1962), not widely held today, was that there was a single early radiation of Australopithecines from Africa into much of Eurasia, followed by the *independent* evolution of *Homo erectus* in Africa and Eurasia and the subsequent independent development of *Homo sapiens sapiens* in Europe and North Africa, sub-Saharan Africa, China, and Java. If true, this evolutionary history would mean that today's Europeans have had little or no genetic exchange with Asians or Africans since about a million years ago—a possibility some have misleadingly used to argue for the superiority of Europeans on the grounds that they show the most "advanced" evolutionary characteristics. Another model of human evolution sees modern humans, *Homo sapiens sapiens,* as evolving in one general area during the Upper Pleistocene (ca. 35,000 years ago), and then radiating over the world to replace all earlier hominid types. A primary issue here is the place of what are popularly known as the *Neanderthals,* people who lived, mainly in Europe, between about 100,000 and 35,000 years ago. Some consider Neanderthals to be side branches on our own ancestral tree while others consider them to be our direct ancestors. These contrasting schemes are not pointless quarrels among overspecialized professionals. They involve fundamental assumptions about the nature of hominid physical and cultural evolution, and to deal with the archaeological remains of this period we must consider various hypotheses about the course of this evolutionary development.

SUCCESSORS TO HOMO ERECTUS

By about 350,000 years ago *Homo erectus* had spread over most of the Old World. Fossil evidence from Vertesszölös in Hungary and from southern France confirms their presence in Europe, and *Homo erectus* remains are well documented in Africa and Asia. Despite considerable local variation, from Java to France these early hominids and their artifacts look quite similar. From about 325,000 to 100,000 years ago, however, there is one of those frustrating gaps in the archaeological record that makes an anthropologist sometimes think the simple Genesis account of our origins has a lot to recommend it. Few fossils and sites have been found to date to this period, but the meager fragments from France, Hungary, and elsewhere suggest that the brain of *Homo erectus* was enlarging and his facial features becoming somewhat more "modern."

Swanscombe

Our earliest well-documented evidence for the initial stages of the evolution of *Homo erectus* into *Homo sapiens* comes from Swanscombe, England, along the Thames River, not far from London. Stone tools and bones of extinct animals have been turning up here for centuries, but hominids were not found until 1935. Workers in a cement plant uncovered a cranial bone from a gravel bank, and a year later another cranial bone fragment was found nearby that articulated perfectly with the first bone (Figure 5.2). Later, during excavations connected with preparations for Allied invasion of France in 1944, another bone from

5.2
The Steinheim (above) and Swanscombe (below) skulls, both of which fall within the range of modern human cranial capacity and probably date to about 300,000 years ago.

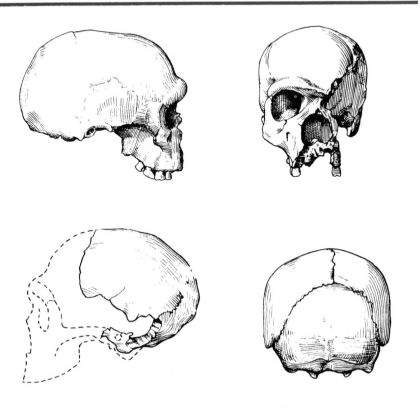

the same skull was found just twenty-five meters from the site of the first find. It is very possible, incidentally, that more hominid bones were included in the gravel used to make concrete for floating docks during the D-Day operation (Pfeiffer 1978: 173).

In the same gravel layers whence these bones came, excavators recovered the bones of extinct forms of elephants, deer, rhinoceroses, and pigs, which, together with subsequent chemical analysis and geological evidence, convincingly dated the Swanscombe fossils to an interglacial period about 225,000 years ago. The climate of England at that time seems to have been somewhat warmer and wetter than it is today, and the abundance of horses, elephants, rhinoceroses, and other big-game species indicates that southern England would have been an ideal place for generalized hunting and gathering groups. Nor is there any problem explaining how these hominids would have gotten there, since Britain and Ireland were physically joined to Europe by a land bridge at various times during the early and Middle Pleistocene.

The Swanscombe cranial remains are probably those of a woman of twenty to twenty-five years of age, with a cranial capacity of about 1,275 to 1,325 cc (Poirier 1973: 158)—well within the range of modern humans. Without the face it is difficult to relate this fossil to the Neanderthals who inhabited Europe about 100,000 years later, and authorities differ as to whether or not the Swanscombe woman should be identified as *Homo sapiens swanscombensis* or as *Homo sapiens neanderthalensis* (Wolpoff 1971). Handaxes roughly similar to those of the Acheulian assemblages of France and Africa are among the most frequent tools in the level where the skull was found, but lower levels contain only flakes and choppers. Similar flakes and choppers have been found elsewhere in England and are commonly referred to as the *Clactonian* assemblage, after the city of that name near London where many such tools have been discovered. A wooden spear fragment found at Clacton is the earliest wooden artifact recovered anywhere in Europe, dating to 400,000 to 200,000 years ago. Stone projectile points are not found at Swanscombe, Choukoutien, or any other site prior to about 150,000 years ago, and thus the wooden spear fragment from Swanscombe may be a clue to how these Middle Pleistocene peoples managed to kill big game without sharp stone-tipped spears. If animals were trapped in bogs, they could have been killed by multiple stab wounds with fire-hardened wooden spears—although it could not have been pleasant work.

Steinheim

A nearly complete skull found in 1933 at Steinheim, Germany, north of Stuttgart, has helped to clarify the taxonomic position of the Swanscombe and Clactonian material (see Fig. 5.2). This cranium, dated to about 250,000 years ago, probably belonged to a young woman whose brain size and facial features place her between *H. erectus* and ourselves. The cranial volume is between 1,150 and 1,175 cc—within the range of *H. erectus*—but the teeth and other parts of the masticatory apparatus are very different from most other *H. erectus* and quite similar to our own. All of the molars, for example, are smaller than the corresponding averages for modern Australian aborigines. Because the brain size falls within the low end of the range of variation of modern European peoples and the facial architecture seems smaller and more "modern" than most *Homo erectus* and Neanderthal individuals, some classify the Steinheim woman as a subspecies of our own species, that is, *H. sapiens steinheimensis*. Others, noting that the all-important lower front part of the face is missing and that the skull itself has been crushed and distorted by the weight of the overburden, prefer to see it as an intermediate form between *H. erectus* and *H. sapiens neanderthalensis*. The important thing here is that we should interpret these fossils in terms of the *range* of variability we might expect from any given population, and in this context it is significant that both the Swanscombe and Steinheim fossils are well within the range of modern humans. Anatole France, one of the most creative minds of his generation, had a cranial capacity of little more than 900 cc, and similar variability exists in contemporary populations. In other words, the Steinheim and Swanscombe individuals probably differed from modern human races little more than these races differ from each other.

Unfortunately, no artifacts were found with the Steinheim skull, so we cannot compare the site with the material from southern England. Nonetheless, the physical differences between this individual and *Homo erectus* indicate that the transition from *H. erectus* to *H. sapiens* was well underway by 300,000 to 250,000 years ago and was taking place in more than one part of western Europe.

Other Middle Pleistocene Hominids

Recently, excavations in a cave site in the French Pyrenees unearthed a skull (the Arago skull) and two mandibles (Figure 5.3) dated to about 200,000 years ago that seemed to fill the gap between the Javanese *Homo erectus* and the European Neanderthals (M.-A. de Lumley 1975). The skull possesses some morphological characteristics of *Homo erectus* in the Far East but lacks the incipient sagittal crest usually found in these populations. The large size of the teeth and mandible and the structure of the chin seem to foreshadow the features of the "classic" (western European) Neanderthal. Analysis of the animal remains and artifacts found with the skull is not complete, but preliminary indications are of much the same type of hunting-foraging economy as was practiced at Terra Amata and elsewhere in Europe in this period.

Few human fossils dating from 400,000 to 100,000 years ago have been found in Asia or Africa, and until they are, we cannot determine whether the emergence of *Homo sapiens* from *H. erectus* was happening worldwide or was a more localized phenomenon, perhaps centered in Europe. Analysis of the artifacts associated with the European

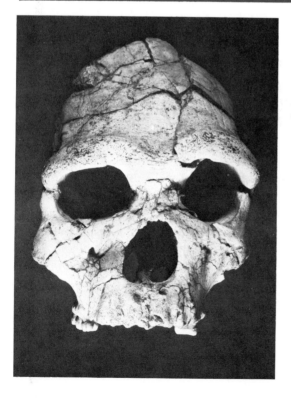

5.3
The Arago skull, from France. This approximately twenty-year-old man had more robust facial features than many Neanderthals and is probably intermediate between *Homo erectus* and *Homo sapiens*.

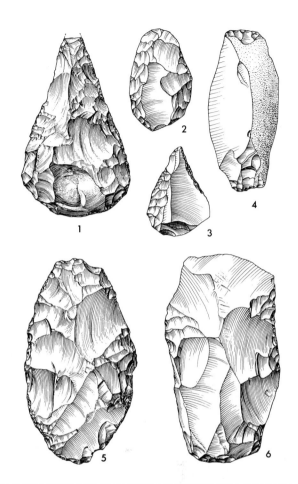

5·4
A sampler of Acheulian tools:
(1) a hand axe from Swans-
combe; (2) (3) (4) sidescraper,
point, and endscraper from
Saint Acheul (France); (5) a
"limande" from Cagny (near
Amiens); (6) an Upper
Acheulian cleaver from
Bihorel, near Rouen (France).

fossils, has been hampered by small samples and the disturbed contexts in which they are usually found, but generally the Middle Pleistocene does not seem a period of substantial change in basic adaptation. Tool technology, diet, site locations, and average group size in Europe about 200,000 years ago do not seem much different from those of several hundred thousand years earlier, as represented at Choukoutien and Torralba-Ambrona. Clearly, however, population densities were increasing, and as people moved into more diverse niches there was an increasing variety in the stone tools associated with them. The basic shape and size of tools (Figure 5.4) vary considerably from site to site in this period, a reflection, no doubt, of different tasks and environmental situations, but there was also increased stylistic variation. The tools found in association with *Homo erectus* activities are termed "Acheulian," after the site at St. Acheul in northern France, and they can be subdivided into groups on the basis of different styles.

In searching for causes of the increasing brain size and other changes between 400,000 and 100,000 years ago, we might note that rates of evolutionary change frequently seem to be higher along the margins of a species' range. This may have been the case with *Homo erectus,* as bands of these hominids probed far into England, northern Europe, and perhaps northern Eurasia, and began to specialize in big-game hunting. Seen in this light, the Swanscombe and Steinheim individuals, with their nearly modern brain size, may be reflections of these developments along the northern periphery. Gene flow in most hunting and gathering societies is sufficiently high that these changes in brain size and facial architecture would probably have been quickly disseminated over a wide area.

It is difficult to determine what factors made increased brain size an advantage, particularly since brain tissue has a relatively high "cost": it consumes great amounts of energy and oxygen. Also, the birth of large-brained offspring requires pelvic bone structure that reduces maternal mobility. Since *Homo erectus* was obviously an efficient hunter, forager, and toolmaker, perhaps the increased brain size was related to increasing emotional capacities, rather than big-game hunting skills or improved rationality. Great advantages would accrue to a Pleistocene hunting and gathering group that could organize itself as part of a social network involving many different bands and hundreds of individuals, and perhaps the increasing brain size had to do with the selective advantage of being able to generalize emotions to scores of "kinsmen." The great variability of cranial capacity among "normal" humans, however, and the fact that human brain size seems generally to have increased quite uniformly up to about 100,000 years ago should warn against simplistic explanations of this phenomenon.

THE NEANDERTHALS

Between about 100,000 and 35,000 years ago Europe, the Near East, and perhaps parts of Africa and Asia were occupied by *Homo sapiens neanderthalensis* ("Neanderthal man"). Fossils classed as Neanderthals or "Neanderthaloids" have come from scores of sites, from China to Germany (Figure 5.5). The characteristics most frequently used to define them are: (1) a receding or virtually absent chin; (2) large cheekbones and prominent brow ridges curving over the eye orbits and connecting across the bridge of the nose; (3) prognathism (relatively large noses); (4) a strong masticatory apparatus, including larger front teeth than are found in most modern human populations; (5) short (average of perhaps five feet) but powerful stature, wih thick and slightly curved long bones; and (6) a cranial capacity some 50 to 100 cc greater than modern European populations.

The Neanderthal physical type is often interpreted as an adaptation to the extreme cold of Pleistocene Eurasia. Even in very moderate climates more than 80 percent of our food is used simply to maintain body temperatures, and one way hominids can adapt to a cold climate is to change body size and shape. Heat loss is directly proportional to the amount of exposed surface, and spheres have the greatest amount of volume in relation to surface area. Thus, within the limits imposed by the advantages of mobility, in cold climates a larger, more spherical

5.5
Some important early *Homo sapiens* sites and the distribution of Mousterian tools.

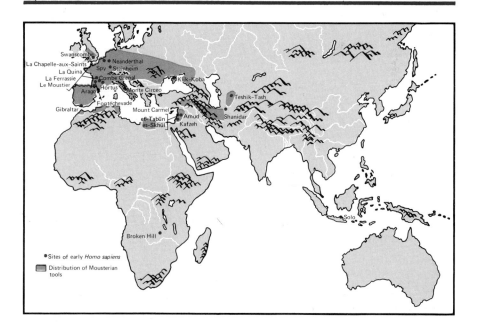

body (like that typical of Eskimos) is thermally more efficient than a long, thin one. Clothing, fire, living in caves, and other cultural adaptations can offset some of this selection, of course, but it is surprising how much we still seem to conform in size and shape to the requirements of the environments in which we live: in a sample of 116 males drawn from all over the world, D. F. Roberts (1953) found a remarkably strong correlation between body weight and local temperature averages (a relationship called *Bergman's Rule*).

Neanderthal facial features also seem to be cold-adapted. One important role of the external structures of the human nose is to warm and filter inspired air, so the large Neanderthal noses would have been an advantage in the frigid climates of Pleistocene Eurasia. Longer noses may also be an advantage in extremely arid areas, because they allow inspired air to be moistened more effectively. People with long noses

5.6
Artist's conception of a Neanderthal band on the move.

today are found in the dry areas of East Africa, in temperate Europe, and in the Near East, which matches the distributions one would expect in terms of warming or moistening requirements. Some apparent contradictions of this principle—the Eskimo and the Kalahari Bushmen, for example—can be explained by the fact that these people are relative newcomers to their niches.

Accordingly, the "classic" or western European Neanderthals are sometimes seen as cold-adapted physical types, who may have been reproductively isolated to some degree from other populations. Thus, some do not think it useful to extend the term *Neanderthal* to populations of Africa and Asia (Howells 1975: 405), where in most cases humans were adapting to less severe Pleistocene climates than in western Europe and may not have been as genetically isolated (Poirier 1973: 175–177).

Neanderthal Subsistence and Social Adaptation

The fossil that gave this stage of human evolution its name was found in the Neander Valley in southwestern Germany in 1856, and because it belonged to the first premodern human identified, the Neanderthals received much of the initial hostility to the concept of human evolution. From the beginning anthropologists, clergy, and others held that the Neanderthals were an aberrant stage in human development, not directly related to our own, presumably superior, ancestors.

C. Loring Brace (1964) has argued that the initial classification of Neanderthals as off the main line of our own evolution was rooted in the errors of nineteenth-century French paleontology. The chief villain in Brace's history of Neanderthal studies is French paleontologist Marcellin Boule who, between 1911 and 1913, published studies that depicted the Neanderthals as bow-legged, slouching, simian-looking individuals who were neither very intelligent nor agile. He didn't actually state that Neanderthals couldn't walk and chew gum at the same time, or that they drooled incessantly, but Boule used the words *apelike, primitive,* and *inferior* so frequently that neither he nor later scholars were anxious to claim Neanderthals as ancestors. And for many years Neanderthals were widely thought to be exactly what Boule said they were: inferior side branches on the human evolutionary tree, who died without issue under the onslaught of modern peoples.

Before and after Boule's publications, however, some scholars concluded that the Neanderthals were the connecting link between *Homo erectus* and at least some populations of *Homo sapiens sapiens*. Once fossils with Neanderthal characteristics were found in western and central Europe and the Near East, it was difficult to see them as a small isolated minority that had developed in its own peculiar and unrewarding direction. In 1957 a conference on Neanderthal problems produced evidence that Neanderthal brain size on the average was *larger* than that of most human groups, and it was demonstrated that there were no grounds for concluding that their brains were structurally inferior or that they did not walk fully erect. In fact, it was suggested that "if he could be reincarnated and placed in a New York subway—provided that he were bathed, shaved, and dressed in modern clothing—it is doubtful he would attract any more attention than some of its other denizens" (Straus and Cave 1957).

With the rehabilitation of the Neanderthals as physical specimens came an increased interest in their subsistence and social adaptations. The Neanderthals are identified with the *Mousterian* stone-tool industry (named after the site of Le Moustier in southern France) (Figure 5.7), which includes several distinctive stylistic and functional elements.

There are scores of Mousterian sites in the Dordogne region of southwestern France, including cave sites, rock shelters, and "open-air" locations. The Dordogne is one of the most beautiful regions of France, where glaciers and rivers have gouged the land surface into hundreds of small valleys and plateaus, all heavily forested and abundantly watered by rivers and streams. The region is a massive limestone formation with caves and rock overhangs, and during the Pleistocene these formations provided warm and dry shelters for generations of people who filled the caves with layer upon layer of debris.

One of the largest and most complex Mousterian sites in this area is a cave in the Combe Grenal Valley, twenty-two kilometers from the village of Les Eyzies, near the Dordogne River. Between 1953 and 1964 archaeologist François Bordes uncovered sixty-four superimposed occupational levels in this cave, spanning the period from about 150,000 to 40,000 years ago, with few long periods of abandonment. The lowest levels contained tools resembling the Acheulian tools found at Swanscombe, but all later levels had the classic Mousterian tools usually associated with Neanderthal. More than 19,000 Mousterian implements were collected and analyzed from this site, and the tools from different levels contrast sharply. Some levels contained many small flake-like pieces of stone, while others had concentrations of scores of "toothed" or "denticulated" tools. Moreover, analysis of the different levels revealed that certain types of tools tended to be spatially associated with a number of other types. That is, levels containing a relatively high number of projectile points ("arrowheads") would usually contain relatively large numbers of scrapers and flakes—but few denticulates. These patterns of spatial correlations pose problems of interpretation that we shall consider in some detail in later sections of this chapter.

There are scores of other Neanderthal sites in western Europe and since most of these sites are located within just a few kilometers of modern roads, it is likely that systematic surveys of less-traveled parts of Europe would reveal many unrecorded sites. Many Neanderthal sites have been destroyed by the advances and retreats of the glaciers, or by torrents of glacial meltwaters.

Analyzing Mousterian Cultures

When we compare the contents of individual Neanderthal sites it becomes apparent that there was great diversity in the types of tools and other artifacts made and used. But what is the significance of this diversity?

No scholars have spent as much time trying to answer this question as Denise and François Bordes. Through years of excavation and analysis, they have built up a classification of Mousterian stone tools that has been the framework for much of the work done on this period. They (e.g., F. Bordes 1961a) have classified all Mousterian tools into four categories, based on the relative frequencies of certain types. These tool kits include the *Mousterian of Acheulian Tradition;* the *Typical Mousterian;* the *Denticulate Mousterian;* and the *Charentian Mousterian,* of which there are two subtypes, the *Quina* and *Ferrassie.* This classificatory scheme has been shown to be valid in the sense that these tools do in fact seem to occur together in these clusters. Individuals well acquainted with Bordes's typology, in fact, can often predict with great accuracy the types of tools that will be found in a particular level of a site simply on the basis of the first ten or twenty lithics recovered. François Bordes observed that these four different assemblages seem to occur in different levels of the same sites, as well as at sites in very different areas, and he originally thought this was because the different assemblages reflected different activities carried out during different times of the year. But he soon rejected this possibility because analysis of bones and botanical evidence showed that each of the four assemblages could be found in deposits representing each season. His second supposition was that different tool assemblages represented activities engaged in during different climatic periods, some having been used during colder millennia of the Pleistocene and then replaced by others during warmer, interglacial periods. Excavations revealed, however, that all assemblages

5.7
A typical Mousterian stone-tool assemblage.

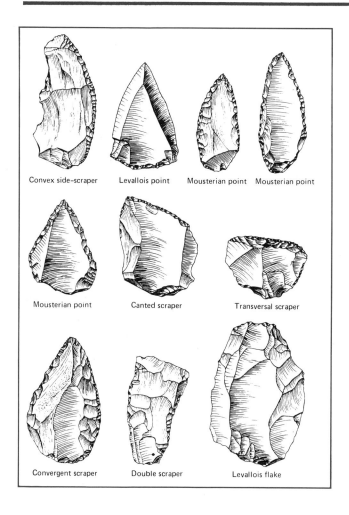

Convex side–scraper   Levallois point   Mousterian point   Mousterian point

Mousterian point   Canted scraper   Transversal scraper

Convergent scraper   Double scraper   Levallois flake

could be found in areas as different climatologically as the Near East, Africa, and western Europe.

Bordes's third and current hypothesis about Mousterian variability is that the four different clusters of tools are the remains of four distinct cultural traditions, or "tribes," which developed certain kinds of tool manufacture and retained these distinctive expressions over the 30,000 years of the Mousterian period. Bordes is quite literal in his interpretation of this hypothesis.

5.8
The Levallois technique. Compared to earlier industries, the *Neanderthals'* Levallois technique allowed more precise control over flake size and shape and more economical use of stone.

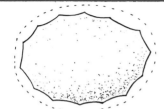

FIRST STEP: trimming edges of nodule.

THIRD STEP: striking platform is made.

Side view of the edge-trimmed nucleus.

Top view of nucleus (*platform, right*).

SECOND STEP: top surface is also trimmed.

FINAL STEP: flake struck from nucleus.

Side view of the fully-trimmed nucleus.

Top view of nucleus (*flake is removed*).

All the history of Europe shows . . . that man exchanges his genes more readily than his customs. Moreover, in primitive societies, conservatism is usually very strong, and if one supposes that a Mousterian of Acheulian Tradition married a Quina woman, she might well have gone on using the thick scrapers to which she was accustomed, but we doubt that her daughters would have done the same. It is, however, possible that the sporadic occurrence of tools which are characteristic of a given type of Mousterian, among the tool kit of another type, may be a trace of such a contact. (Bordes and Bordes 1970: 65)

Bordes's vision of the Mousterian, then, is one in which different tribes of Neanderthals wandered much of the Old World for generation after generation, through tens of thousands of years, each group maintaining its unique styles of tool manufacture and meeting the others infrequently and usually with hostility.

Bordes's analysis of Mousterian variability was questioned by American archaeologists Lewis and Sally Binford, who raise some theoretical issues whose importance transcends the empirical question of the significance of Mousterian tool variability. They argue that studies

in many parts of the world have shown that formal variation in material items that is inexplicable in terms of function or raw materials can be termed *stylistic* variation . . . ; these stylistic variations tend to cluster spatially in direct relationship to the amount of social distance maintained between societies. Spatial clusterings of the Mousterian assemblages are not demonstrable; in fact, in the Dordogne region of France the four types of Mousterian assemblages occur interdigitated at several localities.

In view of the demonstrated alternation of industries, one must envision a perpetual movement of culturally distinct peoples, never reacting to or coping with their neighbors. Nor do they exhibit the typically human characteristics of mutual influence and borrowing. *Such a situation is totally foreign in terms of our knowledge of sapiens behavior.* (1966: 240; emphasis added)

Thus, in contrast to Bordes, the Binfords assume that (1) such things as tool variability are best analyzed in terms of how these different tools enabled individuals to adapt to their environment; and (2) that cultural traditions in close proximity don't become and remain distinct for tens of thousands of years for no reason other than an unexplainable human capacity for this type of behavior. In short, the

Binfords' position is that if we cannot connect the Neanderthals with ourselves in terms of fundamental cultural processes common to both, then the archaeology of the Mousterian and earlier periods can be nothing more than speculative descriptions of these extinct cultures. They assume that Mousterian tool variability was largely a reflection of the different tasks Neanderthals had to perform to meet successfully the demands of their environment. They do not dispute that the Neanderthals expressed themselves stylistically; they simply believe that Neanderthal stylistic expressions would follow patterns similar to those of all other humans.

They tested these ideas through a statistical analysis of Mousterian tools from three widely separated Neanderthal sites: the Jabrud Rock Shelter (near Damascus, Syria); Mugharet es-Shubbabiq Cave, in Israel; and an "open-air" station near Houpeville, France. Each site contained several different levels, representing different occupations, the total number of which for the three sites was sixteen. Lithics from each site were classified in terms of Bordes's system and statistically analyzed to search for evidence that these groups of tools were used for different economic activities, rather than simply representing stylistic traditions. The statistical method used, *factor analysis,* is a procedure for analyzing correlation or covariation matrices (p. 132) and was employed in this case to determine which of the tool types were usually found in close proximity to one another in the various levels of the different sites. If representatives of two or more tool types were frequently found close to one another, the inference was made that they were a tool kit, that is, were used for the same activities.

The Binfords' factor analysis revealed that the sixteen different Mousterian occupations from the three sites could be reduced to five main specialized tool kits (1966: 249–58).

1. Tool Kit I: twelve tool types including borers, end-scrapers, and knives. These may have been used to work bone and wood into shafts or hafts and to work skins for cordage. These tools are associated with toolmaking and maintenance activities.

2. Tool Kit II: twelve tool types, including three kinds of points, scrapers, and burins. The inferred function is hunting and butchering.

3. Tool Kit III: seven tool types, most of them flakes and knives. The inferred function is fine butchering.

4. Tool Kit IV: four tool types, including used flakes and scrapers. The suggested function is preparing wood and plant foods and possibly the scraping of bones.

5. Tool Kit V: six tool types, including a projectile-point type, discs, scrapers, and blades. This kit appears to be a blend of hunting and butchering and perhaps other kinds of tools.

The distribution of the different tool kits at these three sites seems in line with the Binfords' inferences about their uses. The cave site in Israel, for example, is a large well-lighted area that would probably make an excellent base camp for Neanderthal hunters, and the preponderance of tool kits I, II, and III here would seem to support this inference. Tool kit I, supposedly a maintenance and toolmaking assemblage, was particularly frequent at this site, as one would expect if this were a base camp. And several hearths found near the entrance of the cave were surrounded by a high proportion of tool kit III knives and flakes—tools thought to be used for delicate cutting and food preparation and other activities associated with a base camp.

The Syrian rock shelter is much smaller than the Israeli cave and apparently was a temporary work camp used by hunters during forays away from their base camp. Tool kits II and V—both associated with killing and butchering activities—predominated. In contrast to the Israeli site, only one occupation level contained traces of fire, but here too most of the tools close to the ashes were of tool kit III, as they were in the Israeli cave.

The Binfords' work also provides other interesting results. According to their statistical analysis, few of the tool clusters were the results of a single type of activity, such as butchering a particular animal. Most of the samples seemed to reflect combinations of activities, since most included combinations of tool kits. Also, they conclude that the basic distinction in the sixteen levels analyzed was between *maintenance* and *extractive* activities, that is, between *base camps* and *work camps*.

The Binfords' study stimulated interest in statistical analysis of archaeological data and solidified the Neanderthals' position in the evolution of modern humans. The interpretation of stone-tool variability as evidence of different functions may seem an obvious point, but the Binfords' assumptions about culture as an adaptive mechanism and the dynamics of human cultural expression differed from the ideas of many archaeologists at the time. Since then, various people have criticized the specifics of their statistical analyses, but their basic approach has been widely imitated.

François Bordes, however, remains unconvinced. He notes, for example, that some Mousterian tools do not seem to occur at all in some parts of prehistoric France, while they are common in other areas.

> One cannot help wondering what kinds of activities were undertaken in Dordogne . . . which were unnecessary in Provance. The same question can be asked for older times about the scarcity or absence of hand-axes over wide regions of eastern Europe or Asia. And if the answer is that the same activities were being performed in a different way, then we may ask the following question: since there are several ways of performing the same activities with different tool kits, why not admit that the different Mousterian types just represent these different ways, and that the difference is cultural? (Bordes and Bordes 1970: 73)

Neanderthal Cultures and Society

As if the slurs cast on Neanderthal intelligence and posture by early archaeologists were not enough, some anthropologists have recently questioned whether or not Neanderthals were able to produce the range of sounds necessary for normal human language. P. Lieberman and E. Crelin (1971) reconstructed the vocal apparatus of Neanderthals using a computer simulation based on the measurement of a classic Neanderthal found at La Chapelle-aux-Saints. Drawing on studies of the vocal tracts of chimpanzees and human infants for comparison, they concluded that western European Neanderthals would not have been able to make some vowels, such as /e/, and, perhaps, some labial and dental consonants such as /b/ and /d/. Others doubt that the Neanderthals could speak at all. Since parrots have been taught to make most of the sounds of many languages, it is difficult to see much significance in differences between Neanderthal and modern vocal anatomy. Moreover, Lieberman and Crelin's research has recently been reviewed (e.g., D. Falk 1975), and it now appears that their reconstruction may have been based on an inappropriate physical and mathematical model. But aside from the technical problems with Lieberman and Crelin's idea, the enormous selective advantage of having language makes it very probable that even *Homo erectus* was quite proficient in some sort of verbal communication. The complex planning of activities reflected in sites like Torralba-Ambrona argues for a high degree of communication, in any event. Further, the Neanderthal brain was certainly adequate to the task of language, if size is any indication.

Whatever their fluency, the many Neanderthal burials indicate that they invested their life and death with considerable ritual. Excavations at La Chapelle-aux-Saints revealed a corpse laid out in a shallow trench, with a bison leg placed on his chest, and the trench filled in with bones, tools, and other debris—perhaps representing offerings of animal flesh and implements. At La Ferrassie, only a short distance away, a Neanderthal "cemetery" was found, where a man, a woman, two children about five years old, and two infants had been carefully buried. A flat stone slab had been placed on the man's chest, the woman was in a flexed position, and, toward the back of the cave, the skull and skeleton of one of the children were buried in separate holes, about one meter apart. The skull was covered by a triangular piece of limestone whose underside appears to have been engraved with cup-shaped markings. At Le Moustier, in a grave containing tools and animal bones, the body of a young male had been placed in what looks like a sleeping position, with the corpse lying on its right side and the head resting on the arm. At Monte Cicero, in Italy, a Neanderthal skull—with a hole cut into the base, perhaps as a result of cannibalism—was placed in the middle of a circle of stones. At Teshik-Tash, in Siberia, a Neanderthal child was buried in a grave surrounded by six goat skulls whose horns had been jabbed into the ground. At Shanidar Cave in Iraq, a Neanderthal dated to about 60,000 years ago had been buried toward the back of the cave, and the soil around the burial contained massive quantities of flower pollen, mainly grape hyacinth, bachelor's button, and hollyhock. Ralph Solecki, the excavator, and the palynologist, Arlette Leroi-Gourhan, concluded that the skeleton had been buried with garlands of flowers. Some scholars, however, remain unconvinced of this interpretation (Brace 1975: 86).

Beside these mortuary evidences of solicitude, there is evidence that Neanderthals were not insensitive to the plight of their physically disadvantaged comrades. Some Neanderthals evidently suffered terribly from arthritis or had lost limbs and so could not have contributed much to the group's food supply. Yet, they must have been supported by the rest of their society. Despite these rather touching displays of societal concern, there is considerable evidence that they killed, butchered, and ate one another. The Neanderthals had no monopoly on this practice, of course, and their appetites in this direction may have been stimulated by much the same terrible urgency as that experienced by survivors of a recent airplane crash in the Andes. Even recent hunters and gatherers in some places practiced cannibalism, usually in a ritual context in the belief that eating their enemies would help them gain revenge, or protect them from the hostility of their lunch's spirit. But rarely if ever has there been sustained cannibalism as part of normal subsistence strategy, because, compared to a deer or other large animal, a human makes a dangerous but not very rewarding prey. As S. Garn and W. Block (1970) have pointed out, the edible muscle mass of a 110-pound-man would only be about 10 pounds, and thus eating humans does not make much ecological sense under normal conditions in hunting and gathering societies. Still, at Krapina in Yugoslavia, excavations revealed twenty Neanderthals, men, women, and children, whose skulls had been smashed to bits and their long bones split lengthwise and marrow extracted. Many of the bones were charred. Other fossils from Java, Gibraltar, Germany, and France indicate that cannibalism in the Mousterian period was not unique to any specific regional cuisine.

Much has been made of another possible ritual aspect of Mousterian life, the relationship between Neanderthals and the giant cave bears of Pleistocene Europe. Some have argued that Neanderthals had a "cave bear cult" or some ritual involving cave bears, a notion based on early excavations in Switzerland in which stone "chests" containing bear skulls and long bones were reported. Recently, however, Finnish paleontologist Björn Kurtén challenged this "evidence" and questioned the notion that Neanderthals ever worshipped or even systematically hunted cave bears (1976). Most contacts between bears and humans were probably attempts on the part of the people to kill or evict the bears from caves so that the people could move in, and they may have been quite successful at this because of the bears' vulnerability while hibernating. Even a simple "deadfall" trap would have been an efficient way to kill bears with little danger to the hunters.

All Neanderthals were apparently hunters and gatherers, but they must have varied considerably throughout their range in the kinds of resources they exploited. The archaeological record is no doubt biased, because most Neanderthal sites found and excavated are those made evident by masses of animal bones associated with stone tools; the remains of plant foods and wooden tools, of course, do not preserve nearly so well nor are they as easily found.

Neanderthals were probably very like recent human hunters and gatherers in habits and abilities. Population densities appear to have been low, and it is assumed that most Neanderthals lived with the same group of twenty-five or fifty people their whole lives long, from time to time meeting other bands for mate exchanges. They were skilled big-game hunters, locked into seasonal migrations with the animals they hunted, but in most habitats they probably foraged widely for eggs, birds, plants, and other small resources. They competed quite successfully with other predators for game but must have occasionally lost out to the zoological carnival of horrors whose ranges they shared. It is likely that giant cave bears, several species of giant saber-toothed cats, and great packs of wolves occasionally "selected out" an unfortunate Neanderthal: "Some days you eat the bear, some days the bear eats you" was probably no empty cliché in the Mousterian period.

Homo sapiens neanderthalensis and *Homo sapiens sapiens*

Few aspects of Neanderthal existence have aroused such interest as has their demise, primarily because it was originally thought that the Neanderthals "disappeared" as a physical type rather abruptly after about 35,000 years ago. No Neanderthal bones have been found post-dating this time, and in some sites tool types widely believed to be associated with Neanderthals are overlain with levels containing tools of different style and form.

Some think the Neanderthals may have evolved directly into modern European peoples. Few if any reliable hominid fossils from the period between 45,000 and 25,000 years ago in western Europe have been found, so we do not know directly what was happening to the physical form of these populations during this interval. C. L. Brace (1967) has suggested that the improved efficiency of Mousterian tools greatly relaxed the selective pressures for a heavy masticatory apparatus, which is the primary difference between Neanderthal and modern skeletal material. Most Neanderthal dentition shows evidence of extreme wear on the front teeth, so the process may have been only beginning in the early Mousterian period.

Others have argued that the Neanderthals were directly and almost totally exterminated by people very similar to contemporary Europeans. Although popular in the movie industry, this idea has little to recommend it. Where these invaders would have come from is something of a mystery, but beyond that models of predator-prey relationships (Swedlund 1974) show that it would have been virtually impossible for hunters and gatherers to exterminate each other on this scale. Extended, high-casualty warfare has never been observed among peoples living at this stage of cultural evolution, and it is difficult to imagine our ancestors diverging so radically and pointlessly in this direction. If *Homo sapiens neanderthalensis* and *Homo sapiens sapiens* did live at the same time, there was probably a significant amount of genetic exchange between them, rather than warfare. People throughout the ages have expressed a fine democratic spirit in sexual affairs, and wherever different "races" have coexisted, they have interbred.

Some anthropologists have suggested that the extinction of the western Neanderthals may have occurred through the arrival and expansion of *Homo sapiens sapiens* possessing superior linguistic and technological skills. B. Campbell speculates that even if these more modern peoples did not directly kill off the Neanderthals, "natural selection would have worked at maximum efficiency to weed out the slow talkers and foster better speaking skills" (1976: 375). But as noted previously, we really have no solid evidence that the Neanderthals were any less fluent than other people, and it is not at all clear that superior language skills beyond a certain level would be that much of a selective advantage to small groups of hunters and gatherers. Modern human languages seem much more rich and varied than is necessary for the requirements of the Pleistocene way of life.

THE UPPER PALEOLITHIC

To understand the disappearance of the Neanderthals we must consider the period of from about 40,000 to 10,000 years ago, the *Upper Paleolithic*. As indicated in chapter 3, the term *Upper Paleolithic* has been used to refer both to the period of the late Pleistocene and to the evolution of more efficient stone tools—a development that occurred at different times in different areas. For present purposes we are concerned mainly with the period between about 40,000 and 10,000 years ago, during which the last several major glaciations took place.

The major developments of this period, aside from the demise of the Neanderthals and the appearance of anatomically modern people, include: (1) the expansion of humans into most of the world's habitable areas, including the New World and Australia; (2) the relatively sudden and widespread appearance of figurines and other artifacts reflect-

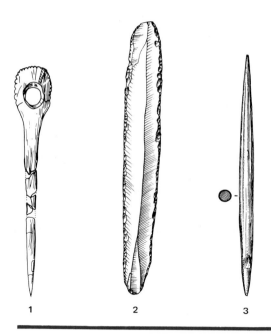

5.9
The specialized tools of the late Pleistocene included: (1) bone points (France); (2) retouched blades (France); and (3) bone pins (Russia).

ing heightened interest in art and ritual; and (3) a wide range of technological innovations, including more efficient methods of stone-tool manufacture, the bow and arrow, bolas, harpoons, and many kinds of fishing equipment (Figure 5.9). In addition, there is some evidence that the Upper Paleolithic was a time of considerable social reorganization. Upper Paleolithic groups in some areas may have been much larger than their predecessors, and some of them appear to have traveled less frequently and shorter distances. There is some evidence that toward the end of the Upper Paleolithic there were changes in the kinds of foods people were exploiting and the ways they were exploiting them, which led in some areas to domestication and agriculture. Finally, some anthropologists think the "racial" characteristics of some contemporary human populations emerged during the Upper Paleolithic—a biologically incidental, but for our age, at least, socially important development.

The "classical" model (Bricker 1976) of the Upper Paleolithic had its origins when, in 1868, five very ancient-appearing human skeletons were found in a rock shelter during a road widening project near Les Eyzies in southern France. The first Neanderthals had been discovered a few years before, and uneasy feelings about our descent from such barbaric-looking creatures had already begun to surface. But the bones from near Les Eyzies—named *Cro-Magnon man* after the rock shelter where they had been found—proved to be from individuals very much like modern Europeans in physical form. Here was an extremely ancient man, but of a race with which nineteenth-century Europeans could feel a strong sense of kinship and even pride.

The discovery of these respectable ancestors stimulated great interest in prehistory, and amateur archaeologists soon began to pillage sites all over Europe. One amateur, a French magistrate named Edward Lartet (1801–1871), took a much more serious and informed interest in the matter and conducted years of relatively careful excavations in France, assisted by an English banker named Henry Christy. Together they published a massive compendium of their researches in which they divided the Paleolithic sites of France into two periods, based on the animal bones found at each site: an initial stage when cave bears and mammoths were the primary game, and a later stage when reindeer were the chief prey and people began carving bone and making different kinds of stone tools. This classificatory scheme was modified by the French prehistorian Gabriel de Mortillet (1821–1898), who labeled Lartet's first stage the *Mousterian,* corresponding to the Neanderthals, and divided the "Age of Reindeer" into three successive epochs: the Aurignacian, the Solutrean, and the Magdalenian. These names, with various additions and subdivisions, are still used by many archaeologists (Figure 5.10). French archaeologists initially defined the Upper Paleolithic in terms of specific types of tools, such as "end-scrapers," "burins," and long blade-like tools, and various kinds of bone, antler, and ivory artifacts; and because these tools were not known in many areas, including Southeast Asia and sub-Saharan Africa, they concluded that these areas did not "have" an Upper Paleolithic, even suggesting that some of these areas were culturally "retarded" (Bricker 1976: 135).

Another aspect of this "classical" model of the Upper Paleolithic was the belief that the Upper Paleolithic archaeological materials were the work of anatomically modern humans and the Mousterian assemblages were the products of Neanderthals or other premodern humans (Bricker 1976: 135). In other words a direct equation between anatomy and technology was made, and the idea soon became widely accepted that one could determine the physical form of the people who inhabited a particular site simply by looking at the artifacts at that site.

A third key element in the classical model of the Upper Paleolithic is the idea that the humans and the technological developments associated with the Upper Paleolithic had come into western Europe from the Near East, Asia, or some other place. Adherents of the classical

TABLE 5.1   Roster of Important *Homo sapiens sapiens* and *Homo sapiens neanderthalensis* Finds

Country	Locality	Remains
Germany	Neanderthal	Parts of skull and skeleton
	Ehringsdorf	Cranium, 2 mandibles, and child's skeleton
	Steinheim*	Cranium
	Heidelberg (Mauer)*	Mandible
	Oberkassel	Parts of skulls and skeletons of 2 individuals
France	La Chapelle-aux-Saints	Skull and nearly complete skeleton
	La Ferrassie	Bones from 6 individuals
	Le Moustier	Parts of skull
	La Quina	Parts of skull
	Montmaurin	Mandible and teeth
	Fontéchevade*	Frontal bone of skull
	Chancelade	Skull and part of skeleton
	Cro-Magnon	Parts of skulls and skeletons of 5 individuals
	Combe-Capelle	Skull and part of skeleton
Belgium	Engis	Skull fragments of infant
	La Naulette	Mandible
	Spy	Parts of 2 skulls
Spain	Cova Negra	Parts of skull
Gibraltar	Forbes' Quarry	Parts of skull
	Devil's Tower	Parts of child's skull
Italy	Saccopastore	Parts of 2 skulls
	Monte Circeo	Parts of skull and 1 mandible
	Grimaldi (Grottes des Enfants)	Parts of skulls and skeletons of 2 individuals
Czechoslovakia	Gánovce	Brain cast
	Brno	Parts of skull
	Predmost	Parts of skulls and skeletons from 20 individuals
Hungary	Vertesszöllös*	One occipital bone
Yugoslavia	Krapina	Fragments of 13 individuals
Great Britain	Swanscombe*	Part of skull
	Bury St. Edmunds?	
	Galley Hill?	
Palestine	Tabūn, Mount Carmel	Skull and adult skeleton

TABLE 5.1 *(Continued)*

Country	Locality	Remains
	Skūhl, Mount Carmel	Nine adult and 1 child's skeletons
	Galilee	Cranial fragment
	Jebel Qafza	Five adult and 1 child's skeletons
	Shukbah	One adult and 6 children's skeletons
Uzbekistan (U.S.S.R.)	Teshik-Tash	Child's skeleton
Crimea (U.S.S.R.)	Starosel'e	Infant's skull
Iraq	Shanidar	Parts of skulls and skeletons of 7 individuals
Iran	Belt Cave	Cranium, skeletal fragments
	Bisitun Cave	Skeletal fragments of 1 individual
	Hotu Cave	Skeletons of 3 adults, many fragments
Morocco	Jebel Ighoud	Two adult crania
	Mugharet El-'Aliya	Juvenile maxilla, several teeth
	Taforalt	Burials, remains of 80 adults, 100 children
Algeria	Afalou-bou-rhummel	Fragments of 15 individuals
	Mechta el-arbi	Skulls and skeletons of 32 individuals
Zambia	Broken Hill*	Skull and skeletal fragments
Ethiopia	Dirédawa	Right mandible
East Africa	Gamble's Cave	Fragments of 4 individuals
South Africa	Saldanha Bay*	Skull
	Fish Hoek	Cranium and skeleton of 1 individual
	Florisbad	Adult cranium
	Border Cave	Skull and skeletal fragments of 2 or 3 individuals
	Cape Flats	Crania, skeletal remains of 3 individuals
	Makapansgat Cave of Hearths	Adolescent mandible, skeletal fragments
	Boskop	Skull and skeletal fragments
Java	Ngangdong*	Fragments of 10 skulls

SOURCE John Buettner-Janusch. 1973. *Physical Anthropology: A Perspective.* New York: Wiley.

* May be Pithecanthropines.

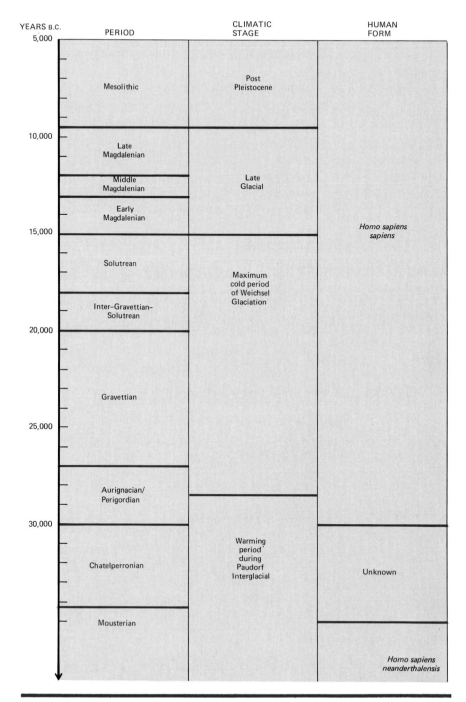

YEARS B.C.	PERIOD	CLIMATIC STAGE	HUMAN FORM
5,000			
	Mesolithic	Post Pleistocene	
10,000			
	Late Magdalenian	Late Glacial	
	Middle Magdalenian		
	Early Magdalenian		
15,000			Homo sapiens sapiens
	Solutrean	Maximum cold period of Weichsel Glaciation	
	Inter-Gravettian–Solutrean		
20,000			
	Gravettian		
25,000			
	Aurignacian/ Perigordian		
30,000			
	Chatelperronian	Warming period during Paudorf Interglacial	Unknown
	Mousterian		
			Homo sapiens neanderthalensis

5.10
Terminology of the French Middle and Upper Paleolithic.

model usually envisioned a single place of origin, from which modern humans had diffused to the rest of the world.

The evidence usually adduced to demonstrate that modern humans swept into Europe and annihilated the Neanderthals is a number of sites where levels containing Mousterian tools are directly overlain by levels containing punch-blades, bone tools, and other artifacts thought to have been made by anatomically modern humans. But this conception is questionable on a number of points. First, it is significant that the earliest industry usually associated with the Upper Paleolithic, the Chatelperronian (ca. 35,000 to 32,000 B.C.), has never been found in unmistakable association with human skeletal material, and, as Bricker notes, the "anatomy of the Chatelperronian artificer must be considered unknown" (1976: 140). Of even greater significance is the now almost certain proof that Mousterian styles of tools were being made by people physically indistinguishable from contemporary Europeans. Most of this evidence comes from outside western Europe (specifically Afghanistan, Israel, and central Europe), but at least one site in Spain, La Cueva de la Cariguela, may show this association. The tools from this site appear to be a very typical *Mousterian of Levallois Facies* (see Figure 5.8) with very few "Upper Paleolithic" types of tools, but the human skeletal remains seem to be from *Homo sapiens sapiens*. Part of a child's skull from the lower levels of this site shows some Neanderthal characteristics, so that this site might reflect the evolution of modern populations from Neanderthals as well as the use of Mousterian tools by *H. sapiens sapiens*. Obviously this conflicts with the traditional view of anatomically "modern" people sweeping into western Europe from elsewhere, carrying with them the tools and techniques associated with Upper Paleolithic cultures.

Although no site has been found in Europe with Neanderthal skeletal remains in direct association with Upper Paleolithic tools, there are no human skeletal remains *of any kind* reliably associated with the precise transitional period when the Neanderthals disappeared—that is, the period associated with the tool types known as the *Mousterian of Acheulian Tradition*. And, as François Bordes observed, it would not be surprising to find in the future *H. sapiens sapiens* in association with this industry (Bricker 1976: 139). Further, it is now apparent that some of the tool types most strongly associated with the Upper Paleolithic, such as the punch-blade technique, were in common use during the period when the classic Neanderthals were thought to be occupying Europe.

Even if these archaeological evidences against the invasion theory were not sufficient, the superpositioning of Upper Paleolithic tools over levels containing Mousterian tool styles simply cannot be interpreted as the "abrupt" displacement of one group by the other. Caves and rock shelters were occupied on a periodic basis throughout the Pleistocene, and even if the classic western Neanderthals evolved directly into Cro-Magnon populations, we would still expect to find many sites where Mousterian tools were overlain by Upper Paleolithic tools, with no evidence of transitional forms separating them.

Let us now consider the archaeological record relevant to the transition from Neanderthal to modern humans, in order to assess the accuracy of the various hypotheses about their relationship.

Central and Eastern Europe

While the classic Neanderthals were living in western Europe, people with some Neanderthal characteristics were also living in Hungary, Czechoslovakia, Yugoslavia, and elsewhere in eastern and central Europe. Our evidence for this is convincing but quite fragmentary. Jaw fragments from Sipka and Ochoz, Czechoslovakia, are apparently a combination of Neanderthal and modern characteristics. An adult's mandible and most of a child's skeleton from Subalyuk Cave, Hungary, resemble the Czechoslovakian fossils in form and were also associated with Mousterian tools. Further to the south, in Petralona Cave, southeast of Thessalonika, Greece, a complete skull was found that also seems to be a combination of classic Neanderthal and modern features.

How are we to interpret these finds? One view is that

> the appearance of *H. sapiens sapiens* in central and eastern Europe (and perhaps other regions) need not be explained in terms of a sudden migration from east to west, but rather as local evolution in populations having basic characteristics in common but differing in intensity and frequency. Such a situation permits relatively rapid morphological change. (Poirier 1973: 178)

The evolution of modern peoples from Neanderthal populations may also be reflected at Krapina, Yugoslavia. Approximately 649 shattered pieces of hominid bone were found there, including 270 teeth, but only 5 skulls are sufficiently complete to be identified. All share many classic Neanderthal characteristics, such as the sloping forehead and powerful jaws, but they vary considerably in other traits and these individuals would appear to be best understood as possessing characteristics of both *Homo sapiens sapiens* and *Homo sapiens neanderthalensis* (Poirier 1973: 164–65). Unfortunately, the more than 1,000 stone tools recovered from the site have not yet been completely studied.

The Near East

The archaeological remains from the Middle Pleistocene in the Near East include hominid fossils that apparently represent transitional forms between Neanderthals and modern humans. The majority of these finds come from Israel, Lebanon, Iraq, and Iran. Particularly important are the fossils from six caves, in Palestine, Zuttiya, near the Sea of Galilee; Tabun and Skhul, near Mount Carmel; Jebel Qafzeh, near Nazareth; Shukba, northwest of Jerusalem; and Amud, near Lake Tiberias.

The fossil finds at Skhul and Tabun were responsible for major revisions in our understanding of hominid evolution. The Tabun cave contained a large mandible and a well-preserved female skeleton, both dated by the C^{14} method to about 41,000 years ago, showing mainly Neanderthal features. The cranial capacity of the female, 1,270 cc, is well within the lower limits of Neanderthal averages, and the low skull profile, arched brows, and other characteristics are indistinguishable from western European Neanderthals. In a few physical characteristics, however, she appears to be somewhat closer to modern populations.

Ten nearly complete hominid skeletons were found at Skhul, dating to approximately 5,000 to 10,000 years later than those from Tabun. The most striking thing about these individuals is their morphological diversity. Some of the skulls are almost indistinguishable from modern *Homo sapiens sapiens,* while others show clear affinities with Neanderthals. Some have argued that the Skhul individuals represent the descendants of intermarriage between Neanderthals and modern individuals, although it is not clear where the modern people were living at this time, since there are no confirmed fossils of this type in levels contemporary with the classic Neanderthals.

One of the few systematic attempts to account for these Near Eastern transitional fossils was made by archaeologist Sally Binford. She observed that, as in Europe, the major change in the archaeological record at the time of the appearance of the first modern humans was radical alterations in the frequencies of various stone-tool types. She assumed that these changes reflected not invasions by different cultural groups, but changing environmental and social adaptations. Binford then analyzed the different environmental zones in which these remains were found to try to analyze the factors that were important in these changes. She defined three basic environmental zones in the Levant (Figure 5.11): (1) the extremely hot and dry Jordan Valley, immediately east of the coastal mountains; (2) the narrow but well-watered coastal plain; and (3) the valleys of the western slopes of the mountains, which because of their abundant rainfall provided lush pastures for grazing animals in spring and early summer. Based on surveys and excavations in each ecological zone, Binford constructed a number of tentative but interesting generalizations. First, in the arid Jordan Valley, the few sites containing Mousterian remains averaged only about 1.5 meters of Mousterian occupational debris, and at only one site was the Mousterian occupation followed by a substantial Upper Paleolithic occupation. Second, the sites on the coastal plain contained relatively thin and intermittent Mousterian deposits—although Binford notes that large parts of the plain have been covered by rising sea levels since the end of the Pleistocene. And, third, the sites on the western slopes of the coastal mountains have by far the thickest Mousterian deposits (twenty-three meters, in one case), and are also frequently overlain with Upper Paleolithic deposits. Moreover, all hominid fossils from this area that seem intermediate between Neanderthals and moderns are found in caves on these western slopes (at the sites of Qafzeh, Skhul, and Ksar Akil). Also, in some sites on the western slopes of the coastal mountains there was a very substantial increase in the remains of wild cow bones in levels dating to the late Mousterian period.

Binford concluded that in the western valleys in the Mousterian period there was a shift in hunting patterns away from the generalized use of animal resources toward a heavy dependence on wild cattle and fallow deer, and she suspects this shift may have been an important step in the evolution of Neanderthals into *Homo sapiens sapiens*.

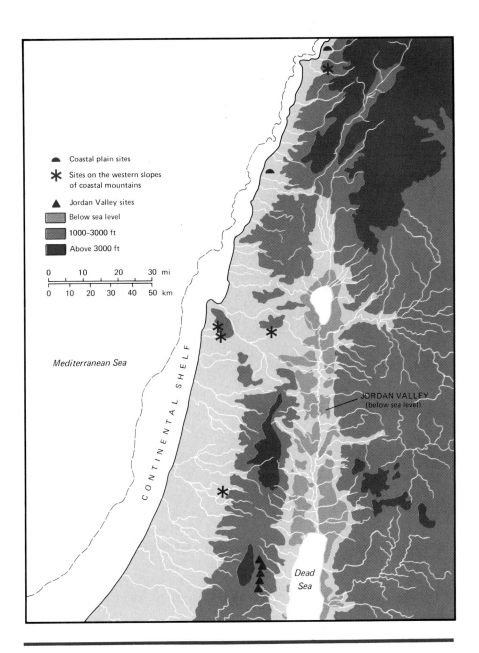

5.11

Ecological zones in Israel and distribution of some important sites. Most of the modern/Neanderthal transitional skeletal finds and the thickest Mousterian deposits are in sites on the western slopes of the coastal mountains.

The cooperative hunting of a few males to capture one or two animals characterized human subsistence from at least [150,000 years ago] . . . but the large-scale systematic exploitation of migratory herd mammals is a qualitatively different kind of activity, one that makes totally different structural demands on the groups involved. This kind of hunting is known to characterize Upper Paleolithic adaptations, and . . . there is evidence to suggest that not only did this hunting pattern appear *before* the Upper Paleolithic, but that the formal changes documented from Neanderthal to modern man and from the Mousterian to the Upper Paleolithic occurred in response to this basic structural change in ecological relationships. (S. Binford 1968: 714)

There are problems of interpretation and sample bias in this analysis, but at least it offers a framework in which other hypotheses can be tested. Unfortunately, few other systematic research designs have been constructed and executed concerning the problem of the relationship of the Neanderthals and modern races.

Africa

Among the most significant African finds are the remains from Broken Hill, Zambia. Discovered during lead- and zinc-mining operations in 1921, these remains resemble western European Neanderthals in the retreating forehead, strongly developed brow ridge, and other characteristics. On the other hand, the postcranial bones are indistinguishable from those of modern populations, and show no Neanderthal traits (Poirier 1973: 184). Because of this mixture of characteristics, the placement of the Zambian fossils on the hominid evolutionary tree is a matter of considerable dispute, some anthropologists seeing them as transitional populations, intermediate between Neanderthals and modern humans, others seeing them as largely unrelated to the Neanderthals. Some, such as Kennedy (1975), see no point in linking the Zambian remains with the Neanderthals at all.

A skull fragment found in 1953 near Hopefield, on Saldanha Bay, South Africa, is very similar to the Zambian specimen, but estimates for its age range all the way from 100,000 to 40,000 years ago. Stone tools found with the fossil resemble in some characteristics the Mousterian assemblages in Europe. Although sites and skeletal materials continue to accumulate, the cultural history of Africa after about 70,000 years ago is still not well understood.

The Far East

Several fossils from China and Java resemble European Neander-thals in some features, but their exact taxonomic status is unclear. Like those in Africa, these are often called *Neanderthaloids*. One important find, from a limestone cave in Kwangtung, China, included only part of the top and side of a skull, making classification difficult, but some authorities place this individual between the classic European Neander-thals and the modern forms elsewhere in Asia and Europe. Unfortu-nately, this fossil has never been adequately dated.

Interesting fossils were also found in Java in terraces along the Solo River (which also yielded the *H. erectus* material discussed in chapter 4). The eleven skulls found here between 1931 and 1941 in deposits very tentatively dated to about 40,000 years ago resemble the classic European Neanderthals in most characteristics, except for cranial capac-ity, which averages between 1,150 and 1,300 cc, or somewhat less than most Neanderthals. Two leg bones found with them, however, are in-distinguishable from those of modern *Homo sapiens sapiens*. Some con-sider these finds to be closely related to the Neanderthals, while others argue that they are linked to earlier *H. erectus* populations. A compli-cating factor in interpreting these hominids is that all of the facial bones had been smashed off, probably in an attempt to get at the brains, and they show other evidences of butchering. So far only a few crude flake tools have been found that may be associated with these fossils.

Elsewhere in the Far East, an important find was made at Niah, in Borneo, where the skull of a fifteen- or sixteen-year-old was discovered in association with stone chopping tools and large flakes in deposits radiocarbon-dated to about 40,000 years ago. The skull is virtually in-distinguishable from contemporary Asian peoples, and it is perhaps sig-nificant that it is quite different in this regard from the Javanese re-mains from the Solo River. Both the Niah and Solo finds seem to date to about 40,000 years ago, but whereas the Solo River skulls approxi-mate closely the classic Neanderthals in some characteristics (Poirier 1973: 183), the Niah skull has no evident Neanderthal characteristics. Taxonomic disputes about these East Asian finds continue.

Generally, Asian tool kits for this period are very different from those of Europe and the Near East, both in the number and kinds of tools. Asian tools, although no doubt well suited to their environments, seem less complex than those of the West, at least based on the few Asian assemblages currently known. These differences may have to do with the greater specialization in Europe and the West on big-game hunting, but more Asian Middle and late Pleistocene sites will have to be researched before we can come to any conclusions as to why these differences emerged.

Neanderthals in the New World?

From time to time human bones or stone tools are found in the New World that some try to connect with Neanderthals, but there has never been a single human fossil found anywhere in this area that does not fit easily into the range of variation of *Homo sapiens sapiens*. Occasionally, stone tools that resemble Mousterian implements have been found, but this is to be expected since some early Americans hunted and gathered their resources in much the same ways as the Neanderthals.

NEANDERTHAL TAXONOMY: CONCLUSIONS

Generally, the Neanderthals would seem to be best understood as a physical type resulting from adaptations to northern climates. They seem to be a case of subspecies variation, and although they are usually inserted in the hominid sequence between *Homo erectus* and *Homo sapiens sapiens,* they are far closer to ourselves than to *Homo erectus*. In fact, physical differences between modern European people and Neanderthals appear to be in relatively trivial characteristics that were free to vary considerably. Neanderthal physical characteristics were probably diffused from the northern periphery through interbreeding, and characteristics similar to those of the Neanderthals apparently evolved independently in some parts of the world, but generally the term *Neanderthal* would seem to be best limited to western, central, and eastern European types, and, perhaps, to some Near Eastern populations.

Where then did modern *Homo sapiens sapiens* evolve? Many anthropologists now believe that modern European races may have evolved through Steinheim and Swanscombe stock, while the Neanderthals—although contributing to the modern European gene pool—were increasingly isolated in the colder areas of Europe (Poirier 1973: 187). Western Neanderthals were probably eventually absorbed as a biological population by other, anatomically modern populations that developed not only in Europe but also in the Near East, Africa, and Asia, and thus many of us probably carry some minor Neanderthal inheritance.

Late Pleistocene Adaptations

With the appearance of modern humans after about 35,000 years ago, hunting and gathering societies began to appear in almost every part of the Old World, and in Australia and the Americas as well.

In Europe, hundreds of sites and over 200 human skeletons have been found that can be reliably dated to the period between 40,000 and 10,000 years ago. One of the most densely occupied areas during this period seems to have been near the confluence of the Dordogne and Vezere rivers in the south of France, where the same resources that attracted the Neanderthals to this location seem to have persisted into the late Pleistocene. The Dordogne is a well-watered, heavily forested, limestone formation, honeycombed with caves and rock shelters offering excellent places to live during the cold winters. Mammoths, horses, wild cattle, and many other animals were hunted by these Upper Paleolithic peoples, but the reindeer was the staff of life: at many sites 99 percent of all the animal bones found belonged to reindeer; reindeer hides provided clothing and coverings for shelters; reindeer antlers were the hammers, or the "batons," used to produce the long elegant blades for which these people are justly famous; and reindeer bone was the raw material for fish gorges, needles, awls, and other important tools. Not surprisingly, the reindeer was a frequent subject in Upper Paleolithic paintings and other artistic expressions.

Reindeer are migrants, traveling long distances each year as they follow the grazing lands from one climatic zone to another. Thus, Upper Paleolithic peoples of southern France could exploit through the reindeer herds land they had never seen: the reindeer would browse their way to the far north each year, and then return to southern France for the winter, at which time they could be harvested. E. Higgs has even argued that as early as 30,000 years ago reindeer may have been domesticated, in the sense that humans were selectively hunting the older adult males and restricting their movements by corraling them in gorges and other natural enclosures (1969: 31–43).

Some reindeer hunters may have migrated with the herds, much as the Laplanders of Scandinavia have traditionally done, but this appears unlikely, given the diversity of resources available in southwestern Europe during the late Pleistocene. The size of human band societies at this time is difficult to estimate, although there are very strict limits on the number of people who can be supported in a single area for any length of time on hunting and gathering, even if that area is extremely productive. Most hunters and gatherers maintain their population level far below what could be supported in most years, often gearing their size to the worst conditions remembered by the oldest living member of the group. Analysis of the age and sex of skeletons from the entire Paleolithic period indicates that only a minimum of infanticide, marriage regulation, or other population control devices would have been needed, because mortality rates were so high that each woman would have had to produce about six children just to maintain the group at its normal size.

Nonetheless, average group size may have been relatively large during the Upper Paleolithic in Europe, the Near East, and other areas because of the requirements of hunting large gregarious mammals such as reindeer, horses, and wild cattle. The Neanderthals apparently specialized in mammoths, rhinoceroses, and other animals whose movements are not easily manipulated by people and whose habits are, in some cases, more solitary than those of reindeer, horses, and wild cattle. With these latter species, an efficient hunting technique is the *drive,* where many people work together to stampede a herd over a cliff or into a bog. Such mass slaughter also requires many people to process the carcasses, else the great majority of the animals would be wasted. Further, a larger group size would have been advantageous in these circumstances as a means of defending particularly favorable places along migration routes.

In addition to increased group size, there apparently was an overall population increase in some parts of Europe—and probably much of Eurasia—during the late Upper Paleolithic. Based on the rather dubious criterion of the density of sites and artifacts of the various subdivisions of the Upper Paleolithic, it has been estimated that the population of France alone rose from 15,000 to 50,000 between about 18,000 and 10,000 B.C.

Several factors were probably important in this population growth, some of which we can reconstruct from changes in technology and diet.

The stone-tool technology of this period, with its indirect percussion and punch-blade techniques (Figure 5.12), was vastly more efficient than previous industries. Spear throwers, or atlatls, were also in common use—a very significant innovation, considering the heavy reliance on big game. It is estimated that an atlatl increases the range of a short spear from about 60 meters, if thrown by hand, to about 150 meters. The bow and arrow would have added significantly to hunting effectiveness, but it is unclear exactly when the first bows were used. Some of the earliest evidence comes from the Stellmoor site, near Hamburg, Germany, where about a hundred wooden arrows dating to approximately 10,000 years ago were recovered. Some were tipped with stone heads while others were untipped and blunted, which accords well with modern use of blunt arrows to hunt small game.

Another important invention was the fish gorge, made by cutting a sliver of bone, sharpening both ends, and baiting it. Once swallowed, the gorge stuck in the fish's throat and the catch could be landed, but except under ideal conditions this method cannot supply enough fish to provide a large part of the diet for mobile hunters and gatherers. What was needed was a way to harvest thousands of fish during their migratory runs, such as the fish traps used by the aboriginal inhabitants of the Pacific coast of northwestern North America. These techniques were not developed in Europe until near the end of the Pleistocene, at about 14,000 to 12,000 years ago.

5.12
A Solutrean "laurel-leaf" spearpoint. The Solutreans introduced "pressure flaking," in which stone is chipped from the tool by pressing hard on it with another stone or bone. Pressure flaking provides better control and finer finishing than "percussion" techniques, where the tool is made by striking it sharply with another stone.

Lewis Binford has argued that the neglect of fish by late Pleistocene people was a result of climatic and geographical barriers that prevented salmon from reaching interior river valleys (1968), but the reason fish were not initially exploited in Europe may be more complex.
This "neglect" has a striking parallel in prehistoric southeastern North
America, where Indians lived for thousands of years subsisting primarily on deer, mussels, and a variety of plant foods, almost totally
ignoring the myriad fish in nearby lakes and streams. Their neglect of
this resource, as well as the Europeans' neglect of salmon, might best be
viewed as a problem of cultural and technological organization, rather
than as the result of unique geological events such as Binford proposes.
That is, even if salmon were present in great numbers in European
rivers during the Mousterian and early Upper Paleolithic, their exploitation may have been blocked by the terms of human adaptation
to reindeer and other animals. Reindeer and other game would have
been a more dependable resource in the sense that at least some of these
animals would have been available year round, while the salmon would
have been sharply seasonal. Salmon runs, in fact, might have conflicted
with the scheduling of reindeer hunting, and as a consequence these
peoples may have been far from the river, exploiting different resources,
at the time the salmon were most available. Perhaps even more important, the successful exploitation of salmon would have required technological readaptation on a major scale. Catching salmon one by one
would not have been especially productive; their real utility probably
came only after nets, fish weirs, drying racks, smoking racks, and other
largely nonportable technology were invented.

In any case, toward the end of the Pleistocene, in the Magdalenian
period (15,000 to 10,000 B.C.), peoples living along the Dordogne River
and elsewhere in France began to exploit salmon intensively. Some sites
contain virtually nothing but several meters of fish scales and vertebrae.
The fish were probably caught in stone weirs or in dams similar to those
used by contemporary Eskimo groups, in which stones are piled in the
stream bed to form an enclosure with an open entrance, and where
migrating fish can be easily speared. The use of nets, although not documented archaeologically, is also likely. There is some evidence from
Magdalenian France suggestive of drying racks and other fish-prepara-
tion paraphernalia, but little material evidence is available concerning
how people prepared and used their catch.

Thus it is apparent from these technological and dietary changes
that we are dealing with another complex situation in which it is diffi-

cult to separate population growth from other changes associated with it. The extremely slow growth of worldwide human population density through most of the Pleistocene would seem to suggest that Upper Paleolithic populations were not in any sense "driven" by growing population size to exploit new resources, such as reindeer and salmon. Rather, it seems more likely that the late Upper Paleolithic social reorganization into larger groups and the development of fishing technologies were the basis on which subsequent human population growth took place.

Eastern Europe

One of the most amply documented Upper Paleolithic cultures in eastern Europe is the Kostenki-Bershevo culture centered in the Don River Valley, about 470 kilometers southeast of Moscow, where Soviet archaeologists have conducted many seasons of well-planned excavations, revealing a detailed portrait of life in this area from about 25,000 to 11,000 years ago. In contrast to western Europe the Kostenki-Bershevo area is an open grassland environment, with no rock shelters, caves, or other natural habitations, and with very little wood available for fires. People here left a variety of archaeological sites, including base camps, where pit houses were constructed by digging a pit a meter or so deep, ringing the excavation with mammoth bones or tusks, and then draping hides over these supports. The savage winters of Pleistocene Russia must have required constantly burning fires, and the great quantities of bone ash found at these sites indicate that these fires were often fed with mammoth bones in lieu of very scarce wood. Some excavated pit houses were relatively large, with many hearths, suggesting that several families may have passed the winter together. The people of Kostenki subsisted primarily through big-game hunting, mainly of mammoths or horses, with an occasional wild cow or reindeer. Numerous wolf and fox bones at these sites probably reflect the hunting of these animals for their fur for clothing. Although this area of the Don River basin probably abounded in fish and wildfowl, the residents of Kostenki apparently made little use of them: only a single pike vertebrae was recovered, and very few bird bones. Like their Upper Paleolithic counterparts elsewhere, the Kostenki culture people manufactured a variety of decorative items, including "Venus" figurines (representations of women,

5.13
This reconstruction of a settlement at Dolni Vestonice (Czechoslovakia) illustrates how people used shelters to colonize the frigid plains of eastern Europe.

usually with exaggerated sexual characteristics) and chalk drawings of animals.

Throughout much of central and eastern Europe big-game hunting was the main subsistence basis for thousands of hunting and gathering bands, much as it had been for tens of thousands of years. But the mammoth hunters of central and eastern Europe probably did not aggregate into relatively large groups, as the people in western Europe and the Near East at this time are thought to have done. Mammoths probably were not as gregarious as reindeer, horses, or wild cattle, and their hunting would not have rewarded any major changes in social organization. The development of a fishing technology, which opened up parts of western Europe to larger groups and more people, apparently did not happen in eastern and central Europe until quite late: these sites by the Don River contained almost no fish remains until the end of the Pleistocene.

Another interesting eastern European site is Dolni Vestonice in south central Czechoslovakia. About 27,000 years ago there was a settlement of five huts here, similar to the pit houses at Kostenki, around which was a palisade of mammoth bones and tusks stuck in the ground and apparently filled in with brush and turf.

The huts at Dolni Vestonice and Kostenki represent a change from the Mousterian cultures. Winter life in the open country of eastern Europe would have been so hard that at least some Mousterian groups here had probably built rough shelters. But the increasing frequency of these shelters in the Upper Paleolithic probably represents increasing human populations in areas previously only sparsely inhabited. There is also some evidence that average group size was perhaps larger than previously: one hut at Dolni Vestonice was fifteen meters long and six meters wide, and included five hearths. Set apart from the other huts was one cut into a hillside that formed its back wall. The hearth inside this structure had been capped with an earthen dome and was used to make ceramic figurines. Earth was mixed with powdered bone to temper the clay, which was then formed into representations of bears, foxes, lions, and other animal heads, and into representations of women. These female figurines adhered to the worldwide Upper Paleolithic pattern of emphasizing sexual characteristics.

Africa

Initially, archaeologists found little evidence that African cultures of the late Pleistocene paralleled European developments in tool-manufacturing techniques and subsistence and social changes. In recent years, punch-blades, bone implements, and other artifacts similar to some of those of late Pleistocene Europe have been found in Africa, but the general pattern of artifacts and sites in Africa contrasts significantly with those of Europe.

Some interesting North African Upper Paleolithic sites were excavated on the Kom Ombo Plain, forty-five kilometers south of the Aswan Dam in Egypt. About 17,000 years ago, when hunters and gatherers apparently first occupied this area, fish, turtles, and hippopotami abounded in the rivers, great herds of gazelles and hartebeest roamed the plain, and enormous flocks of wildfowl from central Europe wintered in the marshes. Archaeological excavations at sites here dating to about 17,000 years ago revealed one of the highest population densities known for the Upper Paleolithic: an estimated one person per 2.6 square kilometers or about 250 for the whole plain. The Kom Ombo people exploited wildfowl and other animals, but, significantly, they also seem to have been among the earliest peoples to exploit wild cereals. Thousands of years later these cereals would be domesticated and form the basis of the revolutionary change to the agricultural way of life, but already in levels dating to 17,000 B.C., archaeologists have found stone sickles and massive grinding stones that almost certainly were used to process grains. More research will be required to establish the amount of the diet supplied by these wild cereals, but, on the available evidence, the people of the Kom Ombo Plain are among the earliest humans to have made intensive use of wild cereals.

Most of sub-Saharan Africa was also occupied during the Upper Paleolithic. A mandible from Makapansgat, South Africa, has been dated to about 40,000 years ago (although the date is somewhat questionable), and a skull from an open-air site at Cape Flats, near Cape Town, falls within the low end of the range of modern human cranial capacity, but its date and taxonomic status are unclear (Poirier 1973: 201). One of the most interesting fossils of late Pleistocene Africa is the Boskop brain case, found in 1913. No faunal remains and only one bladelike tool were found with the skull, but the cranial volume is estimated at between 1,800 and 1,900 cc—some 400 to 500 cc *more* than the modern European average. This emphasizes the importance of looking at cranial capacities in terms of a *range* of variability. The difference between the Boskop skull and most of us is fully as great as between ourselves and *Homo erectus,* yet the Boskop individual is identified as a *Homo sapiens sapiens.*

Generally, in most parts of Africa, hunters and gatherers of the late Pleistocene appear to have been exploiting a diversity of environments and producing technological and cultural innovations parallel in many ways to those occurring in Eurasia.

Asia

Until recently, few Upper Paleolithic sites were known in East Asia. Excavations at Choukoutien revealed levels dating to about 10,000 years ago containing approximately seven individuals—all of whom had been killed, but apparently not eaten. One individual had clearly died from an arrow or small spear wound to the skull, and another had been beaten about the head with a large stone. Elsewhere, two skulls have been retrieved from Wadjah, in central Java, but dating these has proved difficult.

Recent research in India has indicated at least a few "blade and burin" Upper Paleolithic industries. Sites in the Pushkar Basin in northwestern India appear to have been "factory sites" for the production of tools in many ways like the late Upper Paleolithic tools of Europe, and similar types of tools have also been found in eastern India (Bricker 1976: 136). Clearly, more research is needed before we can realistically hope to understand late Pleistocene developments here.

No late Pleistocene human skeletal remains have been found in Japan, but hundreds of sites have been reported (Bricker 1976: 137). Dating these sites is difficult, but the classic European Upper Paleolithic blade and burin industries are well represented in Japan, particularly in the northern areas across from Siberia (ibid.).

Thus, although very little research has been conducted in East Asia, future discoveries will undoubtedly show that the cultural and technological changes of the late Pleistocene occurred in Asia as well as in the more intensively researched areas of Europe and the Near East.

ART AND RITUAL IN THE UPPER PALEOLITHIC

Beginning about 30,000 years ago the peoples of western Europe began to produce works of art that make them today perhaps the best known of all prehistoric peoples. This art was principally of two forms: cave paintings and more portable artifacts of wood, bone, and stone. Some figurines were even made of baked clay, and artistic expressions in more perishable media, such as hides and softer woods, may have been common. The cave paintings are, with good reason, the most famous Paleolithic art.

Altamira

In 1868, near the Spanish port of Santander, a hunter's dog fell into a crevice in some boulders, and in rescuing the animal the hunter moved some rocks, revealing the opening of a cave. The owner of the land in which the cave was located, a Spanish nobleman and amateur archaeologist, eventually began to excavate the cave floor. He found some stone artifacts, but, according to the story, was unaware of the paintings in the cave until his twelve-year-old daughter visited the site and happened to glance at the ceiling. In the glow of her lantern she saw beautiful paintings of animals. Upon closer inspection it was discovered that the central painting was a group of about twenty-five animals, mainly bison, with a few horses, deer, wolves, and boars. Roughly life size, these paintings were done in rich browns, yellows, reds, and blacks, and the natural configuration of the cave ceiling had been used to emphasize the shape of the animals. The rounded haunch of a bison, for example, was painted over a natural bulge in the stone ceiling, creating a three-dimensional, realistic effect (Prideaux 1973: 93–94).

Scholarly reception to the Altamira discoveries was almost uniformly negative. No one believed the paintings to be more than a few decades old, and some respected prehistorians even hinted that Don Marcelino, their discoverer, had hired an art student to fake these paintings, while another scholar dismissed them as simply the expression "of a mediocre student of the modern school." So abused by critics was the Don that eventually he padlocked the cave, and he died in 1888 without having seen his discoveries accepted as true Paleolithic art. Years later, when many more paintings and other art works had been discovered, the antiquity of Altamira was finally acknowledged, and most of these paintings are now given dates between about 34,000 and 12,000 years ago. Analysis shows that the colors were produced by mixing natural mineral pigments, such as ocher and managanese dioxide, with a binder (blood, urine, vegetable juice, or something similar), and that they were either brushed on with an implement made of animal hair or applied by making a kind of crayon from the pigments and lubricant. Some painting may also have been done by using a pipe to blow the powdered pigments on a surface prepared with animal fat or some other binder.

Lascaux

During World War II paintings on a scale comparable to Altamira were discovered at Lascaux Cave, in France. Researchers have agreed upon a date for the cave paintings of from about 34,000 to 12,000 years ago, the consensus being that they were made on many different occasions within this span. Many different animals are depicted here, including some assumed to be imaginary, such as a duohorn (similar to a unicorn, except with two straight horns). The animals are often painted as if they are in motion, and the general effect is very impressive (Figure 5.14). One of the many curious things about these and other Upper Paleolithic cave paintings is that while the animals are depicted in very real, very representational terms, the figures of humans are either simple stick drawings or else weird half-humans, half-animals.

The more than seventy cave paintings in France, as well as those in Spain, have often been treated as "Rorschach tests," in the sense that modern-day observers have tried to read into them the mind and spirit of primitive man. We shall never know exactly why these paintings were made, but their technique and other characteristics offer some clues. Many of the paintings are in small, hidden passages, where work-

5.14
Lascaux Cave painting.

	Oval	Rectangle	Key shape		Hook	Barb	Dot
Normal							
Simplified							
Derived							

5.15
Many cave paintings include realistic depictions of sexual organs, and some scholars interpret some abstract cave paintings as stylized sexual representations. Leroi-Gourhan here illustrates three groups of symbols for each sex in normal, simplified, and derived form.

ing conditions were very cramped, suggesting that these pictures were not created for the pleasure of the general viewing public. Then again many of the paintings are superimposed on one, two, or even more older ones, indicating perhaps that these efforts were ritual in nature, not simply artistic. The conventional wisdom about most of the cave paintings is that they represent forms of sympathetic magic, where, by picturing animals with spears stuck in them or as caught in traps, Upper Paleolithic people thought they increased their chances of killing and trapping these animals. In fact, the most common themes of these Upper Paleolithic artists were food and sex, with food receiving most of the attention.

Sex, or more precisely, fertility, seems to have been the great theme of Paleolithic portable art. Most numerous and famous are the "Venus" figurines (Figure 5.16). Whether these statuettes represented ideals of beauty, magico-religious invocations of fertility, or something else will always remain unknown, as will the purpose of the many small artifacts depicting animals, abstract symbols, or other themes.

A somewhat different perspective on some Paleolithic art is taken by Alexander Marshack, who has analyzed patterns in the lines, notches, dots, and other symbols in Upper Paleolithic paintings and carvings, and he concluded that some of these were used to keep calendars, to plot celestial events, and to record counts of animals and other objects

(1972). It is difficult, of course, to substantiate such inferences, but it would seem only reasonable that hunters and gatherers of the Upper Pleistocene would be aware of, and try to make some record of, the movements of celestial bodies, the sequence of events, and other subjects.

LIFE IN THE UPPER PALEOLITHIC

More than one archaeologist working on the Upper Paleolithic has expressed the opinion that, if reincarnation "works," one could do worse than to come back as an Upper Paleolithic hunter and gatherer. Most such fantasies are set in the ruggedly beautiful mountains of southern France and are based on visions of the simple, healthy life of a con-

5.16
Cast of Venus figurine from Willendorf, Austria.

Location of some important Paleolithic cave paintings in western Europe.

tinual round of reindeer hunting, cave painting, and fertility ceremonies.

The archaeological evidence, however, suggests that life in the Upper Paleolithic was somewhat more stern and earnest than is often imagined. From a sample of seventy-six Upper Paleolithic skeletons drawn from sites in Europe and Asia, Vallois (1961) found that less than half these individuals had reached the age of twenty-one, that only 12 percent were over forty years of age, and that not a single female had reached the age of thirty. In fact, the distribution of ages and sexes represented by these skeletons was not significantly different from what one might expect from a comparable sample of Neanderthals (Vallois 1961). But even worse, many skeletons evidenced dental abscesses of horrifying size as well as rickets, malnutrition, and other diseases and deformities. Not content with nature's provisions for recycling, people of the Upper Paleolithic were also given to slaughtering each other. At the site of Sandalja II (12,000 years ago), near Pula, Yugoslavia, the skeletal remains of twenty-nine people were found in such smashed and splintered condition that there is little doubt they were killed and eaten. Elsewhere, there is much unmistakable evidence of wounds from arrows and spears.

RECENT APPROACHES TO PALEOLITHIC ARCHAEOLOGY

Part of the problem in explaining Middle Pleistocene developments is the way research has been carried out in the past. It has been "inductive" in the worst sense of that term, meaning that it has consisted mainly of finding more and more sites, excavating as many as possible, and speculating on their significance on the basis of what is found in each. There has been little formal theory or even a body of explicit assumptions from which to deduce hypotheses that can be tested archaeologically in any systematic fashion.

In an attempt to improve on this situation, a number of archaeologists have recently turned to a research strategy known as *simulation modeling*.

Simulations are most familiar from fields like forestry, economics, astrophysics, and engineering. In recent moon-rocket flights, for example, scientists modeled the course of the rocket's flight, based on trajectory, speed, and mass, and then were able to correct particular variables if simulation tests showed the rocket leaving the correct course. Somewhat less mechanical, more speculative models are used daily by economists to predict inflation and other economic variables. And rumors abound in computer circles about top-secret government computer-simulation models that regularly fight World War III out on paper. Complex simulation models are possible only with the help of high-speed computers, since the possible variable interactions in complex situations are almost limitless.

The essence of constructing a simulation model is to construct a picture of some aspect of the world and then use this picture to predict the future—or in the case of archaeology, to describe the past. Obviously, simulation models are *simplifications*. It does no good to reconstruct all the complexity of the world: the point is to reduce the complexity to what the researcher feels are the most important factors in a given process, and then to try to determine how these factors interact over time.

One of the most influential simulation models in archaeology was developed recently by H. Martin Wobst (1974a), some aspects of whose work are discussed here, both as an important contribution to Paleolithic archaeology and because his approach exemplifies what may become an important archaeological research method.

Wobst's model was based on several conclusions and assumptions derived from studies of recent hunting and gathering societies and on archaeological data. He assumed that all Paleolithic societies were composed of small bands of perhaps twenty-five related individuals and that some of these bands occasionally aggregated to exchange marriageable females, share food, and to perform other social activities. Wobst called the larger social unit the *maximum band*, and it is an observed fact that all recent human hunting and gathering societies belong to such maximum bands and that they usually spend most of the year in groups of about twenty-five. Wobst also assumed that Pleistocene hunters and gatherers were territorial, to the extent that while they no doubt roamed far from their home bases, they nonetheless spent all or most of their lives in areas of perhaps 100 kilometers' diameter. Because these groups had no beasts of burden or wheeled vehicles, everything they accumulated had to be carried, placing restrictions on the distance covered and ease of movement.

Wobst's third assumption was that Pleistocene hunters and gatherers inhabited roughly hexagonal territories. The basis for this assumption is both empirical and theoretical. Surveys of existing hunting and gathering bands from all over the world show that most of them feel surrounded by approximately six neighboring bands. Laid out on a map, these territories do not look at all like equilateral hexagons, but, as a statistical approximation, it is legitimate to conceive of the territories of hunters and gatherers as hexagonal in shape. There are also theoretical reasons why the territories of hunters and gatherers should be hexagonal:

> Among the regular polygons, only the hexagon combines optimum packing efficiency with minimal movement and boundary costs. . . . While circles provide better accessibility from the center and have the shortest periphery in relation to their area, they cannot be tightly packed without leaving unaccounted voids between neighbors. Triangles and squares can be tightly packed . . . but have poorer accessibility characteristics and longer boundaries per given area. (Wobst 1974a: 153)

Based on these and other assumptions, Wobst then created a world in which there were sixty-one bands, with twenty-five members each, dispersed over an idealized landscape in perfect hexagonal territories (Figure 5.18). Each individual in the population was identified by name, age, sex, place of residence, marital status, and relatives (1974a: 158). Then, employing what is known as the *Monte Carlo technique,* Wobst simulated life in these bands over 400-year periods. He used studies of contemporary hunters and gatherers to estimate the chance each individual had of dying in any particular year, the chance of a married woman giving birth during any particular year, and the chance of any particular birth being a girl or boy. Wobst's simulation program also allowed him to vary social conditions, so that the simulated society could be monogamous, polygamous, endogamous, exogamous, patrilocal, incestuous, or various combinations of these.

The actual simulation procedure was done with a computerized program. The first step was to age each individual by one year. Next, those individuals widowed or of marriageable age entered the "mating loop," where an appropriate mate was found. Each couple was then "moved" to the appropriate band according to the marriage rules and residence patterns then in force. Following mating, each female entered the "procreation loop," where random numbers and probability tables

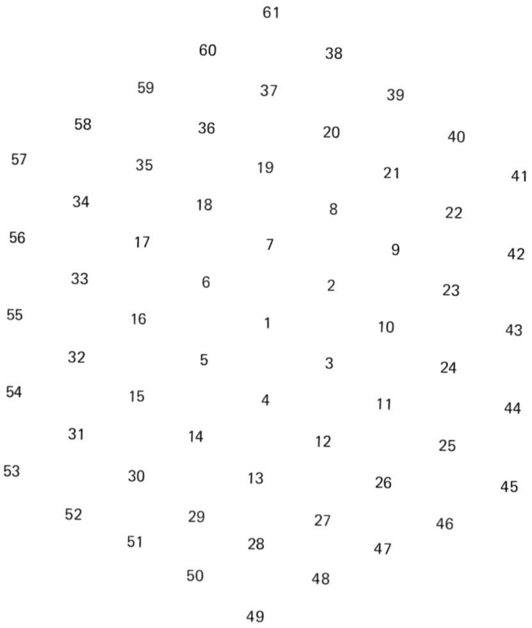

61

60 38

59 37 39

58 36 20

57 35 19 40

34 18 21 41

8 22

56 17 7

33 6 9 42

2 23

55 16 1 10

32 5 3 43

54 15 4 24

31 14 11 44

12 25

53 30 13

52 29 26 45

51 28 27 46

50 48 47

49

5.18
Wobst's basic population for simulation study. Sixty-one bands of twenty-five numbers each, arranged in hexagonal territories.

were used to decide whether the child's sex would be male or female. Other components of the program determined when a group had reached sufficient size to split and move into different territories.

Wobst found that the model had to be simulated for at least 400 years to provide reliable results—a procedure requiring only a few minutes execution time on the computer. He also found that a band of about twenty-five would be close to the optimum size for maintaining marriage networks and group spatial arrangements usually found in hunting and gathering societies. His calculations suggested that incest would not be advantageous to these groups because it would make mate selection much less predictable.

These and other implications of Wobst's model and of similar attempts to model Pleistocene societies await additional research and their implications have not yet been fully analyzed. But they would seem to offer improved methods for planning archaeological surveys and excavations and for reconstructing Paleolithic societies.

Bibliography

Binford, Lewis. 1968. "Post-Pleistocene, Adaptations." In *New Perspectives in Archeology,* eds. L. Binford and S. Binford. Chicago: Aldine.

Binford, Lewis and Sally Binford. 1966. "A Preliminary Analysis of Functional Variability in the Mousterian of Levallois Facies." In *Recent Studies in Paleoanthropology.* American Anthropologist special publication, pp. 238–95.

Binford, Lewis. 1968. "Post-Pleistocene Adaptations." In *New Perspectives in Anthropologist.* 70: 707–17.

Birdsell, J. B. 1972. *Human Evolution.* Chicago: Rand McNally.

Bordes, François. 1961a. *Typologie du paléolithique ancien et Moyen Bordeaux.* Publication de l'Institut de Prehistoire de l'Universite de Bordeaux.

———. 1961b. "Mousterian Cultures in France." *Science.* 134: 803–10.

———. 1968. *The Old Stone Age.* London: Weidenfeld & Nicholson.

———. 1972. *A Tale of Two Caves.* New York: Harper & Row.

Bordes, François and D. de Sonneville-Bordes. 1970. "The Significance of Variability in Paleolithic Assemblages." *World Archaeology.* 2(1): 61–73.

Boule, M. and H. Vallois. 1932. *Fossil Men.* London: Thames and Hudson.

Brace, C. Loring. 1964. "The Fate of the 'Classic' Neanderthals: A Consideration of Human Catastrophism." *Current Anthropology.* 5: 3.

———. 1967. *The Stages of Human Evolution: Human and Cultural Origins.* Englewood Cliffs, N.J.: Prentice-Hall.

———. 1971. "Review of *Shanidar: The First Flower People,* by R. Solecki." *Natural History.* 80(7): 82–86.

Bricker, H. 1976. "Upper Paleolithic Archaeology." *Annual Review of Anthropology.* 5: 133–48.

Brose, D. and M. Wolpoff. 1971. "Early Upper Paleolithic Man and Late Paleolithic Tools." *American Anthropologist.* 73(5): 1156.

Brothwell, D. 1961. "Upper Pleistocene Human Skull from Niah Caves, Sarawak." *Sarawak Museum Journal.* 9: 323.

Butzer, Karl W. and Glynn Isaac, eds. 1975. *After the Australopithecines.* The Hague: Mouton.

Campbell, B., ed. 1976. *Humankind Emerging.* Boston: Little, Brown.

Carlisle, R. C. and M. I. Siegel. 1974. "Some Problems in the Interpretation of Neanderthal Speech Capabilities: A Reply to Lieberman." *American Anthropologist.* 76(2): 319–22.

Chang, K. C. 1962. "New Evidence on Fossil Man in China." *Science.* 136: 749.

Clark, G. 1967. *The Stone Age Hunters.* New York: McGraw-Hill.

———. 1975. *The Earlier Stone Age Settlement of Scandinavia.* Cambridge: Cambridge University Press.

Clark, J. D. 1960. "Human Ecology During the Pleistocene and Later Times in Africa South of the Sahara." *Current Anthropology*. 1: 307.

Clark, J. D. 1969, 1974. *Kalambo Falls Prehistoric Site,* vols. 1 and 2. Cambridge, Mass.: Cambridge University Press.

Coale, Ansley. 1974. "The History of Human Population." *Scientific American*. 231: 41–51.

Coles, J. M. and E. S. Higgs. 1969. *The Archaeology of Early Man*. New York: Praeger.

Constable, George et al. 1973. *The Neanderthals*. New York: Time-Life.

Coon, C. 1962. *The Origins of Races*. New York: Knopf.

Cornwall, I. 1968. *Prehistoric Animals and Their Hunters*. New York: Praeger.

Day, M. 1971. "Postcranial Remains of *Homo Erectus* from Bed IV, Olduvai Gorge, Tanzania." *Nature*. 232: 383.

Denham, W. 1974. "Population Structure, Infant Transport, and Infanticide Among Pleistocene and Modern Hunters and Gatherers." *Journal of Anthropological Research*. 30(3): 101–98.

Divale, William. 1972. "Systematic Population Control in the Middle and Upper Paleolithic." *World Archaeology*. 42(2): 222–41.

Dubois, E. 1921. "The Proto-Australian Fossil Man of Wadjak, Java." Proceedings: Koninklijke Nederlandse Akademie van Wetenschappen. 23: 1013.

Edey, Maitland A. and Editors of Time-Life. 1972. *The Missing Link*. New York: Time-Life.

Falk, D. 1975. "Comparative Anatomy of the Larynx in Man and the Chimpanzee: Implications for Language in Neanderthal." *American Journal of Physical Anthropology*. 43: 123–32.

Freeman, M. 1971. "A Social and Economic Analysis of Systematic Female Infanticide." *American Anthropologist*. 73: 1011–18.

Garn, S. and W. Block. 1970. "The Limited Nutritional Value of Cannibalism." *American Anthropologist*. 72(1): 106.

Gladfelter, Bruce G. 1975. "Middle Pleistocene Sedimentary Sequences in East Anglia." In *After the Australopithecines*, eds. K. W. Butzer and G. Isaac. The Hague: Mouton.

Hewes, Gordon W. 1973. *The Origin of Man*. Minneapolis: Burgess.

Higgs, E. and D. Brothwell. 1961. "North Africa and Mount Carmel: Recent Developments." *Man*. 61: 138.

Higgs, E. and M. R. Jarman. 1969. "The Origins of Agriculture: a Reconsideration." *Antiquity*. 43: 31–43.

Hockett, C. F. 1973. *Man's Place in Nature*. New York: McGraw-Hill.

Holloway, R. 1968. "Cranial Capacity and the Evolution of the Human Brain." In *Culture: Man's Adaptive Dimension*, ed. A. Montagu. Oxford: Oxford University Press.

Howell, F. Clark. 1961. "Isimila: A Paleolithic Site in Africa." *Scientific American.* 205(4): 118–31.

———. 1965. *Early Man.* New York: Time-Life.

Howells, W. W. 1975. "Neanderthal Man: Facts and Figures." In *Australopithecus Paleoanthropology: Morphology and Paleoecology,* ed. R. H. Tuttle. The Hague: Mouton.

Ivanhoe, F. 1970. "Was Virchow Right about Neanderthal?" *Nature.* 227: 577.

Jelinek, J. 1969. "Neanderthal Man and Homo Sapiens in Central and Eastern Europe." *Current Anthropology.* 10: 475.

Kennedy, Kenneth A. R. 1975. *Neanderthal Man.* Minneapolis: Burgess.

Klein, R. 1969. *Man and Culture in the Late Pleistocene.* San Francisco: Chandler.

Klima, B. 1953. "Paleolithic Huts of Dolni Vestonice." *Antiquity.* 27(105): 4–14.

Kummer, H. 1971. *Primate Societies.* Chicago: Aldine-Atherton.

Kurtén, Björn. 1968. *Pleistocene Mammals of Europe.* Chicago: Aldine.

———. 1976. *The Cave Bear Story: Life and Death of a Vanished Animal.* New York: Columbia University Press.

Laughlin, W. S. 1968. "Hunting: An Integrating Biobehavior System and Its Evolutionary Importance." In *Man the Hunter,* eds. R. B. Lee and I. DeVore. Chicago: Aldine.

Leakey, M. D. 1975. "Cultural Patterns in the Olduvai Sequence." In *After the Australopithecines,* eds. K. W. Butzer and G. Ll Isaac. The Hague: Mouton.

Leroi-Gourhan, A. 1968. *The Art of Prehistoric Man in Western Europe.* London: Thames and Hudson.

Lieberman, P. E. and E. S. Crelin. 1971. "On the Speech of Neanderthals." *Linguistic Inquiry.* 2: 203–22.

Lieberman, P. E., E. S. Crelin, and D. H. Klatt. 1972. "Phonetic Ability and Related Anatomy of the Newborn and Adult Human, Neanderthal Man, and the Chimpanzee." *American Anthropologist.* 74: 287.

Luguet, G. 1930. *The Art and Religion of Fossil Man.* New Haven: Yale University Press.

Lumley, Henry de. *French Prehistory, vol. 1: Paleolithic and Mesolithic Culture of France.* Editions Du Centre National De La Recherche Scientifique, Paris.

———. 1969. *Le Paleolithique Inférieur et Moyen du Midi Méditerranéen dans son Cadre Geologique, tome 1: Ligurie Provence.* Editions du Centre National de La Recherche Scientifique. Paris.

———. 1971. *Le Paleolithique Inférieur et Moyen du Midi Méditerranéan dans son Cadre Geologique, tome 2: Bas—Languedoc, Roussillon, Catalogne.* Editions du Centre National de La Recherche Scientifique. Paris.

Lumley, Henry de and M.-A. de Lumley. 1971. "Decouverte de restes humains anteneandertaliens dates du debut du Riss à la Caune de l'Arago (Tautavel, Pyrenees-Orientales)." *Comptes Rendus de l'Academie des Sciences de Paris.* 272: 1739–42.

Lumley, M.-A. de. 1975. "Ante-Neanderthals of Western Europe." In *Australopithe-cus Paleoanthropology: Morphology and Paleoecology*, ed. R. H. Tuttle. The Hague: Mouton.

McBurney, C. B. M. 1960. *The Stone Age of Northern Africa*. Baltimore: Penguin.

Marshack, Alexander. 1972. *The Roots of Civilization*. New York: McGraw-Hill.

Movius, H. 1958. "Tayacian Man from the Cave of Fontéchevade." *American An-thropologist*. 50: 365.

Oakley, K. 1952. "Swanscombe Man." *Proceedings of the Geological Association of London*. 63: 271.

Pfeiffer, John. 1978. *The Emergence of Man*. New York: Harper & Row.

Pilbeam, D. 1975. "Middle Pleistocene Hominids." In *After the Australopithecines*, eds. K. W. Butzer and G. Ll. Isaac. The Hague: Mouton.

Poirier, Frank E. 1973. *Fossil Man*. St. Louis: C. V. Mosby.

Prideaux, Tom and Editors of Time-Life. 1973. *Cro-Magnon Man*. New York: Time-Life.

Roberts, D. F. 1953. "Body Weight, Race and Climate." *American Journal of Physi-cal Anthropology*. N.S. 11: 533–58.

Roper, M. 1969. "A Survey of the Evidence for Intra-human Killing in the Pleisto-cene." *Current Anthropology*. 10(5): 427.

Sampson, Garth C. 1974. *The Stone Age Archaeology of Southern Africa*. New York and London: Academic Press.

Sauer, N. J. and T. W. Phenice. 1972. *Hominid Fossils*. 2nd ed. Dubuque Iowa: W. C. Brown.

Semenov, S. 1964. *Prehistoric Technology*. London: Cory, Adams, and McKay.

Shapiro, Harry, 1974. *Peking Man*. New York Simon & Schuster.

Solheim, W. 1960. "The Present Status of the 'Paleolithic' in Borneo." *Asian Per-spectives*. 2: 83.

Steegman, A. 1970. "Cold Adaptation and the Human Face." *American Journal of Physical Anthropology*. 32: 243.

Straus, Lawrence Guy. 1977. "Of Deerslayers and Mountain Men: Paleolithic Faunal Exploitation in Cantabrian Spain." In *For Theory Building in Archaeology*, ed. Lewis R. Binford. New York: Academic Press.

Straus, W. and A. Cave. 1957. "Pathology and the Posture of Neanderthal Man." *Quarterly Review of Biology*. 32: 348.

Swedlund, A. 1974. "The Use of Ecological Hypotheses in Australopithecine Tax-onomy." *American Anthropologist*. 76(3): 515–29.

Tobias, P. and G. Von Koenigswald. 1964. "Comparison Between the Olduvai Hom-inines and Those of Java and Some Implications for Phylogeny." *Nature*. 204: 515.

Vallois, H. 1961. "The Social Life of Early Man: The Evidence of the Skeletons." In *Social Life of Early Man*, ed. S. Washburn. Chicago: Aldine.

Washburn, S. and J. Lancaster. 1968. "The Evolution of Hunting." In *Perspectives on Human Evolution*, eds. S. Washburn and P. Jay. New York: Holt.

Weinberg, S. S. 1970. "The Stone Age in the Aegean." *Cambridge Ancient History*. 1: 557–618. Cambridge: Cambridge University Press.

Windels, F. 1965. *The Lascaux Cave Paintings*. London: Faber and Faber.

Wobst, H. Martin. 1974a. "Boundary Conditions for Paleolithic Social Systems: A Simulation Approach." *American Antiquity*. 39(2): 147–78.

———. 1974b. "The Archaeology of Band Society—Some Unanswered Questions." *American Antiquity*. 39(4): v–xiii.

Wolpoff, M. 1968. "Climatic Influence on the Skeletal Nasal Aperture." *American Journal of Physical Anthropology*. 29: 405–23.

———. 1970. "The Evidence for Multiple Hominid Taxa at Swartkrans." *American Anthropologist*. 72: 56–57.

———. 1971. "Vertesszölös and the Presapiens Theory." *American Journal of Physical Anthropology*. 35(2): 209.

Woo, J. 1958. "Tzeyang Paleolithic Man—Earliest Representative of Modern Man in China." *American Journal of Physical Anthropology*. 16: 459.

6

The First Americans

At break of day the shore was thronged with people all young . . . all of good stature, fine looking. . . .

I was anxious to learn whether they had any
gold, as I noticed that some of the natives had
rings hanging from holes in their noses. . . . I
tried to get them to go for some, but they could
not understand they were to go.

Christopher Columbus
13 October 1492

Most of the European "discoverers" of the New World in the fifteenth
and sixteenth centuries were at first not surprised to find "Indians"
there, because they thought they had landed in India, China, or even
Japan. But when they finally realized they were not in the Orient and
became aware of the diversity of New World cultures, they began to
grapple with the problem of the origin of the Native Americans. The
Bible, final authority for most Europeans of this era, seemed strangely
silent on the very existence of this "second-earth," so Europeans began
speculating on how the Indians could have reached the New World
from the Garden of Eden, where they were assumed to have originated.
It was widely believed that the Indians were the descendants of Ham,
one of Noah's sons, who was also thought to have been the father of the
Egyptians and other "darker races." Early explorers were greatly impressed by such similarities between Egyptian and aboriginal American

cultures as the pyramids found in Mexico and certain forms of artistic representation (Steward 1973: 60).

Another popular idea was that the American Indians were descendants of the "lost tribes of Israel," Jews who had been evicted from Palestine by the Romans and Babylonians. Some scholars even compiled lists of the physical and cultural similarities between Jews and Indians. The "lost-tribes" idea eventually was incorporated into the doctrines of the Church of the Latter-day Saints (the "Mormons"). The founder of this religion, Joseph Smith, reported that on several occasions between 1823 and 1827 an angel of the Lord showed him golden tablets on which were engraved the *Book of Mormon,* and in this book, in a complicated account, it was explained how the Indians were remnants of tribes of Israel that had come to the New World by ship sometime around A.D. 421.

Equally intriguing are the Atlantis and Mu theories, which hold that the Americans are descendants of people who fled islands in the Atlantic Ocean that were destroyed thousands of years ago by volcanic eruptions.

Over the years many other curious suggestions have been made about the origins of Native Americans, and thus it is interesting that the currently accepted and well-documented ideas about the matter were known as early as the sixteenth century. In 1590 a Spanish Jesuit, José de Acosta, proposed that in the extreme northern part of America there was a land bridge over which many animals had come into the New World. Subsequently, several people announced similar views, and by 1781 the brilliant scholar Thomas Jefferson could describe the peopling of the New World in terms we know today to be largely accurate.

> Late discoveries of Captain Cook, coasting from Kamschatka to California, have proved that if the two continents of Asia and America be separated at all, it is only by a narrow straight. So that from this side also, inhabitants may have passed into America; and the resemblance between the Indians of America and the eastern inhabitants of Asia, would induce us to conjecture, that the former are the descendants of the latter, or the latter of the former: excepting indeed the Eskimaux, who, from the same circumstances of resemblance, and from identity of language, must be derived from the Groenlanders, and these probably from some of the northern parts of the old continent. (Quoted in Steward 1973: 70)

6.1
An early photograph of a
Native American.

In their search for clues to the origins of Native Americans, Jefferson and others of his age were struck by the fact that in physical form the American Indians closely resemble Asian races in having dark brown eyes, black, coarse, straight hair (with little incidence of baldness), and, relative to Europeans, widely spaced cheekbones. But great differences were also apparent: except for the Eskimos and Aleuts, the aboriginal Americans did not have the fleshy eyelid (epicanthic) folds that distinguish East Asian populations, and many Native Americans had relatively prominent noses.

It was soon noted that the New World included an impressive diversity of languages and cultures, that none of the languages of Native Americans, except for the extreme northern populations, bore much resemblance to Old World languages, and that many American languages were unrelated and mutually unintelligible to their speakers. Thus, it seemed certain that although the aboriginal Americans were probably descendants of Asian peoples, they must have lived in America for a long time for such physical and linguistic divergence to have occurred.

Presently the view that the first Americans came from East Asia via a land route is generally accepted, but considerable controversy remains about when the first migrations occurred. Some archaeologists maintain they took place only about 14,000 to 10,000 years ago, while others think it was about 35,000 years ago; still others think that colonization may have begun 70,000 years ago or even earlier. Some clue as to the date of original colonization is suggested by the fact that intensive research has failed to turn up any New World human skeletons that cannot be comfortably fitted within the class *Homo sapiens sapiens*. In fact, the bones of the earliest known Americans cannot be distinguished from those of contemporary aboriginal American populations on the basis of any important skeletal characteristics (Steward 1973: 170). Because the first *Homo sapiens sapiens* appear in the Near East and Europe about 35,000 years ago, we might assume that the aboriginal Americans must have come over since then, but we really don't know when the first *Homo sapiens sapiens* appeared in the East Asian areas from which the first Americans apparently came. Anatomically modern populations may have appeared there long before they did in the Near East or Europe. The alternative view, that there are undiscovered Neanderthal or earlier hominid remains in the New World, has a certain lay popularity, but no informed archaeologist regards this as at all likely.

Although it is uncertain when East Asian populations developed epicanthic folds, small noses, and relatively flat facial profiles, in view of the prominent noses of most Native Americans and their non-Mongolian eye shapes, it is apparent that either the Americans are only distantly related to these populations, or that they emigrated before the Asian populations developed their distinctive features. These differences might also suggest that Americans and Asians had been adapting to very different circumstances for many thousands of years. It is interesting that contemporary aboriginal Americans, from the Yukon to the tip of South America, differ physically much less than, say, contemporary Europeans: Native Americans all have similar hair, eye, and skin coloring and facial features. We have very little evidence on which to estimate rates of evolutionary change in these superficial physical characteristics, but the overall similarity of New World populations suggests that the natural selective pressures that produce variation in these characteristics have not had very long to operate. It is also possible that the physical characteristics of New World peoples were largely determined by "accident" (genetic drift) and isolation. Even in the most temperate periods the northern Arctic would have supported few people, and perhaps only a dozen or so bands of hunters and gatherers and their direct descendants had crossed the land bridge before the rising sea levels isolated them from the Old World populations. Therefore, all Native Americans (except for later migrants, mainly the Eskimo) could have descended from relatively few people, and the "accidental" characteristics of this gene pool would determine the dominent physical characteristics of subsequent Native Americans. Possibly, then, the physical characteristics of Native Americans are not to be understood simply in terms of their adaptiveness.

These various lines of "evidence" are not in any sense conclusive, but, given the absence of Neanderthals in the New World, as well as the physical differences between American and Asian populations and the physical homogeneity of Native Americans, an entry date of about 35,000 years ago (the date of the first known appearance of anatomically modern humans in the Old World) does not seem implausible. We can at least use it as a hypothesis to be evaluated with the archaeological record.

THE BERING LAND BRIDGE

Today, Eskimos using skin boats easily cross the 90 kilometers of open sea separating Siberia and America, but such a sea crossing would not have been necessary during much of the Pleistocene. During periods of glacial advance within the last million years, enormous quantities of water were converted to ice, lowering the sea level sufficiently to expose a 1,500- to 3,000-kilometer-wide expanse of the floor of the Bering Sea. Sea depth here today is only about 55 meters, and sea levels are known to have been lowered by at least this amount several times during the Pleistocene. Formerly this land bridge—usually referred to as *Beringia* (Figure 6.2)—was thought to have existed only at the height of the glacial advance, that is, for several thousand years prior to about 70,000 years ago; from about 50,000 to about 40,000 years ago; and then again from about 29,000 to 10,000 years ago; but there is now evidence that the land bridge may have been available for most of the Pleistocene (Figure 6.3) (Haag 1962: 269).

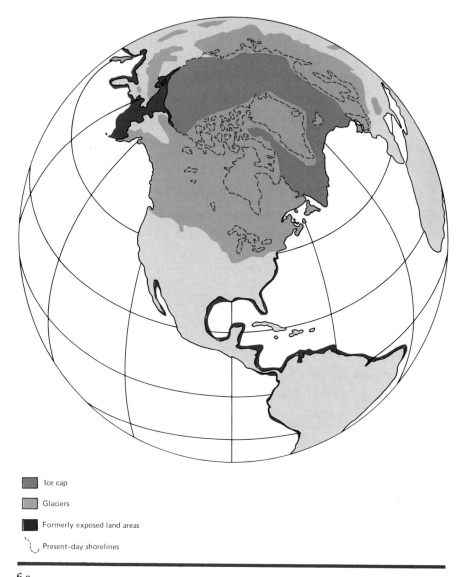

6.2
Formation of a land bridge across the Bering Sea and the extension of shorelines during the second major Wisconsin glaciation. Glaciation may not have been so extensive as represented here.

One might think the ice and cold in Siberia and Beringia would have formed an impassable barrier to hunting and gathering groups, but Pleistocene sediments here reveal that this was not the case. Low precipitation, the flat terrain, and warm ocean currents created an ice-free, tundra-covered connection from eastern Siberia across the land bridge and into central Alaska. These conditions are reflected in the

Legend:
- Ice cap
- Glaciers
- Formerly exposed land areas
- Present-day shorelines

many non-Arctic adapted animal species that crossed from Asia to America during the Pleistocene. Prior to 10,000 years ago, species of deer, bison, camels, bears, foxes, mammoths, moose, caribou, and even rodents crossed from Siberia into the New World. Going the other way—from America to Asia—were foxes, woodchucks, and, during the early Pleistocene, the ancestors of modern forms of horses, camels, and wolves. Nor were animals the only migrants: a wide variety of plant species also made the crossing, supporting the geological evidence that the Bering land bridge must have been at least 1,500 kilometers wide and in existence for long periods (Haag 1962: 269).

THE ROUTE SOUTH

It is not difficult to imagine the first Americans crossing the ice-free land bridge, and them or their descendants eventually reaching central Alaska. But how could they have survived the ice and snow of inland Pleistocene Alaska and Canada and reached the lower latitudes of North and South America?

An influential early hypothesis (reviewed in Hopkins, ed., 1967) was that these southward migrations could have occurred only a few times, because it was thought that for most of the Pleistocene the way would have been blocked by coalescing ice sheets. Even if these ice sheets did not completely bar the way south, most authorities thought that a narrow open corridor between them would have had too little food to support groups of hunters and gatherers—who require large territories to support even low population densities. Until recently, it was widely accepted that a route southward would have been available only during periods when the glaciers retreated: that is, intervals of a few thousand years shortly after the warmer periods of 70,000 years ago, 40,000 years ago, or, perhaps, only after the last glacial retreat, some 12,000 to 10,000 years ago.

Some archaeologists continue to believe that humans entered the lower reaches of the New World only after the last glacial retreat, but this interpretation has a number of problems. Ten thousand years would not seem sufficient time to account for the tremendous linguistic and cultural diversity evident in the New World cultures, and more important, except possibly for a period of a few thousand years, the corridor southward appears to have been open for almost all of the Pleisto-

American Sequence

Holocene time	Hypsithermal warm time (4–7500 B.P.)
Wisconsin Ice Age	Valders ice adv. (± 11,000 B.P.)
	Mankato ± 22,000
	± 28,000
	Tazewell ± 45,000
Sangamon Interglacial	± 60,000 B.P.
Illinoisian Ice Age	warm
Yarmouth Interglacial Age	cold
	Temperature curve
Kansan Ice Age	warm
Aftonian Interglacial Age	cold
Nebraskan Ice Age	

Eurasian Sequence

Recent	Upper Pleistocene
Würm Ice Age	
Third Interglacial	Middle Pleistocene
Riss Ice Age	
Second Interglacial Age	
Mindel Ice Age	Lower Pleistocene
First Interglacial Age	
Günz Ice Age	

pre-projectile points stage?

6.3
Late Pleistocene chronology.

cene (Reeves 1971). Also, as we shall see, there is archaeological evidence of human occupation prior to 12,000 years ago.

The exact path the first Americans took is not known but the most likely would be along the coast of the land bridge, then into Alaska north of the Brooks range, up the Yukon River Valley, then into the Mackenzie River Valley, and from there southward, along the eastern slopes of the Rockies and on into the Dakotas (Figure 6.4), and then southward. Along the coast of the land bridge were probably abundant resources in the form of fish, birds, eggs, invertebrates, and many plant foods. If groups did come this way, it is unlikely that we shall ever be able to document their journey archaeologically, for the rising seas of the post-Pleistocene era have submerged the ancient shoreline.

We might expect that if the immigrants crossed the land bridge primarily along the coast, then the groups migrating south would have retained some elements of the generalized hunting, fishing, and foraging economies required in the intertidal zone. If, on the other hand, they came across the middle of the land bridge, a greater reliance on big-game hunting would have been essential.

These different adaptations should be expressed in the archaeological record, particularly if the main adaptation was inland big-game hunting. Siberian cultures that specialized in this way of life had a developed blade and point technology, as well as huts of mammoth hides and tusks, and if these peoples were the progenitors of the first Americans, we might expect similar implements and adaptations in the New World. The coastal foraging route, however, may not have required a very specialized tool kit.

Whatever their adaptation, the migrants were almost certainly not constantly on the move southward; no doubt these population movements were achieved by *budding-off,* as groups grew to certain numbers, split, and one group moved some distance from the parent group. This pattern is the usual one in cases when new species move into empty niches, and many thousands of years may have passed between the time the first human set foot on the land bridge and the year the first groups arrived in the Continental United States.

PLEISTOCENE NORTH AND SOUTH AMERICA: RESOURCES

North winds blowing off the kilometer-high glacial ice sheets made the climate of much of Pleistocene North America much different from today's. Much of Nevada and Utah was covered by Lake Bonneville, of which only a shrinking remnant (Great Salt Lake) remains. Wyoming, Iowa, and other parts of the Great Plains were vast pine, spruce, and tamarack forests, except in the higher elevations, where there were lush open grasslands. To the south, the area between the Mississippi River and the Rockies was a verdant mosaic of grasslands, lakes, and birch and alder forests. In eastern North America huge expanses of coniferous forests stretched from the edge of the glacial ice sheets to the lower Ohio River Valley, and in the South were virgin forests of oak, beech, and other deciduous trees.

The animals inhabiting this wilderness of 14,000 to 12,000 years ago closely approximate a modern hunter's vision of paradise (Figure 6.5). Giant moose, three meters and more in height, could be found in many of the wetter areas, along with *Castoroides,* a type of beaver as large as a modern bear. Along the woodland edges of the southeastern United

6.4
Possible migration routes into North America.

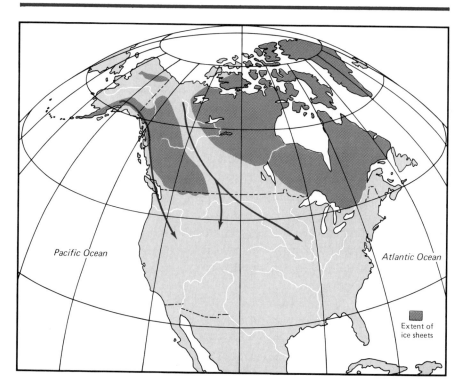

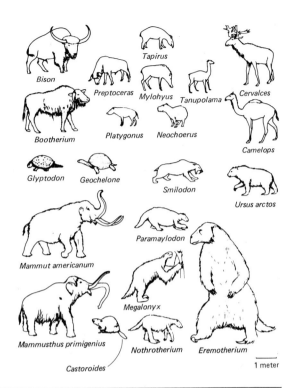

6.5
Some large mammals of
Pleistocene America. The
scale preserves relative size.

Bison
Preptoceras
Tapirus
Mylohyus
Tanupolama
Cervalces
Bootherium
Platygonus
Neochoerus
Camelops
Glyptodon
Geochelone
Smilodon
Ursus arctos
Paramaylodon
Mammut americanum
Megalonyx
Mammusthus primigenius
Castoroides
Nothrotherium
Eremotherium
1 meter

States were large populations of giant ground sloths, ungainly creatures fully as tall as modern giraffes. In more open country were vast herds of straight-horned bison, caribou, musk-oxen, and mammoths—some species of which stood four meters high at the shoulders. In the more forested areas of the East and South were the mammoth's cousin, the mastodon, a more solitary animal than the mammoth and apparently a browser rather than a grassland grazer (Martin and Guilday 1967). Amid all these large creatures were rabbits, armadillos, birds, camels, peccaries, and other animals. And the carnivores that such a movable feast attracted were equally impressive. Packs of dire wolves roamed most of the New World, as did panthers as large as modern lions and two species of saber-toothed cat, one about the size of a lion but with heavier forequarters and enormous teeth. Jaguars larger than modern lions also ranged from Alaska to Mexico (Martin and Wright 1967: 32–33). Thus, the first Americans were hardly entering an "empty niche," as these ferocious predators no doubt provided stiff competition for people trying to specialize in hunting.

Central and South America were also rich game preserves during and just after the Pleistocene, but in the rainforests of the Amazon

Basin, the great coniferous forests of the North American South and East, and a few other locations so much energy was in the form of inedible and unnutritious vegetation (cellulose) that there would have been few resources for primitive hunters and gatherers.

The First Americans: The Archaeological Record

Given the probable southward migration routes, we might expect to find a long trail of archaeological sites stretching from northeastern Siberia along the sea floor of the now submerged land bridge into central Alaska, and then southward, between the ice caps. If these early immigrants were big-game hunters, we would expect many of the sites to be concentrations of animal bones, hearths, and flint tools appropriate for killing and preparing these animals.

Alas, the gap between the real and ideal—so persistent in all archaeological research—is particularly great in this case. Some sites do fit this expected pattern, but the evidence is far from conclusive. First of all, adequate surveys of northeastern Siberia have never been completed. Aside from the rigors of the Arctic climate, the politics of staging an archaeological expedition to Siberia have deterred most Western scholars. Soviet scholars, however, have recently been working in these areas, and we may soon have more data. Present evidence suggests that before about 30,000 years ago, Siberia had extremely low population densities or was unsettled altogether. The Ural Mountains, the intense cold, and the great interior swamps and forests of Siberia may have barred human colonization, at least until huts had been developed. In any case, the earliest known sites in northeastern Siberia date to about 23,000 years ago and reflect a life focused on the hunting of mammoths and other large animals. Projectile points, scrapers, and burins—tool types associated with big-game hunters all over the Old World—are the most frequent implements at Mal-ta, Afontova gora II, and other sites of this period. To the east, on the Aldan River, Diuktai Cave has yielded crude pebble tools, including scrapers and points, some of which apparently resemble early American artifacts, but it has not yet been possible to date this site with any confidence.

Some archaeologists see similarities between these pebble and flake tools of Siberia and the earliest artifacts in the Americas, but others dispute this. As we shall see, the earliest American sites seem to contain crude pebble tools, not projectile points or finely worked blades or scrapers. Thus it is difficult to tie them to these big-game hunting cultures of late Pleistocene Siberia.

The evidence is also somewhat sketchy on the American side of the land bridge. The Alaskan and northern Canadian climates make surveys very difficult, and farther south the constant waxing and waning of the glacial ice sheets and the vast riverine systems that drained them have thoroughly chewed up much of the land along the Canadian corridor. No doubt many sites in these areas have long since been scoured away by ice or water. In any case, these extreme environments would have supported only comparatively light population densities, and thus we would not expect to find many sites.

Some crude bone tools from the Old Crow site in the Yukon have been radiocarbon-dated to between 28,000 and 23,000 years ago, but the bones may have been deposited many thousands of years before they were made into tools. Occasionally, other Alaskan and northern Canadian sites are reported in the 20,000 years and older time range, but so far none has been conclusively demonstrated to be of this age.

Although there are presently no well-dated sites in the "corridor" through Canada, where glacial and water activity was most destructive, the situation improves somewhat south of the Canadian-U.S. border. For example, human bones found in 1936 during a construction project near Los Angeles have been datad by amino-acid racemization methods, based on analysis of chemical changes in bones, to more than 50,000 years ago. Skeletal fragments from other southern Californian sites have given comparable dates, and some archaeologists provisionally accept their accuracy (Bada and Helfman 1975). But the disturbed contexts of these finds and lingering questions about the accuracy of the dating method have engendered debate. Other sites have also been dated to before 30,000 years ago, such as American Falls, Idaho, and Calico Hills, California, but in every case the evidence is ambiguous.

The oldest widely accepted dates for a New World site come from Pikimachay Cave in Peru, where archaeologist Richard MacNeish excavated crude stone tools and animal bones that have been radiocarbon-dated as early as 22,000 years ago (MacNeish 1978: 203). The association between these stone tools (Figure 6.6) and some forms of extinct animals is unmistakable in 12,000-year-old levels of the site, but some archaeologists doubt that its earliest levels represent human occupation.

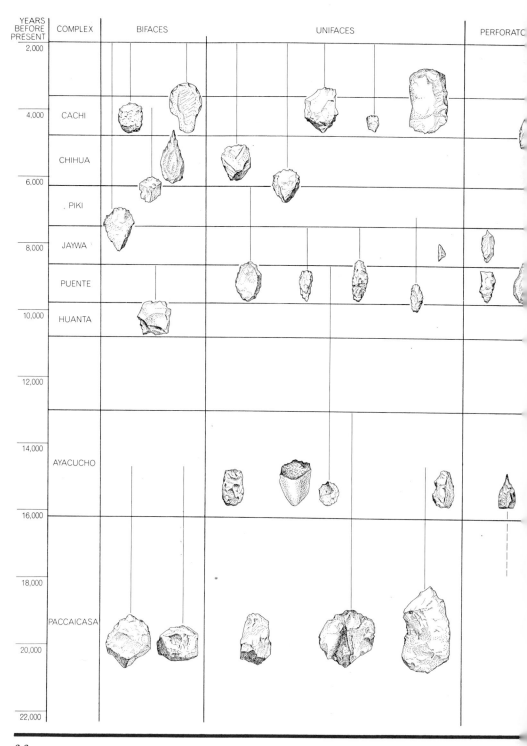

6.6

Kinds of tools found in various excavations in the Ayacucho Valley, Peru. The earliest tools resemb

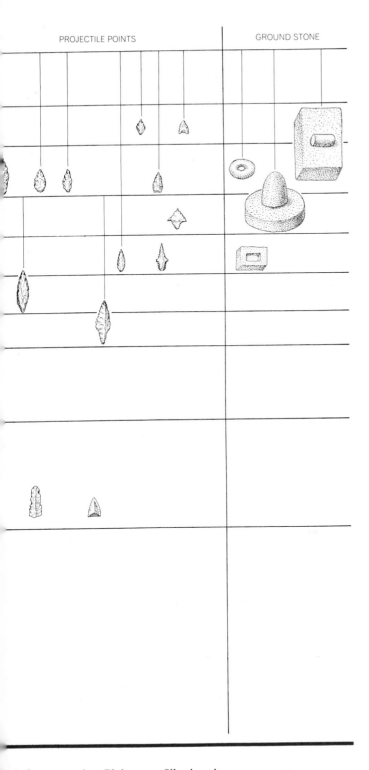

PROJECTILE POINTS

GROUND STONE

ols from some late Pleistocene Siberian sites.

Whatever the specific earliest date for Pikimachay, we would obviously expect to find earlier sites north of Peru, but for this the evidence is not overwhelming. At Valsequillo, Hueyatlaco, and a few other sites in the Mexican state of Puebla, there are nondescript concentrations of flakes, chips, and choppers that may date to between 40,000 and 20,000 years ago. The different dating methods applied to these sites (which are buried in rough gravels) have produced varied results, and at present all that seems clear is that these tools were deposited sometime before 11,000 B.C. We know this because elephant bone from one of these sites was incised with pictures of mammoths, and these animals became extinct shortly after 10,000 B.C.

Early dates for the colonization of Mexico are suggested by several other finds, including a camel's sacrum that had been carved to represent a dog's or wolf's face (recovered in a gravel formation thought to have been deposited 40,000 years ago), and the site of Tlapacoya, just outside Mexico City, where some stone tools found beneath tree fragments were radiocarbon-dated to about 24,500 years ago. The tools are blades of a type not used elsewhere in Mexico until many thousands of years later, however, and thus many archaeologists do not consider this site significant.

Several other sites dated to about 11,000 B.C. have been found in Mexico, most of them composed of the debris from killing and butchering mammoths. The consistency with which mammoths are found in these sites may seem to reflect an economy specialized in hunting large animals, but most of the people of Mexico at this time were probably generalized hunters and gatherers and only because of the great size and preservation of the mammoth bones do we find so many of these sites. As MacNeish noted, these early hunters probably killed one mammoth in a lifetime—and never stopped talking about it.

Some of the other sites thought to date between 30,000 and 20,000 years ago are shown in Figure 6.7, and although none of them are unequivocal, as a group they suggest that people entered the New World no later than 30,000 to 25,000 years ago.

The artifacts found at the earliest sites differ greatly, but most sites lack the projectile points that in later periods are among the most frequent types of tools. This has led to the characterization of the earliest New World cultures as the *Pre-projectile Point Stage* (Krieger 1964). The absence of projectile points and the simplicity of these early artifacts probably mean that the earliest immigrants were not highly specialized big-game hunters, which suggests that they came over during the warmer periods of the Pleistocene as generalized hunters and gatherers. We cannot be certain, of course, because successful big-game hunters (like *Homo erectus*) used crude stone tools; but these early American tool complexes do not look as if they were specialized killing or butchering implements. Nor have they been found with butchered animal bones or in environmental circumstances suggesting specialized hunting.

If people entered the New World 30,000 or more years ago, it might seem surprising that more archaeological sites have not been found dating to this period; after all, hundreds of Old World sites date to this age. But population densities in Europe and other parts of the Old World had been slowly building for hundreds of thousands of years before people entered the New World. In addition, most European sites of this age are found in caves and rock shelters, and there are relatively few of these along the probable route into the New World. There are caves in Nevada and Oregon, but most were submerged under the lakes that dotted these areas throughout the Pleistocene. There are also great caves in Kentucky and Tennessee, but none of these have yielded evidence of Pleistocene occupation, possibly because these areas were largely vast coniferous forests at this time, and since such forests support very few animals or edible plants, these areas would not have been hospitable for hunters and gatherers. Alternatively, the first Americans may have worked out adaptations to cold climates that did not require caves. Their ancestors must have done this, because there are no caves along the Siberian-Beringia-Alaska route.

Another problem in locating early sites in eastern North America is that in much of the lower Mississippi area, alluviation has been so great that many such sites would be buried under tens of meters of soil. And in the rest of the South and East, because the glacial ice sheets never reached these areas, the present land surface is millions of years old. Thus, soft-drink bottles and ancient artifacts can be found in virtually the same soil, because accumulation of soil over these areas has been so slow for millions of years. Additionally, bones and other datable materials do not preserve well under these humid, exposed conditions.

In conclusion, people certainly had entered the New World by at least 14,000 to 12,000 years ago, and they were probably here long before that. It is thought that they reached interior Alaska and Canada by 40,000 or more years ago, most likely as generalized hunters and gath-

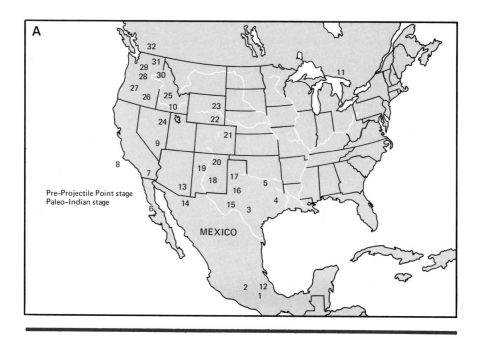

6.7

Location of some possible early American occupations. Some are of questionable date or are not demonstrated to be of human origin. The "Pre-Projectile Point Stage" is widely considered to be the earliest.

Map A: North American sites and complexes: (1) Valsequillo; (2) Tequixquiac; (3) Friesenhahn Cave; (4) Malakoff; (5) Lewisville; (6) Lake Chapala Basin; (7) Scripps Campus; (8) Santa Rosa Island; (9) Tule Springs; (10) American Falls; (11) Sheguiandah; (12) Iztapan; (13) Lehner (14) Naco; (15) Scharbauer; (16) Lubbock; (17) Blackwater Draw; (18) Lucy; (19) Sandia Cave; (20) Folsom; (21) Lindenmeier; (22) Hell Gap; (23) Brewster; (24) Danger Cave; (25) Crane Creek; (26) Fort Rock Cave; (27) Cougar Mt. Cave; (28) Five-Mile Rapids; (29) Indian Well; (30) Ash Cave; (31) Olcott; (32) Yale.

Map B: South American sites and complexes: (1) Pozo de Muáco; (2) Manzanillo; (3) Chocó; (4) Garzón; (5) Ghatchi I; (6) José Vieira; (7) Gruta de Wabeto; (8) Barracao; (9) Quarai; (10) Catalán, (11) Ampajango; (12) Aceguá; (13) Potraro Sucio; (14) Carro de Montevideo; (15) Playa Verde; (16) Taltal.

erers with simple pebble and flake tool kits. For many thousands of years after people reached mid-continental and southern latitudes in the New World, population densities were probably extremely light and most bands no doubt stayed in the same general mixed forest and grassland environments their ancestors had adapted to in more northern areas. By about 12,000 years ago, however, they began to display greater diversity in subsistence strategies as they evolved adaptations to a greater range of environments.

B

1
2
Venezuela
Guyana
Surinam
Fr. Guiana
3
Columbia
4
Ecuador
Brazil
Peru
Bolivia
Paraguay
5
6
7
8
11
9
Chile
10
12
16
13
14
Uruguay
Argentina
15

Pre-Projectile Point stage

EARLY AMERICAN ADAPTATIONS

In 1926 a black cowboy named George McJunkin was riding along the edge of a gully in New Mexico, near the town of Folsom, when he discovered some "arrowheads" and animal bones protruding from a layer of soil about six meters beneath the surface of the plain. Eventually, his find came to the attention of J. D. Figgins, director of the Colorado Museum of Natural History, who began a long series of excavations at this site. The bones associated with the artifacts turned out to be those of a species of bison that had been extinct for about 10,000 years, and so skeptical were most archaeologists and other people of the idea that humans had been in the New World that long that Figgins insisted on

TABLE 6.1   Sites in the New World with Radiocarbon Dates Greater than 13,000 B.P.

Site	Date B.P.	Remarks and Associations
1. Trail Creek, Alaska	13,070 ± 280	Bison bone worked by man.
	15,750 ± 350	Horse bone associated with worked bison bone
2. Lamb Spring, Colorado	13,140 ± 1000	Mammoth bone associated with worked camel toe bone.
3. Ft. Rock Cave, Oregon	13,200 ± 720	
4. Pikimachay Cave, Peru, Ayachucho Level	14,150	Core tools, flake tools, and bone tools
5. Lucy Site, New Mexico	14,300 ± 650	Caliche overlying Sandia level
6. Muaco, Venezuela	9030 ± 240	Bones
	10,490 ± 100	Soil
	14,290 ± 500	Charred bones
	16,365 ± 400	Charred bones
7. Taima Taima, Venezuela	13,010 ± 280	Bones
	14,440 ± 435	Bones
	12,580 ± 150	Soil
	11,860 ± 130	Wood
	9,650 ± 80 to 14,010 ± 140	Soils
8. Wilson Butte Cave, Idaho	14,500	
9. Laguna Beach, California	14,800	Skeletal fragments
	17,150 ± 1470	Skull
10. Manix Lake, California	19,290 ± 400	Dates on tufa of high lake stand, crude choppers, and large leaf-shaped points occur only above dated level.
	19,490 ± 400	
11. Santa Rosa Island, California*	15,820 ± 280	Wood from mammoth beds
	16,700 ± 1500	Charcoal from mammoth beds
	29,700 ± 3000	Charred mammoth bones
12. Pikimachay Cave, Peru, Paccacaisa Level	19,600	Crude core tools, extinct fauna
13. Sandia Cave, New Mexico	20,000	Dates on tusk have been questioned (Bryan 1965: 144).
14. Scripps Campus, La Jolla, California	21,500	

TABLE 6.1 *(Continued)*

Site	Date B.P.	Remarks and Associations
15. Hueyatlaco, Mexico	21,850 ± 850	Shell date, associated with butchered horse, camel, mastodon, etc. Flake or blade point industry. Recent geologic dates are of the surprising antiquity of 200,000–250,000 years.
16. Tlapacoya, Mexico	21,700 ± 500	Charcoal from hearth
	22,400 ± 2600	Charred log
	23,400 ± 950	Tree above blade
	24,000 ± 4000	Charcoal from hearth
	24,200 ± 400	Soluble organics
	24,500 ± 900	Wood
17. Old Crow, Canada	23,000–28,000	Bone tools
18. Calico Hills, California	34,000	Date is on calcium carbonate cementation in the alluvial fan. Haynes (1973) believes the "artifacts" are rocks broken by natural geologic action.
19. Lewisville, Texas	37,000	Dates are much older than Clovis point found in hearth would imply. Findings are controversial.
	38,000	
20. American Falls, Idaho	30,000	Charcoal, peat
	43,000	Bison bones have holes punched with wooden spears.

SOURCE   J. J. Hester. 1976. *Introduction to Archaeology.* New York: Holt.

NOTE   Numerous additional sites, at least several dozen, are thought to have great antiquity. This group is best summarized in Krieger (1964) and Bryan (1965). The list includes sites of undoubted importance such as Freisenhahn Cave, Texas; Sheguiandah site, Level V, Ontario; and the Camare complex, Venezuela. Other sites are less accepted, such as the San Marcos complex, Texas, and the Texas Street site, San Diego, California. These sites are not listed above because none of them have radiocarbon-dated levels earlier than 13,000 B.P.

* Dates for the Santa Rosa Island and some other samples are probably not associated with human occupation. Many dates are controversial.

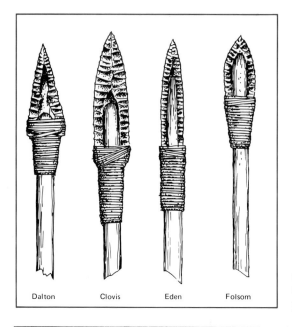

Dalton Clovis Eden Folsom

6.8
Some types of early American
projectile points.

excavating the site with a committee of archaeologists there to watch
his every move, so that no one could claim the evidence had been faked.

In 1932 another important find was made, this time near the town
of Clovis, New Mexico, and here too large blade tools were associated
with extinct animals. But at this site artifacts somewhat different from
those at Folsom (Figure 6.8) were found in a layer *beneath* some "Folsom points." Analysis suggested a date of about 12,000 years ago for the
earliest Clovis-style artifacts, and within a few years artifacts similar in
size, shape, and style to the Clovis points were discovered at many different places in North America. Since then, stone points resembling
Clovis artifacts have been found in every state of the Union, as well as
far north into the Arctic and deep into South America.

It is difficult to reconstruct the subsistence systems of the people
who made these points. The easiest archaeological sites to find are those
with large stone tools and the bones of large animals, and most of the
sites in the grasslands of North America are of this type: dozens of stone
tools intermixed with mammoth, bison, and other bones, often near
streams or bogs where hunters ambushed these animals (Figure 6.9). But
there may be many less obvious sites—sites not yet found because they
are not marked by masses of animal bones.

Many archaeologists question the presumption that even the Clovis
and Folsom peoples were mainly big-game hunters. They note that large

points have been found in many areas where there would probably not have been large herds of big game, such as the deciduous forests of the North American South and East. In addition, it is curious that although the mastodons and other large animals are known to have roamed the woodlands of southeastern North America, none have ever been found in association with these large stone points—even though many such points have been found in these areas. The poor preservation of ar-

6.9
Occurrences of animal species and tool types at various western U.S. sites. Most sites were occupied between 10,000 and 5000 B.C. Data and format after Jennings, 1974. Llano culture is earliest, Folsom next, and Plano is the latest.

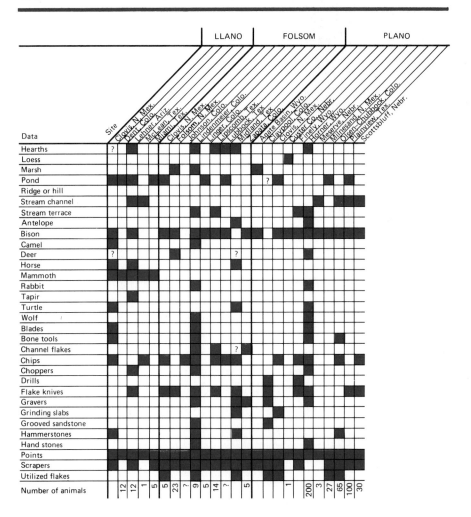

6.10
Bones of some of the hundreds of bison killed at the Olsen-Chubbock site, Colorado, at about 6500 B.C. Many of the carcasses were butchered, while others were left untouched. Twenty-seven large projectile points and some other tools were found amid the bones.

chaeological remains in the East may explain part of this; in addition, the woodlands of the East were quite different from the open plains of the West, and eastern hunters may have hunted in smaller groups, pursuing single animals.

Shortly after 8000 B.C., however, at least some groups in the American West were undoubtably specializing in hunting big game. They often practiced "jump hunting," in which many people cooperate to stampede bison herds or other animals over a precipice, killing them by the score. Where there were no convenient precipices, animals were driven into natural cul-de-sacs, where they could be easily killed. In sites reflecting these practices, archaeologists find the bones of hundreds of bison (Figure 6.10), many showing clear butchering marks. By drying the meat, these hunters could accumulate large food reserves, and the skin, hide, and bones of the bison had many uses. It is difficult to determine the length of time and the area in which this specialized big-game hunting was a primary subsistence method, but it seems to have been largely a phenomenon of the Great Plains, lasting for at least several thousand years after 8000 B.C.

The appearance of the Clovis, Folsom, and other cultures has been interpreted in several different ways. Some archaeologists suggest that they developed from groups arriving in the New World as early as 30,000 years ago, but those who do not accept the entry of humans to the lower latitudes of the New World before about 12,000 years ago believe these "big-game hunters" adapted to the hunting way of life on the Bering land bridge, and then migrated south about 12,000 to 10,000 years ago when the glaciers began their retreat.

The problem is complicated by evidence that big-game hunting cultures of the Great Plains may have developed out of the more ancient, generalized, hunting and gathering cultures in the North American East. It used to be widely believed that the first wave of immigrants to the New World stayed mainly on the western side of North America, colonizing the area east of the Mississippi River only about 10,000 years ago, but recent archaeological evidence suggests that the East may be a much earlier cultural center. Of particular interest are the so-called "pebble-tool" complexes that have been found in Tennessee, Alabama, the Ohio Valley, and elsewhere. These crude tools (Figure 6.11) have been found in both open-air sites and rock shelters, and occasionally in levels containing the Clovis-type points dated to about 12,000 years ago in the Great Plains. Some archaeologists think these pebble tools were used by people entering the North American East 20,000 or more years ago (Dragoo 1976). We have noted that the land surfaces of much of the East are millions of years old and that preservation is generally poor, so it is not surprising that we do not have good carbon-14 dates for these early cultures. The ancient date given to these tools is based on their simplicity and extreme patination in comparison to other artifacts, and also on their resemblance to crude pebble tools and other implements found in Peru and dated to between 19,600 and 14,150 B.C.

The earliest well-dated site known in the North American East is at the Meadowcroft Rock Shelter, near Avella, Pennsylvania. Radiocarbon samples yield dates of from 15,130 to 9,280 years ago for hearths in lowest cultural level; lithic artifacts in association with this feature have not been assigned to any known type. The earliest distinctive and widely distributed tool complex found in the North American East (but not found at Meadowcroft) is distinguished by the presence of large stone projectile points. Most such points are between twelve and thirty centimeters long and occasionally have been "fluted" by detaching flakes along the long axis of the core. Formerly, many archaeologists thought these eastern points were imitations of the Folsom and Clovis points, but it is now evident that these larger points occur as early—and probably earlier—in the eastern woodlands as on the Plains and are more numerous in the East: Alabama alone has yielded more points than the entire western half of North America (Dragoo 1976).

A particularly interesting eastern site containing Clovis-type artifacts is St. Albans, in West Virginia, where stratified occupations to a depth of eleven meters have been found. Radiocarbon dates ranging around 7900 B.C. have been derived from deposits at depths of about nine meters, and further excavations may help clarify many details of early eastern occupations.

Archaeological surveys of many areas are not yet complete, but it appears that late Pleistocene—early Holocene eastern North America contained many small groups of hunters and gatherers, who arrived by at least 15,000 years ago and lived at low population densities, pursuing a variety of resources, but deriving most of their calories from generalized hunting and foraging.

By about 5000 B.C., the glaciers had retreated to the point that the flora and fauna of the eastern United States were very similar to what they are today—except where changed by human activity—and there was a broad cultural readaptation to the changing environments. In the Ohio, Cumberland, and Tennessee River valleys, for example, there are huge middens containing the refuse of centuries of shellfishing. At Koster in lower Illinois, excavations revealed that Middle and Late Archaic people (the Archaic period is about 7000 to 5000 B.C.) here subsisted principally on fishing, deer hunting, and gathering wild plants. To the north in the "Lake Forest" areas of Michigan, Wisconsin, and Ontario, hunting was still the major protein source, with deer, elk, moose, and bear getting most of the attention. Farther to the north, in the Canadian Shield area, subsistence was based even more on the hunting of large herd mammals as people followed the retreating glaciers and tundra-adapted game northward.

Along the coasts of eastern North America a variety of specialized adaptations evolved, based on the exploitation of seals, sea birds, and, along the southern coast, fish and shellfish. In all these "specialized" adaptations, however, the people were actually exploiting a great diversity of plant and animal foods.

At about 2,500 B.C., pottery first appeared in the North American East, in eastern Georgia and South Carolina, and over the next 2,000 years the use of ceramics spread over the entire East. Primitive agricul-

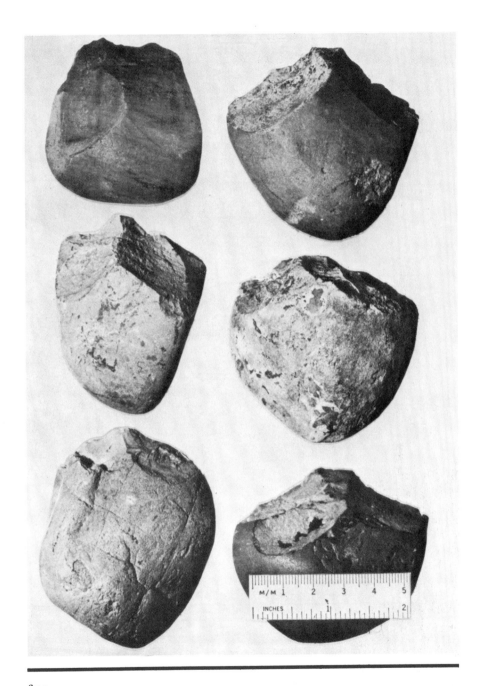

6.11
These tools of the Lively complex, from Alabama, may be more than 20,000 years old.

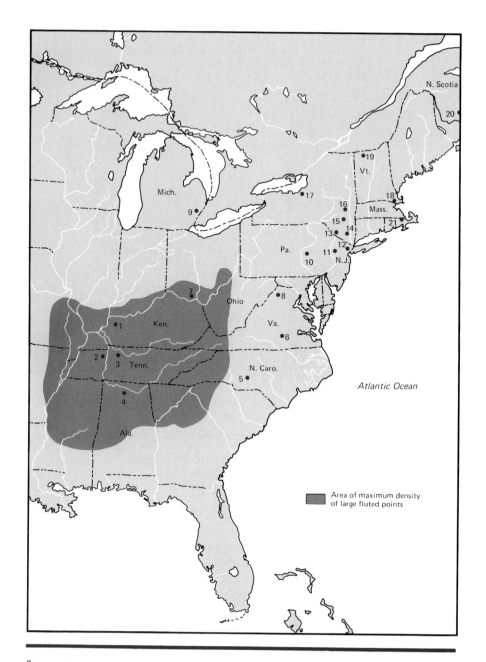

6.12

Some early sites in eastern North America. (1) Parrish; (2) Nuckolls; (3) Wells Creek; (4) Quad; (5) Hardaway; (6) Williamson; (7) Adams Co.; (8) Flint Run; (9) Holcombe Beach; (10) Shoop; (11) Plenge; (12) Port Mobile; (13) Ziert; (14) Dutchess Quarry; (15) West Athens Hill; (16) Kings Road; (17) Potts; (18) Bull Brook; (19) Reagen; (20) Debert; (21) Wapanucket.

tural systems also appeared during this period, and a number of plants, including sunflowers, marsh elder, and goosefoot weed, were domesticated. We shall consider these developments and the rise of sedentary, complex communities in eastern North America in chapter 16.

THE DESERT WEST

The *Desert West* refers to the area between the Rocky Mountains and the Sierra Nevada and Cascade Mountain ranges, extending from Canada to southern Mexico. About 12,000 years ago, when the glacial ice sheets were still a kilometer high along the northern border of the United States, some of the Desert West was probably cooler and wetter than it is today and had many large lakes and marshes. Then, between 12,000 and 10,000 years ago, the lakes shrank, rivers ceased to flow, and springs began to dry up (Mehringer 1977: 28). Since that time there have been important climatic variations, but the ecological variation in much of the Desert West over the last 10,000 years probably has not been great: the area has been, and remains, quite arid, averaging about twenty-five centimeters of rain per year.

The Desert West has less diverse flora and fauna than most other parts of North America, but for most of the last 10,000 years it has supported large populations of squirrels, rabbits, marmots, wood rats, peccaries, and other small animals, as well as localized herds of deer, bison, elk, and big-horn sheep. Sunflowers, pickleweed, yucca, piñon nuts, and other vegetable foods are available seasonally in most of this area. Resource diversity is particularly great as one moves up and down the hills and ridges of the Desert West: a single day's climb can take one from a desertic environment to Arctic-Alpine environments in the uplands. An especially important element in the subsistence of prehistoric peoples of the Desert West was the lakes and marshes probably present here during much of the Pleistocene. Fish, waterfowl, invertebrates, marsh plants, and many other resources were exploited as soon as colonization began and have played an important part in determining human settlement here to the present. Generally, then, the Desert West offers archaeologists an opportunity to study the many ways prehistoric populations in this area have adapted their subsistence strategies, population densities, technologies, and seasonal movements to the nuances of a somewhat extreme physical environment.

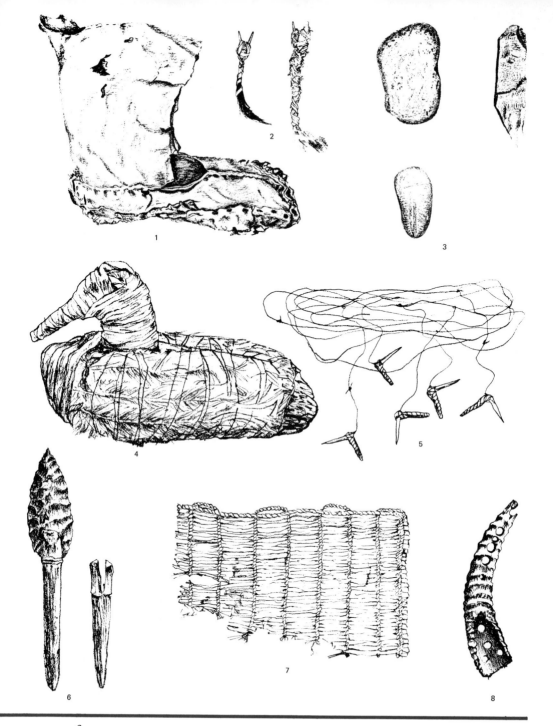

6.13
Assorted artifacts of the Desert West Archaic tradition: (1) moccasin (2) feather effigies (?) and (3) etched stones from Hogup Cave, Utah; (4) duck decoy of tule and feathers; (5) fishhooks on setline; (6) hafted knife and knife handle; (7) twined tule mat; and (8) worked sheep horn from California-Nevada.

If we accept the 30,000 to 15,000 year dates for other early sites in the Americas, we might suspect that bands were also in the Desert West at this time, but we have little evidence. The earliest reliably dated sites are all between 12,000 and 10,000 years old, although remains of earlier occupations will probably be found when the archaeology of the Desert West is better known. Many of the rock shelters and caves in the Desert West were submerged by lakes during the late Pleistocene, so most of the early sites may be "open-air" sites and thus difficult to find and date.

The first well-documented Desert West cultures are represented by lithic artifacts very like the Clovis points that appeared in the Great Plains about 12,000 years ago. These artifacts have been found at many locations in the Desert West, but almost all were surface finds, with no associated animal or plant remains that could tell us much about either the age or the economy of these cultures. Often associated with these points are stone artifacts usually interpreted as gravers, borers, and other types of projectile points. On the basis of these tools' inferred functions, and because they are usually found on the shores of extinct Pleistocene lakes, some argue that they reflect a period of "big-game" hunting (Tuohy 1968: 31). There is little evidence, however, to support this position.

From about 11,000 to 8,000 years ago, many of the Desert West peoples apparently organized their economies around the resources of lakes and marshes, while groups in more arid areas probably adopted a more generalized hunting and gathering strategy. Remains of pole-and-thatch huts have been found in some areas, but the size, location, and contents of most sites of this period suggest that for most of the year Desert West peoples lived in small bands and followed complex seasonal rounds, exploiting different resources as they became available.

Between 9,000 and 2,500 years ago these cultures worked out a marvelous array of subsistence technologies and strategies, and the aridity of the Desert West has preserved artifacts so well that we can reconstruct their way of life in considerable detail. Scraps of fur clothing have been found, as well as hide moccasins, woven sandals, wooden clubs, twined basketry, grinding stones, atlatl points, and many other items (Figure 6.13).

Analysis of the animal and plant remains from sites dated between 9,000 and 2,500 years ago reveals an extremely diverse diet. Rabbits, rats, and squirrels were trapped—probably with twined nets—and bison, antelopes, and mountain sheep were also occasionally taken. At sites near bodies of water, grebes, pelicans, herons, ducks, swans, geese, and even hawks and ravens appear to have been eaten (Jennings 1975: 143). The number of grinding stones and digging sticks found in Desert West sites suggests that, as with most hunters and gatherers, much of the diet was supplied by plant foods. At Hogup Cave, in Utah, for example, human feces contain masses of pickleweed seeds, and the archaeological deposits are stained yellow by pickleweed chaff (Aikens n.d.: 24). *Quids,* the fossilized expectorated fibers of succulent plants, have also been found in great numbers in Desert West sites, and their numbers suggest they may have been a source of both food and water.

The generalized hunting and gathering way of life persisted in the Desert West into the present century, except in a few favored areas where, beginning about 2,000 years ago, a horticultural way of life, based on domesticated maize, beans, and squash, was possible.

PLEISTOCENE EXTINCTIONS

The spread of human hunting and gathering societies over the New World after the last glacial period coincides with the extinction of many animal species, and by about 8,000 years ago, all or most of the mammoths, mastodons, long-horned bison, tapirs, horses, giant ground sloths, dire wolves, camels, and many other creatures had disappeared. Extinction is, of course, a natural evolutionary development and can be accounted for by known biological processes. But the number of animal species that became extinct in the New World and their apparent rate of extinction has led some to conclude that human hunters forced many New World animals into extinction shortly after the Pleistocene. Those who argue for the role of humans in causing these extinctions point out that the bones of these animals are found in great numbers at archaeological sites, and they suggest that New World animals, unlike their Old World relatives, had developed in the absence of humans and were therefore less wary—and consequently more easily killed. Through mass-slaughter drives and jumps, these scholars suggest, humans extinguished at least some animal species. They also point out that more recently people have caused the extinction of several animal species (such as the passenger pigeon) and that even such large and numerous animals as the bison were driven to the brink of extinction. Vance Haynes, one of the most influential students of the problem of Pleistocene extinctions, believes that people first entered the lower latitudes of the New World only about 12,000 years ago (he questions the accuracy of earlier C^{14} dates). He proposes that the rich resources encountered led to such phenomenal rates of population growth that within 1,000 years people had reached the tip of South America and had killed off so many animal species that they were "forced" into new subsistence adaptations based on hunting smaller game and collecting a greater variety of plant foods (Haynes 1974).

The importance of the problem of Pleistocene extinctions goes beyond the simple question of whether or not the late Pleistocene and early Holocene peoples were major factors in the demise of some animal species. At issue here is the important problem of the *general* nature of the relationship of humans and other animals in any place and time. If it could be shown that people really were the major cause of most animal extinctions in the New World in the immediate post-Pleistocene period, this would indicate that the hunters of post-Pleistocene America were virtually unique in their ecological relationships. For in no other case in prehistory or history has it ever been shown that humans caused a comparable range of animal extinctions within so short a time. Even with the growth of industrialization and population of the last two centuries, Americans have not been able to drive into extinction the number and range of animals that became extinct after the Pleistocene. And in the Old World, although humans had hunted varied animal species in Europe and elsewhere for many millennia, the animals we know archaeologically to have been the most intensively hunted—such as reindeer and horses—were never threatened with extinction.

Generally, the evidence does not seem to support the view that humans were important elements in the extinction of New World species. Figure 6.9, for example, shows that the animal bones found at a sample of thirty-five early sites in North America were mainly those of mammoths and bison—species that did in fact become extinct; but that many of the other large animals which became extinct during this period are either not found at all in these sites or are found in very limited numbers. Perhaps even more significant, game species were not the only ones to die out. Grayson (1976) has shown that numerous bird species also became extinct at this time, and it is difficult to believe that people could have played any role in this. Also, some "big-game" species such as the mastodon lived in the North American South and East while humans were there and are known to have perished shortly after the end of the Pleistocene, but their bones have never been found in association with artifacts of any kind. Thus, it would seem that at least

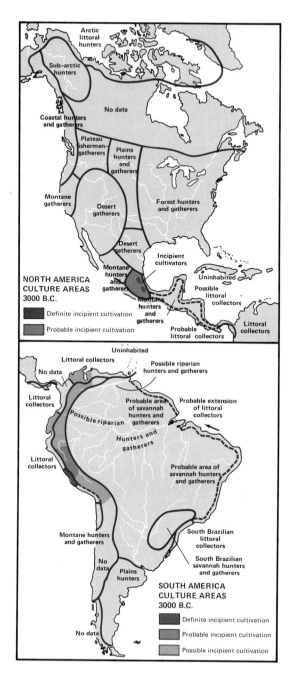

NORTH AMERICA CULTURE AREAS 3000 B.C.

Arctic littoral hunters
Sub-arctic hunters
No data
Coastal hunters and gatherers
Plateau fishermen-gatherers
Plains hunters and gatherers
Montane gatherers
Desert gatherers
Forest hunters and gatherers
Desert gatherers
Incipient cultivators
Uninhabited
Montane hunters and gatherers
Possible littoral collectors
Montane hunters and gatherers
Probable littoral collectors
Littoral collectors

■ Definite incipient cultivation
▨ Probable incipient cultivation

SOUTH AMERICA CULTURE AREAS 3000 B.C.

Uninhabited
Littoral collectors
No data
Possible riparian hunters and gatherers
Littoral collectors
Probable area of savannah hunters and gatherers
Probable extension of littoral collectors
Possible riparian
Hunters and gatherers
Littoral collectors
Probable area of savannah hunters and gatherers
Montane hunters and gatherers
South Brazilian littoral collectors
South Brazilian savannah hunters and gatherers
No data
Plains hunters
No data

■ Definite incipient cultivation
▨ Probable incipient cultivation
▨ Possible incipient cultivation

6.14
Varieties of American adaptations at about 3000 B.C.

some of the larger animals became extinct without much human assistance. Finally, we might also note that there is no archaeological evidence that the hunting practices most likely to lead to animal extinctions, such as drives and jumps, were ever used during the period, some 10,000 to 8,000 years ago, when most of the larger species became extinct.

If we rule out human hunting as the most important factor in these extinctions, what alternative explanation can we give? Many have been suggested, but none are really very satisfactory. Clearly, the immediate post-Pleistocene period was one of radical climate change, and no doubt this was of some importance. Of thirty-one genera of mammals that became extinct, however, only seven had entered the New World during the last 70,000 years, and thus all the others had managed to adapt to the climatic changes of previous interglacial periods, which were fully as dramatic as those after the last glacial retreat. Why did they become extinct after the last glacial period? On the other hand, we do not know the rates at which animal genera became extinct, and thus it is difficult to say that the diversity or number of genera that became extinct in the New World was far more than would be expected by "natural" processes.

Some have suggested that New World animals might have been decimated by diseases introduced from the Old World during one of the later intervals when the Bering land bridge route was open—a situation reminiscent of the frightful casualties inflicted on aboriginal Americans by smallpox, measles, and other diseases introduced by the Europeans. Such epidemics, however, usually do not cause species to become extinct: they decimate local populations over a large area, but generally leave small pockets of resistant individuals who eventually reestablish the species.

In summary of the problem of Pleistocene extinctions, perhaps the best we can do at present is repeat Charles Lyell's comment of more than a hundred years ago.

> It is probable that causes more general and powerful than the agency of Man, alterations in climate, variations in the range of many species of animals, vertebrate and invertebrate, and of plants, geographical changes in the height, depth, and extent of land and sea, or all of these combined, have given rise, in a vast series of years, to the annihilation . . . of many large mammalia.

OTHER EARLY AMERICAN CULTURES

Although the cultures of the Desert West, Great Plains, and eastern North America are the best known examples of the late Pleistocene-early Holocene in the New World, there were many other specialized hunters and gatherers during this period (see Figure 6.14). Along the Pacific coast of California, for example, the combination of sea and land resources supported very dense human population concentrations. In Tierra del Fuego, near the tip of South America, Indians with a very limited stone-tool technology developed an effective adaptation to the berries, fruit, shellfish, and fish abundant in these areas. In the Arctic, bands focusing on the hunting of sea mammals and caribou appeared between 7,000 and 5,000 years ago, and the Eskimo cultures go back at least 2,000 years.

Generally, then, the early Holocene in the Americas was a time of cultural specialization, as technologies, social systems, and subsistence systems were evolved to meet diverse and changing environments. Human population densities rose in many parts of the New World, and, as we shall see in chapter 16, by 7,000 years ago some hunting and gathering societies were already in the process of domesticating plants and beginning the transition to the agricultural, complex cultures of late prehistoric America.

Bibliography

Aikens, C. Melvin. 1970. *Hogup Cave*. University of Utah Anthropological Papers, no. 93. Salt Lake City.

Anderson, Douglas D. 1968. "A Stone Age Campsite at the Gateway to America." *Scientific American*. 218(6): 24–33.

Arellano, A. R. V. 1951. "Some New Aspects of the Tepexpan Man Case." *Bulletin of the Texas Archaeological and Paleontological Society*. 22: 217–25.

Asch, Nancy B., R. I. Ford, and D. L. Asch. 1972. *Paleoethnobotany of the Koster Site*. Illinois State Museum, Reports of Investigations, no. 24. Springfield.

Baby, Ramond S. 1972. "Interim Report. Teocintli, No. 76." Knoxville. Mimeographed.

Bada, Jeffrey L. and Patricia M. Helfman. 1975. "Amino Acid Racemization Dating of Fossil Bones." *World Archaeology*. 7(2): 160–73.

Berger, Rainer. 1975. "Advances and Results in Radiocarbon Dating: Early Man in North America." *World Archaeology.* 7(2): 174–84.

Bettinger, Robert L. 1977. "Aboriginal Human Ecology in Owens Valley: Prehistoric Change in the Great Basin." *American Antiquity.* 42(1): 3–17.

Birdsell, Joseph B. 1951. "The Problem of the Early Peopling of the Americas as Viewed from Asia." In *Papers on the Physical Anthropology of the American Indian,* ed. W. S. Laughlin. New York: Viking Fund Inc.

Brennan, Louis A. 1976. "Coastal Adaptations in Prehistoric New England." *American Antiquity.* 41(1): 112.

Broyles, Bettye J. 1971. "The St. Albans Site, Kanawha County, West Virginia." Report of the Archaeological Investigations no. 3, West Virginia Geological and Economic Survey. Morgantown.

Bryan, A. L. 1965. *Paleo-American Prehistory.* Occasional Papers of the Idaho State University Museum, no. 16. Pocatello.

———. 1969. "Early Man in America and the Late Pleistocene. Chronology of Western Canada and Alaska." *Current Anthropology.* 10(4): 339–65.

Bushnell, G. and C. McBurney. 1959. "New World Origins Seen from the Old World." *Antiquity.* 33(130): 93–101.

Campbell, John M. 1963. "Ancient Alaska and Paleolithic Europe." In *Early Man in the Western American Arctic: A Symposium,* ed. F. H. West. Anthropological Papers of the University of Alaska. 10(2): 29–49.

Carter, George F. 1957. *Pleistocene Man at San Diego.* Baltimore: Johns Hopkins Press.

Chard, Chester S. 1956. "The Oldest Sites of Northeast Siberia." *American Antiquity.* 21(4): 405–9.

———. 1960. "Routes to Bering Strait." *American Antiquity.* 26(2): 283–85.

Claiborne, Robert and the Editors of Time-Life. 1973. *The First Americans.* New York: Time-Life.

Cushing, E. J. and H. E. Wright, Jr., eds. 1967. *Quaternary Paleoecology.* New Haven: Yale University Press.

DeJarnette, D. L. 1967. "Alabama Pebbletools: The Lively Complex." Eastern States Archaeological Federation Bulletin 26.

deTerra, Helmut. 1949. "Early Man in Mexico." In *Tepexpan Man,* by H. deTerra, J. Romero, and T. Dale Stewart. New York: Viking Fund Publications in Anthropology. 11: 11–86.

Dragoo, Don W. 1976. "Some Aspects of Eastern North American Prehistory: A Review 1975." *American Antiquity.* 41(1): 3–27.

Driver, Harold E. 1969. *Indians of North America.* Chicago: University of Chicago Press.

Figgins, J. D. 1927. "The Antiquity of Man in North America." *Natural History.* 27: 229–31.

Frison, George C., Michael Wilson, and Diane J. Wilson. 1976. "Fossil Bison and Artifacts from an Early Altithermal Period Arroyo Trap in Wyoming." *American Antiquity*. 41(1): 28–57.

Giddings, J. L., Jr. 1960. "The Archaeology of Bering Strait." *Current Anthropology*. 1(2): 121–38.

———. 1964. *The Archaeology of Cape Denbigh*. Providence, R.I.: Brown University Press.

Grayson, Donald K. 1976. Personal communication with author.

Greenman, E. F. 1963. "The Upper Paleolithic in the New World." *Current Anthropology*. 4(1): 41–91.

Griffin, James B. 1960. "Some Prehistoric Connections Between Siberia and America." *Science*. 131(3403): 801–12.

———. 1967. "Eastern North American Archaeology: A Summary." *Science*. 156(3772): 175–91.

Haag, William G. 1962. "The Bering Strait Land Bridge." *Scientific American*. 206(1): 112–23.

Haynes, C. V., Jr. 1969. "The Earliest Americans." *Science*. 166(3906): 709–15.

———. 1971. "Time, Environment, and Early Man." In Papers from a Symposium on Early Man in North America, New Developments: 1960–1970. ed. Richard Shutler, Jr. *Arctic Anthropology* 8(2): 3–14.

———. 1974. "Elephant Hunting in North America." *New World Prehistory: Readings from Scientific American*, eds. E. Zubrow, et al. San Francisco: W. H. Freeman.

Hopkins, David, ed. 1967. *The Bering Land Bridge*. Stanford: Stanford University Press.

Huddleston, Lee E. 1967. "Origins of the American Indians: European Concepts, 1492–1729." Institute of Latin American Studies, monograph, no. 11. Austin: University of Texas Press.

Irwin-Williams, Cynthia, ed. 1968. *Early Man in Western North America*. Portales: Eastern New Mexico University Press.

Jennings, Jesse D. 1964. "The Desert West." In *Prehistoric Man in the New World*, eds. Jesse D. Jennings and Edward Norbeck. Chicago: University of Chicago Press.

———. 1975. *The Prehistory of North America*. 2nd ed. New York: McGraw-Hill.

Jennings, Jesse D. and Edward Norbeck, eds. 1964. *Prehistoric Man in the New World*. Chicago: University of Chicago Press.

Krieger, Alex D. 1964. "Early Man in the New World." In *Prehistoric Man in the New World*. eds. Jesse D. Jennings and Edward Norbeck. Chicago: University of Chicago Press.

Leakey, Louis S. B., R. E. Simpson, and T. Clements. 1970. "Man in America: The Calico Mountains Excavations." *1970 Britannica Yearbook of Science and the Future*, pp. 64–79. Chicago: Encyclopedia Britannica.

Leonhardy, Frank C. 1966. "Domebo: A Paleo-Indian Mammoth Kill in the Prairie-Plains." Contributions of the Museum of the Great Plains, no. 1. Lawton, Oklahoma.

Lively, M. 1965. "The Lively Complex: Announcing a Pebble Tool Industry in Alabama." *Journal of Alabama Archaeology.* 11(2): 103–22.

Lyell, C. 1863. *Principles of Geology.* London: J. Murray.

MacNeish, Richard S. 1971. "Early Man in the Andes." *Scientific American.* 4: 36–46.

————, ed. 1973. *Early Man in America.* San Francisco: W. H. Freeman.

————. 1978. *The Science of Archaeology?* North Scituate, Mass.: Duxbury Press.

Madsen, David B. and Michael S. Berry. 1975. "A Reassessment of Northeastern Great Basin Prehistory." *American Antiquity.* 40(4): 391–405.

Martin, Paul S. 1973. "The Discovery of America." *Science.* 179: 969–74.

Martin, Paul S. and J. E. Guilday. 1967. "A Bestiary for Pleistocene Biologists." In *Pleistocene Extinctions: The Search for a Cause,* eds. P. S. Martin and H. E. Wright, Jr. New Haven: Yale University Press.

Martin, Paul S. and H. E. Wright, Jr., eds. 1967. *Pleistocene Extinctions: The Search for a Cause.* New Haven: Yale University Press.

Mehringer, Peter, Jr. 1977. "Great Basin Late Quaternary Environments and Chronology." In *Models in Great Basin Prehistory: A Symposium,* ed. Don D. Fowler. Desert Research Institute Publications in the Social Sciences. (12): 113–68.

Müller-Beck, H. J. 1966. "Paleo-Hunters in America: Origins and Diffusion." *Science.* 152: 1191–1210.

Reeves, Brian O. K. 1971. "On the Coalescence of the Laurentide and Cordilleran Ice Sheets in the Western Interior of North America." In *Aboriginal Man and Environments on the Plateau of Northwest America,* eds. A. Stryd and R. A. Smith. Calgary: University of Calgary Archaeological Association.

Steward, T. D. 1973. *The People of America.* New York: Scribner's.

Tuohy, D. R. 1968. "Some Early Lithic Sites in Western Nevada." In *Early Man in Western North America,* ed. C. Irwin-Williams. Portales: Eastern New Mexico University Press.

Warren, Claude, and Anthony Ranere. 1968. "Outside Danger Cave: A View of Early Men in the Great Basin." In *Early Man in Western North America,* ed. C. Irwin-Williams. Portales: Eastern New Mexico University Press.

Wheat, Joe Ben. 1972. "The Olsen-Chubbuck Site. A Paleo-Indian Bison Kill." *Memoirs of the Society for American Archaeology.* No. 26. 37, pt. 2.

Williams, B. J. 1974. "A Model of Band Society." *American Antiquity.* 39(4) pt. 2, memoir 29.

Wright, H. E., Jr. and D. G. Frey, eds. 1965. *The Quaternary of the United States.* Princeton: Princeton University Press.

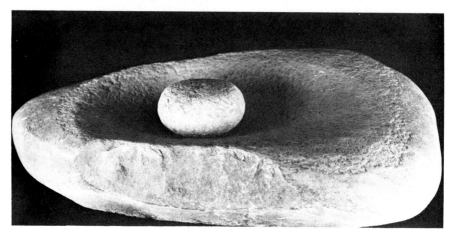

7

The Origins of Domestication, Agriculture, and Sedentary Communities

> The greatest events come to pass without any design; chance makes blunders good. . . . The important events of the world are not deliberately brought about; they occur.
>
> George C. Lichtenberg

The several million years separating the first tool users from the hunters and gatherers of the late Pleistocene was a time of tremendous change. Human brain size trebled, stone-tool technologies became more complex and people colonized most of the Old and New Worlds. But in one important respect all Pleistocene societies were alike: they made their living through hunting and gathering, that is, through *nonagricultural* subsistence systems. While minor trade contacts did take place among bands, every Pleistocene society hunted and gathered its own food, made its own tools, and generally replicated the economic activities of every other society.

We have already commented on the impressive durability of hunting and gathering as a subsistence adaptation. Hunters and gatherers managed to adapt to a wide variety of resources and environments and have persisted in many areas despite great pressures from more complex societies. But about 10,000 years ago the first domesticated plants and animals were beginning to appear in Southwest Asia, Mesoamerica, Peru, and elsewhere, and over the next ten millennia these domesticates were incorporated into agricultural economies that in many environments were able to produce much greater amounts of food than hunting and gathering could. Although hunters and gatherers occupied much of the world as recently as two or three centuries ago, today they exist only in the Kalahari Desert, the Arctic, and the few other places where hunting and gathering is still more productive than agriculture.

One of the most significant aspects of the origins of agriculture is that the correspondence between agriculture and the towns, cities, and other cultural elaborations we call *civilization* is absolute. All civilizations have been based on the cultivation of one or more of just six plant species: wheat, barley, millet, rice, maize, and potatoes. The critical advantage of modern industrial peoples over hunters and gatherers is not so much in energy conversions through water power, fossil fuels, or atomic power as it is in *food production:* if, for some reason, the world's present population were required to resume our ancestors' reliance on undomesticated plants and animals, most of us would surely starve, despite our automobiles, nuclear energy, and hydroelectric plants.

For millions of years our ancestors had subsisted solely on the proceeds of hunting and gathering, yet within just a few thousand years, between about 10,000 and 3,500 years ago, domesticated plants and agricultural economies independently appeared in several different parts of the Old and New Worlds. What conditions elicited these parallel cultural responses, and why did these conditions exist only within this relatively short period of time? Is the coincidence of domestication and agriculture in both the Old and New Worlds explainable as a result of contacts between peoples in these different places, or does it have to do with local, ecological, or cultural circumstances?

Domestication, Agriculture, and Sedentary Communities

We have been using the terms *domestication, agriculture,* and *sedentary communities* very generally, but careful distinctions should now be made. Most definitions of *domestication* appeal to the active interference by people in the life cycles of plant and animal species such that subsequent generations of these organisms are in more intimate association with, and of more use to, people. Domestication is thus often measured in terms of the *loss of fitness* of domesticated species relative to their wild relatives. Domesticated maize, for example, no longer has an effective natural mechanism for seed dispersal, because the seeds are all clustered on a cob that, without human intervention, usually remains tightly attached to the plant. Similarly, a variety of sheep in Southwest Asia has been selectively bred over the last several thousand years so that its tail is a five-to-eight-pound mass of fat, making it necessary, it is said, for people to help these animals mate.

Archaeological evidence indicates that the physical changes associated with domestication in wheat, barley, maize, rice, and many other plants developed, initially at least, not out of the desire or intention of making these plants more useful to people, but rather out of relatively simple changes in exploitation patterns, brought on by rising population densities and changing ecological and cultural conditions. Any plant or animal regularly eaten or used by people—or any other animal—will reflect this relationship in its genetic characteristics, and thus all through the Pleistocene hunters and gatherers had some effect on the genetic makeup of various plant and animal species. But the low Pleistocene population densities and mobile way of life prevented people from exploiting plant and animal populations with sufficient intensity to maintain and further the kinds of mutations represented by maize, fat-tailed sheep, and other modern domesticates. Domestication, then, is not an event, but a process in which the physical characteristics of plant and animal species change as these species' relationships to their human consumers change. Obviously, some species are more likely to be domesticated than others. Oak trees have such long life cycles that even tens of thousands of years of human consumption of their acorns have not greatly altered their form; in contrast, most grains and vegetables each year offer a new generation that can be manipulated.

Agriculture is a particular kind of subsistence system in which efforts are made to modify the environments of plants so as to increase their productivity and usefulness to people (Dunnell 1977). Here too people modify the environments of plants and animals simply by collecting and eating them; but agriculture is the systematic modification of environments in order to increase productivity. This definition of agriculture, like that of domestication, is a relative one. At the one extreme are the simple efforts a group might make to suppress weeds near a stand of wild wheat or barley; at the other extreme are contemporary agribusinesses where crops are grown on precisely leveled fields and treated with pesticides and fertilizers, and where chickens live out their lives in computer-regulated environments. One of the most important consequences of agriculture is that it concentrates food resources and makes them somewhat predictable, allowing large population densities.

Sedentary communities are composed of people who are domiciled in the same place for all or most of every year. Such communities probably first appeared in Southwest Asia as much as 1,000 years before agriculture or domesticated wheat or barley, while in Mesoamerica at least five plant species were in the process of domestication several thousand years before the first sedentary or agricultural communities appeared. Sedentary life usually involves the construction of permanent structures. We have seen that huts of sticks and stones and brush go back at least 300,000 years, but sedentary peoples typically build more substantial buildings. It is possible, of course, to be sedentary and yet not build permanent structures, but such adaptations are limited to a very few highly productive niches where the climate is such that permanent constructions are, at least initially, not particularly advantageous.

Early Domestication and Agriculture:
The Background

All cultures involve the interaction of countless social and environmental variables, and to understand a particular development we must often know something about the system at a point long before the first appearance of the phenomenon to be explained. If we wish to comprehend the origins of the Industrial Revolution, for example, it is necessary to analyze political, social, and economic factors going back to the sixteenth century, at least. Thus, it is not surprising that to understand the appearance of the first domesticated plants and animals and the first agricultural communities, we must look at developments during the several thousands of years preceding these events.

This period, between 15,000 and 8,000 years ago, was a time of major cultural and climatic change. In western Europe population densities shifted as the herds of reindeer and horses that once supported many hunting bands moved northward with the retreating glaciers.

Some people moved with them, but others worked out subsistence strategies stressing plants, smaller game, and fish. Salmon became especially important in Europe as nets, traps, drying racks, and other tools were developed to make salmon exploitation a reliable way to make a living. In Southwest Asia, parts of Africa, and parts of the Americas, some late Pleistocene and early post-Pleistocene human groups increased markedly their consumption of smaller game, fish, waterfowl, invertebrates, and plants, although in many areas the earlier big-game hunting specializations persisted. In North America, for example, the Folsom hunters centered their lives around vast bison herds, while hunters and gatherers in the Mexican highlands diversified their subsistence base.

Where a shift to smaller, more varied resources was made, there was a consequent change in technologies, as the bow and arrow and throwing stick replaced the stabbing spears, and as new tools were developed to dig plants, trap wildfowl, and prepare a more diverse range of foods. Small, simple geometric stone tools predominated in many areas of the world (Figure 7.1). The world of about 8,000 years ago, then, was probably more culturally diverse than in the Pleistocene, with more and different subsistence adaptations, as some groups remained big-game hunters while others took up fishing, intensive foraging, and other pursuits.

Some of these subsistence changes have often been interpreted as a response to the changing climates and sea levels attendant on the retreat of the glaciers some 10,000 years ago, but the increasing emphasis on fish, fowl, and small game in some areas seems to occur several thousand years *before* the glaciers began to retreat, and the shift seems to have occurred in Africa and India and Mexico as well as in the colder parts of the world. Thus, although the climatic change may have been an important part of the *eventual* evolution of domestication and agriculture, it does not appear to be a complete explanation, either for the shift to fish, fowl, and other resources, or for *initial* domestication and agriculture.

Besides, as L. Binford (1968) has pointed out, we run into severe logical problems when we try to explain the changing subsistence practices in terms of climatic change. There had been several periods of glacial retreat prior to the most recent one; why didn't permanent major subsistence changes occur during any of these?

One major difference between the relationships among plants, animals, and people at the end of the last glacial period and those relation-

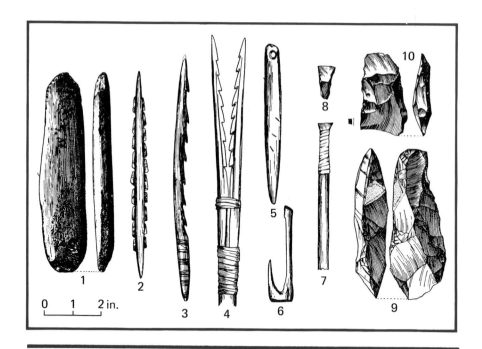

7.1
Mesolithic fishing and hunting equipment: (1) limpet hammer; (2) bone fish-spear with microlith barbs, so. Sweden; (3) barbed point in red deer antler, ca 7500 B.C., Star Carr, Yorkshire; (4) leister prongs of Eskimo fishermen (shows how (3) may have been used); (5) net-making needle (?) and (6) bone fish hook, Denmark; (7), (8) microliths or transverse arrowheads, one found in peat hafted in wood with sinew binding, Denmark; (9) core-axe with transversely sharpened edge, Sussex; (10) flake-axe, Denmark.

ships in earlier interglacials was simply that there were more people in the latter period. Archaeological surveys are incomplete and any estimates would be premature, but it is clear that about 15,000 to 10,000 years ago the world contained more people than ever before. From this fact, some (Cohen 1977; Harris 1977) have argued that domestication and agriculture were direct results of the food shortages and consequent pressures to exploit new, perhaps less desirable food sources, as these "overpopulation" stresses mounted.

Growing population densities probably played an important role in the evolution of agricultural economies and domestication, but there is little hard evidence about what this role was. And it is puzzling, given the "overpopulation" hypothesis, that, as we shall see, some of the earliest domesticates and agricultural villages around the world appeared in areas of extremely low, and apparently stable, population densities.

How, then, are we to account for the widespread and momentous late Pleistocene and post-Pleistocene cultural changes? To attempt to answer this, let us consider in detail the evidence from the two areas of the world where substantial research has been done on the origins of domestication and agriculture: Southwest Asia and Mesoamerica (southern and central Mexico, Guatemala, Belize, Honduras, and El Salvador). In addition, we shall briefly survey some of the evidence from other early centers of domestication and agriculture, and perhaps by

7.2
Early archaeological occurrences of some important Old World and New World domesticates. Domestication is a process, not an event, and these specific sites represent only some early occurrences of species domesticated over wide areas.

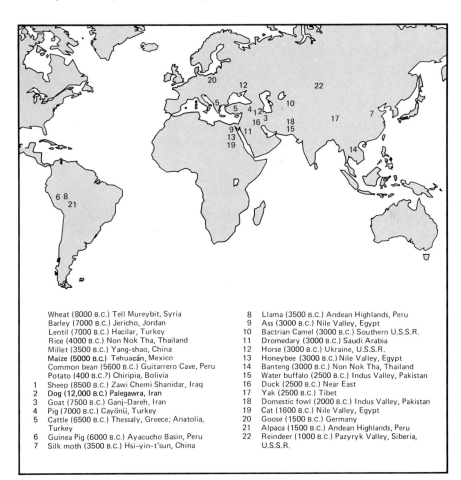

	Wheat (8000 B.C.) Tell Mureybit, Syria	8	Llama (3500 B.C.) Andean Highlands, Peru
	Barley (7000 B.C.) Jericho, Jordan	9	Ass (3000 B.C.) Nile Valley, Egypt
	Lentil (7000 B.C.) Hacilar, Turkey	10	Bactrian Camel (3000 B.C.) Southern U.S.S.R.
	Rice (4000 B.C.) Non Nok Tha, Thailand	11	Dromedary (3000 B.C.) Saudi Arabia
	Millet (3500 B.C.) Yang-shao, China	12	Horse (3000 B.C.) Ukraine, U.S.S.R.
	Maize (5000 B.C.) Tehuacán, Mexico	13	Honeybee (3000 B.C.) Nile Valley, Egypt
	Common bean (5600 B.C.) Guitarrero Cave, Peru	14	Banteng (3000 B.C.) Non Nok Tha, Thailand
	Potato (400 B.C.?) Chiripia, Bolivia	15	Water buffalo (2500 B.C.) Indus Valley, Pakistan
1	Sheep (8500 B.C.) Zawi Chemi Shanidar, Iraq	16	Duck (2500 B.C.) Near East
2	Dog (12,000 B.C.) Palegawra, Iran	17	Yak (2500 B.C.) Tibet
3	Goat (7500 B.C.) Ganj-Dareh, Iran	18	Domestic fowl (2000 B.C.) Indus Valley, Pakistan
4	Pig (7000 B.C.) Cayönü, Turkey	19	Cat (1600 B.C.) Nile Valley, Egypt
5	Cattle (6500 B.C.) Thessaly, Greece; Anatolia, Turkey	20	Goose (1500 B.C.) Germany
6	Guinea Pig (6000 B.C.) Ayacucho Basin, Peru	21	Alpaca (1500 B.C.) Andean Highlands, Peru
7	Silk moth (3500 B.C.) Hsi-yin-t'sun, China	22	Reindeer (1000 B.C.) Pazyryk Valley, Siberia, U.S.S.R.

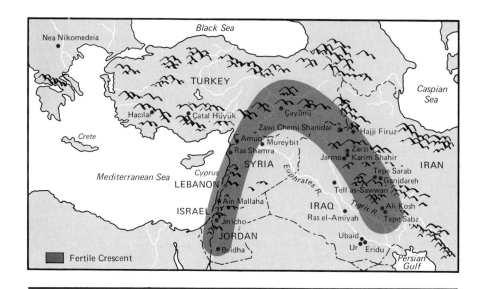

7.3
The "Fertile Crescent" and some important early pre-agricultural and agricultural sites.

comparing developments in these diverse areas we can come to a more precise understanding of the overall subsistence and cultural changes that began in the late Pleistocene, intensified in the immediate post-Pleistocene period, and matured in the last several millennia.

The Origins of Domestication, Agriculture, and Sedentary Communities in Southwest Asia

Although domestication probably began much earlier, the earliest archaeological evidence of it in Southwest Asia dates to shortly after 9000 B.C., when the domestication of wheat, barley, lentils, sheep, goats, pigs, cattle, and other genera was already underway. By 6000 B.C., when most of the rest of the world was still inhabited by nonagriculturalists, Southwest Asia was dotted with thousands of agricultural villages whose inhabitants subsisted mainly on domesticated plants and animals. And by about 3000 B.C. these cultures had developed to the point that the people differed little in social organization, subsistence, or technology from most of the peoples who inhabited these same areas just a century ago.

THE ECOLOGICAL SETTING

The development of domestication, agriculture, and sedentary communities in Southwest Asia involved complex regional processes that crystallized over a large area of the "Fertile Crescent" (Figure 7.3). The physical characteristics of this zone were formed millions of years ago when movements of the earth's crust forced the Arabian Peninsula toward the stable Iranian Plateau, compressing the land in between so that it is pleated like the folds of an accordion. The high points of these folds are the Zagros Mountains, which rise in places to over 4,200 meters. Other areas were forced downward, and rivers running down from the newly formed mountains began covering this sunken region with silt, forming what we know today as the Mesopotamian Alluvium.

At the end of the Pleistocene, the uplands of the Fertile Crescent supported large herds of wild sheep, goats, cattle, and pigs, and, in many areas, dense stands of wild wheat and barley. In lower elevations and wetter regions were lakes and streams with abundant supplies of waterfowl, fish, and other resources. Neither the Fertile Crescent nor the rest of Southwest Asia is as ecologically complex as, for example, southern Mexico, but plants, animals, and climates here vary considerably, especially at different altitudes. As we shall see, most early domesticates appeared at the intersections of complex ecological zones—not in more homogeneous areas like the temperate forests of Europe or the hot lowlands of Mesopotamia.

CEREAL DOMESTICATION

The domestication of wheat and barley—economically the most important plants in Southwest Asia—involved a complex series of changes in at least four native wild grasses, including wild barley (*Hordeum spontaneum*), wild einkorn (*Triticum boeoticum*), and wild emmer wheat (*Triticum dicoccoides*), each with different habitats and characteristics. Domestication of these plants, as elsewhere, was a long process in which certain kinds of mutations were perpetuated through changing patterns of exploitation.

In most of these wild grasses, the *rachis,* the segment of the stalk to which the kernels are attached, becomes extremely brittle as the wild wheat and barley plants ripen. This brittleness is essential to the suc-

cessful propagation of these plants because it allows the seeds to be separated from the plant and dispersed by the merest touch of an animal or
simply the force of the wind. The head of the plant becomes brittle
gradually, from top to bottom, and the seed dispersal is spread over one
to two weeks. Although this is advantageous for the plant because it
prevents the seeds from sprouting in a dense mass of competing seed-
lings, it poses problems for the human collector. If the grain is gathered
when quite ripe, the slightest contact will cause the rachis to fall off, so
harvesting with a sickle is difficult—although holding the stalk over a

7.4
Wild and domestic emmer wheat (A) and detail (B) of the wheat spike. The cultivated emmer wheat spike is somewhat shorter on the average than that of un-
cultivated emmer, and the grains are somewhat larger and more densely packed.
At maturity, wild emmer spikelets break off from the rachis at the nodes, while in
cultivated emmer the spikelets remain intact.

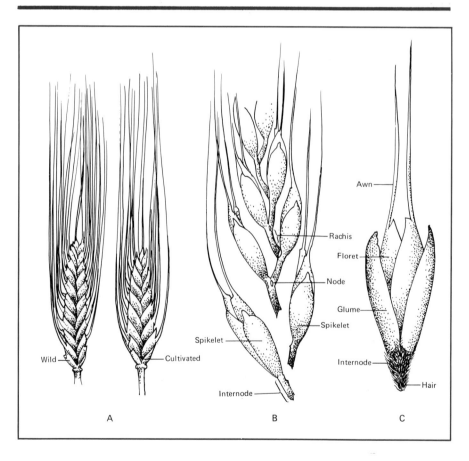

basket and tapping it with a stick works. If, on the other hand, the grain is harvested before it is fully mature, excess moisture in the unripe kernels will cause them to rot in storage or become very unpalatable. A plant with a tougher rachis and on which the kernels ripen at about the same time would clearly be more useful to people.

A second problem with some wild cereals as a food source is that the kernels are enclosed in very tough protective husks, called *glumes*. These protect the seeds from frost and dehydration, but primitive threshing often will not separate the seeds from the glumes, and the human digestive tract cannot break down their tough fibers. Thus a cereal with less tough and less developed glumes would be more useful.

A third problem is that each stalk of grain has only two rows of kernels. Domesticated varieties have six rows, rendering them much more productive as a food resource, and wild species had to change in this direction before it was profitable to invest energy in sowing, cultivating, and harvesting wheat and barley in many areas—particularly in those areas where natural conditions were not optimal for wild cereals.

One other difficulty with wild wheat and barley as foods is that their distribution is sharply limited by temperature, soil, and moisture. As a result, stands of these grains can be widely scattered and therefore difficult to harvest. Much greater efficiency could be attained if these plants could be adapted to a greater variety of temperature, soil, and moisture ranges—especially the hot conditions of the flat lowlands.

In addition to these botanical limitations, wild wheat and barley posed a number of technological and social problems for the peoples who subsisted on them. Tools for cutting and transporting the grain, for example, would have been of great use. Some people in Southwest Asia still harvest wild grains by stripping the seeds from the plants by hand, but this is laborious and inefficient. Moreover, storage technology was required, for, as Flannery (1973) observes, where could one go with a metric ton or so of clean wheat seed, no matter how nutritious? Finally, a sedentary lifestyle would have been advantageous, because of the cost of moving large quantities of grain and because successful harvesting requires that collectors be near stands at very precise times. In contrast to many plants, wild grain can be collected only during the few days when the plants are ripening, and even then there is considerable competition from birds and other predators. Another consideration is that women and children in collection societies could contribute a great

TABLE 7.1   Important Cereals of Southwestern Asia

Species	Characteristics
Hordeum spontaneum (wild barley)	Most tolerant and widespread of wild cereals in Southwest Asia. Primary range in uplands of much of the Fertile Crescent. Tolerates disturbed habitats very well and follows seasonal stream beds from the mountains out onto hot steppes and arid plains.
Triticum boeoticum (wild einkorn wheat)	Tolerates cold better than wild barley. Found in extremely dense stands between 1500 and 2000 meters in the Taurus and Zagros mountains of Turkey, Iraq and Iran.
Triticum dicoccoides (wild emmer wheat)	Most sensitive of common wild cereals in Southwest Asia. Does not tolerate cold or aridity well. Its range is split into two distinct segments, a robust, large-seeded race occurring in dense stands in Palestine, and a smaller-seeded variant occurring in the lower oak woodlands of the Zagros and Taurus ranges. The Palestinian race forms fertile hybrids with cultivated emmer wheat (*Triticum dicoccum*), suggesting that it may be the ancestor of today's domestic emmer wheats, and focussing attention on the Israel-Lebanon area as a center of early emmer domestication and cultivation.
Aegilops squarrosa (goat-face grass)	A wild grass growing principally near the Irano-Turkmenistan border, near the Caspian, and flourishing in disturbed habitats. This species may have hybridized with emmer wheat to produce "bread-wheats." Most forms of early wild and domestic wheat were unsuitable for making bread and were used mainly in porridge.

SOURCE   After Flannery 1973.

deal to the food supply, whereas in societies specializing in hunting, women and children—beyond a certain minimum—are not good "investments."

We shall review the archaeological evidence concerning how and when these wild cereals were domesticated, but first it is important that we examine some aspects of animal domestication in Southwest Asia, for these were parallel and complementary processes.

ANIMAL DOMESTICATION

Domesticated animals were a crucial part of the overall transition to sedentary and agricultural communities, and animal domestication may well have preceded grain domestication in Southwest Asia. In some

areas, such as the southern Mesopotamian Alluvium, permanent settlement was not possible until domesticated animals were available to
supply the fats and proteins that were not readily obtainable from any
other source. Domesticated animals also provided a way of converting
highland grasses, weeds, shrubs, surplus grain stubble, and other plants
into storable, portable, high-quality foods and other usable products,
and, later, some animals, such as cattle, horses, and donkeys, provided
draught and transport power.

The earliest, most important domesticated animals in Southwest
Asia were sheep, goats, cattle, and pigs, all of which were domesticated
between about 9000 B.C. and 6000 B.C. Domesticating these—and
other—animals involved breeding controls through selective slaughter,
castration, and directed matings, such that the genetic composition of
an animal population was altered (G. Wright 1971: 463).

Detecting the process of animal domestication on the basis of archaeological data is a complex problem usually entailing three primary
classes of evidence (Perkins and Daly 1968): (1) the presence of an animal species outside its natural range, such as the pig in the New World
or the presence of highland species of sheep in lowland environments;
(2) morphological changes in the bones and other preserved parts of the
animal, such as the loss of horns in female domestic sheep or the reduced bone size of domestic cattle (morphological changes can also occur at the microscopic level); and (3) abrupt increases in the number of
some species relative to others that cannot be accounted for by natural
causes (for example, at many sites in Southwest Asia at about 8000 B.C.
the proportion of sheep and goat bones increased dramatically). Obviously, none of these kinds of evidence is an infallible reflection of
domestication, and every archaeological faunal collection must be analyzed in terms of as many classes of evidence as are available.

The dog (Canis familiaris) is no doubt the oldest animal domesticate in Southwest Asia, probably having been fully domesticated between 22,000 and 10,000 B.C. The general consensus is that dogs are
descended from the great wolf packs that inhabited all of temperate
Eurasia during the late Pleistocene, although later interbreedings with
jackals probably occurred in the semiarid subtropics. Turnbull and
Reed (1974) report the skeleton of a fully domesticated dog from Palegawra Cave in Iran in levels dating to about 12,000 B.C. Domesticated
dogs from Jaguar Cave in Idaho have been dated to 8370 B.C., and others of about this same age have been reported in such disparate places
as England, Illinois, and Japan.

Hunters and gatherers the world over are known to have remarkably unsentimental ideas about pets, and we should probably see the early domestication of dogs as a result of a symbiotic, utilitarian relationship. Dogs probably served as watchdogs, assisted in the hunt, and were likely eaten as a starvation food, for they efficiently convert garbage into at least tolerable meat, and hunters and gatherers from the Arctic to Southwest Asia are known to have eaten them on occasion.

In economic terms the most important domesticated animals in Southwest Asia are sheep (*Ovis*) and goats (*Capra*). From about 9000 B.C. to the present most meat, milk, and hide products used in Southwest Asia have come from these animals. Because of their form, goats can reach higher than sheep and apparently can tolerate somewhat coarser plants, so that in Southwest Asia they often feed on the thorny plants sheep tend to shun.

Horn size and shape in wild populations is a major determinant of reproductive success, since the larger males fight with their horns to establish breeding rights. As humans domesticated these animals, however, they relaxed selective pressures for large, strong horns. Thus, domestication altered horn size and shape in males and largely eliminated them in females (Figure 7.5). The increase in woolliness in domestic sheep is interesting because, as Flannery notes, on the one hand it efficiently insulates the sheep against the extreme heat of the agricultural lowlands, but on the other hand, it increases their problems with *Stipa* grass, which can lodge in the wool and eventually penetrate the skin, with much attendant discomfort and infection (Flannery 1971: 74–77).

Intensive hunting of wild sheep and goats was an important part of life in Southwest Asia by at least 10,000 B.C., but this subsistence pattern probably goes back much earlier. The first evidence of *Ovis* domestication may be the presence of sheep bones in Neolithic (ca. 9000 to 6000 B.C.) settlements in the Jordan Valley. These bones reflect no morphological changes in the direction of domestication, but sheep and goats are not native to this area and their presence here probably reflects intentional introduction.

Ethnographic studies of modern pastoralists suggest that they typically sell or eat 50 percent or more of the animals born each year, principally the males, since the females can be kept for reproduction and only a few males are required to service the breeding population. Once a male has reached two years of age, any further investment of food or time in him yields little additional return.

7.5

Goat-horn cores changed shape as domestication proceeded, from roughly quadrilateral to a twisted form. Cores here are classified by type of cross section and listed by stratigraphic zone at Tepe Ali Kosh and Tepe Sabz, Deh Luran, Iran.

Phase	Site	Zone	Cross section quadrilateral	Cross section lozenge–shaped	Medially flat, but untwisted	Medially concave, helical twist	Too young or too broken to diagnose
Bayat	TS	A$_1$				1	
Bayat	TS	A$_2$				1	
Bayat	TS	A$_3$			1	3	1
Mehmeh	TS	B$_1$			1		
Mehmeh	TS	B$_2$				1	1
Mehmeh	TS	B$_3$					1
Khazineh	TS	C$_1$					1
Khazineh	TS	C$_2$					
Khazineh	TS	C$_3$					3
Sabz	TS	D			2	1	6
Mohammad Jaffar	AK	A$_1$	4	1		1	7
Mohammad Jaffar	AK	A$_2$					8
Ali Kosh	AK	B$_1$		1	2		3
Ali Kosh	AK	B$_2$	11	7	8		27
Bus Mordeh	AK	C$_1$	2?	2			
Bus Mordeh	AK	C$_2$		2			7

Type of Horn Core

Ca. 3700 B.C.

Ca. 7500 B.C.

Evidence from two sites near Zawi Chemi Shanidar in Iraq indicates that this selective slaughtering may have been underway as early as 9000 B.C. Prior to 12,000 B.C., only about 20 percent of the animals killed and eaten at one of the sites were immature, but by 8650 B.C., 44 to 58 percent of the sheep and 25 to 43 percent of the goats eaten were immature when butchered. And at the other site (dated to about 8900 B.C.), the percentage was approximately the same (G. Wright 1971: 463).

Some of the earliest hornless sheep skulls—in some cases an indication of domestication—come from Ali Kosh, in southwestern Iran, in levels dating to shortly after 7000 B.C. By 6000 B.C. there is evidence of domestic sheep and goats at sites all over Southwest Asia and even into Greece and southern Europe, and it appears that once domestication was well advanced, the spread of sheep and goat raising was very rapid. The importance of sheep and goats in this context lies not so much in their meat as in their milk, hair, and hides. The milk can be converted and stored as cheese and yogurt, both excellent sources of protein, and a well-kept animal can supply many times its own weight in these products over the course of a year. In every agricultural community there are hedgerows, thorny plants, clippings, and stubble that are perfectly acceptable to the rather undiscriminating sheep and goats, and these animals, with their heavy fleece, are well protected against the sun and thus are among the few animals that can withstand the heat of Mesopotamia.

Domestic cattle were herded on the Anatolian Plateau (central Turkey) by about 5800 B.C., and were probably present in the Balkans by 6500 B.C. As with sheep and goats, cattle domestication seems to have been a widespread phenomenon, probably beginning sometime after 9000 B.C. and occurring in many areas from China to western Europe. Domestication of cattle focused on reduced size, increased docility and milk production, and increased tolerance of climatic conditions.

The importance of cattle in the upland areas was considerable, and some sites have "shrines" with paintings, cattle skulls, and other evidence that cattle played a vital part in the religion as well as the economy of these societies. But cattle were probably even more important to the first settlers on the southern Mesopotamian Alluvium. During the dry, hot summers in this region few reliable protein sources are available to primitive agriculturalists, and cow meat and milk apparently provided a crucial nutritional component. Sheep and goats were part of this development, but cattle apparently contributed something that sheep and goats couldn't. Possibly, this was the use of oxen (castrated bulls) to pull plows and carts. In many areas of Southwest Asia where rainfall is sufficient for cereal cultivation, plowing is essential because natural vegetation is so thick it would not be possible to sow the cereals. Later, the horse, donkey, and mule were also used as draught animals.

Another important domesticated animal was the pig. The bones of this animal have been recovered in the thousands from sites all over Southwest Asia by 6000 B.C., and even as late as 2700 B.C. pig bones represent 20 to 30 percent of all animal remains at many large sites. Curiously, however, sometime after about 2400 B.C. pork apparently was religiously proscribed in most Mesopotamian cities, as well as in Egypt and elsewhere in Southwest Asia. Pigs are quite useful in some agricultural systems because they eat and convert into high-grade food some of the garbage, human and animal wastes, and other materials discarded by farmers. Pork, if not injected with water, soaked in nitrosamines and other carcinogens, and plasticized by commercial packers, is one of the most nutritious, storable, and versatile of meats. Why should the poor peasants of prehistoric Southwest Asia reject such an important food?

Marvin Harris (1977: 133) dismisses the notion that this prohibition had anything to do with the common infection of pigs with trichinae, the small parasites that can infect and kill people. Recent studies have shown that pigs raised in hot climates seldom transmit this disease; moreover, Southwest Asian farmers ate cattle, sheep, and goats, which carry anthrax, brucellosis, and other diseases as dangerous or more so than anything pigs can transmit.

Instead, Harris explains prohibitions of pork in terms of the cost-benefit ratio of the animal in early subsistence agricultural systems. Pigs, unlike sheep, goats, and cattle, cannot subsist on husks, stalks, or other high-cellulose foods; their natural diet is tubers, roots, nuts, and fruits, and they completely lose their advantages over cattle as a converter of plant foods if forced to subsist on high-cellulose diets. Also, pigs are native to woodlands and swamps and do not tolerate direct sun and open country well. Thus, the clearing of land and felling of forests coincident with the spread of agriculture in Southwest Asia greatly reduced the habitat and natural foods available to pigs, and, increasingly, pigs had to be fed on grain, which brought them into competition with people; they also had to be provided with artificial shade and considerable water. Moreover, in contrast to other domesticates, as Harris points out, pigs cannot be milked, sheared, ridden, or used to pull a plow. In short, they lost their cost effectiveness relative to sheep, goats, and cattle, and their eventual proscription made excellent economic "sense."

The Archeological Record of Plant and Animal Domestication

Archaeological sites throughout Southwest Asia during the late Upper Pleistocene, from about 20,000 to 16,000 B.C., are monotonously alike in their concentrations of stone tools, ash, and the bones of large, hoofed mammals. Almost all the meat eaten by people came from just a few species of *ungulates* (hoofed mammals), mainly gazelles and wild cows. Based on the tools and other artifacts from Southwest Asian sites of this period, it appears that the basic social unit was a band of about fifteen or twenty people, comprising several families, who season after season moved through this area hunting animals and gathering plants. Sometime after about 16,000 B.C. in Southwest Asia there was a subtle but fundamental shift in subsistence strategies that is termed the *broad-spectrum revolution*. At this time some groups gradually increased their exploitation of resources that previously had been largely ignored, such as mollusks, birds, snails, and a variety of wild plants. Whether wild wheat and barley were also exploited is not yet known, since not a single wild wheat or barley seed has ever been recovered from these Upper Pleistocene sites—perhaps because the archaeologists who excavated these sites were usually not interested in recovering them.

Alternatively, the wild ancestors of domesticated wheat and barley may not have existed in Southwest Asia until about 11,000 years ago, toward the end of the Pleistocene (H. E. Wright 1976). If true, this would certainly simplify the problem of why these plants were not domesticated here during previous interglacials. On the other hand, it does not explain why these plants were not previously domesticated in their native areas (Wright suggests they would have been native to Morocco and the eastern Mediterranean during the Pleistocene), and, in any case, we run into difficulties when we try to explain the timing of cereal domestication in terms of changes in the geographical distribution of grain. For the worldwide range of plants that were being domesticated at roughly the same time as those in Southwest Asia includes rice, potatoes, maize, and many other diverse plants, and it is difficult to explain each of these radically different domestication processes as resulting from habitat changes brought on by the end of the Pleistocene.

Not every hunting and gathering group in Southwest Asia increased its exploitation of snails, mollusks, and these other "minor" resources. Sites in the Khorramabad Valley in Iran, the Mount Carmel area of Israel, and elsewhere dating from this period still contain the classic late Pleistocene accumulations of large animal bones, and there is no evidence of increased eating of invertebrates. Even at those sites indicating a shift to a broader range of resources, large ungulates still provided approximately 90 percent of the meat consumed. Thus, we should see the broad-spectrum revolution as a subtle shift that occurred at many places over a large and ecologically diverse region.

Accompanying the broader diet of the late Pleistocene was the appearance of a more diverse technology. Barbed spears and arrows, bows, knives made by setting obsidian and flint flakes into bone or wood, and other tools bespeak a broadening range of subsistence activities. Some animal species were exploited systematically for the first time, and the grinding stones, "sickles," and other new tools indicate that vegetable foods, including wild cereal grasses, may have been important parts of the diet. Minor local trade in obsidian and sea shells was carried on, and substantial huts appeared in some areas. Apparently, population densities were slowly increasing in some areas—although the archaeological evidence for this is not at all clear (Mellaart 1975: 22–28).

The changing diet of the late Pleistocene and early post-Pleistocene may not be totally understandable as a result of climate changes, but certainly the great reduction in the numbers of large herd animals occasioned by these climatic changes was an important factor in stimulating new subsistence strategies. As the wild cattle, reindeer, and other large herbivores retreated north, hunting cultures in Southwest Asia were forced to make up for lost protein by increasing their exploitation of plant foods, smaller animals, and, perhaps, by making the initial attempts to domesticate sheep, goats, cattle, and pigs.

Shortly after 10,000 B.C. there were still no agricultural economies in Southwest Asia, but sedentary communities appeared for the first time, such as those of the *Natufian* culture, represented by scores of sites located in a wide strip of land running from southern Turkey to the edge of the Nile delta. At about 10,000 B.C. intensive collectors and hunters in this area subsisted largely on gazelle hunting, fishing, and the

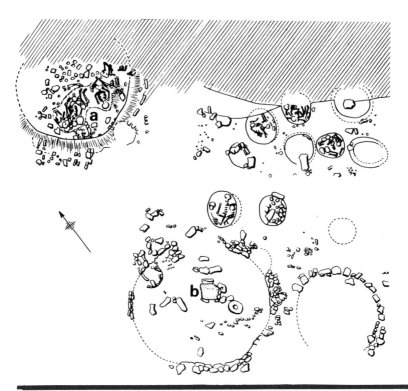

7.6
Above, simplified plan of an early settlement at Ain Mallaha (Israel). Below, an "idealized" rectangular house from Jarmo (Iraq). Compounds of circular huts such as those at Ain Mallaha were widespread in Southwest Asia after about 8000 B.C., but by 6000 B.C. had been superseded largely by villages of rectangular units.

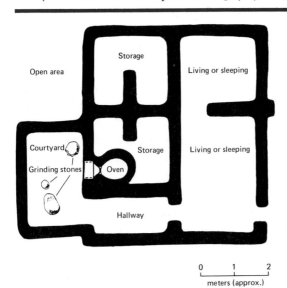

Storage

Open area

Living or sleeping

Courtyard

Storage

Living or sleeping

Grinding stones

Oven

Hallway

0   1   2

meters (approx.)

collection of wild cereals. The importance of cereals in these communities is reflected in large numbers of sickle blades, many of which have been worn to a glossy finish by continued contact with the rough stems of cereal plants.

Some Natufian peoples retained a mobile way of life, but others established sedentary communities, such as at Ain Mallaha, near Lake Huleh, Israel (Figure 7.6A), which between 9000 and 8000 B.C. comprised about fifty huts, most of them circular, semisubterranean, and rock-lined, and from 2.5 to 9 meters in diameter. Mortars and pestles litter the site and occur in most huts, and storage pits were found both in individual huts and in the interior of the compound.

This same basic housing pattern, compounds of circular huts, has a wide distribution in Southwest Asia, occurring at Nahal Oren in Israel, Beidha in southern Jordan, and Tell Mureybit in Syria. Kent Flannery (1972) has noted that many contemporary African peoples also live in compounds of circular huts and that most such societies share several characteristics: only one or two people are usually housed in each hut; many of the huts are not residential, but are used for storage, kitchens, stables, and the like; huts are often placed in a circle around a cleared space; food storage is usually open and shared by all occupants; and, perhaps most important, the social organization of the typical compound, like that of hunting and gathering groups, usually consists of six to eight males, each associated with from one to three women and their respective children, and there is a strong sexual division of labor.

Flannery argues that settlements of adjacent rectangular buildings—which he calls *villages*—have advantages over settlements of circular buildings—which he calls *compounds* (Figure 7.6B). The former are more expandable because rooms can simply be added on, whereas increasing the number of circular residences rapidly increases the diameter of the settlement to an unwieldy size. Villages are also more defensible than compounds for a number of reasons. But the primary difference is in their respective capacities for intensification of production. In compounds, storage facilities are open and shared and the basic economic unit is the group; but in villages the basic unit is the family, which maintains its own storage of supplies, and thus has greater incentives for intensification of production (Flannery 1972: 48).

If Flannery is correct, the transition which occurred between 9000 B.C. and 7000 B.C. from compounds of circular structures to villages of rectangular rooms is a reflection of changes in the social organization of the Greater Mesopotamian peoples, with the nuclear family gradually replacing the hunting and gathering group as the unit of economic production. And although the circular-building tradition continued for several thousand years in parts of Southwest Asia, it was eventually entirely supplanted by rectangular-unit villages.

To return to the archaeological evidence for early domestication, it is evident that Natufian culture contrasted in many ways with its predecessors. Sickles, querns (hand mills), mortars, pestles, pounders, and other ground stone tools occur in abundance at Natufian sites, and many such tools show signs of long, intensive use. Fish hooks and gorges and net sinkers attest to the growing importance of fish in the diet in some areas. Vessels made of limestone and marble indicate an increased need for containers, but there is no evidence of Natufian clay-working or pottery.

Compared to the Pleistocene cultures of the Levant, there appears to have been considerable social change in the Natufian. Cleverly carved figurines of animals, women, and other subjects occur in many sites, and Natufian period cave paintings have been found in Anatolia, Syria, and Iran (Mellaart 1975: 34–35). Trade in shell, obsidian, and other commodities appears to have been on the rise, and we suspect that exchange of perishables, such as skins, foodstuffs, and salt, was also increasing. As Mellaart notes, with the increased importance of wild cereals in the diet, salt probably became for the first time a near necessity, perhaps for food preservation and to compensate for the lowered salt content of the diet (1975: 33).

More than 200 Natufian burials have been found, most of them simple graves set in house floors. Grave goods are infrequent, but some burials indicate concern with the philosophical implications of death: at Ain Mallaha skeletons were buried with their heads wedged between two stones and their joints covered with large stones, "to ensure perhaps that the deceased would not rise from his grave" (Mellaart 1975: 37).

Some of the earliest evidence for domesticated grain cultivation in the Levant comes from lower levels of Jericho (ca. 8350 to 7350 B.C.), next to the springs in the center of this oasis. At some time during this period domestic forms of wheat and barley were cultivated in quantity here. Neither wild wheat nor barley appears to have been native to the arid wastelands that surround this site, so these grains were probably brought down from the uplands of the Jordan Valley and grown at Jericho, perhaps as wild species initially (Mellaart 1975: 50). No domes-

7.7
Early Natufian house, situated on virgin soil at Tell as-Sultan, Jericho. The round shallow pits in the floor were probably storage pits, and the stone querns to the left were probably used for grinding cereals.

tic animals were used in this period, but wild gazelles, goats, cattle, and boars were intensively hunted. Two thousand or more people probably lived at Jericho at any time between 8350 and 7350 B.C., and although the earlier communities were apparently unwalled, around 7350 B.C. the inhabitants built a massive stone wall, 3 meters thick, 4 meters high, and perhaps 700 meters in circumference (ibid.: 49). Asphalt, sulphur, salt, and a little obsidian seem to have been traded, but in moderate quantities. The apparent destruction of the settlement without obvious violence at about 7350 B.C. is unexplained (ibid.: 51).

While the Natufian and early agricultural cultures were developing in Palestine, groups in and around the flanks of the Zagros and Taurus mountains were also making the transition to sedentary communities based on intensive plant collection. One of the earliest such communities was at Tell Mureybit, on the Euphrates River east of Aleppo, Syria. There, at about 8200 to 8000 B.C., people built circular stone huts, similar in almost every respect to the circular huts at Ain Mallaha and Beidha. Charred wild einkorn seeds have been recovered from Tell

Mureybit, as well as the remains of wild barley, lentils, bitter vetch, pistachios, toad rush, and possibly peas. Most of these plants can be found locally, but the wild einkorn and barley are not native to this area and in fact can be found in natural stands no nearer than the Anatolian hills some 100 to 150 kilometers to the northwest (Mellaart 1975: 46). The impracticality of moving large amounts of grain this distance suggests that Tell Mureybit may be one of the earliest agricultural settlements in Southwest Asia, that here and in adjacent areas intensive collectors first tried to plant, cultivate, and harvest their own fields of grain. Tell Mureybit is a deep site and its many levels of construction, first of circular compounds of rude huts, then larger rectangular villages, suggest the success of this experiment (ibid.: 46–47).

7.8
Common implements for grinding and preparing grain in Iraq, between 7000 and 4000 B.C. The ceramic husking tray above was used to strip grain from chaff; the heavy stone quern and round pestle below were used to grind grain to flour.

Soon after 8000 B.C. sedentary communities and domestic plants and animals had appeared at several places along the flanks of the Zagros. At Ali Kosh, situated on the arid steppe of western Iran, at about 7500 B.C. people hunted gazelles, onagers (wild asses), and pigs, fished in the Mehmeh River, collected shellfish, and snared wild fowl. They also collected vetch and other plants, and between 8000 and 6500 B.C. they began growing domestic, two-rowed, hulled barley and emmer wheat. These early farmers lived in crude clay huts furnished with reed mats, and they had stone bowls and a few other small household goods, but this settlement was neither rich nor impressive. Possibly the people came here only in the winter, since summers are unearthly hot and the cooler mountains would have provided many plant and animal products. Wild wheat is not native to the Ali Kosh area, but wild barley is available within a few kilometers (Hole 1971: 473), and the people here may have been growing grains that had been domesticated elsewhere.

Other evidence of early agriculture in the Zagros zone has been found at Ganj Dareh, Asiab, and elsewhere (Table 7.2), and by shortly after 7500 B.C. the transition to sedentary life and agricultural economies seems to have been well underway. At 6500 B.C. domestic plants and animals were providing much of the food for people at Jarmo, Ali Kosh, Tepe Guran, and many other sites, and most of these early farmers had the full range of agricultural tools and the mud-brick houses that were the mainstays of the agricultural revolution.

Further north, in eastern Anatolia, intensive collectors and hunters made the transition to sedentary life some time shortly before 7000 B.C. and within a few centuries had developed a primitive but efficient agricultural system. They still hunted and gathered many wild resources, but they also began to use domesticated sheep, goats, and pigs, and by about 6400 B.C. were eating large amounts of wheat. At Çayönü, houses were mainly mud-brick structures built on stone foundations, but in one area there is a grill-like stone foundation of what may have been a fairly elaborate structure, or a grain-storage depot.

Hypotheses about the Origins of Domestication, Agriculture, and Sedentary Communities

We have described the botanical and cultural changes involved in plant and animal domestication in Southwest Asia, noting in the process some

TABLE 7.2 Archaeological Evidence of Early Cereal Cultivation and Animal Herding in the Near East

Sites and stratigraphy	Approximate dates B.C.	Barley	Einkorn	Emmer	Bread wheat	Sheep	Goat	Cattle	Pig	Dog
AEGEAN AREA										
Argissa (Thessaly), Aceramic	6500	x	x	x		x	x	x	x	?
Nea Nikomedeia (Macedonia)	6200	x		x		x	x	x	x	?
Knossos (Crete), stratum X	6100	x		x	x					
Khirokitia (Cyprus), Aceramic	6000					x	x			
Sesklo (Thessaly), Aceramic	6000–5000	x		x						
Ghediki (Thessaly), Aceramic	6000–5000	x	x	x						
ANATOLIA										
Haçilar, Aceramic	7000			x						?
Haçilar, Ceramic	5800–5000	x	x	x	x					?
Çayönü	7000					x			x	x
Çatal Hüyük, VI–II	7000		x	x	x	x		?		
LEVANT										
Tell Ramad (Syria)	7000	x	x	x	x					
Jericho, Prepottery Neol. A.	7000–6500	x		x						
Jericho, Prepottery Neol. B.	6500–5500	x	x	x						
Beidha (Jordan), Prepottery	5850–5600			x			x			

Ali Kosh, Bus Mordeh	7500–6750
Ali Kosh, Ali Kosh	6750–6000
Ali Kosh, M. Jaffar	6000–5600
Tepe Sabz, Sabz	5500–5000
Tell as-Sawwan	5800–5600
Hassuna	5800
KURDISTAN-LURISTAN	
Zawi Chemi, Karim Shahir	8900
Jarmo	6750–6500
Tepe Sarab	? 6500
Tepe Guran	6200–5500
Matarrah	5800

SOURCE Karl W. Butzer. 1971. "Agricultural Origins in the Near East as a Geographical Problem," in *Prehistoric Agriculture*, ed. Stuart Struever. Garden City, N.Y.: Natural History Press, pp. 224-25. Based on Hole, Flannery, 1967; Mellaart, 1965; Reed, 1959, 1961, 1969; Renfrew, 1969; and others.

of the relevant archaeological evidence. At this point let us consider some ideas about how and why domestication, agriculture, and sedentary communities appeared in the area.

THE OASIS HYPOTHESIS

Among the first such hypotheses was the so-called *Oasis hypothesis,* also known as the *Propinquity hypothesis,* which was an attempt to explain the origins of agriculture in terms of the climate changes associated with the end of the Pleistocene some 10,000 years ago.

> With the gradual shrinking in dimensions of habitable areas and the disappearance of herds of wild animals, man, concentrating on the oases and forced to conquer new means of support, began to utilize the native plants; and from among these he learned to use seeds of different grasses growing on the dry land and in marshes at the mouths of larger streams on the desert. With the increase of population and its necessities, he learned to plant the seeds, thus making, by conscious or unconscious selection, the first step in the evolution of the whole series of cereals. (Pumpelly 1908: 65–66)

In 1904 geologist R. Pumpelly led an expedition to Turkestan in central Asia to test his ideas. He chose Turkestan because it was thought to be the ancient homeland of the Aryan peoples and Pumpelly was interested in the hypothesis that the great post-Pleistocene drought forced the Aryans to emigrate to Europe.

At two mounds in an oasis named Anau he found the remains of a sedentary agricultural community whose date he estimated as about 5000 B.C. He felt this supported his hypothesis because at that time it was the earliest known agricultural settlement, and since he found no walls or weapons at this site, he concluded that these people had had no need for defense and had developed in virtual isolation from the rest of the world. In short, he saw agriculture as a direct result of the great desiccation and of the inventive genius of the Aryan peoples.

The Oasis hypothesis found many supporters after Pumpelly's excavations. Most prominent was V. Gordon Childe, who accepted much of what Pumpelly argued but who thought that agriculture first appeared in Egypt, along the Nile Valley, where the soil was so rich and the climate so conducive to plant growth that little would have been required to encourage humans to begin cultivation.

The Oasis hypothesis was accepted in whole or in part for many years, but a number of empirical and logical problems were obvious from the first. Already by 1926, for example, it had been demonstrated that the wild ancestors of wheat and barley did not grow in the areas of the central Asian oases, but rather were native to the uplands of Southwest Asia. In addition, excavations by G. Caton-Thompson in 1934 suggested that settled agricultural communities had existed in Egypt by 5000 B.C., making it doubtful that the oases of central Asia were the first to evolve agriculture; and by the 1950s there was also evidence that there had not been a major climate change in Southwest and central Asia at the time domestication began—a devastating blow to the Oasis hypothesis.

THE NATURAL HABITAT HYPOTHESIS

Harold Peake and Herbert Fleure suggested in 1926 that the first domesticates and agriculturalists would have appeared in the upper valley of the Euphrates River, or at the point where the river passes through the last ranges of foothills on the edge of the Mesopotamian Plain, mainly because they knew that wild species of wheat and barley were native to these areas. Accordingly, in the early 1950s Robert Braidwood of the University of Chicago organized a series of excavations to evaluate post-Pleistocene climatic changes and to look for early farming communities in northern Mesopotamia. His expeditions were among the first to include specialists in botany, geology, and zoology as well as archaeology, and this "multidisciplinary" approach has proven to be a highly successful research strategy. To derive the most information from archaeological projects it is necessary to have more specialized knowledge than one individual could hope to control, and the improved quality of archaeology, in Southwest Asia in particular, owes a great deal to Braidwood's pioneering efforts.

Palynologists and geologists attached to Braidwood's expedition concluded that there had not been a climate change of any significance during the period when domestication and agriculture first appeared, and therefore Braidwood rejected the Oasis hypothesis. More recent evidence indicates that, in fact, Southwest Asia *was* somewhat cooler and drier than it is today, but not sufficiently to resurrect the Oasis hypothesis.

Braidwood's excavations (1960) at *Jarmo* in the hill country of northern Iraq revealed an agricultural settlement dating to about 6500 B.C.—much earlier than had been found either at Anau or in the Fayum (a lake area west of the Nile) area of Egypt. About 6500 B.C. Jarmo was a settlement of a few dozen mud-walled huts inhabited by about 150 people who relied partly on wild plants and animals, such as snails, pistachios, and acorns, but who also seem to have been herding domesticated goats and, perhaps, sheep. But Braidwood also found at Jarmo the remains of partially domesticated wheat in association with grinding stones, sickle blades, and storage pits.

Braidwood conducted excavations at a number of other sites within the natural habitat zone of wild wheat and barely and eventually became convinced this was indeed the home of the first agriculturalists. As an explanation of why domestication, agriculture, and sedentary villages first appeared in this area, Braidwood formulated his *Natural Habitat hypothesis.*

> In my opinion there is no reason to complicate the story with extraneous "causes." The food-producing revolution seems to have occurred as the culmination of an ever increasing cultural differentiation and specialization of human communities. Around 8000 B.C. the inhabitants of the fertile crescent had come to know their habitat so well that they were beginning to domesticate the plants and animals they had been collecting and hunting. At slightly later times human cultures reached the corresponding level in Central America and perhaps in the Andes, in southeastern Asia, and in China. From these "nuclear zones" cultural diffusion spread the new way of life to the rest of the world. (1960: 74)

Braidwood's research into agricultural origins was one of the few systematic investigations into this problem at the time, and his work has had substantial and positive influences on subsequent investigations in this area, but as L. Binford pointed out (1968), Braidwood's account of the factors responsible for the appearance of domestication and agriculture was not complete. Why, for example, didn't agriculture develop during previous interglacial periods? Braidwood's answer, that "culture was not ready to achieve it," is less than compelling. For hundreds of millennia hunters and gatherers had been living in these mountains and yet none had ever "come to know their habitat so well" that they began to domesticate plants or animals. Why were these people such slow learners?

There were also empirical problems with Braidwood's hypothesis. Frank Hole, Kent Flannery, and James Neeley (1969) conducted excavations at several sites on the Deh Luran Plain in southwestern Iran and found evidence that by 6700 B.C. domestication and agriculture were already evolving in this area, which is just outside the natural habitat of wheat and barley (wild barley grows quite close by, but very sparsely) (F. Hole 1971).

Also damaging to the basic premise of the Natural Habitat hypothesis was a series of experiments performed by J. Harlan in eastern Anatolia in 1966, in which, using a crude sickle made with flint blades set in a wooden handle, he was able to harvest wild emmer wheat at the rate of about 6.25 pounds per hour (Harlan and Zohary 1966). A family of four or five could probably have collected a year's supply of grain with only a few weeks labor, and this would seem to suggest that the people who lived in the natural habitat of wheat and barley had perhaps the *least* incentive to farm it, because they could collect more than enough from wild stands.

Because of these and other problems with the Natural Habitat hypothesis, archaeologists in the 1960s began to try to formulate a more comprehensive and defendable hypothesis about the origins of domestication and agriculture in Southwest Asia, and they also attempted to explain how and why sedentary communities could have appeared so long *before* domestication or agriculture occurred.

THE EDGE-ZONE HYPOTHESIS

Lewis Binford's approach to the problem of the origins of domestication and agriculture was based on his idea of culture as an adaptive device. "If we seek understanding of the origins of agriculture or 'of the spread of the village-farming community,' we must analyze these cultural means as adaptive adjustments in the variety of ecosystems within which human groups were participants" (1972: 431). Thus, Binford attempted to describe the selective environments that would favor domestication and cultivation. He assumed that prior to the first agriculture, hunting and gathering bands were in equilibrium with their natural environment, using wild plants and animals, but not altering them in ways we recognize as domestication.

What could have upset this ancient equilibrium? Binford's answer begins with his rejection of the attractively simple idea that domestication and agriculture were the result of population growth that forced people to domesticate or starve, for if prehistoric hunting and gathering populations always grew until their food requirements outstripped available resources, "no population could ever achieve a stable adaptation since its members would always be under strong selective pressure to develop new means of getting food" (1972: 433).

Recent studies have shown that human hunters and gatherers—and indeed, all animal populations—normally regulate their population size quite precisely. This is, of course, the only way a population can have a reasonable chance of survival over many generations, for if population levels were too close to the limits of the food supply, even minor fluctuations in this supply, such as a colder than average winter, could result in the starvation of the whole group.

In this context Binford also rejects the idea that agriculture and domestication could be explained simply as a result of humanity's quest for more food and more free time. Various studies have shown that many primitive groups exist in circumstances where, by exerting themselves just a bit more, they could support much larger populations; yet these groups show no inclination to make such investments, usually regarding them as an unnecessary infringement on their leisure time and social life.

Similarly, Binford dismisses the idea that primitive peoples are so preoccupied with the quest for food that they have no leisure time to create technologies, arts, sciences, and the other hallmarks of civilization. In fact, some hunting and gathering groups have been shown to have more leisure time than many subsistence farmers (Lee 1969), although there is considerable dispute about how frequent and under what conditions this disparity existed in prehistory.

If hunters and gatherers are not constantly breeding themselves into disaster and they have sufficient leisure time and some security, what kinds of stresses would upset this equilibrium and favor the adoption of new subsistence systems involving agriculture, domestication, and sedentary communities? Binford argues that this was essentially a case where changes in the demographic structure of one region resulted in the impingement of one group on the territory of another, upsetting the equilibrium and increasing the population density in some areas to the point that manipulation of the natural environment in new ways in order to increase productivity would be favored. He notes that Southwest Asia is an ecological mosaic, with close juxtapositioning of very different climates and plant and animal communities, and suggests that late Pleistocene hunters and gatherers in such an area would fall into one of two categories: (1) *closed systems,* groups whose population size was regulated by their mobile way of life, infanticide, abortion, marriage rules, and other practices, with very little emigration or immigration; or (2) *open systems,* groups that used budding-off as the primary mechanism for population-size control. This phenomenon, noted in many parts of the world, involves a group slowly increasing its size up to a certain number, at which point, because of squabbling or insufficient resources, the group splits, with half the people emigrating to another, usually adjacent, territory.

Population control through emigration is common when a new territory has been opened up for colonization, such as when the first groups moved into the New World. Alternatively, budding-off can also become the primary population control mechanism if a new resource or subsistence technique—such as domestication and agriculture—opens a new niche. Binford notes that budding-off usually happens before any substantial overcrowding or major food shortages occur and that

> the shift to the exploitation of highly seasonal resources such as anadromous fish and migratory fowl did not occur until the close of the Pleistocene. This shift . . . established for the first time conditions leading to marked heterogeneity in rates of population growth and the structure of the ecological niche of immediately adjacent sociocultural systems. (1968: 334)

Given these varying population growth rates, Binford argues that budding-off would have certain consequences that could have led to domestication and agriculture.

> From the standpoint of the populations already in the recipient zone, the intrusion of immigrant groups would disturb the existing density equilibrium system and might raise the population density to the level at which we would expect diminishing food resources. This situation would serve to increase markedly for the recipient groups the pressures favoring means for increased productivity. The intrusive group, on the other hand, would be forced to make adaptive adjustments to their new environment. . . . There would be strong selective pressures favoring the development of more efficient subsistence techniques by both groups. (1968: 331)

Thus, Binford is particularly concerned with describing situations that would select for, or *reward,* a cultural innovation like domestication or agriculture. He assumes that for at least the last several hundred thousand years, people had the mental and physical abilities to interact with and domesticate plants and animals and that domesticable plants and animals have always been available. But domestication did not occur in these earlier periods because situations that would reward these innovations did not exist. Once the population-to-resources balance was disturbed, however, there was a premium on every resource, and domestication might have come about in a number of ways. Perhaps the immigrant groups, in an attempt to regain the resources of their former habitats, would have tried to introduce wild wheat and barley into these marginal, "edge" zones. This would have exposed these plants to different selective environments, and domestication might have occurred as people manipulated these plant communities in these new environments.

Binford's *Edge-Zone hypothesis* provoked much discussion and research relating to the origins of Southwest Asian domestication and agriculture, but the hypothesis has run up against some logical and empirical problems. Flannery has summed these up as follows:

> The Near East is a mosaic of "favorable" habitats (e.g., oak-pistachio woodland) and "marginal" habitats (e.g., gravel desert); the wild cereals have definite "optimum" zones in which they grow densely and marginal zones in which they do poorly. If one follows Binford's model to its logical conclusion, the "optimum" habitats should have been the centers for population growth, with the marginal areas receiving the emigrant overflow. It is in these marginal zones that man-land disequilibrium and stress would have been felt first. Thus in 1969 I suggested that farming might have begun first, not in the optimum area of wild cereal growth (where, as Harlan and Zohary point out, wild wheat already does as well as it would in a cultivated field), but around the margins where it was necessary to raise the available food per capita. . . .
>
> Let me now raise some objections to this model. First, although it has won an alomst frightening acceptance among some of my colleagues, it is still unproven and highly speculative. Second, . . . our archeological data (such as they are) do not show strong population increases in "optimum" areas like the Lebanese woodland, but the very opposite—some of the most striking increases are in "marginal" habitats like the Negev! Clearly, there were a number of very interesting processes at work in the late Pleistocene Levant which could only be handled by a more multi-

variate model. Finally, the model comes too close to making population growth and climatic change into prime movers. It may be that the "demographic change" which made cultivation seem like a good idea in Southwest Asia was an increase in sedentary communities—and the latter may have begun in response to changes in socio-political organization which had nothing to do with either climate or population density. (1973: 284)

As we shall see, Flannery's summary is still essentially accurate. Post-Pleistocene climate changes, variable rates of human population growth, and rising population densities no doubt played important roles in the appearance of the origins of agriculture, but the mechanisms and other variables are still far from clear, and the developmental process was likely somewhat different in various parts of the world.

Whatever the ultimate causes of these developments, by 6000 B.C. agricultural villages had appeared over almost all of Southwest Asia where it was possible to raise wheat and barley without artificial irrigation, and densities were such that most villages were within a day's walk of another settlement. Excavations at a sample of these villages reveal them to have been simply organized with no palaces, rich tombs, occupational specialists, or complex economies. Each appears to have been largely self-sufficient and politically and economically independent. The story of how these peasant villages were transformed and incorporated into the great Southwest Asian civilizations of antiquity is taken up in chapter 9.

The Diffusion of Southwest Asian Domesticates

The domesticates and allied agricultural economies developed in Southwest Asia proved both successful and adaptable to the extent that within centuries of their appearance they had spread far outside the Fertile Crescent. Already by 7000 B.C. farmers at Argissa-Maghula in Greek Thessaly were subsisting on cultivated emmer wheat and barley, as well as domestic cattle and pigs. Shortly thereafter these same staples began replacing other adaptations in temperate Europe and southern Russia. Recent recalibration of carbon-14 dates for scores of early European sites reveals that the basic wheat-barley/cattle-pigs-sheep complex diffused at a rate of about a mile a year, reaching Bulgaria about 5500

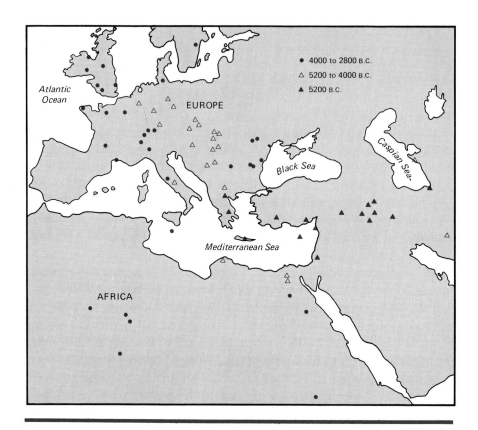

7·9
Radiocarbon dates for early agricultural settlements, showing the slow northwestern spread of agriculture into the temperate woodlands of Europe. Recent re-analysis suggests that these dates are probably underestimated by 500–1000 years.

B.C., southern Italy about 5000 B.C., and Britain and Scandinavia between 4000 and 3000 B.C. (Figure 7.9) (Ammerman and Cavalli-Sforza 1972). To the east, domestic wheat and barley reached the Indus Valley by at least 3000 B.C. (and probably much earlier), and by the late first millennium B.C. domestic wheat was in cultivation in northeastern China.

The processes by which these domesticates and their associated agricultural techniques replaced hunting and gathering economies in much of the Old World are not well known, but appear to have involved both the replacement of hunters and gatherers by agriculturalists and the conversion of hunters and gatherers to agricultural ways of life.

The grasslands and forests of temperate Europe and Eurasia contrast sharply with the steppes and arid plains of the Fertile Crescent, and the spread of agriculture northward and eastward required new strains of plants and animals and different social and technological adaptations. Methods had to be developed to clear the dense northern forests; and in some areas the rich hunting, gathering, and fishing resources formed such a productive food base that there was considerable "resistance" to the introduction of agriculture, with its unpredictability and heavy labor expenses. But along the loess (wind-blown soil) plains of the Danube and the other major European rivers, cultivated barley and wheat and domestic cows and pigs were combined with intensive hunting and gathering to form a rich and reliable economy that by the fifth millennium B.C. was the basis for dense sedentary populations throughout much of the temperate North. These early European and Eurasian cultures are considered in more detail in chapter 10.

Early Agriculture and Village Life in Asia and Africa

Ferreting out the complex ecological and cultural changes associated with the domestication process and the rise of agricultural economies requires extensive fieldwork and laboratory analyses, and no Old World areas have received as much research as Southwest Asia in this context. But recent work indicates that East Asia will prove to be an extremely early center for these kinds of developments.

EARLY DOMESTICATION AND AGRICULTURE
IN NORTH CHINA

One of the world's most important cereals, millet, was apparently domesticated and first cultivated on the great Yellow River flood plain, in North China (see Figure 7.2). The alluvial soils in this area are extremely fertile and are sufficiently arid that there was little vegetation to clear for agriculture in many areas. By about 4000 B.C. there were scores of villages in North China, most of them subsisting on millet and a few other domesticates and considerable hunted and gathered food. These villages usually contained about two or three hundred inhabitants housed in wattle-and-daub houses that looked very much like the circular houses and compounds that marked the evolution of agricultural communities in Southwest Asia some 3,000 years earlier.

Wheat and barley were apparently introduced to North China in late prehistoric times (early Chinese written characters for *cereal plant* were written with another character that indicated it was not a native plant), but when these other crops were introduced and where exactly millet was first domesticated will require much additional research. Another crop of considerable importance in North China was soybeans, several wild varieties of which are native to this area. The little evidence available suggests soybeans were in cultivation by at least 1600 B.C. Soybeans are a remarkably versatile crop that can replace meat, cheese, and milk with little loss in food value. In addition, they are good "green manure," enriching the soils on which they grow through nitrogen fixation. The substitution of soybeans for milk and meat in early Chinese diets may have to do with the fact that many oriental populations never evolved the enzymes necessary to digest milk products, causing them to suffer intestinal upsets if they eat these foods. Similar intolerances are found in Africa, South America, and elsewhere.

EARLY DOMESTICATION AND AGRICULTURE
IN SOUTHEAST ASIA

In the last few years there have been several sensationalist accounts of archaeological discoveries in Thailand and other parts of Southeast Asia, suggesting that plants were domesticated and in cultivation here many thousands of years earlier than in Southwest Asia. Available evidence is so limited that it is unwise to give much weight to these claims, but it is at least obvious that Southeast Asia was an important core area for early domestication and agriculture.

In terms of dietary contribution, rice is the most important domesticate of Southeast Asia, but several varieties of beans and cucumbers were also domesticated. Many authorities believe that rice (*Oryza sativa*) was domesticated in India, but recent evidence points to Thailand and other tropical areas of Southeast Asia as the place of origin. Less is known about the domestication of rice, however, than about any other major cereal.

Many varieties of wild rice still grow throughout Southeast Asia, and from these we can determine that the principal changes brought about by the process of domestication were: (1) a tougher rachis; (2) larger seed size; and (3) the conversion of the plant from a perennial into an annual.

Imprints from rice-grain husks have been found in potsherds from the site of Non Nok Tha in central Thailand in levels dating to between 6800 and 4000 B.C., but it is difficult to determine whether these represent domesticated rice. The use of the husks as tempering in ceramic manufacture may suggest domestication, but they may have been from collected wild species of rice. Other than this, the earliest known domesticated rice is from a site near Shanghai in levels dating to about 3000 B.C. (K. C. Chang 1976). Rice cultivation may go back much earlier than this in other parts of Southeast Asia, but to date we lack any solid evidence on this point.

We do know, however, that by about 8700 B.C. some groups in Southeast Asia were intensive plant collectors. Excavations at Spirit Cave in northwestern Thailand revealed the remains of five different kinds of nuts, a bean (*Vigna* or *Phaseolus*), bottle gourds, water chestnuts, black pepper, and cucumber. None of these plants showed any convincing signs of domestication (Flannery 1973).

One form of agriculture, *vegeculture,* may have developed very early in Southeast Asia—perhaps far earlier than rice domestication. In vegeculture plants are propagated not from seeds, but from cuttings taken from leaves, stems, or tubers of plants like manioc, yams, potatoes, and taro. As Flannery has pointed out, vegeculture often produces complex ecosystems because many different species of plants are frequently grown in the same fields, and although these crops are often less productive than seed crops, they are more stable ecologically because they more closely resemble the natural vegetation in warm, moist environments (1973: 273). They also require relatively little work once the plantings have been made.

Domestication of these crops is accomplished simply by making cuttings from plants which have the desired characteristics, since the new plant will be an exact genetic replica of the parent plant. Occasionally an accidental variant with desirable characteristics may appear and it can quickly be incorporated into the system. In many plants propagated this way, the long-term inattention to selection for seeds has resulted in plants that can no longer propagate themselves sexually.

Because of the warm, moist environment of Southeast Asia, not a single vegecultural remain of any antiquity has been recovered. It has been suggested that many of these crops were domesticated first in eastern India, near the Bay of Bengal, but the evidence for this is very tentative. Perhaps the only way we shall ever discover the origins of vegeculture in this region will be through careful analysis of changes in tool assemblages and in the locations of sites, but to date few efforts have been made in this direction.

In any case, vegeculture does not seem to have led to an early development of sedentary communities, and the origins of vegeculture and the origins of seed-crop cultivation are probably not related in Southeast Asia. Vegeculture apparently developed in those parts of Southeast Asia where seed-crop cultivation would have been most difficult with a primitive technology: the hot, humid areas where land clearance and weeding would have been laborious (Flannery 1973).

OTHER OLD WORLD CENTERS OF AGRICULTURAL ORIGINS

Egypt, North Africa, sub-Saharan Africa, Polynesia, and other areas of of the Old World gave rise to their own distinctive suites of domesticated plants and animals over the last several thousand years (see Figure 7.2), and apparently a great deal of intentional domestication through selective breeding occurred in many of these later processes. We shall consider the development of agricultural economies in Egypt, Pakistan, and China in subsequent chapters of this book, but first let us compare these Old World developments with similar processes in the New World.

The Origins of Domestication, Agriculture, and Sedentary Communities in the New World

Many scholars formerly believed that New World agriculture resulted primarily from contacts with Old World peoples who, arriving by ship centuries ago, had instructed the Native Americans in these arts. Traces of these quaint diffusionist ideas linger, but it is now almost certain that New World domesticates and agricultural economies were entirely the products of local processes that occurred in several parts of the New World independently. And while the sequence and form in which these practices appeared in the New World contrast in some respects with Old World developments, the parallels are sufficiently strong as to suggest that both cases can be understood in terms of the same general principles.

New World agriculture appeared very early in several ecologically distinct areas from the tropics of South America to the woodlands of North America and involved many different species. *Maize,* or corn, the most important domesticate, first appears in the archaeological record in southern Mexico, in deposits dating to about 7,000 years ago, but it may have been domesticated somewhat earlier in the tropical lowlands of Ecuador and adjacent areas. Complementing maize in most early agricultural communities were beans, squash, pumpkins, and peppers, the earliest domestic varieties of which come from Peru, Mexico, and several points in between. Gourds—grown mainly to use as containers— may have floated to the New World from Africa but may also have been domesticated in the New World. Manioc, sweet and white potatoes, other root crops, peanuts, and cotton were apparently first domesticated in South America, perhaps in the tropical forests, while sunflowers, amaranths, tobacco, and several other plant species were domesticated in the North American East.

Compared to the Old World, few American animal species were domesticated. Domestic dogs were in evidence at least 10,000 years ago, and early Peruvians domesticated the llama, which provided meat, wool, and transport power, but New World people never domesticated native bison or any other animals for draught power. Turkeys and ducks substituted to some extent for Old World fowl, and the guinea pig filled the role of the Old World rabbit in some areas, but generally the Americans relied much less on domesticated animals than did Old World peoples.

DOMESTICATION AND AGRICULTURE IN
PREHISTORIC MESOAMERICA

The earliest evidence of New World plant domestication and agriculture comes from the arid highlands of central Mexico, but to understand these agricultural origins we must look at a much wider area, including much of Mesoamerica (Figure 7.10).

Mesoamerica, even more so than the centers of domestication in Southwest Asia, is a mosaic of different ecological zones, where sharply contrasting climates, land forms, flora, and fauna are encountered within very short distances, as one traverses towering mountains, deep valleys, and high arid plateaus. At the same time, the latitude of Mesoamerica is such that along the coasts there are hot, humid rainforests as well as shallow coastal waters teeming with fish and other marine resources.

Mesoamerica differs sharply from Southwest Asian centers of domestication, however, in that it has few permanent large rivers and, consequently, no great alluvial plains; and variations in altitude and land form are even more pronounced than they are in Mesopotamia and probably were a much greater barrier to trade and communication between different parts of this area.

Little is known about Mesoamerican cultures prior to about 8000 B.C., and the few early sites we have are largely concentrations of stone tools with the bones of mammoths or other extinct animals. The overall human population density does not appear to have been high.

With the end of the Pleistocene at about 8000 B.C., there may have been a slight overall increase in temperature for much of Mesoamerica,

7.10
Mesoamerican and Peruvian areas of early domestication and agriculture.

as well as shifts in rainfall patterns, with significantly increased aridity in some highland areas.

Post-Pleistocene Mesoamerica

Using remains from dry caves in Tehuacán and Oaxaca (see Figure 7.10), Kent Flannery has reconstructed much of the way of life of the hunters and gatherers who roamed the uplands of Mesoamerica between 8000 and 2000 B.C., when initial maize and other plant domestication took place. According to Flannery (1968), shortly after 8000 B.C. the areas of Mesoamerica between 900 and 1,900 meters elevation encompassed a diversity of environments, including cool-temperature oak woodlands, cactus deserts, and semitropical thorn forests. Hunters and gatherers here made their living by moving from zone to zone in different seasons to exploit a wide range of plant and animal resources, including annual grasses like teosinte and fox-tail, avocados, wild onions, acorns and piñon nuts, and several varieties of pigweed. Of all the different plants exploited, however, three genera seem to have been especially important, regardless of altitude: (1) the maguey cactus or century plant, a large succulent that reaches three meters in height and grows year-round in most parts of Mesoamerica; (2) other succulent cacti, including "organ cactus" and prickly pear, whose small fruits are seasonal, but whose leaves are available year-round; and (3) a number of related genera of tree legumes, known locally as mesquites and guajes, which bear edible pods during the rainy season only. Complementing these plant foods were several animal species, most importantly white-tailed deer and rabbits, but also peccaries, raccoons, squirrels, skunks, and gophers.

Flannery has shown that between 8000 and 2000 B.C. the hunters and gatherers of Mesoamerica had developed an intricate pattern of relationships with these plants and animals. Maguey, for example, is hardy enough to flourish in many different climates and soils, even in the cold, arid highlands where little else will grow. But its flesh is unbearably bitter unless cooked for about twenty-four to seventy-two hours, and today maguey is still prepared as it was in prehistoric times, by digging a pit about 90 to 120 centimeters in diameter, lining it with stone, and filling it with slow-burning wood. When the stones are red hot the maguey leaves are placed in layers in the pit and covered with earth and grass. One to three days later the pit is opened and the leaves can be eaten, except for the stringy fibers, which are expectorated in the form of a quid—the remains of which are found in great numbers in dry cave sites.

The best time to eat maguey is just after the plant has sent up its *infloresence,* the spike-like growth bearing the reproductive structures. This happens in the sixth to eighth year of the plant's growth and soon afterward, in a process taking several days, natural fermentation begins in the plant, increasing its sugar content. Within a few weeks of this, the plant begins to die.

As Flannery notes, by eating maguey after the plant has infloresced, the harvesters would be removing only the dying plants which would have already have pollinated and contributed their genetic characteristics to the maguey population. Thus, in spite of substantial harvesting, the characteristics of the plant did not change much, and later agricultural practices have effected only minor increases in its productivity.

Similarly, cactus fruits ripen in the dry season and thus are available only during a short time each year, but their young leaves can be eaten any time. In order to harvest these fruits, the early Mesoamerican hunters and gatherers had to collect the fruits soon after they became ripe because of considerable competition from fruit bats, birds, and small mammals, and also because the fruit begins to rot soon after the rains begin. But no matter how intensively humans harvest these fruits they do not diminish the numbers of plants, because the human intestinal tract is incapable of digesting cactus fruit seeds. As Flannery points out, human consumption actually aided the distribution of these plants —at least until the arrival of modern plumbing.

Like the maguey and the cactus fruit, the exploitation of white-tailed deer and rabbits—the principal game between 8000 and 2000 B.C.—was usually a balanced relationship beneficial to both the humans and the animals. The legendary fecundity of rabbits would have kept them very numerous despite the heaviest predation rates. In fact, in Australia and elsewhere it has been shown that rabbits can withstand continuous mass slaughter by guns, cars, and poisons with no long-term population declines.

White-tailed deer, although not as prolific as rabbits, are also highly resistant to population declines through predation. Analysis of deer bones from early Mesoamerican sites indicates these hunters did not practice any conservation, killing young, old, and pregnant animals alike. Deer herds can stand—and even benefit from—annual predation rates of 30 to 40 percent, and therefore, rather than causing population diminishment through overhunting, prehistoric hunters and gatherers very likely made a positive contribution by thinning the herds. Thus, some of the major food sources for prehistoric Mesoamerican hunters and gatherers were linked to these people by subsistence practices that kept the overall ecological adaptation in a state of equilibrium.

Flannery sees two primary mechanisms that operated to enhance this stability. The first of these is *seasonality*. The most important division of the Mesoamerican year is between the dry winter season (October to May), and the summer (June to September), when most of the rain falls. Many of the plants and animals were available only during one season or the other, and even deer, which were present year-round, were probably most easily hunted when the winter drought reduced vegetation and increased visibility. Also, as noted, the exploitation of plants like the cactus fruits must be accomplished in a matter of days, because of the competition from animals or the rot induced by the summer rains.

One effect of this seasonality is to make it impossible for hunting and gathering groups to be large all year long, because during the dry season there was not enough food to support large concentrations of people. This seasonal pattern "effectively counteracted any trends toward population increase which might have been fostered by the intensive harvests of the rainy season macrobands" (Flannery 1968: 78). For example, archaeological data show that as late as 3000 B.C. the entire Tehuacán Valley, an area of 3,600 square kilometers, is estimated to have supported only 120 to 140 people (MacNeish 1964).

In addition to *seasonality*, Flannery sees *scheduling* as an important mechanism in maintaining the stability of the adaptation of these early Mesoamerican hunters and gatherers. Scheduling refers to the decisions these hunters and gatherers had to make about which resources to exploit during different periods of the year. So many plant and animal resources were available to them that they could not exploit them all with equal intensity, and they had to make a series of important decisions about where to invest their time and labor. Among contemporary hunting and gathering groups these decisions are often made on the basis of "scouting reports" that kin-related bands pass on to them. If a group finds a particularly thick stand of wild fruit or has great success with game in a particular area, it often gives this information to relatives in other bands as they pass each other on their rounds. But because these groups are of different sizes and are coming into areas at different times, there is a great variability in the decisions they make about the resources they will exploit. And, as Flannery notes:

> Because scheduling is an opportunistic mechanism, it promoted survival in spite of annual variation, but at the same time it supported the status quo: unspecialized utilization of a whole range of plants and animals whose availability is erratic over the long run. In this sense scheduling acted to counteract deviations which might have resulted in either (1) starvation, or (2) a more effective adaptation (1968: 76)

INITIAL DOMESTICATION IN MESOAMERICA

Despite effective mechanisms that maintained the hunting and gathering way of life for so long in Mesoamerica, sometime after 8000 B.C. these people—probably unintentionally—began to domesticate maize, beans, squash, peppers, and other plant species. Domesticated maize was the most important food through much of later Mesoamerican prehistory, and at present it is the only domesticated plant from this area whose evolutionary history we know in any detail. A few fragments of early forms of beans, squash, and peppers have been found, but not enough to reconstruct recent changes in their morphological characteristics.

Until about 1970 the most widely accepted view of maize domestication was that advanced by geneticist Paul Mangelsdorf, who argued that domesticated maize evolved from a "wild maize," now extinct, with small cobs topped by small tassels. This would have been a "pod-corn"—that is, the individual kernels would have been enclosed in chaff rather than the cuplike fruit case of domesticated varieties (Figure 7.11). Mangelsdorf (1967) explained the extinction of this wild maize as a result of overgrazing by European-introduced cattle and as a result of its having been genetically "swamped" by continual hybridization with emerging species of domesticated maize.

In the early 1960s, Richard MacNeish excavated several sites near Tehuacán, Mexico, and his findings seemed to confirm Mangelsdorf's hypothesis: the earliest corn cobs found (dating to about 5000 B.C.) were very small, and the tassels did indeed emerge from the tops of the fruits. And the discovery, shortly thereafter, of "maize" pollen in sample cores from 60,000-year-old levels of the lake in the Valley of Mexico seemed to be conclusive evidence of the validity of Mangelsdorf's hypothesis. But the early maize found by MacNeish seemed to have many morphological similarities to another wild perennial grass common in the semiarid, subtemperate regions of Mesoamerica, a grass called *teosinte* (*Zea Mexicana*), and some botanists felt somewhat uneasy about the whole reconstruction proposed by Mangelsdorf, partially because the placement of kernels on a cob such as wild and domesticated maize were supposed to have had would seem a very inefficient mechanism for seed dispersal.

In 1972 plant geneticist George Beadle reasserted his argument of some decades previous: that there had never been a "wild maize," that domesticated corn, instead, was a descendant of teosinte (Beadle 1972). Teosinte is a tall (up to two meters) annual grass found throughout the semiarid and subtropical zones of Mexico and Guatemala, where it thrives in disturbed areas and rapidly invades open areas such as abandoned cornfields. Teosinte can be found growing in fields that also include wild beans and squash, with the beans twining around the teosinte stalk. Thus, the three staffs of life for Mesoamerica, maize, beans, and squash, are a "natural" association.

Chemical analyses of teosinte and maize and studies of their genetic characteristics (Galinat 1971) have recently seemed to support Beadle's view of teosinte as the major ancestor of maize—although Man-

7.11
Three possible ancestors of domestic maize (corn): "Wild maize" (reconstructed, left), which some doubt ever existed; *teosinte* (center) which grows abundantly in Mesoamerica and may be the ancestor of maize, although some believe domestic maize was produced by hybridization of wild corn, teosinte; and *Tripsacum* (right).

gelsdorf has recently mounted a spirited counterattack (1974). Beadle's supporters claim that the 60,000-year-old pollen from the Basin of Mexico has been shown to be indistinguishable from teosinte pollen (Galinat 1971), and the "wild maize" cobs from Tehuacán can just as easily be viewed as representatives of an early stage in the transformation of teosinte to maize.

If we accept teosinte as the ancestor of domesticated maize (and some do not—e.g., R. E. Adams 1977: 66; Mangelsdorf 1974), the primary changes in the domestication process were: (1) the development of a less brittle rachis, followed by the evolution of the cob; (2) the development of a soft fruit case, so that the kernels could be shelled free of the cob; and (3) the evolution of larger cobs and more rows of kernels. A single gene—the so-called *tunicate allele*—controls to some extent the brittleness of the rachis and the toughness of the fruit case, and thus these features could easily have been produced by direct selection of mutants with these characteristics. The third change, increased cob size, was very gradual and probably differed sharply from area to area. The cobs from Tehuacán dating to about 5000 B.C. averaged a little less than 2 centimeters in length and were remarkably uniform. Cobs dated to between 3400 and 2300 B.C. averaged 4.3 centimeters, and by A.D. 700 the average size was still less than 4.4 centimeters. Between A.D. 700 and 1536, however, the maize cobs from Tehuacán reached an average of about 13 centimeters in length.

Other Mesoamerican Cultivars

While maize is an excellent food source, it is deficient in a number of important proteins and vitamins, and the evolution of agricultural economies in Mesoamerica derived considerable impetus from the domestication of other species, the most important of which were beans and squash. Three species of beans (common beans, runner beans, and tepary beans) have wild ancestors in Mesoamerica, and changes in their morphological characteristics began to appear at about the same time as those of maize. Wild bean remains recovered in caves in Tamaulipas date to 7000 to 5500 B.C., and in Oaxaca from 8700 to 6700 B.C., but the earliest known domesticated beans don't make their appearance in these areas until between 4000 and 3000 B.C.

The domestication of beans seems to have involved: (1) increased seed permeability, so that the beans need not be soaked so long in water before being processed; (2) a change from a corkscrew-shaped, brittle pod that shatters easily to straight, limp, nonshattering pods; and (3) in some cases, a shift from perennial to annual growth patterns (Flannery 1973: 300). The primary importance of beans is that they are rich in lysine, which maize is deficient in; thus the two are nutritionally complementary.

The domestication of squash and pumpkins, members of the genus *Cucurbita,* seems to have been aimed at improving the seeds (rather than the flesh), since wild *Cucurbita* have flesh so bitter or thin that they have little food value. The earliest cucurbit seeds are found in cave deposits in Oaxaca and Tamaulipas dating to 8000 to 7000 B.C., but since only seeds and a few stems are preserved, we know relatively little about recent morphological changes in this genus. Even less is known about the various peppers and other plants domesticated in Mesoamerica during this period.

MECHANISMS OF EARLY MAIZE DOMESTICATION

Given the botanical problems of maize domestication and the seasonality and scheduling mechanisms that kept Mesoamerican highland hunters and gatherers in stable, low-density, foraging adaptations, what factors could have produced not only domesticated maize and other plants, but also sedentary agricultural communities?

There are several schools of thought on this question, none of which, unfortunately, can be put to any rigorous test with present archaeological data. The traditional view is that those same hunters and gatherers who were domesticating maize and other plants in the highlands at this time somehow gradually reached a point where it was possible and preferable to become village agriculturalists. Clearing the mesquite and other vegetation on the bottom lands where maize would be the most productive would require considerable effort, as would seeding, protecting the crop from predators, harvesting, and processing it. Geographer Anne Kirkby has calculated that maize did not achieve a cob size and overall productivity sufficient to make it worth this effort until sometime between 2000 and 1500 B.C.—precisely the time when the first sedentary occupations occurred (Kirkby 1973).

But while mobile hunters and gatherers may have domesticated these plants, the actual transition to sedentary communities based on agriculture could well have been made by groups on the coasts who had achieved a sedentary way of life based on intensive exploitation of fish, mussels, and other marine and terrestrial resources (Zevallos et al. 1977). Coastal peoples were probably in the best position to take advantage of the increasingly productive plants at about 1600 B.C., because the rich littoral resources supported a sedentary community structure that was already "preadapted" in social organization, settlement systems, and technology to the agricultural village way of life.

Resolution of this problem would be assisted if we had a large sample of excavated sites from all over Mesoamerica between 4000 B.C. and 1500 B.C. so that we could look for a pattern of change, perhaps consisting of an overall increase in settlement size, indications of population nucleation, or botanical and faunal evidence that people were spending more of each year in the same general area as they became increasingly reliant on domesticated plants. So far, however, all we have are sites in the Tehuacán Valley, the Valley of Mexico, the Valley of Oaxaca, Guerrero, and a few other places.

The Tehuacán Evidence

The Tehuacán Valley, in the central Mexican highlands, is a high, dry basin where the desertic vegetation, soils, and climate are ideal for the preservation of organic remains. In fact, Tehuacán may contain remains of early domesticated plants not because they were first domesticated here, but because this is one of the few areas where they would preserve well.

Most of the Tehuacán excavations (MacNeish 1964) were in thick rock shelter deposits, but some were in open air sites (Figure 7.12). In the *Ajuereado phase* (10,000 to 7200 B.C.) the inhabitants of Tehuacán were generalized hunters and foragers, subsisting on rabbits, gophers, turtles, rats, and other small game, and an occasional deer. There are few obvious plant-preparation implements, but no doubt plants were an important part of the diet. Ajuereado sites are small, suggesting seasonal movements of microbands.

During the *El Riego phase* (7200 to 5200 B.C.), there were significant shifts in the subsistence and settlement practices in the Tehuacán Valley. Tools and bones reveal that hunting was still an important activity, but ground-stone and pecked-stone implements, particularly mortars and pestles, appeared for the first time, and many of the artifacts showed wear patterns consistent with grinding and milling—probably of plant foods. In addition, some of the earliest evidences of weaving and woodworking in Mesoamerica come from these levels, mainly in the form of knotted nets, twined blankets, coiled baskets, dart shafts, and animal traps. The types of stone implements found here and the fragments of wild squash, chiles, avocados, and other plant remains suggest that a shift may have been underway to a more intensive utilization of plant foods. At what point "domestication" could be said to have begun is somewhat arbitrary, but compared to the peoples of the Ajuereado phase, MacNeish believes, the El Riego inhabitants may have been exerting more of the kinds of selective pressures important in eventual domestication.

Despite MacNeish's belief that population increased significantly in the Tehuacán Valley during the El Riego phase, the vagaries of preservation and sampling make this difficult to establish with any certainty.

7.12
Excavations at Coxcatlán Cave, Tehuacán.

Excavations at Tehuacán occupations dating to the *Coxcatlán phase*
(5200 to 3400 B.C.) reveal that people at this time still hunted and
trapped small mammals but had turned increasingly to an intensive
exploitation of plants. Remains of small corn cobs, chiles, avocados,
gourds, beans, amaranths, and other plants were recovered, and some of
these were clearly in the process of being domesticated. If Beadle's reconstruction of maize domestication is accurate, these first corn cobs indicate that maize domestication was already well advanced by 5000 B.C.
Unfortunately, no teosinte seeds have been recovered from Tehuacán—
the plant does not now occur there naturally—so we cannot use the
Tehuacán data to resolve disputes about the ancestors of maize. The

7.13
The cultural sequence in the Tehuacán Valley, showing hypothesized changes in
settlement patterns, population, and farming technology. Revisions of this chart
are expected on the basis of current research in Tehuacán.

implements of Coxcatlán phase included grinding stones—*metates* and *manos*—as well as projectile points, blades, scrapers, and choppers.

MacNeish has interpreted the remains from the *Abejas phase* (3400 to 2300 B.C.) occupations of Tehuacán as evidence for the beginnings of sedentary village-based agricultural life in Mesoamerica. His conclusion is based on two structures he regards as "pit houses," found at two different sites dating to this phase. As reconstructed by MacNeish, one pit house was an oval shelter, 3.9 by 5.3 meters in extent, with its base dug about 60 centimeters into sterile clay (Flannery 1971: 37). The floor of the shelter would have had an area of only about 6 square meters. The second pit house, located some 4.5 kilometers west of the

7.14
The evolution of maize cob size at Tehuacán. Smallest cob (left) dates to about 5000 B.C. Dates, successively (left to right), are 4000 B.C., 3000 B.C., 1000 B.C., and (far right) an entirely modern variety dating to about B.C./A.D.

first, was defined on the basis of slabs of stones that projected above the surface of the site and seemed to form rough ovals. Because the area was in cultivation MacNeish could not excavate the structure.

But as Flannery (1973) notes, there is little evidence that either of these structures was actually a year-round residence. There is no similarity between these structures and the permanent villages that appear all over Mexico about 1,500 years later, in layout or method of construction. The pit houses have floor space for only about one person at a time, and thus would seem to resemble a temporary shelter more than a residence. In addition, neither the plant remains nor any other evidence from the site demonstrate year-round habitation.

Even if we discard the notion that these people had adopted sedentary life, it is noteworthy that their diet included significant quantities of domesticated plants, including maize, beans, pumpkins, cotton seeds, and perhaps dogs. Analysis of human feces, however, reveals that more than 70 percent of the diet during this period still came from wild plants and animals.

MacNeish feels settlement patterns changed dramatically during the Abejas phase. In addition to the pit houses, at least eight of the sites from this period were what he calls *macroband* camps on river terraces. "Macrobands" refer here to groups of microbands that came together seasonally to exploit resources or to engage in social activities. He intimates that these macrobands probably occupied the pit houses (assuming that there are other pit houses here), perhaps engaging in minor cultivation along the river banks.

The artifacts in this level, however, remain essentially the same as in previous levels, and in view of the questions about the significance of the pit houses, it may be that the Abejas phase occupants of this area were not very different from the hunters and gatherers who preceded them.

The *Purron phase* (2300 to 1500 B.C.) is poorly represented in the Tehuacán sequence: only a few floors have been excavated. The plant and animal remains and the technology seem to have been basically the same as in the previous period, with the addition of pottery. Some of the earliest known pottery in Mesoamerica comes from these levels, and some have interpreted its appearance as a sign that village agriculture had begun, but this is not a legitimate inference. Pottery dating to 2200 B.C. and earlier has been found not only at Tehuacán but also at Puerto Marquez, near Acapulco (Brush 1965), in Ecuador and Colombia, and several other areas, and in at least some of these places pottery precedes the appearance of village agriculture by several centuries. Pottery may reflect an increased emphasis on plant foods, but it is not an indispensable part of either domestication or agriculture. Nor is it likely that pottery was introduced by Japanese fishermen who drifted off course, landed in Ecuador, and showed the natives how to make ceramics, as has been suggested (Meggers 1975). The multiple independent origins of New World ceramics indicate they were a response to changing subsistence adaptations, not the product of some prehistoric genius or random trans-Pacific contact.

There are archaeological remains in Tehuacán from the period between 1500 B.C. and the present, but our interests in this chapter are the origins of domestication, agriculture, and sedentary life, and by 1500 B.C. all of these had appeared in Tehaucán.

Tamaulipas

MacNeish has also excavated some important sites in the southwestern part of Tamaulipas (see Figure 7.10), a setting very much like Tehuacán in terms of aridity and desert-adapted vegetation.

The earliest occupation (7200 to 5200 B.C.) here is very similar to that of the El Riego phase in Tehuacán, the most common artifacts being stone projectile points and other tools and a great variety of woven materials, such as mats, baskets, and nets. Fibers from the agave and yucca plants were used for these woven goods, and considerable diversity in design and technique was achieved. Wooden artifacts are also numerous, including darts, atlatls, traps, snares, and tongs.

Food remains found included agave, prickly pear, runner beans, domesticated gourds and peppers, and possibly domesticated pumpkins. Maize does not appear in this area until after about 3000 B.C.

The Evidence from Southern Mexico

Excavations in caves and rock shelters near Mitla in the state of Oaxaca indicates that life here during the El Riego (7200 to 5200 B.C.) and Coxcatlán (5200 to 3400 B.C.) phases was similar to that in Tehuacán. In the oldest levels deer and rabbit bones are associated with projectile points and the other stone implements common to most of Mexico at this time. The Guila Naquitz Cave near Mitla, occupied from about 7840 to 6910 B.C., contains the remains of acorns, maguey, prickly pear, organ cactus fruits, and, in the later levels, some squash seeds and small black beans. Another cave nearby, Cueva Blanca, which was occupied during the Coxcatlán phase, contained similar food remains. Domestication of squash and beans, at least, seems to have been underway by about 7000 B.C. in this area.

Elsewhere, Santa Marta Rock Shelter in Chiapas contains a number of flint-tool concentrations dating to between 7000 and 5360 B.C. but no evidence of domesticated maize or other plants. In fact, until at least 2000 B.C. most Mesoamerican peoples apparently subsisted mainly on undomesticated plants and animals.

Early Sedentary Coastal Communities

As noted, some scholars think that maize, beans, squash, and perhaps other plants were domesticated over a wide area of highland, and perhaps lowland, Mesoamerica, but that the stimulus for the adoption of the agricultural and village way of life came from coastal areas. There, rich resources in the littoral/terrestial interface may have provided sufficient food for nonagricultural but sedentary communities (Flannery and Coe 1968). In time, these sedentary communities could have incorporated the new domesticated plants into their "preadapted" economies and social organizations, forming the first agricultural communities. From that point on, the superior productivity of village-based agriculture would have ensured its rapid spread over all the areas where these crops could be grown successfully. Presently, there are not sufficient data to evaluate this reconstruction rigorously, but recent evidence indicates that it may be correct. Large mounds of shellfish remains and cracked rock and stone tools have been found on both the Gulf and Pacific coasts of Mesoamerica, but few have been excavated or firmly dated. Radiocarbon dates as early as 2900 B.C. have come from shell middens at Sanja and Puerto Marquez, along the coast of Guerrero, but the humid climate probably has destroyed much evidence of earlier occupations. Other coastal communities dating to between 7000 and 5300 B.C. and based on shellfish collecting and other foraging activities have been found at Islona de Chantuto, on the Pacific Coast, and

El Viejon, in central Veracruz, and elsewhere, but none have been extensively excavated and little is known of their subsistence or settlement practices.

Some interesting evidence has recently come from Ecuador, however, where several sites, both along the coast and further inland, may be the remains of sedentary communities where maize and other crops were grown by 3000 B.C. or even earlier. These settlements were part of the *Valdivia* and *Early Cerro Narrio* cultures, both of which have been securely radiocarbon-dated to between 4000 B.C. and 2000 B.C. Many sites appear to have been located in order to exploit both coastal and floodplain environments, but some are in the highlands. At sites in lower elevations large middens often contain shellfish remains, fish bones, and other refuse, and at several sites near the coast investigators have found what they believe to be the impressions of corn kernels in the surfaces of ceramics. Other ceramics appear to have been decorated with applied clay effigies of maize cobs (Figure 7.15). Significantly, these kernel and cob decorations appear on ceramics quite securely dated to about 2900 B.C., and the type of maize apparently reflected is an eight-rowed, large-kernel variety that, if dated correctly, would have been far more "advanced" than the maize of a 1,000 years later at Tehuacán. Roasted snail shells, which may have been used as lime to prepare corn, were also found at these sites, as were many large storage pits and tools that may have been used to grind corn. The humid conditions make it

7.15
Representations and impressions of maize in pottery from Valdivia, Ecuador.

difficult to recover botanical remains, but at least one corn cob has been
tentatively identified.

In view of these various lines of evidence, the investigators of these
occupations suggested that

> maize was first brought to a high level of productivity in some place in
> the moist tropics of northern South America. But our data shed no light
> on the zone in which maize was first domesticated. We believe the pre-
> cocious occurrences of efficient maize cultivation in the coast and high-
> lands of Ecuador had marked effects on population growth rates and the
> development of more complex societies. We further suspect that the de-
> mographic imbalances triggered by the efficient level of agriculture in
> early Ecuador impinged on both Mesoamerica and Peru. (Zevallos et al.
> 1977: 389)

CONCLUSIONS: MESOAMERICAN AGRICULTURE

The domestication of maize, beans, squash, and other plants seems to
be linked to the climate changes and increasing population densities
during the last 10,000 years. Despite the scheduling and seasonality
mechanisms that perpetuated early hunting and gathering adaptations
in Mesoamerica, human population densities were probably slowly
growing and this, coupled with an increasingly arid climate, may have
changed the pattern and intensity of teosinte, wild bean, and squash
exploitation sufficiently to initiate domestication. Although there is no
evidence that hunters and gatherers were at the mercy of starvation because of overpopulation, a very subtle change in exploitation patterns
may have been sufficient to begin the domestication process, particularly
with a genetically plastic plant like teosinte. At what point people intentionally began to select for certain characteristics in maize is impossible to determine, but it may have been quite early. Domestication
probably proceeded at different rates and in different directions in various areas of Mesoamerica, Central America, and South America, but if
the Valdivian material has been correctly interpreted, the primary center of maize domestication may have been the tropical lowlands and
highlands of Central and South America. On the other hand, teosinte
may have been domesticated to a certain extent in more arid northern
areas, and then incorporated into the productive lowland and coastal
wetlands.

The rapid and uniform spread of the village farming way of life over both highland and lowland Mesoamerica after about 1600 B.C. perhaps resulted from increasing population densities in the lowlands and subsequent emigration into the highlands, but in no area of either Mesoamerica or northern South America has archaeological evidence of rapidly expanding population densities been found (Flannery 1973: 296). Thus, the applicability of the Edge-Zone hypothesis of agricultural origins remains unclear. Once both lowland and highland maize farming communities appeared, the developmental advantage may have swung to the more arid highlands, where maize and other crops would have less competition than in the heavily vegetated coastal and lowland areas.

Whatever their origins, by about 1500 B.C. sedentary agricultural communities began appearing all over Mesoamerica, from the Valley of Mexico to the Guatemalan lowlands. Most of the communities were composed of ten to fifteen small clay and reed houses which show little evidence of activity specialization. Each community apparently made its own pottery, stone tools, and implements of wood and bone and generally replicated the economic activities of every other village. Hunting remained a major food source for most early villagers, and in the coastal and lake environments collecting shellfish and fishing were important activities. The Ocos complex, for example, centered in the Isthmus of Tehuantepec and coastal Veracruz-Tabasco, reflects an early adaptation to the rich interface between terrestial, marine, and aquatic resources, the productivity of which was reflected in relatively high population densities. The Ocos people are particularly noted for their fine early ceramics, and the wide distribution of specific styles of pottery manufacture and decoration indicate some social cohesion and contact immediately after the transition to sedentary, agricultural life had been made.

We shall consider the later development of these early Mesoamerican communities in chapter 14.

DOMESTICATION IN THE ANDES

A primary problem in the analysis of New World domestication, agriculture, and early sedentary communities is the relationship between developments in Mesoamerica and those in Peru, Bolivia, and other

TABLE 7.3 The Archaeological Evidence for the Domestication of Some of Mesoamerica's Important Plants*

Name of plant	Oldest archaeological occurrences	Comments	Subsequent archaeological occurrences
Setaria (foxtail grass)	0.5 oz. in level XXIII (7000 B.C.?), Coxcatlán Cave, Tehuacán	Smith believed *Setaria* domestic at Tehuacán by ca. 6000 B.C.; Callen saw size increase by 3500 B.C. in Tamaulipas	About 45 oz. from later levels (7000–5000 B.C.) in Tehuacán caves
Zea mexicana (teosinte)	Pollen grains in levels B-C (7400–6700 B.C.), Guilá Naquitz Cave, Oaxaca	It is still disputed whether teosinte pollen can be distinguished from that of maize	Seeds from 5000 B.C. level at Tlapacoya, Valley of Mexico
Zea mays (corn)	18 cobs in Level XIII (5050 B.C.), Coxcatlán Cave, Tehuacán, Mexico	Good sample. Mangelsdorf says "wild"; Beadle says "domestic."	74 more cobs, later levels (5000–3000 B.C.) in Tehuacán caves
Cucurbita pepo (pumpkin)	1 "pepo-like" seed in level D, (+8000 B.C.), Guilá Naquitz Cave, Oaxaca, Mexico; bigger sample at 7000 B.C. in Ocampo, Tamaulipas	All specimens are seeds (and should be treated with caution) prior to the first peduncle frags. Even so, most specimens look "wild" prior to 5000 B.C.	14 seeds and peduncles in levels B-C (7400–6700 B.C.), Guilá Naquitz; 1 "wild" specimen from level XIV (5200 B.C.?) Coxcatlán Cave
Cucurbita mixta (squash)	3 specimens (2 dubious) in levels XIV–XIII (5000 B.C.), Coxcatlán Cave	All specimens prior to 3000 B.C. should be treated with caution	5 specimens including peduncle from level VIII (3010 B.C.), Coxcatlán Cave
Wild runner beans	100+ in 8700–6700 B.C. levels, Guilá Naquitz; 14 between 7000 and 5500 in Ocampo, Tamaulipas	These wild varieties were gradually replaced by cultivars through time	
Phaseolus vulgaris (common bean)	6 pod valves dating to between 4000 and 2300 B.C., Ocampo, Tamaulipas	Small sample but very similar dates from Tehuacán and Tamaulipas	Single pods from levels XI (4000 B.C.?) and VIII (3010 B.C.), Coxcatlán Cave

Persea americana (avocado)	1 seed in level XXIV (7200 B.C.?), Coxcatlán Cave, Tehuacán, is wild type	Larger seeds show avocado to be domestic by 1500 B.C., but when first cultivated is not known	31 seeds in later levels (7000–5000 B.C.) in Tehuacán Caves are also wild type
Capsicum annuum (chile)	1 pod from level XIX (6500 B.C.?), Coxcatlán Cave, probably wild	Smith feels chiles domestic by level XI (4121 B.C.) at Coxcatlán Cave on basis of pendulous fruit	7 more specimens from later levels (6000–5000 B.C.) at Coxcatlán Cave, probably wild
Gossypium hirsutum (cotton)	2 bolls from level XVI (5625 B.C.), Coxcatlán Cave, Tehuacán	Both found in an area of disturbed stratigraphy; Stephens is skeptical	2 bolls from level D (3300 B.C.) San Marcos Cave, Tehuacán; earliest cotton yarn is a "questionable" frag. from level IX (3183 B.C.) at Coxcatlán Cave

SOURCE Kent V. Flannery. 1973. "The Origins of Agriculture," *Annual Review of Anthropology*. 2: 271–310.

* Note comments on the nature and reliability of the evidence.

parts of northwestern South America (see Figure 7.10). Domestication in this area involved three very different *biomes* (ecological environments), each with its own archaeological problems. The Amazon jungles and the tropical slopes of the eastern Andes contain the wild ancestors of several South American domesticates, including manioc, peanuts, guavas, cocoa, and lima beans, but little is known about their domestication because the humid environment does not preserve botanical remains well. The second biome, the Andes Mountains, contributed the wild ancestors of potatoes, the starch-yielding herb quinoa (*Chenopodium quinoa*), oca (*Oxalis tuberosa*), and olluco (*Ullucus tuberosus*), but the scarcity of caves and high humidity make it difficult to recover botanical remains here also. The third biome, the coastal deserts of Peru, offers excellent preservation of archaeological materials, but does not appear to have been the natural habitat of any important South American domesticates (Flannery 1973: 302–03).

The earliest domesticated maize reported from Peru, dating to about 3000 to 2500 B.C., comes from Rosamachay Cave in the Ayacucho region of the south central highlands, and resembles in some characteristics a Mexican tesosinte-influenced race called Nal Tal. Since this was some 2,500 years after maize was present at Tehuacán, and since no teosinte has ever been found in South America, some conclude that domestic maize was introduced to South America from Mesoamerica (Flannery 1973: 302). The possibility that domesticated maize was being cultivated in Ecuador by shortly after 3000 B.C. may alter this hypothesis somewhat, particularly if additional research shows that this maize was, as is now claimed, a much more developed form than that at Tehuacán (Zevallos et al. 1977). Even if maize were being cultivated in the Peruvian highlands prior to 2000 B.C., there is no evidence that it was important in coastal areas until some centuries later. Coastal peoples prior to about 1800 B.C. were able to establish large sedentary communities on the basis of a mixed fishing, foraging, and agricultural strategy; maize became sufficiently productive to replace shellfish and other littoral resources only comparatively late.

Another important South American domesticate is the common bean (*Phaseolus vulgaris*), the oldest examples of which in Peru come from Guitarrero Cave in the north highlands and are radiocarbon-dated to about 5600 B.C.—at least 1,500 years earlier than the first Mesoamerican domesticates of the same species. Thus, it is likely that beans were domesticated at several different places in the New World.

The domestication histories of cotton, chili peppers, squash, potatoes, and other crops in South America are poorly known. Much of the available evidence is summarized in Table 7.3. On the basis of this evidence, Flannery concludes that domestication and agriculture in Peru began too early to have been stimulated initially by a diffusion from Mesoamerica and that from the very beginning the Amazonian slopes must have played an important role, despite our lack of archaeological evidence from that region (1973: 303).

The role of animal domestication in early Peru is unclear, but llamas and guinea pigs were certainly domesticated in central Peru by 3500 B.C. As in Mexico, however, hunting continued to play an important role in many areas until quite late (Table 7.4).

The relationship of plants and animals, agriculture, and sedentary communities in northwestern South America in general suggests that domestication and sedentary communities preceded specialized agricultural economies in some areas by many centuries, particularly on the coast, where small sedentary communities of fishers, foragers, and part-time bean and squash cultivators were established before maize cultivation was of any importance. Flannery questions whether this could be another "Edge-Zone" situation, where village life began with a wild food base, populations rose, and "agriculture began in response to disturbances of density equilibrium around the margins of an expanding coastal population" (1973: 303), but surveys along the Peruvian coast show that until at least 3000 B.C. there were only sparse and largely seasonal occupations—long after people in the Andes were cultivating beans and other plants.

Eventually, domesticated plants and animals and agriculture became the bases for human settlement in most of the prehistoric New World, as maize, beans, squash, and other plants were adapted to environments as far north as Canada and as far south as the tip of South America. The cultural developments made possible by these subsistence changes in Mexico, Peru, and North America are considered in chapters 14, 15, and 16.

Domestication, Agriculture, and Sedentary Communities: Conclusions

In summarizing the problem of agricultural origins, Kent Flannery noted that all of the seed crops, such as maize, wheat, barley, and rice,

TABLE 7.4 The Archaeological Evidence for the Domestication of Some of Peru's Important Plants*

Name of plant	Oldest archaeological occurrences	Comments	Subsequent archaeological occurrences
Lagenaria (bottle gourd)	Rind frags (11,000 B.C.), Pikimachay Cave, Ayacucho, Peru	Probably not domestic (Pickersgill); could even be intrusive, as 11,000–6000 B.C. levels have no preserved plants	5500–4300 B.C. Ayacucho; 3000 B.C. (?) Chilca, Peruvian coast; used as floats, Huaca Prieta (2500 B.C.)
Phaseolus vulgaris (common bean)	5600 B.C. at Guitarrero Cave, C. de Huaylas, Peru	Not yet known whether locally domestic or introduced from Mexico (Kaplan)	4700 B.C., northern Chile; 2800 B.C., Ayacucho, Peru
Phaseolus lunatus (lima bean)	5600 B.C. at Guitarrero Cave, C. de Huaylas, Peru	Native to the Amazon side of the Andes	2500 B.C., Huaca Prieta, Peruvian Coast
Zea mays (corn)	Level D (3100–2500 B.C.) Rosamachay Cave, Ayacucho, Peru	A teosinte-derived, Nal-Tal-like race of Mexican origin	Huarmay, Peruvian Coast 1950 B.C.
Cucurbita moschata	Pampa site (>3100 B.C.?); Ayacucho (2800–1700 B.C.)	Possibly introduced from Mexico?	
Gossypium (cotton)	3100 B.C.? Chilca Site, Perusian Coast	Exact level of earliest cotton is not yet clear	2500 B.C., Huaca Prieta, Peruvian Coast
Capsicum (chile)	2500 B.C. on Peruvian Coast (Huaca Prieta, Punta Grande, Yacht Club)		
Chenopodium quinoa (quinoa)	2 seeds (5500–4300 B.C.), Pikimachay Cave, Ayacucho, Peru	Pickersgill recommends caution, as these are the only quinoa seeds from the whole sequence	
Manihot (manioc)	1800–1500 B.C. on Peruvian Coast	Native to the Amazon side of the Andes	

Arachis hypogaea (peanut)	1800–1500 B.C. on Peruvian Coast		
Solanum tuberosum (potato)	400 B.C., Chiripa, Bolivia?	Andes	A.D. 1000, coastal Peru; as both unprocessed and freeze-dried (*chuño*) potatoes
		Towle is not certain whether these tubers are potatoes or one of the other highland root crops	

SOURCE Kent V. Flannery. 1973. "The Origins of Agriculture," *Annual Review of Anthropology.* 2: 271–310.

* Note comments on the nature and reliability of the evidence.

appear to have derived from wild ancestors that were *third-choice foods:* plants that were usually more difficult to gather and process than other wild plants and thus were probably first eaten in quantity because the people had to, not because they wanted to (1973: 307). On the other hand, all of these wild plant species have characteristics that help explain why these particular species were domesticated: most are annuals, yield a high return, tolerate a wide variety of habitats, store easily, and are genetically plastic. The disadvantages of these foods are mainly that they require more work to gather and process than other food sources and they also tend to produce unstable ecosystems because they replace complex, varied ecosystems with simplified ecosystems dominated by just a few species.

We have seen that neither the Edge-Zone hypothesis (Binford) nor any of the other hypotheses about agricultural origins have been substantiated in all independent centers of agricultural origins. The Edge-Zone hypothesis, while offering some stimulating ideas and concepts, simply does not seem to "work" in Peru, Southwest Asia, and perhaps elsewhere. Much additional research will be required, however, before we can make any final judgments on the accuracy of this concept and similar demographic models.

Some scholars have suggested that the very different sequences in which domestication, agriculture, and sedentary communities appeared in Mesoamerica and Southwest Asia resulted from the gross differences between these areas in the amount of available animal protein. Marvin Harris (1977), for example, notes that in both Mesoamerica and Southwest Asia the end of the Pleistocene was accompanied by a great reduction in the large herd animals that had previously been the basis for subsistence in both areas, but that in Southwest Asia there were wild sheep, goats, cattle, and pigs that could be domesticated and combined with cereals to replace and extend the Pleistocene food base. In Mesoamerica, in contrast, according to Harris, there were few or no large, domesticable animal species, and sedentary life based on agriculture was delayed until a complex cropping strategy and coordinated interregional exchange achieved sufficient economic productivity to support village life.

We might ask why New World peoples never domesticated the native species of wild sheep and goats, as was accomplished in Southwest Asia, but this may have to do with behavioral characteristics of the New World animals. The reduced availability of animal protein in Mesoamerica may in fact explain to a great extent why sedentary agricultural communities were established in Mesoamerica so long after initial domestication, but considerable additional research will be required to test this hypothesis.

Generally, we seem to be left with two major variables as potentially important factors in the origins of agriculture: climate change and increasing population densities. Despite the limitations on these factors as explanatory devices, it remains true that the environmental changes and climatic changes of the late Pleistocene and early post-Pleistocene periods are not well documented for all areas of independent agricultural origins, and thus we cannot be certain of their effects (H. E. Wright 1976). Still, on a general scale it also seems true that the only unique aspect of the period when domestication and agriculture appeared is that there were more people and higher population densities than in previous interglacials (Cohen 1977).

Generally, we have no evidence that people of the immediate post-Pleistocene era experienced recurrent periods of starvation, or that they "invented" domesticates and agriculture as a way of addressing their immediate food supply problems. Instead, the situation may well have been one in which, as population densities slowly rose, people gravitated into various niches where exploitation of wild wheat and barley, teosinte, and other third-choice plants was marginally increased. Even if they were not forced into these areas by expanding population densities and were not under the dire threat of imminent starvation so that they radically increased their consumption of these third-choice foods, the plasticity of some of these species was such that minimal changes in selective pressures might have quickly and directly rewarded this increased exploitation.

In this sort of reconstruction it does not seem likely that the timing of wheat and barley domestication, for example, was the result mainly of "lucky" mutations, or that the distribution of the ancestors of these plants was vastly different before the last glacial period. All over the post-Pleistocene world so many diverse animal and plant species were domesticated that explaining them in terms of "lucky" mutations would require coincidences of a highly unlikely nature. Nor was this a technological revolution: the first intensive cereal collectors required only minimal tools—implements certainly no more complex or imaginative than the fish traps, bows, and arrows of the late Pleistocene.

Finally, while agriculture on any significant scale requires sedentary communities, sedentary communities are not dependent on agriculture. The Natufian settlements in favored areas of the Levant, as well as coastal communities in Mesoamerica and Peru, indicate that the over-all productivity of an environment rather than the specific type of food production determines when and where sedentary communities will appear. Harpending and Davis (1976) have recently presented mathematical models describing how sedentary communities are cost-efficient in environments where the food resources are distributed evenly and are of many different species—such as the littorals of Mesoamerica and Peru. Such models do not explain why sedentary communities did not appear in these areas (as far as we know) in the Pleistocene or previous interglacials (in the case of the Old World), but they do outline some of the conditions of productivity for sedentary life.

Bibliography

Adams, Richard E. W. 1977. *Prehistoric Mesoamerica*. Boston: Little, Brown.

Adams, Robert McC. 1964. "The Origins of Agriculture." In *Horizons of Anthropology,* ed. Sol Tax. Chicago: Aldine.

Ammerman, A. J. and L. L. Cavalli-Sforza. 1972. "A Population Model for the Diffusion of Early Farming in Europe." In *The Explanation of Culture Change: Models in Prehistory,* ed. Colin Renfrew. London: Duckworth.

Athens, J. Stephen. 1977. "Theory Building and the Study of Evolutionary Process in Complex Societies." In *For Theory Building in Archaeology,* ed. L. R. Binford. New York: Academic Press.

Beadle, G. W. 1972. "The Mystery of Maize." *Field Museum of Natural History Bulletin.* 43(10): 2–11.

Belyaev, D. K. 1969. "Domestication of Animals." *Science Journal.* 5: 47–52.

Binford, Lewis R. 1968. "Post-Pleistocene Adaptations." In *New Perspectives in Archaeology,* eds. S. R. Binford and L. R. Binford. Chicago: Aldine.

———. 1972. *An Archaeological Perspective.* New York: Seminar Press.

Birdsell, J. B. 1968. "Some Predictions for the Pleistocene Based on Equilibrium Systems Among Recent Hunters-Gatherers." In *Man the Hunter,* eds. R. B. Lee and I. DeVore. Chicago: Aldine.

Bökönyi, S. 1969. "Archaeological Problems and Methods of Recognizing Animal Domestication." In *The Domestication and Exploitation of Plants and Animals,* eds. P. J. Ucko and G. W. Dimbleby. Chicago: Aldine.

Boserup, E. 1965. *The Conditions of Agricultural Growth.* Chicago: Aldine.

Braidwood, Robert J. 1960. "The Agricultural Revolution." *Scientific American.* 203: 130–41.

————. 1973. "The Early Village in Southwestern Asia." *Journal of Near Eastern Studies.* 32: 34–39.

Braidwood, Robert J. et al. 1960. *Prehistoric Investigations in Iraqi Kurdistan.* Chicago: University of Chicago Press.

Braidwood, Robert J., Halet Cambel, and Patty Jo Watson. 1969. "Prehistoric Investigations in Southeastern Turkey." *Science.* 164: 1275–76.

Brush, C. 1965. "Pox Pottery: Earliest Identified Mexican Ceramic." *Science.* 149: 194–95.

Butzer, Karl W. 1971. "The Significance of Agricultural Dispersal into Europe and Northern Africa." In *Prehistoric Agriculture,* ed. S. Struever. Garden City, N.Y.: Natural History Press.

Byers, D. S., gen. ed. 1967. *The Prehistory of the Tehuacán Valley: Environment and Subsistence,* vol. 1. Austin: University of Texas Press.

Carneiro, R. 1970. "A Theory of the Origin of the State." *Science.* 169: 733–38.

Carneiro, R. and D. Hilse. 1966. "On Determining the Probable Rate of Population Growth During the Neolithic." *American Anthropologist.* 68: 177–81.

Caton-Thompson, G. and E. W. Gardner. 1934. *The Desert Fayum.* London: Royal Anthropological Institute.

Cauvin, J. 1972. "Nouvelles fouilles à Tell Mureybet (Syria): 1971–1972. Rapport preliminaire." *Annales Archeologiques de Syrie.* 22: 105–15.

Chang, K. C. 1976. *Early Chinese Civilization: Anthropological Perspectives.* Cambridge, Mass.: Harvard University Press.

Childe, V. Gordon. 1952. *New Light on the Most Ancient East.* 4th ed. London: Routledge and Kegan Paul.

Clark, J. G. D. 1952. *Prehistoric Europe: The Economic Basis.* London: Methuen.

Coe, M. D. 1960. "Archaeological Linkages with North and South America at La Victoria, Guatemala." *American Anthropologist.* 62: 363–93.

Cohen, N. M. 1977. *The Food Crisis in Prehistory.* New Haven and London: Yale University Press.

Dunnell, Robert C. 1977. Personal communication with author.

Ekholm, G. F. 1964. "Transpacific Contacts." In *Prehistoric Man in the New World,* eds. Jesse D. Jennings and E. Norbeck. Chicago: University of Chicago Press.

Flannery, Kent V. 1965. "The Ecology of Early Food Production in Mesopotamia." *Science.* 147: 1247–56.

————. 1968. "Archeological Systems Theory and Early Mesoamerica." In *Anthropological Archeology in the Americas,* ed. Betty J. Meggers. The Anthropological Society of Washington: Washington, D.C.

————. 1971. "Origins and Ecological Effects of Early Domestication in Iran and the Near East." In *Prehistoric Agriculture,* ed. Stuart Struever. Garden City, N.Y.: Natural History Press.

————. 1972. "The Origins of the Village as a Settlement Type in Mesoamerica and the Near East: A Comparative Study." In *Man, Settlement and Urbanism*, eds. P. J. Ucko, Ruth Tringham, and G. W. Dimbleby. London: Duckworth.

————. 1973. "The Origins of Agriculture." *Annual Review of Anthropology*. 2: 271–310.

Flannery, Kent V. and M. D. Coe. 1968. "Social and Economic Systems in Formative Mesoamerica." In *New Perspectives in Archeology*, eds. S. R. Binford and L. R. Binford. Chicago: Aldine.

Galinat, W. C. 1971. "The Origin of Maize." *Annual Review of Genetics*. 5: 447–78.

Garrod, Dorothy. 1957. "The Natufian Culture: The Life and Economy of a Mesolithic People in the Near East." *Proceedings of the British Academy*. 43: 211–17.

Gorman, Chester F. 1969. "Hoabinhian: A Pebble-tool Complex with Early Plant Associations in Southeast Asia." *Science*. 163: 671–73.

Harlan, Jack and Daniel Zohary. 1966. "Distribution of Wild Wheats and Barley." *Science*. 153: 1074–80.

Harner, Michael. 1970. "Population Pressure and the Social Evolution of Agriculturalists." *Southwestern Journal of Anthropology*. 26: 67–86.

Harpending, Henry and Herbert Davis. 1976. "Some Implications for Hunter-Gatherer Ecology Derived from the Spatial Structure of Resources." *World Archaeology*. 8(3): 275–86.

Harris, Marvin. 1977. *Cannibals and Kings*. New York: Random House.

Helback, Hans. 1964. "First Impressions of the Çatal Hüyük Plant Husbandry." *Anatolian Studies*. 14: 121–23.

————. 1969. "Plant Collecting, Dry-farming, and Irrigation Agriculture in Prehistoric Deh Luran." In *Prehistory and Human Ecology of the Deh Luran Plain*, eds. Frank Hole, Kent V. Flannery, and James A. Neely. Memoirs of the Museum of Anthropology, University of Michigan, no. 1.

Higgs, E. S. and M. R. Jarman. 1969. "The Origins of Agriculture: A Reconsideration." *Antiquity*. 43: 31–41.

Ho, Ping-Ti. 1969. "The Loess and the Origin of Chinese Agriculture." *American Historical Review*. 75: 1–36.

Hole, Frank. 1962. "Archeological Survey and Excavation in Iran, 1961." *Science*. 137: 524–26.

————. 1971. "Comment on 'Origins of Food Production in Southwestern Asia' by G. Wright." *Current Anthropology*. 12(4–5): 472–73.

Hole, Frank, Kent V. Flannery, and James A. Neely. 1969. *Prehistory and Human Ecology of the Deh Luran Plain*. Memoirs of the Museum of Anthropology, University of Michigan, no. 1.

Johnson, F., ed. 1972. *The Prehistory of the Tehuacán Valley*, vol. 4. Austin: University of Texas Press.

Kirkbride, Diana. 1968. "Beidha: Early Neolithic Village Life South of the Dead Sea." *Antiquity*. 42: 263–74.

Kirkby, Anne. 1973. *The Use of Land and Water Resources in the Past and Present Valley of Oaxaca, Mexico*. Memoirs of the Museum of Anthropology, University of Michigan, no. 5.

Kovar, A. 1970. "The Physical and Biological Environment of the Basin of Mexico." In *The Teotihuacan Valley Project. Final Report*, vol. 1, eds. William Sanders et al. Occasional Papers in Anthropology. Pennsylvania State University.

Lange, F. W. 1971. "Marine Resources: A Viable Subsistence Alternative for the Prehistoric Lowland Maya." *American Antiquity*. 73: 619–39.

Lee, Richard B. 1969. "!Kung Bushman Subsistence: An Input-Output Analysis." In *Environment and Cultural Behavior*, ed. A. P. Vayda. Garden City, N.Y.: Natural History Press.

MacNeish, Richard S. 1964. "Ancient Mesoamerican Civilization." *Science*. 143 (3606): 531–37.

————. 1966. "Speculations about the Beginnings of Village Agriculture in Mesoamerica." *Actas y Memorials del 35a Congreso Internacional de Americanistas*. 1: 181–85.

————, gen. ed. 1972. *The Prehistory of the Tehuacán Valley: Chronology and Irrigation*, vol. 4. Austin: University of Texas Press.

Mangelsdorf, Paul. 1974. *Corn: Its Origin, Evolution, and Improvement*. Cambridge, Mass.: Harvard University Press.

———— et al. 1967. "Prehistoric Wild and Cultivated Maize." In *Prehistory of the Tehuacán Valley*, vol. 1. Austin: University of Texas Press.

Martin, P. S. and P. J. Mehringer, Jr. 1965. "Pleistocene Pollen Analysis and Biography of the Southwest." In *The Quaternary of the United States, Biogeography: Phytogeography and Palynology, Part II*, eds. H. E. Wright, Jr. and D. G. Frey. Princeton: Princeton University Press.

Meggers, Betty. 1975. "The Transpacific Origins of Mesoamerican Civilization: A Preliminary Review of the Evidence and Its Theoretical Implications. *American Anthropologist*. 77(1): 1–27.

Mellaart, James. 1966. *The Chalcolithic Early Bronze Ages of the Near East and Anatolia*. Beirut: Khayats.

————. 1975. *The Neolithic of the Near East*. London: Thames and Hudson.

Mortensen, Peder. 1972. "Seasonal Camps and Early Villages in the Zagros." In *Man, Settlement, and Urbanism*, eds. P. Ucko, Ruth Tringham, and G. W. Dimbleby. London: Duckworth.

Munchaev, R. M. and N. Y. Merpert. 1971. *New Studies of Early Agricultural Settlements in the Sinjar Valley*. VIII Congress International des Sciences Prehistoriques et Protohistoriques. Belgrade.

Palerm, A. and E. Wolf. 1960. "Ecological Potential and Cultural Development in Mesoamerica." *Social Science Monographs*. 3: 1–38.

Perkins, Dexter, Jr. 1973. "The Beginnings of Animal Domestication in the Near East." *American Journal of Archaeology*. 77: 279–82.

────── and Patricia Daly. 1968. "A Hunter's Village in Neolithic Turkey." *Scientific American.* 210: 94–105.

Pumpelly, R. 1908. *Explorations in Turkey, the Expedition of 1904: Prehistoric Civilization of Anau,* vol. 1. Publications of the Carnegie Institution, no. 73. Washington, D.C.

Reed, Charles A., ed. 1977. *Origins of Agriculture.* The Hague: Mouton.

Reichel-Dolmatoff, G. 1965. *Columbia.* New York: Praeger. Ancient Peoples and Places Series, no. 44.

Renfrew, C., J. E. Dixon, and J. R. Cann. 1966. "Obsidian and Early Cultural Contacts in the Near East." *Proceedings of the Prehistoric Society.* 32: 30–72.

Sahlins, Marshall. 1968. "Notes on the Original Affluent Society." In *Man the Hunter,* eds. Richard B. Lee and Irven DeVore. Chicago: Aldine.

Sanders, W. T. 1965. *Cultural Ecology of the Teotihuacan Valley.* Department of Sociology and Anthropology. Pennsylvania State University.

────── and B. J. Price. 1968. *Mesoamerica: The Evolution of a Civilization.* New York: Random House.

Sauer, Carl O. 1952. *Agricultural Origins and Dispersals.* New York: American Geographical Society.

Smith, C. Earle, Jr. 1969. "From Vavilov to the Present—A Review." *Economic Botany.* 23: 2–19.

Smith, P. E. L. 1967. "New Investigations in the Late Pleistocene Archaeology of the Kam Ombo Plain (Upper Egypt)." *Quaternaria.* 9: 141–52.

──────. 1972. "Ganj Dareh Tepe." *Iran.* 10: 165–68.

Solecki, Ralph S. 1964. "Zawi Chemi Shanidar, a Post-Pleistocene Village Site in Northern Iraq." VI International Congress on the Quaternary, *Reports.* 4: 405–12.

──────. 1964. "Shanidar Cave, a Late Pleistocene Site in Northern Iraq." VI International Congress on the Quaternary, *Reports.* 4: 413–23.

Tringham, Ruth. 1971. *Hunters, Fishers, and Farmers of Eastern Europe 6000–3000 B.C.* London: Hutchinson University Library.

Turnbull, P. F. and C. A. Reed. 1974. "The Fauna from the Terminal Pleistocene of Palegawra Cave." *Fieldiana,* Field Museum of Natural History. 63(3).

Van Loon, Maurits. 1968. "The Oriental Institute Excavations at Mureybit, Syria: Preliminary Report on the 1965 Campaign." *Journal of Near Eastern Studies.* 27: 265–90.

Vavilov, N. I. 1949–50. "The Origin, Variation, Immunity, and Breeding of Cultivated Plants." *Chronica Botanica.* 13.

Vita-Finzi, C. and E. S. Higgs. 1970. "Prehistoric Economy in the Mount Carmel Area of Palestine, Site Catchment and Analysis." *Proceedings of the Prehistoric Society.* 36: 1–37.

Waterbolk, H. T. 1971. "Food Production in Prehistoric Europe." In *Prehistoric Agriculture,* ed. S. Struever. Garden City, N.Y.: Natural History Press.

Wendorf, Fred and Anthony E. Marks, eds. 1975. *Problems in Prehistory: North Africa and the Levant*. Dallas: SMU Press.

Western, C. 1971. "The Ecological Interpretation of Ancient Charcoals from Jericho." *Levant*. 3: 31–40.

Wright, Gary, 1971. "Origins of Food Production in Southwestern Asia: A Survey of Ideas." *Current Anthropology*. 12(4–5): 447–77.

Wright, H. E., Jr. 1968. "Natural Environment of Early Food Production North of Mesopotamia." *Science*. 161: 334–39.

———. 1976. "The Environmental Setting for Plant Domestication in the Near East." *Science*. 194(4263): 385–89.

Zeist, W. van. 1970. "The Paleobotany (Mureybit)." *Journal of Near Eastern Studies*. 29: 167–76.

Zeist, W. van and W. A. Casparie. 1968. "Wild Einkorn Wheat and Barley from Tell Mureybit in Northern Syria." *Acta Botanical Nederlandica*. 17: 44–53.

Zevallos M., Carlos et al. 1977. "The San Pablo Corn Kernel and Its Friends." *Science*. 196(4288): 385–89.

8

The Origins of
Complex Societies

I should like to see, and this will be the last and
most ardent of my desires, I should like to see the
last king strangled with the guts of the last priest.

J. Messelier (clause in a will, Paris, 1733)

Although many people have echoed Messelier's sentiments, the appearance of priests, kings, and other elites seems to mark one of the most profound cultural transformations of all time. Several thousand years ago in Southwest Asia, Egypt, the Indus Valley, China, Peru, and Mesoamerica, the economic and social structuring of some communities became sufficiently complicated that no person, or small group of people, could perform all the activities required to keep these communities in operation. In hunting and gathering societies virtually any family can and does perform all the activities of every other family, but in these first complex societies this was not possible. And once this economic and social differentiation and interdependence appeared, these communities inevitably seem to have evolved social and economic elites, relatively high population densities, the elaboration of arts, crafts, and architecture, and many other characteristics we associate with "civilization." Moreover, although such societies have existed for only the last five or six millennia, they have almost completely replaced the simpler cultural forms in which our ancestors had lived for a million years or more. Today, in the Arctic, the Kalahari Desert, and a few other places, hunting and gathering bands still follow the ancient ways, but soon they will be extinct and the "victory" of complex societies complete.

Scholars are not in agreement regarding the definitional characteristics of complex and simple societies: hierarchical elites, urbanism, intensity of agricultural and craft production, writing systems, dense populations, and many other criteria have been used to measure cultural complexity, and different authorities attach primary significance to different criteria. But no matter how they are defined, the origins and development of complex societies involve some of the most fascinating and significant problems of anthropology and archaeology. For, as in the case of early agricultural communities, complex societies evolved independently or almost independently in both the Old and New Worlds, and once formed, they followed similar developmental patterns. And although there are many points of contrast among these societies, their similarities require some explanation. Why, after millions of years, did the successful and resilient band form of human social organization give way to more complex forms so decisively and in so many places?

In this chapter we shall consider these and related questions by examining several explanatory models, which in later chapters we shall test with archaeological data. Because of the nature of archaeological data, we shall have to limit ourselves primarily to the artifacts of these extinct civilizations, the bones and stones and houses that have survived them. But we might note in passing the tremendous impact of evolution of cultural complexity has had on the way people view themselves and the world. People have apparently always had ambivalent feelings about living in complex societies. Even some of the earliest writings of the first complex societies, those in Mesopotamia in the fourth and third millennia B.C., contain complaints about poverty, taxes, oppressive rulers, governmental harassment, and other ills of cultural complexity. Today there are still many who want to go back to a simpler place and time, when political, religious, and economic hierarchies did not exist, when all people were considered of equal worth, where all had an equal share, and where no one had power over any one else.

This theme of the loss of the "purity" that was ours in simpler societies is recurrent in all literatures, and the idea of alienation for self and community because of the nature of cultural complexity is the wellspring for major philosophical movements. As anthropologist Marshall Sahlins (1968) expressed it, our hunting and gathering ancestors took the "Zen road to affluence": whereas people living in complex sedentary communities seem to live in the eternal economic dilemma of unlimited wants and limited means, simpler societies have adjusted to their limited means by having few wants. Hunters and gatherers can't accumulate many goods because they are frequently moving, and they live in such small and scattered groups that social hierarchies are of little use. Thus, for millions of years our ancestors probably lived with comparatively little of the crime, class consciousness, alienation, anxiety, and other ills of modern societies. It would seem difficult, therefore, to support the argument that complex societies evolved because people saw that they represented an obviously superior way of life. Indeed, we might suspect that the transition to social complexity was made in spite of its effect on lifestyle, and that its causes are not to be found in the choices of individuals or groups about how they want to live, but in more basic, material factors of ecology, economics, and technology.

Social and Cultural Taxonomies

In order to analyze the origins of cultural complexity, it is useful to classify societies according to their relative complexity. Recent approaches to cultural and social taxonomies have been heavily influenced by anthropologists Morton Fried (1967) and Elman Service (1962), and although their schemes were formulated principally to classify the diversity of extant and recent cultures, their ideas have been widely applied by archaeologists to prehistoric societies. The use of ethnographic data to categorize ancient societies that exist only as rubble and discarded artifacts can, of course, be misleading, particularly since most of the ethnographic record was collected during the last two centuries when most "primitive" societies had already long since been influenced by more complex ones. If we use contemporary hunters and gatherers as models of Pleistocene bands, we can therefore expect at least some distortions. Nonetheless, the ethnographic taxonomies of Fried, Service, and others are explicit or implicit in so much of recent archaeology that we must consider them briefly here.

Both Fried and Service divide societies into four classes. Service calls his divisions *bands, tribes, chiefdoms,* and *states,* while Fried labels his *non-ranked, non-stratified societies; ranked societies; stratified societies;* and *states.* Fried and Service differ on important aspects of these classifications and their terms are not strictly equivalent; further, both have recently questioned the archaeological utility of some of their own distinctions. Nonetheless, archaeologists still frequently use these concepts when discussing the archaeological record, especially Service's arrangement, which will be considered here.

BANDS

The Copper Eskimo, Kalahari Bushmen, Australian aborigines, and most other contemporary hunting and gathering societies are examples of this type of social organization. Based on archaeological evidence discussed below, it appears that prior to the appearance of agriculture almost all people lived in bands, which are very simply organized. There are minor differences among members of the group in terms of prestige, but no one has any greater claims to material resources than anyone else. In most of these societies older males who are good providers gain the most respect, but they have no political power. Band members spend most of their lives in groups of fifteen to forty people, moving often as they exploit wild plants and animals. Territoriality, ceremonialism, and descent reckoning are usually very weakly developed. Division of labor is along basic age and sex lines and the economic structure is very simple: money is not used and exchange usually takes place between people who consider themselves friends or relatives. This gift giving is usually done very casually and relationships are frequently cemented by offers of reciprocal hospitality, the granting of sexual access to wives, or some similar procedure (Fried 1967: 58–66). One of the most impressive things about bands is their stability and long-term success. For millions of years they were the only form of cultural organization.

TRIBES

Tribes are seen as differing from bands in several respects, the most obvious of which is size. People living in tribes are often subsistence farmers, such as the Pueblo Indians of the American Southwest, or the New

Guinea highlanders. Tribes often have a nominal leader who acts to redistribute food and perform a few minor ceremonial activities, but, as in band societies, he has no privileged access to wealth or power. He can lead only by example, and serves at the pleasure of the tribe. Exchange in such societies is still usually accomplished through reciprocal trading within a kinship structure. Typically, tribal societies are larger, more territorial, have more elaborate ceremonialism and kinship systems, and make more distinctions in terms of prestige than band societies (Flannery 1972). Service now asserts that for archaeological purposes at least, a distinction should no longer be made between tribes and bands (1975).

CHIEFDOMS

While in many cases tribes seem little more than large bands, chiefdoms represent a quantum change in social organization. Chiefdoms are based on the concept of *hereditary inequality:* differential status is ascribed at birth, and members of the society are classed as "chiefly" or "common" regardless of their individual abilities (Flannery 1972). These differences in prestige usually correlate with preferential access to material resources, so that chiefs and their families can claim the best farmlands or fishing places, as well as more food and more exotic and expensive items than "commoners." They are often regarded as divine and typically marry only within noble families. The economies of these societies typically show a greater degree of specialization and diversification than those of tribes or bands. Craftsmen exist, but they are usually also farmers, and there is no permanent class of artisans as there is in states. Chiefdoms are much larger than tribes, often involving thousands of people. Examples of chiefdoms include the precontact Nootka of British Columbia, early Hawaiian societies, and the Tonga of Africa.

STATES

States typically have centralized governments composed of political and religious elites who exercise economic and political control. In addition to being larger in population and territory than other societal forms, states are characterized by having full-time craftsmen and other specialists, and residence within a settlement is often determined more by occupational specialization than by kinship ties (Flannery 1972). The state codifies and enforces laws, drafts soldiers, levies taxes, and exacts tribute. States have powerful economic structures, often centered upon market systems, and they typically have a diversity of settlement sizes, such as villages, hamlets, towns, and sometimes, cities.

Early states formed essentially independently in at least six areas of the ancient world: Mesopotamia, Egypt, the Indus Valley, China, Mesoamerica, and Peru.

EMPIRES

A still more complex societal division is the empire, which has more people, controls more territory, exploits more environments, and has more levels of social, economic, and political stratification than early states (Eisenstadt 1963). Many of the early states seem to have been involved in competitive relationships with adjacent states, and for long periods this factor apparently limited their size and power. Eventually, however, in all the early centers of state formation these competitive relationships broke down and one state was able to increase its size and influence drastically—usually so rapidly that it had few competitors. In fact, its ultimate size seems to have been limited only by the level of its communications technology and its administrative efficiency.

Empires of this type first appeared in Mesopotamia toward the end of the second millennium B.C., and within 1,000 years thereafter in Egypt, the Indus Valley, and China. The Inca state of Peru and the Aztec state of Mexico also seem to have achieved imperial dimensions just before the arrival of the Europeans, in the sixteenth century A.D.

CULTURAL COMPLEXITY AND CULTURAL RELATIVISM

One of the oldest and commonest human errors has been to confuse cultural complexity and cultural worth. Already by 2500 B.C. a haughty citizen of a city state in Iraq disparagingly described his nomadic neighbors as "[barbarians], who know no house or town, the boor of the mountains . . . who does not bend his knees [to cultivate the land]

. . . who is not buried after his death" (Roux 1964: 161). Even in our own age it is difficult to avoid the notions that civilizations have emerged because of the special gifts and vitality of their populaces; that simpler societies are incompletely developed; and that all the world's cultures are at various points along a gradient whose apex is the modern Western industrial community.

The above classification of societies in terms of their social stratification, size, and the complexity of information, matter, and energy exchanges is a research tactic that has as its goal the elucidation of the processes that produce these forms of complexity, and we should not consider these measures as ultimate criteria. If we categorized human societies in terms of filial piety, aesthetic sensibility, social cohesiveness, "justice," or other abstract but important concepts, an ordering of societies very different from that having to do with "cultural complexity" would probably result.

Archaeology and Social Taxonomies

Archaeologists regularly talk about the band societies of the Middle Pleistocene and the early chiefdoms of prehistoric Mesopotamia, but we do not have these societies trapped in amber; we have only the bones and stones and other artifacts, and we use the words *bands, tribes,* and *states* to describe them only with some license. To deal with this problem, archaeologists typically equate these terms with specific categories of physical evidence, such as the appearance and frequency of certain types of houses, irrigation canals, monumental buildings, and mortuary complexes and the various spatial relationships of ancient settlements.

At the heart of most conceptions of cultural complexity is the idea of changing forms and levels of matter, energy, and information exchange. Each person and each society exists because it is able to divert energy from the natural world, through food sources and technology. And as a general rule, cultures follow essentially the same principles of competition and dominance that one can observe in the biological sphere. Our definition of cultural complexity is firmly tied to the principle of the *Natural Selection of Cultures:* cultures are constantly changing and being changed by their physical and social environments, and some of these changes are selective advantages. The greater the amount of energy a culture can capture and efficiently utilize, the better its competitive chances. And we can measure this in part by measuring such variables as the population density supported and agricultural and commodity productivity.

ARCHITECTURAL EVIDENCE OF CULTURAL COMPLEXITY

Perhaps the most obvious differences between the archaeological record of the Pleistocene and that of the last five or six millennia is the presence in the latter period of massive amounts of residential and public architecture. Pleistocene hunters and gatherers occasionally built huts and shelters, but only with the increasing population densities and altered subsistence strategies of the post-Pleistocene period did some intensive collectors and hunters and agriculturalists alike take up life in sedentary communities comprised of permanent buildings.

The appearance of residential and other buildings, then, is mainly a reflection of economic productivity: if a group produces or gathers sufficient resources within a small enough area it can become sedentary, and in some climates shelter is worth the cost and effort required to build houses.

Soon after permanent communities appeared in both the Old and New Worlds, the architecture of these settlements began to reflect changing levels of cultural and social complexity. Whereas the first houses in all communities were built very much alike and had the same contents, later communities were composed of residences that varied considerably in expense of construction and furnishing. Ethnographic evidence leaves little doubt that this architectural variability reflects economic, social, and political differentiation within the community, but the essential point is that, relative to earlier societies, there was a change in patterns of investment of societal energy and resources. Similarly, once residential architectural variability appeared in many of these early communities, "monumental" architecture also appeared. Pyramids, earthen or brick platforms, "temples," "palaces," and other constructions protrude from the ruins of ancient settlements from North China to the high mountain valleys of Peru, and here, too, the important thing is that the ability and incentive to make these investments are radically different from the capacities of Pleistocene bands or simple agriculturalists.

EVIDENCE OF FUNCTIONAL DIFFERENTIATION
AND INTERDEPENDENCE

A particularly important part of cultural and social complexity is occupational specialization, the division of a community into functionally interdependent entities of such complexity that no small group of people can maintain all that community's activities. To translate this into archaeological terms, we must look for concentrations and distributions of artifacts indicating a certain level of activity specialization. In early agricultural villages, each house and each group of houses had approximately the same contents in terms of numbers and types of ceramics, stone tools, figurines, and garbage. But in later societies we find concentrations of artifacts that clearly represent such things as pottery workshops and stone tool-manufacturing workshops, indicating that people specialized in these activities. Again, we infer that they were specialized, but the significant point archaeologically is that certain classes of artifacts are found in places, volumes, and diversities far different from that which would be produced by, say, a hunting and gathering group. Certain differences will also be evident if we compare the contents of settlements. Some settlements might specialize in saltmaking, or barley agriculture, or pottery manufacture. This variability in the artifacts found within discrete but contemporary sites is a key element in our definition of cultural complexity.

SETTLEMENT PATTERN EVIDENCES

In addition to the intrasite variables used to measure cultural complexity, we can look at other aspects of settlement patterns.

First, we can look at variability in settlement size and configuration. Early agricultural villages in Southwest Asia were almost all of approximately the same size, but settlements in the region several thousand years later were of many different sizes, ranging from a few hundred square meters in area to several square kilometers. Similarly, the basic shape of the settlements changed; some were apparently fortified rectangular compounds, while others were sprawling, amorphous collections of small detached units. Thus, any archaeological analysis of cultural complexity will involve measuring the variability in site size and shape in a large sample of contemporary sites.

Second, we can look at the placement of settlements relative to the environment and to each other. A major part of the cost of exploiting any resource is the distance it must be transported. This applies equally to the deer hunted by Paleolithic bands and the irrigated rice of ancient China. It also applies to the cost of making decisions about resource production, movement, and storage. With primitive communications systems, for example, an official in one settlement cannot make many timely decisions about the agriculture or craft production of thirty or forty other settlements many kilometers away, because the cost of gathering the relevant information and accurately and rapidly acting on it and disseminating it is too high. As a consequence, some arrangements of settlements are more common than others under certain conditions, and we can tell something about the relationships between settlements by analyzing their respective locations. On a relatively broad agricultural plain, settlements, under some economic conditions, tend to be placed so as to form a pattern of interlocking hexagons (see Figure 9.13), because this arrangement is especially efficient if there is a high level of movement of goods and people among the various settlements (Berry 1967). We will see several instances in our discussion of the archaeological record relevant to the origins of cultural complexity where ancient settlements in fact fit neatly into a lattice of hexagons or some other pattern. Here too it is relatively unimportant whether or not the distribution of ancient settlements corresponds exactly to the patterns observed among present ones. What is important is that we know there has been a major change in settlement patterning over time. Paleolithic hunters and gatherers and early agriculturalists lived in locations determined largely by the availability of material resources. But later in some areas of the ancient world, settlements began to be located with less regard for natural resources and more concern for trade routes, political frontiers, and administrative networks. Again, these changes occurred in settlements that were also building monumental structures, achieving denser population concentrations, and evolving some or all of the other elements of cultural complexity.

MORTUARY EVIDENCE

For much of its history archaeology has been almost synonymous with graverobbing. Its early practitioners were primarily concerned with finding ancient burials in order to loot the beautiful and curious goods that people so often have lavished on their departed. The importance of mortuary evidence to archaeologists is still considerable, partly because the preservation of items carefully enclosed in burials is usually much better than those in houses or toolmaking sites. Also, death for our earliest ancestors, as for ourselves, was invested with more ritual than any other cultural aspect, and in many burials we have, so to speak, the crystallization of complex religious and social forces, as well as reflections of social status. These ideas, attitudes, and forces can be expressed in many ways in mortuary practices, and ethnographers have detailed these for hundreds of cultures. Corpses can be buried, burned, ritually exposed, or entombed; they can be laid out flat, on their sides, flexed, or oriented to the cardinal points of the compass; and placed in earth, in caves, in crypts, in trees, or on refuse heaps. Burial contents can range from nothing to the tombs of early Mesopotamia with their enormous quantities of jewelry and furnishings and scores of sacrificed human attendants and animals.

It is a fundamental archaeological assumption that a correlation exists between the level of social complexity of a people and the way they treat their dead. In a test of this relationship, Lewis Binford (1971) examined the burial customs of forty "primitive" societies, including hunters and gatherers, nomads, pastoralists, shifting agriculturalists, and sedentary agriculturalists. There was considerable variation within this group but as a general rule, the correlation between subsistence strategy, social organization, and mortuary practices was very direct: bands and tribes differed comparatively little in mortuary practices, while sedentary agriculturalists varied their practices according to a wide range of age, sex, and status distinctions.

The presence of juveniles buried with rich grave goods has been given considerable importance in defining the cultural complexity of ancient societies, because such burials are considered indications of ascribed status: it is assumed that young individuals could not have earned these goods on their own. Similarly, some ancient cemeteries have three or four distinct classes of burials. Some types are well constructed of stone, have rich grave goods, and are centrally located, while others are simple graves with little in them except the corpse. And it is a reasonable inference that these divisions correspond to different economic and social classes.

To summarize archaeological approaches to complex cultures, we have several specific lines of evidence: we can look for changes in architecture, technology, settlement size and location, and mortuary complexes, and we can attempt to link these changes to different levels and forms of energy and information usage and overall thermodynamic capture.

Explaining the Origins of Cultural Complexity: The Search for Causes

Most ancient scholars believed the rise of cities and states and other elements of evolving cultural complexity required no explanation, because they assumed these developments to be mainly or entirely the work of the gods. Even the Greeks, as we noted in chapter 1, tended to explain the diversity of sociocultural forms in terms of the preferences and habits of the people who lived in them. The scholars of the Enlightenment and subsequent centuries usually explained the origins of cultural complexity in evolutionary terms. Drawing a parallel with the biological world, they felt that competition between human societies was inevitable, and that "progress," both intellectually and socially, would be the result. A hundred years ago, Darwin stated that "civilized nations are everywhere supplanting barbarous nations, excepting where the climate opposes a deadly barrier; and they succeed mainly, though not exclusively, through their arts, which are the products of the intellect. It is, therefore, highly probable that with mankind the intellectual facilities have been gradually perfected through natural selection" (1871: 154).

And because these evolutionary ideas placed western European civilization at the apex of human development, the cultural evolution of the whole world was viewed to some extent as an offshoot of Western traditions. The ancient states of China, India, and even the Americas were thought to have been prodded to higher achievements by contacts with the European/Near Eastern core areas. Thor Heyerdahl's *Kon-Tiki* and *Ra* expeditions perpetuate this notion that all civilizations are derived from a Near Eastern or, at least, Old World source.

Within the last half century, students of the origins of cultural complexity have been much influenced by archaeological evidence indicating that all the earliest complex societies developed in similar physical environments, followed similar developmental trajectories, and yet had negligible contact with each other. To some this has suggested that the explanation of the appearance of complex cultures must be quite simple, perhaps consisting of one or two key factors operating in each of these early cases.

The coincidence of the village farming way of life with the rise of cultural complexity represented to some a sufficient explanation of the evolution of cultural complexity. People then finally had enough leisure time and sedentary habits, it was argued, to develop architecture, art, writing, cities, and the rest of "civilization." The problems with this explanation are apparent upon even a superficial examination. Many agricultural groups apparently never developed into "states," while at least one early complex culture (in Peru) may have developed without an agricultural basis. In any case, many hunters and gatherers have more leisure time than primitive agriculturalists. Although agriculture is the foundation of almost all early complex cultures, it is not a sufficient explanation in and of itself, and within the last several decades a number of attempts have been made to combine agriculture or particularly abundant environments with other specific factors in order to explain the general process of the evolution of cultural complexity.

RESOURCE VARIABILITY AND CULTURAL COMPLEXITY

Anthropologist J. Athens (1977) contends that while we may not be able to explain the rise of complex cultures as the direct and inevitable result of agriculture, there is an immediate causal relationship. Agriculture, he notes, is an effort to maintain an artificial ecosystem, and in some climates, such as arid or temperate environments, the plowing, hoeing, irrigating, and other efforts needed to maintain agricultural ecosystems are so great that it is doubtful that "the more intense forms of agricultural production would be developed or become adopted unless there was a compelling reason to do so" (1977: 375). Athens maintains (as does Ester Boserup [1965]) that the only reason sufficient to account for the enormous efforts required to maintain agricultural systems would be an imbalance between the population and available food supply.

In arid and temperate environments annual agricultural production can vary greatly because of crop disease, weather, and other factors, and there is some incentive to try to stabilize production in these areas by augmenting the irrigation system, intensive weeding, land leveling, and other tasks that require a lot of work. In arid, semiarid, and temperate regions, the growing season is often sharply restricted by the weather, and thus "cultivation . . . does not permit cycling of plantings in such a way as to equalize the labor requirement throughout the year" (Athens 1977: 366). Each spring, for example, many different activities might have to be performed in order to avoid poor harvests, and under these conditions, according to Athens, there is a strong selection for certain kinds of cultural complexity. Increasing the territorial size of the cultural system would help meet crises brought on by a flood or some other disaster striking a single village; individuals and villages might also become specialized in trades and crafts to make production more efficient; and perhaps most important, it would be advantageous to have a hierarchical administrative organization, so that work and production could be closely and efficiently administered.

Athens's argument, which draws heavily on the work of other scholars (e.g., Boserup 1965; Service 1962), involves complex ecological concepts, and it has not been rigorously applied to the archaeological record. Nonetheless, he demonstrates that any comprehensive explanation of cultural complexity will almost certainly require a detailed examination not just of the productivity of ancient agricultural systems, but also of the precise details of planting schedules, water requirements, disease patterns, and hundreds of other variables.

IRRIGATION AS A PRIMARY CAUSE OF THE EVOLUTION OF SOCIAL COMPLEXITY

Perhaps the most obvious common denominator of ancient complex societies is the presence of extensive irrigation systems. Even today aerial photographs of the Yellow River Valley, Mesopotamia, the Indus and Nile valleys, Mesoamerica, and Peru clearly show the massive remnants of these ancient structures, and similar constructions were built in many other centers of evolving social complexity, including Hawaii and southwestern North America.

This evidence led some scholars to conclude that it was the construction and operation of complex irrigation systems that was at the heart of the origins of complex societies. A particularly influential proponent of this view is Karl Wittfogel, whose *Oriental Despotism* (1957) is a detailed excursion into comparative history and sociological analysis.

Wittfogel spent decades studying China and much of his analysis is based on this work, but he generalized his scheme and saw it as applicable to all the early complex societies in both the Old and New Worlds. He begins by noting that in most early complex societies the core agricultural areas were arid or semiarid, with insufficient rainfall for productive unirrigated agriculture but with the advantages of wide areas of flat fertile land adjacent to large perennial streams and rivers. Once domestication had been accomplished—a development Wittfogel does not attempt to explain—people in these areas were "encouraged" by potentially productive environments to divert rivers and streams into irrigation works. At this point in his argument Wittfogel is something of a "mentalist," for he says of these people: "History offered them a genuine choice, and man proceeded not as the passive instrument of an irresistible and unilinear developmental force but as a discriminating being, actively participating in shaping his future" (1957: 17). What they chose, according to Wittfogel, was to engage in intensive irrigation. This involved an intricate series of actions and decisions that transformed societies into highly complex "despotic" states.

Wittfogel places considerable emphasis on the special characteristics of water as the key to this process. He notes that high agricultural productivity is the basis of most social complexity and that in all environments the limiting factors on agriculture are soil conditions, temperature, and the availability of water. Of these, water is the most easily manipulated, but its weight and physical characteristics impose limitations on this manipulation. To divert water to agricultural fields requires canal systems, dams, and drainage constructions that can only be built efficiently with organized mass labor; and once built, irrigation systems require enormous investments of labor and resources annually to clean and maintain them. In addition, these systems necessitate complex administration and communication, because crucial decisions have to be made about construction and repairs, water allocation, and crop harvesting and storage. Thus, a complex irrigation system under ancient conditions required cooperation and centralized hierarchical decision-making institutions.

Irrigation systems also have the intrinsic capacity to create another element in the process of the evolution of complex societies: wealth and status differentials. Fields closer to main rivers are better drained, more easily irrigated, and possess a higher natural fertility, and thus control of such lands would create immediate wealth differentials. Correspondingly, wealth and status would most likely accrue to the elites of the decision-making hierarchies. Wittfogel concludes that irrigation-based agriculture has many other effects on a society. It encourages the development of writing and calendrical systems, so that records can be kept of periods of annual flooding, agricultural production statistics, the amounts of products in storage, and the allocations of water. Construction of roads, palaces, and temples would also be encouraged, because the mobilization of labor for the canal works could be generalized to these other endeavors very easily, and roads would contribute to the movement of agricultural produce and to the communication required for efficient operation of the systems. The construction of temples and palaces would also serve to reinforce the position of the hierarchy. The creation of standing armies and defensive works would also likely follow, because irrigation systems are extremely valuable but not very portable, and they are easily damaged by neglect or intentional destruction.

All societies had not evolved equally in Wittfogel's scheme, and he suggests that the relative evolution of each could be measured by calculating the percentage of the society's land irrigated by a single integrated system, and by estimating the percentage of irrigated to unirrigated land in that society's entire domain. Wittfogel argues repeatedly, however, for the multilinear aspect of the evolution of social complexity: he does not see the oriental despotic state as the only possible outcome of specific geographic and historical circumstances. People could develop states through other mechanisms, and people living in areas that could environmentally support a typical oriental despotism did not inevitably have to develop into such a society. It was, to some degree, a matter of free choice.

The actual steps by which social complexity increases in this scheme are approximately as follows (Figure 8.1): (1) a large number of *separate* community irrigation systems emerge in a particular region; (2) a *hydraulic region* develops, irrigated by a single integrated system, and dominated by a community; and (3) the hydraulic region establishes control over other areas that include societies that either don't irrigate at all or irrigate only a small proportion of their land. This last stage Wittfogel terms an *empire*.

Obviously, no society necessarily goes through all stages. The deciding factor in moving societies from (1) to (2) and (3) is the amount of irrigated land and the amount of rainfall. Wittfogel considers Peru

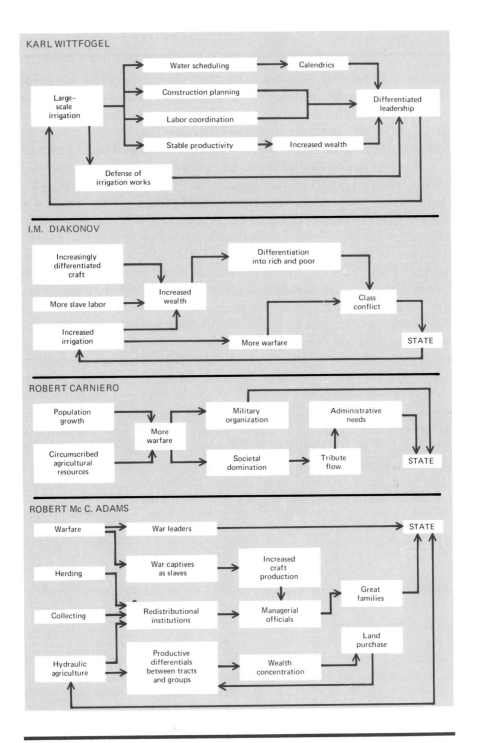

8.1

Several models of the evolution of cultural complexity. (Source: Wright 1977)

a classic of "oriental despotism" because civilization there arose initially in the desertic plains of the alluvial coast; on the other hand, he sees Mesoamerican civilization as a "loose hydraulic" society because, although the key to success there was still the irrigation systems of the Valley of Mexico, only part of the area was actually artificially irrigated.

While Wittfogel's hydraulic hypothesis still has some currency among contemporary archaeologists (e.g., Sanders and Price 1968), there are a number of logical and empirical problems with his ideas as a *general* model of the origins of cultural complexity. A minor but recurrent problem is that it is based on arguable assumptions about human nature and relies for some of its explanations on the free will of people. There is no a priori reason, for example, why community irrigation systems could not have evolved without the simultaneous appearance of despotic religious and social systems. In fact, low-level chiefdoms in several parts of the world have recently been observed operating extensive irrigation works with no perceptible despotic administrative systems or rapid increases in social complexity (Woodbury 1961). More damaging to Wittfogel's hypothesis is the absence of any archaeological evidence of complex irrigation systems dating to before, or to the same time as, the appearance of monumental architecture, urbanism, and other reflections of increasing cultural complexity in Southwest Asia and perhaps other areas where complex societies appeared independently and early. Nonetheless, irrigation systems were important in the *later* stages of cultural evolution in some areas, and we shall consider these cases in subsequent chapters.

HUMAN POPULATION GROWTH

Another persistent candidate for the prime mover in the evolution of cultural complexity is human population growth. The central idea in most of these schemes is

> that a pervasive and powerful factor in human history has been the strong tendency of human populations to increase up to the point where serious shortages of important resources are in the offing; and that experience or anticipation of such shortages has been a major factor, or even the dominant factor, in stimulating intensification of agricultural production and other technical and social innovations. In extreme versions, the entire history of complex societies and civilizations is seen as

hardly more than the outcome of measures that began as ways of coping with problems posed by relentless human fertility—what might be called the "strictly from hunger" point of view of developmental processes. (Cowgill 1975)

It is easy to see the attractiveness of these ideas, for if one examines history, a strong positive statistical correlation between population growth and cultural complexity is evident. The relationship between human population growth and cultural complexity may not be one of direct cause and effect, however, for correlation does not necessarily demonstrate causation. Moreover, even if the relationship is in some sense causal, it may be that the evolution of cultural complexity leads to rising population densities, rather than the reverse. Empirically, too, there seem to be some problems with the idea that human population growth somehow caused the evolution of cultural complexity. All societies have evolved mechanisms like abortion, infanticide, marriage rules, and contraceptive techniques in order to control population growth, and thus we might expect people faced with stresses because of overpopulation to impose population controls, rather than "invent" cultural complexity. Further, there is no evidence human populations have ever increased at anything approaching the biologically feasible rate. If the world's population 5,570 years ago were only one thousand people and their annual rate of increase since then were four per thousand people—a relatively moderate growth rate—the world's present population would be between 7 and 8 *trillion*. Obviously, human populations in the past have been under fairly stringent natural and cultural controls, and if we are to link population growth to increasing cultural complexity, we must specify additional factors or principles whereby this relationship operated.

POPULATION GROWTH, WARFARE, AND ENVIRONMENTAL FACTORS IN THE EVOLUTION OF CULTURAL COMPLEXITY

"War is the father of all things" said Heraclitus, and given its frequency in human affairs, we should not be surprised that many scholars see warfare as a natural adjunct of population growth in effecting cultural evolution.

Anthropologist Robert Carneiro argues that warfare was the primary mechanism for the evolution of social complexity in ancient

Peru, Mesopotamia, Egypt, Rome, northern Europe, central Africa, Polynesia, Mesoamerica, Colombia, and elsewhere. He believes, however, that warfare

> cannot be the only factor. After all, wars have been fought in many parts of the world where the state never emerged. Thus while warfare may be a necessary condition for the rise of the state, it is not a sufficient one. Or, to put it another way, while we can identify war as the mechanism of state formation, we need also to specify the conditions under which it gave rise to the state. (1970: 734)

Carneiro sees two such conditions as essential to the formation of complex societies in concert with warfare: *population growth* and *environmental circumscription*. He notes that human population densities have been increasing in many areas for millennia, but that only in certain *environmental zones* can population growth join with warfare to produce highly complex early civilizations. These environmental zones are exceptionally fertile areas "circumscribed," or surrounded, by areas of lesser productivity such as deserts, mountains, or oceans. As an example, Carneiro points to the coast of Peru where approximately seventy-eight rivers run from the Andes to the ocean through an eighty-kilometer stretch of some of the driest deserts on earth. Here, he says, are fertile, easily irrigated strips of land along the rivers, but in any direction one soon encounters desert, mountains, or the ocean. Similar conditions, he asserts, prevailed in Mesopotamia, Egypt, and the other centers of early civilizations.

How does warfare combine with population growth and environmental circumscription to produce social complexity? Again using Peru as an example, Carneiro suggests that shortly after the accomplishment of domestication and the adoption of the village farming way of life, these fertile riverine areas were thinly occupied by small autonomous villages. For reasons not specified he concludes that village populations grew and, as these populations increased, villages tended to divide because of internal conflicts and pressure on agricultural lands. Some of the inhabitants would then establish a new community some distance away. Such movements were easily accomplished in this early period because there was no shortage of land, the few stone tools used were easily portable, and there was little investment in terracing or irrigation systems. As a consequence, the number of villages increased faster than village size and all communities remained essentially the same in political and social organization.

Eventually, however, given this constant population growth and the proliferation of villages, all the land that could be irrigated and exploited easily became occupied, and the expanding population rapidly began to outrun the available food supplies. Since they could not move into the sea or deserts or easily colonize the mountains, early Peruvian farmers chose the only other alternative: agricultural intensification. They built terraces and irrigation canals and tried to keep pace with their population growth rates, but they were caught in the classic Malthusian dilemma: food supplies can be increased, but not nearly as quickly as population increases. At this point, Carneiro concludes, they turned to warfare as the only alternative to starvation. The village under the most stress would attack the weakest adjacent village, and the victor would expropriate the land and harvests of the loser. The conquered people not killed in the fighting could not simply move away and reestablish their villages, and they could not emigrate to the highlands because their whole culture was based on the village farming way of life. They were either taken back to the victors' village, where they became slaves or artisans, or else they were left as serfs who were taxed so heavily that they had to reduce their own consumption and intensify their production still further.

These developments encouraged the formation of an institutionalized bureaucracy to administer the taxes and slaves, and the establishment of the bureaucracy in turn intensified wealth and status differentials, as the most successful military men were given the administrative posts. In addition, the defeated peoples came to constitute a lower class, and thus the stratification of society increased as the level of warfare rose. Carneiro believes that warfare continued in Peru until all of each river valley was under the control of one integrated center, a development he terms a *state*. Subsequently, again because of the never-ending pressure of population, these states contended with each other until a whole series of river valleys was controlled by a single dominant center.

While Carneiro uses ancient Peru as an example of this developmental pattern, he argues that it applies almost point-for-point to the other major centers of early development. And even in those areas where environmental circumscription was not so pronounced as on the Peruvian coast, Carneiro feels that resource circumscription and warfare were still at the heart of cultural evolution. He observes that along the Amazon, the land is very productive because of fertile alluvial soils, at least compared to the soil of the adjacent rainforests, and that population growth and warfare generated some rise in the level of social complexity in societies along the river system.

In fact, Carneiro believes that even in the relatively undifferentiated Amazon rainforests there was some pressure toward cultural evolution because of *social circumscription:* some villages were at the center of these undifferentiated areas and were surrounded by relatively high population densities, restricting their ability to divide and send out daughter communities. This, Carneiro suggests, eventually led to warfare and some of the social transformations toward complexity, but at a much lower level and a much slower rate than seen in those communities in environmentally circumscribed areas.

Carneiro's ideas are diagrammed in Figure 8.1, where it can be seen that the whole structure rests on two "causal" factors: (1) the assumption that constant population growth among early village agriculturalists would inexorably demand increases in food production; and (2) the assumption that warfare is the most likely response to these conditions. Carneiro infers that other elements of social complexity, such as political structures, occupational specialization, and public construction projects, emerged from the mix of warfare, population growth, and sedentary agriculture.

Since many primitive societies had remarkably precise control of their population-to-resources balance, population growth cannot be regarded as automatic. There is no demonstrated and inevitable reason why these populations could not have maintained their size below the stress level rather than resorting to agricultural intensification or warfare. Thus, to strengthen Carneiro's hypotheses we must stipulate other factors that encouraged or allowed these presumed growth rates.

One other aspect of Carneiro's scheme should be stressed here: his assumption that conflict and warfare are inevitable. Again, there is no reason why this should be so, given that it is within the capacity, if not the experience, of human beings to aggregate for their mutual benefit and to unite peacefully as they evolve increasingly complex forms of government. This is not to suggest that Carneiro is wrong, but only that his appeal to the effects of warfare in societal evolution is incomplete. His theory would be more persuasive and more amenable to empirical testing if he detailed the specific reasons why warfare was chosen, rather than population regulation, peaceful cooperation, or some other alternative.

In a recent reconsideration of Carneiro's model, David Webster (1975) maintains that warfare's principal importance in the evolution of the first states was the role it played in breaking down the kinship ties that organized early chiefdoms. He notes that chiefdoms apparently are kept from evolving into states partially because the chief's power and prestige are tied to his role as a redistributive head, and if he begins to hoard wealth or exploit people, the chief begins to lose the support of his kinsmen and deputy rulers. Thus, it is difficult for the monopolization of force, or great wealth differences, or other "state-level" features of social organization to appear in chiefdoms. Webster proposes that warfare produces a potent environment for evolutionary change to state-level societies by rendering ineffective many of the internal constraints that keep chiefdoms in a stable sociopolitical status. Continued warfare between chiefdoms would place great adaptive value on a stable military leadership, thereby dampening the constant petty squabbles between rival rulers. A chief who is successful in warfare can also claim more wealth in the form of booty than he could on the basis of his redistribution of his own society's production.

It is difficult to test archaeologically Webster's and Carneiro's ideas about the interrelationship of population growth, warfare, and cultural change, because we must find evidence of conflict and demonstrate that it is linked to pressures exerted on resources by increasing population densities. If Carneiro is correct, we should find that the first complex societies appeared only after a long period of population growth in circumscribed environments, and that monumental architecture, irrigation systems, urbanism, land terracing, and other aspects of "civilization" emerged only at population density peaks and are associated in time and space with defensive constructions, mass burials, burned settlements, concentrations of weapons, and other evidences of conflict.

To the extent that it is possible to test these associations, it appears that population densities in sedentary agricultural communities do tend to increase under many circumstances; and the use of social complexity in many early areas of development probably did involve some population growth. But warfare and relatively high population densities seem to have emerged *after* the development of complex societies in most cases.

CLASS CONFLICT AND THE ORIGINS OF SOCIAL
COMPLEXITY: RECENT MARXIAN APPROACHES

For many of today's social scientists there is really no doubt about the answer to the problem of the evolution of social complexity. Friedrich Engels's remarks at Karl Marx's grave express this certainty: "As Darwin discovered the law of evolution in organic nature so Marx discovered the law of evolution in human history" (quoted in Harris 1968: 217).

The critical part of this law is the Marxian dictum that the social, legal, religious, and ideological spheres of societies are determined by their economic, environmental, and technological foundations (cf. Legros 1977). Despite attempts by many to discard Marx's ideas on this point as simplistic and wrong, and despite the interweaving of Marx's economic analysis with dubious political polemic, there is no denying the tremendous influence Marx's contributions have had on the analysis of social systems.

Marx himself, however, had very little to say specifically about the origins of complex societies. He seems to have been largely unacquainted with the anthropology of nonindustrial cultures, and his primary attention was given to detailing the problems of capitalism and the dynamics of the transition from feudalism to capitalist societies. Much more attention was paid to the problem by later followers of Marx, particularly Engels and Lenin. More recently, the Russian economic historians V. V. Streuve and I. Diakonov have studied the prehistory of Mesopotamia with the specific purpose of giving a Marxian interpretation to the rise of ancient state societies.

Until the origins of agriculture, these scholars suggest, all societies were classless, all goods were shared, no one really owned anything, and all were treated equally. But gradually, after the achievement of domestication and the agricultural way of life, some people managed to control more than their fair share of the land, which is of course the basic source of wealth in an agricultural community. By controlling land these elites were able to enslave others and to force these people to work the land for them. In time the ruling classes developed the state, laws, and the church to justify, protect, and perpetuate their economic and political privileges. The state then is seen as an exploitative mechanism created by the elites to control and oppress the workers.

According to Marxian theory, every economic system based on the division of society into socioeconomic classes and on exploitation carries within itself the seeds of its own destruction, because generally the means of producing wealth constantly improve, technologically and otherwise, and at a certain stage outgrow the social system constructed on them. Thus, slave societies would eventually give way to feudal societies, and eventually, Communist societies will replace capitalist societies.

Given this perspective, how did the first complex societies develop? Predictably, Marxian prehistorians argue that this transition was the inevitable result of a specific combination of changes in the means of production in early Egypt and Mesopotamia. Streuve (1969) proposes that the first inhabitants of these riverine systems came there retreating from hostile tribes and, once there, adopted ways of obtaining food and supplies that culminated in the evolution of a slave class. For example, external trade for wood and stone for agricultural implements would have been crucial because these resources were not locally available, and this, according to Streuve, would inevitably have resulted in wealth differentials as some traders prospered more than others. Similarly, agriculture would have led to a slave class because it would have rapidly rewarded the construction of irrigation systems with increased productivity, and these irrigation systems would likely have been built with slave labor. Fishing too was extremely important and would have created a slave class, because coerced labor would have been necessary (for reasons not explained) to make nets and process the fish. The slaves themselves either would have been captured in war or would have emerged internally as wealth differentials increased and some people were economically forced into servitude. Once slavery and wealth differentials had developed, the administrative, political, and economic structures of state societies emerged as a means by which the upper classes maintained their exploitative control over the workers.

Diakonov's model (1969) of early Mesopotamian state formation (Figure 8.1) rests on the assumption that if wealth differentials can arise, they will, and that once these differentials exist, antagonism between socioeconomic classes will follow and eventually the state will form to promote and protect the vested interests of the ruling class.

These various assumptions are unproven, and it certainly also would have been feasible for early agricultural communities to have developed into societies in which the wealth and the work were equitably shared. We do know, however, that once sedentary communities were established, social and economic stratification and conflict everywhere replaced cooperative egalitarian ways of living. Evidence from early Mesopotamian and Egyptian societies does support some aspects of the Marxian reconstruction: wealth differentials developed early and were impressive, and slavery existed, as did communal labor pools, warfare, irrigation systems, trade networks, and other elements integral to the Marxian scheme. But that is not to say that this scheme is correct or complete. Much of it was constructed on the basis of evidence from early documents, and there is considerable evidence that the Mesopotamian states, at least, evolved several hundred years prior to any significant writing systems; thus the textual evidence might be of only limited relevance to the origins of social complexity. More important, it is very difficult to test the Marxian reconstruction with archaeological data. We cannot demonstrate class conflict or slavery in the absence of written records, and nowhere in early states do we find documentary or archaeological evidence that force was used to maintain the position of the elites over the masses (Service 1975: 285).

The rather simplistic rendering here of the Marxian approach to problems of cultural change should not, however, obscure the fact that there may yet be important advances made in archaeological analyses through the implementation of Marxian ideas. Marx and his interpreters' contributions to historical analyses have not always been properly interpreted by American anthropologists because their conception of mode of production, social formation, and other Marxian ideas have been wrong (Legros 1977). Recent reinterpretations of the relationship of Marxist economics and cultural evolutionary theory (Legros 1977), for example, have attempted to show that Leslie White, Julian Steward, Marvin Harris, and other prominent "cultural materialists" (who claim to derive much of their inspiration from Marxist thought) have misinterpreted the relationship of technology to cultural evolution, the appropriateness of classifications involving "states," feudalism," etc., and many other important concepts. Thus, whether or not Marxian theory can be used to advance greatly the analysis of history must still be considered unresolved.

MULTIFACTOR APPROACHES TO THE ORIGINS OF COMPLEX SOCIETIES

Carneiro, Wittfogel, and the Marxian prehistorians do not believe only one variable accounts for the rise of social complexity; but each considers one factor (warfare, irrigation, or class conflict) more important in these developments than others. Given the extreme complexity of human affairs generally, it might seem quixotic to attempt to explain momentous social transformations primarily in terms of a single factor, but at a certain level these attempts are understandable. There *are* strong resemblances among the various early complex societies, and they did all seem to develop in similar ecological circumstances and at about the same time. After all those millions of years of relatively static social-form, such coincidences tantalize one with the possibility that single variable, perhaps just a change in the weather or the appearance of a new plant resource was the driving force behind these changes.

Archaeological research has revealed, however, that none of these single factors, such as irrigation, population growth, trade, or warfare, was equally important in all of the early independent cases of cultural evolution. For this reason, several researchers have recently tried to formulate more general explanations of the origins of cultural complexity, explanations that involve principles applicable to all geographic areas and time periods in which this phenomenon occurred.

Systems Theory and Cultural Complexity

Kent Flannery (1972) has recently proposed an analysis of the problem of the origins of cultural complexity based on general *systems theory*. The fundamental premise of general systems theory is that there are processes so basic to all living systems that all such systems can be compared on criteria having to do with these processes.

Two such processes are *centralization* and *segregation* (Flannery 1972). Centralization is the degree of linkage between the various subsystems and the highest order of controls in society, while segregation is the amount of internal differentiation and specialization of the subsystems of a general system—whether it be a mold culture or an ancient state. To illustrate this hypothesis, let us consider a typical community of simple agriculturalists living on the northern Mesopotamian plains at about 6000 B.C. These villagers grew wheat and barley, herded sheep and goats and perhaps a few cattle, did some hunting, and gathered several kinds of wild plants. Each of these *economic subsystems* would have required control and administration. Someone had to make decisions about when to plant, when and where to hunt, as well as what products to trade, and so forth. These decisions were made by comparing results with goals: the amount of wheat harvested, for example, was compared with the needs and expectations of the community members, and if there was too little wheat, additional planting would be done the next year; if there was a surplus, it might have been invested as feed for sheep and goats—an idea storage mechanism under these conditions, because sheep and goats are portable and turn the grain into high-grade protein.

The point is that this society was—and all societies are—composed of economic, religious, political, and social subsystems, and that all of these constantly require monitoring and control.

In a hunting and gathering society this monitoring and controlling can be done by a single headman or a few older adults, because they are able to acquire the knowledge to make correct decisions about the relatively simple operation of the group. They are essential to the society's survival and they are "cheap" because they process information without taking any "overhead" in the form of larger portions of food or the palaces, thrones, jewels, and other items which are often the trappings of power in more complex societies.

But if we consider the early agricultural villages, it is apparent that the subsystems and the monitoring and control apparatus needed by such communities are more numerous and complexly related than in the hunting and gathering groups. A hunting and gathering headman may be able to make decisions and control a group of at most about seventy-five people, but an early agricultural village probably required a hundred or more people just for existence, because its economy was more complex. Animals had to be cared for at the same time as grain had to be harvested, storage facilities had to be built and administered, irrigation systems required constant repair, decisions had to be made about water allocation, and pottery manufacture required planning and organization. No one could make all the decisions or acquire and store all the knowledge needed to make the best decisions about all sectors of community life. The person who spent his time herding sheep and goats was in the best position to make decisions about when and where to pasture them and which to slaughter, but he was not in the best position to make decisions about irrigation or cultivation.

Under these conditions a society would profit by investing more of its resources in administrators and control systems. One person might be charged with the administration of cultivation, another with the administration of the animals, a third with the religious sector, and so forth. To make the system operate efficiently, a single individual would have to be placed over these lower-level administrators, so that the activities of the various sectors of the community would be integrated. It would be vital, for example, to make decisions about how many animals to keep in the context of how much grain would be available for feed.

To translate this example into Flannery's terminology and the concepts of centralization and segregation, we can see that, compared to hunters and gatherers, village agriculturalists were more *segregated:* their economy involved more subsystems than did that of the hunters and gatherers. The concept of *centralization,* the degree of linkage between the various subsystems and the highest order controls in a society, is more relevant to people living in states and empires than to the hunters, gatherers, and primitive agriculturalists of our example. To take one modern instance of this concept, in the contemporary United States every person deals with local governments (property taxes, traffic laws, etc.), state governments (automobile registration, etc.), and federal governments (income tax, social security, passports, etc.), and these three levels of administration are highly integrated. The citizens of many countries, however, especially in the "third world," have contact only with local governments and have little interest in or knowledge of the federal government; that is, they have a lower level of centralization.

Thus, we can measure every society in terms of its centralization and its segregation, and to some extent this can be seen as a measure of evolutionary level. As mentioned earlier, evolutionary level in no way correlates with how "good" a society is in some moral sense, but it is certainly true that increasing amounts of territory and people are being aborbed into more segregated and centralized societies at the expense of less developed ones.

Now for the crucial question: how does a society become more segregated and centralized? Flannery has proposed two evolutionary mechanisms and suggests that there are others. The two he considers are *promotion* and *linearization.*

> In promotion . . . an institution may rise from its place in the control hierarchy to assume a position in a higher level. . . . Alternatively a new institution may arise out of what was simply one role of a pre-

viously existing institution, as the office of chieftainship presumably rose out of the leadership role of the informal headman in a simpler society.

. . . In linearization . . . lower order controls are repeatedly or permanently bypassed by higher order controls, usually after the former have failed to maintain relevant variables in range for some critical length of time. (1972: 413)

In explaining *promotion*, Flannery uses as an example some economic and social developments in an agricultural village in Oaxaca, Mexico. During the late nineteenth century there was little concentration of power or wealth in this community because of two regulatory mechanisms: the *cargo* system, in which the village governmental offices were rotated among the more important members of the community; and the *mayordomia*, an arrangement whereby the cost—and prestige—of sponsoring the annual religious festivals was rotated among the richer families.

In the late 1880s an enterprising villager named Marcial Lopez managed to subvert this nicely balanced system. With the help of some friends in the clergy he forced the council of elders to appoint the sponsor of the festivals without regard to ability to meet the heavy expenses of these affairs. Social and religious pressures were such that few could turn down an offer to sponsor the fiestas, and Lopez astutely began offering loans to such individuals—providing they put up their land as collateral. Debts in this culture pass from father to son, and by 1915 the Lopezes and a few other families owned about 92 percent of the village's arable land. And because they staunchly backed the clergy, their privileged position was soon institutionalized and religiously "validated."

In systems-theory terminology, the rise of the Lopez family is a case in which a special-purpose institution, the church, was *promoted* to a general-purpose system, in that it took over the function of appointing the *mayordomia*—which had formerly been accomplished by another general-purpose system (the town government).

In the end, the concentration of wealth and privilege in the hands of a few great families produced such stresses, and the *mayordomia* and *cargo* systems were so ineffective in maintaining the equilibrium of the society, that these systems were bypassed by a higher-order control system—in this case the Mexican Revolution with its policy of land reform and the abolition of the power of the clergy.

Thus, Flannery's example indicates how a new institution—which he calls a *great family*—and an economy with preferential access to strategic resources can evolve out of a stable, relatively egalitarian society. Flannery is not suggesting that all ancient complex societies began in this way—only that we can analyze each case of cultural evolution in the same general framework: specifically, in terms of the changing levels of control institutions and the socioeconomic stresses that select for specific administrative and social responses.

Similarly, in explaining the mechanism of *linearization,* Flannery describes a situation in which village agriculturalists in rural Mexico formerly ran their own primitive irrigation systems by informally working together to maintain the canals and by rotating the job of allocating the water each year among the responsible citizenry. Each village knows intimately its own requirements and irrigation system and can adapt to seasonal changes in rainfall, stream flow, or cropping strategies. No prestige or privilege is attached to the office of water allocation, and no sophisticated administrative system is required to operate it.

Under the development program of the central Mexican government, however, state engineers, designers, and administrators come into rural areas and take over local irrigation systems. They built expensive dams and other facilities, and when they have modernized the whole irrigation system they are understandably reluctant to leave it in the hands of the peasants. Instead, the government generally leaves control in the hands of its own agents. "Centralization, therefore, represents a linearization of the linkage between the special purpose arm [the irrigation development administration] of a higher-order system [the central government] and an important variable (water) in a lower-order system (the local village ecosystem); response is direct rather than buffered by the village government" (Flannery 1972: 417).

Flannery argues that promotion and linearization are just two of the mechanisms whereby the processes of cultural evolution (that is, centralization and segregation) are effected, and he notes that these mechanisms can be set in motion by any one or combination of *socio-environmental stresses,* such as irrigation agriculture, warfare, population growth, or trade.

Thus, Flannery has "solved" the problem of not being able to find common denominators or prime movers which can be shown to be responsible for the evolution of cultural complexity in the various Old and New World locations where largely independent developments occurred. He does this by rephrasing his explanation so that it is no longer necessary to find the same specific factors in all the early independent complex societies. Irrigation may have been critically important in Mesopotamia, but not in Mesoamerica, while population growth may have been vital in ancient Mesoamerica, but not in Mesopotamia. In Flannery's scheme all that's really important is that there be some socioenvironmental stress that triggers promotion or linearization or some other evolutionary mechanism, resulting in increased segregation and centralization. The socioenvironmental stresses may vary from place to place and time to time, but the evolutionary mechanisms and processes remain constant and are applicable to all living systems.

Flannery has suggested fifteen "rules" which he argues are just some of the many general principles that may be required to simulate—and thereby explain—the origins of complex societies. The following sample is sufficient to convey the flavor of this approach:

1. Should lower-order controls fail to maintain certain variables within specified goal ranges, higher-order controls are activated. Repeated activation may lead to "linearization," or "evolution" through centralization.

2. Linearization weakens the buffers between subsystems, and consequently leads to simplification or lack of subsystem autonomy.

3. Maintaining such simplification requires more management.

4. More management requires more formal institutions. (1972: 423)

Some scholars (e.g., Buck 1956) have argued that systems theory is perhaps a useful *description* of the process of cultural evolution, but that it is not an analysis or an *explanation*. Science, these scholars assert, searches for laws that relate phenomena in meaningful patterns; we cannot then have a "law" about the evolution of cultural complexity which uses in different places irrigation, or warfare, or drought, or some other "socioenvironmental stress," because it is the essence of scientific laws that they use units which are the same in each application of the law (cf. Athens 1977). Other scholars, however, have suggested that systems-theory explanations are ultimately reducible to the same form as "hypothetic-deductive" laws—it's just the vocabulary which obscures this (LeBlanc 1974).

Despite these disagreements on the utility of systems-theory approaches to the problem of cultural evolution, there is currently considerable research activity involving these concepts. British archaeologist Colin Renfrew (1972) has analyzed the rise of Minoan and Mycenaean civilizations in terms of a complex systems-theory framework that draws on ideas similar to those proposed by Flannery. Renfrew stresses the self-generating nature of complex societies, in which administrative hierarchies and complex economic relationships create an "artificial environment" that moves the operation of these cultural systems far beyond the simple ecological determinants of a particular geographical area.

Generally, however, while systems-theory approaches to the problem of cultural complexity show some promise, their application to the archaeological record is still largely incomplete.

Bibliography

Athens, J. Stephen. 1977. "Theory Building and the Study of Evolutionary Process in Complex Societies." In *For Theory Building in Archaeology*. New York: Academic Press.

Berry, Brian. 1967. *Geography of Market Centers and Retail Distribution*. Englewood Cliffs, N.J.: Prentice-Hall.

Binford, Lewis. 1971. "Mortuary Practices: Their Study and Their Potential." In *Approaches to the Social Dimensions of Mortuary Practices,* ed. James A. Brown. Memoirs of the Society for American Archaeology. 25: 6–29.

Boserup, E. 1965. *The Conditions of Agricultural Growth*. Chicago: Aldine.

Buck, R. C. 1956. "On the Logic of General Behavior Systems Theory." In *The Foundations of Science and the Concept of Psychology and Psychoanalysis,* eds. Herbert Feigl and Michael Scriven. *Minnesota Studies in the Philosophy of Science*. 1: 223–28. Minneapolis: University of Minnesota Press.

Carniero, Robert. 1970. "A Theory of the Origin of the State." *Science*. 169: 733–38.

Cowgill, George. 1975. "On the Causes and Consequences of Ancient and Modern Population Changes." *American Anthropologist*. 77(3): 505–25.

Darwin, Charles. 1871. *The Descent of Man and Selection in Relation to Sex*. New York: Appleton.

Diakonov, I. ed., 1969. *Ancient Mesopotamia*. Moscow: "Nauka" Publishing House.

Eisenstadt, S. N. 1963. *The Political Systems of Empires*. New York: Free Press of Glencoe.

Flannery, Kent V. 1972. "The Cultural Evolution of Civilizations." *Annual Review of Ecology and Systematics.* 3: 399–426.

———. 1973. "Archeology with a Capital S." In *Research and Theory in Current Archeology,* ed. Charles L. Redman. New York: Wiley.

Fried, Morton H. 1960. "On the Evolution of Social Stratification and the State." In *Culture in History,* ed. Stanley Diamond. New York: Columbia University Press.

———. 1967. *The Evolution of Political Society.* New York: Random House.

———. 1975. Public lecture at the University of California at Santa Barbara. Spring 1975.

Hammond, Mason. 1972. *The City in the Ancient World.* Cambridge, Mass.: Harvard University Press.

Harris, Marvin. 1968. *The Rise of Anthropological Theory.* New York: T. Y. Crowell.

———. 1977. *Cannibals and Kings.* New York: Random House.

Howe, John Emil. 1976. "Pre-Agricultural Society in Soviet Theory and Method." *Arctic Anthropology.* 13(1).

LeBlanc, Steven. 1973. "Two Points of Logic Concerning Data, Hypotheses, General Laws, and Systems." In *Research and Theory in Current Archeology,* ed. C. L. Redman. New York: Wiley.

Legros, D. 1977. "Chance, Necessity, and Mode of Production: A Marxist Critique of Cultural Evolutionism." *American Anthropologist.* 79(1): 26–41.

Marx, Karl. 1973. *Grundrisse. Foundations of the Critique of Political Economy.* New York: Vintage Press. Original manuscript 1857–58.

Marx, K. and F. Engels. 1970. *Selected Works,* in three volumes. Moscow: Progress Publishers.

Renfrew, C. 1972. *The Emergence of Civilization.* London: Methuen.

Roux, George. 1976. *Ancient Iraq.* Baltimore: Penguin.

Sahlins, M. 1968. "Notes on the Original Affluent Society." In *Man the Hunter,* eds. R. Lee and I. DeVore. Chicago: Aldine.

Sander, William T. and Barbara J. Price. 1968. *Mesoamerica.* New York: Random House.

Scheffer, Charles. 1971. "Review of *The Conditions of Agricultural Growth* by E. Boserup." *American Antiquity.* 36(3): 377–79.

Service, Elman. 1962. *Primitive Social Organization.* New York: Random House.

———. 1975. *Origins of the State and Civilization.* New York: W. W. Norton.

Spengler, Oswald. 1932. *The Decline of the West.* New York: Knopf.

Spooner, Brian, ed. 1972. *Population Growth: Anthropological Implications.* Cambridge, Mass.: MIT Press.

Streuve, V. V. 1969. "The Problem of the Genesis, Development and Disintegration of the Slave Societies in the Ancient Orient," trans. I. Levit. In *Ancient Meso-potamia,* ed. I. M. Diakonoff. Moscow: "Nauda" Publishing House.

Trigger, Bruce. 1972. "Determinants of Urban Growth in Pre-Industrial Societies." In *Man, Settlement and Urbanism,* eds. P. J. Ucko, Ruth Tringham, and G. W. Dimbleby. London: Duckworth.

Webster, David. 1975. "Warfare and the Evolution of the State: A Reconsideration." *American Antiquity.* 40(4): 471–75.

Wittfogel, Karl. 1957. *Oriental Despotism.* New Haven: Yale University Press.

Wolf, Eric R. 1966. *Peasants.* Englewood Cliffs, N.J.: Prentice-Hall.

Woodbury, Richard B. 1961. "A Reappraisal of Hohokam Irrigation." *American Anthropologist.* 63(3): 550–60.

Wright, Henry. 1977. "Recent Research on the Origin of the State." *Annual Review of Anthropology.* 6: 379–97.

9

The Evolution
of Complex Societies
in Southwest Asia

Royal power rests upon the army, and the army
upon money, and money upon the land-tax, and
the land-tax upon agriculture, and agriculture
upon just administration, and just administration
upon the integrity of government officials, and the
integrity of governmental officials upon the reliability of the vizier, and the pinnacle of all these
is the vigilance of the king in resisting his own in-
clinations, and his capacity so to guide them that
he rules them and they do not rule him.

Attributed to Chosroes I,
a Persian king of the sixth century A.D.

Late in the fourth millennium B.C., when most of the Old World was
inhabited by hunters, gatherers, and simple agriculturalists, and when
the peoples of the New World were still 2,000 years from village life,
there existed in Iraq, Iran, and other parts of Southwest Asia a cosmopolitan world of cities, libraries, schools, shops, international commerce, roads, taxes, temples, and many of the other elements we identify with the "civilized" way of life. Indeed, it is no exaggeration to say
that most of us today are still living in social patterns laid out in these
Southwest Asian cities over 5,000 years ago.

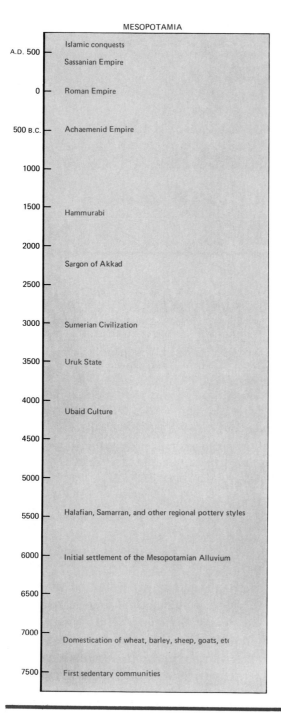

MESOPOTAMIA

A.D. 500	Islamic conquests
	Sassanian Empire
0	Roman Empire
500 B.C.	Achaemenid Empire
1000	
1500	Hammurabi
2000	
	Sargon of Akkad
2500	
3000	Sumerian Civilization
3500	Uruk State
4000	
	Ubaid Culture
4500	
5000	
5500	Halafian, Samarran, and other regional pottery styles
6000	Initial settlement of the Mesopotamian Alluvium
6500	
7000	
	Domestication of wheat, barley, sheep, goats, etc
7500	First sedentary communities

9.1
Chronology of early agriculture and complex societies in Mesopotamia.

These Southwest Asian civilizations have been studied for well over a century, and the resulting books, articles, and excavation reports fill many library shelves. We know in great detail how these people constructed their buildings, what they ate, with whom they traded, what things they made, and what they wrote about life, death, war, taxes, love, and other basic human concerns. It has proved somewhat more difficult, however, to explain why and how these societies developed as they did, why this part of the world was the first to produce complex cultures, and why the basic pattern of cultural development in ancient Southwest Asia was repeated in most of its essentials in Egypt, the Indus Valley, China, Mesoamerica, Peru, and, perhaps, elsewhere.

The Ecological Setting

The world's first complex societies developed in a relatively small area of southern Iraq and Iran, but the factors that produced them involved a much larger area, "Greater Mesopotamia," which can be divided into at least four ecological zones: the Zagros and Taurus mountains, the Piedmont, the northern Mesopotamian Plains, and the southern Mesopotamian Alluvium (Figure 9.2).

The Taurus and Zagros mountains extend in a great arc from southern Iran through Anatolia, and it will be remembered from chapter 6 that the wild ancestors of wheat, barley, sheep and goats are to be found in this "Fertile Crescent." Substantial rain falls here, and in ancient times the area was covered with oak and pistachio forests interspersed with grasslands; but today it has been largely stripped of its forests and severely overgrazed. Because of the rugged topography there are few villages in northern areas of the zone, but in the South where there is less relief, a few well-watered valleys have soils and precipitation favorable for agriculture.

Although human occupation of the Zagros and Taurus regions has always been sparse, these mountains have played a crucial role in the cultural history of all of Southwest Asia. The first complex societies arose on the alluvial lowlands, but early on they used the gold, silver, copper, stone, and animal and plant resources of the mountain areas, and today there is still no more efficient way to bring these areas into the regional agricultural economy than by using sheep and goats to convert mountain vegetation into milk, meat, and hides, which can then be exchanged for lowland products.

The Piedmont, the foothills and rolling plains adjacent to the Taurus and Zagros mountains, was the location of some of the earliest agricultural villages. Annual rainfall is adequate for reliable dry farming and good grazing conditions part of the year, and oak and pistachio trees thrive in the higher elevations of this zone. The greatest extent of the Piedmont is in the North, since in the South the alluvium extends almost to the base of the mountains.

North and northwest of the Iraqi cities of Hit and Samarra lie the dry, undulating northern Mesopotamian Plains. Rainfall here is insufficient for unirrigated agriculture, except between the Tigris and Euphrates rivers, along the east bank of the Tigris between the river and the Piedmont zone, and near the Taurus Mountains. Since late prehistoric times these zones have been thick grasslands suitable for grazing and, with the invention of the plow, for agriculture. The Tigris and Euphrates flow rapidly through the northern Mesopotamian Plains and have cut deeply into the land surface, so that irrigation here requires sophisticated damming and canalization.

9.2
Southwest Asia. The world's first complex societies evolved in the alluvial plains of the Tigris and Euphrates rivers and their tributaries.

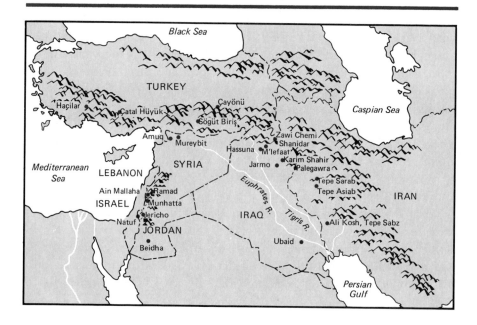

Much of the plains is very arid, but the construction of large irrigation systems in early historic times and the high productivity of those areas where rainfall agriculture is possible made the northern plains an important sector of some of the greatest empires of antiquity.

The most important area, however, is the southern Mesopotamian Alluvium. In the 1940s the historian Arnold Toynbee argued that civilizations first evolved in physical circumstances that challenged the inhabitants to overcome severe problems of climate and resources. His ideas have been largely abandoned, but the modern visitor to the southern Mesopotamian Alluvium, the lower courses of the Tigris and Euphrates, might come to have considerable sympathy for Toynbee's point of view.

Nothing in this region appears to account for its pivotal role in human history. It is an unprepossessing few thousand square kilometers of flat, hot plains, with essentially no usable stone, metal, or lumber, and with a climate whose extremes of heat and humidity have been the main topic of conversation for the generations of archaeologists who have worked there. Rainfall is insufficient for dry farming in most years and occurs in adequate amounts only during winter and spring; during the rest of the year unirrigated areas are brown and very, very dusty. And because of millennia of intensive farming and poor drainage, some parts of the lower alluvium are too saline for productive cultivation.

The Tigris and Euphrates rivers created the alluvium with annual deposits of flood-borne fertile silt and clay, and they provide the irrigation water that makes agriculture possible here. The swamps and wetlands formed by the rivers support a variety of usable wild plants, such as flax for textiles and rushes for basketry, but in addition to irrigation water the major gift of the rivers is fish. The vegetation cannot support many game animals, and thus fish—and later domestic cattle—furnished the protein indispensable to survival on the alluvium. Vegetarianism was not an option for the ancient agriculturalists, because the varieties of vegetable proteins necessary to substitute for animal protein were not widely available. Fish fill this lack admirably, however, and there are many clues to its importance for the early inhabitants: "altars" in buildings dating to the fifth millennium B.C. have been found covered with layer upon layer of fish bones; and the earliest texts make it clear that there were many full-time fishermen.

Another major resource of the alluvium is the climate. From May to October, the average daily high temperature is over 40°C (104°F), and arid winds dry the soil to a depth of about a meter and darken the sky with clouds of choking dust. No rain falls for about four or five months. Winters are cooler and wetter, but with insufficient rainfall to support crops or pastures in most areas. But with adequate irrigation, the long hours of bright sunlight and the intense heat are ideally suited for plant growth. Wheat, barley, millet, date palms, olive trees, citrus fruits, sesame, mustard, cumin, onions, garlic, and many other crops thrive under these conditions, and throughout history this region has been celebrated for its fecundity.

When the first farmers came to the alluvium in the sixth millennium B.C. the rivers were in an *aggrading regime,* meaning they were depositing most of their annual burden of silt and clay on their own beds. Frequently, however, through either particularly violent flooding or the activities of man, the rivers broke through their banks and cascaded across the plains, forming new channels. Centuries of such flooding and the leveling action of wind had covered the area with a thick blanket of fertile soil, requiring only irrigation to become lush croplands and pastures. And because the river banks were above plain level in many areas, irrigation could be accomplished simply by digging a small trench through the river bank, and then closing it when enough water had been diverted. This pattern began to change at about 2000 B.C., when movements of the earth's crust caused the rivers to cut down through the alluvium. Today they are many meters below plain level and irrigation requires dams to raise the water to points where it can be diverted. But by the time down-cutting commenced, the cities of the plains were thousands of years old.

The Archaeology of Early Southwest Asian
Complex Cultures (8000 to 2350 B.C.)

Southwest Asian peoples have lived in agricultural communities for almost ten millennia, and there is hardly a square meter of large parts of central Mesopotamia that does not contain a few sherds, stone tools, bones, old irrigation canal banks, or some other evidence of human activity. Nevertheless, the most common unit of analysis in Southwest Asian archaeology is still the site, which usually takes the form of a mound, referred to as a *tell* or *tapeh*. These tells are a result of the con-

9.3
A typical Near Eastern village near Dezful, Iran. Most archaeological sites in
Southwest Asia are composed of successive rebuildings on the same spot of villages
like this one. The photo was taken from atop a mound site just outside the village
walls.

struction and continual reconstruction of buildings on the same spot.
For thousands of years people here have used clay as their basic building material, and their settlements have taken the form of closely
packed small rectangular structures (Figure 9.3). Although ideally
suited to the climate and resources of the area, such buildings become
so dilapidated after fifty or a hundred years that it is easier to rebuild
than to repair them, and because there are incentives to rebuild on the
same spot (less land is lost to cultivation and higher elevation gives
better drainage and protection against floods and attack), settlements
become mound-shaped as they are constantly reconstructed.

Hundreds of thousands of such mounds dot the landscape of
Southwest Asia, some of them rising fifty meters or more in the air,
while others—occupied for only a few decades or so—are only imper-
ceptibly higher than the surrounding plains. Thousands more have

9·4
Excavating a typical mound site, at Chogha Sefid, Iran. Note outlines of mudbricks.

been leveled for agricultural purposes, eroded by wind or water, or buried beneath the alluvium. Those which do survive are very similar in appearance: their surfaces are littered with stone tools, rock rubble, broken pottery, broken clay bricks, collapsed walls, eroding ovens and pottery kilns, and corroding metal. Animal burrows, well and terrace construction, and erosion constantly mix the layers of these mounds so that usually one finds the remnants of every phase of a site's occupation on its surface. This allows archaeologists to estimate a site's periods of occupation simply by inspecting the surface artifacts.

Besides the mounds, the most obvious archaeological features of Southwest Asia are irrigation canals. Seven millennia of irrigation agriculture have resulted in a landscape criss-crossed with canals and marked by collapsed dams and dikes. It is not unusual to find abandoned irrigation canals several thousand years old with banks still two or three meters high. Aerial photographs are particularly useful in charting these ancient waterworks, even when they are no longer visible at ground level.

This richness of the Southwest Asian archaeological record is at once a problem and a blessing. Because of the time and expense of archaeological excavation and the destruction of sites, far fewer than 5 percent of all sites dating from 8000 to 2350 B.C. have been, or will ever be, properly excavated, and thus our analyses must be tempered with some tentativeness. On the other hand, the rich archaeological remains provide ample opportunity to use sampling procedures and to test hypotheses; and by using aerial reconnaissance and surface surveys, archaeologists can fit many unexcavated sites into their approximate periods of occupation.

EARLY AGRICULTURE (CA. 8000 TO 6000 B.C.)

By about 6000 B.C., village agriculturalists were living in virtually every part of Greater Mesopotamia where rainfall cultivation of wheat and barley was possible.

It is difficult to estimate rates of population growth between 8000 and 6000 B.C. Part of the apparent "population increase" of the period probably involved the gradual settling of formerly nomadic peoples—in other words, a redistribution of populations, not an absolute increase in their numbers. But it is also likely that concurrently there was an absolute and significant increase in human population, for the mobile way of life imposes strict population controls, and these controls may have been relaxed when the sedentary way of life was adopted and children became economically productive through their agricultural labors.

The Levant

At Jericho, even though the populace was still hunting and gathering wild resources to complement their primitive agriculture, soon after 7000 B.C. they had built a stone wall some 1.5 meters thick and more than 3.5 meters high around a complex of stone houses (Figure 9.5). An essential element in cultural complexity is activity specialization to the point that large populations are socially and economically interdependent, and in these terms Jericho was certainly not a complex community; but the construction of the wall indicates that its people were beginning to direct their energies in a way quite different from that of most hunters and gatherers.

But most sites in the Levant dating between 8000 and 6000 B.C. were small simple farming communities with little to distinguish them from each other; each was composed of tiny single-room mud or stone houses with mud-plastered walls and perhaps a few woven mats on the floor. In and around the houses were numerous hearths, storage pits, ovens, grinding and threshing floors, and garbage pits, and at most settlements the only "public architecture" was a retaining wall or a modest stone platform. At Munhata, north of Jericho in the Jordan Valley, the people built a large plaza, at the center of which was a platform of large basalt blocks carved with water channels (Mellaart 1975: 58), and a small room at Jericho included a niche in which was placed a standing stone, suggesting, perhaps, a cult room. But nowhere are there palaces, pyramids, or the like.

The disposal of the dead, usually an excellent reflection of changing cultural complexity, suggests that people at Jericho and perhaps elsewhere were not much different socially from their predecessors. Forty headless adult bodies were found buried beneath one room at Jericho, and further excavations revealed a cache of skulls that had been reconstructed with plaster, painted, and then decorated with "eyes" made from seashells. Whether these represent ancestor worship, war trophies, or some other ritual is unclear. Similar corpses have been found in Beidha and other Levantine sites. Hunters and gatherers in various parts of the world have exhibited an equivalent degree of mortuary ritual, however, and generally, these early Levantine societies seem quite simply organized.

Anatolia

"It may be said without undue exaggeration that Anatolia, long regarded as the barbarous fringe to the fertile crescent, has now been established as the most advanced center of neolithic culture in the Near East. The neolithic civilization revealed at Çatal Hüyük shines like a supernova among the rather dim galaxies of contemporary peasant culture" (Mellaart 1965: 77).

There is some question, as we shall see, whether or not Çatal Hüyük (pronounced rather like "Chatal Huooyook") merits all the superlatives its excavators have showered on it, but it is undoubtedly one of the most interesting sites in all of Southwest Asia. Located in eastern Anatolia and first occupied at about 6250 B.C., Çatal Hüyük was probably inhabited continuously until its complete abandonment at about 5400 B.C., and during some of this time it may have extended over thirteen hectares and had a population of about 4,000 to 6,000—several times larger than any other known site in this period (Mellaart 1975).

Situated at the base of the Taurus Mountains, Çatal Hüyük controls access to a critical resource: the obsidian sources at the Hasan Dag volcano. Each obsidian source is chemically distinctive, and thus we know that after 7000 B.C. great quantities of obsidian from the Çatal Hüyük area were distributed throughout Anatolia, the Levant, and Cyprus. Beautiful obsidian artifacts were found in Çatal Hüyük itself, but so far no obsidian storage or workshop areas have been found in the less than one hectare of the site that has been excavated.

Most of the 138 structures uncovered at Çatal Hüyük are little different from their contemporaries elsewhere in Southwest Asia: each is built of shaped mud and composed of rectangular rooms with plastered walls and floors, and most houses are one or two stories high and abut

9.5
Millennia of rebuilding at Jericho formed many superimposed layers containing stone walls.

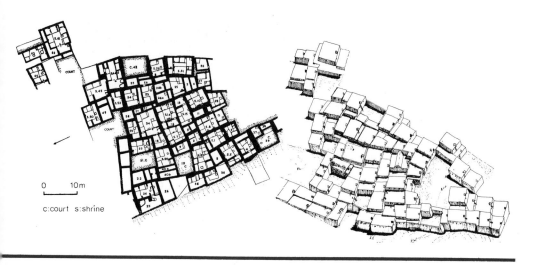

9.6
Houses at Çatal Hüyük.

one another, except where they are occasionally separated by an open courtyard (Figure 9.6). Inside most rooms are two raised platforms, probably for sleeping, and an occasional rectangular bench. Straw mats covered the floors, and the walls were decorated with simple geometric designs. Only two aspects of these buildings distinguish them from their contemporaries at most other sites: access to each is only by ladder through the roof—there are no front doors—and there are about forty structures that are larger and more richly furnished and decorated than the others. The roof access may reflect a need for defense, for once the inhabitants had pulled up the ladders on the outside walls, the settlement would be very difficult to attack successfully. Other Southwest Asian sites had walls at this time, but most settlements were small unfortified hamlets.

In terming Çatal Hüyük a city, Mellaart placed considerable emphasis on the more than forty *shrines,* to use his term, found at this site. These buildings have essentially the same floor plan as the others, but their walls are more richly decorated with paintings, reliefs, and engravings expressing many naturalistic themes, most concentrating on the two staples of Paleolithic and Neolithic art—fertility and death. Vultures are portrayed ripping apart headless human corpses, women give birth to bulls and ride leopards, and other symbols such as breasts, navels, deer, vultures, bulls, and rams abound. Some of the rooms have intricate arrangements of cattle skulls and horns (Figure 9.7) that no doubt served a ritual function.

But are these buildings quantitatively and qualitatively different from those at contemporary sites? With so few excavations it is not pos-

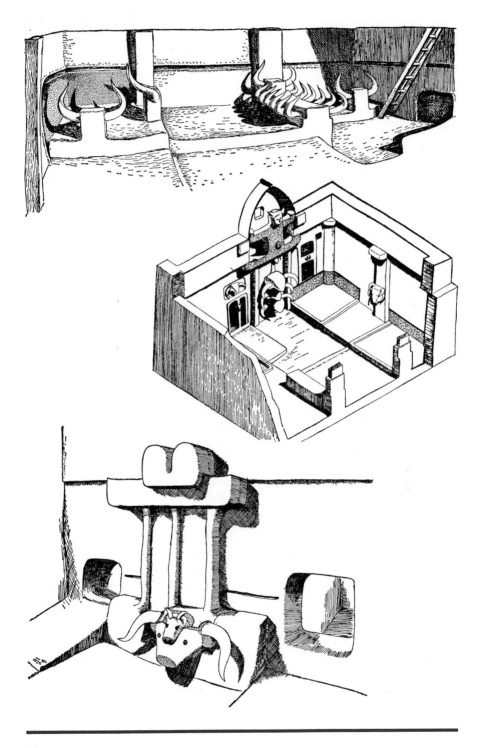

9·7
Motifs in the shrines at Çatal Hüyük stressing fertility and the importance of cattle.

sible to answer definitively, but it would appear that while there are more "shrines" at Çatal Hüyük than elsewhere, they do not represent a major departure from the patterns of the seventh and sixth millennia. They do not seem to have required the expenditure of vast amounts of labor and resources for essentially noneconomic purposes, as did the monumental constructions of later periods. Nor do they enclose radically different amounts of expensive goods, indicating great wealth disparities. Little about them, in fact, conflicts with the interpretation that they were kinship-cult centers in an egalitarian or simple ranked society.

Such a conclusion would be strengthened if we found only minor variability in mortuary practices, and indeed this seems to be the case. Many corpses appear to have been taken outside the settlement and exposed to the vultures and the elements until the flesh was gone, after which the bones were interred in the house floors. Men, women, and children were buried in much the same way, either in baskets or simply in holes. Most of the graves contained no goods, but some women and children were accompanied by shell and stone necklaces, armlets and anklets, and, occasionally, obsidian mirrors and bone cosmetic implements. Some men were buried with mace heads, flint daggers, obsidian projectile points, clay seals, and other items. Textiles and wooden artifacts were found with both sexes, but neither pottery nor figurines were found in any graves. Interestingly, most of the burials were women and children and few were middle-aged individuals—a reflection, perhaps, of high infant and maternal mortality rates, or of differential mortuary ritual.

In one complex of rooms, the so-called *Vulture Shrine,* six individuals were buried in the floor with significantly richer grave goods than were found in the residential burials (Mellaart 1975: 101–05). However, we do not find any infants at Çatal Hüyük buried with disproportionately rich or numerous grave goods, nor do we find any significant variation in construction expense of the graves themselves; there are no stone coffins, tombs, or the like. This may indicate the absence of inherited or ascribed status.

The people of Çatal Hüyük subsisted on the typical late Neolithic combination of agriculture, hunting, and gathering. Emmer, einkorn, a bread wheat, barley, pea vetch, and other crops were grown in quantity, but with simple techniques. There was considerable trade but mainly in small quantities of exotic items. Shells from the Mediterranean (160 kilometers distant) and Syrian flint were found here, perhaps taken in trade for obsidian artifacts (Figure 9.8). But there is no evidence of voluminous trade in agricultural products, or even in large amounts of obsidian, and there are no obvious workshops for goods, no stores of obsidian, no complex technologies.

Thus Mellaart's conception of Çatal Hüyük as a "supernova" among the contemporary dim, drab peasant communities elsewhere in Southwest Asia must be viewed with some skepticism—at least until more excavations are conducted and reported.

Settlements dating to between 7500 and 6000 B.C. have also been found at Asikli, Çayönü, Hacilar, Suberde, Can Hasan, and elsewhere, but all of these are very simple, undifferentiated farming communities with little discernible public architecture, intense occupational specialization, or elaborate mortuary practices. Even pottery seems to have come into use at these settlements relatively late (Mellaart 1975: 96–98).

9.8
The circulation of obsidian throughout Southwest Asia was an important economic process that may have contributed to the evolution of political and economic institutions.

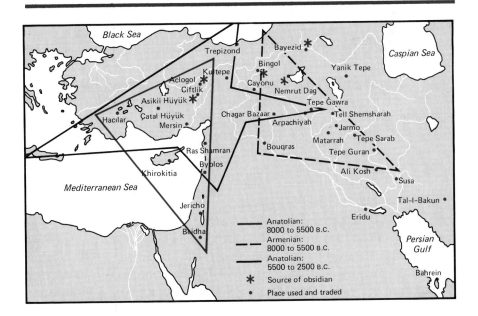

The Zagros Mountains

Jarmo, in Iraqi Kurdestan, is an excellent example of the drab peasant culture that Mellaart invidiously compared to Çatal Hüyük. Jarmo was first settled sometime before 6750 B.C. and was occupied intermittently to 5000 B.C., and thus it overlaps with Çatal Hüyük for perhaps as much as 1,000 years. But unlike Çatal Hüyük, Jarmo was probably home to no more than 200 people, and for most of its existence it consisted of only twenty to twenty-five small, rectangular mud houses.

Burials at Jarmo are quite uniform, as are the contents of the houses. There is not nearly the diversity of aesthetic expression found at Çatal Hüyük, nor wall paintings, masses of finely worked obsidian, or the like; just a few clay figurines of pregnant women and some animals. There are no fortified walls or large, nonresidential buildings, and the technology seems to have been mainly devoted to the processing of plant foods. Perhaps the most significant difference between the two sites is that Çatal Hüyük controlled a localized and important resource (obsidian), whereas Jarmo didn't. Until additional excavations are conducted at Çatal Hüyük, however, it will be difficult to determine how significant its obsidian trade was.

Elsewhere in the Zagros, northern Mesopotamia, and the Iranian Plateau, communities established between 8000 and 6000 B.C. were undeviatingly simple, undifferentiated farming villages, with little public architecture, elaborate mortuary cults, or obvious occupational specialization. Some of the ceramics of this period were beautifully crafted and painted, and there was some minor production of turquoise, shell, marble, and alabaster ornaments, but no evidence exists of differential access to wealth, power, or prestige.

THE FORMATIVE ERA (6000 TO 3500 B.C.)

By about 6000 B.C. agricultural villages existed in most parts of Southwest Asia where rainfall farming was possible, and densities were such that most settlements were within sight—or at most a day's walk—of one another. If, as some have suggested, cultural change is in part a function of increasing numbers of people living in close proximity, it is little wonder that 6000 B.C. marks a transition point in Southwest Asian culture history.

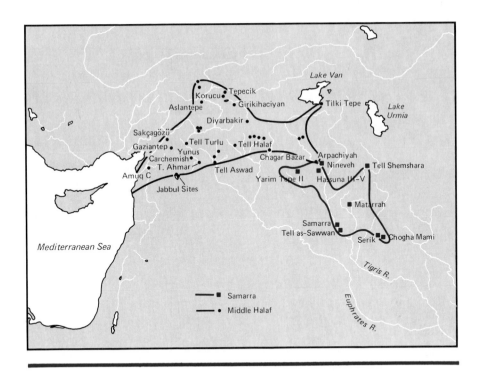

9.9
Areal distribution of Middle Halafian and Middle Samarran pottery styles.

An early indication of social change in Southwest Asia is evident in the distribution of pottery styles. As with agriculture, the invention of pottery seems to have occurred independently in many areas of Southwest Asia, where clay had previously been used for figurines and storage pits for centuries. The multiple origins and rapid spread of pottery after about 6500 B.C. no doubt reflect the increasing importance of containers in these agricultural economies—initially probably largely for water transport and food storage and preparation.

Soon after ceramic vessels came into general use in Southwest Asia, the first sophisticated uniform pottery styles appeared, and by about 5500 B.C. two distinctive styles, the *Samarran,* and somewhat later, the *Halafian,* had achieved wide distribution (Figure 9.9), as had distinctive pottery styles in highland Iran and elsewhere. Each involved many different types of vessels, all painted with pleasing geometric designs. Before 5500 B.C. some figurine types, architectural styles, and other designs had equally wide regional distributions, but Halafian and Samarran ceramics differ from these earlier artifact distributions in that they are found at most settlements within a large area, occur in massive quantities, and are quite uniform stylistically.

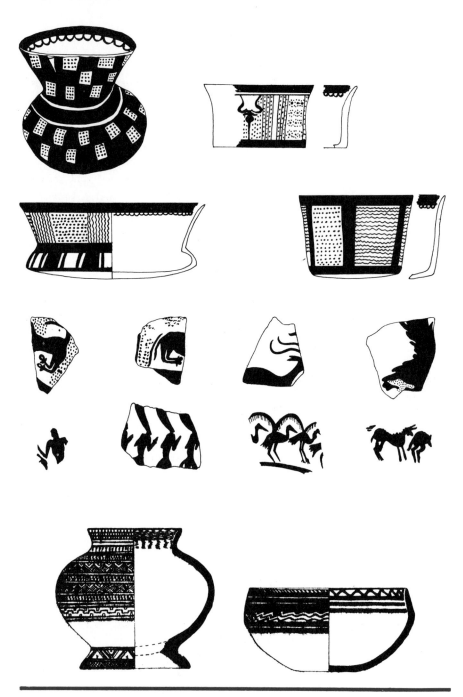

9.10

Halafian, Samarran, and contemporary pottery styles were the first instances in which complex uniform styles were widely distributed in Southwest Asia. This development may mark the evolution of interregional social and religious systems. Above, Halafian pottery, and fragments showing human and animal representations. Below, examples of Samarran pottery.

The artistry of these richly painted ceramics suggests at least some occupational specialization—perhaps at a higher level than among earlier communities. Each village, or each extended family, may have had one or two specialists who, while they probably also farmed, spent much of their time in ceramic arts. On the other hand, despite the wide geographical distribution of these design elements, there is little evidence that ceramic production was centrally organized and administered or that there was a large volume of regional trade in ceramics. Most sites from this period have one or more pottery kilns as well as other evidence of local pottery production, and it appears that the styles, not the actual pots, were usually exchanged. Indeed, the distribution of these pottery styles may simply be a more obvious and better preserved reflection of regional exchange and contact networks that had been at about the same level of intensity for centuries before this, but previously had moved only obsidian and other products (R. McC. Adams 1955: 9).

The distribution of Halafian and Samarran ceramics coincides with the extension of cultivation to the arid lowlands and the consequent accelerating pace of cultural evolution. A significant site of this period is Tell as-Sawwan (Abu es-Soof 1968; Yasin 1970), located in north central Iraq, at the juncture of the northern arid steppe country and the alluvial plains extending south from Samarra to the swamps of the Persian Gulf coast. Agriculture here has always been marginal without some sort of artificial irrigation because rainfall is low and unpredictable.

Preliminary excavations indicate that from 6000 to 5000 B.C. Tell as-Sawwan was a farming community of several hundred people, most of whom were engaged in simple irrigation farming of wheat, barley, linseed, and other crops. They also kept domestic goats, sheep, and cattle; hunted onagers, antelopes, and other animals; and gathered fish and mussels from the Tigris, which ran close to the site.

In most ways, this settlement resembled other early agricultural villages: granaries, kilns, ovens, and small rectangular T-shaped mudbrick houses are arranged around open courtyards. A large ditch or moat was constructed around the site by cutting into the natural conglomerate rock strata on which the site was located. This ditch averaged 2.5 meters wide and 3 meters deep, narrowing to less than .50 meters wide at the bottom, and was buttressed, in one period, by a thick clay wall. The discovery of many hardened clay balls ("sling missiles") in

9.11
A "Susa A" style (early fourth
millennium B.C.) beaker from
the ancient city of Susa in
southwestern Iran. The decoration around the rim shows
long-necked water birds in
formalized, abstract design.
The central figure is a stylized ibex with curving horns.

the ditch led its excavators to suppose it was a defensive structure, reminiscent of the fortifications at Jericho.

The residential architecture of Tell as-Sawwan (Figure 9.12) contrasts somewhat with that of other settlements of the period, consisting mainly of huts with stone foundations (possibly used as granaries) in addition to the more common rectangular clay structures, although there is still little variability in building size or apparent construction cost.

9.12
Plan of level IIIA at Tell-as Sawwan, showing circuit wall and multi-roomed houses.

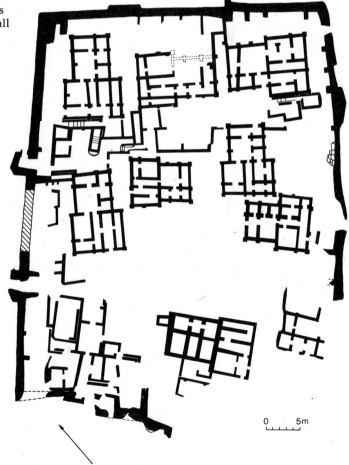

0   5m

At least 128 burials at Tell as-Sawwan date to approximately 5500
B.C., and they contain the richest assortment of grave goods for this
period of any site known in Southwest Asia. Of the classifiable skeletons, fifty-five were infants, sixteen were adolescents, and thirteen
adults. Given the probable infant mortality of the period, these percentages are not surprising, but only certain people may have been formally buried and the rest simply abandoned outside the settlement.
Or, others might have been buried in areas of the site not yet excavated. The graves differ little in orientation, location, or construction.
Most bodies were placed in a contracted position, facing west, in simple shallow oval pits dug into house floors. Although most rooms had
many burials (one had up to twenty-three), one room contained only
an adult male's burial, whose relatively rich grave goods may reflect
emerging status ascription.

Almost all graves had at least one associated craft item, and most
had several. There is a significant difference in the distribution of

9.13
Distribution of some early sites on the Mesopotamian Alluvium.

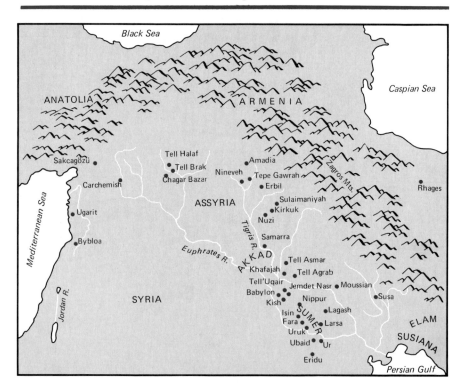

these goods, with burials of adults and juveniles having, on the average, more numerous and varied goods than infants. The range of variability is great, however. If we require great diversity in the construction of graves and the interment of infants with rich grave goods as indications of social stratification, it is clear that the inhabitants of Tell as-Sawwan do not provide this evidence. Nonetheless, these graves are very rich, compared to those of contemporary sites, and the disparity among graves may indicate emergent ranking and status ascription. On the other hand, there is nothing at this site not consonant with either an essentially egalitarian or, perhaps, a "big-man" society, where one person is charged with coordinating various activities and redistributing agricultural and craft production. Such an individual, however, usually does not have any formally constituted authority, police power, or control over the means of production.

Another important early Mesopotamian community was located at Yarim Tepe, in northwestern Iraq (Figure 9.13). Communities here between 6000 and 4000 B.C. constructed many rectangular residences, cattle pens, kilns, storage facilities, and other buildings, as well as some larger, better-constructed, "public" buildings that may reflect some minor centralization of community authority. But there is little evidence of social stratification in the scores of burials excavated at this site, and the economic organization seems to have been based on the simple farming, fishing, and unspecialized craft production typical of the period.

In summary of Mesopotamian developments up to about 5300 B.C., we cannot point to any physical evidence of radically increasing cultural complexity, but the archaeological record may be deceptive: the extension of Halafian and other pottery styles may correlate with the extension of belief systems that, while not organized religious or political systems of great complexity, were initial steps in the transition to complex organizational structures. Belief systems, as we shall see, are remarkably powerful ways of coordinating and organizing societies to accomplish the public constructions and hierarchical arrangements typical of early states.

Early Complex Cultures in Southern Mesopotamia

Shortly after the appearance of Halafian, Samarran, and other pottery styles, the developmental focus shifts to the southern Mesopotamian Alluvium. As we have noted, developments here may initially have been limited by the lack of game animals and edible wild plants, but eventually fishing, cattle raising, and irrigation agriculture solved these problems. Subsistence in most parts of the alluvium is more complex than in the highlands, involving a series of complex decisions in which floods must be anticipated and controlled, land irrigated and drained, and cattle pastured, tended, and milked. Fishing adds to this complexity because it is seasonal to some extent, and requires coordination to be maximally effective. Even getting sufficient stone for simple agricultural implements necessitates considerable organization in the lowlands, for such stone often had to be traded for in the mountains far from lowland settlements.

All of the decisions about trade and organization may have "selected for" somewhat more complex social organizations, and very early in this process differences in social authority may have been intensified by the capacity of the alluvial areas to produce wealth differentials. The limits of agricultural production in the highlands are determined by rainfall, which is of course uncontrollable, but in the South irrigation water is the limiting factor and those areas closest to the rivers are much more fertile and easily watered than more distant areas. The fields far from the rivers are the first to suffer in a water shortage and require the most labor to bring into cultivation and maintain. Also, because cattle must be pastured on irrigated land for much of the year, the most profusely irrigated land supports the most cattle and other animals, intensifying the differential productivity of the two areas. The fact that animal droppings were used as fertilizer probably added to these differences. Thus, the advantage would lie with societies that evolved administrative institutions to coordinate the many facets of these economies and to redistribute products so as to deal with the grossly unequal productivity of different parcels of land within the community's territory.

In the Sumerian account of the creation of the Universe (written at about 3000 B.C.), the city of Eridu was the first to have emerged from the primeval sea that covered the world before the creation of man. Eridu is in fact the earliest known settlement on the southern Mesopotamian Alluvium, having been established at about 5400 B.C. Virtually no other contemporary sites have been found here, but the lowest levels of many large ancient mounds have not been excavated and some may contain occupations contemporary with the earliest levels at Eridu. Many sites on the alluvium have been eroded by wind and water while others are covered with sand dunes, and thus it is difficult to calculate population densities, or to estimate how they have changed since initial settlement, especially since nonsedentary populations may have exploited this region long before agriculturalists moved in. The lack of local sources of stone may have forced farmers to rely principally on wooden tools that have long since vanished, making their settlements difficult to detect.

At Eridu, the earliest known structure is thought to have been a temple. Archaeologists have been accused of bestowing this term on virtually any structure large enough to stand upright in, but the earliest building at Eridu is very similar to others known through texts and other evidence to have been temples. A single small room (3.5 by 4.5 meters) with an "altar" faces the entrance and there is a pedestal in the center, and in these specifics the building is nearly identical to the temples of later periods. The ceramics found here resemble those of Halaf and Samarra, but there were few other artifacts. This "temple" may reflect a low level of social complexity, perhaps including an institutionalized religion and the capacity to organize construction of minor public architecture. But we can say little on the basis of this single occupation.

In occupations dating to just after 4500 B.C., however, we finally find solid evidence of evolving cultural complexity. "Overnight," relatively speaking, the southern Mesopotamian Alluvium—and only a little later the northern Plains—are dotted with full-fledged cities, massive public buildings, and all of the other characteristics we associate with early complex societies. The name usually associated with this period of transformation is the *Ubaid*, a term used to refer both to a time period and a complex of artifact forms. By 4350 B.C. the Ubaid culture was remarkably uniform over most of the alluvium: all the settlements seem to have been located on reliable water courses and almost all were less than ten hectares in size (most of them only one or two).

The spread of the Ubaid culture is remarkable for many reasons, particularly its apparent extent. Ubaid-style ceramics are found as far north as the Taurus Mountains, as far west as Mersin in Cilicia, southwest onto the Arabian Plateau, north into highland Iran, and east to Iran's Susiana Plain—an area much greater than that encompassed within the Halafian and Samarran stylistic zones.

Virtually every Ubaid settlement had a large nonresidential building, probably a temple, built of mud-brick on platforms of clay or imported stone. Access typically was by a flight of stairs, to a room about ten meters in length, with a broad platform at one end and a table or small "altar" at the other. Smaller rooms were built on both sides of the main room, and ladders in these would sometimes give access to a second story (Mellaart 1965: 132). The exteriors of the buildings were often decorated with projections and recesses, with which light and shadows created pleasing effects. In later periods, mosaics of colored ceramic cones and bitumen were used as decorations.

At Eridu, seventeen such "temples" were found superimposed, giving the later ones considerable elevation. Such structures are found all over Greater Mesopotamia soon after their appearance on the southern alluvium. At Tepe Gawra and other sites in the North, however, the co-occurrence of "temples" and *tholoi*—circular buildings—perhaps indicates the persistence of ancient local traditions.

The temple architecture of the Ubaid period raises an important point. As we shall see in surveying other early complex cultures around the world, one of the most consistent signs of evolving cultural complexity is the diversion of enormous amounts of energy and materials into pyramids, ziggurats (stepped pyramids), palaces, platforms, and other essentially nonutilitarian constructions. Why would people who could just as easily and certainly more profitably build irrigation canals, terrace slopes, weave wool, or do other productive tasks instead "waste" their labors on these mammoth construction projects?

Some have suggested the answer to this question lies precisely in the fact that these constructions are, in a limited sense, "wasteful." They may, for example, have prevented high and unstable rates of population growth, either directly, by cutting back food production, or indirectly, by drawing women into manual labor and thereby decreasing fertility and increasing infant mortality. "It would appear that the ruling class was frequently confronted with the problems of over-production and the threat of technological unemployment or a surplus of population among the lower classes. Their great public works programs, the wholesale disposition of wealth in mortuary customs, etc., enabled them to solve both these problems with one stroke" (White 1949: 383).

Just as importantly, monumental construction programs could serve to train and legitimize administrative elites. The building and maintenance of such constructions require complex decisions and mechanisms to carry out these decisions, and the bureaucracies and labor forces organized for such projects could then be used, if necessary, for defense or subsistence-related activities.

Until about 5000 B.C., settlements seem to have been located primarily with regard to the availability of resources, not on the basis of the political and economic relationships between them. We have noted that all over the world and in many different levels of cultural complexity, people tend to organize their territories in patterns reflecting changing social and economic conditions. Thus, when the movement of people and goods between settlements becomes important, and the area is agricultural and relatively flat, these settlements often are quite regularly spaced, as is evident in both the Warka area and the Susiana Plain—two areas of early Mesopotamian complex society formation where detailed archaeological reconnaissance has been accomplished (Figure 9.14).

By 4000 B.C. the number of small settlements had increased dramatically in many areas, and there was increasing variability in their arrangement and composition. At Uruk, for example, population may have reached 10,000 as early as 3800 B.C. (Adams 1972), and for some distance around the town there were many smaller villages and towns, whose sizes and distribution suggest they may not have been tightly integrated into Uruk's political and economic systems. Then, at about 3000 B.C. the city of Uruk apparently grew rapidly, and had about 50,000 people living behind substantial defensive walls. There is also evidence of widespread simultaneous abandonment of almost all the rural settlements surrounding Uruk—leaving little doubt, as Adams notes (1972: 739) that the growth of the city was a result of the immigration or forcible transference of the population from the hinterlands into the city.

In contrast, while initial settlement around Ur may have been earlier and denser than around Uruk, Ur never reached even one eighth the size of Uruk (ibid.). It also seems to have developed considerably later than Uruk, but when Ur's population size was increasing significantly, Uruk seems to have been in a period of decline, leading Adams to speculate that populations may have moved from one to the other as the cities' respective political fortunes advanced or declined.

Developmental patterns were even more variable in other parts of Mesopotamia. In the Diyala region, north of Baghdad, true urban areas developed only many centuries after they had appeared in the South; most people lived in small towns and villages until about 2000 B.C. Despite these variations, however, the general trend in Greater Mesopotamia was toward increasingly larger settlements—many of them fortified—and a reduction in rural population densities.

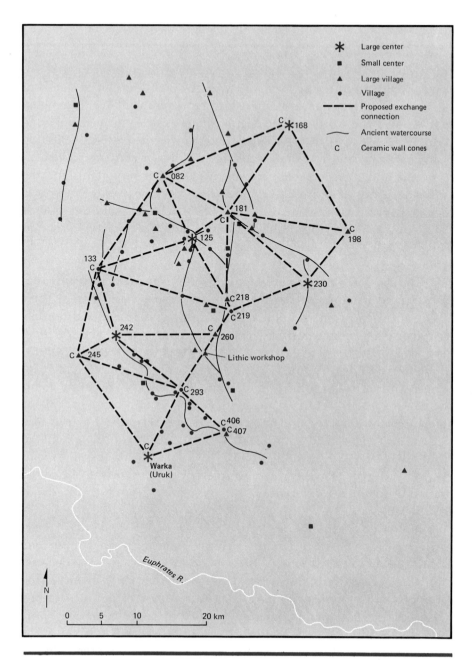

9.14

The late Uruk settlement system (ca. 3200 B.C. in the Warka area, southern Iraq). As political and economic administration centralized and became more complex, the arrangement of settlements became more regular. The location of ceramic wall cones is indicated because these objects were often used to decorate administrative buildings.

The urbanization of this period is difficult to explain. Toward the end of the Ubaid period almost all major settlements were fortified, and the earliest documents speak at length of conflict between the people of Ur, Uruk, Umma, and the other city-states. In subsequent chapters we shall see that urbanization in other parts of the world also seems to be related to defensive needs. Egypt, which was protected from hostile outside forces by the deserts and the sea, developed urban societies only comparatively late, while in the Indus Valley, much more of a crossroads for nomadic and other groups, urbanism was present almost from the very first. In this context, Adams argues that early Mesopotamian urbanization may have been imposed on a rural populace by a small, politically conscious superstratum that was motivated principally by military and economic interests (1972: 743).

Because of defensive considerations and the cost of transporting labor and products, agricultural land nearest the urban areas would have been most intensively exploited, and this may have stimulated the construction of large irrigation systems. The outlying settlements may eventually have been superseded to a degree by small temporary camps for city-dwelling seasonal agriculturalists who went out during some months to farm distant areas.

Another important possible effect of urbanism is that it might have created—and to some extent have been created by—the large nomadic populations thought to have been present in Southwest Asia perhaps as early as 6000 B.C. Most of these people were probably similar to the present-day Bakhtiari of western Iran, who herd sheep and goats in the uplands during much of the year but come down to the lowlands in the winter to sell their animals' wool, meat, and milk products, and to buy craft items, food, and other products. The relationships between these upland nomadic and lowland sedentary groups are varied and complex. Historically, when central governments have weakened in Southwest Asia, some marginal cultivators, in times of war or poor harvests, revert to nomadic pastoralism, while some pastoralists become laborers or marginal farmers if they lose too many sheep. One of the effects of urbanism suggested by the archaeological record—the depopulation of the countryside—may have given nomads and semisedentary populations a new niche. By working the mountain areas and highlands for most of the year, the nomads could have come down and exploited the marginal areas between urban centers—peacefully most of the time, but other times with hostility—and then interacted with the townsmen.

THE RISE OF CITY-STATES (3500 TO 2350 B.C.)

The ancient settlement of Uruk (known as *Warka* in Arabic and *Erech* in the Bible), located in the heart of the southern Alluvium between the Tigris and Euphrates rivers, is one of the oldest cities in the world and may have been the center of one of the earliest states.

Initially settled before 4000 B.C., by the late fourth millennium B.C. Uruk was already an impressive settlement of perhaps several thousand people and many large temples. Between about 3200 and 3100 B.C. the "White Temple" at Uruk was built on a ziggurat some twelve meters above ground level (Mallowan 1965: 40). Made of white-washed mud-brick and decorated with elaborate recesses, columns, and buttresses, it must have been an impressive sight—especially to peasants coming into the city on market days. Inside the temple were tables and altars, all arranged according to the same ritual plan evident at Eridu some 2,500 years previously.

The residential architecture of Uruk indicates a diversity of occupational, economic, and social classes. All the buildings were mud-brick, but some were larger, better-built, and more elaborately decorated. Many of the people lived in small rectangular buildings built along narrow winding streets through which ran both above- and below-ground drainage canals. Apparently, houses were one story high for the poor and two stories for the wealthier, but both types were essentially very similar. Built of mud-brick and whitewashed, they represent an ideal architectural adaptation to the climate. Similar houses today are comfortable and attractive, their whitewashed walls contrasting effectively with beautiful dyed rugs and textiles.

A

B

9.15
Warka (Uruk) period pottery of the fourth millennium B.C. In contrast to the handmade, highly painted pottery of earlier periods, the pottery of lowland Mesopotamia in the fourth millennium was largely mold-made and mass-produced, such as the beveled-rim bowls (A); fourth millennium buildings were often decorated with painted clay cones (B) set in mosaic patterns.

9.16
Stamp seals, hard stones engraved with representations of animals, abstract symbols, and other motifs, were used from the fifth millennium B.C. on. Bales and jars of commodities were often tied with rope and the knot covered with a lump of clay which was stamped with these seals. Untying the rope broke the seal.

By the middle of the fourth millennium B.C. the population of Uruk included specialists in scores of arts and crafts. Potters, using molds and mass-production techniques, turned out enormous quantities of pottery, including both highly decorated specialized wares and crude utilitarian forms. In earlier periods great numbers of beautifully painted vessels were made at most larger settlements, but by the middle and late fourth millennium pottery manufacture had become a centralized, administered activity at Uruk and many other settlements. Millions of beveled-rim bowls (Figure 9.15), for example, were made in a common pattern and in regularly graduated sizes—possibly reflecting standard amounts of food (perhaps grain or yogurt) being rationed out from centralized warehouses. Other specialists apparently included stonecutters, metalsmiths, bricklayers, farmers, fishermen, shepherds, and sailors. Writing did not come into general use in Mesopotamia until about 3000 B.C., but at Uruk and other sites in levels dating from about 3500 B.C. onward archaeologists frequently find stamp seals (Figure 9.16) and cylinder seals, which were used to impress clay sealings on bales of commodities and documents. Some of these seals convey in picture form the economic specialization of the community. Boats, domestic animals, grain, deities, and many other motifs are portrayed; and these seals may have been used to denote ownership—by individuals, perhaps, but more likely by kin-groups or religious associations—of craft goods and agricultural produce. Even without written documents it is obvious that the highly specialized and integrated economy of a city like Uruk in the mid-fourth millennium could not have functioned without scores of administrative specialists to oversee social, religious, economic, and political affairs. Wall paintings, seal impressions, and other evidence indicate that these administrative elites were embedded in a religious matrix and that political and religious authority was combined in a "god-king."

9.17
Major Sumerian cities. As indicated, there may have been a large freshwater lake north of Basra in the early historic period.

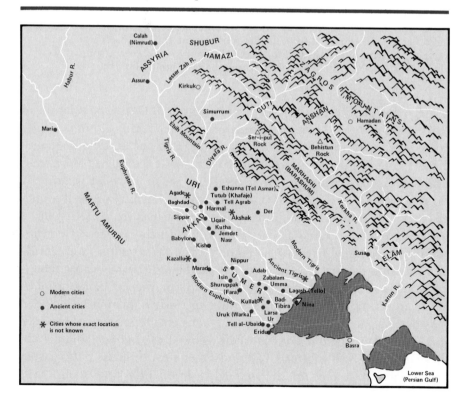

The increasingly complex economy and administrative structure of Mesopotamia during the middle and late fourth millennium B.C. is reflected very dramatically in changing settlement patterns. Five hundred years earlier there had been comparatively little diversity of settlement sizes and types—most people lived either in small towns or villages—and communities were located principally in regard to the agricultural potential of a given tract of land. But in the mid-fourth millennium major cities appeared all over the alluvium, and most were surrounded by dependent towns and villages. Analysis of the placement of these settlements and their contents indicates that much of the alluvium was parceled up among autonomous city-states, in each of which one or two cities served as "central places" that provided goods and services to thousands of people living in smaller communities in the countryside. Subsequently, the establishment of settlements was determined in part by economic and political factors. We shall consider these settlement pattern changes in greater detail (pp. 423–433) when we try to explain why cities and states first appeared in Mesopotamia.

Sumerian Civilization (3000 to 2350 B.C.)

Approximately thirteen roughly contemporary city-states made up the Sumerian "civilization" between about 3000 and 2350 B.C. (Figure 9.17). Through most of their history these city-states were politically autonomous, but they belonged to the same cultural tradition and by 3000 B.C. had collectively developed many of the classical elements of Southwest Asian civilization, including ziggurats, brick platforms, the potter's wheel, wheeled carts, metalworking, sailboats, and writing.

The fact that the Sumerian language was essentially unlike those of the contemporary but less-developed "Semitic" cultures that surrounded the Sumerians has led some to place Sumerian origins in Turkey, Iran, Bahrain, or even outer space. The Sumerians thought of themselves as a distinct and superior culture (as do most groups), and their myths speak of origins in some distant land; but we shall probably never determine the ethnic origins of the Sumerians, and in a sense this is an unimportant problem. The achievements of cultures cannot be explained in terms of the special characteristics and mental gifts of the people of these cultures: people are constants in the equations of cultural evolution, and it is their circumstances and position in place and time that determine their cultural "achievements."

Sumerian city-states were made up of one or more cities surrounded by smaller rural towns and villages. City-states frequently competed with one another economically and militarily, although cooperation and trade also occurred. We have a remarkably detailed picture of life in these Sumerian city-states because shortly before 3000 B.C. they began to develop a written language. Many prehistoric peoples conveyed information by using written signs, such as those on the stone stamp seals used in Mesopotamia since the seventh millennium B.C. or the "pictographs" of African hunters. But the Sumerians vastly increased the utility of such sign systems by developing a way to convey much of their *spoken* language with written symbols. What we know about the Sumerian language is derived from the thousands of clay tablets on which they wrote. Their script is known as *cuneiform,* from the Latin for *wedge-shaped,* a reference to the fact that Sumerian was written by

9.18
Photograph of cuneiform text on baked brick.

EARLIEST PICTOGRAPHS (3000 B.C.)	DENOTATION OF PICTOGRAPHS	PICTOGRAPHS IN ROTATED POSITION	CUNEIFORM SIGNS CA. 1900 B.C.	BASIC LOGOGRAPHIC VALUES		ADDITIONAL LOGOGRAPHIC VALUES		SYLLABARY (PHONETIC VALUES)
				READING	MEANING	READING	MEANING	
	HEAD AND BODY OF A MAN			LÚ	MAN			
	HEAD WITH MOUTH INDICATED			KA	MOUTH	KIRI₃ ZÚ GÙ DUG₄ INIM	NOSE TEETH VOICE TO SPEAK WORD	KA ZÚ
	BOWL OF FOOD			NINDA	FOOD, BREAD	NÍG GAR	THING TO PLACE	
	MOUTH + FOOD			KÚ	TO EAT	ŠAGAR	HUNGER	
	STREAM OF WATER			A	WATER	DURU₅	MOIST	A
	MOUTH + WATER			NAG	TO DRINK	EMMEN	THIRST	
	FISH			KUA	FISH			KU₆ HA
	BIRD			MUŠEN	BIRD			HU PAG
	HEAD OF AN ASS			ANŠE	ASS			
	EAR OF BARLEY			ŠE	BARLEY			ŠE

9.19
The evolution of Sumerian writing. Fourth millennium B.C. tablets were inscribed vertically with pictographs, but in the early third millennium, the direction of the writing and the pictographs was rotated to the horizontal. In succeeding millennia the symbols were stylized and given phonetic meanings.

impressing wet clay with end of a reed, leaving wedge-shaped marks. When baked, these clay tablets are extremely durable and can survive thousands of years buried in garbage pits, abandoned houses, and collapsed palaces (Figure 9.18). The Sumerians may have also written on paper, bark, or other long-since decayed vegetable material.

Our knowledge of the earliest Sumerian language comes mainly from the site of Uruk, where excavators found a cache of about 1,000 tablets inscribed with a kind of picture writing (Figure 9.19) in which over 900 unique symbols were used to represent such things as *sun, river, man,* and so forth. The ability of such a system to convey abstract concepts or the spoken language was quite limited, but in the centuries after 2900 B.C. the Sumerians devised ways to generalize and improve the information-carrying capacity of their script. The symbol for the sun, for example, was generalized to mean not only the sun but also *day* and *time*. More importantly, the process of *phoneticization* was underway, so that some signs came to represent distinct words and syllables of the spoken language. Thus, the sign of an arrow came to mean both *arrow* and the Sumerian word for *life,* the connecting link being that the spoken word for both was *ti* (Diringer 1962). Eventually much of spoken Sumerian was represented by written symbols, and the pictographic elements slowly lost their representational character as the scribes stylized them to make writing more rapid. Unique signs were developed for most Sumerian vowels and syllables, but the language was never reduced to an *alphabetic* system where every distinct sound in the language is represented by a unique sign. Instead, it remained a confusing welter of signs that represented pictographs of concrete objects, signs that represented syllables of speech, and signs that represented ideas. This made reading the script a complicated process, requiring the memorization of hundreds of different characters. One sign, for example, which ultimately derived from a pictograph representing a mountain, acquired a total of ten possible phonetic values—*gin, kur, kin, lat, mat, mad, nat, nad, shat,* and *shad*—and four ideographic values as well (ibid.: 40). At first the reader had to infer the exact meaning of the word by considering its context, but eventually the Sumerians devised a system of *determinatives*—signs placed before or after a word to indicate the general category to which the word belonged, such as, birds, numbers, male proper nouns, or deities.

Over the centuries the Sumerians' successors managed to reduce the complexity of the written language still further, but even as late as about 1900 B.C. the written language had between six and seven hundred unique elements. At this stage it was similar to Chinese and a few other modern languages, which faithfully represent the spoken language and are adequate for most purposes, but which, compared to alphabetic systems, are very cumbersome. It is almost impossible to construct typewriters or computers for languages with hundreds of unique elements, and even minimal literacy in such languages is the product of long and arduous training. It is estimated that to become literate in modern Chinese one must memorize between five and seven thousand characters.

The first truly alphabetic written languages appear to have developed toward the end of the second millennium B.C. among Semitic-speaking peoples in Palestine and northern Syria. In the tenth or ninth centuries B.C. the Greeks adapted the Syrian or Phoenecian variant of these early alphabets to their own language, reducing the number of signs to less than twenty-five and making several major refinements in the process. The Greek alphabet was thus the basis for all modern European writing systems, including the Cyrillic alphabet of eastern and central Europe.

The role of writing in early Mesopotamian societies was largely economic. Simple pictographs and the spoken language are adequate to communicate, process, and store information in a hunting and gathering society or a community of farmers, but they cannot efficiently meet the requirements of a society that has surpluses to be stored and redistributed, water to be allocated, land rights to be assigned and adjudicated, ritual prayers to be said, and all the other elements we find in complex cultures. In fact, only the Inca of Peru managed to develop states and empires without developing a written language, but they had a fairly efficient substitute in the form of a vast bureaucracy and the *quipu,* a system of knotted strings in which the length of strings and placement of knots was used as a device to assist the memory of the record keeper.

The way of life described by the Sumerian texts, and by texts of other Southwest Asian cultures of the third millennium B.C., is still recognizable to anyone who has traveled in these areas. Sheep, goats, and cattle are tabulated, taxed, and exchanged; children are shepherded to school—as always, much against their will—by concerned parents; and a council of elders meets to consider grievances against the inhabitants of an adjoining city-state while a politician attempts to win the favor of the populace with tax reductions. Explicit instructions were drawn up for irrigating crops, making medicine, and working metal. And Sumerian proverbs express ideas recognizable in many human societies:

> Upon my escaping from the wild ox,
> The wild cow confronted me.
>
> My wife is in church
> My mother is down by the river
> And here am I starving of hunger.

You go and carry off the enemy's land;
The enemy comes and carries off your land.

You can have a lord, you can have a king,
but the man to fear is a "governor."

When a poor man dies do not try to revive him.

(Hamblin 1973: 104–05)

Other Sumerian texts include myths about the creation of the world, theological treatises, legal documents, bills, songs, tax lists, and school texts.

The prosaic, essential human activities reflected in these texts tempt one to see the Sumerians very much in our own terms, but this would be a distortion. As one scholar put it, "we are all Greeks"—meaning that our perspective is deeply influenced by the philosophies first propounded in ancient Greece, philosophies very different from those of ancient Sumer. Thus, we see the world in terms of beginnings and ends, causes and effects, and the importance and "will" of the individual. We cannot completely reconstruct Sumerian philosophy on the basis of fragmentary texts, but it seems evident that the Sumerians saw a much more static and magical world than we do. Although their technology and complex organizations demonstrate that they were shrewd, rational people, there seems to have been little emphasis or analysis of human motivation or the physical world. They saw the earth as a flat disk under a vaulted heaven and believed that a pantheon of anthropomorphic gods guided history according to well-laid-out plans and that the world continues without end and with little change. Each god was in charge of something—the movements of the planets, irrigation, or brickmaking, for example—and each was immortal and inflexible. As with humans, the deities were hierarchically arranged in power and authority and were given to power struggles and many vices.

The economy of Sumerian city-states was based on intensive agriculture. Wheat, barley, vegetables, and dates were the major crops, while cattle raising and fishing were of almost equal importance. Cattle were raised for draught power, hides, and milk, and only incidentally for their flesh. Fish was a staple, as were pigs. Few economies in history or prehistory have been as organized as the Sumerian. Tablet after tablet records endless lists of commodities produced, stored, and allotted. Ration lists, work forces, guild members—all are recorded in numbing detail. Even the city's snakecharmers were organized.

Although the evidence is not clear, the temples seem to have dominated the community's social and economic life by serving as collection and redistribution centers. At Lagash, a city close to Uruk, documents from about 2400 B.C. record that temple personnel rationed out bread and beer for 1,200 people each day, ran textile shops employing hundreds of women and children, and controlled a variety of other specialists, such as fishermen, smiths, scribes, and potters.

There is some question about the exact nature of the political and economic hierarchies at this time, but religious and political authority were probably in large part combined. The temples seem to have held a great deal of land in the names of specific gods, and the produce of this land was set aside for the priests and members of the temple communities; other land was assigned to individuals or individual families and appears to have been sold occasionally.

Although this society was still structured through kinship, people also belonged to and acted through occupational and social classes. In the event of war, for example, members of different guilds, such as silversmiths or potters, would be under the command of their guild "president." One of the major trends in the evolution of complex societies generally was the change from a kinship-based society to one based on divisions along occupational, social, and economic class lines, and by 3000 B.C. there is evidence that this trend was developing in Mesopotamian societies. Even so, throughout the history of Southwest Asia kinship ties have been powerful social forces.

At the pinnacle of Sumerian society was a god-king, assumed to be a descendant of and in contact with the gods. Beneath him was a leisured class of nobles, who could command a disproportionate share of the wealth. We know from the records that there was also a class of wealthy businessmen who lived in the larger, better houses of the city; beneath them were the many artisans and farmers, including smiths, leatherworkers, fishermen, bricklayers, weavers, and potters. Scribes apparently held fairly important positions, and literacy was an admired accomplishment. At the bottom of society were the slaves, often war captives or dispossessed farmers. In later periods at least, slavery in these cities meant harsh exploitation, but slaves had rights and were apparently not nearly so destitute as in many other societies.

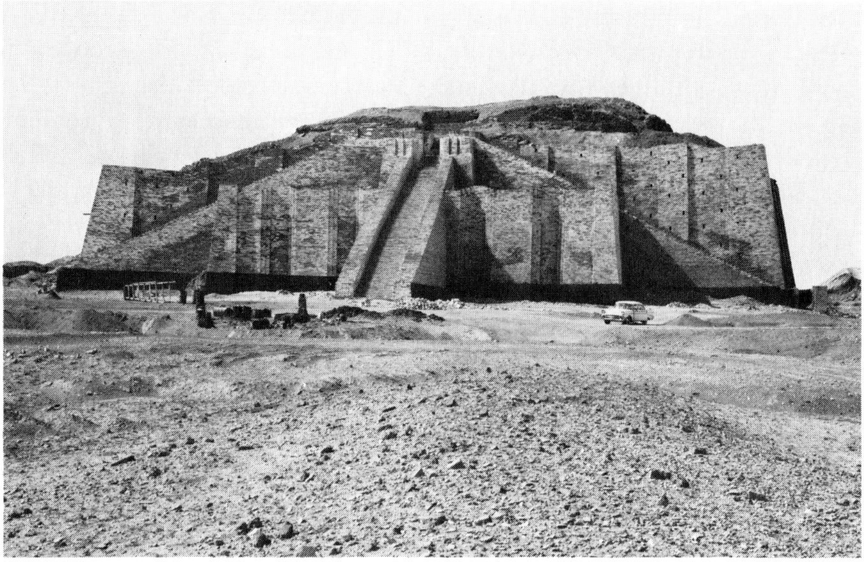

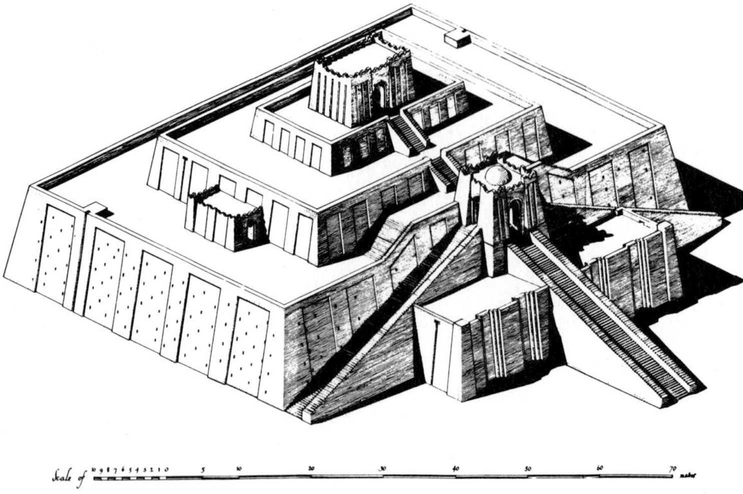

9.20
Temple precincts in Sumerian cities often included a large mudbrick "ziggurat," or stepped pyramid. The extant remains (rebuilt) and an artist's reconstruction of the ziggurat at Ur, in southern Mesopotamia, are shown here.

Money, as we know it, did not exist in ancient Sumer; most exchange was "in kind," the trading of products for other products. Local and long-distance trade was voluminous, however, and ships sailed up the rivers from the gulf carrying shell, carnelian, lapis lazuli, silver, gold, onyx, alabaster, textiles, and food and other produce.

Dress, as depicted in art and literature, was typically a simple full-length garment, sometimes wrapped around the waist and clasped with silver or gold pins. Artistic representations and analysis of skeletons indicate that these early people were a typical "Mediterranean" population, with relatively long skulls and an average height of 5'6".

One of the most spectacular differences between Sumerian societies after 3000 B.C. and their predecessors is in mortuary practices. At the end of the Ubaid period (3800 B.C.) graves varied little, even at the largest settlements; but after 3000 B.C. there was a radical shift. The famous death pit at Ur (Figure 9.21), is an impressive display of wealth and pomp. Excavating here in 1927–1928, Sir Leonard Woolley (1965) came upon five bodies lying side by side, each with a copper dagger and a few other items. Beneath them was a layer of matting on which the bodies of ten women were encountered, lying in two rows, each individual richly ornamented with gold, lapis lazuli, and carnelian jewelry. Laying nearby was a gold- and jewel-encrusted harp, across which were the bones of the gold-crowned harpist. At this point it was evident that the bodies were lying on a ramp, and as the excavators continued down this they encountered a heavily jeweled chariot, complete with donkeys and grooms. Then the investigators began unearthing masses of gold, silver, stone, and copper vessels, as well as additional human bodies, weapons, and other items. Nearby another set of six male skeletons equipped with copper knives and helmets was found, as well as the remains of two four-wheeled wooden wagons—also decorated with harnesses of gold and silver and accompanied by the skeletons of grooms and drivers. Other arrangements of human skeletons, harps, wagons, and model boats appeared as the excavations continued. Finally, at the end of the tomb was a wooden bier containing the remains of the queen. The entire upper part of her body was hidden by a mass of beads of gold, silver, lapis lazuli, carnelian, agate, and chalcedony. Her headdress and other furnishings were lavishly ornamented with gold, silver, and precious jewels. Liberally strewn about the chamber were human bodies, jewelry, vessels of precious metals,

9.21
The great death pit at Ur, where scores of people were sacrificed and entombed near the king's crypt.

silver figurines, silver tables, cosmetics, seashell ornaments, and a number of other treasures (Figure 9.22).

All together some sixteen royal burials were found at Ur, all of them distinguished from the myriad common graves by the fact that each was not merely a coffin but a structure of stone, or stone and mudbrick, and by the inclusion of human sacrifices—up to eighty in one case. In fact, at least three distinct categories in burials seem evident, ranging from the sixteen royal graves to less elaborate but still richly furnished graves to the simple graves in which presumably the common people were placed.

The expenditure of such vast quantities of wealth and effort in the burials at Ur and elsewhere at this time may have acted to maintain the integrity of the economic system. Gold, silver, and other commodities are precious in most economies because of their relative scarcity and because they have to be brought in from distant places, often at great transport and processing cost. By periodically taking these items out of circulation—as in burials—the elites not only solidify their superior position by impressing the populace with their ability to com-

9.22
Crushed skull of female attendant in the death pit at Ur. Note gold jewelry and precious stones.

This Sumerian model of a goat and a tree is made of wood, lapis, and gold, and is about 51 cm high. It was found at Ur and dates to about 2600 B.C.

mand these luxuries, but also prevent devaluation of these materials through oversupply. It may have been essential for political and economic reasons that the trade routes and exchange networks established to provide these precious commodities be maintained, and if too great a surplus of these items accumulated, there would be no incentive to maintain these contacts. Whatever the conscious motives and economic and social effects of mortuary "waste," it apparently is an important element in cultural evolution, because it appears in every center of early cultural complexity.

SOUTHWEST ASIA AFTER 2350 B.C.

For centuries after 3000 B.C. the Sumerian city-states engaged in an almost constant round of internecine warfare, with first one and then another gaining temporary ascendancy. With the rise to power of Sargon of Akkad at about 2350 B.C., however, the political fabric of ancient Southwest Asia was forever changed. Sargon and his several immediate

9.23
Gypsum statuettes of an aged couple, residents at about 2500 B.C. of Nippur, one of the largest cities in southern Mesopotamia during this period.

successors used the city of Akkad as a military base from which they mounted spectacularly successful attacks in all directions. Akkadian historical documents recount thirty-four battles fought by Sargon against the southern city-states, during which he moved down the alluvium, capturing many kings, smashing city walls, and, finally, "cleansing his weapons in the sea." Sargon appointed Akkadians to administrative posts in the conquered city-states and then began expanding his other frontiers, invading Syria, Lebanon, and western Iran.

Sargon may have established an empire, in the sense of having political control over much of this area, or he may have only been able to exact tribute from the conquered people and never succeeded in achieving direct political administration. Sargon's successors, according to the texts, were forced repeatedly to reconquer areas he had invaded, indicating perhaps that only nominal control was ever exerted over the provinces.

After 2200 B.C. quarrels arose among rival claimants to the Akkadian throne, and the "empire" fragmented under the onslaught of the Martu, the Gutians, and other seminomadic peoples moving in from the highlands on the margins of the empire. We know little about this "dark age" until about 2100 B.C., when one or more Sumerian kings were able to evict the invaders and reestablish political control over much of the southern Alluvium under what has come to be known as the *Ur III dynasty*. One ruler, Ur-Nammu, established a political center at the ancient city of Ur and from there aggressively extended his influence into much of the area formerly encompassed by the Akkadians. Ur-Nammu and his successors established an orderly legal system, reorganized the political and religious administrations, and instituted many public projects to build roads, dams, and irrigation systems. Provincial governors were charged with local administration but were responsible to the central government. Great volumes of obsidian, lapis lazuli, copper, and other commodities are thought to have passed into central Mesopotamia from as far away as India and the Aegean, and local economies seem to have been highly regulated. Legal texts of the late third millennium describe in detail problems of land use, irrigation, rights, compensation for bodily injury, penalties for adultery, and many other elements of daily life.

Despite its apparent stability, the Ur III political system of the late third millennium was constantly under pressure from internal political rivalries, as well as from the incursions of nomads and rival

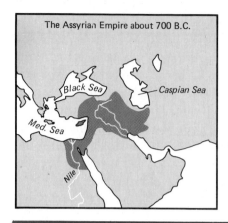
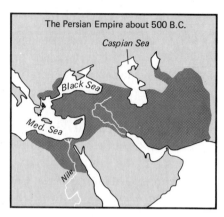

9.24
The extent of the Assyrian and Persian (Achaemenid) empires.

groups along the empire's frontiers. The coup de grace was administered at about 2004 B.C., with the invasion from western Iran of the
Elamites, who led the king of Ur away in captivity.

From about 2000 to 1800 B.C. Greater Mesopotamia was politically fragmented, as kings at Isin, Larsa, Susa, and elsewhere established contending petty states. Numerous documents from this period,
particularly from the rich archives of the city of Mari, describe endless
political maneuvers, treaties, and conflicts. Eventually the ancient city
of Babylon became the most powerful political entity and by 1792 B.C.
Hammurabi established the Babylonian Empire, based mainly on the
southern Alluvium. The many documents of his reign reflect a skillful
politician who was equally adept at bureaucratic and military means of
gaining and using political power, and his famous law code, although
not particularly enlightened by contemporary standards, was a model of
efficient social administration. Both Hammurabi and his successors encountered political and military opposition from insurgent southern
city-states and from a rival state in Assyria, to the north. As always, the
nomads and other peoples on the empire's periphery, in this case the
Kassites and Hurrians, made inroads as soon as the central government weakened, and eventually they overran much of the Babylonian
Empire.

After about 1600 B.C. the political history of Southwest Asia becomes extremely complicated, with frequent political realignments
and, overall, the gradual extension of imperial power (Figure 9.24).
Assyrians, Elamites, and other cultural groups established empires, and
eventually the political and military scale became distinctly interna-

9.25
Two bas-reliefs from Iraq, seventh century B.C. Above, a wounded lioness. Below, relief commemorating Assyrian defeat of the Elamites.

tional, as empires centered in Egypt, Anatolia, and Iran met and, more often than not, came into conflict.

Beginning in the sixth century B.C., Cyrus, Darius, Xerxes, and other kings of the *Achaemenid Empire* reached out from their homelands in highland Iran and through military conquest and astute civil administration managed to alter fundamentally the political organization of Southwest Asia. With their mobile armies, efficient bureaucracies, and nationalistic fervor, the Achaemenids conquered and placed under some degree of imperial control an area extending from India to the Aegean. Although defeated by the Greeks in several famous battles, the Achaemenids eventually used trade and political means to annex Greece and other areas that had resisted them militarily. The Achaemenid Empire was at times only a loose confederation of largely self-governing principalities, but Achaemenid kings made many innovations in civil administration and under their reigns the arts and crafts flourished. Thousands of commodities flowed across the empire along imperial highways, whose traces are still evident. So well ordered was the Achaemenid state at its peak in the fourth and fifth centuries B.C., that it was said that "a virgin with a sack of gold" could walk unmolested throughout the empire.

Like its many predecessors, the Achaemenid Empire eventually crumbled under a variety of internal and external pressures, as rival claimants to the throne warred against one another and wars of national liberation broke out among many of the diverse ethnic groups subjugated by the Achaemenids.

After about 350 B.C. the Hellenistic world had its revenge on the dynasts of the East, as first Philip and then Alexander the Great established large empires. Alexander conquered and spread Greek culture over most of the "civilized world," from southern Yugoslavia to central India. Alexander's empire, a cosmopolitan world of literature, high art, huge metropolises, an established currency, and an elaborate administrative structure, eventually fell victim to the same pressures that had dismantled empires from the time of Sargon—insurgent vassal states, nomadic incursions, and general corruption in the imperial hierarchy.

Between 300 B.C. and A.D. 225 Southwest Asia came under the control successively of the Seleucids and the Parthians, who reestablished political control over much of the areas controlled centuries previously by the Achaemenids. The Parthians, and their successors, the

Sassanians (A.D. 225–640), rose to prominence first in Iran and then through wars of conquest and political maneuvers put together empires that extended from the Mediterranean to the Indus River. Both the Parthians and Sassanians eventually came into conflict with the Roman Empire, and the numerous wars between East and West that mark the period between 150 B.C. and A.D. 650 also signal the beginnings of a truly international era in which the Old World was largely divided between three world powers: Rome, the Sassanians, and the great empires of China.

THE ORIGINS OF COMPLEX SOCIETIES IN SOUTHWEST ASIA: SUMMARY AND CONCLUSIONS

Having reviewed the evidence from Southwest Asia, let us consider how well the archaeological record accords with the various hypotheses advanced in chapter 8 to explain the origins of complex societies in general.

Agriculture

There is no indication in the Southwest Asian archaeological record that the agricultural way of life by itself led inevitably to cultural complexity. For several thousand years villagers farmed the uplands of Mesopotamia with no apparent increases in cultural complexity; only after settlement was established on the alluvium was there clear evidence of change. Moreover, as we shall see, in ancient Peru, North America, and perhaps other places there is evidence that some aspects of cultural complexity appeared before either domesticated plants and animals or agricultural economies.

Nonetheless, it is apparent that the great agricultural productivity of the southern Mesopotamian Alluvium was a primary factor in the evolution of complex cultures. Agriculture in this environment had the potential for enormous amounts of surplus food, it required a complex series of administrative decisions that could best be met by a hierarchical bureaucracy and social stratification, and along with other subsistence strategies on the alluvium, it quickly and richly rewarded occupational specialization (Athens 1977).

Thus, the analysis of the evolution of complex Mesopotamian cultures is essentially a problem of determining the factors that, *in addition* to agriculture, were responsible for this development.

Complex Irrigation Systems

A frequent nominee for the crucial link between agricultural economies and cultural complexity is complex irrigation systems, but our review of the evidence from Southwest Asia suggests that, at least as conceived by Wittfogel (p. 352), irrigation cannot be said to be the "primary cause" of early Southwest Asian cultural complexity. Activity specialization, monumental architecture, changes in settlement spacing and size hierarchies, architectural variability, mortuary stratification—in short, the whole range of physical evidence of cultural complexity—appears *before* evidence of significant extension of irrigation systems. This is true for both the heartland of Sumer and for the Susiana Plain—the two areas for which we have the best archaeological data.

In much of Southwest Asia, in fact, increased investments in irrigation systems appear to be the result of the phenomenon of urbanism (Adams 1972). Population agglomeration (urbanism) requires that the surrounding areas be particularly productive, because it is not feasible for the city dwellers either to farm or to defend areas more than several kilometers from the city. Irrigation was absolutely necessary for any sedentary existence on the alluvium, but if the spread, integration, and construction of irrigation systems were the mechanisms whereby complex societies first evolved and developed, we would expect to see a direct and positive correlation between the size and complexity of irrigation systems and the complexity of cultures based on them.

Instead, we find that Ubaid, Uruk, and early dynastic settlements subsisted on the produce of fields irrigated by relatively simple, *autonomous* canal works. Only many centuries after the appearance of the first complex societies were there complex, integrated irrigation systems.

Population Growth

Many scholars have tried to explain the origins of cultural complexity in Southwest Asia and elsewhere as mainly the result of human population growth. The persistence of this view must be seen in large part as a result of the fact that if one graphs the approximate population of Greater Mesopotamia from about 8000 B.C. to about 3000 B.C. against evidence of activity specialization, monumental architecture, agricultural productivity, and the other evidences of cultural complexity, then an impressively close correlation is apparent. In the *long run* there *is* an obvious statistical relationship between these variables. One can't have an empire with 250 people. Furthermore, it makes a sort of intuitive sense that as you get more people, communities need more and more complex structures to feed and organize them.

But how can population growth be *directly* related to the evolution of cultural complexity?

> Eventually, though there were important local variations in the pattern, the inhabitants of Greater Mesopotamia began to reach the limits of colonization as a solution to the population problem given existing subsistence systems. At this point a trend toward intensification on all levels appeared, including improvements in the irrigation system and a shortened fallow period. In time and in certain circumstances the amount of land available for cultivation actually began to decline. Conflict became more common. Both factors accelerated the need for intensification. When and where the pressures were the greatest urbanism appeared on the scene as a means of organizing and controlling the increased population, and the labor force which made that intensification possible. In time there followed royal kings and empires. (Young 1972: 838–39)

Thus Young's hypothesis rests on both population growth and on environmental circumscription (as defined by Carneiro, p. 357). Young sees Carneiro's concept of environmental circumscription as providing the immediate reason why intensification of production and, eventually, conflict occurred, and with them, cultural complexity. This explanation has at least the virtue of having straightforward test implications. If it is correct, we should expect to find the following categories of archaeological evidence in Greater Mesopotamia:

1. There should be an increase in population density in and adjacent to those areas where the first complex communities developed.

2. The first complex societies should occur in environmentally circumscribed areas.

3. Technological innovations and intensification of agriculture should correlate with increasing population density.

4. Population declines should be rare except as a result of epidemic disease, large-scale warfare, or massive environmental deterioration.

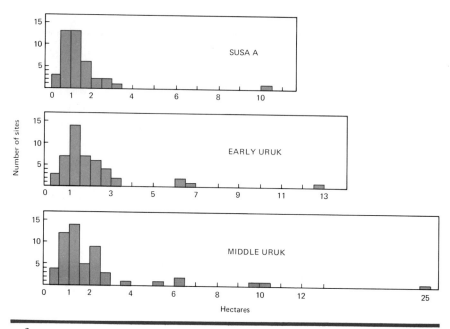

9.26

Histograms of site sizes on the Susiana Plain (southwestern Iran) during the periods of early state formation. Note the larger number of intermediate and large settlements during the Early and Middle Uruk periods, when the first states evolved.

> 5. We should find walled settlements, mass burials, and other evidence of conflict, and these should correlate in time and place with increasing population densities (Cowgill 1975).

Although it is difficult to estimate ancient populations, some careful attempts have been made, and they seem to indicate that the proposed relationship between population densities and cultural complexity in ancient Southwest Asia does not occur. Consider Wright and Johnson's settlement statistics for the Susiana Plain in southwestern Iran (Table 9.1, Figure 9.26) truly a circumscribed area, where some of the earliest Near Eastern complex societies occurred.

> The available data show that there was a period of population decline prior to state formation. States emerged perhaps during a period of unsettled conditions as population climbed back toward its former level. As Carneiro suggested, warfare may have a role in state formation, but in this case, increasing population in a circumscribed area cannot be the sole or direct cause of such warfare. If the hypothesis that population increase was the primary cause of state formation were correct, the state should have emerged in Susiana times [before 4000 B.C.] because population in that period seems to have been as high as in early Uruk times [3700 B.C.]. (1975: 276)

The Susiana Plain, however, is an area where rainfall agriculture is possible, and there are some questions about the reliability of Wright and Johnson's population estimates (Weiss 1975). What about the southern Mesopotamian Alluvium, the Sumerian heartland? On the basis of more than two decades of archaeological survey in Mesopotamia, Robert Adams concluded that

> possibly the attainment of some minimal population level was necessary to set the process [of urbanization] into motion. But such evidence as there is suggests that appreciable population increases generally followed, rather than preceded, the core processes of the Urban Revolution. Particularly in Mesopotamia, where the sedentary village pattern seems to have been stabilized for several millennia between the establishment of effective food production and the "take-off" into urbanism, it may be noted that there is simply no evidence for gradual population increases that might have helped to precipitate the Urban Revolution. (1966: 44–45)

Adams here is principally concerned with the phenomenon of urbanism, rather than complex societies in general, but his "Urban Revolution" includes many of the essential transitions we have defined as the basis for the evolution of complex societies.

What about agricultural intensification? In Carneiro's scheme this is a direct result of population pressure; thus we should find evidence of increasingly intensive irrigation and of farming of marginal lands just before, and along with, the evolution of cultural complexity. In-

TABLE 9.1   Environment and Settlement Characteristics of Three Lowland Plains in Southwestern Iran*

	Deh Luran	Susiana	Ram Hormuz
Area in Square Kilometers	940	2280	445
Hectares Site/100 km² Level Land			
Susiana d (c. 5000 B.C.)	6.4	6.2	4.0
Susa A	2.7	3.9	1.0
Terminal Susa A	.5	2.2	.3
Early Uruk	3.0	6.5	.5
Middle Uruk	3.2	8.5	1.0
Late Uruk (c. 3200 B.C.)	1.0	3.5	.5

* The first states, as defined by Wright and Johnson, appeared in the early Uruk period.

Source   H. T. Wright and G. A. Johnson. 1975. "Population, Exchange, and Early State Formation in Southwestern Iran," *American Anthropologist.* 77: 276.

sufficient research has been done here to decide the issue absolutely, but major investments in irrigation and land reclamation seem to have occurred *after* the emergence of urbanism and other evidences of cultural complexity, and, as Adams notes, urbanization seems to have involved the widespread *abandonment* of large areas of formerly intensively farmed lands. Furthermore, there is no evidence that any of the areas of early state formation ever approached their agricultural limits: that is, with only minor investments in additional irrigation systems they could have enormously increased the numbers of people who could be supported; yet the population size remained quite stable. In short, agricultural intensification seems to have been more a result than a cause of the emergence of complex societies.

What about evidence of warfare, the other component in Carneiro's hypothesis? Given the ambiguities of the archaeological record and the difficulty in demonstrating the existence of warfare from archaeological data, perhaps the most significant thing we can point to is the presence or absence of substantial city walls. One might expect that with the cheapness of clay construction there would be many more walled settlements in the early civilizations, if warfare were a frequent curse. The walling of towns does occur very soon after the emergence of urbanism, and warfare may have played a significant role in the major increases of cultural complexity that *followed* the earliest "states," but extensive circumvallation of sites is common on the southern Alluvium mainly after about 2900 B.C.—some centuries after the appearance of other evidence of cultural complexity.

Given the difficulties of demonstrating warfare archaeologically, however, its importance in the formation of the first Southwest Asian complex societies must remain moot.

Class Conflict—The Marxian Model

According to some Marxian economic historians (p. 362), the first Southwest Asian states formed because (1) differential fertility of farming land and technological progress produced wealth differentials and increased trade; (2) agricultural surpluses and increased production of craft goods intensified wealth differences between people and produced *classes* of traders, entrepreneurs, profiteers, and exploited workers; and (3) the state developed as a coercive instrument to protect the rich from the more numerous poor, and the rich subverted law and religion to prop up their privileged position (Service 1975: 269).

The state of archaeological research does not permit us to evaluate all aspects of the Marxian paradigm, but on balance it does not seem to agree with what we know of ancient Mesopotamia, or of other areas of early complex society formation. After an extensive review of the problem, Service concluded that

> there is absolutely no evidence in the early archaic civilizations themselves, nor in archaeologically or historically known chiefdoms and primitive states, of any important private dealings—i.e., evidence of the dominance of capitalism. There are, to be sure, important exchanges of goods, but these are accomplished by primitive reciprocities and complex redistribution, not by entrepreneurs. The bureaucracy itself manages the important production and exchange, and of course uses a proportion of the production to maintain itself and to subsidize its own court-temple economy. (1975: 283)

The disparity between the Marxian position and the position of Service is partly definitional. The criteria we consider essential to complex societies, such as settlement pattern changes, monumental architecture, and occupational specialization, were already fully developed in central Mesopotamia by about 3500 B.C. Diakonov and other Marxian scholars, however, base their definition of the emergence of "states" on information from written texts, which appear in quantity only after 3000 B.C. To be sure, these texts do record some "capitalistic" elements in these societies, such as the sale of land from one person to another for silver, barley, or some other commodity; but this does not mean that the same "capitalistic" elements were present between 4500 and 3500 B.C. when other elements of cultural complexity first appeared.

Even if there were some private sales of land in the period between 4500 and 3500 B.C., this would not prove the Marxian thesis. In the years after 3000 B.C., for example, private land ownership—if it existed at all—was only a limited part of the agricultural system. Most land was apparently owned by the temple community and by kinship groups, and the amount of actual private enterprise and entrepreneurship was very limited. The picture many scholars draw of these communities, even after 3000 B.C., is one of a great deal of cooperation and redistribution of goods through the temples and palaces and not of armed insurrections against exploitative profiteers.

It should be noted that according to the Marxian model, a successful state is one in which actual physical class conflict is suppressed—that is, people in different classes are antagonistic but do not actually

fight. The difficulties of dealing with such potential conflicts archaeologically are obvious, but, to repeat, most information suggests that
early states were tied by religious and kinship bonds, not coercion or
conflict.

Trade

Recently some theorists (e.g., Rathje 1973) have argued that long-
distance trade in material goods was a key to the initial evolution of
cultural complexity in at least some areas. Most hypotheses about the
importance of trade imply the following sequence: (1) people move
into some areas, begin farming, and develop needs for materials that
can only be obtained by importing them from distant places (for example, the need for flint and grinding stone on the southern Alluvium); (2) such trade becomes essential to the economy, because trade
is necessary to deal with the pressure of population growth—or for some
other reason—and it becomes so voluminous and vital that administrators are needed to control and direct it; (3) these administrators either
become wealthier than their fellow citizens or have more political
power, and eventually gain control of all aspects of the society, and
thus complex societies are born.

Besides being incomplete as an explanation of the origins of cultural complexity, there is little in Southwest Asian prehistory to support this syllogism. In a survey of sites from several places on the Mesopotamian Alluvium and in western Iran, Wright and Johnson found
that bitumen, copper, shell, basalt, alabaster, obsidian, copper, chert
(flint) and other imported commodities appeared in increased quantities only *after* state-level political systems had appeared (1975: 277–79).
If trade were ever the driving force behind cultural evolution, one
would expect it to have been so in Mesopotamia, since even the stone
needed for simple agricultural implements had to be imported; but
there is no evidence that trade volumes increased drastically before the
emergence of complex societies. The early Mesopotamian cities imported enough chert to make sickle blades, but they used baked clay
for the sickles—and for virtually everything else. Once the complex administration institutions were developed, however, trade became extremely important, and with the first texts we get impressive accounts
of trade in hundreds of commodities. As early as 3000 B.C., sailing
ships probably worked the rivers and the coast, perhaps as far as Bahrain, Iran, and Afghanistan.

Although there is no evidence that the need for long-distance trade was the key to the development of Southwest Asian societies, we cannot dismiss regional trade as of *no* importance in this process. Products such as salt or the meat, milk, and hides of the animals of the highland pastoralists may have been extremely important in the evolution of lowland societies, but it would be very difficult to demonstrate this archaeologically: most of the products involved simply wouldn't survive in material form. Wright (1977) and Hole (1977) are currently involved in trying to gauge the level of lowland-highland economic interaction at the crucial period of complex society formation, and these studies may help us resolve this question.

Decision-Making and the Evolution of Mesopotamian Cultures

Recently, Wright and Johnson (1975) have introduced a model for the evolution of Southwest Asian cultures that differs in several respects from those we have discussed. First, instead of trying to formulate a model for the change from simple agriculturalists to fully developed complex societies, they have been principally concerned with the origins of the "state," which they define as a society with at least three levels of hierarchically arranged, specialized administrators. For example, in a simple agricultural village such as still exists in many parts of Southwest Asia, Latin America, and elsewhere, there are many decisions to be made about what crops to plant, how much of the harvest is to be stored, who gets what share of the land, who marries whom, and so forth. Many of these decisions are made by individuals, but some of those which directly affect the whole community are made by a village headman. We might say, then, that this village headman represents the first level of the decision-making hierarchy—he directs the activities of others who do the work. A second level of administrative hierarchy would exist if there were people charged with coordinating the activities of these village headmen and correcting or approving their decisions—perhaps government agents charged with taxing and administering local affairs. Such agents would be under a third administrative level, and additional levels may exist above this.

Wright and Johnson suggest that: (1) the ancient state can be defined as a society with at least three such levels of specialized administrators; (2) the effectiveness of such societies and their dominance over other societal forms is tied to their ability to store and process information and make correct decisions at specific points along the control hierarchy; and (3) it is possible to demonstrate archaeologically the initial changes from societies with one or two levels of decision-making institutions to those with three or more.

In a series of extensive archaeological survey programs they have examined some of the areas where the first Mesopotamian states developed, trying to locate specific evidence for this change. One type of evidence was the actual administrative "documents" themselves. In most of Mesopotamia at this time the administration of people and goods was facilitated by using pieces of inscribed stone to impress clay with signs of authorization. These stones were usually either in the form of "stamps," used like the rubber stamps of today, or cylinders that were rolled across the clay to make an impression, and they varied in size and in the complexity of the symbols incised on them. Fortunately, the clay impressed with these seals, and the seals themselves, are often preserved in archaeological sites, and they can be used to infer the levels of administration in these extinct societies. The impressed clay can be divided into two classes. *Commodity sealings* were used to prevent the opening of a container such as a vessel, basket, bale, or storeroom. They were made by placing a lump of clay over a knot which had to be untied to gain access to the container, so that unauthorized entry could be detected. Discarded commodity sealings indicate the receipt of stored or redistributed goods. Other seals are termed *message sealings* and convey or store facts about goods or people. Some of these are plain counters whose shape indicates a numerical unit, others (*bullae*) are small spheroidal jackets which were once wrapped around sets of counters, and still others are flat rectangular "tablets" stamped with numerical symbols (Wright and Johnson 1975: 271). Writings, as we know it, did not exist until after the state, as defined by Wright and Johnson, emerged, but these stamps and seals obviously conveyed a great deal of information.

In one study focusing on the Susiana Plain, Wright and Johnson used the number of commodity or message sealings found at specific sites to reconstruct some aspects of the production, transport, and administration of goods. They concluded that they could determine when the change was made from one- and two-level decision-making institutions to the three levels which define the state.

Wright and Johnson also analyzed the locational arrangement of the settlements in southwestern Iran and found that after about 3600

B.C. there were trends toward more regular spacing of settlements and the emergence of distinctive site size groupings—both of which are consistent with the change from a two-level to a three-level control hierarchy. They concluded:

> This pattern of developing settlement arrangements correlated with changes in the technology of administration is apparently not unique to southwestern Iran. The transition seems to occur in several adjacent regions in Iraq between [3700 B.C. and 3250 B.C.] around the ancient centers of Nippur, Nineveh, and Uruk. . . . Thus rather than one case of state emergence, there was a series of emergences of individual states in a network of politics. (1975: 273–74)

In trying to explain why this shift came about, Wright and Johnson propose that several factors were probably involved. Decisions involving problems posed by drought, overpopulation, conflict, or some other single factor could probably be handled by a two-level hierarchy—something on the order of a chiefdom, perhaps—but a combination of problems would require additional decision-making capacity. They suspect that one important factor in early Southwest Asian state formation may have been the economic interactions between nomadic pastoralists and lowland farmers, probably in the form of the exchange of cheese, rugs, meat, and other highland resources for pottery, grain, and other lowland commodities. Economic models suggest that fluctuating demand for certain craft products in relatively simple economies often stimulates the centralization of workshops and economic administration (Kochen and Deutsch 1970), and Wright and Johnson believe that in prehistoric Mesopotamia the economic demands of nomads on lowland economies may have fluctuated sufficiently to produce a similar effect, with the eventual emergence of a three-level hierarchy.

Generally, then, Wright and Johnson propose a multifactor model for early state formation in Southwest Asia, a model that examines the conditions under which the gathering, storage, retrieval, and implementation of information took place. They suggest that the factors operating to change these levels of information processing may vary from place to place, but that the essence of complex society formation is the evolution of these administrative institutions.

In this regard their analysis is very similar to one proposed earlier (1964) by Robert McC. Adams, who stressed the multivariate nature of the evolution of Mesopotamian cultures. Adams laid particular emphasis (Figure 8.1) on the importance of administrative systems in meeting the demands of herding, food collecting, fishing, and farming, and he attempted to chart how these activities, in concert with warfare, could have produced "great families" and class-based, rather than kin-based, societies. Adams's model is difficult to test archaeologically, because it involves so many elements in complex patterns of interaction, but it may very well be an accurate description of at least some of the important variables in the appearance of the first Mesopotamian states.

In conclusion, then, our review of the evidence and hypotheses relating to the first complex Mesopotamian societies indicates that no single factor "explains" these origins, and it is beginning to appear that this problem will be resolved only through more research and perhaps a drastic rethinking of our hypotheses about the general origins and mechanics of cultural complexity.

Bibliography

Abu es-Soof, B. 1968. "Tell Es-Sawwan Excavations of the Fourth Season (Spring 1967). Interim Report." *Sumer.* 24: 3–16.

Adams, Robert McC. 1955. "Developmental Stages in Ancient Mesopotamia." In *Irrigation Civilizations: A Comparative Study,* ed. Julian H. Steward. Washington, D.C.: Pan-American Union, Social Science Monographs.

———. 1965. *Land Behind Baghdad.* Chicago: University of Chicago Press.

———. 1966. *The Evolution of Urban Society: Early Mesopotamia and Prehispanic Mexico.* Chicago: Aldine.

———. 1972. "Patterns of Urbanization in Early Southern Mesopotamia." In *Man, Settlement and Urbanism,* eds. P. G. Ucko, R. Tringham, and G. Dimbleby. London: Duckworth.

———. 1975. "The Mesopotamian Social Landscape: A View from the Frontier." In *Reconstructing Complex Societies.* Supplement to the Bulletin of the American Schools of Oriental Research, no. 20.

Adams, Robert McC. and H. Nissen. 1972. *The Uruk Countryside.* Chicago: University of Chicago Press.

Athens, J. Stephen. 1977. "Theory Building and the Study of Evolutionary Process in Complex Societies." In *For Theory Building in Archaeology.* New York: Academic Press.

Bloomfield, Leonard. 1956. *Language History.* New York: Holt.

Bottero, Jean, Elena Cassin, and Jean Vercoutter, eds. 1967. *The Near East: The Early Civilizations,* trans. R. F. Tannenbaum. New York: Delacorte Press.

Buck, R. C. 1956. "On the Logic of General Behavior Systems Theory." In *The Foundations of Science and the Concept of Psychology and Psychoanalysis,* eds.

Herbert Feigl and Michael Scriven. Minnesota Studies in the Philosophy of Science. 1: 223–28.

Butzer, Karl W. 1971. *Environment and Archaeology: An Ecological Approach to Prehistory.* Chicago: Aldine.

Cowgill, George. 1975. "On Causes and Consequences of Ancient and Modern Population Changes." *American Anthropologist.* 77(3): 505–25.

Daniel, G. 1968. *The First Civilizations.* London: Thames and Hudson.

Diakonoff, Igor M., ed. 1969. *Ancient Mesopotamia.* Moscow: "Nauka" Publishing House.

Diringer, David. 1962. *Writing.* New York: Praeger.

Eliot, Henry Ware, Jr. 1950. *Excavations in Mesopotamia and Western Iran: Sites of 4000–5000 B.C.* Special Publication of the Peabody Museum of American Archaeology and Ethnology. Cambridge, Mass.

Flannery, Kent V. 1972. "The Cultural Evolution of Civilizations." *Annual Review of Ecology and Systematics.* 3: 399–426.

Frankfort, Henri. 1956. *The Birth of Civilization in the Near East.* Garden City, N.Y.: Doubleday.

Gelb, Ignace J. 1952. *A Study of Writing: The Foundations of Grammatology.* Chicago: University of Chicago Press.

Gibson, McGuire. 1972. "Population Shift and the Rise of Mesopotamian Civilization." In *The Explanation of Cultural Change: Models in Prehistory,* ed. C. Renfrew. London: Duckworth.

Hamblin, Dora Jane, et al. 1973. *The First Cities.* New York: Time-Life.

Hole, Frank. 1977. "Pastoral Nomadism in Western Iran." In *Explorations in Ethnoarchaeology,* ed. R. A. Gould. Albuquerque: University of New Mexico Press.

Jacobsen, T. and R. Adams. 1958. "Salt and Silt in Mesopotamian Agriculture." *Science.* 128: 1251–58.

Jawad, Abdul Jalil. 1965. *The Advent of the Era of Townships in Northern Mesopotamia.* Leiden: E. J. Brill.

Johnson, Gregory A. 1973. *Local Exchange and Early State Development in Southwestern Iran.* Museum of Anthropology, Anthropological Papers, University of Michigan, no. 51. Ann Arbor.

———. 1975a. "Locational Analysis and the Investigation of Uruk Local Exchange Systems." In *Ancient Civilization and Trade,* eds. J. Sabloff and C. Lamberg-Karlovsky. Albuquerque: University of New Mexico Press.

———. 1975b. "Early State Organization in Southwestern Iran: Preliminary Field Report." *Proceedings of the 4th Annual Symposium on Archaeological Research in Iran.* Teheran.

———. 1977. "Aspects of Regional Analysis in Archaeology." *Annual Review of Anthropology.* 6: 479–508.

Kenyon, Kathleen. 1969–70. "The Origins of the Neolithic." *The Advancement of Science.* 26: 1–17.

King, Leonard W. 1968. *A History of Sumer and Akkad.* New York: Greenwood Press.

Kochen, Manfred and Karl W. Deutsch. 1970. "Decentralization and Uneven Service Loads." *Journal of Regional Science.* 10: 2.

Kramer, Samuel Noah. 1959. *History Begins at Sumer.* Garden City, N.Y.: Doubleday.

Lamberg-Karlovsky, C. C. 1975. "Third Millennium Models of Exchange and Modes of Production." In *Ancient Civilization and Trade,* eds. J. Sabloff and C. Lamberg-Karlovsky. Albuquerque: University of New Mexico Press.

Lees, G. M. and N. L. Falcon. 1952. "The Geographical History of the Mesopotamian Plains." *Geographical Journal.* 68(2): 24–39. London: Royal Geographical Society.

Lees, Susan H. and Daniel G. Bates. 1974. "The Origins of Specialized Nomadic Pastoralism: A Systematic Model." *American Antiquity.* 30(2): 187–93.

Lloyd, Seton. 1963. *Mounds of the Near East.* Edinburgh: Edinburgh University Press.

Mallowan, Sir Max E. L. 1965. *Early Mesopotamia and Iran.* London: Thames and Hudson.

Mellaart, James. 1965. *Earliest Civilizations of the Near East.* London: Thames and Hudson.

————. 1975. *The Neolithic of the Near East.* London: Thames and Hudson.

Mitchell, W. 1973. "The Hydraulic Hypothesis: A Reappraisal." *Current Anthropology.* 4: 532–34.

Nissen, Hans. 1972. "The City Wall of Uruk." In *The Explanation of Cultural Change: Models in Prehistory,* ed. C. Renfrew. London: Duckworth.

Oates, Joan. 1976. "Prehistory in Northeastern Arabia." *Antiquity.* 50(197): 20–31.

Oppenheim, A. L. 1964. *Ancient Mesopotamia: Portrait of a Dead Civilization.* Chicago: University of Chicago Press.

Perkins, Ann Louise. 1949. *The Comparative Archaeology of Early Mesopotamia.* Studies in Ancient Oriental Civilization, no. 25. Chicago: University of Chicago Press.

Polanyi, Karl, Harry Pearson, and C. M. Ahrensburg. 1957. *Trade and Market in the Early Empires.* New York: Free Press of Glencoe.

Rathje, William L. 1973. "Classic Maya Development and Denouement: A Research Design." In *The Classic Maya Collapse,* ed. T. P. Culbert. Albuquerque: University of New Mexico Press.

Renfrew, Colin. 1975. *The Emergence of Civilization.* London: Methuen.

Renfrew, Colin, ed. 1972. *The Explanation of Cultural Change: Models in Prehistory.* London: Duckworth.

Roux, George. 1976. *Ancient Iraq.* Baltimore: Penguin.

Sabloff, J. and C. C. Lamberg-Karlovsky, eds. 1975. *Ancient Civilization and Trade.* Albuquerque: University of New Mexico Press.

Sanders, James A., ed. 1970. *Near Eastern Archaeology in the Twentieth Century* (Essays in Honor of Nelson Blueck). Garden City, N.Y.: Doubleday.

Service, Elman R. 1962. *Primitive Social Organization.* New York: Random House.

———. 1975. *Origins of the State and Civilization.* New York: W. W. Norton.

Smith, Philip E. L. and T. Cuyler Young, Jr. 1972. "The Evolution of Early Agriculture and Culture in Greater Mesopotamia: A Trial Model." In *Population Growth: Anthropological Implications,* ed. Brian Spooner. Cambridge, Mass.: MIT Press.

Spooner, Brian, ed. 1972. *Population Growth: Anthropological Implications.* Cambridge, Mass.: MIT Press.

Steward, Julian H. 1949. "Cultural Causality and Law: A Trial Formulation of the Development of Early Civilizations." *American Anthropologist.* 51: 1–27.

Tosi, Maurizio. 1972. "The Early Urban Revolution and Settlement Pattern in the Indo-European Borderland." In *The Explanation of Cultural Change: Models in Prehistory,* ed. C. Renfrew. London: Duckworth.

Ucko, P., G. Dimbleby, and R. Tringham, eds. 1972. *Man, Settlement and Urbanism.* London: Duckworth.

Webb, M. 1975. "The Flag Follows Trade: An Essay on the Necessary Integration of Military and Commercial Factors in State Formation." In *Ancient Civilization and Trade,* eds. J. Sabloff and C. C. Lamberg-Karlovsky. Albuquerque: University of New Mexico Press.

Weiss, Harvey and T. Cuyler Young, Jr. 1975. "The Merchants of Susa." *Iran.* 13: 1–17.

Wheeler, Mortimer. 1959. *Early India and Pakistan.* London: Thames and Hudson.

White, Leslie. 1949. *The Science of Culture.* New York: Grove Press.

Wittfogel, Karl W. 1957. *Oriental Despotism: A Comparative Study Total Power.* New Haven: Yale University Press.

Wolf, Eric. 1966. *Peasants.* Englewood Cliffs, N.J.: Prentice-Hall.

Woolley, Sir Leonard. 1965. *Excavations at Ur.* New York: T. Y. Crowell.

Wright, Henry T. 1969. *The Administration of Rural Production in an Early Mesopotamian Town.* Museum of Anthropology, Anthropological Papers, University of Michigan, no. 38. Ann Arbor.

———. 1977. "Recent Research on the Origin of the State." *Annual Review of Anthropology.* 6: 379–97.

Wright, Henry T. and Gregory A. Johnson. 1975. "Population, Exchange, and Early State Formation in Southwestern Iran." *American Anthropologist.* 77(2): 267–89.

Yasin, Walid. 1970. "Excavation at Tell Es-Sawwan, 1969 (6th season)." *Sumer.* 26: 3–11.

Young, T. Cuyler, Jr. 1972. "Population Densities and Early Mesopotamian Origins." In *Man, Settlement and Urbanism,* eds. P. J. Ucko, R. Trigham, and G. W. Dimbleby. London: Duckworth.

10

Early Complex Societies
in Anatolia, Greece, and
Temperate Europe

Agricola gave . . . official assistance to the building of temples, public squares, and . . . man-
sions. . . . He trained the sons of the chiefs in
the liberal arts. . . . And so the Britons were
gradually led on to the amenities that make vice
agreeable—arcades, baths, sumptuous banquets.
They spoke of such novelties as "civilization,"
when really they were only a feature of enslave-
ment.

Tacitus

"Civilization" is sometimes imagined as having developed independently in Mesopotamia and Egypt and subsequently having spread
through trade contacts, military expeditions, and cultural borrowing
to Anatolia, the Aegean and Mediterranean countries, and western Europe. But it is now apparent that, important as Mesopotamian and
Egyptian influences were, the early complex societies of Anatolia,
Greece, and temperate Europe must also be understood as the results
of local and regional factors, not solely as faint imitations of the ancient
civilizations of the East.

The rise of these societies in the West is a many-faceted subject,
and a detailed review of the relevant archaeological evidence is far be-

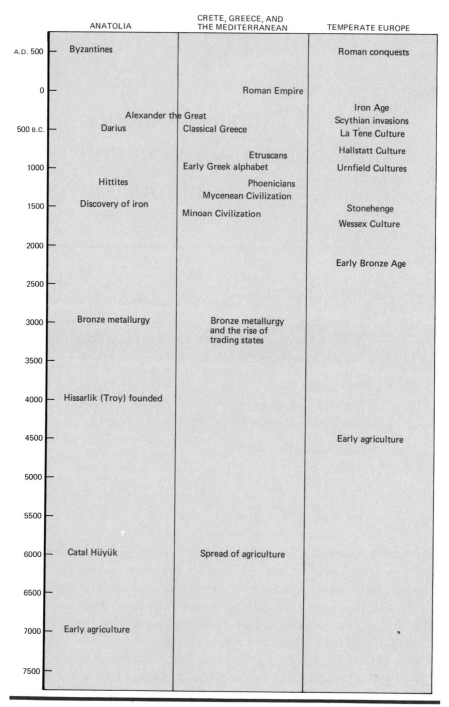

	ANATOLIA	CRETE, GREECE, AND THE MEDITERRANEAN	TEMPERATE EUROPE
A.D. 500	Byzantines		Roman conquests
0		Roman Empire	
500 B.C.	Alexander the Great Darius	Classical Greece	Iron Age Scythian invasions La Tène Culture
1000	Hittites	Etruscans Early Greek alphabet Phoenicians	Hallstatt Culture Urnfield Cultures
1500	Discovery of iron	Mycenean Civilization Minoan Civilization	Stonehenge Wessex Culture
2000			Early Bronze Age
2500			
3000	Bronze metallurgy	Bronze metallurgy and the rise of trading states	
3500			
4000	Hissarlik (Troy) founded		
4500			Early agriculture
5000			
5500			
6000	Catal Hüyük	Spread of agriculture	
6500			
7000	Early agriculture		
7500			

10.1

Chronological correlation of cultures in the Aegean area, Egypt, and Europe.

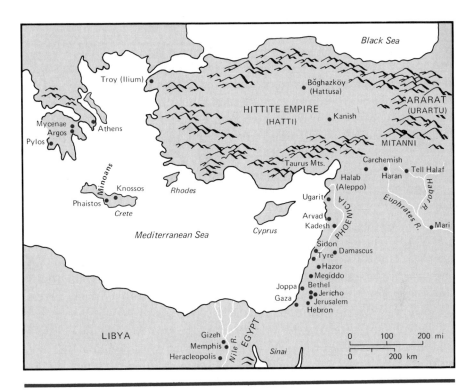

10.2
Anatolia and the Levant evolved complex societies shortly after comparable developments in Mesopotamia.

yond the scope of this chapter; nonetheless, these early Western complex societies provide in some aspects instructive contrasts and comparisons with parallel developments in Mesopotamia.

Anatolia and the Levant

As we noted in the previous chapter, the early farming villages of Anatolia and the Levant, such as Çatal Hüyük and Jericho, were among the largest and architecturally most impressive agricultural communities in the world for their time; even as late as 4000 B.C., some Anatolian communities were only slightly less complexly structured than their Mesopotamian contemporaries. At Hissarlik (ancient Troy) in northwestern Anatolia (Figure 10.2), for example, the settlement at 4000 B.C. was equipped with a sizable "public hall" and impressive stone fortifications. Later, between about 3000 and 2000 B.C., the *Early Bronze Age,* Anatolian peoples, while not matching the brilliant developments of the contemporary Sumerian civilization, were nevertheless evolving increasingly complex societal and economic forms. They conducted an extensive trade in bronze, copper, silver, obsidian, and many other raw materials, which they worked into extraordinarily beautiful artifacts for export to Mesopotamia and more distant regions. At Troy, Alaca Hüyük, and other Early Bronze Age settlements, the populace constructed large assembly halls, rich tombs, and other elements indicative of evolving cultural complexity. The contents and location of many of these settlements suggest that a powerful factor in their evolution was long-distance trade, coordinated by a class of rich warrior chieftians whose military and commercial interests ranged from Cyprus, across Anatolia, and far into Mesopotamia (Renfrew 1972).

During and after the *Middle Bronze Age* (ca. 2000 to 1700 B.C.), Anatolia was linked to the states and empires of Mesopotamia by large trading outposts, such as the one at Kanesh (Kultepe), where many cuneiform tablets documenting a flourishing trade in copper and other commodities have been recovered (Özgüç 1972).

The first large state in Anatolia was probably created by the Hittites, toward the end of the second millennium B.C. Through warfare, alliances, and administrative innovations they managed to put together a wealthy and powerful empire, centered at the city of Boghazkoy (see Figure 10.2). Hittite archives, written in cuneiform script in the Hittites' Indo-European language, record their complex relationships with neighboring powers, including their devastation of Babylon and their wars with Egypt for control of the Levantine coast.

The rise of civilization along the Levantine coast, or "Palestine," was somewhat belated, at least compared to developments in Greater Mesopotamia. Pottery manufacture, copperworking, and other crafts were not common in Palestine until late in the fifth millennium B.C., and written languages there were heavily influenced by Mesopotamian scripts. As the Old Testament and other documents tell us, the Israelites were able to establish an independent kingdom in Palestine between about 1000 and 900 B.C. But for the most part Palestine was a pawn in power struggles between the Egyptians and the Hittites, and later the Assyrians. In northern Palestine, the Phoenicians, the coastal branch of the Canaanite peoples who originally settled Palestine, erected a major state based on their control of trade along the eastern Mediterranean shore.

There were many rich and powerful Phoenician cities in the first and early second millennia B.C., but the arid, mountainous terrain of Palestine did not have the agricultural productivity to support regional empires capable of competing directly with the power centers in Egypt, Anatolia, or Mesopotamia.

Greece and the Aegean

The Aegean world, including the southern Greek mainland, the Peloponnese, central Greece, Thessaly, Crete, the Cyclades, and other Aegean islands (Figure 10.3), is an extraordinarily beautiful area that also produced civilizations of great creativity and influence. But compared to Mesopotamia and Egypt, the Aegean world has little fresh water or fertile land, and this limited agricultural potential is the major reason cultural complexity came relatively late here and was based mainly on trade and craft production.

Between 6000 and 3000 B.C. the agricultural way of life spread throughout the Aegean area, and the general trend of cultural development apparently paralleled that in Mesopotamia: some villages, mainly those in the more productive agricultural areas or along important trade routes, became larger and more complex socially. In Thessaly in the fourth millennium, for example, several settlements included centrally located houses that were larger and more elaborate than others—implying some status distinctions—and some of these communities were protected by fortification walls and ditches, reflecting, perhaps, increasing competition for land and control of trade networks.

Between 3000 and 2000 B.C. (the Early Bronze Age), while Sumerian civilization was flourishing on the Mesopotamian Alluvium, communities on the Greek mainland, Crete, and other large islands were also evolving wealthy, highly stratified societies. The introduction (perhaps from Anatolia) of bronze metallurgy at about 3000 B.C. may have been a factor in this process, but bronze was only one of many commodities of great commercial importance at this time. Gold, silver, salt, marble, obsidian, lapis lazuli, ceramics, and many other commodities were being circulated in large quantities all over the Aegean, at

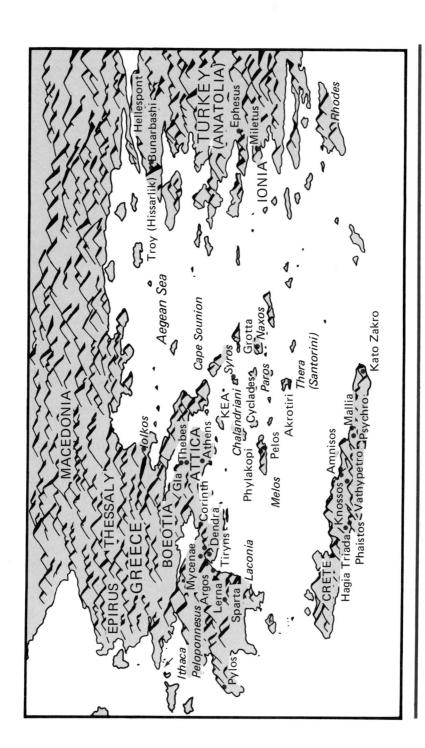

10.3
Important sites in the Aegean world.

first on simple oar-driven boats, but by the late third millennium B.C. on large merchant vessels equipped with sails.

At Lerma and elsewhere on the Greek mainland massive defensive walls and towers protected towns and their centrally located "palaces," which were large one- or two-storied rectangular buildings that apparently functioned as residences for chiefs and as centers for the collection, storage, and redistribution of agricultural produce and craft goods. Early Bronze Age settlements on Crete and the other islands were also impressive, and throughout the Aegean world during the third millennium B.C. investments in public architecture increased and status differences in residential quarters were elaborated. Occupational specialization, too, was on the rise, as potters, stonemasons, sailors, bronzesmiths, farmers, herders, and other specialists were required to support individual communities, in turn giving rise to administrative hierarchies to coordinate these complex local economies.

Wealth and status distinctions are also reflected in burial practices during the late third millennium B.C., particularly on Crete, where large communal tombs were built out of cut stone blocks. The dead of successive generations of large families were deposited in the same mortuary centers, often with rich collections of personal items, such as seals, bronze jewelry and weapons, and beautifully painted pottery (Figure 10.4).

Late in the third millennium B.C., many settlements on the southern mainland and on some of the islands were destroyed by fire, perhaps following severe earthquakes, and the radically different architectural and mortuary styles of the next construction phase at these settlements may indicate an invasion by northern people or else simply a change in local styles.

In the first half of the second millennium B.C. the developmental focus of the Aegean was the *Minoan* culture on Crete, whose rich cities controlled a major share of the lucrative Aegean and Mediterranean trade routes. Crete seems to have escaped the foreign incursions that disrupted life on the Greek mainland toward the end of the third millennium, and while it was no doubt influenced by the many cultures with which it traded, Minoan civilization did not develop as an "introduction" from the outside (Renfrew 1972).

Large settlements with elaborate palaces and elite residences were constructed at Knossos, Phaestus, Mallia, and elsewhere on Crete shortly after 2000 B.C., and Cretan ships carried ceramics and other

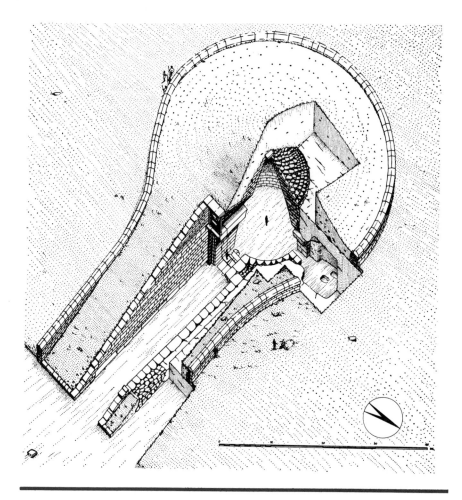

10.4
The Treasury of Atreus reflects the extravagant mortuary cults of early Aegean civilizations. Mycenean kings were buried with masses of gold and other precious commodities in these royal tombs.

local products to Syria, Cyprus, and Egypt. Cretan bronzeworking in ornaments and weapons was also known and admired throughout the Mediterranean and Aegean worlds.

At about 1700 B.C., the palaces at Knossos, Mallia, Phaestus, and other Cretan cities were either damaged or destroyed by a variety of calamities, including perhaps earthquakes (recorded in stratigraphy at Levantine sites of this period) or invasions. Rebuilding and expansion of surviving centers commenced soon after these disasters, however, and over the next 200 years Crete was the center of a powerful, wealthy, and creative civilization. Great palaces, several stories high, were con-

structed with cut stone and mud mortar and surrounded with elite residences, wide-paved public squares, and storehouses. Larger settlements
were equipped with cobblestone streets, sidewalks, and municipal
drainage systems. Cretan society of this period boasted master artists
in bronze and gold working, gem-stone cutting, and, especially, wall
painting. Using brilliant primary colors and painting directly on still
wet plaster walls, Cretan artists covered palace walls and perhaps ceil-
ings with images of leaping bulls, birds, monkeys, goats, flowers, and
imaginative depictions of goddesses and people (Figure 10.5).

   In the middle centuries of the second millennium B.C. Crete was
probably self-sufficient in most agricultural and craft goods, and its
powerful navy carried Cretan cloth, ceramics, and metal products to

10.5
A youth of Thera holds
strings of mackerel. Frescoes
such as these were done in
brilliant colors on freshly
plastered walls.

10.6
A Minoan goddess (?) of
about 1600 B.C. This grace-
ful, naturalistic faience statu-
ette is representative of Cretan plastic arts.

10.7
The stylized octopus on this
painted ceramic jar of the
fourteenth century B.C. is
representative of the naturalistic artistic traditions of the
ancient Aegean.

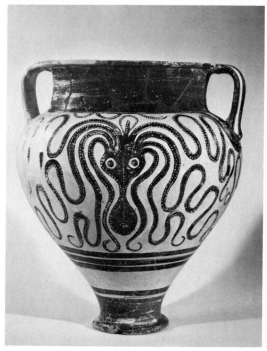

distant Mediterranean ports and also acted as a middleman in the flourishing Mediterranean trade in gold, silver, obsidian, ivory, and salt.

Long-distance trade does not somehow automatically metamor-
phose a simple society into a more complex form, and in fact the
mechanisms whereby long-distance trade led to cultural complexity
have never been satisfactorily identified for a single prehistoric society.
Nonetheless, after 1700 B.C., Crete certainly had the advantage of a
central, easily defendable location on the Mediterranean trade routes,
and its agricultural productivity, given precise administration, was
substantial. The domestication and cultivation of olive trees and grapes
in the Aegean area contributed greatly to Crete's food production, for
both these plants do well in dry, rocky areas that might otherwise not
be worth cultivating, and olives and grapes supply nutritious, versatile,
and easily storable products (Zohary and Speigel-Roy 1975).

Compared to those of Crete, cultural developments on the mainland and on other islands were somewhat slower, perhaps because of
greater disturbances through foreign invasions. The destruction of
Lerma, Eutresis, and other mainland settlements shortly after 2000
B.C. may have been the work of nomads from the Balkans and northern Greece.

The dominance of Cretan culture in the Aegean between 1700
and 1450 B.C. is evident in the use of Cretan styles and motifs in pottery and ornaments found at mainland settlements, and in the fact that
the peoples of the mainland adopted the fast potter's wheel, writing,
and other arts and crafts several centuries later than did the people of
Crete. But already by 1600 B.C. the growing power and wealth of mainland cultures is evident in large public building complexes (Figure
10.9) and sumptuous mortuary cults. At Mycenae Heinrich Schliemann
discovered and excavated a group of "shaft graves," deep rectangular
pits leading to stone-walled burial chambers roofed with timbers. In
each were the remains of what must have been several generations
(both men and women) of kin groups accompanied by priceless troves
of gold and silver jewelry, necklaces of amber and amethyst beads,
bronze swords, knives, and spear heads, gold death masks, and many
other spectacular items. The discoveries of further complexes of shaft
graves at Mycenae and other settlements vividly reflect a wealthy,
highly stratified society. At this time Mycenae and other mainland settlements were trading extensively with cities along the western Mediterranean littoral, and by the fifteenth century B.C. Mycenae was able

to dominate trade with Egypt, Cyprus, and the Levant as well (Hutchinson 1962: 305).

The commercial importance of Mycenae as well as the city's plentiful fresh water, natural resources, and strategic location produced a wealthy community, led by a warrior king who controlled trade routes extending far into Europe and the Mediterranean world. The Mycenaeans transshipped tin—used for alloying copper to produce bronze—from mines in Europe and Cyprus to consumers in many parts of the Mediterranean world and they also dealt extensively in Baltic amber, a yellow-brown translucent fossilized amber that can be polished into jewelry. Static electricity produced by rubbing amber may also have resulted in its being prized for its "magical" properties.

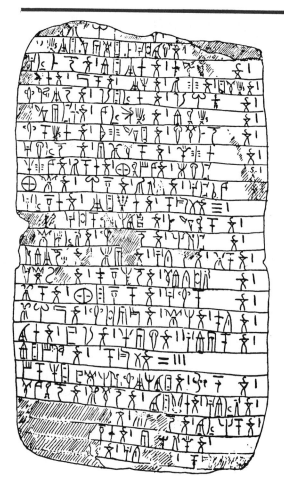

10.8
This clay tablet from Knossos was written in Minoan Linear B script, which was probably an early mixture of hieroglyphic and syllabic characters. Most of the Knossos texts are simple accounts of goods and labor.

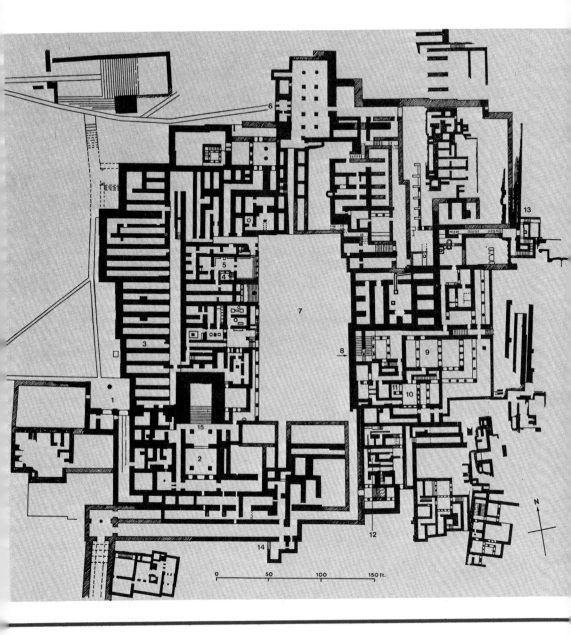

10.9
The Minoan palace at Knossos was a complex of shrines, residential units, storage rooms, and other buildings arranged around a large central courtyard. Such constructions were typical of the powerful trading states of the Aegean area in the second and third millennia B.C. (1) west entrance; (2) south anteroom; (3) west storerooms; (4) lustral chamber; (5) throne room; (6) north entrance; (7) central court; (8) grand staircase; (9) king's megaron; (10) queen's megaron; (11) queen's bath; (12) Shrine of the Double Axes; (13) east entrance; (14) south entrance; (15) stairway to second story.

THE DECLINE OF EARLY AEGEAN CIVILIZATION

Around 1500 B.C. the various Aegean city-states began to break up under the onslaught of natural calamities and warfare. At about 1500 B.C. the volcano on the island of Thera, about 110 kilometers off the northern coast of Crete, erupted and covered cities on Thera under many meters of ash and debris (perhaps the origin of the "Atlantis" story), and it is thought that either the force of the eruption, or perhaps earthquakes or tidal waves (estimated at more than nine meters high) accompanying the explosion, also destroyed Knossos and other Minoan settlements. In most cases, however, the Cretans rebuilt the palaces and enjoyed general prosperity for some decades, but in the middle of the fifteenth century B.C. most of the settlements on Crete were destroyed by fire; this time the destruction extended to houses, farms, and smaller shrines. Subsequent rebuilding was much slower and more sporadic, and it appears that Crete was invaded by warriors from the Greek mainland at this time. Whether the destruction of Cretan civilization was an aftereffect of the eruptions and earthquakes of the fifteenth century or of these massive invasions, or both, is unclear. The new rulers of Crete rebuilt Knossos and other settlements, but sometime after 1400 B.C. there was another wave of destruction and the balance of power in the Aegean swung permanently to the mainland. Mycenae, which controlled lucrative trade routes, became a large, fortified, rich city after 1400 B.C., as did Tiryns, Pylos, and other settlements. Texts of the late second millennium B.C. describe highly stratified societies, led by kings and their ministers and supported by vassal-like lords, craftsmen, peasant farmers, and a slave class.

Mycenae and other large settlements on the mainland were often apparently under military pressures from people to the north, and toward the end of the thirteenth century many major mainland settlements were destroyed by fire, and widespread depopulation and the cessation of writing, wall painting, gem carving, and other arts and crafts followed. Various factors have been suggested in explanation of this period of disruption and decline, including long-term droughts, revolutions, invasions, and internecine warfare among cities. That conflict was an important element in this pattern of cultural disintegration is suggested by the fortifications and massive quantities of bronze and iron weapons appearing in thirteenth- and twelfth-century sites. This may have been an instance where warfare, rather than leading to

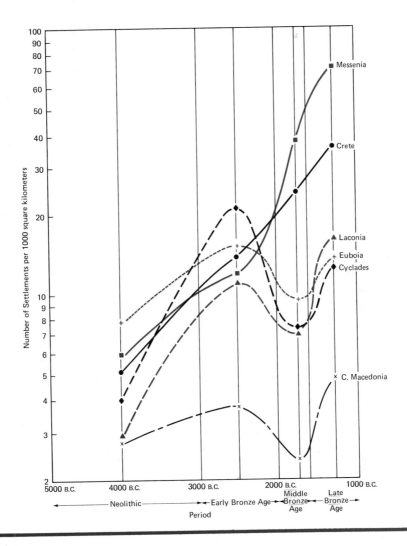

10.10
Trade and new agricultural techniques stimulated a great expansion of settlement in the Aegean area. The plot shown is semi-logarithmic. The different graphs represent different geographical regions.

the formation of a great empire, as in the case of Sargon of Akkad, resulted instead in the mutual destruction of competing petty states. The presence of artifacts in foreign, mainly northern, styles at Mycenaean sites of the late twelfth century suggests that interregional warfare may have been exacerbated by waves of foreign invaders, among whom, perhaps, were the first Greek-speaking peoples, coming probably from Anatolia or the north.

Greek cultures of the first millennium B.C. and later are beyond the scope of this book, except to note their extraordinary creativity. To take a single example, in a period of about 250 years the small city-state of Athens, with a cumulative population in this period of just a few hundred thousand, gave birth to Solon, Themistocles, Aristides, Pericles, and other statesmen, to the dramatists Aeschylus, Sophocles, Euripides, Aristophanes, and Menander, to the historian Thucydides, to Demosthenes, the incomparable orator, to Mnesicles and Ictinus, the architects of the Acropolis, to Phidias and Praxiteles, among the most influential sculptors of all time, and to Socrates and Plato, the fundamental philosophers of Western civilization (Kitto 1951: 95). In addition, the Greeks of the late first millennium B.C. created forms of social and political organization and a world and life view of such balance and productivity that many scholars still regard the Greek city-states of this period as models of the best arrangement for meeting human needs and potential (Kitto 1951; Hamilton 1930).

It is an article of faith with almost all anthropologists that all races have essentially identical innate potential, and thus explanations of the unique Greek contributions have focused on the general environmental and historical context of Greece in the late fi. ` millennium B.C. Greece was then in a sense at the crossroads of the world, because through its dependence on trade and the great volume of shipping around the Aegean and Mediterranean shore, it was constantly exposed to a great diversity of languages, styles, and ideologies. Also important were the low agricultural potential and mountainous terrain of most of Greece, which proved effective barriers to political confederation and consequent cultural homogeneity.

Those intimately familiar with the Greek achievement, however, will find such "explanations" ultimately incomplete.

Temperate Europe

Julius Caesar and other Roman authors were united in their praise of the courage of the Celts, Gauls, Germans, Britons, and other northern Europeans in their empire, but they were totally unimpressed by the standards of European culture. Even as late as 2,500 years ago, Europe, from the plains of Russia to Ireland, was mainly inhabited by violent tribes who lived without benefit of cities, writing, money, or bureaucracies. Life revolved around simple farming communities, where cattle herding, primitive grain and vegetable agriculture, and substantial hunting and fishing were the major occupations, and the only developed crafts were pottery making and bronze and iron metallurgy.

European cultures have dominated the world so thoroughly in the last 1,000 years that it might seem surprising that northern Europe was a cultural backwater while great civilizations flourished in Egypt, Mesopotamia, and elsewhere, but there are compelling ecological and other reasons for the course of European development.

As we noted in chapter 7, domestic plants and animals and the agricultural way of life came relatively late to temperate Europe, at least several millennia after these same developments took place in Southwest Asia. The rate and direction of the spread of agricultural economies from Southwest Asia was a direct function of their effective-

10.11
The distribution of some important sites and cultures in Europe during the 5th millennium B.C.

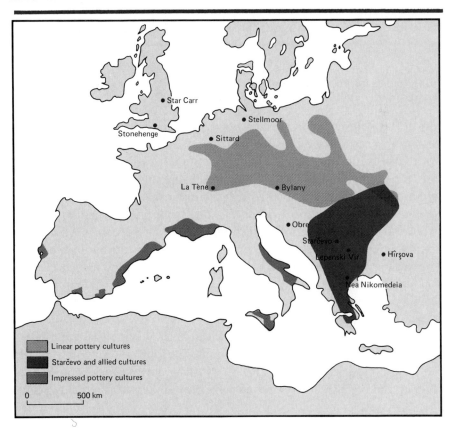

10.12
Stonehenge is the most famous of ancient European stone monuments, but burial vaults, "observatories," and other large stone constructions were erected over much of northwestern Europe in the last several millennia B.C.

ness in the different ecological zones of Europe. Not only was the Mediterranean coastal zone the first to receive domesticates from the East; it was also itself a nuclear zone for the domestication of various plant and animal species and for the evolution of some of the first farming communities. The temperate zone, extending from southern Russia to northern France, the Low Countries, and Britain, is marked by deciduous forests, and in these zones farming was at first successful only when combined with considerable stock raising and hunting and gathering. The circumpolar areas of Scandinavia and European Russia were settled by farmers only comparatively late, because the thick pine and birch forests and the tundra and short growing season make agriculture there only marginally effective.

By the end of the fourth millennium B.C., a mixed farming economy had spread over much of temperate Europe, as far north as Poland, the Netherlands, and southern Norway and Sweden, and at this time we can see the emergence of some minor degree of cultural complexity. Excavations of waterlogged deposits in Swiss lake sites and elsewhere reveal specialization in weaving, leatherworking, embroidery, ceramics, and metallurgy. About this time too, people in France, Britain, and adjacent areas began building large cut-stone monuments (Figure 10.12) and burial chambers, some of which represented considerable work and planning. At Carnac in northwestern France, for example, over 3,000 stone monoliths were arranged in many parallel rows extending from five to six kilometers. Many burial chambers of this period were decorated with complex pictographs, perhaps reflecting a growing interest in religion, astronomy, and theology, and the rich grave goods of some of the tombs imply wealth and status differences among members of the same communities. There is no evidence in either the distribution of artifact styles or in settlement patterns that European peoples at about 3000 B.C. were organized in anything more complex than tribes or simple chiefdoms, but the presence of monumental architecture and the spread of regional artifact styles suggest that the pace of cultural evolution was quickening.

An important developmental stimulus was provided shortly after 3000 B.C., when the domestic horse, wheeled vehicles, plows, bronze metallurgy, and other innovations came into use, beginning in the Mediterranean areas and slowly spreading north and west. Whether this technological complex was directly introduced by foreign invaders or was in part an independent European invention is a question of unremitting controversy, but no doubt invasions, diffusions, and independent inventions each played some role.

Although the use of copper slowly accelerated in Europe after 3000 B.C., at first it was probably of no greater importance than fine-grain stone. This may be because unalloyed copper is so soft that a warrior or woodsman armed with copper implements would not find felling either an enemy or a tree appreciably easier than if he were working with traditional stone tools. Flint tools have surprising durability, and Neolithic flint axes have been used without resharpening to fell hundreds of trees.

Throughout the third millennium B.C. the stable European farming cultures appear to have been influenced by invading tribesmen from the steppe region north of the Black Sea (Gimbutas 1970). These invaders, commonly called *Kurgans,* after the Russian word for the small mounds under which they buried their leaders, were a highly mobile people who used metal weapons, wheeled carts, and perhaps horses to subjugate much of the area between Europe and central Russia and south to the Aegean.

BRONZE AGE EUROPE (CA. 2500 TO 650 B.C.)

Shortly after 2500 B.C. a flourishing industry in bronze appeared in Czechoslovakia and over the next millennium bronzeworking evolved into a highly sophisticated craft practiced over much of temperate Europe. The raw ores needed for bronze production were widely traded, as were bronze artifacts, especially in the form of axes, knives, and ornaments, and paralleling the bronze trade was vastly increased regional and international trade in amber, salt, glass beads, and other products. As these trade networks were extended and increased in volume, there was a concurrent reshaping of the demographic and economic landscape of temperate Europe. In the third and second millennia B.C., settlement was extended into many areas, particularly the sandy wastelands previously avoided. Fortified settlements appeared on hilltops along the major central European river valleys—probably as a defensive tactic but also perhaps linked to the vast amount of sheep and cattle pasturage these zones would provide (Sherratt 1972: 534). Coupled with these settlement changes were agricultural shifts made possible by the increased use of wheeled carts and plows during the second half of the third millennium, resulting in increased agricultural productivity.

Competition for arable land also apparently intensified as people moved into a more diverse range of environments, and the great numbers of fortified sites and weaponry found dating to this period may reflect wars fought for land control. Intensified agricultural strategies may have, for the first time, removed large amounts of cropland from production as rains leached materials from upper sandy soils (Sherratt 1972: 535).

A. G. Sherratt has suggested that these various economic changes may have contributed to the formation of centralized redistributive centers and an administrative hierarchy to administer metal trade, coordinate textiles and other crafts, and deal with complex agricultural problems—developments perhaps reflected in the proliferation of burial mounds in Europe at this time (1972: 535). Occupational specialization, in the form of religious shamans, metalsmiths, weavers, and many others, no doubt also intensified throughout the third and second millennia B.C.

EUROPE IN THE IRON AGE (CA. 650 B.C. TO CA. A.D. 100)

At about 700 B.C. ironworking was introduced into northern Europe, and this innovation was associated with—and to some extent was a cause of—major subsequent cultural changes. Iron-bearing ores are much more common in Europe than the copper and tin needed to make bronze, and iron artifacts are much more durable and versatile than those of bronze or copper. Under conditions of primitive technology, making iron implements required that iron ore be hammered repeatedly while red hot and in contact with charcoal, so that carbon would slowly be added to the metal (J. G. D. Clark 1966: 199). The inventors of this smelting process appear to have been the Hittites of fifteenth century B.C. Anatolia, and it is widely supposed that the great advantage of iron for the manufacture of military armaments caused the Hittites to guard their secret jealously, until about 1200 B.C., when Hittite power faded. Succeeding centuries saw the passing of the secrets of iron technology into the Aegean world, and by the middle of the seventh century B.C., iron technology was practiced as far north as France and Germany. Iron artifacts made clearing forests and cultivating land much easier, and iron weapons, being much cheaper and more durable than bronze, may have heightened the ferocity of conflict between European chiefdoms. Iron technology may also have contributed to social and political change in Europe by encouraging the formation of new and expanded trade routes to move iron ores and artifacts and the establishment of centralized administration to oversee iron production. It must be remembered, however, that even before the introduction of iron, there was a long-term trend toward increasing cultural complexity in Europe, a trend that iron technology may have accelerated but did not set in motion.

One of the best-known Early Iron Age European cultures is the *Hallstatt* culture, which spread from Poland to Spain, as far south as Yugoslavia, and north into the Low Countries (Figure 10.13). The definition of this culture is based on the wide distribution of very similar ceramic, architectural, and mortuary styles, but it is likely that the people sharing these styles were organized only in chiefdoms, with a population totaling no more than several thousand. Hallstatt sites at Heuneberg, near the Danube, Biskupin, in Poland, and elsewhere were heavily fortified communities built on commanding hills, and some of these communities were social and economically quite complex. But most rural peoples still lived much as their forefathers had, in simple farming villages.

Hallstatt chieftains were frequently buried in timbered chambers under large earthen mounds along with massive quantities of bronze and iron weapons, metal ornaments, bronze shields, and, occasionally, four-wheeled horse-drawn carts. The fortified sites and weaponry suggest extensive conflict among rival chiefdoms, but there was also considerable trade and an increasingly productive agricultural economy. Ceramic wine bottles and other artifacts of Greek manufacture demonstrate continual cultural contacts with the more complex societies to the south.

The later stages of the pre-Roman European Iron Age take their name from the Swiss site of *La Tène*. From its original focal area, La Tène culture spread northeast into Scandinavia, south into Cisalpine

10.13
From the seventh through the fifth centuries B.C., the Hallstatt culture (shaded area) spread over much of north-central Europe. This and similar culture areas are based on the distribution of similar pottery and other artifact styles; they do not represent areas of direct political control.

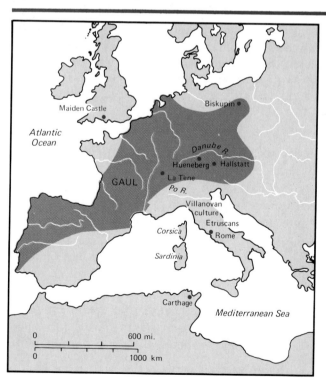

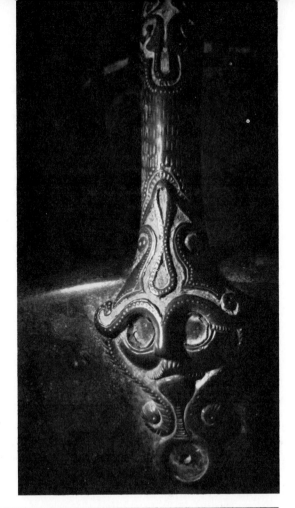

10.14
Detail of a bronze flagon handle from fifth century B.C. France. La Tène period artifacts include remarkable decorative arts in bronze, wood, stone, and other materials.

Gaul, and north and west over France, the Low Countries, and the British Isles. As with the Hallstatt complex, La Tène culture was marked by similar art and architectural styles, but there were few large political or social confederations. The area occupied by the La Tène peoples was divided among hundreds of aristocratic chiefdoms whose local rulers amassed large personal fortunes by taxing their dependents and raiding their neighbors. The La Tène people borrowed extensively from their neighbors in Greece and Rome, from whence came chariots, rotary lathes and querns, coinage, and other important technological innovations.

The La Tène peoples and their descendants were eventually incorporated into the Roman Empire, but Roman authority outside the major cities was often weak and the ancient ways of life persisted long into the historic era. Eventually, Rome itself fell victim to the incompletely civilized European tribesmen to the north, who repeatedly invaded and devastated the Italian cities.

Nomads of Eurasia

An important element of the evolution of complex cultures in Europe, the Mediterranean, and Southwest Asia alike was the continual infringement by Eurasian nomads (often called *Scythians*) on the margins of agricultural societies. By the beginning of the first millennium B.C.—and probably much earlier—the vast rolling grasslands and steppe country of Eurasia, from southern Russia to China, were inhabited by resilient, mobile tribes living at very low population densities and subsisting mainly on mare's milk and cheese and a few hunted and gathered resources. To meet the climatic extremes of this region, these people created an elegant, superbly adapted material culture, including beautifully woven and dyed rugs, wool tents, and leather boots and gloves.

The flavor of Eurasian nomad society is extraordinarily well preserved in the frozen tombs at Pazyryk, in northeastern Siberia, where warrior chiefs were buried with their weapons, horses, wives, and other provisions for the hereafter (Figure 10.15).

The archaeology of nomads is almost a contradiction in terms, since they generally leave little physical evidence, but historical records from China to western Europe indicate that these Eurasian nomadic peoples were important catalysts in cultural evolution. Often the rela-

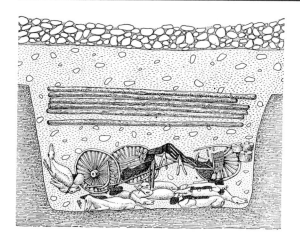

10.15
An ancient horse sacrifice in a Scythian burial mound at Pazyryk, Siberia.

tionship among settled and nomadic peoples was an antagonistic one, as nomads preyed on agricultural communities. Alternatively, nomads sometimes took up the agricultural way of life along the margins of established farming societies, adding to the administrative problems of these societies. Even when relationships between nomads and sedentary agriculturalists were peaceful, the presence of the former no doubt stimulated the development of administrative hierarchies to coordinate economic exchange.

Bibliography

Ammerman, A. J. and L. L. Cavalli-Sforza. 1971. "Measuring the Rate of Spread of Early Farming in Europe." *Man*. N.S. 6(4): 674–88.

Atkinson, R. J. C. 1960. *Stonehenge*. Baltimore: Pelican.

Bruce-Mitford, R., ed. 1975. *Recent Archaeological Excavations in Europe*. London: Routledge and Kegan Paul.

Chadwick, John. 1972. *The Mycenaean World*. Cambridge: Cambridge University Press.

Childe, V. Gordon. 1925. *The Dawn of European Civilization*. London: Routledge and Kegan Paul.

————. 1940. *Prehistoric Communities of the British Isles*. Edinburgh: Edinburgh University Press.

————. 1958. *The Prehistory of European Society*. London: Pelican.

Clark, J. G. D. 1966. *Prehistoric Europe: The Economic Basis*. Stanford: Stanford University Press.

Daniel, G. and J. D. Evans. 1975. "The Western Mediterranean." *Cambridge Ancient History*. 2(2): 713–72. Cambridge: Cambridge University Press.

Desborough, V. R. d'A. 1972. *The Greek Dark Ages*. London: Ernest Benn.

Dow, S. and J. Chadwick. 1973. "The Linear Scripts and the Tablets as Historical Documents." *Cambridge Ancient History*. 2(1): 582–626. Cambridge: Cambridge University Press.

Escalon de Fonton, M. 1967. "Origine et développement des civilisations néolithiques Méditerranéennes en Europe occidentale." *Palaeohistoria*. 12: 209–47.

Evans, Sir Arthur. 1921–28. *The Palace of Minos*, vols. 1–4. London: Macmillan.

Evans, John D. 1971. "Neolithic Knossos: The Growth of a Settlement." *Proceedings of the Prehistoric Society*. 37(2).

Gimbutas, Marija. 1956. *The Prehistory of Eastern Europe. American School of Prehistory Research Bulletin,* vol. 20. Harvard University.

———. 1970. "Proto-Indo-European Culture: The Kurgan Culture During the Fifth, Fourth, and Third Millennia B.C." *Indo-European and Indo-Europeans.* Philadelphia: University of Pennsylvania Press.

Guilaine, J., ed. 1976. *La préhistoire française.* Paris: Éditions du centre national de la recherche scientifique.

Hamilton, Edith. 1930. *The Greek Way.* New York: W. W. Norton.

Hawkins, Gerald. 1965. *Stonehenge Decoded.* New York: Souvenir Press.

Hood, Sinclair. 1967. *Home of the Heroes: The Aegean Before the Greeks.* New York: McGraw-Hill.

———. 1971. *The Minoans.* New York: Praeger.

Hutchinson, R. W. 1962. *Prehistoric Crete.* London: Penguin.

Kitto, H. D. F. 1951. *The Greeks.* Harmondsworth: Pelican.

MacQueen, J. G. 1975. *The Hittites and Their Contemporaries in Asia Minor.* London: Thames and Hudson.

Modderman, P. J. R. 1975. "Elsloo, a Neolithic Farming Community in the Netherlands." In *Recent Archaeological Excavations in Europe,* ed. R. Bruce-Mitford. London: Routledge and Kegan Paul.

Özgüç, Tahsin. 1972. "An Assyrian Trading Outpost." In *Old World Archaeology: Foundations of Civilization.* San Francisco: W. W. Freeman.

Palmer, L. R. 1965. *Mycenaeans and Minoans.* 2nd ed. London: Faber and Faber.

Piggott, Stuart. 1954. *The Neolithic Cultures of the British Isles.* Cambridge: Cambridge University Press.

———. 1965. *Ancient Europe.* Chicago: Aldine.

Renfrew, Colin. 1967. "Cycladic Metallurgy and the Aegean Early Bronze Age." *American Journal of Archaeology.* 71: 1–26.

———. 1969. "The Autonomy of the South-East European Copper Age." *Proceedings of the Prehistoric Society.* 35: 12–47.

———. 1972. *The Emergence of Civilization. The Cyclades and the Aegean in the Third Millennium B.C.* London: Methuen.

———. 1975. Beyond a Subsistence Economy: *The Evolution of Social Organization in Prehistoric Europe.* Boston: MIT Press.

Rodden, Robert J. 1965. "An Early Neolithic Village in Greece." *Scientific American.* 212(4): 82–93.

Rudenko, Sergei I. 1970. *Frozen Tombs of Siberia: The Pazyryk Burials of Iron Age Horsemen,* trans. M. W. Thompson. Berkeley: University of California Press.

Sherratt, A. G. 1972. "The Interpretation of Change in European Prehistory." In *The Explanation of Culture Change,* ed. C. Renfrew. Pittsburgh: University of Pittsburgh Press.

Sieveking, Gale. 1963. "The Migration of the Megaliths." In *Vanished Civilizations of the Ancient World,* ed. Edward Bacon. New York: McGraw-Hill.

Tringham, Ruth. 1971. *Hunters, Fishers and Farmers of Eastern Europe 6000–3000 B.C.* London: Hutchinson University Library.

Wailes, Bernard. 1970. "The Origins of Settled Farming in Temperate Europe." In *Indo-European and Indo-Europeans.* Philadelphia: University of Pennslyvania Press.

Zohary, D. and P. Speigel-Roy. 1975. "Beginnings of Fruit Growing in the Old World." *Science.* 187: 319–27.

11

The Origins of
Cultural Complexity
in Africa

Concerning Egypt I shall extend my remarks to
a great length, because there is no country that
possesses so many wonders, nor any that has such
a number of works which defy description. Not
only is the climate different from that of the rest
of the world, and the rivers unlike any other
rivers, but the people also, in most of their man-
ners and customs, exactly reverse the common
practice of mankind.

Herodotus, c. 440 B.C.

Egypt

Ancient Egyptian civilization came into full flower centuries later
than Mesopotamian cultures and may have been affected to a minor
degree by them, but the rise of Egypt to cultural complexity was
largely an independent process so distinctive and brilliant that ancient
Egypt is the most widely renowned of all ancient civilizations.

There are of course many common denominators linking Egypt with ancient Mesopotamia, China, and the other early complex cultures: early Egyptians, too, intensively cultivated and irrigated crops, organized themselves in hierarchies of wealth, power, and prestige, built massive structures, and engaged in international wars, alliances, and commerce. But the distinctive aspects of their art, architecture, character, and ideology set the Egyptians off from the rest of the world.

We ought to know more about Egypt than any other ancient culture. Archaeologists have worked there for centuries, Egyptian writing developed early and has been largely deciphered, the arid climate has preserved many artifacts in excellent condition, and the geographic isolation of Egypt sheltered it from many of the interregional influences that made Southwest Asian developments so complex. In addition, the stable climate and all-important role of the Nile River in determining the patterns of Egyptian culture would seemingly make for a situation in which an ecological analysis of cultural development would be especially simple and revealing.

But centuries of looting (which continues) and well-intentioned development programs have destroyed a significant portion of the archaeological record, and a fanatical preoccupation by archaeologists with tombs and palaces, to the virtual exclusion of other aspects of the archaeological record, has made the origins of cultural complexity in ancient Egypt one of the least understood examples of this developmental process.

THE ECOLOGICAL SETTING

Every spring, torrential rains in central Africa send silt-chocked floods pulsing down the 6,500-kilometer-length of the Nile Valley, depositing along the way innumerable tons of rich soil, and emptying finally into the Mediterranean in late autumn. Along the river's course this natural alluviation has produced one of the world's richest agricultural niches, which with even the simplest tools supports as many as 450 people per square kilometer (Wilson 1949: 40). These alluvial soils are high in nitrogen, require no deep plowing, and are replenished each year.

Although highly productive, agricultural areas comprise only about 3.5 percent of the total area of the modern state of Egypt (Figure

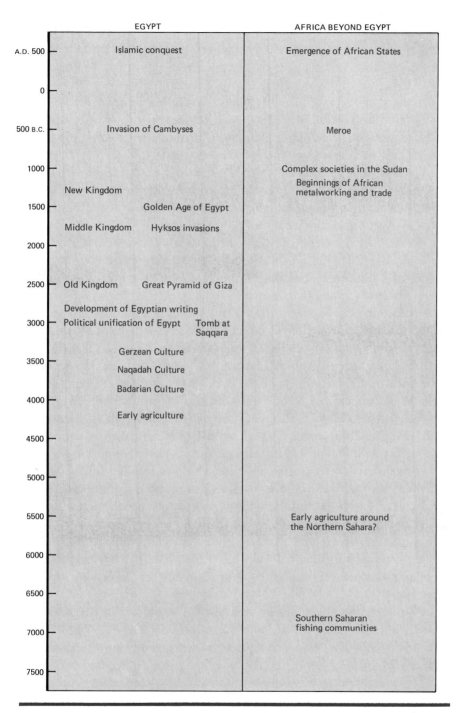

EGYPT   AFRICA BEYOND EGYPT

A.D. 500 — Islamic conquest   Emergence of African States

0 —

500 B.C. — Invasion of Cambyses   Meroe

1000 —   Complex societies in the Sudan

New Kingdom   Beginnings of African metalworking and trade

1500 —   Golden Age of Egypt

Middle Kingdom   Hyksos invasions

2000 —

2500 — Old Kingdom   Great Pyramid of Giza

Development of Egyptian writing

3000 — Political unification of Egypt   Tomb at Saqqara

Gerzean Culture

3500 — Naqadah Culture

Badarian Culture

4000 — Early agriculture

4500 —

5000 —

5500 —   Early agriculture around the Northern Sahara?

6000 —

6500 —

7000 —   Southern Saharan fishing communities

7500 —

11.1
Chronology of ancient Africa.

11.2), and they are sharply circumscribed in most regions by rocky deserts. From the Sudanese border to Cairo, the cultivable strip along both banks of the river is only about three kilometers wide in most places and rarely exceeds twenty-two kilometers width. And so sharp is the demarcation between desert and cultivable land that one may literally stand with one foot on the red desert sands and the other foot on the black, irrigated croplands (Wilson 1949: 39). But north of Cairo, the Nile breaks up into many smaller, slower streams, and over the millennia the river has created a delta area, about 250 by 160 kilometers, of flat, well-watered, and exceptionally fertile land.

Temperatures along the Nile regularly exceed 100°F, and rainfall is sparse: irrigation is required almost everywhere in the country for agriculture. The heat and humidity can often be oppressive, but the climate is perfect for plant growth, allowing the harvesting of two and even three crops a year and the cultivation of a wide range of plants. From antiquity, the principal crops have been spelt (a kind of wheat), barley, legumes, onions, radishes, cucumbers, melons, and figs, and the pastures and gardens of the alluvium have long sustained the standard Near Eastern array of sheep, goats, pigs, cattle, and fowl. Even without agriculture, the Nile itself is extraordinarily productive, supporting great quantities of fish, wildfowl, crustaceans, hippopotami, and other game animals, dense stands of rushes and reeds for basketry and netted goods, flax for linen and canvas, and papyrus for cordage and paper.

The deserts that parallel the Nile are dotted with a few oases, but elsewhere they provide barely enough to support a few nomads. They are, however, rich in building stone, and copper can be found in the Sinai Desert, while immense gold and silver reserves used to be available in the Arabian Desert. In addition, their heat and aridity provide the perfect place for grain storage and, incidentally, the preservation of human corpses and other organic remains so important for archaeology.

Although the enormous agricultural productivity of the alluvium and the mineral reserves of the desert were the base on which was erected ancient Egyptian civilization, some specific ecological factors gave this civilization its distinctive character. The bleak and inhospitable desert and the lack of any natural harbors in the Delta protected Egypt from foreign influences and invasions until well after the first Egyptian states had formed, and such characteristics as very late and

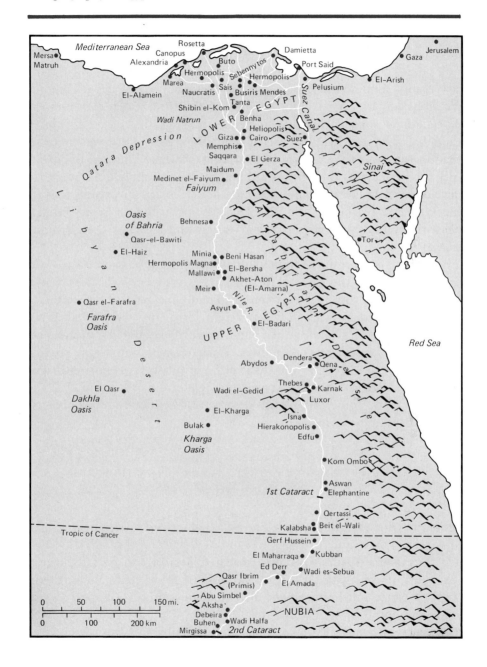

Mediterranean Sea

Mersa•
Matruh

Rosetta
Canopus
Alexandria
Buto
Hermopolis
Marea
Sais
Naucratis
El-Alamein
El-Alamein
Shibin el-Kom
Tanta
Wadi Natrun
Benha
LOWER EGYPT
Qatara Depression
Heliopolis
Giza• Cairo
Memphis•
Saqqara
Maidum
Medinet el-Faiyum
Faiyum

Damietta
Gaza
Jerusalem
Port Said
Sebennytos
Hermopolis
El-Arish
Busiris Mendes
Pelusium
Suez Canal
Suez
El Gerza
Sinai

Oasis
of Bahria
Behnesa•
• Qasr-el-Bawiti
• El-Haiz
Minia
Beni Hasan
Hermopolis Magna•
El-Bersha
Mallawi
Akhet-Aton
(El-Amarna)
Meir•
Nile R.
• Qasr el-Farafra
Asyut•
UPPER EGYPT
Farafra
Oasis
• El-Badari

Libyan

Tor•

Red Sea

Desert
Abydos
Dendera
Qena
El Qasr•
Wadi el-Gedid
Thebes
Karnak
Dakhla
Oasis
• El-Kharga
Luxor
Bulak•
Hierakonopolis•
Isna
Kharga
Oasis
Edfu•

Kom Ombo•
Aswan
1st Cataract
Elephantine
Qertassi
Kalabsha
Beit el-Wali
Tropic of Cancer
Gerf Hussein
El Maharraqa
Kubban
Ed Derr
Wadi es-Sebua
Qasr Ibrim
(Primis)
El Amada
Abu Simbel
Aksha
NUBIA
Debeira
Buhen
Wadi Halfa
Mirgissa
2nd Cataract

0   50   100   150 mi.
0   100   200 km

weakly developed urbanism in Egypt may have derived mainly from this isolation (Butzer 1976: 226). Ancient Egypt was thus "a hermetically sealed tube containing a concentration of life close to the saturation point" (Wilson 1949: 40).

Another important environmental factor was the efficient communications and transport route provided by the Nile, which over most of its length is sufficiently wide and slow moving that since antiquity there has been considerable and dependable boat traffic—even more so than in the case of the Tigris and Euphrates rivers. This was undoubtedly a key factor in the centralized and precisely controlled states that developed in later Egyptian antiquity, and it is not surprising that in the southern reaches of the Nile, where five cataracts (steep rapids) constitute impassable barriers to navigation, the power of the Egyptian states weakened.

Although there have been major fluctuations in the annual volume of the Nile—there were, for example, catastrophically low water levels in some of the years between 2250 and 1950 B.C.—the Nile floodplain has existed in essentially its present form since about 3800 B.C. (Butzer 1976: 28). On the other hand, the average annual rainfall has varied considerably, and there was a particularly important drying trend during the whole of the third millennium B.C., resulting in environmental changes that very well may have reduced pasturages, interrupted trade routes across the deserts, and reduced the number of nomads (ibid.: 39–40).

EARLY EGYPTIAN AGRICULTURE: THE PREDYNASTIC PERIOD (5200 TO 3100 B.C.)

People have no doubt lived in the Nile Valley and adjacent areas for hundreds of thousands of years, but most evidence of this is buried under deep layers of silt. The few excavated sites of this period suggest that hunting and gathering was the basis of human life in northern (Lower) Egypt until about 6000 B.C., and in southern (Upper) Egypt as late as 4000 B.C.

It was once assumed that domesticated plants and animals and agriculture were introduced into Egypt from Southwest Asia, but Egyptian strains of many animal species are so distinctive as to suggest that they were at least partially domesticated there; also, the Egyptians partially domesticated some animals that almost no one else did, such as the oryz, addax, hyena, and mongoose (Butzer 1976). Moreover, a "protoagricultural" economy seems to have developed in at least some areas as early as 12,500 B.C.: Wendorf and Schild report numerous grinding stones and lustrous-edged blades (probably from sickles) at sites near Isna and elsewhere, some in association with what appears to be barley pollen (1975). Such settlements were apparently much less numerous after 9500 B.C., however, and they did not lead directly to a widespread agricultural economy (Butzer 1976).

In trying to account for Egyptian agriculture, Karl Butzer hypothesizes that the hunting and gathering potential of much of the Nile Valley was so great that hunters and gatherers there, although aware of agricultural and pastoral practices, at first had no incentive to give up their ancient way of life (1976: 9). He also interprets the archaeological, botanical, linguistic, and physical anthropological evidence to suggest that agriculture was introduced to the Nile Valley from *northwestern* Africa, not Southwest Asia or southern Africa. He nominates the oases of the northern Libyan desert and the Mediterranean coastal areas as possible sources of these introductions (ibid.: 11).

Whatever the origins of Egyptian domesticates and agriculture, in the mid-fifth millennium B.C. people were living along the lake shores of the Fayum region, subsisting primarily on fishing, hunting, and gathering, but also growing grain, which they stored in straw silos. They also made artifacts from flint, bone, and pottery. At the same time, settlers in the Delta had essentially the same subsistence basis and technological skills, but were culturally distinct (Smith 1976).

By the mid-fourth millennium B.C. the people of the *Badarian* culture in Upper Egypt were producing high-quality pottery as well as the first metal implements in Egypt—simple, small copper tools.

The Badarians' successors in Upper Egypt, the people of the *Nagadah* cultures, made some advances in stoneworking and other arts and crafts, but the economic and subsistence base probably remained much the same, with hunting, gathering, and pastoralism more important than plant cultivation (Butzer 1976: 107). Little is known about the social and political nature of either Upper or Lower Egypt at this time, although artifacts indicate that there were at least several major stylistic zones. Badarian and Naqadah settlements seem to have been restricted to the desert margins of the alluvium, perhaps to take advantage of seasonal pastures the desert would have provided during this somewhat moister era (ibid.: 14). Of course, settlements now buried beneath silt may also have been directly on the alluvium, and other explanations of these settlement patterns are possible (Hoffman 1970: 54–56); but the evidence here is far too incomplete to support any detailed reconstruction.

There is, however, some evidence that may reflect evolving cultural complexity in the late *Predynastic period*. One settlement near Hierakonpolis, often called the *Gerzean town,* was very large, with perhaps as many as 50,000 square meters of occupation (Hoffman 1970: 44). Near this site and elsewhere in the valley are some large structures that may have been ceremonial public buildings, and in some locations there are cemeteries and tombs that vary considerably in construction costs and grave goods. On the basis of this and other evidence, including a few sketchy historical documents, some Egyptologists have suggested that by the late Predynastic period there were two "kingdoms" in Egypt, one in the North with its capitol at Buto, the other in the South, centered at Hierakonpolis. The basic political and settlement unit in both areas appears to have been the *nome,* a Greek name for sets of many small hamlets arranged around one or two larger towns. During periods of anarchy, these nomes often became almost autono-

11.3
A Gerzean pottery vessel
(fourth millennium B.C.)

mous, and even during the most centralized governments they were probably largely self-sufficient economically and administratively (Aldred 1961: 73).

Toward the end of the Predynastic era two very significant developments occurred: the importation of a few artifacts and craft techniques from Mesopotamia, and the use of the first rudimentary hieroglyphic writing. Little evidence exists of any substantial sustained connections between Egypt and Southwest Asia at this time, although it is possible that the Mediterranean was regularly crossed by ships from the Levant, some of which may have called at Egyptian ports (Aldred 1961: 73).

THE EARLY DYNASTIC PERIOD: THE FIRST EGYPTIAN COMPLEX SOCIETIES (CA. 3100 TO CA. 2686 B.C.)

The *Early Dynastic period* was the great formative era of Egyptian civilization, the time when Upper and Lower Egypt were first united politically and the distinctive Egyptian forms of writing, architecture, administration, and ideology emerged.

Traditional sources record that Menes (also known as Narmer), a minor official from Upper Egypt, rose to power and conquered Lower Egypt at about 3100 B.C., and that he and his successors established a theocratic political system over the entire navigable length of the Nile (Figure 11.4). Menes is recorded as having built a capital at Memphis, diverting the stream of the Nile to create a strategic position at the junction of Upper and Lower Egypt, and he is also credited with leading military expeditions against the nomads in the southern desert. His next several successors were also powerful kings, but there is some evidence of internal dissension at about 2900 B.C. Later, peace appears to have been restored and major construction projects were undertaken in the centuries before 2700 B.C.

The archaeological evidence from the Early Dynastic period is limited to some badly looted tombs, several monuments, and a few excavated sites. From these have been recovered beautiful artifacts of diorite and other varieties of hard stone, as well as skillfully fashioned copper implements and a few items of gold. Such distinctive Egyptian materials as faience (a glassy substance made from molded and fired crushed quartz) and papyrus paper were in use at this time, and contemporary documents written on this paper show that the Egyptians were already skilled in astronomy, geometry, accounting, surgery, and other arts and sciences.

At this same time there was a gradual shift from hunting and gathering to grain and vegetable farming, and some irrigation works were already in use by the beginning of the Early Dynastic period (Butzer 1976: 107). It appears that the economic sphere was now quite complex, involving long-distance trade to Syria and beyond and considerable local exchange of craft goods and foodstuffs; but most Egyptians of the Early Dynastic period continued to live in unwalled, largely self-sufficient villages (ibid.). Apart from Memphis there were few towns or cities, a situation that may have contributed to the political integration of the country, since there were no urban power centers to resist incorporation (Service 1975: 228). Large areas of the Middle Nile Valley were only sparsely settled, and population growth was no doubt quite slow, with little competition for agricultural land or irrigation water (although many new settlements appear to have been founded in the Delta) (Butzer 1976: 94). Apparently, the slow population growth during the Early Dynastic period (Butzer estimates an annual rate of 0.8 per 1,000) eventually did begin to exert some pressure on available resources toward the end of the period, since large game almost disappeared from the alluvium and contemporary documents describe a shift away from pastoralism to a greater reliance on grain agriculture (ibid.: 1976).

The appearance of writing, monumental architecture, varieties of settlement sizes, large tombs, intensified agriculture and trade, and historical mentions of a powerful ruler make it clear that by the Early Dynastic period, Egypt was a complex society, one that we might label a *theocratic chiefdom* (Service 1975: 229). Until a great deal more archaeological research is accomplished, however, we shall not be able to account for the evolution of these first complex Egyptian societies, except perhaps to note that the available evidence makes it highly unlikely that human population growth, the requisites of irrigation agriculture, warfare, long-distance trade, or conflict between economic classes had much if anything to do with this initial transformation (Butzer 1976). Finally, some scholars consider later Early Dynastic Egypt to have been a state-level society, but Egypt at this time probably did not have the complex bureaucracy that marked the evolution of later Egyptian states—as well as that of all other ancient states.

THE FIRST EGYPTIAN STATES: THE OLD KINGDOM AND THE
FIRST INTERMEDIATE PERIOD
(CA. 2686 TO CA. 2040 B.C.)

The last half of the third millennium B.C. was for Egypt a marvelous age in which many of the greatest pyramids and palaces were built, an integrated royal bureaucracy was formed, and numerous arts and crafts were brilliantly executed. Because of the relatively comprehensive documents from this period, we know many of its political and social details.

Djoser, the second king of the *Old Kingdom period,* was able to organize the people and economy of Egypt to the extent that he, or his grand vizier, Imhotep, could arrange construction of the great step pyramid at Saqqarah as a tomb for Djoser. The actual crypt was built in-

11.4
The Palette of Narmer, an engraved thin sheet of stone that was possibly a symbol of the political unification of Egypt. From Hierakonopolis.

side the pyramid, whose six levels rose over 60 meters into the air and were surrounded by large buildings and monuments. The entire complex was encircled by a stone wall more than 9 meters wide with a perimeter of more than 1.6 kilometers (Aldred 1961: 84–85). The pyramid complex at Saqqarah was the world's first large-scale stone building and one of the most beautiful, and in terms of the effort and materials required for its construction, it dwarfs the monumental architecture of all other early complex societies. It truly must have been an impressive sight, forty-five centuries ago when it was new, with its crisp white limestone facing contrasting with the cobalt sky and green palm groves.

Djoser's successors, particularly those of the Fourth Dynasty (ca. 2613 to ca. 2494), also built massive pyramids and experimented with designs and constructions until the "perfect" pyramid form was achieved by King Khufu—as exemplified by the pyramids at Giza (Figure 11.5). It is not just the massive size of this and other pyramids of the era that is so impressive, but also the complex engineering, the deft execution of stone sculpture, and the precise planning such projects would have required. And the pyramids were accompanied by massive tombs hewn out of living rock, by monumental sculpture, such as the Sphinx, by funerary temples, and by various roads, ramps, and platforms constructed to service the larger buildings.

The Great Pyramid of Giza required the quarrying, transport, preparation, and laying of 2,300,000 stone blocks, each with an average weight of 2.5 tons, and it is estimated to have required a labor force equivalent to about 84,000 people employed for eighty days a year for twenty years. It is not known how these people were mobilized and administered, but many think the construction was done by the peasantry during seasons when little agricultural activity was required. What appear to be barracks, with a capacity of at least 4,000 people, have been found near one of the pyramids, and the administration, feeding, direction, and planning required to control such a work force, which included many highly trained craftsmen as well as laborers, would obviously argue a high degree of political and bureaucratic centralization. The king was apparently able to call on all the resources of the country, and direct them and the people to virtually any end, and at times the entire national economy was probably focused on these projects. The absolute control of the monarch is directly reflected in the texts and in the mortuary complexes of the various levels of high-

11.5
The pyramids of Giza, seen from the air.

ranking administrators who served him, many of whose tombs are laid out around the king's own tomb, perpetuating the king's control over them even into eternity.

Shortly after 2495 B.C. there was a change in dynasties, as well as in the religious and political texture of the Old Kingdom. The worship of the sun god, Re, emerged as the dominant religion, and the devolution of kingly power seems to have been matched by increasing power among the nobility and provincial authorities. There was a greater degree of upward mobility in the administrative hierarchy. Provincial rulers apparently even led expeditions against hostile nomads and administered foreign trade to some extent, and although these activities were done in the name of the king, Egypt was clearly heading toward political decentralization.

11.6
The well-preserved corpse of
Seti I (d. 1304 B.C.). In the
Cairo Museum.

The breakup came in the *First Intermediate period* (ca. 2160 to
ca. 2040 B.C.), a century and more of political and religious upheaval.
The increasing prominence of the god Osiris cut away at the foundation of the old authoritarian state religion of Re in which the king was
central and absolute, and at the same time there was a rapid succession
of weak kings and consequent insurrections. At various times one or
another province was able to dominate some of the others, but revolt
and rebellion convulsed the country. Despite periods of peace and
prosperity, the lack of a centralized, efficient administration began to
be felt in the agricultural sector, as the complex irrigation systems fell
into disrepair, and at the end of the Old Kingdom Egypt was ripe for
the reestablishment of a powerful monarchy.

As a whole, the political and economic structures of the Old Kingdom are those of a highly complex civilization, but some important
characteristics distinguish it from Mesopotamian and other early complex societies. For example, there seem to have been no standing armies during most of the Old Kingdom and no economically significant

As Egyptian writing evolved, the original hieroglyphics were assigned phonetic values and the characters became highly stylized to facilitate writing.

EGYPTIAN SCRIPTS (Alphabet)

Hieroglyphic sign		Meaning, transcription, sound value		New Kingdom Hieratic	Demotic	Coptic
	vulture	ꜣ	glottal stop			omitted or ει
	flowering reed	ỉ	I			ε ι or ε
	forearm & hand	ꜥ	ayin			omitted
	quail chick	w	W			oγ
	foot	b	B			π or ß
	stool	p	P			π or ß
	horned viper	f	F			ϥ
	owl	m	M		ꝫ or ꞌ	м
	water	n	N			N
	mouth	r	R			ρ or λ [ε]
	reed shelter	h	H			8
	twisted flax	ḥ	slightly guttural			8 or omitted
	placenta (?)	ḫ	H as in "loch"			8 or ϧ
	animal's belly	ẖ	slightly softer than h			8
	door bolt	s, z	S			c
	folded cloth	s, ś	S			c
	pool	š	SH			ϣ
	hill	ḳ	Q			κ, ϭ
	basket w. handle	k	K			κ, ϭ
	jar stand	g	G			ϭ
	loaf	t	T			τ, θ
	tethering rope	ṯ	TJ		ꞌ (ρϛ)	ϫ, τ
	hand	d	D		ꞌ (α δ)	τ
	snake	ḏ	DJ			ϫ

EGYPTIAN ROYAL TITULARY

Horus Name (srḫ)	Nebty Name (nbty)	Golden Horus Name (Ḥr nbw)	Prenomen (ny-sw bit)	Nomen (s3 Rꜥ)

slavery. In some ways the economic system—although highly administered—was a simple redistributive, almost chiefdom-like system, quite different from that of early Mesopotamian states.

Economic exchange was apparently controlled almost entirely through the king; there were no "merchants," in the capitalistic sense at least, until 1,000 years after the end of the Old Kingdom. Craftsmen, scribes, peasants, and everyone else were required to perform some services in the name of the king and were liable for military and civil conscription, but there is a clear contrast here with the partially capitalistic, multitiered, highly differentiated economic system characteristic of the later Mesopotamian states.

11.8
Limestone statues of the steward Memy-Sabu and his wife. Height about 61 cm. From Giza, about 2340 B.C.

In early Mesopotamia there appeared to have been a "natural" cycle of expansion and collapse of the economic and political systems, and the same seems true of Egypt, even in the Old Kingdom, when periods of extreme centralization followed eras of fragmentation. The developmental cycles of Egypt through the end of the Old Kingdom may have been in part a direct result of dramatic climatic changes. Rainfall decreased in much of Egypt after about 2900 B.C., and Butzer notes that decreasing rainfall would have reduced the resources and numbers of desert nomads, as well as eliminating much of the seasonal pastoral movements of valley sedentary folk out into the deserts. It may even have interrupted travel between the Nile and the Red Sea and the Libyan oases (1976: 26–27).

THE MIDDLE KINGDOM (2040 TO 1570 B.C.)

The political and social history of the *Middle Kingdom* contains the same cycles of expansion and collapse that can be seen in all the great ancient empires. Periods of well-regulated trade, an expanding economy, and brilliant advances in art, architecture, and literature were followed by revolution, poverty, and political fragmentation; and toward the end of the period Egypt finally fell under the power of foreign invaders.

The Middle Kingdom originated in the great civil unrest of the twenty-first century B.C., when conditions in Egypt were probably at least half as bad as the following hyperbolic contemporary account suggests.

> Corn has perished everywhere. . . . People are stripped of clothing, perfume, and oil. . . . Everyone says, "Three is no more." . . . Strangers have come into Egypt everywhere. . . . Men do not sail to Byblos today: What shall we do for fine wood? Princes and pious men everywhere as far as the land of Crete are embalmed with the resins of Lebanon, but now we have no supplies. . . . The dead are thrown in the river. . . . Laughter has perished. Grief walks the land. (Aldred 1961: 102)

Conditions began to improve radically after 2040 B.C., when Mentuhotep II, the first king of the Middle Kingdom, brought Upper and Lower Egypt once again under the rule of a single royal house. Mentuhotep and his next several successors reorganized the country with considerable energy, undertaking expeditions into Nubia, Libya, and Syria, reopening trade routes to the Red Sea, and commencing again the construction of monumental buildings.

In about 1999 B.C. Amenemhet came to power, and he and his successors inaugurated one of the most brilliant periods of Egyptian civilization. The capital was reestablished near Memphis, from which both Upper and Lower Egypt could be ruled effectively, trade routes were extended, fortresses were built along the country's frontiers, territories were annexed, and various administrative innovations were made, including the tradition of co-regency, in which sons were made co-rulers toward the end of their fathers' reigns, thereby eliminating some of the bloody battles for succession that had plagued previous dynasties. Amenemhet and his successors, notably Sesostris II and Amenemhet II, also restructured and expanded the economy by extending irrigation systems in the Fayum, increasing trade with Nubia, and by opening Egypt to the skills and ideas of foreign craftsmen and agents. Concurrently, they vastly reduced the power of the nobles, and thus probably retarded the recurrence of the civil wars that had afflicted Egypt during previous millennia.

There were also major advances in Egyptian art and architecture during this period, many literary classics were composed, and the cult of Osiris completed its replacement of the colder, sterner religion of Re and gave the common people some hope of the glorious afterlife that in the past had been restricted to royalty.

Anthropologist Elman Service notes that the ability of Egyptian dynasts of the first millennium B.C. (some of whom came from relatively unimportant noble families) to reform Egyptian society so brilliantly and fundamentally has strong parallels in Sargon's conquest of Mesopotamia, and also in the imperial designs of the rulers of Tiahuanaco in Peru and the rise to power of the Aztecs in Mesoamerica (1975: 235). He suggests that this might be a common evolutionary pattern, where economically less-developed and less-specialized groups along the margins of established civilizations have more "evolutionary potential," in the sense that they have more freedom in working out solutions to problems that have locked more specialized cultures into unprogressive adaptations (1975: 235).

From about 1786 to about 1720 B.C., various kings managed to remain in general control of most of Egypt, but gradually the power of enclaves of Asiatic peoples in the eastern Delta increased as they took advantage of the weakening monarchy. The ancient origins of these foreigners, collectively referred to as the *Hyksos,* are uncertain, as is the manner in which they took over Egypt and the extent of their domination. But at about 1674 B.C. they captured Memphis and the Hyksos king adopted the trappings of Egyptian royalty. Artifacts made in the manner of the Hyksos have been found all along the Nile Valley and as far south as Karmah, but it is not clear how directly they were able to control most of the population. Also, it appears that the Hyksos were "conquered" by the Egyptian culture in much the same way that the "barbarians" on the periphery of China lost their ethnicity as they adopted the Chinese way of life.

Shortly after 1650 B.C. the rulers of Thebes, a local Egyptian dynasty, were able to expand their area of control at the expense of the Hyksos, and within a short time the stage was set for the final expulsion of the hated foreigners.

THE NEW KINGDOM AND LATER PERIODS (1570 TO 330 B.C.)

King Ahmose, a native of Thebes, began at about 1570 B.C. to expel the Hyksos from the northern Delta, and after several successful battles he managed to drive them beyond the eastern frontier. He even attacked and captured the city of Sharuhen, in southern Palestine, and the rich spoils from this city were the basis for the creation of an influential social class, as military officers were made administrators of the conquered territories. Ahmose and his successors reformed the bureaucracy established by the Hyksos, modeling it after that of the Middle Kingdom.

Perhaps the greatest ruler of this period, and in the whole of Egyptian history, was Thutmose III, who established Egypt's Asiatic empire with his conquest of much of the eastern Mediterranean coastal areas. Even powerful Assyria paid material tribute to the Egyptian Empire, as did the Babylonians and the Hittites. Thutmose III was a master military strategist, and his surprise attack on Megiddo and amphibious operation against the Mitanni, a powerful kingdom in Southwest Asia, established Egypt as a world power. By about 1450 B.C. Egypt had commercial contacts on a large scale, exchanging products with Phoenecia, Crete, the Aegean Islands, and its traditional African trading partners. Military pacification programs were extended far into Nubia, and vast quantities of Nubian gold and building stone were shipped to the Nile Valley cities.

One of the most famous monarchs of the *New Kingdom* was Akhnaton, who altered the basic religious structure of Egypt by introducing a semi-monotheistic religion and trying to eradicate vestiges of older polytheistic elements. He built many marvelous temples to Aton, the new god, and constructed a new capital at Tell el-Amarna in central Egypt, complete with many magnificent religious and administrative buildings. Akhnaton's influence on art and architecture was substantial, but soon after his death the old religions were reestablished by Smenkhkare and the famous Tutankhamen. Another famous pharaoh of the late New Kingdom was Ramses II, the oppressive king who held the Israelites in bondage. Apparently it was his successor, Merneptah, who refused to let the Israelites leave and gave Charlton Heston such a difficult time.

Egypt's society and religion remained quite stable throughout the second millennium B.C., although its internal cohesion and ability to exert itself internationally fluctuated considerably. At about 1000 B.C. Egypt lost military control of Nubia, and the breakup of its Asiatic empire brought it into confrontation with the Israel of David and Solomon. The Egyptians captured a city on the border of Israel and agreed to peace upon the marriage of the pharaoh's daughter to Solomon. But

11.9
Estimated population changes in Egypt between 5000 B.C. and A.D. 1000.

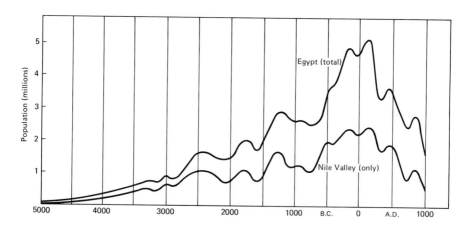

five years after Solomon's death Seshonk I invaded Israel, plundered Jerusalem, and reestablished Egypt's Asiatic empire.

During the first millennium B.C. Egypt had various periods of resurgence when particularly strong kings were able to reassert Egyptian influence in Palestine and Africa, but increasingly Egypt slipped under foreign domination, and it never really recovered its autonomy. At about 525 B.C. Cambyses, a Persian king, conquered Egypt and reduced it to a vassal kingdom, proclaiming himself pharaoh. In 332 B.C. Alexander the Great marched into Egypt, evicted the Persians, and built the city of Alexandria. Later, the Romans, Arabs, and British would complete the conquest of Egypt, submerging almost entirely this distinctive civilization that was for so many years the light of the ancient world.

THE ORIGINS OF EGYPTIAN CIVILIZATION: CONCLUSIONS

Many simplistic notions about the general origins of cultural complexity have foundered on the evidence from Egypt. The idea that large-scale irrigation is a key to state formation, for example, does not hold for Egypt, where the first states developed many centuries before there were any unified large irrigation systems and where irrigation remained largely a local concern until the recent past. Similarly, the hypothesis that population growth in circumscribed environments leads to increasingly wider spheres of warfare and increasing cultural complexity finds no support in the Egyptian record. As Figure 11.9 illustrates, population growth in ancient Egypt was extremely slow, with no land or water shortages until long after the first states and empires had already emerged. Here too, as in Mesopotamia, dense populations seem more a *result* than a cause of evolving cultural complexity (cf. O'Connor 1972). Nor is there any evidence that systematic warfare was a first cause in the evolution of the earliest complex Egyptian cultures (although later it was important), and much the same can be said of the Marxian idea that class struggle transformed these societies. Early Egyptian societies appear to have been cemented by mutually supportive bonds of kinship, religion, and economics, and there were few capitalistic elements until very late in the Middle Kingdom.

The pressure of nomads and others on the Egyptian periphery seems to have been an important factor occasionally, but there is not much of a parallel here with the situation in ancient China, where nomad-farmer relationships were a central theme in imperial developments.

A comparison of Mesopotamian and Egyptian settlement patterns underscores the fact that urbanization is just one strategy, not an indispensable condition, of cultural complexity. Whereas the people of Mesopotamia early and dramatically aggregated into fortified towns and cities, from which they conducted agricultural, industrial, religious, and administrative operations, the Egyptians did not even have a permanent capital until late in the second millennium, when Thebes emerged as a center—although recent excavations reveal a greater degree of urbanization than was previously thought to have existed. The comparatively slow development of Egyptian urbanism probably had many causes, including: (1) the absence of any powerful foreign peoples on Egyptian borders; (2) the uniformity of the environment all along the Nile, so that there was little to be gained from large-volume, interregional exchange of food or craft products; and (3) the pronounced political centralization, which inhibited development of secular, economic differentiation.

When the largest pyramids and other structures were built, population growth rates were slow, there was apparently little pressure on the country's resources, and there were large areas of uninhabited but fertile land. If we view these pyramids as mechanisms to mobilize and train a large work force, we must ask why such a work force would be an advantage, because when the first pyramids were built there were few large irrigation works and little demand for a standing army. If we view the vast expenditures of wealth in the funerary complexes as a means of "balancing" the economy by taking out of circulation inordinate amounts of gold, silver, or craft items, there is some difficulty in explaining why this would have been necessary in a society whose economic system and long-distance trade were strictly controlled by the monarchy and where there were few large markets and almost no free enterprise or capitalism of any kind.

The Egyptian Character

The rich Egyptian tombs and literature irresistibly seem to elicit theories about Egyptian "character," even though we know that not all Egyptians thought alike and that the Egyptian world view and life view were not static. Nonetheless, there are some persistent, deeply embedded themes in Egyptian culture. For one thing, Egyptians seem to have been a God-intoxicated people, "half in love with easeful death." Herodotus noted that they were the most "religious" people he had encountered and that they were given to incessant and elaborate religious rituals and supported an enormous priestly bureaucracy. Their concern with death, and the vast energies and richness they invested in preparing for it, are manifestly evident.

To our own, essentially Greek, minds, the Egyptians were badly confused about the nature of reality. They seemed unable to distinguish between things and their substances. J. Wilson notes (1946: 72) that the Egyptians saw no difference between supplying a dead king with real loaves of bread, wooden models of bread, or loaves painted on the walls; it was not the actual thing that mattered, it was the idea. Nor did they see any problem in combining several gods into a single entity, or according the same god different characteristics in different parts of the country. Again, the substance, not the incidental manifestation, was important. The Egyptians also apparently felt justified in threatening a god who did not grant their wishes, particularly if they had made expensive sacrifices to him. They seemed to feel that causality in the physical world was not impersonal and inevitable. If the Nile did not rise to its most productive height, it was not because of some sort of alteration in rainfall patterns in central Africa; it was because the river *refused* to rise, and some action, some kind of propitiation, was in order (ibid.: 24). Of course, this perspective can be found in many other cultures, both ancient and modern, but the Egyptians seem to have been particularly inclined to a denial of "natural" forces.

Many eminent scholars (e.g., Frankfort 1949; Hamilton 1930; Kitto 1951) have commented on the different values and perspectives of the Egyptians compared to those of the Greeks, but one need only look at the lyric poetry and other fine literature of ancient Egypt to see that these people were very like people in every place and time. Poem after poem celebrates the physical beauty of young men and women, the eroticism of adolescence, the natural wonders of the Egyptian world, and the pleasures of food, drink, and play (see Kaster 1968 for particularly rewarding translations). And like most people, the ancient Egyptians looked toward an afterlife made perfect by the absence of all the troubles and turmoils of life.

The Evolution of Complex Societies in Sub Saharan Africa

Except for pharaonic Egypt and adjacent areas, complex societies and intensive agricultural economies did not develop on the vast African continent until the last 1,000 years, and even then these developments were in large part the result of trade with the more complex cultures of the Near East and the Mediterranean littoral.

Africa had been center stage for human physical and cultural evolution for millions of years, and thus the question naturally arises as to why it so decisively lost its developmental preeminence. The answer, obscured by centuries of archaeological neglect and racist interpretations of history, is at last emerging.

THE ECOLOGICAL SETTING

Africa is so rich in gold, silver, iron, jewels, ivory, palm oil, and other resources that it is difficult to appreciate its formidable ecological barriers to the origins and spread of domestication, agriculture, and complex cultural organization. The enormous Sahara Desert, expanding and contracting with Pleistocene and post-Pleistocene climatic changes, has almost always isolated most of Africa from the critical mass of Near Eastern and Mediterranean cultures. And even in the more humid sub-Saharan regions the dense vegetation, poor soils, and unpredictable rainfall make large-scale intensive agriculture unproductive for the primitive cultivator. Nor do the great rivers, like the Niger, have the regular regimes, large semiarid alluvial plains, or latitude that make the Nile, Tigris and Euphrates, and Yellow river valleys so productive. To make matters worse, Africa has a veritable horror show of diseases, including a tsetse-fly-borne cattle illness that barred pastoralists from many areas and malaria, which recurrently wiped out human populations in the more tropical areas.

Given these and other ecological problems, the surprising thing about African cultural evolution is not that complex societies failed to develop there as independently and early as they did elsewhere; it is that early African societies managed to produce sophisticated arts, crafts, and religious and political systems as early and as brilliantly as they did. Indeed, post-Pleistocene Africa's cultural history is an object lesson in human inventiveness and adaptability in the face of an extreme environment.

EARLY AFRICAN DOMESTICATION AND AGRICULTURE

The extent to which Egypt and North Africa participated in the transition to agriculture that was occurring all over the Southwest Asian and Mediterranean world of the sixth and seventh millennia B.C. is unclear. Domestic cattle bones dating to about 5500 B.C. have been found in caves on the periphery of the Saharan Desert, and domestic sheep and goats were being raised in some Libyan coastal areas by 4600 B.C. Some cereals may have been domesticated in the wetter areas of the northern edge of the Sahara long before 6000 B.C. (Butzer 1976: 11), and recent radiocarbon dates from the Nile Valley suggest that domestic plants and animals may have been there even earlier (Posnansky and McIntosh 1976).

Domestication and early agriculture in both North Africa and sub-Saharan Africa were directly linked to the complex climatic changes of the post-Pleistocene period. A relatively humid environment was established shortly after 9000 B.C., and there were particularly wet periods during the seventh and eighth millennia B.C. (Butzer et al. 1972). The increased rainfall at these times enlarged many lakes, swamps, and rivers and created many new ones (Sutton 1974: 528). Lake Chad, for example, covered 300,000 square kilometers during these rainfall peaks. The lush vegetation supported by this additional moisture provided an excellent game habitat, and all across the south Saharan fringe from the Atlantic to the Nile Valley, and from there south into the African Rift valleys, the landscape—which today is very dry—teemed with giraffes, elephants, buffalos, antelopes, and other animals.

The presence of thousands of serrated bone "harpoon" points and other archaeological evidence indicates that the shores of many of these lakes and rivers were occupied by fishing communities, and radiocarbon dates suggest that by no later than the seventh millennium B.C. fishing, complemented by hunting and gathering, was the basic subsistence strategy of thousands of communities along the southern Saharan fringe (Sutton 1974: 529). Pottery appears at some of these fishing communities as early as 6000 B.C., sometimes in association with the harpoon points, and this use of ceramics probably points to largely sedentary populations. These sites show no evidence of agriculture at this time, but ceramics were probably useful in the aquatic economy. Unfortunately, few traces of actual residences or community settlement patterns remain, because most constructions were probably of reeds and mud.

Little is known about the possible interactions of these central African fisherfolk and the peoples of the tropical forests and savannas of eastern and southern Africa, areas which were probably still inhabited mainly by highly mobile groups of hunters and gatherers.

Shortly after 3000 B.C. Saharan and sub-Saharan climates grew increasingly arid, and some pastoral and lake-adapted societies may have been forced southward, perhaps bringing with them domesticated plants. The domesticated wheat and barley of the North may not have done well initially in the greater heat of the South, and these people probably experimented with native central African plants like sorghum, millet, and yams. Regional sub-Saharan economies diversified in succeeding millennia, as the climate fluctuated, and with the return of an arid climate shortly after 1100 B.C. large agricultural villages began to appear around the margins of the few remaining lakes. Munson's research in central Mauritania (West Africa) demonstrates that early in the first millennium B.C. sedentary agriculturalists, growing mainly millet, had achieved substantial population densities and were living in large, heavily walled villages (1976).

The peoples of the southern edge of West Africa and the lush vegetation zones of central Africa may have domesticated and cultivated yams and other root crops by 3000 B.C. or even earlier, but this is difficult to document. Such crops are propagated by simple vegeculture, the planting of a cutting, and their technological requirements are only a primitive digging stick and perhaps a few tools to clear and burn vegetation. And because such crops grow best in humid climates and disturbed areas, there is often little for the archaeologist to recover that indicates this sort of subsistence. A few traces of ash layers, ground stone tools, and ceramics in West Africa, however, suggest early *swidden* cultivation; that is, farmers here cut down vegetation and then burned it off in order to prepare areas for vegeculture of yams and other root crops (Clark 1972: 136) (Fig. 11.10).

CENTRAL AFRICA'S FIRST COMPLEX SOCIETIES

By about 900 B.C. complex societies had formed in the Sudan, far to the south of the Egyptian heartland, and at about 590 B.C. a non-Egyptian but urban and sophisticated society was ensconced at Meroe, on the fertile floodplain between the Nile and Atbara rivers. The peo-

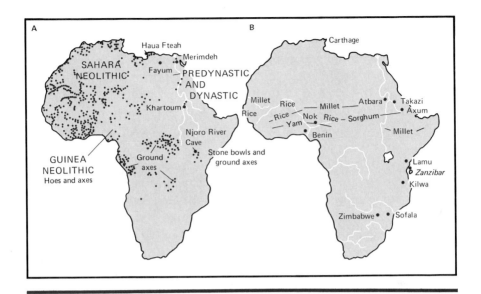

11.10
The widespread distribution of hoes and axes in Africa may indicate the spread of early vegeculture and agriculture; (Map A) Dots indicate concentrations of Neolithic artifacts and sites. (Map B) Millet, yams, sorghum, perhaps rice and other crops were probably domesticated or introduced into cultivation in Africa in the last several millennia B.C.

ple of Meroe traded with both south Saharan and Mediterranean societies, acting as middlemen in the lucrative trade in slaves, iron, ivory, gold, and possibly copper. Great slag heaps from copper smelting have been found near Meroe, but most of these seem to date to early in the first millennium A.D., by which time the Meroe state had disintegrated (Posnansky 1976).

Beyond this northeastern corner, Africa's first complex societies seem to have been directly stimulated by two factors: (1) the involvement of the whole of the continent in trade networks feeding the rich, advanced civilizations of the Mediterranean and the Near East; and (2) the migrations of Bantu-speaking peoples, who brought with them ironworking.

The beginnings of long-distance trade in Africa are probably connected to the exploitation of metals (Posnansky 1973: 150). Copper was likely being shipped north from mines in Mauritania sometime before 1000 B.C., and the presence of many large Greek and Roman towns along the North African coast may be a reflection of trade in gold, skins, and ivory during the several centuries before and after the birth of Christ.

On many stone outcroppings in the Sahara and adjacent areas there are rock engravings and paintings of horses and horse-drawn chariots, and the location of these is thought to mark two trade routes, both connecting West Africa with the North African shore. The chariots depicted—which were of a military, not a transport type—suggest a date of about A.D. 500 (Posnansky 1973: 150), and trade in slaves, salt, gold, ivory, skins, and many other African commodities was probably well established by this date. This trade may have been in part responsible for some signs of embryonic cultural evolution in the Senegambian region, where about A.D. 750 the populace built more than 150 groups of megaliths, most of them circles or lines of stone blocks. Some of the circles are eight meters across and up to four meters high. Posnansky thinks these structures "clearly indicate a rapid increase in wealth in the area, with the megaliths serving for long-forgotten rituals for chiefs whose power was perhaps derived from controlling the wealth obtained from the exploitation of nearby iron reserves and local gold deposits" (ibid.: 151). There are other indications of evolving cultural complexity in West Africa at this time, such as the more than 4,000 burial mounds, some as much as five meters high and forty meters across, that have been found in Senegal. Most of these contain multiple burials, with highly variable collections of copper, gold, carnelian, and iron grave goods (ibid.: 152).

Sometime before the trans-Saharan trade routes were fully established, population migrations and the development of ironworking were changing the character of much of sub-Saharan and West Africa. Iron artifacts dating to the fourth century B.C. have been found in several parts of West Africa, although it is uncertain whether these were of local production or had arrived via the Saharan trade routes. About 2,000 years ago, cereal farmers, who made pottery and worked with iron, appeared in Zambia, whence they fanned out in a few centuries over most areas of the subcontinent where rainfall was sufficient for dry farming of cereals.

The spread of Iron Age cultures has traditionally been associated with the migrations of Bantu-speaking peoples, whose ancestral homeland may have been the forests of Zaire. Bantu-derived languages such as Zulu are now spoken by almost all black Africans south of a line extending from the Niger delta to the Kenyan coast (Pfeiffer 1977: 264). It was thought at one time that invading hordes of Bantu speakers had swept into southern Africa and exterminated the natives with iron weapons, but as elsewhere, archaeological evidence indicates that this "invasion" was more likely a long, slow process of short-range migrations, intermarriage, and cultural absorption. In fact, ironworking and agriculture may have been adopted in some areas long before the Bantu arrived.

At first, Iron Age communities in southern and central Africa shared many cultural elements, but over the centuries great diversity developed. Iron hoes and other implements, and possibly also pottery, were produced by specialists and exchanged between communities, and there is archaeological evidence of continuing trade between hunters and gatherers and these sedentary ironworking agriculturalists. After about A.D. 500, copper, tin, and gold mining were added to the economic repertoires of many areas, particularly in Rhodesia where there are more than 1,100 prehistoric gold mines and 150 copper mines. The subsistence basis of these people was probably swidden cultivation of sorghum, millet, and other plants, complemented by cattle, goat, and sheep raising, as well as considerable hunting and gathering.

As early as the first century A.D., traders of the Greco-Roman and Arab worlds knew of the riches of coastal East Africa, and by the eighth century A.D. Arab traders were visiting the coastal ports of southern Africa in pursuit of the gold trade. Between the eleventh and fifteenth centuries A.D., thirty-seven new towns were founded along the coast as part of the trade in gold and other products. In the fourteenth and fifteenth centuries A.D., three large centers evolved as control points for most of the coastal salt and metal trade: Zimbabwe in southwestern Zimbabwe Rhodesia, Ingombe Ilede in Zambia, and Mapungubwe, in the northern Transvaal. These communities shared many characteristics and appear to have been largely contemporary, but their political or economic connections, if any, are not at all clear.

Graves at Zimbabwe and Mapungubwe differ sharply in their richness, some containing only a corpse and a few trinkets while others are swamped with gold and copper ornaments, imported beads, and cloth. There seems little reason to doubt the widely accepted view that these settlements were the capitals of societies stratified by rank and wealth, but it is unlikely that there was much economic specialization, either in production or administration.

Zimbabwe has perhaps the most imposing public architecture in all of Iron Age Africa. Its twenty-five hectares of ruins (Figure 11.11) appear to be the remains of several periods of construction, the most impressive of which was probably completed shortly before A.D. 1450. The rulers of this city apparently lived in an exclusive precinct on a hill, from which they controlled the city's religious and commercial activities as well as the rural villages that surrounded it. Zimbabwe lost its importance shortly after A.D. 1450, and in the same century Portuguese merchants and support troops arrived and within a short time came to dominate much of East and South Africa.

After about A.D. 500 the increasing trade across the western Sahara in gold, kola nuts, slaves, and salt, plus the establishment of agriculture and an iron technology in much of southwestern Africa, eventually resulted in the appearance along the southern edge of the Sahara of three large states: Ghana, Mali, and Songhai (Figure 11.12). Each of these reached its peak in the first half of the second millennium A.D.,

11.11
The "Great Enclosure" at Zimbabwe, Zimbabwe Rhodesia, was probably built as an administrative and trade center shortly before A.D. 1500.

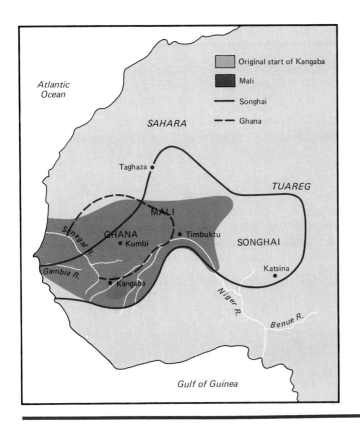

11.12
The African kingdoms of Mali, Ghana, and Songhai.

when the power of Near Eastern Islamic states was also expanding, and much of what we know about Ghana, Mali, and Songhai comes not from archaeological research, but from the writings of al-Bakri and other Islamic scholars—most of whom never saw the African states, but compiled their accounts from travelers' reports.

The kingdom of Ghana, situated in the Upper Niger and Sengal river valleys, is thought to have begun forming in the fifth and sixth centuries A.D., and by A.D. 1000 it was a powerful state with a large army equipped with iron weapons. The capital, at Kumbi, is estimated to have had a population of 30,000 and the rulers could apparently call on the services of a rural population numbering in the hundreds of thousands. The economic basis of the state was principally trade in gold and ivory, as well as in salt, kola nuts, slaves, and iron weapons. The demise of the Ghanian state, beginning at about A.D. 1000, was probably tied to the incursions of the Berbers, who at that time were also invading Spain.

The largest trade state of medieval Africa was Mali, which began at about A.D. 1250 to fill the vacuum left by the eclipse of Ghana. The state was initially centered at the city of Mali on the Niger River, but its control was eventually extended over much of sub-Saharan West Africa, from the Atlantic almost to Lake Chad. The Mali state reached its peak under Mansa Musa, a Muslim potentate. Its capital was Niani,

11.13
West African trade routes in the early second millennium A.D.

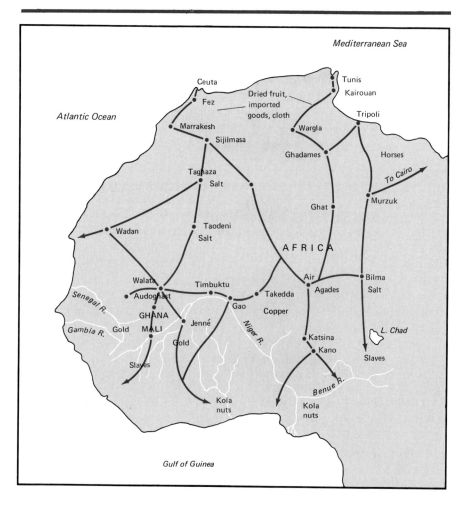

but its greatest city was Timbucto, already famous for its university, book trade, and wealth. Mali went into a period of decline after Musa's death, late in the fourteenth century A.D.

Songhai, a state based at the town of Gao on the Niger River, began to expand at about A.D. 1340, and by A.D. 1492 the militaristic Muslim leaders of Songhai had extended their control into the area formerly controlled by Mali, and far north into the Sahara as well. Trans-Saharan trade, as in the case of Mali and Ghana, was the economic mainstay of the Songhai state. Although this state collapsed under the Berber invasion of A.D. 1591, the Songhai people still exist as an ethnic group living along the Niger River.

After the sixteenth century, Africa fell increasingly under the control of non-Africans, and only in the last fifty years have most Africans retrieved their autonomy. They were held in thrall for so long by outsiders because of their inferior economic position, but also because European-introduced diseases killed many people and because of slavery: the African slave trade was organized and profited from by Africans well before the sixteenth century; some have estimated that nearly as many African slaves were shipped north into the Near Eastern and Mediterranean areas as were eventually carried to the New World.

CONCLUSIONS

If we take as our main criterion of cultural complexity the specialization of the economic and social organizations to the point that no small group of people can maintain that particular cultural system, then obviously many African societies were complex. Ceramics, gold mining, trade administration, and many other specialized functions are clearly evident in much of sub-Saharan Africa early in the first millennium A.D. (Maggs 1977). That cultural complexity remained for the most part at a very low level in virtually all of Africa, however, is also quite evident. Except for small burial mounds and a few specialized centers like Zimbabwe, monumental architecture was never a major part of African developments. In settlement patterns we can discern the effects of trade routes and evolving rank and wealth stratification, but only very late do complexly structured, multilevel settlement-size hierarchies appear. In fact, even the largest African settlements in the early states were essentially just large villages, with scores of mud-thatch houses and very little variation in residential architecture. Kin ties were, and continue to be, the principal bonds of African societies, and even to-day class-structured societies in most of black Africa are in their infancy.

The evolution of cultural complexity in most of Africa has been determined by the generally low agricultural productivity and the cultural isolation that was broken only by relatively late transportation innovations like the triangular (lateen) sail, used on boats carrying traders from the Indian Ocean ports, and the systematic use of camels to bridge the great deserts. As important, perhaps, was the discovery of the antimalaria drugs such as quinine, which opened areas to settlement (Shaw 1971: 53).

If past patterns of cultural change are any guide, it may well be that Africa will soon be one of the world's power centers, despite its past centuries of "underdevelopment." Cultural dominance is a some-time thing, and Africa's vast natural wealth and cultural heterogeneity give it great evolutionary potential.

Bibliography

Aldred, Cyril. 1961. *The Egyptians.* New York: Praeger.

Arkell, A. J. 1966. "The Iron Age in the Sudan." *Current Anthropology* 7(4): 451–52.

Arkell, A. J. and P. J. Ucko. 1965. "Review of Predynastic Development in the Nile Valley." *Current Anthropology.* 6: 145–66.

Baumgartel, E. J. 1970. "Predynastic Egypt." In *Cambridge Ancient History.* Rev. ed. 1(1): 463–97.

Brothwell, D. R. and B. A. Chiarelli, eds. 1973. *Population Biology of the Ancient Egyptians.* London: Academic Press.

Budge, Sir E. A. Wallis. 1972. *The Dwellers on the Nile.* New York: Benjamin Blom.

———. 1960. "Archeology and Geology in Ancient Egypt." *Science.* 132: 1617–24.

————. 1976. *Early Hydraulic Civilization in Egypt*. Chicago: University of Chicago Press.

Butzer, K. W., G. U. Isaac, J. L. Richardson, and C. K. Washbourn-Kamau. 1972. "Radiocarbon Dating of East African Lake Levels." *Science*. 175: 1069–76.

Caton-Thompson, G. 1931. *The Zimbabwe Culture*. London: Oxford University Press.

Clark, J. Desmond. 1971. "A Re-Examination of the Evidence for Agricultural Origins in the Nile Valley." *Proceedings of the Prehistoric Society*. 37(2).

————. 1972. "Mobility and Settlement Patterns in Sub-Saharan Africa: A Comparison of Late Prehistoric Hunter-Gatherers and Early Agricultural Occupation Units." In *Man, Settlement and Urbanism*, eds. P. Ucko, R. Tringham, and G. Dimbleby. London: Duckworth.

————. 1976. "Prehistoric Populations and Resources Favoring Plant Domestication in Africa." In *Origins of African Plant Domestication*, eds. J. R. Harland et al. The Hague: Mouton.

Connah, H. 1975. *The Archaeology of Benin*. London: Oxford University Press.

Davidson, Basil. 1966. *A History of West Africa to the Nineteenth Century*. New York: Anchor.

————. 1971. *African Kingdoms*. New York: Time-Life.

Edwards, I. E. S. 1961. *The Pyramids of Egypt*. London: Max Parrish.

Fagan, Brian. 1967. *Iron Age Cultures in Zambia*. London: Chatto & Windus.

Fagg, Bernard. 1969. "Recent Work in West Africa: New Light on the Nok Culture." *World Archaeology*. 1(1): 41–50.

Frankfort, Henri. 1956. *The Birth of Civilization in the Near East*. Garden City, N.Y.: Doubleday.

Frankfort, H., J. Wilson, and T. Jacobsen. 1949. *Before Philosophy*. Baltimore: Penguin.

Hamilton, Edith. 1930. *The Greek Way*. New York: W. W. Norton.

Harland, J. R., J. M. de Wet, and A. B. Stemler, eds. 1976. *Origins of African Plant Domestication*. The Hague: Mouton.

Harris, J. E. and Kent R. Weeks. 1973. *X-Raying the Pharaohs*. New York: Scribner's.

Hoffman, Michael. 1970. "Culture History and Cultural Ecology at Hierankonpolis from Paleolithic Times to the Old Kingdom." Unpublished doctoral dissertation, University of Wisconsin.

Kaster, Joseph, trans. and ed. 1968. *Wings of the Falcon*. New York: Holt.

Kemp, B. J. 1977. "The Early Development of Towns in Egypt." *Antiquity*. 51(203): 185–200.

Kitto, H. D. F. 1951. *The Greeks*. Harmondsworth: Pelican.

Maggs, Tim. 1977. "Some Recent Radiocarbon Dates from Eastern and Southern Africa." *Journal of African History*. 18(2): 161–91.

Munson, Patrick J. 1976. "Archaeological Data on the Origins of Cultivation in the Southwest Sahara and Its Implications for West Africa." In *Origins of African Plant Domestication,* eds. J. R. Harland et al. The Hague: Mouton.

O'Connor, P. 1972. "A Regional Population in Egypt to Circa 600 B.C." In *Population Growth: Anthropological Implications,* ed. Brian Spooner. Cambridge, Mass.: MIT Press.

Oliver, Roland and Brian M. Fagan. 1975. *Africa in the Iron Age.* London: Cambridge University Press.

Pfeiffer, John E. 1977. *The Emergence of Society.* New York: McGraw-Hill.

Posnansky, Merrick. 1973. "Aspects of Early West African Trade." *World Archaeology.* 5(2): 149–62.

———. 1976. "A Review of *Africa in the Iron Age: c. 500 B.C. to A.D. 1400* by Roland Oliver and Brian Fagan." *Journal of African History.* 17(4): 629–31.

Posnansky, Merrick and Roderick McIntosh. 1976. "New Radiocarbon Dates for Northern and Western Africa." *Journal of African History.* 17(2): 161–95.

Service, Elman. 1975. *Origins of the State and Civilization.* New York: W. W. Norton.

Shaw, Thurstan. 1971. "Africa in Prehistory: Leader or Laggard?" *Journal of African History.* 12: 143.

———. 1975. "Those Igbo-Ukwu Radiocarbon Dates: Facts, Fictions, and Probabilities." *Journal of African History.* 16(4): 503–17.

———. 1976. "Early Crops in Africa: A Review of Evidence." In *Origins of African Plant Domestication,* eds. J. R. Harland, et al. The Hague: Mouton.

Shinnie, P. P., ed. 1971. *The African Iron Age.* London: Oxford University Press.

Smith, Philip E. L. 1976. "Stone Age Man on the Nile." *Scientific American.* 235(2): 30–45.

Stuiver, M. and N. van der Merwe. 1968. "Radiocarbon Chronology of the Iron Age in Sub-Saharan Africa." *Current Anthropology.* 9(1): 53–59.

Sutton, J. 1974. "The Aquatic Civilization of Middle Africa." *Journal of African History.* 15(4): 527–46.

Trigger, Bruce G. 1969. "The Myth of Meroe and the African Iron Age." *African Historical Studies.* 2(1): 23–50.

———. 1976. *Nubia.* London: Thames and Hudson.

Wendorf, Fred. 1976. "The Use of Ground Grain during the Late Paleolithic of the Lower Nile Valley, Egypt." In *Origins of African Plant Domestication,* eds. J. R. Harland et al. The Hague: Mouton.

Wendorf, Fred, R. Said, and R. Schild. 1970. "Egyptian Prehistory: Some New Concepts." *Science.* 169: 1161.

Wendorf, Fred and R. Schild. 1975. "The Paleolithic of the Lower Nile Valley." In *Problems in Prehistory: North Africa and the Levant,* eds. F. Wendorf and A. Marks. Dallas: SMU Press.

White, Leslie. 1949. *The Science of Culture*. New York: Grove Press.

Wilson, John A. 1946. "Egypt: The Nature of the Universe." In *Before Philosophy,* eds. H. A. Frankfort et al. Baltimore: Penguin.

————. 1951. *The Culture of Ancient Egypt*. Chicago: University of Chicago Press.

————. 1960. "Civilizations Without Cities. In *City Invincible,* eds. C. H. Kraeling and R. McC. Adams. Chicago: University of Chicago Press.

12

Early Complex Cultures
in the Indus Valley

As a civilization [the Harappan] had not been
very remarkable, its techniques being imported
and never improved, its buildings utilitarian and
its artifacts unattractive, and the completeness of
its destruction its only claim to fame.

C. McEvedy (1972)

Since the discovery of its archaeological remains in the 1920s, the *Harappan* "civilization" that flourished in the Indus Valley late in the third millennium B.C. has been considered a sort of poor relation to the civilizations that graced the Mesopotamian Alluvium and the Nile Valley. Not only did the Indus Valley cultures mature thousands of years later than those in Egypt and Southwest Asia, but they also neglected to leave much in the way of the pyramids, tombs, and palaces prized by the archaelogical fraternity. Nor was the Harappan a particularly long-lived civilization, having appeared, matured, and "died" all within the space of a few centuries.

Thus, it is hardly surprising that until quite recently most archaeologists believed that Indus Valley developments were directly stimulated by the great civilizations of ancient Mesopotamia. But it has now become quite evident that the development of cultural complexity in the Indus Valley was a largely independent phenomenon that drew on the resources and cultures of a wide area, but was little influenced by

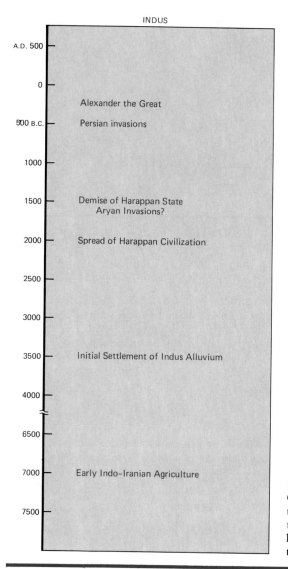

INDUS

A.D. 500

0

Alexander the Great

500 B.C. — Persian invasions

1000

1500 — Demise of Harappan State
Aryan Invasions?

2000 — Spread of Harappan Civilization

2500

3000

3500 — Initial Settlement of Indus Alluvium

4000

6500

7000 — Early Indo-Iranian Agriculture

7500

12.1
Chronology of early agriculture and complex societies in the Indus Valley. Little is known about most areas of the Valley.

any other complex culture. It is also clear that the Indus Valley cultures are of great interest for the study of the origins of cultural complexity: (1) they developed a writing system that has never been adequately deciphered; (2) they constructed massive cities laid out on very "modern"-looking grid systems, with broad avenues, carefully planned residential areas, and perhaps the ancient world's most advanced municipal water and sewage system; (3) their area of cultural and political influence and control extended over almost 1,300,000 square kilometers—considerably more territory than any other Old World civilization of this period; and (4) the distribution of wealth appears to have been much more equitable in the Indus cities than in other early Old World civilizations.

The Ecological Setting

Fifty million years ago, movements of the earth's crust forced the Indian subcontinent against the main Eurasian land mass with such enormous pressure that the land in between was squeezed upward, creating the dramatic Himalayan Mountains. Every spring melting snow in these highlands sends floods racing down the mountains and across the lowlands to the sea. Mixed with this average annual flow of 210 billion cubic meters of water are large amounts of silt and clay, and over the centuries the deposition of these has created the large Indus River Plain, a broad, flat, fertile area of enormous agricultural potential.

So little rain falls on most of this plain during the average year that large-scale, reliable agriculture is possible only through irrigation from the river, but—unlike the Nile—the Indus is very unpredictable. From year to year there can be great fluctuations in its volume and course. Much of the silt carried by the river is deposited in its own bed, raising the river above the level of adjacent plains so that it frequently breaks through its banks, flowing across the countryside in devastating floods. Countless centuries of this have left the Indus flood plain a maze of old river channels and great deposits of silt, all smoothed down into a fairly level surface by the action of wind and water. The great fertility of these soils is complemented by the arid, hot climate, which, like that of Egypt and Mesopotamia, supports several crops a year and a great diversity of plant species—as long as there is sufficient water.

The Indus River has probably always been rich in fish and other aquatic life, and there is evidence as well that until quite late in antiquity large forests and grasslands covered much of the plain. And because the river is navigable over much of its length, it no doubt contributed to the political integration and economic success of ancient Indus Valley cultures.

While the Indus Valley was the focus of the first complex communities in the subcontinent, adjacent areas also played an important role. To the west, the foothills and mountains of Pakistan, Afghanistan, and Iran sharply limit the extension of agriculture, but they provide valuable minerals, metals, animal products, and other goods, and they are also the homelands of pastoral and nomadic peoples who exerted great influence on lowland civilizations. The diffusion of new ideas, objects, and peoples into the Indus Valley was mainly along routes through these western borderlands, or along the thin coastal strip on the Arabian Sea, since the Himalayas to the north were a formidable barrier to influences coming from that direction. The Great Indian Desert to the east of the Indus Valley reduced contacts with the rest of the subcontinent.

Thus, the Indus Valley was, like Egypt, an area of rich agricultural lands sharply bounded by highlands and desert.

Early Indo-Iranian Agriculture

As in the case of the Tigris and Euphrates, the arid lands along the Indus River appear to have been largely uninhabited for many centuries after agricultural villages appeared in adjacent highland areas. Domesticated wheat and the remains of domesticated sheep and goats have been found in levels dating to about 7000 B.C. in several sites in Afghanistan and Baluchistan (Agrawal and Kusumgar 1974: 63), and the evidence suggests that thereafter the agricultural and pastoral ways of life spread gradually throughout highland areas where rainfall and perennial streams provided enough water for dry farming of wheat and barley (most such areas are found between 500 and 1,500 meters elevation). Although the extent to which the spread of domestication, agriculture, and pastoralism was due to diffusion from the west or was a result of independent evolutions is difficult to assess, the evidence points to many different centers of domestication and subsistence shifts all along the highland arc from northern Greece to the Indus Valley (Flannery 1973).

Many settlements in the highlands west of the Indus at about 3500 B.C. were probably based on simple wheat farming, supplemented by sheep and goat raising and some hunting and gathering. These farmers made pottery and used a few copper tools, but some of the villages are so insubstantial that they suggest a relatively mobile population and perhaps only seasonal occupation (F. R. Allchin 1974: 337).

Between 3500 and 2500 B.C. the number of highland farming villages increased, as did their average size, and there was a marked regional diversification of pottery; accompanying these trends was an overall increase in the permanence of the villages and a more important agricultural component in village economies. Even today, however, many tribes in northwestern Pakistan are quite mobile, growing a few crops but traveling with their flocks for part of the year (ibid.).

Initial settlement of the Indus flood plain apparently began near the end of the fourth millennium B.C., when a few sites, such as the hamlet at Amri (Figure 12.2), were established at the juncture of the plain and the foothills. Some very early agricultural settlements in this area, however, may lie under the ruins of the massive cities of the early second millennium B.C., such as Mohenjo-daro, where the water table is so high that remains earlier than about 3000 B.C. are inaccessible.

12.2
The central focus of Harappan civilization was the Indus Valley, an area of almost 300,000 square kilometers. Almost all archaeological work has been concentrated on the large Harappan cities (black squares), but there were also numerous smaller communities (small black dots).

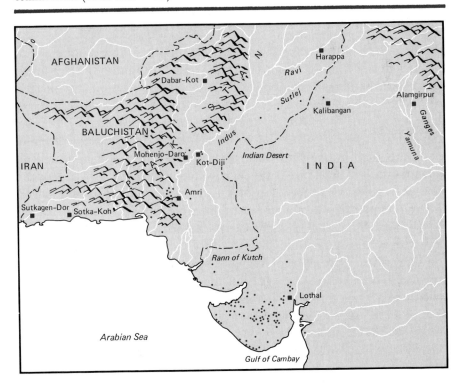

Between 3000 and 2400 B.C. settlements appeared at Kot Diji, Harappa, Kalibangan, and elsewhere, perhaps founded by people moving in from the western highlands. The few excavated settlements of this period reveal a very simple agricultural way of life, with the people residing in mud-brick houses in small villages scattered in areas where no extensive irrigation would have been necessary. Some villages were walled, though there was certainly no shortage of land or pressure on other resources at this time. At Kalibangan ancient plow marks indicate that fields were plowed in a manner similar to that of the recent past, but there are also many stone projectile points and other evidences of considerable hunting and gathering.

These various lowland settlements prior to 2400 B.C. show some stylistic uniformity and a great deal of economic and architectural similarity, but they appear to have been economically and politically independent and self-sufficient, and they reflect none of the rigid planning typical of later settlements here.

The Indus Civilization

Within a few centuries after 2400 B.C., the simple, scattered agricultural societies of the Indus Valley were transformed and united into a large, complex, urban-based sociopolitical system that we might legitimately call a state society. Once again the archaeological evidence is so meager that we can only speculate on how this transition was effected. Population densities began increasing in the southern delta area in the middle of the third millennium B.C., after which settlements appeared all along the Indus, but there is no evidence of intensive competitive pressure on resources. At Kot Diji and Amri, thick layers of ash suggest the transformation was not a peaceful one, but this is not at all clear. It may be significant that the emergence of Indus Valley urban cultures occurred at the same time that the first Near Eastern empires were forming, since there appears to have been increased trade and other contacts between these two areas at this time, but there is no evidence that these Mesopotamian contacts somehow induced the Indus Valley peoples to form states or aggregate in cities. More frequent incursions from highland peoples occurred during this period, raising the possibility that urbanization in the Indus Valley, as it seems to have been in

China, Mesopotamia, and elsewhere, was in part a defensive response to these external pressures.

HARAPPAN URBANISM

The appearance of large planned cities shortly after 2200 B.C. and the associated spread of a distinctive constellation of artifact and architectural styles over much of the Indus Valley marked the emergence of *Harappan* civilization, a political system that survived only about 500 years but which managed to weld much of Pakistan into an integrated political and cultural unit.

More than 200 Harappan sites are known, but almost all research has been devoted to the largest settlements, especially Mohenjo-daro, Harappa, Chanhu-daro, Pathiani Kot, Judeirjo-daro, Kalibangan, and Lothal. At least two cities about as large as Mohenjo-daro have been located but not yet excavated (Pfeiffer 1977: 205), and doubtless many Harappan settlements are buried beneath silt or have been washed away by floods.

The spatial extent of Harappan civilization has been defined on the basis of the location of the precisely planned cities and the rigid stylistic uniformity of its settlements, and these evidences tell us that, at its maximum, the Harappan culture area reached from the Arabian Sea to the foothills of the Himalayas, and from the eastern Iranian frontier to the Ganges River Valley—an extent far larger than any other Old World political system at this time.

The largest Harappan settlement, Mohenjo-daro (Figures 12.3–4), covers about 2.5 square kilometers of the Indus Plain, of which less than 30 percent has been excavated. Unlike early Mesopotamian cities, where shops, homes, and stores were jumbled together and connected by a maze of tiny, winding streets, Mohenjo-daro and the other major Harappan cities were laid out on a precise grid, with broad thoroughfares and straight, evenly spaced cross-streets. At Mohenjo-daro the central north-south street was 9 meters wide and flanked by well-designed open drainage ditches virtually identical to those still found in many Near Eastern cities. There were also public toilets, underground sewage lines with "manholes" for service access (Fairservis 1975: 247), and row upon row of comfortable homes. Many residences were constructed of fired brick, with several rooms arranged around an open courtyard, and the majority appear to have had private showers and toilets drained by municipal sewage systems. Some houses were two stories high and larger and more elaborate than others, but the overall impression is one of uniformity. If gross differences in wealth divided the inhabitants, these are not reflected in residential architecture, at least not to the extent that they were in Mesopotamia.

At Mohenjo-daro and the other two largest Harappan sites, Harappa and Kalibangan, the carefully arranged residential areas were flanked on the west by a great fortified "citadel" mound. Mohenjo-daro's citadel is about 150 meters to the northwest of the main settlement, separated from the residences by land that seems to have been devoid of any settlement and perhaps was regularly flooded by a branch of the river. It has even been suggested that this flooding may have been deliberate, to create a pool of water for bathing, fishing, or some other activity (Fairservis 1975: 243). The northwest complex at Mohenjo-daro is dominated by a brick platform some 12 meters high.

12.3
Street plan of a residential quarter at Mohenjo-daro. The city was laid out in a grid, with wide streets.

12.4
A main street and adjacent houses at Mohenjo-daro. Entrances to houses were usually on smaller alleyways leading off the major streets.

That this was built higher during successive periods and was made of baked bricks and fill raises the possibility that this platform was erected as a refuge from floods (F. R. Allchin 1974: 340).

One of the most interesting structures at the northwest complex is the "Great Bath," a swimming-pool-like structure about 12 by 7 meters and 2.5 meters in depth, constructed of baked brick and lined with bitumen (Figure 12.5). Flanking the pool are what appear to have been dressing rooms. They were carefully staggered to give maximum privacy, and some were equipped with toilets (Fairservis 1975: 246–47). The Great Bath probably figured in some religious activities, although it contained no obvious icons or other religious elements, and it may have been mainly just a public bathing facility.

Adjacent to the bath was a cluster of platforms and rooms, variously interpreted as granaries, assembly halls, and garrisons. Overall, the complex was about 450 meters long and 90 meters wide at its maximum extent—representing a major investment of labor and materials. Thus, while there is nothing at Mohenjo-daro or any other Indus city to compare with the Egyptian pyramids or the White Temple at Uruk, the Indus city dwellers nonetheless were also diverting considerable energy and resources to building projects. The major difference seems to have been that, in contrast to the largely ceremonial public architecture in Mesopotamia and Egypt, the Indus Valley constructions provided some return in the way of administrative buildings, better defenses, and more storage space. There is at least a possibility that Harappan civilization was "cut off" in the midst of its development by invasion, flood, interrupted trade routes, or some other factor, and that

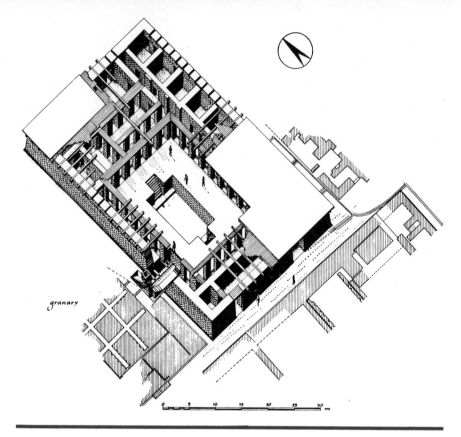

granary

12.5
Reconstruction of the Great Bath at Mohenjo-daro.

more "wasteful" monumental architecture might eventually have appeared at the Indus cities had they been allowed to develop for a longer period. The absence of easily accessible building stone may also account for the comparatively utilitarian and drab Harappan monumental architecture.

About 35,000 to 40,000 people probably lived at Mohenjo-daro, and the populace included farmers, herdsmen, goldsmiths, potters, weavers, brickmasons, architects, and many other specialists; streets were lined with stores and shops. Wheat and barely were the basis of the economy, supplemented by dates, melons, sesame, peas, mustard, and other crops. Cattle, sheep, goats, pigs, and domestic fowl were the major animal foods, and buffalos, camels, asses, dogs, and cats were also kept. A few elephant bones have been found, but there is no proof that these animals were domesticated. The horse was apparently rarely used until the very end of the Harappan period.

Most of the larger Harappan settlements were similar to Mohenjo-daro in architecture and economy, but at the site of Lothal there was also a great brick basin about 219 meters long and 37 meters wide, with extant brick walls 4.5 meters in height (F. R. Allchin 1974: 341). There are varied interpretations of the basin's function; some scholars believe it was a dock to which ships could be brought from a nearby branch of the river (Leshnik 1968).

We know little about the smaller Harappan settlements. The few that have been examined seem to have brick walls around a district within the site, perhaps in imitation of the citadels at the larger cities, and the basic arts and crafts and subsistence practices also appear to have been patterned after those of the cities.

Harappan settlements, with their precisely administered character, would seem to be excellent subjects for the systematic analysis of settlement patterns to try to discern the economic and political forces

12.6
General view of the Citadel at Mohenjo-daro. A stupa (Buddhist shrine) was built on the Citadel many centuries after the site was abandoned.

that dictated where people lived, but generally archaeologists have not competed with each other for a chance to survey systematically the intensely hot, heavily populated Indus Plain. What we do know of Indus settlement patterns suggests at least four different size categories, with about six large centers, twenty smaller centers, and about two hundred large and small villages. Doubtless there are many more settlements to be discovered, but from this sample it is clear that Harappan settlement patterns are comparable to, for example, those of Mesopotamia in the third millennium B.C., and if we consider three or more administrative levels to be evidence of state-level political organization (cf. pp. 426–429), then the Harappan civilization was certainly a state. In fact, the Harappan population at the beginning of the second millennium B.C. was probably at least 200,000, and the tightly organized fabric of their lives suggest an empire-like (pp. 343–344) political system.

The great similarity of cities, towns, and villages of the Harappan civilization bespeaks a high degree of centralization and contact among communities, but it is difficult to demonstrate this archaeologically. Clay and metal models of wheeled carts and river boats may reflect transport of goods along the Indus. Pottery, some kinds of flint tools, and other artifacts were mass produced at a few locations and distributed from place to place. The considerable degree of occupational specialization evident in these artifacts suggests intensive local trade, but there is a strong possibility that this was a kind of administered, noncapitalistic redistribution, rather than a free-enterprise or peasant marketing system. One possible key to the Harappan economic system is the hundreds of Harappan stamps and seals (Figure 12.7), which may have been used to denote ownership or make records of transactions. The apparently ritual scenes depicted in so many of these might argue against this interpretation, but the question will remain unresolved as long as Harappan script is undeciphered.

Almost all Harappan writing is in the form of inscriptions on these seals. The estimated number of unique symbols is between 350 and 425 (Fairservis 1975: 279), which would seem to rule out the possibility that the writing is alphabetic. The writing system was complemented by a standardized system of weights and measures. Small, precisely cut pieces of chert in both binary and decimal arrangements were used as counterweights in balances, and several measuring sticks marked off in units of about 33.5 centimeters have been found; apparently this unit was the common measure of length, much like the English "foot,"

12.7
Harappan seals may have been used to mark ownership on commodities. The symbols are undeciphered.

12.8
This figure (11.4 cm high) of a dancing girl is one of the few bronzes discovered at Mohenjo-daro.

for many of the buildings are precisely constructed to this scale (F. R. Allchin 1974: 343).

Harappan art and religious architecture cannot compare with that of the same period in Mesopotamia, but they have a certain affecting quality. The most popular art was in the form of terra-cotta figurines, the majority of which were standing females, heavily adorned with jewelry. A large share of Harappan aesthetic expression seems to have been lavished on seal and stamp carvings, and even those that appear to have been nothing more than commercial stamps are often executed with great delicacy.

Some Harappan items persist in Indian and Pakistani culture today, including styles of residential architecture, baths, and drains, the use of bangles, nose ornaments, and other personal decoration, and the religious significance of the bull, elephant, tiger, and composite animals; even the boats and carts found all over the subcontinent today are little changed from those depicted in models from Harappan sites (F. Allchin 1974: 339).

The Decline of Harappan Civilization

As with the Maya of Mesoamerica, much of the interest in Harappan civilization concerns the possibility that it was suddenly destroyed by flood, drought, famine, invasion, or some other calamity. The principal archaeological evidences relating to the demise of Harappan civilization are (1) the increasing heterogeneity of pottery and other artifact styles within the same area that in earlier centuries had been so uniform stylistically; (2) the "degradation" of art and architecture toward the end of the Harappan period—which has led some imaginative scholars to suppose that the Harappans had lost their sense of cultural unity and purpose; and (3) the discovery of about a score of human skeletons "sprawled" in the streets of Mohenjo-daro (Figure 12.9), supposedly in the aftermath of an invasion.

Hydrologist Robert Raikes suggests that Harappan civilization was terminated by destruction of their fields and settlements through floods brought on by major shifts of the earth's crust near the mouth of the Indus River (1965). Raikes notes the lack of settlements in the area near the mouth of the river and also that the fossil beaches are many miles inland from the present coast, which one would expect if the river's route to the sea were blocked by an uplift of land near the mouth, since water would have been backed up into a large lake that eventually could have inundated the Harappan area. He believes that the late Harappan building projects for increasing the height of some of their larger structures may have been an effort to compensate for rising water levels.

A more romantic suggestion is that the Harappan civilization was destroyed by repeated invasions of seminomadic peoples coming out of central Asia and Iran. The *Rig Veda,* the oldest surviving Vedic Sanskritic literature, describes the conquest of the dark-skinned natives of the Indus Plain by lighter-skinned Aryan invaders, and the Harappans have traditionally been associated with the former. The translation of Sanskritic literature, first accomplished in the sixteenth century, revealed major similarities between Sanskrit, Latin, Greek, and many European and central Asian language families. These similarities were eventually traced to origins in the Caucasus Mountains of southern Russia and adjacent areas and associated with tall, long-headed, fierce peoples collectively referred to as *Aryans* or *Indo-Europeans,* who shortly after 1900 B.C. apparently invaded and influenced the cultures of India, central Asia, western Asia, and Europe. How they were able to do this is one of the great unresolved problems of history.

Bronze weapons and other artifacts traditionally associated with the Indo-Europeans have been found in the upper levels of some Harappan sites, and some scholars have identified these with the invaders referred to in the *Rig Veda.* It is difficult to substantiate these invasions, and many now believe that such invasions would have been at most only a minor part of the Harappan collapse.

The "invasion" of largely pastoral peoples into agricultural areas in the Harappan case and in similar circumstances elsewhere probably was more a gradual infiltration than a brutal massive invasion of the sort so often led by Yul Brynner and his colleagues in cinematographic histories. Overall, there may have been a gradual shift of power away from the Harappan heartland to peripheral groups in the South and East, where the "evolutionary potential" may have been higher because of the emergence there of rice agriculture, which is an extraordinarily productive crop. Political and cultural influence may well have gravitated to those areas outside the primarily wheat-growing regions of the Harappan sphere of influence (Fairservis 1975: 311).

Generally, the most productive way to look at the termination of Harappan civilization may be as the product of multiple causes. Continued pressure from peripheral groups, altering courses of the Indus River, droughts, floods, earthquakes—all may have contributed to the gradual abandonment of Harappan centers, and the final collapse probably resulted from the coincidence of several of these factors.

THE DEVELOPMENT OF INDIAN CIVILIZATION AFTER 1500 B.C.

After the Harappan downfall, many diverse cultures appeared throughout India and Pakistan, ranging from hunters and gatherers to highly sophisticated urban-based civilizations. The centers of power and influence gradually shifted from the Indus Valley to the great Ganges River Valley where, after about 1100 B.C., large cities were built and state-level political systems were formed. Many Harappan elements ac-

12.9
Skeletons lying in public areas of Mohenjo-daro.

companied this transfer of power, including aspects of metallurgy, architecture, pottery styles, and agriculture.

To the present day, India and Pakistan have remained rich blends of both urban and rural ways of life, with sprawling cities surrounded by hundreds of thousands of agricultural villages, most of whose inhabitants are still tied to the land in patterns of subsistence and settlement that emerged in the Harappan period.

THE INDUS VALLEY CIVILIZATION: CONCLUSIONS

There is far too little archaeological evidence from the Indus area to support an elaborate analysis of the evolution of cultural complexity there, but a few tentative summary points can be made.

The rigid planning and execution of Harappan settlements bespeaks a powerful centralized authority, perhaps rivaling that of ancient Egypt, but there is no evidence of the great tombs, palaces, and pyramids that accompanied theocratic states in Egypt and elsewhere. Some have suggested that the familiar Indian caste system was already in effect during the Harappan period and that this would have conferred the social control evident in the architecture (Service 1975: 246), but the overall similarity of residences and grave contents suggests few major class distinctions—or at least few distinctions that entailed differential access to wealth or prestige.

The great extent of the Harappan sphere of influence and its widely spaced and largely unwalled cities may reflect a stable and secure state, but there is no evidence in the way of masses of weapons or forts that the extension of Harappan influence was achieved or maintained through military might.

Long-distance trade, particularly the flow of goods from the Indus Valley to Mesopotamia, has frequently been suggested as a key factor in the development—and decline—of Harappan civilization. Harappan seals and seal impressions have been found in limited quantities in Mesopotamia and along the Persian Gulf, and there clearly was some commerce between these areas, perhaps by way of ships sailing along the coast and caravans transversing the Iranian Plateau. Exactly which commodities would have been shipped from the Indus Valley westward is unknown, although steatite and a few other minerals and semiprecious stones would have been likely trade items. Commerce appears to have been very one-sided, however, with little going from Southwest Asia to the Indus area, and this has suggested to some that Harappan civilization may have been established and maintained mainly by Mesopotamian or Iranian states. Indeed, there are some Mesopotamian elements in the Indus cultures, such as carved stone boxes, dice, faience, wheeled vehicles, shaft-hole axes, religious art motifs, and the "ram-style" sculptural motif (Fairservis 1975: 296–97). But taken as a whole, long-distance trade seems to have had little importance in the evolution of cultural complexity in the Indus Valley. The volume of product exchange was very low and mainly in luxury items, and the movement of goods appears to have been accomplished through intermediaries in the Iranian Plateau, rather than through deliberate and direct administered trade between Harappans and Mesopotamians (ibid.: 297–98).

It has also been argued that a key element in the evolution of Harappan culture was the necessity of constructing and maintaining flood control and irrigation works, but, as in Egypt and Mesopotamia, there is little evidence of this. Major constructions of this sort seem only to have appeared long after the initial transformation was well underway.

As in the case of Egypt and Mesopotamia, rates of population growth in the Indus Valley appear to have been slow, and there is no evidence of pressure on the agricultural systems until long after the Harappan civilization had collapsed. The present large areas of salinized land in the Indus Valley are the result of mismanagement during the recent past, not the outcome of "overexploitation" of land because of uncontrolled increases in ancient human population densities. Nor are there evidences of the class conflict and other elements that would be expected under the Marxian model.

In conclusion, the only factor we can be certain played a key part in Indus Valley developments was, of course, the great agricultural potential of the rich riverine environment. From the beginnings of agriculture in this environment to the evolution of Harappan civilization, we are confronted with a complex and very subtle process of cultural evolution, and it will require much additional research to separate the many factors that combined to produce Harappan civilization.

Bibliography

Agrawal, D. P. 1971. *The Copper Bronze Age in India.* New Delhi: M. Manoharlal.

Agrawal, D. P. and S. D. Kusumgar. 1974. *Prehistoric Chronology and Radiocarbon Dating in India.* New Delhi: M. Manoharlal.

Allchin, Bridget and Raymond. 1968. *The Birth of Indian Civilization.* Baltimore: Penguin.

Allchin, F. R. 1960. *Piklihāl Excavations.* Hyderabad: Government of Andhra Pradesh.

———. 1961. *Utnūr Excavations.* Hyderabad: Government of Andhra Pradesh.

———. 1963. *Neolithic Cattle-keepers of South India.* Cambridge: Cambridge University Press.

———. 1968. "Early Domestic Animals in India and Pakistan." In *Man, Settlement and Urbanism,* eds. P. J. Ucko, R. Tringham, and G. W. Dimbleby. London: Duckworth.

———. 1974. "India from the Late Stone Age to the Decline of Indus Civilization." *Encyclopaedia Britannica.* 9: 336–48.

Clauson, Gerard and John Chadwick. 1969. "The Indus Script Deciphered?" *Antiquity.* 43(171): 200–207.

Dales, George F. 1966. "Recent Trends in the Pre- and Protohistoric Archaeology of South Asia." *Proceedings of the American Philosophical Society.* 110(2): 130–39.

Fairservis, Walter A., Jr. 1956. "Excavations in the Quetta Valley, West Pakistan." Anthropological Papers of the American Museum of Natural History, 45(2). New York.

————. 1967. "The Origin, Character and Decline of an Early Civilization." *American Museum of Natural History Novitates,* no. 2302, October 20, 1967.

————. 1975. *The Roots of Ancient India.* 2nd ed. rev. Chicago: University of Chicago Press.

Flannery, K. V. 1973. "The Origins of Agriculture." *Annual Review of Anthropology.* 2: 271–310.

Hammond, Norman, ed. 1973. *South Asian Archaeology.* Park Ridge, N.J.: Noyes Press.

Lal, B. B. 1954–5. "Excavations at Hastinapura and Other Explorations in the Upper Ganga and Sutlej Basins, 1950–2." *Ancient India,* nos. 10–11.

Lamberg-Karlovsky, C. C. 1967. "Archaeology and Metallurgical Technology in Prehistoric Afghanistan, India and Pakistan." *American Anthropologist.* 69(2): 145–62.

Leshnik, Leon S. 1968. "The Harappan 'Port' at Lothal: Another View." *American Anthropologist.* 70(5): 911–22.

McEvedy, Colin. 1967. *The Penguin Atlas of Ancient History.* Harmondsworth: Penguin.

MacKay, E. J. H. 1938. *Further Excavations at Mohenjo-Daro.* New Delhi: Delhi Manager of Publications.

Malik, S. C. 1968. *Indian Civilization: The Formative Period.* Simla: India Institute of Advanced Study.

Masson, V. M. 1972. "Prehistoric Settlement Patterns in Soviet Central Asia." In *The Explanation of Cultural Changes: Models in Prehistory,* ed. Colin Renfrew. London: Duckworth.

Mughal, Mohammad Rafique. 1970. "The Early Harappan Period in the Greater Indus Valley and Northern Baluchistan." Unpublished doctoral dissertation, University of Pennsylvania.

————. 1974. "New Evidence of the Early Harappan Culture from Jalilpur, Pakistan." *Archaeology.* 27(2): 106–13.

Perttula, T. 1977. "Between the Indus and Euphrates: The Comparison of the Evolution of Complex Societies." Seattle. Mimeographed.

Pfeiffer, John E. 1977. *The Emergence of Society.* New York: McGraw-Hill.

Piggott, S. 1950. *Prehistoric India.* London: Pelican.

Possehl, Gregory L. 1974. "Variation and Change in the Indus Civilization." Unpublished doctoral dissertation, University of Chicago.

————. 1976. "Lothal: A Gateway Settlement of the Harappan Civilization." In *Ecological Backgrounds of South Asian Prehistory,* eds. Kenneth A. P. Kennedy & G. L. Possehl. *South Asia Occasional Papers and Theses* 4: 118–31. Ithaca.

Raikes, Robert. 1965. "The Mohenjo-Daro Floods." *Antiquity* 39: 196–203.

Van Lohnizen-de Leeuw, J. E. and J. M. M. Ubagns, eds. 1974. *South Asian Archaeology.* Leiden: E. J. Brill.

Wheeler, Sir Mortimer. 1966. *Civilizations of the Indus Valley and Beyond.* New York: McGraw-Hill.

————. 1968. *The Indus Civilization.* 3rd ed. Supplementary volume to the *Cambridge History of India.* Cambridge: Cambridge University Press.

Wheeler, R. E. M. 1950. *Five Thousand Years of Pakistan.* London: Royal India and Pakistan Society.

13

From Tribe to Empire
in North China

"Let the past serve the present."

Mao Tse-tung

At about 1800 B.C., just a century or so after the Babylonian king Hammurabi had established a great empire in Southwest Asia, the people of North and central China began a period of development that was to take them from simple agricultural tribes to one of the most brilliant and complex civilizations of antiquity. Because scientific archaeology in China is only a few decades old and has often been interrupted by wars and revolution, we still know only the outlines of these developments. Nonetheless, in terms of basic processes, the evolution of Chinese civilization appears to be yet another variation on the same developmental theme we have noted in Mesopotamia, Egypt, and the Indus Valley.

The Ecological Setting

The modern political boundaries of China incorporate vastly different environments, ranging from the Himalayas to the Pacific shore, and people from many of these areas came to play some role in shaping Chinese civilization. But the initial transition from simple farming com-

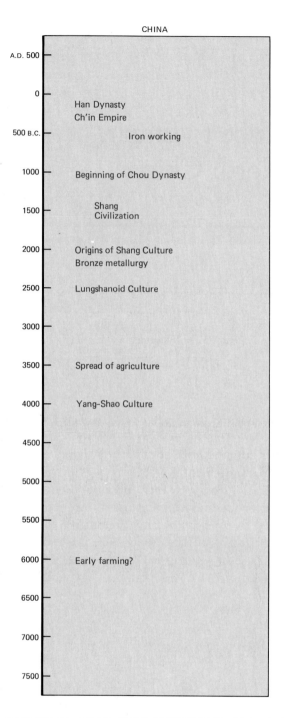

CHINA

A.D. 500

0

Han Dynasty
Ch'in Empire

500 B.C.   Iron working

1000   Beginning of Chou Dynasty

1500   Shang
        Civilization

2000   Origins of Shang Culture
        Bronze metallurgy

2500   Lungshanoid Culture

3000

3500   Spread of agriculture

4000   Yang-Shao Culture

4500

5000

5500

6000   Early farming?

6500

7000

7500

13.1
Chronology of early agriculture and complex societies in North China.

munities to complex societies had two principal centers: a primary focus in the middle Wei and Hsiang-ho river valleys and a secondary
focus in the middle Yangtze Valley (Lattimore 1951: 27). Developments in these areas eventually overlapped and both areas were affected
to some extent by the tens of thousands of nomads that throughout
early Chinese history interacted with the peoples along the margins of
the agricultural zones.

North China's developmental leadership was closely tied to its
agricultural potential. Late in the Pleistocene, winds blowing off the

13.2
The distribution of Yang-shao, Lungshanoid, and early Shang cultures in North
China.

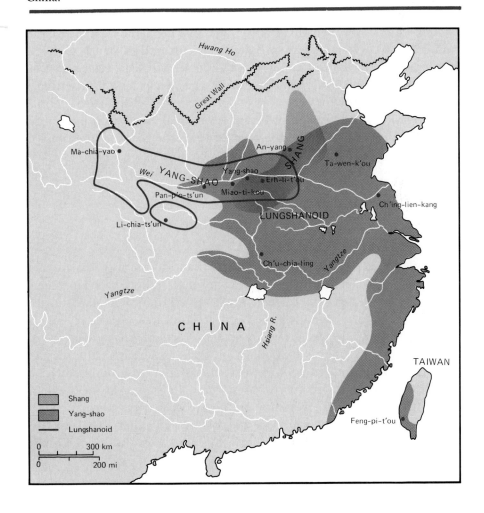

Gobi Desert covered parts of North China with a layer of loess that in some places reached a depth of several hundred meters. The Hwang Ho (or "Yellow River"—whose name comes from the color given it by the loess it carries) cuts through these loess plains, frequently changing its course, and through flooding and draining it has created a rich agricultural zone of lakes, marshes, and alluvial fields. Loess is the agricultural soil par excellence: it is organically rich, requires little plowing or cultivating, and by capillary action manages to retain near the surface much of the sparse rain that falls on North China. Moreover, it can yield large crops with little fertilization, even under intensive cultivation, because rainwater that is absorbed into lower levels collects mineral nutrients that are then brought back to the surface through this same capillary action. Perhaps even more important, the sparse rainfall, cold climate, and soils of many areas of North China do not support forests or even thick grasslands, making land clearance either unnecessary or very easy for primitive agriculturalists. Much of North China is mountainous, but there are large areas of flat, relatively well-watered land, and while winters can be very harsh here, the setting is generally favorable for agriculture—provided there is sufficient rainfall for irrigation. The climate of North China may have been more moderate in ancient times, but the evidence on this point is questionable (Wheatley 1971: 21–22).

Early Agriculture

We have already briefly considered the domestication of plants and animals and early agriculture in China (p. 301), and it will be remembered that millet was the earliest important domesticated staple in this region. Millet may actually have been domesticated elsewhere, but by about 3500 B.C. it was grown over the North China plains (K. C. Chang 1963: 94–95). Nutritionally as rich as wheat, millet is also quick-maturing and drought-resistant—making it admirably suited to the cold, arid plains of North China—and its stems can be used for food, fuel, and fodder. Sorghum and a few other crops were also cultivated in the early agricultural period, but it was millet, and later, rice and wheat, that provided the energy basis for the evolution of Chinese civilization.

The many polished stone axes and adzes found in the earliest agricultural settlements in North China are a reflection no doubt of land-clearing operations to extend the range of these plants into the aboriginal grasslands and forests. Fire probably was also used for this purpose, but we lack any archaeological evidence of this (Triestman 1972).

The first farmers here also depended for much of their food on hunting, gathering wild plants, and fishing—as evidenced by the hundreds of hooks, fish gorges, and net weights found. Pigs, a few domestic fowl, and later, cattle, sheep, and goats were eaten, but until very late in prehistoric times, hunting and gathering remained important sources of food.

THE YANG-SHAO CULTURE (CA. 3950 TO CA. 1700 B.C.)

By about 3900 B.C. many of the people of North China lived in small villages, consisting of a few dozen wattle-and-daub pit houses scattered along the ridges overlooking fertile river valleys. Hunting and gathering were still important, but millet cultivation was probably becoming the base of subsistence. Millet was apparently first grown on a shifting schedule, in which fields were cleared (by the slash-and-burn technique) and worked for at most a few seasons, then fallowed for long periods while other nearby areas were farmed. Most villages appear to have been inhabited for only a few years, then abandoned, and then re-settled after a lapse of some time, as cultivation was shifted from field to field. The apparently planned arrangement of houses in these villages suggests that the people were organized on the basis of clans (K. C. Chang 1976: 28).

These *Yang-shao* villages were not much different from those of a thousand years earlier, but they have some interesting variations. As in earlier times, stone hoes and knives, wooden digging sticks, and baskets were the primary agricultural implements, but there is also some slight evidence of the growing of silkworms at this time. In later periods silk-making was a highly specialized craft and became a major part of the Chinese economy, and its early appearance here may signal the first movements away from simple subsistence farming. Also, compared to early European and Near Eastern farming villages, Yang-shao villages were comparatively large. The significance of this is obscure, except that it may be a reflection of the greater productivity of the loess, and

13.3
Reconstruction of a round house at Pan-p'o-ts'un. Digging the floor of the house a meter or more into the earth protected the inhabitants from cold winter winds.

possibly a harbinger of later trends in Chinese history when population densities in some areas became very high.

A large but fairly typical example of a Yang-shao village is Pan-p'o-ts'un, in Shensi province. Including its cemetery and pottery kilns on the periphery, Pan-p'o-ts'un covered about 70,000 square meters and was home to perhaps 600 people at its largest extent. It was enclosed within a ditch (perhaps for defense, but more likely for drainage) and comprised scores of wattle-and-daub houses, all facing south and half-buried (doubtless to avoid the icy winter winds) (Figure 13.3). In the center of the village was a much larger structure (about 160 square meters), built on a foundation of packed earth and somewhat more elaborately and expensively made. Predictably, Western archaeologists have usually interpreted this as a "big-man's house," implying a ranked society, while Chinese excavators interpret it as a communal meeting hall (Watson 1974: 26).

Around the houses were many deep pits, presumably for storing millet and other commodities. No doubt most villagers were full-time agriculturalists, but some people engaged in silkworm cultivation, pottery manufacture, jade carving, and leather and textile production, and there may have been some minor degree of occupational specialization. But based on the similarity of residential units and their contents, the absence of any monumental architecture or apparent intensive craft specialization, and the uniform graves, it is likely that there was little differential access to wealth, power, or prestige in Pan-p'o-ts'un.

The almost uniform absence of walls, fortresses, mass burials, and weapons suggests a peaceful era of low-level and infrequent contacts between villages. But the Yang-shao seem to have differed from their predecessors in that at this time many people began using the same basic stylistic elements in decorating their pottery and other artifacts. We have seen that in the Samarran and Halafian periods in Mesopotamia the rise of complex cultures was immediately preceded by the widespread distribution of a few pottery types, and a similar process may have been underway in China at this time. Perhaps the spread of Yang-shao style pottery reflects the extension of a sense of community outside the village—a primary step in the formation of complex political systems.

LUNGSHAN AND LUNGSHANOID CULTURES
(?2000 B.C. TO CA. 1850 B.C.)

The transformation of the simple farming communities of third millennium B.C. China into more complex social and political forms began shortly after 2400 B.C., with the emergence of the *Lungshan* culture (variants of which are called *Lungshanoid*) in North and central China. Lungshan cultures, like the Yang-shao, are defined on the basis of similar styles of artifacts. Lungshan settlements are distinguished by a highly burnished, wheel-made, thin-walled black pottery ware that occurs in many different vessel forms and is found, with minor stylistic variations, from the southeastern coast of China to the northern provinces of Shantung and Hupei (see Figure 13.2). The "nuclear" or core area of the Lungshan culture appears to have been in Shantung and Hupei, but very early Lungshan pottery and other diagnostic artifacts are found over most of the old Yang-shao heartland (K. C. Chang 1976: 29).

As with the Yang-shao, the Lungshan peoples lived mainly in villages made up of pit houses arranged around a central "long house," and virtually every Lungshan adult male was probably still a millet farmer who supplemented the family fortunes with hunting, collecting, and part-time craft production of pottery, jade, and a few other commodities. But Lungshan villages were, on the average, significantly larger than those of the Yang-shao period, and were likely occupied for longer periods of time. Lungshan agriculture, although still based on millet and a few domestic animals, seems to have been more intensive than that of the Yang-shao. The slash-and-burn, shifting agricultural system of Yang-shao times probably gave way to a permanent field system in the Lungshan period. Domestic poultry, sheep, and cattle became more important, and there is evidence of the increasing significance of rice agriculture in some southern areas (K. C. Chang 1976: 30–31).

There are also signs of change in social organization. Compared to Yang-shao graves, Lungshan burials exhibit significantly more variation in richness of grave goods, and there is greater specialization reflected in jade carving, pottery manufacture, and other crafts. These are inferences, based on scanty archaeological data, but Lungshan pottery and jade ornaments are so sophisticated and beautiful that they suggest at least some semispecialized craftsmen. In addition, Lungshan people sought knowledge through scapulimancy, the art of writing signs on bones, applying heat to the bone to crack it, and then interpreting the pattern of cracking to foretell the future. Archaeologist K. C. Chang interprets the appearance of this art in Lungshan times as a reflection of the rise of at least a semiprofessional class of shamans (1976), an interpretation made credible by the fact that the character meaning *book* already appears on these bones and may signify the existence of specialized scribes.

At least one other significant development in Lungshan communities is the appearance of large walls of pounded earth around many settlements. Arrowheads, spears, daggers, and clubs appear frequently in Lungshan sites, some skeletons show evidence of beheading and scalping (K. C. Chang 1976), and, collectively, this evidence would seem to argue a relatively intense level of conflict.

Paul Wheatley concludes that the Lungshan cultures were a "stratified society in Service's sense of the term" (1971: 89), but in economic and technological terms, the Lungshanoid communities were probably still largely self-sufficient and independent. Settlement patterns of this period are poorly known, but there is little evidence of population aggregation or regular spacing of settlements according to economic or administrative principles. Nonetheless, the transition to life in permanent villages and established agricultural fields was made over much of

North China in the Lungshan period, from the western highlands into
the northern Manchurian highlands and well into southern China.

Early Bronze Age China: The Shang Dynasty
(1850 to 1112 B.C.)

Much of what we know about *Shang* China comes from approximately
thirty sites near the present city of Changchou (Figure 13.4), where excavations have revealed deposits extending from the Lungshan period
to late Shang times. During the Shang dynasty China really became
"China," in the sense that this period marked the first widespread use
of the distinctively Chinese forms of writing, architecture, art, and
ideology. Also during this period all the correlates of cultural complexity, such as monumental architecture, large population concentrations,
occupational specialization, written records, gross differences in wealth,
power, and prestige, and large public-works projects, appeared in full
force.

13.4
The walled complex at Chengchou and the workshops and residential quarters
around it reflect the growing complexity of north Chinese administrative and
economic systems.

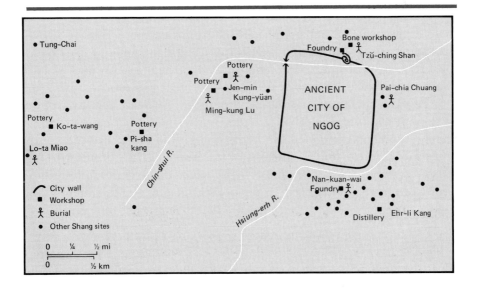

So impressive are Shang achievements, in fact, that until recently many elements of their civilization were widely believed (by European scholars) to have been introduced from elsewhere, perhaps from central Asia or the Near East. But research indicates that the evolution of Shang civilization was almost wholly an independent and regional development in North China—although it no doubt drew on the resources of many diverse ethnic groups in this area.

ERH-LI-T'OU PHASE (CA. 1850 TO CA. 1650 B.C.)

The transition from the Lungshanoid cultures in North China to Shang civilization has often been perceived as a "sudden" development, but there are now several known sites where the transition has been documented as having been a very gradual process. Here, too, our evidence comes mainly from the middle Yellow River Valley.

At the site of *Erh-li-t'ou,* for example, in levels dating to shortly after 1800 B.C., the persistence of the Lungshan level of cultural complexity is clearly evident: there were no monumental buildings, no written documents, no elaborate tombs, and the people still lived in wattle-and-daub pit houses arranged around a larger, more elaborately constructed long-house. As in the late Lungshan period there is some evidence of walls around settlements, and there was also sophisticated and beautiful craftsmanship in pottery, carved jade, and turquoise. Some burials have richer collections of grave goods than others, but these differences are not significantly more pronounced than in Lungshan settlements. And, again like in the Lungshan, some human skeletons show signs of mutilation, and, in at least one case, an individual's hands were tied at the time of death or interment (Triestman 1972: 59).

Perhaps the most significant difference between the Erh-li-t'ou phase cultures and Lungshan peoples was in metals. Some Erh-li-t'ou phase settlements contained fish hooks, bells, pins, and projectile points made from bronze; and for the rest of the Shang period, bronzeworking was to become one of the most highly developed crafts and bronze items were consistently used to denote status and wealth differentials.

ERH-LI-KANG PHASE (CA. 1650 TO 1400 B.C.)

With the *Erh-li-kang phase* we move into the historical period in ancient China, and from the end of this period on there are some written documents to supplement the archaeological record. As with the earlier phase of the Shang period, the Erh-li-kang phase is best documented archaeologically at the cluster of settlements near Chengchou. Few inscribed oracle bones have been found in levels of this period here, but archaeological research has been quite informative. The central area of Erh-li-kang phase settlement was a roughly rectangular arrangement of buildings extending about 3.4 square kilometers (see Figure 13.5), much of which was enclosed by a pounded-earth wall some 36 meters wide at the base and 9.1 meters in height—as estimated from the segments still remaining (K. C. Chang 1976). The central area of the site is thought to have been the residence and ceremonial center of the ruling elite, and surrounding it and spread over a large area were thousands of pit houses, animal pens, shops, storage pits, and other features whose contents make it clear that life in Shang China differed considerably from that of Neolithic times. Based on the number and quality of the artifacts found, there must have been hundreds of skilled, full-time craftsmen at Chengchou. In one area thousands of pieces of animal and human bone were recovered, much of it already fashioned into fish hooks, awls, axes, and hairpins. In another area were more than a dozen pottery kilns, each surrounded by masses of broken and overfired pottery. No jade, leather, or textile workshops have been found, but the circulation of these products at this time is well documented, and they were probably being produced somewhere near Chengchou. This settlement even had a distillery (Wheatley 1971).

But the Chengchou craftsmen really displayed their skill in working bronze. Large areas were given over to workshops for casting fish hooks, axes, projectile points, and various ornaments. A kind of "mass-production" was achieved by using multiple molds, made by impressing a clay slab with the forms of six arrowheads, each impression connected by a thin furrow to a central channel. A second clay mold was placed over the first, the two bound together, and then molten bronze was poured in. After cooling, the individual points could be sawn off from the central stem.

There may also be some indication in the mortuary practices that social organization was becoming more complex. Several tombs and graves have been excavated and have been reported to include human sacrifices and masses of luxury items; but, unfortunately, the details of these excavations have never been published.

Both archaeological evidence and ancient documents written after the Shang period indicate that society during the Erh-li-kang phase was headed by a king, who ruled through a hierarchically arranged nobility. Commoners were conscripted for public works and military service; there were highly organized and incessant military campaigns; and many settlements were apparently integrated into an organized inter-village system of commerce (Wheatley 1971). It has not been determined if there were large-scale irrigation systems, but at Chengchou at least a canal system was in use, perhaps to carry water to the settlement, or else to carry drainage water or sewage out of the complex (ibid.).

The great mass of Shang people, however, lived much as they did before, in villages of pit houses located along river systems, subsisting on the same kinds of crops and agricultural technology as had people of previous millennia. And despite the vastly increased use of bronze among the nobility, almost no agricultural implements or craft tools were made from metal of any sort. As K. C. Chang observed: "The transition from neolithic Lungshan culture . . . to the Shang civilization is a quantum jump of the highest order in the quality of life for the elite, yet there is no discernible corresponding change in the technology of food production" (1976: 10).

YIN PHASE (CA. 1400 TO 1123 B.C.)

The last and most brilliant phase of Shang civilization, the *Yin phase,* seems to have begun about 1384 B.C., when the Shang king, P'an-kèng, is reported to have moved his capital to the city of An-yang, in Honan province.

Excavations at An-yang and contemporary sites in this area have been conducted intermittently since the 1920s, but the publication of this research is far from complete. Scores of sites within an area of about twenty-four square kilometers have been tested, and the evidence suggests that the complex at An-yang included a large ceremonial and administrative center surrounded by smaller dependent hamlets and craft centers (Wheatley 1971: 93). True to tradition, most peasants still lived in small pit houses a few meters in diameter—most of them not very different from those of 2,000 years earlier. Scattered throughout the settlement were hundreds of granaries, pottery kilns, storage pits, bone and bronze workshops, animal pens, ditches, and familiar features of ancient Chinese life.

No city wall has been found at An-yang, but apparently for the first time in Chinese history monumental buildings appear. The largest of these was about sixty meters long, rectangular in form, with large stone and bronze column bases, and founded on a large platform of compacted earth. There were at least fifty-three structures of this type (though somewhat smaller) in one group at An-yang, arranged in three main clusters. Although not lavish in construction, these buildings are surrounded by scores of human and animal sacrificial burials as well as many pits containing royal records written on oracle bones and numerous small structures thought to be for service personnel (K. C. Chang 1976: 48). Near the cluster of buildings is a cemetery with eleven large graves, replete with lavish, expensive burial goods and many human sacrificial burials—the whole complex surrounded by 1,200 smaller, much less lavish burials. Elsewhere, a complex of ceremonial buildings at Hsiao-T'un was dedicated with the sacrifice of 852 people, 15 horses, 10 oxen, 18 sheep, 35 dogs, and 5 fully equipped chariots and charioteers (Wheatley 1971).

The Shang ceremonial and administrative structures are perhaps not as impressive in size or cost as the ziggurats and temples of Mesopotamia, but the level of occupational specialization, the immense wealth of the burials, and the intensity of organization of the agricultural and economic systems reminds one of the Mesopotamian city-states of the late fourth millennium B.C.

Little urbanism and only a thin distribution of bronzeworking and a few other Shang cultural traits appear in most of non-Shang China at this time, and most of these non-Shang cultures were probably still at a predominantly Neolithic level of development (Wheatley 1971: 96).

Late in the Yin phase of the Shang dynasty (about 1200 B.C.) the written language had evolved to the point that texts from this period give us a detailed portrait of Shang life. Over 3,000 phonetic, ideographic, and pictographic characters were in use, of which about 12,000 have been identified, and more than 160,000 inscribed shells (of which only 15,000 or so have been translated) and numerous inscriptions in bronze or stone date to this period. Although the vast majority of these texts are from only a few sites and largely concern the activities of the elites, they are nonetheless illuminating.

According to the texts, the late Shang rulers held sway over a territory extending from the Pacific shore to Shensi province in the West, and from the Yangtze River in the South to southern Hupeh in the North. At the apex of Shang society was the king, who ruled directly on many affairs of state and who was assisted by a complex hierarchy of nobles possessing considerable local autonomy in their respective territories. These lords were charged with defending the homeland, supplying men for armies and public-works projects, and with collecting and contributing state taxes. Toward the end of the Shang period, many nobles apparently achieved almost feudal status in the sense that they were no longer required to attend the royal court and were virtually independent in their own domains. But the king was still considered to have superior supernatural powers and to be the pivot of all ritual procedures, and the Shang kingdom retained many theocratic elements. The kingdom was ringed with "barbarians," and Shang kings often granted them almost complete autonomy in exchange for peaceful relationships. Royal powers waxed and waned, and there were many times when the king and nobles were able to exert power only a short distance away from their ceremonial complexes and walled towns (Wheatley 1971: 63).

On occasion, royal armies of up to about 30,000 men were conscripted and led by the nobles against insurgent "barbarians" and neighboring principalities. The basis of the army was the horse-drawn chariot, supported by infantrymen equipped with bronze-tipped arrows and laminated bows, and royal records indicate that military campaigns often incurred and inflicted frightful casualties. Staggering quantities of plunder were often taken, along with thousands of prisoners, most of whom were apparently sacrificed or enslaved (Wheatley 1971).

The agricultural system seems to have been essentially the same as previously, with millet, wheat, rice, and vegetables the major crops, and cattle, sheep, pigs, and poultry, the only "new" domestic animal being the water buffalo. The proportions of these crops and animals may have been shifted somewhat, with wheat and rice expanding their range at the expense of millet, but the evidence for this is questionable. There is little evidence of large irrigation systems anywhere in the Shang domain, and hunting and gathering still supplied a large part of the diet. Apparently intravillage trade in foodstuffs was considerable,

13.5
Royal Shang tomb at Hou Chia Chuang, Honan province. Note multiple human sacrifices.

and documents and utensils indicate that already the justly famed Chinese cuisine was well developed.

The crafts of late Shang times included bronzeworking, jade and turquoise carving, leather and textile production, and of course massive production of ceramics. There is some evidence that Shang craftsmen had somewhat higher status than farmers, and local occupational specialization was considerable. Many villages lacked one or more of the more important handicraft workshops, suggesting that products were exchanged among these settlements (Wheatley 1971: 76). The discovery of large caches of agricultural implements (3,500 stone sickles, new and used, in a single pit at one site, for example) may indicate a degree of centralized management of both agriculture and craft production (ibid.).

Toward the end of the Shang period there were many walled towns and villages in North and central China, and, compared to earlier periods, a much greater proportion of the populace lived in these semiurban settings. But if we compare the settlement size distribution of late Shang China—or rather what we estimate it to have been—with those of Mesopotamia or Mesoamerica at a comparable level of development, it is clear that Shang China was a much less urbanized society. There were no settlements the size of Ur or Teotihuacán, nor were there any pyramids, ziggurats, or temples to compare with buildings at these other sites. Wheatley argues that the primary difference between the Shang and earlier cultures was economic. "Although Shang civilization had evolved uninterruptedly from the matrix of Lungshan culture, there had supervened between these two phases a major economic transformation, in which a predominantly reciprocal integration oc-

13.6
The evolution of Chinese script involved the stylization of original pictographs and the assignment of phonetic values.

| 土 | 水 | 鼎 | 示 | 田 | 就 | 祖 | 逆 | 天 | 祝 |

curring spontaneously at village level had been subsumed into a super-ordinate, politically institutionalized, dominantly redistributive pattern" (1971: 77).

The Chou Dynasty (1122 B.C. to 221 B.C.)

According to legend, the *Chou dynasty* was founded by Tan Fu, who settled his people in the fertile Wei Ho Valley in Shensi province. Shang documents occasionally refer to the Chou, sometimes as a friendly neighbor, other times as a hostile one, but the level of cultural development of the Chou during the Shang period is not well known. In any case, through political maneuverings and warfare the Chou were eventually able to replace the Shang as the dominant force in North China, finally and decisively defeating the remnants of the Shang in battle about 1122 B.C.

Generally, the Chou built on and expanded the cultural base evolved during the Shang period; there is no archaeological evidence

13.7
A Shang ceremonial bronze vessel.

suggesting any major changes in the basic pattern of Chinese civilization in North China immediately after the Chou conquest (K. C. Chang
1963: 221). The area controlled by the Chou fluctuated, and not until
the end of the Chou period were the cultural borders of China greatly
expanded (Figure 13.8).

The Chou political system was composed of a king and royal court
supported by a highly stratified society of nobles, scholars, warriors,
craftsmen, farmers, and slaves. Most parts of the Chou territory were
administered by semifeudal lords, themselves organized in at least five
different ranks, and these lords had almost independent control over
their territories. Royal power over vassal states fluctuated considerably
during the Chou period, and occasionally feudal lords expelled tyran-
nical kings. The vassal states and the royal court usually cooperated in

13.8
China under the Chou and Han dynasties.

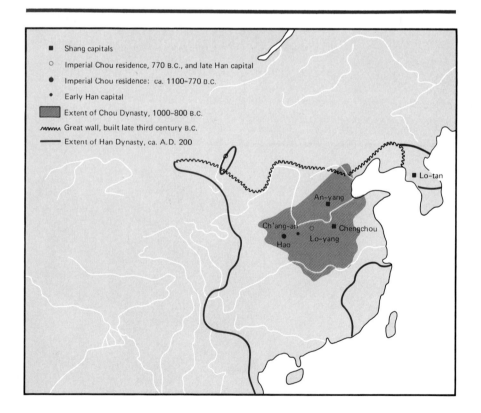

the defense and development of the state, but pressure from northern nomads and competing principalities often made substantial inroads on Chou territory, and on more than one occasion provincial capitals had to be abandoned to the invaders.

The Chou were great city builders. In many cases settlements built in the Shang period were increased in size, garrisons and towns were established in formerly nonurban areas, and tribal villages previously outside the periphery of Shang dominance were fortified and brought into the national economic system. Prior to the Chou period, larger settlements seem to have been primarily administrative and military in nature, and the major crafts conducted there involved the production of prestige items of bronze, jade, and pottery, while most agricultural implements and goods were still produced and circulated at the village

13.9
The evolution of urban-centered settlement patterns was well underway by the eighth to fifth centuries B.C. Note that this distribution is approximate and cumulative, representing settlement over about two-and-a-half centuries.

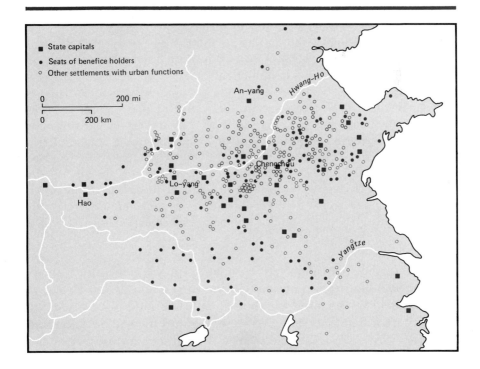

level (Wheatley 1971: 176). But during the late Chou period the city became the base of operations of an emerging merchant class and their capitalist operations, combining "the economic and social functions of the *agora* of the Greek *polis* and the *forum* of the Roman city" (ibid.: 178). Like the citizens of ancient Ur in Mesopotamia, however, the vast majority of city dwellers in Chou and even later times were cultivators who went out daily to work their fields (ibid.).

From the Chou period to the present, the same written character has been used to denote *wall* and *city*, and archaeological evidence confirms that all larger Chou cities were walled (ibid.: 182). Many Chou cities were exceptionally large, such as G'a-to, with maximum dimensions of 8,300 meters by 3,930 meters (and a population estimated at 270,000) (ibid.: 183). Most of the settlements were square or rectangular in layout, with many important buildings constructed on large platforms of pounded earth. Toward the end of the Chou period, more and more residences and craft workshops were enclosed within the city walls. In the suburbs many of the dwellings were constructed of thatch and clay, and records indicate that fast-moving fires were a constant danger here. Often the ceremonial nucleus of the settlement was marked off by interior walls.

The emergence of these "compact cities" is truly a major development in Chinese history and seems to presage profound alterations in the fabric of Chinese society. But as Wheatley notes, there are no obvious explanations of this phenomenon.

> I have been unable to correlate the advent of the compact city with . . . any change in political status such as the expansion from city-state to territorial empire, or with any mutation in the organization of government such as that from religious oligarchy to kingship. Nor does it seem invariably to be directly or clearly related to any specific method of warfare, or, somewhat surprisingly, to specific advantages in transportation technology. Possibly, it may in some instances reflect the emergence of a new mode of economic exchange, but this topic is at present . . . obscure. (1971: 480)

One of the other important economic changes at this time was the rise of private ownership of land. In the early Chou period almost all land was held by the nobility, who allowed their land to be worked by peasants according to a tenantry system. Toward the end of the period, however, a direct system of taxation was instituted and private ownership of land became common. Through usury, the purchase of land by rich merchants, and ruinous taxation, thousands of peasants were forced off their land and had no option but to become slave labor for rich landowners.

At the same time, warfare became much more infantry-based, augmented with charioteers and cavalry, and battles took place between armies of tens of thousands of men. The crossbow was invented and used against nomads who plundered border settlements. Agriculture also changed as wheat gradually became more important than millet, and rice was extended into the drier northern areas. Cultivation became much more labor intensive, with frequent weedings and careful rotation of rows and crops. Concurrently, investments in irrigation and drainage systems were greatly increased, and while some of these systems were quite complex, most appear to have been relatively small, requiring perhaps no more than local administration. Trade in many commodities was considerable, and was greatly facilitated by a regulated coinage. Ironworking became very important, and to a certain extent iron replaced bronze for many purposes. For the first time, metal tools became available to most of the peasantry.

The Chou period was also the "classical" period in Chinese intellectual history, producing Confucius, Mencius, and other scholars who were usually attached to academies supported by rich nobles. Some intellectuals of this age saw the ordering of the Chinese state system as a natural extension of the harmony, cooperation, and deference that ideally prevailed among members of extended families.

Most of the Chou administrative units were feudal states, many of which were not even contiguous geographically. There were frequent insurrections by people who lived in areas between these feudal states, and nomads applied pressure on Chou states along the northern frontier. The balance of power in Chou China changed frequently, as loose confederacies of states formed for short periods, only to give way eventually to other, more powerful states or confederacies.

The Ch'in Empire (221 to 202 B.C.)

The period of about 481 B.C. to 221 B.C., known as the *warring-states period*, was a long nightmare of struggle during which the Chou state was fragmented into seven major powers and about as many minor ones. The Chou royal house and territory itself had sunk to the level of a small autonomous state, distinguished only by its claims to a superior ritual role.

During this period of continual warfare, the small principality of *Ch'in* in western China had probably been a largely independent entity, but through warfare and strategy it began a rise in preeminence in the third century B.C. After a decisive battle against a competitor in 260 B.C., the Ch'in expanded their domination, and in 221 B.C. the Ch'in king claimed control over most of the old Chou territory, and extended the imperial borders west to Szechwan and south to the Canton delta. Shih Huang Ti ("first emperor") abolished the feudal system completely, entirely revised the administrative system, and sent investigators to every part of the empire to administer local affairs. Highways were constructed, a "Great Wall" about 2,250 kilometers long was completed along the northern frontier, millions of men were conscripted for other public-works projects, the written language was standardized and laws codified, and many other projects and reforms instituted. There is also evidence that Shih Huang Ti stifled dissent and killed many intellectuals.

13.10
The burial clothes of a princess of the late second century B.C. The suit was made of over 2000 jade tablets tied together with gold wire.

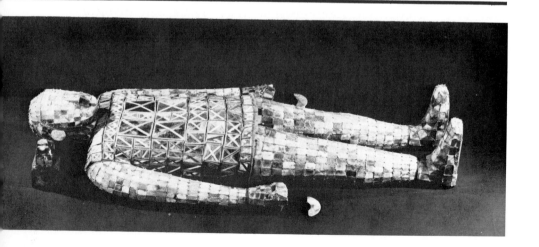

When Shih Huang Ti died in 210 B.C. his empire immediately fell into disarray, with many revolutions and counterrevolutions, and the empire was not restored until the Han dynasty was established.

The Han Dynasty (202 B.C. to A.D. 220)

The *Han dynasty* was founded by Liu Pang, a native of Huai, in 202 B.C., and except for brief lapses, imperial power was vested in his descendants for the next four centuries. The Ch'in dynasty had lasted only about nineteen years, and thus the Han period represents the first long-lasting unification of China. Also, despite continual pressure from nomads along the northern borders and occasional flareups of insurgency among vassal states, the Han extended their area of control to approximately the modern borders of China proper and were even able, through trade and travel, to influence the cultures of Japan, central Asia, and the Near East.

The Han administration was a complex hierarchy imposed on a vast peasant society. Below the emperor were tens of thousands of ranked administrators, many of them belonging to royal families or recruited on the recommendation of the nobility. This enormous bureaucracy spent much of its time in record keeping and organizing public works. A census taken in A.D. 1, for example, lists the number of households and total population (57 million individuals), and calendrical records, tax receipts, labor assignments, and myriad other documents attest to a well-functioning state administration. Coins of several denominations circulated, weights and measures were standardized, public transport was available for officials, labor was conscripted and supported for public works, and populations were resettled.

Later historians have tended to look back on the Han era as a time of great peace, tranquillity, equality, and justice, and compared to other periods this was sometimes so. But the documents make it clear that corruption existed, revolts occasionally flared, and there were enormous differences in wealth.

Still, the cultural achievements of the Han are impressive. Paper appears to have been invented shortly after A.D. 105—no doubt partly in response to the bureaucratic proliferation that afflicted the Han no less than ourselves. And for the same reason, perhaps, the Chinese script was reformed and dictionaries compiled during the late Han period, as were textbooks in mathematics and medicine. Waterclocks, sundials and even a kind of seismograph were invented and widely used. In the philosophical realm, Buddhism was brought into China from India in the first century A.D., and the basis of the Taoist religion was established in the second century A.D.

Internationally, the Han empire occasionally came into conflict with the nomadic and semisedentary peoples living to the north and west, in the great reaches of East and central Asia. From time to time the Han were obliged to mount invasions into the steppe country, none of which were successful in permanently extending imperial control.

The Origins of Cultural Complexity in North China: Conclusions

If we compare the origins of cultural complexity in North China to similar developments elsewhere, several points of contrast are apparent. Perhaps most obvious is the initial lack of any monumental architecture during the Lungshan and early Shang periods, stages of development at which most other early complex communities were building massive pyramids, platforms, or buildings.

If, as has been suggested here, monumental construction projects in these early societies functioned to control population growth, to provide a focus for the important administrative and ritual ties that bound these communities together, to "verify" in some manner the societal elite, and to mobilize and discipline a large labor pool that could be used for other purposes, then we can only conclude that the early Chinese communities managed to meet these needs in ways that did not require monumental construction projects.

Another contrast between China and other areas that developed complex cultures is the relatively late and diffuse appearance of urbanism. There were no cities in ancient China on anything like the scale of Ur or Teotihuacán until long after full-fledged states had appeared. In this regard the Chinese were like the ancient Peruvian cultures, where urbanism was also a late development.

The literature on the causes and consequences of urbanism is enormous, and many hypotheses have been suggested to account for why people aggregate in settlements of different sizes under different conditions. Unfortunately, the archaeological evidence from China during the critical periods is not sufficiently complete to evaluate the several possibilities. Some have suggested that warfare was extremely important in determining the settlement size distribution in ancient China, and, in fact, warfare did have a profound influence on Chinese developments. But warfare, too, seems to be simply another—and somewhat variable—expression of more fundamental changes going on within societies as their complexity and differentiation increase.

Karl Wittfogel hypothesized that Chinese cultural developments could be explained largely in terms of the necessities and consequences of large-scale, unified irrigation systems (p. 352). Certainly, irrigation systems became highly integrated and important in ancient China, beginning at least by about 250 B.C., and no doubt these developments were in part the cause and in part the result of evolving cultural complexity, but the transition to state-level societies in ancient China was already well developed before irrigation systems developed much complexity (K. C. Chang 1976: 59).

Turning to the major similarities between ancient Chinese developments and those elsewhere, in China too one of the first steps was an increasingly intensive and productive agricultural system, coupled with sedentary village communities. As elsewhere, this stage was followed by the rapid extension of pottery styles over a large region and a concurrent increased variability in residential architecture and mortuary complexes. And while monumental architecture may have been somewhat minimized and belated in ancient China, the great wall around Chengchou and other features are examples of at least some investment in "wasteful" monumental projects.

Ultimately, China fell into the same cyclical pattern of expansion and collapse we documented in the other ancient civilizations (Lattimore 1951). It is as if some internal limiting factors exist that restrain growth past a certain point, at least until certain alterations can be made within a culture. In China, at least, the early appearance of writing, the largely superficial role of bronze in the economy, and the great constancy in agricultural practices seem to suggest that the limiting factors on early Chinese developments were not directly tied to technological matters. It may have been simply that a certain amount of time and trial-and-error were necessary to evolve the administrative institutions that, in the final analysis, are the heart of cultural complexity.

Bibliography

Barnard, N. 1972. "The First Radiocarbon Dates from China." Monograph on Far Eastern History: 8, School of Pacific Studies, A. N. U. Canberra.

Chang, K. C. 1963. *The Archaeology of Ancient China.* New Haven: Yale University Press.

———. 1970. "The Beginning of Agriculture in the Far East." *Antiquity.* 44: 175–85.

———. 1976. *Early Chinese Civilization: Anthropological Perspectives.* Cambridge. Mass.: Harvard University Press.

Chang, Sen-Dou. 1963. "The Historical Trend of Chinese Urbanization." *Annals of the Association of American Geographers.* 53(2): 109–43.

Chêng, Tê-K'un. 1957. *Archaeological Studies in Szechwan.* Cambridge: Cambridge University Press.

———. 1963. *Archaeology in China, vol. 3: Chou China.* Cambridge: Heffer.

Creel, Herrlee G. 1937. *The British of China.* New York: Reynal & Hitchcock.

———. 1937. *Studies in Early Chinese Culture.* Baltimore: Waverly Press.

Fairservis, Walter A., Jr. 1959. *The Origins of Oriental Civilization.* New York: New American Library.

Lattimore, Owen. 1951. *Inner Asian Frontiers of China.* Boston: Beacon Press.

Li, Chi. 1957. *The Beginings of Chinese Civilization.* Seattle: University of Washington Press.

Nai, Hsia. 1957. "Our Neolithic Ancestors." *Archaeology.* 10: 181–87.

Service, Elman. 1975. *Origins of the State and Civilization.* New York: W. W. Norton.

Skinner, G. W. 1964. "Marketing and Social Structure in Rural China." *Journal of Asian Studies.* 24(1): 3–43.

Stover, Leon E. 1974. *The Cultural Ecology of Chinese Civilization.* New York: Pica Press.

Toynbee, Arnold, ed. 1973. *Half the World.* New York: Holt.

Triestman, Judith. 1972. *The Prehistory of China.* Garden City, N.Y.: Natural History Press.

Watson, William. 1960. *Archaeology in China*. London: Max Parrish.

———. 1971. *Cultural Frontiers in Ancient East Asia*. Edinburgh: Edinburgh University Press.

———. 1974. *Ancient China*. Greenwich, Conn.: New York Graphic Society.

Wheatley, Paul. 1971. *The Pivot of the Four Quarters*. Chicago: Aldine.

Wittfogel, Karl A. 1957. *Oriental Despotism*. New Haven: Yale University Press.

14

The Origins of Complex Cultures in Mesoamerica

"The Near East," Sir Mortimer Wheeler once remarked, "is the land of archaeological sin." Such a statement could have been made only by a man who had never worked in Mesoamerica.

Kent V. Flannery

Introduction

In Easter week of the year 1519 the Spanish lawyer-soldier Hernán Cortez landed on the coast of Veracruz, Mexico, and began a military campaign that would end in the crushing defeat of Aztec civilization. For perhaps 40,000 years before Cortez's arrival, the peoples of the Old and New Worlds had had so little contact that they were physically different and spoke entirely different languages. But here is the curious thing: when Cortez traveled the road from Veracruz to the Aztec capital near Mexico City, he passed through cities, towns, villages, markets, and irrigated fields; he saw slavery, poverty, potentates, farmers, judges, churches, massive pyramids, roads, boats, pottery and textiles; in short, he encountered a world whose almost every aspect he could understand in terms of his own experience as an urban Spaniard of the sixteenth century.

There were of course many dissimilarities between the Spanish and Aztec peoples. Neither the Aztecs nor their predecessors had horses, ocean-going ships, steel, or alphabetic writing systems. And the psychological differences between the Aztecs and their European conquerers were probably particularly profound. The Spanish, despite their imperialism and murderous ferocity in warfare, viewed the Aztecs' preoccupations with death and human sacrifice with abhorrence, and the Aztecs found many aspects of Christianity both evil and incomprehensible.

Yet despite profound differences in their respective morals and ideas, the Spanish and the Aztecs were fundamentally culturally alike: they lived in hierarchically organized, class-structured, complex, expansionistic empires, with state churches, intensive agricultural and industrial systems, and many other features in common.

Complex societies are not an automatic or necessary step in cultural evolution; they are, rather, the products of specific factors and conditions. Thus, the appearance of Mesoamerican complex societies that paralleled those of Mesopotamia and other areas suggests that similar processes and factors were operating in these different areas, and this coincidence can be used to evaluate the several hypotheses about the *general* process of the formation of complex societies.

The Ecological Setting

At one time or another almost every part of Mesoamerica (southern and central Mexico, Guatemala, Belize, Honduras, and El Salvador) played a part in the evolution of complex societies there, but four specific areas seem to have been developmental centers (Figure 14.2): the South Gulf Coast, the Valley (or Basin) of Mexico, the Valley of Oaxaca, and the Mayan lowlands. The evolution of complex Mesoamerican cultures was much influenced by three general ecological conditions: (1) the millions of years of mountain-building volcanic activity, which left Mesoamerica a still trembling land of towering mountains and circumscribed valleys, and which in many areas compressed extremely different flora, fauna, and climates into close proximity, making

MESOAMERICA

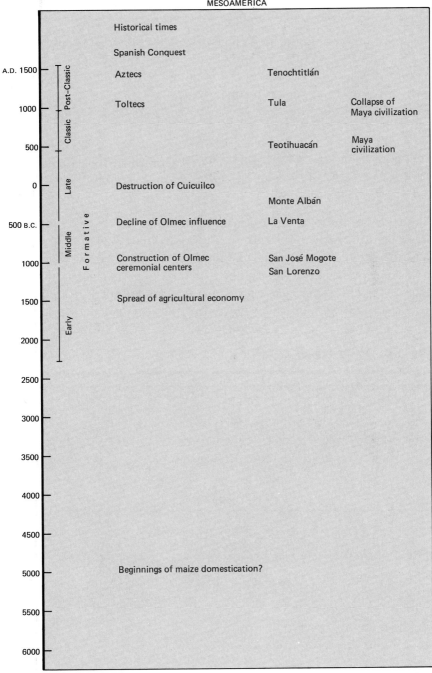

Historical times

Spanish Conquest

Aztecs	Tenochtitlán	
Toltecs	Tula	Collapse of Maya civilization
	Teotihuacán	Maya civilization
Destruction of Cuicuilco		
	Monte Albán	
Decline of Olmec influence	La Venta	
Construction of Olmec ceremonial centers	San José Mogote San Lorenzo	
Spread of agricultural economy		
Beginnings of maize domestication?		

Post-Classic · Classic · Late · Middle · Early

Formative

A.D. 1500
1000
500
0
500 B.C.
1000
1500
2000
2500
3000
3500
4000
4500
5000
5500
6000

14.1
The chronology of Mesoamerica.

transport and communication difficult; (2) the absence of any domesticable animal suitable for providing milk, transport, or draught power; and (3) the virtual absence of large river systems that could be used year-round to irrigate crops.

The Archaeological Record of Early Complex Mesoamerican Societies (ca. 1600 B.C. to A.D. 1519)

Although the domestication of maize, beans, squash, peppers, and other Mesoamerican plants was well under way by 4000 B.C., the first documented sedentary agricultural communities date to only about 1600 B.C. Among the interesting aspects of these first villages is that they appeared at about the same time in many different areas, from the lowland coasts to the highland valleys, and they seemed to appear quite

14.2
The geography of Mesoamerica.

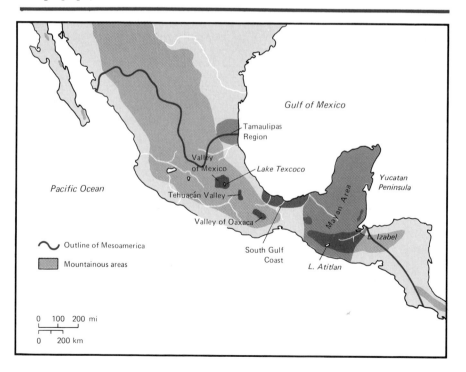

14.3
Mexico's first agriculturalists probably lived in wattle-and-daub houses thatched
with straw, much like these in a village of Nahuatl-speakers in Morelos, Mexico.

suddenly. This suddenness is no doubt partly an illusion: presently we
can't distinguish the ages of these early settlements with sufficient precision to be able to see short-term changes. Still, there are no known
villages at 1700 B.C. in Mesoamerica, and yet by 1300 B.C. there were
probably thousands—a rapid change by archaeological standards.

A second intriguing aspect of this period is the similarity of these
early villages. From the hot, wet Guatemalan lowlands to the arid Tehuacán Valley, the earliest villages were made in essentially the same
way, were of approximately the same size, and their inhabitants apparently led very similar lives (Flannery 1976a: 13–15). Almost invariably,
houses (Figure 14.3) were built using the wattle-and-daub method—
walls were constructed of woven reed sheets, plastered with mud, and
dried by the hot Mexican sun. Roofs did not preserve well but were
apparently made of thatched materials. Houses were seldom larger than
four by six meters, with a tamped clay floor on which fine sand was
scattered; often, the walls were whitewashed or plastered with limed
clay.

Plan of a house in an agricultural village in Oaxaca, Mexico. Late San José phase, ca. 900 B.C.

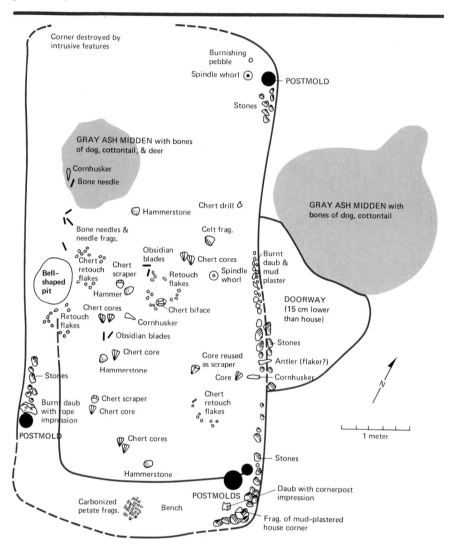

About 90 percent of all known *Early Formative* (1600 to 1100 B.C.) sites were two hectares or less and contained ten to twelve houses inhabited by a total of about fifty to sixty people (Figure 14.4), but some settlements were larger, such as San Lorenzo at about fifty-three hectares and Chimalhuacán at about forty-five hectares.

These settlements also have similar contents. Every extensively excavated Early Formative household has yielded all of the following items: fragments of grinding stones; storage pits; pieces of large ceramic storage jars; bones of cottontail rabbits; carbonized maize fragments; and broken pieces of ceramic charcoal braizers (Flannery and Winter 1976: 36). In addition, ovens, middens, and graves are very common. While the proportion of plant and animal foods varied somewhat, all villages probably grew maize, beans, squash, peppers, and some other crops, and hunted deer and rabbits. Each village, or each extended family, may have had a specialist who did pressure flaking of stone, leatherworking, or a similar craft, and individual villages may have concentrated on specialities like salt production, feather weaving, shellworking, grinding stone manufacture, and the like (ibid.: 38).

These early villages also show some evidence of a level of cultural complexity one might not expect if these were recently transformed hunters and gatherers. The very first villages seem to have some minor "public architecture" and variable distributions of exotic and craft items.

THE EVOLUTION OF COMPLEX SOCIETIES
ON THE SOUTH GULF COAST (CA. 1500 TO 400 B.C.)

The earliest and most radical break with the simple village farming tradition of Mesoamerica apparently occurred in the sweltering lowlands of the South Gulf Coast in Tabasco and Veracruz. Here, shortly after 1350 B.C., people began to engage in activities reflecting increasing cultural complexity: they built massive pyramids and other nonresidential structures, aggregated in relatively large settlements, engaged in a variety of specialized arts and crafts, and began to invest considerable energy and resources in drainage channels and terraces in order to intensify agricultural production. These people are known to us as the *Olmec,* a name derived from an Indian word meaning *rubber people*—doubtless a reference to the rubber trees that grow in this area.

The Olmec were not the only people in Mesoamerica to develop a complex culture more or less independently, and some question exists as to whether or not they were even the first, but they were undeniably one of the most influential of all early Mesoamerican societies. The Olmec worked jade and stone and made pottery in styles that were copied in Oaxaca, Puebla, the Valley of Mexico, and elsewhere, and although it is uncertain whether the peoples of the South Gulf Coast actually invented these styles, they do seem to have reached an expressive climax there. Some scholars have argued that the Olmec culture was the *cultura madre* (mother culture) of all later complex societies in Mesoamerica, and that they were directly responsible for transforming their neighbors by military, political, religious, or economic means into complex societies. Others have argued that the Olmec represent only one of several largely independent cases of the evolution of social complexity in Mesoamerica, and that their connection with their neighbors was mainly through limited economic exchange networks.

The Ecological Setting

The *Olmec Heartland* or *Climax Area,* as it is sometimes called, is a coastal strip approximately 350 kilometers in length, extending inland about 100 kilometers. It was created by the alluviation of several rivers that run to the sea from the highlands of Oaxaca, Chiapas, and Orizaba. Toward the coast, as the gradient lessens, the rivers become sluggish and eventually lose themselves in the thick mangrove swamps that border the ocean. Except for the Tuxtla Mountains in the center of the heartland or where vegetation has been cleared for grazing, the region is thickly forested. Rainfall is extremely heavy but regionally variable, with some areas getting as much as 2,500 millimeters annually, while others receive as "little" as 1,500 millimeters. The rainfall is also quite sharply seasonal, falling almost entirely during the summer, an essential condition for swidden or slash-and-burn agriculture, the predominant agricultural system here prehistorically and currently. Swidden agriculture is common in tropical vegetation zones and is one of the few effective ways to exploit these areas agriculturally. It involves cutting down all the vegetation in a particular area and then waiting for the dry season so that the cut vegetation can be burned off. Swidden agriculture is therefore restricted to areas where there is a suf-

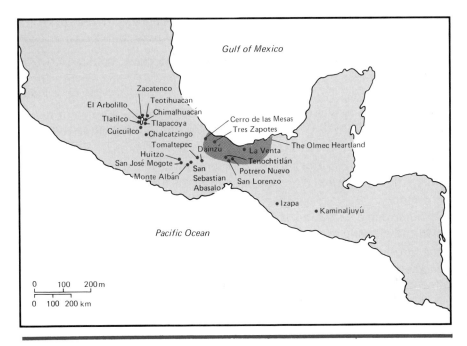

14.5
Some Mesoamerican Formative sites of the first millennium B.C.

ficiently long and consistent dry season to allow this. The burning of the vegetation is essential because it returns nutrients to the soil—a particularly important contribution in areas where artificial fertilizers are not available. After burning, the land is sown and the crops germinate and come to maturity in the rainy season. After one or two years of exploitation, however, the land must be left fallow for variable lengths of time, sometimes for twenty years or more. If the cycle is speeded up, productivity falls rapidly, and most villagers avoid this by keeping to a complex fallowing system. Because of soil conditions and underground limestone formations (which continually add lime to the soils) (Ferdon 1959: 13), the agricultural lands in this area are relatively productive and not as susceptible to the leaching that plagues some other tropical areas (for example, the Amazon Basin). In the flat lowlands of the Olmec Heartland as much as 70 to 90 percent of the land is fallow at any one time, and it is estimated that population densities of about twenty people per square kilometer can be supported on such a system (Pelzer 1945). Maize, beans, and squash were probably agricultural staples in Early Formative times, as they are here today, but the Olmec also supplemented their diet by hunting deer and pigs, by intensively fishing the many rivers and ponds of the region, and by collecting wild plant foods. In coastal areas they could also collect mussels and other rich resources of the marine interface. And some river levees near the coast are annually inundated with water-borne silt of such fertility that two crops a year are possible using swidden techniques. Indeed, it is probable that the precocity of the Olmec in developing the first complex Mesoamerican culture was tied directly to the great agricultural potential and rich floral and faunal resources of these riverine environments. At the same time, this area is also subject to fires, floods, storms, tropical plant diseases, and other natural limiting factors.

Some have suggested that the Olmec Heartland was much drier during the Formative period and that some areas now forested were open grasslands as late as 900 A.D.; but the weight of evidence suggests that the Olmec Heartland at 1500 B.C. to 900 B.C. was very much like it is today.

The Archaeological Record

The Early Formative cultures of the South Gulf Coast have been the subject of research since the 1870s, but only a few studies have directly addressed the problem of the origins of complex societies. Substantial archaeological excavations have been conducted at some of the larger sites, and a few surveys have been made in rural areas (Sisson 1970), but we do not have the two essentials for studying culture change: systematic settlement surveys of large areas and extensive excavations of a diversity of settlement types and sizes. Instead we have whole library shelves full of books of drawings, descriptions, and photographs of Olmec sculpture, stonework, and architecture—all beautifully done and a pleasure to peruse, but an incomplete source for analyzing the problem of the origins of complex societies.

OLMEC CEREMONIAL CENTERS   At San Lorenzo, in southern Veracruz, the Olmec carried thousands of tons of clay, sand, and rock in baskets to make a large platform and ceremonial complex. Excavations have not been substantial enough to date precisely much of the construction at San Lorenzo, but Michael D. Coe suspects that at least one stepped platform of sand and clay and some of the cruder stone reliefs might date to before 1200 B.C. (1968: 46, 64).

San Lorenzo actually refers to a group of sites within a diameter of about five kilometers, including, besides San Lorenzo, the sites of Te-

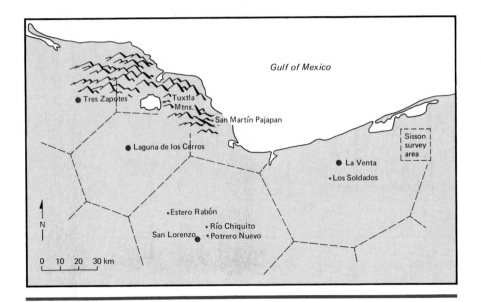

14.6
The regular spacing of major Olmec ceremonial centers may reflect their economic
and administrative dominance over hexagonal-shaped (dashed lines) rural territories.
It is unlikely that these centers were politically federated.

nochtitlán and Potrero Nuevo. The architectural sequence at San Lorenzo is somewhat confusing, and we really don't know how much was
accomplished in the critical period between 1200 and 900 B.C., but the
most impressive artifacts there, the sculpted heads and monuments, almost certainly date to this period (Coe 1968). These artifacts include
free-standing figures of kneeling men and carved stelae and "altars," all
carefully executed from massive basalt blocks. On them are myriad engraved figures, often fantastic mythical creatures representing hybrids
of snakes, jaguars, and humans.

The remains of houses and other occupational debris have been
found in the area of San Lorenzo, and Coe estimates that at about 950
B.C. the population of the site of San Lorenzo was approximately
1,000, while another 1,000 lived at Tenochtitlán, and perhaps 250 at
Potrero Nuevo (1968: 57). Only a few test excavations of these residential areas have been conducted, but fragmentary evidence suggests
maize was the primary staple, frequently supplemented with fish, turtles, deer, and other animals.

The agricultural system was probably swidden-based, since analysis of plant remains in hearths indicates that the area was then covered
by a thick tropical forest. The twenty or more artificial ponds and la-

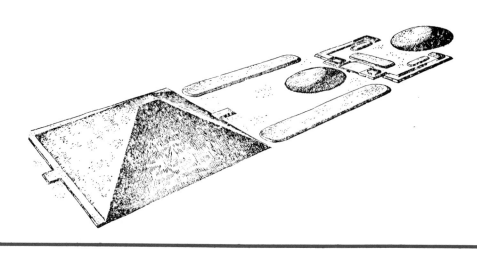

14.7
Reconstruction of Complex A at La Venta.

gunas built at San Lorenzo before 900 B.C. were apparently drained by an elaborate system of deeply buried basalt troughs covered with slabs. Several possible uses have been suggested for these ponds, ranging from water storage to intensive hydraulic agriculture (Sanders and Price 1968: 57). Strangely, the remains of thousands of toads (*Bufo marinus*) were found at this site, and it may be significant that eating parts of these animals produces hallucinations. These toads are restricted to the very moist environments of coastal areas, and the discovery of their remains in Oaxaca—a very dry area several hundred kilometers distant—suggests that they may have been a trade item in the Early Formative.

At La Venta, on a small island in a coastal swamp near the Tonalá River, the Olmec constructed a series of mounds, platforms, courts, and pyramids covering more than five square kilometers (Figure 14.7). Much of this has been destroyed by looters and an oil well/processing installation, but excavations in the 1940s revealed a large portion of this site's plan. Dominating the area is a pyramid of clay, 128 by 73 meters at the base and 33.5 meters high. Two long, low mounds extend out to the north from the pyramid, with a circular mound between them. All these mounds are oriented 8° west of true north.

Different colored clays were used to achieve contrasts among these various constructions, and the whole complex was studded with monumental stone sculpture. The most impressive of these are the famous "Olmec heads," of which four were found at La Venta. These heads are as large as 3 meters in height and invariably depict a human head with a serious, not to say sneering, facial expression, and they usually are shown wearing a "football helmet." The basalt from which they were made was transported to the site from a source at least 130 kilometers to the west, probably by floating it down the river on rafts. Since the Olmec had no metal tools, we assume they worked with grinding and pecking stone implements, and it is difficult to believe that these sculptures were made by anyone other than skilled specialists.

Other works in stone are almost as impressive as the heads. Massive basalt slabs were engraved with human and animal forms and erected at various points around La Venta and other Olmec sites, and the highly stylized designs on these monoliths may represent the first steps toward a writing system. Large stone "altars" were also carved with bas-reliefs of kneeling men, jaguars, and other subjects.

Among the spectacular discoveries at La Venta were many unique jade and serpentine objects and three superimposed pavements, each composed of about 485 serpentine blocks (about the size of small construction bricks), laid out in a traditional Olmec design, a jaguar mask.

Unfortunately, the acidic, damp soils here do not preserve bones well, and the only burial information we have from La Venta comes

14.8
Scores of these huge stone heads were produced by the Olmec and transported many miles to ritual positions near ceremonial centers.

from a tomb in a large mound near the central pyramid. The tomb was elaborately constructed of basalt slabs, and on its limestone floor two juveniles were laid out in fabric bundles heavily coated with red paint. Buried with the bodies were jade figurines, beads, a shell ornament, a stingray spine (elsewhere known to have been used in ritual contexts and traded in some quantities in Mesoamerica), and a few other items.

Other types of evidence relating to social complexity, such as residential architecture and settlement patterns, are not well represented at La Venta. There is little residential debris there except for pottery and a few clay figurines (mainly female, some male). Apparently, most of the people who built La Venta did not live there permanently.

Other Olmec ceremonial centers have been found at Laguna de los Cerros, and similar sites in the Papaloapan River Basin have been reported, but we have little archaeological evidence about them.

By 900 B.C. Olmec culture had reached its peak on the south Gulf Coast. There was considerable trade (Figure 14.9) in jade, iron ore, obsidian, bitumen, magnetite mirrors, shark teeth, stingray spines, and perhaps cocoa and pottery, with goods circulating in complex patterns between the Olmec Heartland and highland Mexico and as far south as Guatemala. The large volume of trade items found in the Olmec Heartland, in fact, suggests that the Olmec imported so many commodities that they may even have had, on occasion, a balance of payments problem (R. E. Adams 1977: 88).

An analysis of Olmec settlement patterns is difficult because adequate archaeological surveys have not been made of the rural areas, and thus we know little about the types of communities that may have supported the large centers. One survey (Sisson 1970) discovered many small undifferentiated villages that did not evidence the regular spacing we would expect if they were economically or politically interdependent. The dates of these settlements are not well established, however, making it difficult to interpret their spatial patterns, although it seems evident that the major ceremonial settlements drew their labor and resources from these rural populations. Analysis of the major centers' locations revealed a regular spacing (see Figure 14.6), which archaeologist Timothy Earle (1976: 216) concluded may have been due to competitive, perhaps antagonistic relationships among them, but it is difficult to estimate their populations at specific times.

"Olmec" ceramic and sculptural designs have been found far outside the borders of the South Gulf Coast. Some bas-relief rock carvings

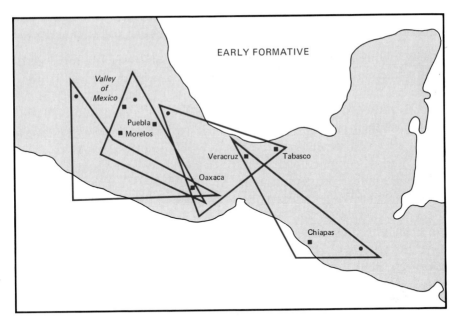

EARLY FORMATIVE

Valley
of
Mexico

Puebla
Morelos

Veracruz   Tabasco

Oaxaca

Chiapas

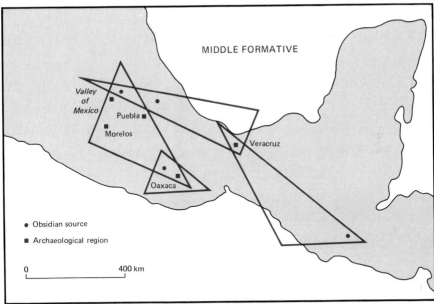

MIDDLE FORMATIVE

Valley
of
Mexico

Puebla
Morelos

Veracruz

Oaxaca

• Obsidian source

■ Archaeological region

0   400 km

14.9
Obsidian was one of many commodities traded in Formative Mesoamerica. The triangles enclose sites and areas linked in exchange networks.

at Las Victorias in highland El Salvador strongly resemble those at La
Venta, and similar sculptures have been discovered in the highlands of
Guerrero and Morelos in western Mexico. At Chalcatzingo, in Morelos,
cliff sculptures include a standard Olmec motif of a man seated in what
may have been meant as the mouth of a cave. Also in Morelos, at the
burial sites of San Pablo Pantheon and La Juana, David Grove has
found hollow ceramic "baby" figurines and other ceramics that closely
resemble those from San Lorenzo. Olmec styles of pottery, worked
stone, jade, and other artifacts have also been found at several sites in
the Valley of Oaxaca, at Tlatilco and Tlapacoya near Mexico City, in
Guatemala, and elsewhere in Mesoamerica.

The nature of the political and social relationships among these
various trading partners and the significance of the borrowing of Olmec
motifs by peoples outside the South Gulf Coast are considered below.

14.10
Olmec "baby" figurine in red-
painted clay.

Between 900 and 400 B.C. the Olmec civilization seems to have come to an end as a distinctive entity in Mesoamerica. The appearance at San Lorenzo at about 700 B.C. of new pottery wares, figurines, and art styles, and the intentional destruction of the Olmec monuments has been interpreted to mean that the settlement was overrun by non-Olmec invaders. More plausibly, the Olmec themselves, recognizing the collapse of their religious and economic systems, may have intentionally defaced these monuments—which may explain why some of the heads were carefully buried after having been mutilated (Drennan 1976: 362–63; Weaver 1972: 52).

Olmec culture continued for hundreds of years after 700 B.C. at Tres Zapotes, La Venta, and other sites, suggesting that all the ceremonial centers were not part of a unified system. But by 400 B.C. the Olmec Heartland had lost its earlier prominence, and, although inhabited continuously to the present, since the collapse of the Olmec it has been a cultural backwater.

Olmec Art

The Olmec apparently had no developed writing system, so what we know of their world and life views comes from their sculpture, figurines, pottery, and other artifacts. The Olmec apparently believed that at some distant time in the past a woman mated with a jaguar and gave issue to a line of half-human, half-feline monsters, or "were-jaguars." These are portrayed in pottery, stone, and other media in a highly stylized way, usually as fat infants of no discernible sexuality. Their snarling mouths, toothless gums, and cleft heads give them a strikingly bizarre quality that some have explained as an imitation of a birth defect known as *spina bifida*. M. D. Coe suspects that the Olmec saw in such deformities the characteristics they would expect of a mating between a human and a jaguar (1965a).

One of the most common themes in Olmec art is violence. The Olmec are often depicted with clubs and occasionally in the act of beating prisoners. The execution of these artifacts is pleasing to many people today, and Olmec art commands high prices on the illegal art market, particularly in the United States. Through such dealings has come the rape and destruction of many Olmec sites by the looters who feed these criminal art markets.

Some have called the Olmec complex a "state," but it would seem premature to conclude that the Olmec had a fully differentiated and hierarchically arranged social, political, and religious organization. Their settlement patterns are not well known, but there is little evidence of the hierarchical arrangement of villages, towns, and cities that we saw in the case of state societies elsewhere. Neither residential architecture nor mortuary complexes are sufficiently documented that we can infer several levels of socially and economically differentiated classes, and even the degree of occupational specialization is questionable, except, perhaps, as represented by rock-carving specialists and officials to plan and coordinate construction projects. Sanders and Price, in fact, conclude that nothing about the Olmec is inconsistent with a "chiefdom" level of organization, by which they mean that there was probably no class stratification or elaborate control hierarchy (1968: 127).

However we classify the Olmec, they are clearly different from previous cultures in Mesoamerica in their capacity to organize massive amounts of resources and labor and in their investment of these in monumental architecture and other nonsubsistence activities. The obvious question is, Why did they develop in this way? Again, neither population pressure, irrigation, nor other single factors seem to work as "prime movers" here. Until surveys are completed we won't know precise population figures, but the Olmec probably rarely encountered severe imbalances between population size and resources. The swidden agricultural systems they apparently used would have been quite productive in the frost-free heartland area, and there is no evidence of massive investments in drainage canals, land terraces, or other forms of agricultural intensification. Warfare also seems an unlikely "prime mover," because there is no evidence of substantial walling or fortifications at either the large ceremonial centers or the rural villages.

Possibly, the initial stimulus for Olmec developments was the great fertility of the river levees near the coast, where, once maize had been domesticated, two crops a year were possible without fallowing. Sanders and Price (1968) and others suggest that where agricultural lands differ sharply in their productivity, a certain "selection" for cultural change exists, in that "variations in productivity within small zones and between adjacent zones would place some groups in an advantageous competitive position. In such a setting egalitarian tribal society could be transformed quite readily into a ranked or stratified one" (1968: 132).

Once the Olmec sphere of influence included larger areas, how-ever, its economic base became increasingly "redundant" in the sense that the swidden cultivation of the same three or four crops was the economic basis for most of this area. Under such conditions there would have been an advantage to the collection and redistribution of food, so as to even out any ecological disaster that might befall any par-ticular region of the heartland—an area where drought, disease, rain-storms, and other problems are a constant threat to agriculture. The enormous constructions of La Venta and the other sites, then, may have served as the religious focus under which this redistribution took place, and may also have served to control population growth and commodity exhange in ways we have detailed elsewhere. On the other hand, while these local factors may have been important in Olmec developments, there is some evidence that Olmec cultural changes cannot be under-stood without reference to other areas of Mesoamerica, particularly the Valley of Mexico.

THE DEVELOPMENT OF CULTURAL COMPLEXITY
IN THE VALLEY OF MEXICO (1500 B.C. TO A.D. 700)

The Ecological Setting

The Valley of Mexico is a large basin with no external drainage and rimmed on three sides by high mountain walls cut by only a few passes. These impressive mountains rise to 5,000 meters in some areas, and even in the North where there are no actual mountains, the valley is delimited by a series of low hills. The valley has often been consid-ered a "natural" analytical unit, bounded as it is by such impressive natural barriers, but archaeological research has revealed that almost from their arrival here the people of this area interacted with cultures far beyond the valley itself (Parsons 1974: 83).

Of the roughly 7,500 square kilometers area of the Valley of Mex-ico, 3,000 square kilometers are high rugged terrain, much of it beyond the temperature limits of maize agriculture. Until the last 400 years a large lake covered the low central portion of the valley, and much of the adjacent areas were covered by marshes. The maximum depth of the lake was probably never more than a few meters, and it provided rich lacustrine/swamp resources, such as fish, fowl, turtles, algae, and reeds.

There is not a single navigable stream or river in the whole Valley of Mexico today, and most natural channels contain water only during part of the year. There were probably many permanent streams in the prehispanic period, prior to deforestation and slope erosion, but such streams would have been relatively small, although useful for irrigating agricultural areas.

Water availability was an important element in the cultural evolution of the Valley of Mexico, because rainfall is limited and sharply seasonal and varies considerably from north to south. If the land is not artificially irrigated, the rainfall may be insufficient to make the plants germinate until late June, by which time they cannot mature before the fall frosts destroy them. Crop failure in nonirrigated areas for this and other reasons is frequent, and thus there is a strong incentive to irrigate crops where possible.

The upper slopes of the Valley of Mexico, the areas above 2,500 meters in elevation, are today thinly settled. Rainfall maize agriculture can be done in a few areas, but failure rates are high. The forests and meadows here provide today, as they did in the past, many wood products, and in earlier times they supported large deer herds that were an important part of the prehistoric and early historic diet. Other resources of the Valley of Mexico include several obsidian sources, which were of considerable importance in prehistoric periods, and a diversity of plants, animals, and mineral commodities.

Formative Settlements in the Valley of Mexico
(1100 B.C. to 200 B.C.)

Between 1100 and 800 B.C., when the Olmec were rapidly developing relatively high population densities, monumental architecture, and spectacular art, there were still relatively few settlements in the Valley of Mexico, and most of these were simple small villages and hamlets. Only a few sites, such as Tlatilco and Cuicuilco (Figure 14.11), were of any size, the last estimated to have included approximately twenty-five hectares (and contained 500 people) (Parsons 1974: 91).

Cuicuilco was covered with lava by a volcanic eruption around 150 B.C., and therefore little is known about it, Tlatilco has been largely destroyed by looters and the activities connected with a modern brick factory built on the site. How much of the occupation there dates to the period between 1100 and 800 B.C. will probably never be known, but apparently it was somewhat larger than that of the few other settlements in the valley at this time.

Thus, little in the settlement patterns of this period indicates social complexity. The two-tiered site size hierarchy is consistent with a simple, perhaps tribal, organization, and the distribution of settlements does not point to any political or social spacing. Settlements seemed to be located principally around the edge of the great lake, although there were a few small villages in the highlands in areas where the soil is particularly rich and deep. Most of the settlements were concentrated at the juncture of the lake shore and the gently sloping, fertile soil of the valley floor, or in the areas of heaviest rainfall, suggesting, no doubt, the importance of lacustrine resources and rainfall maize agriculture (Parsons 1974: 93). Differences in settlement size seem to be a result of local variations in agricultural potential.

Nor is there much evidence of complex architecture at these settlements. A few small mounds and platforms may date to before 800

14.11
Some important early sites in the Valley of Mexico.

B.C., but none are on the scale of the pyramids, platforms, and other structures found on the South Gulf Coast. No evidence of elaborate residential structures or monumental sculptures has been found.

The contrasts between the settlements on the South Gulf Coast and those in the Valley of Mexico are thus principally in the respective presence and absence of monumental architecture; the actual residential areas appear to have been quite comparable in that most people on the South Gulf Coast at this time were probably living in small rural hamlets which, if anything, were less impressive than the Valley of Mexico settlements. This is significant because, as we have noted, the primary function of monumental architecture may have been to control populations and organize disparate peoples for collective economic and military action. The relatively homogeneous environment of the South Gulf Coast—compared to the Valley of Mexico—conceivably offered greater inducement to the construction of massive public buildings because of the necessity to integrate relatively large areas in order to guard against economic disaster.

In short, when we compare the Olmec and the occupants of the Valley of Mexico up to about 400 B.C., it is perhaps misleading to see the Olmec as more complex than the societies of the Valley of Mexico. Perhaps the Olmec were more hierarchically organized, but in occupational specialization, technological development, differential access to wealth, power, and prestige, and other aspects of cultural development, these peoples may have been quite similar. Even the most obvious difference between these groups, monumental construction, may be more apparent than real: there may be at least some smaller version of the constructions at La Venta and San Lorenzo under the lava at Cuicuilco.

The cemetery at Tlatilco provides little evidence that the occupants of the Valley of Mexico were living in complex cultures. Burial goods include pottery, shell ornaments, obsidian tools, figurines, bone tools, and jade and serpentine objects, and there is some evidence that a number of women were buried with more numerous and more expensive objects than other people in the cemetery, perhaps even with sacrificed men and children. But there are no lavish mortuary cults.

The presence of Olmec design elements on some of the ceramics found in graves at Tlatilco, along with other evidence, has led some to argue that settlements in the Valley of Mexico were becoming more complex as a result of contact with the Olmec. The "Olmecness" of the artifacts in the Tlatilco graves is somewhat dubious, however, and the vast majority do not look anything at all like Olmec material (Porter 1953).

From about 800 B.C. to about 500 B.C., the population density of the Valley of Mexico increased considerably. At least ten sites were larger than fifty hectares (each inhabited by about 1,000 people), and one, Cuicuilco, probably had a population of about 2,500, but the lava obscures the site to the point that it is impossible to make reasonable estimates. All of the larger sites are located along the lake margin, while scattered small hamlets are found in the highlands. The economic basis of these lakeside settlements appears to be similar to that of the preceding period, with a focus on agricultural, lacustrine, and marsh resources.

The pattern of these settlements may suggest some degree of political, religious, or economic interrelationship, as they are fairly evenly spaced at eight to ten kilometer intervals along the lake shore. We also infer considerable contact among these people because the degree of similarity in their pottery and other stylistic expressions is high. Site placement here, however, seems to be largely determined by food resource concentrations, not by political or economic boundaries.

Few of the excavated sites of this period have substantial public or monumental structures. Some unexcavated sites seem to have small mounds on them, but most appear residential in function (Parsons 1974: 93). El Arbolillo and Zacatenco, two of the larger settlements at this time, were found to have only simple wattle-and-daub constructions, but more substantial architecture may be in the unexcavated portions of these sites.

For the period between about 500 and 200 B.C. there is persuasive evidence of changing cultural complexity in the Valley of Mexico. Population density rose considerably, and people were now living in larger settlements. Cuicuilco may have had as many as 7,500 people at this time—an unmanageable size without considerable social organization and control. Many other settlements of eighty to a hundred hectares existed, and intermediate and small settlements also increased in number. In addition, there is evidence of substantial public architecture toward the end of this period. Small "temple" platforms of stone and clay, some three to four meters high, appeared in several areas, and there were substantial stone structures at Cuicuilco and other sites. Unfortunately, little burial evidence relevant to this period exists (except at Tlatilco).

THE EVOLUTION OF CULTURAL COMPLEXITY
IN ANCIENT OAXACA (CA. 1600 TO 200 B.C.)

The Ecological Setting

The Valley of Oaxaca, like Mexico's other mountain valleys, includes a diversity of ecological zones. On the valley floor are large fertile alluvial areas of flat land that have a sufficiently high water table
for irrigation to be easily accomplished. Grading up into the mountains, the piedmont areas are less fertile than the alluvium, but they
can be productively farmed by diverting water from the perennial
streams that run toward the valley floor. The higher mountains are
cooler and wetter than the other zones and are still covered with pine
and oak trees. Little agriculture is practiced in the mountains today,
but, as in antiquity, the area is exploited for wood, nuts, berries, and
other resources (S. Lees 1972).

Oaxaca is generally warmer than the Valley of Mexico and more
arid. Frost is not nearly the limiting factor on agriculture it is in the
Valley of Mexico, although it can be a significant determinant of productivity. Since Formative times irrigation by means of canals and
wells has been an important aspect of agriculture in Oaxaca.

Several natural resources are important to an understanding of
the evolution of complex cultures here. The bedrock which underlies
parts of the valley is travertine, a smooth, hard stone that can be fashioned into ornaments; and there is evidence that this material was
traded at least as far away as the Valley of Mexico and the South Gulf
Coast. Also, some of the streams in the valley have extremely high salt
content and were used for salt production until about 1910; presumably this production (and trade) would have been possible in the Formative period as well.

Finally, some of the most important resources of Oaxaca were the
native iron ores, including magnetite, ilmenite, and hematite. Small
pieces of these materials were polished and used as mirrors and ornaments, which were then traded widely over Mesoamerica and used as
marks of status.

The Archaeological Record

OAXACA (1400 TO 850 B.C.) Shortly after 1400 B.C. the most productive areas of the piedmont and the alluvium in the Valley of Oa-

xaca were occupied by small villages composed of perhaps fifty people living in tiny wattle-and-daub structures. There is little evidence for ranking or stratification at this time, although it is entirely conceivable that these villages were organized along tribal lines.

The first significant deviation from this pattern of egalitarian farmers occurred sometime between 1350 and 1150 B.C., when the inhabitants of at least one site (San José Mogote) built several "public buildings" which together covered about 300 square meters. Although these structures average only 5.4 x 4.4 meters each, they are interpreted as "public buildings" because the floors were carefully covered with a distinctive white lime plaster and swept clean, in contrast to the average house of this period whose floors are usually stamped clay and sand and covered with household debris.

Other evidence suggests that these buildings at San José Mogote may have been intended for special functions: they are oriented 8° west of true north, about the same as the major monumental constructions at La Venta, in the Olmec Heartland; they were repaired and reused over longer periods of time than the obviously residential structures; and at least one of them has an "altar" or step against one wall.

Most of the other Formative villages in Oaxaca lack such public structures, although one, Tomaltepec, was found to have a large prepared mud-brick platform (Whalen 1976). In the area which would have been the floor of such a structure was a storage pit, considerably larger than any of the others at the site, containing relatively large quantities of obsidian, ornamental seashell, and deer and rabbit bones.

Between 1400 and 1000 B.C., overlapping in time with the construction of this platform, a large cemetery was created at Tomaltepec. Eighty burials containing a total of about 100 individuals were found, and most of these burials had almost exactly the same goods, including ceramics and a few other small items. In four of the burials, however, small quantities of obsidian, magnetite, and jade were found, but these differences in grave goods seem fairly small in view of the overall similarity. And, interestingly, no juveniles or infants were buried here; all were adults, suggesting that this society had not yet achieved significant social stratification.

Analysis of trade items in the valley between 1400 to 1000 B.C. also reinforces this impression of low-level community organization. A few items, such as obsidian, were traded, but in small amounts, and the trade was probably organized through individual households (Winter 1976). But archaeological evidence after 1000 B.C. suggests major

changes in the cultural organization of Oaxacan society. The largest
site of this period, San José Mogote, had several successive public
buildings of earth and adobe construction (Flannery 1976d: 335). One
of these, at Huitzo, was also oriented 8° west of true north, and like the
structure at Tomaltepec, it was built and decorated in a way that
suggests something more than a simple residential building: it had an
elaborate staircase, thickly plastered walls, and was crowned by a large
wattle-and-daub building.

More crafts were apparently performed at San José Mogote than
at other settlements in the valley at this time. Debris from working obsidian, jade, magnetite, shell, and other substances are found here in
concentrations proportionately greater than at other sites. There was a
major increase in the volume of "exotic" traded materials in Oaxaca at
this time also, perhaps in response to increasing social stratification;
these materials seem to have been used most frequently to make ornaments that reflect differences in social rank. There are clear resemblances between Olmec figurines and ones of comparable age from Oaxaca, particularly the baby-face style. In addition, some pottery with
Olmec motifs is found in Oaxaca. Certainly, magnetite and obsidian
were moved in substantial volumes between Oaxaca and the South
Gulf Coast between 1100 and 850 B.C.

Flannery (1976a: 178–79) concludes that between 1000 and 850
B.C. the spacing of villages along the main river, the Atoyac, was determined much more by social factors than agricultural ones, because
the spacing does not seem to reflect differences in physical features,
such as the amount of available farmland. Significantly, some villages
at this time specialized somewhat in salt production and ore mining
(Flannery 1976b: 166–67).

Burial evidence during the period from 1100 B.C. to 850 B.C. also
implies some low-level ranking (Pyne 1976). Winter (1972) reports that
of fifty Formative burials in the valley, decorated "Olmec" pottery defi-
nitely occurs with adult male burials, but rarely or never with female
burials.

OAXACA (850 TO 600 B.C.)   After about 850 B.C., variation in settlement size was greater than earlier. San José Mogote, for example,
grew to fifteen times the size of the next largest occupation by 550 B.C.
Many of the settlements excavated have public architecture, and their
distribution seems to mirror the growing importance of social and political factors in determining site location.

There is also evidence of considerable contact between the Olmec of the South Gulf Coast and the inhabitants of the Valley of Oaxaca at this time. There are enormous quantities of Olmec-style pottery and figurine fragments imitating Olmec designs in Oaxaca, while metallic ores and travertine from Oaxaca are found in the major Olmec sites on the South Gulf Coast.

OAXACA (600 TO 200 B.C.) Between 600 and 200 B.C. many of the elements we associate with complex cultures appeared in the Valley of Oaxaca. At the site of Monte Albán, on a high bluff in the middle of the valley, large stone buildings were flanked by stone slabs engraved with nude male figures that, because of the position of their limbs, have been called the *Danzantes*—the dancers (Figure 14.12). These have sometimes been thought to be "Olmec" in inspiration and proof of Olmec control of this region, but they are only superficially like the Olmec stone carvings. The Danzantes are portrayed with sexual organs, for example, and such representations do not appear in the surviving Olmec art from the South Gulf Coast. Besides, the constructions at Monte Albán probably date to about 200 B.C.—centuries after the Olmec had gone into a period of decline. The stone carvings at Monte Albán are also significant because of the hieroglyphics carved on these slabs—hieroglyphics that were the elements of a calendar system later common in more advanced Mesoamerican cultures.

Other major settlements in the Valley of Oaxaca at this time also indicate great cultural change. At Dainzú, a large pyramidal platform was constructed and ornamented with fifty stone carvings representing a variety of themes.

In settlement patterns, too, this period saw the emergence of more complex arrangements, which included "hilltop elite centers, densely occupied valley floor sites which could be classified as 'semi-urban' and piedmont villages and towns on key tributary streams" (Flannery: 1968: 98).

The Colonial Olmec Hypothesis

The belated appearance of monumental architecture and sculpture in Oaxaca, the Valley of Mexico, and elsewhere in the highlands (at least compared to that of the Olmec Heartland) has led some to the conclusion that the Olmec stimulated the development of complex so-

14.12
Above, one of the "Danzante" (dancer) reliefs from Monte Albán, Oaxaca, Mexico. Below, monumental architecture at Monte Albán.

cieties all over Mesoamerica. This interpretation goes back at least to the 1940s and 1950s (Covarrubias 1946, 1957), when the monumental complex at La Venta first came to the attention of archaeologists, and for the last twenty years it has had forceful proponents. Coe argues that from about 1300 B.C. to at least 200 B.C. most development in Mesoamerica as a whole was the direct result of contact with the peoples of the Olmec Heartland, and that "there is now not the slightest doubt that all later civilizations in Mesoamerica, whether Mexican or Mayan, ultimately rest on an Olmec base" (1962: 84). Elsewhere Coe has said, "it is no longer a competitive question of priority, but of discovering the mechanisms of how the pattern set by the Olmec was transferred from them to later peoples" (1968: 63).

This "pattern" is the distribution, from central Mexico to El Salvador, of "Olmec" styles of pottery and figurines, pyramid constructions, astronomical orientation of ceremonial centers, monumental sculpture, ball courts, the religious significance of jade and sophisticated techniques for working it, various forms of calendars, and the inscribing of signs and symbols on raised stelae (Grennes-Ravits and Coleman 1976: 196).

Several mechanisms have been proposed to account for the origin and dissemination of these traits. Coe discounts environmental factors ("No one acquainted with the Olmec achievement is likely to remain an environmental determinist very long" [1968: 86]), since he does not think the hot humid areas of the Olmec Heartland possess any exceptional agricultural productivity that could explain their rise to power and prominence. Regarding the spread of the Olmec culture to other areas, Coe at various times has argued that Olmec missionaries, jade traders, military expeditions, or a combination of these were responsible. He proposes that the superior organization and religious traditions of the Olmec allowed them to send out civilizing elites who brought the secrets of complex social organization to the barbarians in the outlands, perhaps imposing this organization first on the elites of these provincial areas, possibly through a "convert-or-die" religious subjugation. Alternatively or concurrently, Coe suggests, the jade traders could have peacefully or militarily established themselves along routes into other areas, so that the barbarians came into contact with the superior religion and social organization of the Olmec, with more distant regions being affected to a lesser degree (Coe 1965a). Some have even suggested that the rise of complex societies in ancient Peru was a result of direct stimulus by the Olmec, who may have arrived by ship.

The idea that the Olmec were a potent "civilizing" influence on the rest of Mesoamerica has been attacked on both theoretical and empirical grounds (e.g., Flannery 1968; Grennes-Ravitz and Coleman 1976; Sanders and Price 1968). Some archaeologists see the *Colonial Olmec hypothesis* as a remnant of the old and discredited idea that major cultural advances are frequently the accomplishment of a particularly gifted people who, for reasons unexplained or unexplainable, are able to transform their own and neighboring cultures. In contrast to this perspective, some archaeologists have argued that we must look for local, ecologically based factors to explain the origins of complex cultures in various parts of Mesoamerica, viewing the Olmec influences as somewhat superficial and incidental (Sanders and Price 1968).

Criticisms have also been made of some of the specific points of the Colonial Olmec hypothesis. For example, perhaps the most difficult idea to accept in this regard is that the Olmec accomplished their empire by military power. Even given the maximum population estimates for the Olmec Heartland, it is hard to see how armies from the tropical lowlands could have marched into the difficult terrain of central Mexico, defeating as they went the many diverse groups of Puebla, Oaxaca, Morelos, Mexico, and other regions, with perhaps even an expeditionary force to central Peru. There is no evidence that the Olmec had a superior military technology, and military annals, from the Peloponnesian War to Vietnam, are replete with examples of the difficulties of fighting a guerrilla war far from home among a hostile citizenry. This would be especially difficult for the Olmec since they had no pack animals or modern weaponry.

Other criticisms of Coe's interpretations are based on the archaeological record. Sanders and Price (1968) see clear differences between the Olmec Heartland and the rest of Mesoamerica in terms of architecture, burial practices, and settlement patterns, and they suggest that these differences reflect societies that were fundamentally distinct. As an example they cite the burials at Tlatilco in the highlands, where women appear to have been buried with sacrificed men and children, as a sharp contrast to the superior status of men in the Olmec Heartland (as inferred from sculptures and other depictions). Such evidence is of course inconclusive, but Sanders and Price argue that if the Olmec really recast the highland cultures in their own image, this transformation should have extended to the allocation of wealth and prestige in these societies. Also, Sanders and Price contend that although there are

14.13
Three bodies were buried with many ceramic vessels and other goods in this grave at Fabrica San José, Oaxaca (ca. 100 B.C. to A.D. 100). Note that two of the skulls were separated from their bodies and placed on the stone ledge.

some "Olmec" artifacts in these various highland areas, the vast majority of items found show no trace of Olmec influence, including many items with supposed religious and status significance, such as masks, stone carvings, and highly decorated ceramics (see also Weaver 1967).

Other archaeological evidence relevant to the Colonial Olmec hypothesis comes from Oaxaca and Chalcatzingo, both several hundred kilometers from the San Lorenzo-La Venta region. Flannery has demonstrated that the real peak of power at San Lorenzo and La Venta occurred for the most part much earlier than in comparable constructions at Monte Albán in Oaxaca. Thus, the similarities between the architecture and sculpture of Oaxaca and the South Gulf Coast are difficult to interpret as direct results of contacts between the two (Flannery 1968: 79–80). At Chalcatzingo, on the southern edge of the Valley of Mexico, the figurines and rock carvings have long been thought to show direct Olmec contacts (Grove 1968, 1976), but recent research indicates that many of these may date to about 1200 B.C., making them contemporary with the oldest settlements on the South Gulf Coast. This has led some scholars (Grennes-Ravits and Coleman 1976: 204–05) to hypothesize that many of the cultural features thought to have originated in the early Olmec occupation in the Gulf Coast region instead come from some third, and as yet unknown, area. In fact, they suggest that the great complexes at La Venta and San Lorenzo can be best understood as probably nonmilitary religious complexes, serving a large region of Mesoamerica as great market/pilgrimage centers. This would account for the wide distribution of Olmec and Olmecoid artifacts, because pilgrims and traders going to these market shrines would likely circulate figurines and ceramics.

Kent Flannery has suggested that while the Olmec may have originated various stylistic elements, these styles and other cultural elements were only diffused to Oaxaca, and the highlands, and other areas where complex cultures were already developing in response to mainly local conditions. Flannery stresses the importance of trade in shell, magnetite, and other commodities among the South Gulf Coast, Oaxaca, and other areas, and concludes that the "spread of [Olmec] style was not a primary *cause* of Formative Mesoamerica's unity, but one reflection of the fact that it already was united, in an economic sense" (1968: 108).

The Rise of States in Mesoamerica (ca. 200 B.C. to A.D. 900)

TEOTIHUACÁN

By 200 B.C. developments were underway in the *Teotihuacán* area of the Valley of Mexico (see Figue 14.11) that were to culminate in the evolution of the first true states in Mesoamerica. Previously the Teotihuacán area had been relatively unimportant culturally, despite its large areas suitable for irrigated agriculture and large natural springs capable of supplying small irrigation systems. Obsidian is also available nearby, and the area is thought to have supported large stands of edible maguey cactus and nopal, a plant species which is home to an insect that can be rendered into a red dye that was highly prized in prehispanic Mexico. Moreover, Teotihuacán stands along a natural trade route to eastern Mesoamerica—an important advantage given the difficult terrain of this region.

Between about 500 and 150 B.C. Teotihuacán supported a few small villages with a combined population of at most 3,000, but between 150 and 1 B.C. the growth rate exceeded that of any other period, and a city extending some six to eight square kilometers formed and reached about one third its eventual maximum size (G. Cowgill 1974: 4). Between about A.D. 1 and 150 the growth rate was still high but perceptibly slower; the average population during this period was probably between 60,000 and 80,000 (ibid.: 5). At this same time work was completed on the massive pyramids of the Sun and the Moon (Figure 14.14) and on at least twenty other important temple complexes (Millon 1974: 42).

Evidence of increasing cultural complexity at Teotihuacán correlates closely with population growth. Already by about A.D. 100 there were hundreds of workshops specializing in items of obsidian, pottery, stone, and many other commodities; massive public constructions were underway; considerable variability existed in mortuary complexes and residential architecture; and the settlement patterns in the surrounding areas were heavily influenced by the city.

Elsewhere in the Valley of Mexico in the first century A.D. were many clusters of small hamlets and towns, but none approached the size of Teotihaucán. Some of the larger settlements had modest public architecture (platforms and buildings), but they differed little from previous settlements, except perhaps in their geographical location: for the first time some of these settlement clusters were in the rugged high areas on the volcanic hills and cinder cones which ring the valley (Parsons 1974).

Teotihaucán population rose from perhaps 80,000 at A.D. 100 between 100,000 and 200,000 at A.D. 500. By A.D. 100 both the Pyramid of the Sun and the Pyramid of the Moon were probably approaching their final heights (G. Cowgill 1974: 388). The Pyramid of the Sun is over 200 meters long on each side of its base—as large as the great pyramid of Cheops in Egypt—and it rises 60 meters (half the height of the Cheops pyramid). The interior is filled with approximately 1 million cubic meters of sun-dried bricks and rubble. In volume, this probably equalled 2 million cubic meters of uncompressed fill, which would have required the excavation, transport, and shaping of the soil in an area 1.4 kilometers square to a depth of 1 meter—a considerable effort by any standards. The Pyramid of the Moon is somewhat smaller (150 meters at the base, 45 meters high), but of greater architectural sophistication, with a series of inset trapezoidal platforms. Pottery fragments in the fill of these pyramids indicate that the pyramids were constructed by using material from earlier occupations near the city. Considering the size of these structures it is little wonder that the Aztecs believed that the pyramids had been constructed by giants and that some of the gods were buried beneath them (Coe 1962: 107–08).

The rest of the city, although not so spectacular, is perhaps even more significant in terms of its evidence of cultural complexity. It was laid out in quadrants, formed by the Street of the Dead intersected by streets running east to west. Some of the quadrants were more densely occupied than others, and very different architectural styles and artifacts are found in various zones of the city. Along the main north-south street are elaborate residences, presumably for societal elites, as well as large and small temple complexes. Many of the more impressive buildings are built on platforms and often face inward on patios and courtyards. Most buildings are one story high. In some temple complexes the walls are decorated with beautiful murals depicting religious themes, warfare, imaginary animals, and scenes from daily life.

The hundreds of workshops found at Teotihuacán suggest that perhaps as much as 25 percent of its population consisted of craft specialists, turning out a variety of products in obsidian, ceramics, precious stones, slate, basalt, seashells, feathers, basketry, leather, and other materials (R. E. Adams 1977: 200). Many people at Teotihuacán were farmers and hunters, but food was also imported from Tula, Xochicalco, Maquixco, and other settlements in the valley. In some of these satellite settlements the houses and civic buildings are arranged in a rather faint imitation of Teotihuacán ibid.: 199).

The basic residential unit of Teotihuacán appears to have been the large, walled, windowless compound, made of adobe bricks and broken-up volcanic rock, and faced with a fine plastered clay. Many such compounds measured 50 meters or more on a side and internally

14.14
The Pyramids of the Sun (upper left) and the Moon were the ceremonial heart of Teotihuacán. Hundreds of buildings and plazas lined the Street of the Dead, the main avenue leading to the Pyramid of the Moon. At the city's peak the population probably numbered far in excess of 100,000 and there were thousands of workshops, residential units, and public buildings.

were divided into many rooms, porticoes, patios, and passageways. In some, open patios let in sun and air and drained the compound through underground stone troughs. Many walls were brilliantly decorated with frescoes of jaguars, coyotes, trees, gods, and people in naturalistic settings (Coe 1962: 107). Who lived in these compounds is not known; possibly they were members of large kinship groups or guild-like associations of artisans and their families. Whatever their relationships, these people must have constantly been in close contact, since entrance to these compounds was often through only one or two small exterior doors.

Curiously, some residential complexes at Teotihuacán were found to have concentrations of artifacts characteristic of distant areas of Mesoamerica. The *Oaxaca Barrio*, for example, included ceramics, funeral urns, burials, and other elements indistinguishable from the artifacts used in Oaxaca—over 400 kilometers to the south—and very much in contrast to the distinctive artifacts of the Teotihuacán natives.

It has been suggested that the rulers of Teotihuacán forced their vassals in other parts of Mesoamerica to come to the capital city for certain periods so as to forestall revolutions, or that these "barrios" were trade enclaves. Whatever their significance, the foreign "barrios" appear to have remained culturally distinct and intact for at least several centuries.

The city's people apparently ate large quantities of nopal and other kinds of cactus, as well as maize, beans, squash, and a variety of other domesticated and nondomesticated plants and animals. Even at Teotihuacán's peak, however, there was considerable hunting, as evidenced by about 80 percent of the animal remains found being deer bones. The discovery of many burned and cracked human bones in settlements near Teotihuacán and the depiction of human sacrifice in Teotihuacán murals suggest that the diet may have been agumented occasionally with human flesh (R. E. Adams 1977: 201).

Although irrigation agriculture was possible because of the natural springs, there is little evidence that the Teotihuacanos built complex canals. Later, in the Aztec period, irrigation agriculture became quite intensive.

By the time Teotihuacán reached its maximum size it had apparently depopulated much of the rest of the Valley of Mexico: only one other major settlement appears in the valley at about A.D. 500, and it is but a small fraction of the size of Teotihuacán. In fact, the abandonment of rural sites correlates so closely with Teotihuacán's growth that it appears likely that populations were either drawn or coerced directly into the city; overall population growth in the Valley of Mexico at this time (A.D. 100 to 600) was probably very minor and absorbed by Teotihuacán. Also, sometime in the first or second century B.C. the city of Cuicuilco was buried under five meters of lava and the surrounding agricultural areas rendered worthless by layers of volcanic ash, an event which may have contributed to the rapid growth of Teotihuacán by removing its only large competitor (Parsons 1974).

By A.D. 500 the influence of the civilization at Teotihuacán had spread over most of Mesoamerica. Elegant vases made at Teotihuacán are found in the richly furnished burials of apparently high-status individuals on the Gulf Coast, in Oaxaca, and elsewhere. At Kaminaljuyú, a particularly significant site 650 kilometers to the southeast in the highlands of Guatemala, a small city was built that imitated the layout and architecture of Teotihuacán itself, and some of the tombs there contained great masses of luxury items from Teotihuacán.

Although it dominated the Valley of Mexico, Teotihuacán was not the only complex culture in Mesoamerica at this time: to the south, the Valley of Oaxaca and the southern lowlands of the Mayan areas were developing competing civilizations. It seems unlikely that the few hundred thousand people at Teotihuacán were able to extend military control over the millions of people living in the rest of Mesoamerica; fighting a military campaign in the rough terrain of these distant areas would have been suicidal. More likely, the Teotihuacanos were tied to the many other areas through trade networks. The city has no major defensive fortifications, but it does have what appear to be large market areas, and the ecological diversity of Mesoamerica would have put a high premium on large volume trade in basic agricultural and technological commodities. By circulating these many products people would have had a much higher standard of living and much greater protection against food shortages.

Sometime before A.D. 600 Teotihuacán's size and influence began to decline. As the city shrank in population, new centers and settlements appeared throughout the Valley of Mexico, particularly on its edges. Coe suggests that the city met its end through deliberate destruction and burning by outside invaders (1962: 116) shortly after A.D. 600, but we cannot be certain of this. Significantly, after A.D. 600 Teotihuacán styles in pottery, architecture, and other artifacts come to an abrupt end in the rest of Mesoamerica. It is as if a complicated exchange network had been beheaded, and local cultures began developing their own distinctive traditions.

Archaeologist George Cowgill has persuasively argued that Teotihuacán stopped growing in size and power after A.D. 600 because it had reached the limits of productivity of its sustaining area. There are only a few thousand hectares of land near Teotihuacán suitable for canal irrigation, and once populations at the city reached about 100,000, much of the food would have had to have come from riskier, less productive forms of agriculture and from collecting and hunting wild plants and animals (1976: 8–9).

Thus, Teotihuacán may have been outcompeted by other political systems based on more productive agricultural and economic resources; there is some evidence that at least part of its sphere of influence was encroached upon by emerging states in the Mayan areas. Even closer to home, political systems centered at Tula, Xochicalco, and elsewhere in the Valley of Mexico (Figure 14.15) may have begun to block Teotihuacán's access to needed raw materials and foodstuffs (Sanders 1965).

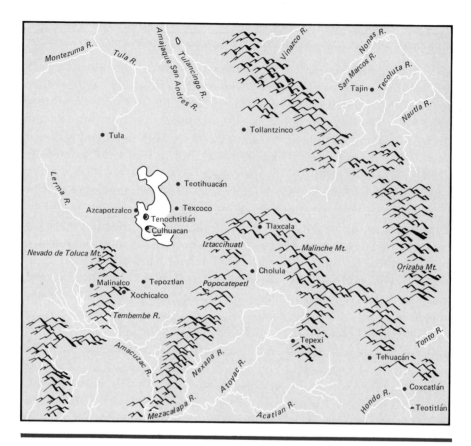

14.15
Major settlements in the Valley of Mexico in the Toltec period.

THE MAYA

At about the same time the civilization of Teotihuacán was developing in the Valley of Mexico (200 B.C. to A.D. 600), another major civilization, the *Maya,* was emerging in southern Mexico, Guatemala, Belize, and Honduras (Figure 14.16).

Early Mayan civilization was influenced to some degree by Teotihuacán, but it was also an independent and unique state. The Maya devised a complex writing system, their temples and palaces are spectacularly beautiful monumental constructions, and they are thought to have organized vast areas and many peoples under a centralized government. It was formerly believed that the Maya never developed large population concentrations, but at the great Mayan site of Tikal 3,000 structures have been located within an area of 16 square kilometers, and only 10 percent of these appear to have been nonresidential, major ceremonial buildings. Estimates of Tikal's population range as high as 5,000, and other centers like Dzibilchaltún seem to have had a population of many thousands at various times (Sjoberg 1965). But these settlements never had the hundreds of thousands of people of Teotihuacán, and they had less diversity in residential architecture and perhaps less occupational specialization than existed in Teotihuacán or Oaxaca at a comparable time.

14.16
Ecological setting of the Mayan area.

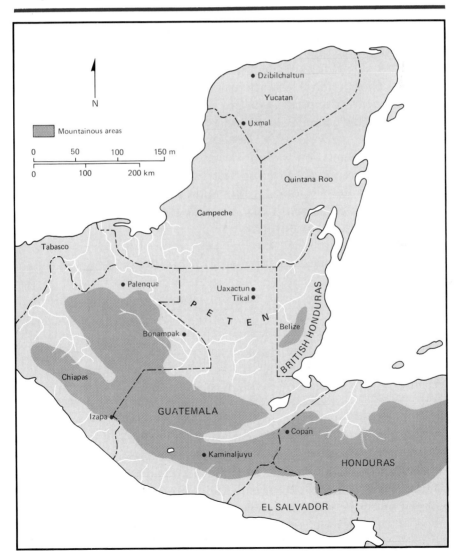

Ecological Setting

Most of the Mayan homeland is a hot, semitropical forest, but large areas are highlands created by a string of volcanoes that rise over 4,000 meters and extend from southeastern Chiapas toward lower Central America. In the highlands volcanic ash and millennia of wind and water erosion have created a rich thick layer of soil spread over a convoluted landscape of deep ravines, ridges, and a few gentler valleys. Rainfall is substantial but sharply seasonal. Population density has historically been low in these highlands.

The tropical lowlands that form the heartland of the Mayan civilization cover the immense area of the Petén and the Yucatán Peninsula, a massive limestone shelf built up out of the seas over millions of years. The land is rugged toward the southern part of the Petén, but most of the peninsula is flatter. There are few rivers or lakes because the porous limestone quickly drains away surface water.

The lowland climate is hot and humid for most of the year, but drought can be a severe problem because the rainfall is seasonal and localized. The vegetation is quite varied, with low thorny jungle areas, humid mangrove forests covering vast tracts but interspersed with savanna, and xerophytic scrub as one approaches the coast. Deer, peccaries, tapirs, monkeys, and turkeys are plentiful in the area and were intensively exploited in antiquity.

Some have argued that the thick vegetation of the Petén is largely a result of the intensive exploitation of the area by the Maya and their successors, and that the climate and vegetation were less tropical during the Mayan era than they are today. But most authorities maintain that this area during the Mayan period was similar to what it is today, and that the Mayan agricultural system must therefore have been largely swidden-based, but recent research has revealed large irrigation systems in some areas, and during at least some periods, permanent field agriculture with annual cropping was probably very important economically. In much of the Mayan lowlands the fields used for maize, beans, squash, tomato, and pepper cultivation must be fallowed for four to eight years after about three years of production. Even then, the Mayan homeland is sufficiently productive that some estimates of the land's carrying capacity on the basis of traditional swidden agriculture are up to 60 to 80 people per square kilometer (U. Cowgill 1962). Also, exploitation of the nuts of the ramón tree (*Brosimum alicastrum*) may have been a major part of the Mayan agricultural strategy. Ramón nuts are highly nutritious and widely available in the Mayan area, and their harvests are not severely affected by even prolonged droughts (R. E. Adams 1977: 140–41). Underground chambers (*chultún*) may have been used to store these nuts for up to eighteen months (Puleston 1971), and surveys indicate that in some areas, the correlation of Mayan house mounds and ramón tree groves is very high.

Most peasant cultivators use animals, whether wild or domestic, to convert brush and hedgerow vegetation into usable form, and the small Yucatec deer apparently filled this role in the Mayan lowlands.

The Culture History of the Maya

People have probably lived in various parts of the Mayan home-land for many thousands of years, but few sedentary settlements appeared there until quite late, and most of the early material is in the highlands. At Izapa, near the Mexico-Guatemala border on the Pacific coast, there may have been some mounds and plazas as early as 1500 B.C. Population growth over much of the highland Mayan areas seems to have been slow but steady after about 200 B.C., and at about this same time the first elements of the Mayan civilization appeared. At Izapa over eighty temple mounds were built, many of them faced with cut stone, and some of the core elements of Mayan art appeared: the carvings of various designs on stone stelae, the depiction of certain deities, and the use of a two-dimensional art style emphasizing histori-cal and mythical themes with great attention to costumes and decora-tion (Coe 1966: 61).

Another highland center was Kaminaljuyú, now ravaged by the expansion of Guatemala City. Kaminaljuyú was apparently a large set-tlement by about 800 B.C., and between 100 B.C. and A.D. 200 it reached its zenith. Beautiful sculpture in the style of that at Izapa was executed, some bearing glyphs, or signs, that are assumed to convey his-torical and calendrical information. Most of these glyphs were inten-tionally destroyed in antiquity and none have been translated, although it is thought they might be direct antecedents of the Mayan scripts de-veloped elsewhere between A.D. 1 and A.D. 600. Kaminaljuyú also contained many temple mounds and rich burials, suggesting that it was a ceremonial center for many small dependent hamlets in the surrounding countryside.

One of the most important early sites in the Mayan lowlands was Chiapa de Corzo, located in Chiapas. Already occupied at 1400 B.C., Chiapa de Corzo appears to have been almost continuously occupied for about 3,300 years (R. E. Adams 1977: 114). By 550 B.C. small pyramids and other civic buildings were under construction at the site, and by 150 B.C. there is clear evidence of gross wealth and status differences in residential architecture and mortuary complexes. Pottery and other artifacts indicate that very early on the people at Chiapa de Corzo were in contact with their neighbors at Kaminaljuyú and in the Valley of Oaxaca, and a piece of Izapa-style inscribed stele from Chiapa de Corzo seems to bear the date 36 B.C. in the Mayan calendar (ibid.: 116).

Settlement in the Petén, the Yucatán Peninsula, and other lowland areas may have been inhibited by the thick vegetative cover of this area and by other environmental factors. Xe (pronounced *shay*) on the Pasion River and a few other sites have evidence of occupation as early as 1000 B.C., but they have no monumental buildings or advanced artistic traditions.

Between 550 and 300 B.C. population densities increased markedly in the lowlands, and villages with some ceremonial architecture appeared at Dzibilchaltún, Becan, Tikal and elsewhere. The ceramics found in the lowlands at this time are quite similar, suggesting that the people were participating in at least some generalized exchange systems, but there is little evidence of political federation or voluminous economic exchange. As we have seen in the case of the Harappan (Indus Valley) and Halafian (Mesopotamian) ceramics, however, the spread of a distinctive, uniform ceramic style over large areas often precedes rapid and fundamental cultural change. By about A.D. 1, a distinctively styled pottery was in use over the entire 250,000 square kilometers of the Mayan lowlands, and pyramids, platforms, and other large public buildings were being constructed at Yaxuná, Dzibilchaltún, Uaxactún, and elsewhere.

In the so-called *Proto Classic period* (A.D. 150 to 450) population growth continued, as did the construction of many large ceremonial buildings, and the essentials of the Mayan calendrical and writing systems appeared. Some of these developments may have been stimulated by population and cultural intrusions from Central America and the Mayan highlands.

The Classic Maya

Between A.D. 300 and 900, Mayan civilization reached its climax, as hundreds of beautiful pyramids, temples, and other buildings were completed, and painting and sculpture flourished.

The first part of this period corresponds to the florescence of Teotihuacán, and some see the Maya as developing principally under Teotihuacán's stimulus (Sanders and Price 1968). We know that the Teotihuacán civilization had a tremendous influence at this time and that trade between the Mayan area and Teotihuacán may have been considerable, but much of Mayan development was autonomous and distinctive. After A.D. 600, when Teotihuacán apparently began rapidly to lose influence and population, the Maya began a 300-year period of intense development. Hundreds of temple complexes were constructed and beautiful stone sculptures executed—many of them dated and inscribed. Many tombs have been found, some containing adults and adolescents with massive quantities of expensive and exotic goods.

But despite these material indications of their brilliant achievements, the Mayan peoples themselves seem to have lived much as their ancestors had. They still had not aggregated in cities, and although thousands of people must have cooperated to construct these great projects, most still lived in small undifferentiated rural hamlets that closely followed the natural terrain, favoring ridges where flood waters could be avoided and where adequate drinking water and well-drained soils were located.

These dispersed agricultural hamlets were grouped around small ceremonial centers that included a small temple pyramid and a few other stone constructions. Several districts of small ceremonial centers were congregated around the major ceremonial centers of Tikal, Uaxactún, Palenque, Uxmal, and other sites. It is difficult to convey the aesthetic brilliance and diversity of these many Mayan centers. Figure 14-17 shows the complexity of construction at one of the major sites, and all over southern Mesoamerica at this time there were beautiful, gleaming white limestone pyramids and temples surrounded by marvelously executed stone sculpture and decorated with brilliant wall paintings. Most centers also had ball courts made of stucco-faced rock where, apparently, people played a game in which a rubber ball was meant to be thrown or batted through a stone ring protruding from one of the inclined walls of the court.

14.17
The Mayan ceremonial center at Tikal. The Maya constructed hundreds of temples, plazas, and public buildings.

The major Mayan centers had unique architectural arrangements. At Copán there is a large temple with a stone staircase, each of whose sixty-three steps is inscribed with a hieroglyphic legend. Tikal contains an extremely large pyramid-temple complex (seventy meters tall), many inscribed stelae, and several rich tombs, while one of the greatest of all known Mayan frescoes is at Bonampak (Figure 14.18). Here, in several rooms of murals, the paintings tell a story of warfare, the torturing of prisoners of war, and a celebration. The carefully drawn mutilated bodies, richly dressed figures, and men with weapons convey an extraordinarily vivid sense of militarism, royalty, and religion.

Themes of military triumph, the torture of captives, and the power of the ruling classes were also commonly depicted in bas-relief sculpture throughout the *Classic* period—even in the Valley of Oaxaca and the peripheral areas of the Mayan sphere of influence. Individuals of presumably higher status were juxtaposed in stone carvings with persons of lower status, and differences of dress, bearing, and position sharpened the contrast. In some cases, representations of prisoners and commoners were carved into the facings of stone steps, so that they were trod on by the nobility—a not too subtle visual pun (Marcus 1974: 92).

In the settlement patterns too are signs of increasing cultural complexity. The major Mayan ceremonial centers approximate the regular spacing we have previously associated with substantial intersettlement exchange of goods and information (p. 348) (Figure 14.19) (Hammond 1976; Marcus 1973). Robert Fry and Scott Cox used mathematical studies to show that some product exchange (particularly in ceramics) was accomplished through major ceremonial centers. They suggest that

14.18
In this wall painting from Bonampak, a Mayan center, the ruler of Bonampak is presiding over the removal of fingernails and other tortures of captives.

most of the utilitarian pottery used by the people living within about twenty-two kilometers of Tikal was made and sold at trade fairs at that city, and that the many people living within this area focused most of their economic activities on Tikal and had little contact with other large ceremonial centers (1974: 222–23). This does not necessarily demonstrate that these settlements were coordinated by a single authority, but it does suggest considerable contact between these groups. Still, the bulk of the people lived in the small rural hamlets of their ancestors, and there were no large cities.

The Post-Classic Maya

Although we do not yet fully understand why and how Mayan civilization declined, we do know when it happened. Each new monumental building of the Maya was usually accompanied by a stone stele engraved with the date of its construction, and thus we know that while many buildings were completed during the eighth and ninth centuries A.D., by A.D. 889 only three sites were under construction, and by about A.D. 900, construction seems to have ended for good. On the basis of ceramics and other information, we know that depopulation of the countryside and centers apparently followed quickly.

Shortly after A.D. 900 there was an invasion of sorts by the Toltecs, a people whose culture was centered at Tula in the Valley of Mexico

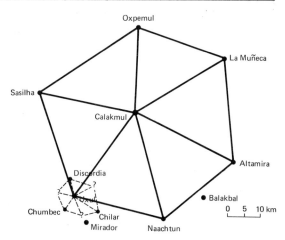

14.19
These six major Mayan centers were almost equally spaced and hexagonally arranged around the major center of Calakmul, suggesting that they were all parts of the same administrative system. Secondary centers may have formed around each of these larger settlements. Similar spacing of settlement patterns probably existed in most of the Mayan heartland as the power and centralization of the government evolved.

and who apparently established feudal control over some areas of the lowlands—an event setting off many years of internal dissension and local revolt. During this time various centers were built and some major population concentrations developed; but in population density, construction projects, art styles, inscribed stelae, settlement patterns, and mortuary complexes, the developmental period of Mayan culture was at an end.

The Mayan area remained isolated and relatively independent for centuries, and revolutions against the central Mexican government occurred as late as 1847 and 1860. Even today it is sparsely settled and in some ways a more primitive place than it was in the eighth and ninth centuries A.D.

The Rise and Collapse of Mayan Civilization: The Search for Causes

Many diverse factors have been suggested as causes of the development, and also the collapse, of Mayan civilization, and new interpretations sporadically appear. Not surprisingly, many involve the ecology of the Mayan homeland, which seems at first glance to be a major barrier to cultural evolution. Archaeologist Betty Meggers believes that the limits on agriculture in the Mayan areas were so stringent that Mayan civilization had to have been introduced from elsewhere fully developed, and that it probably began to decline almost immediately (1954: 809).

But as an explanation of why the Mayan culture evolved, the simple idea of its intentional introduction or its introduction by contact is not very satisfactory. What reason could another civilization have for installing and supporting at great expense a developed civilization in a rainforest? What reason could there be for the independent development of a sophisticated writing system, if the Mayan culture were introduced and sustained from outside? And if, as others have suggested, the Maya simply imitated other cultures, how do we account for their distinctive written language and unique and brilliant art?

William Rathje argues that the Maya, at least those in the central lowlands, could have prospered only if they were able to import several basic commodities, including obsidian, stone, and salt (1973). He contends that if these essential commodities were to reach each household, a complex administrative structure had to be developed to co-ordinate this trade and get people involved in transport and redistribution activities. The pyramid-temple complexes and their resident elite hierarchies would then develop out of these administrative requirements.

Others have argued that there probably was no need to trade for these commodities in most of the Mayan area. The region is in fact littered with flint that could be substituted for most uses of obsidian, and only in a few areas was there a shortage of stone suitable for manufacturing grinding implements. Salt, too, is thought to have been readily available from the Yucatán coast. Overall, it appears that trade for some commodities may have been an important part of evolving cultural complexity in the Mayan areas, but trade certainly does not represent a complete explanation.

Ray Matheny (1976) has recently altered our whole concept of Mayan agricultural systems by his discoveries of large-scale irrigation works. Working from aerial photographs he surveyed parts of Campeche and found canals, reservoirs, and moats radiating out from the ceremonial center at Edzna; he estimates that the collective effort required for these constructions was greater than that represented by the great pyramids at Teotihuacán. Some canals are about 1.6 kilometers in length, 30 meters in width, and 3 meters deep. We do not know how many such irrigation systems exist out in the tropical forests of the Mayan lowlands, and thus we cannot estimate how important they may have been in the evolution of Mayan cultural complexity, or even what the water carried by the canals was used for. Matheny proposes drinking water, irrigation water for small garden plots, and a source of mud for renewing soil fertility as possible uses, and Marvin Harris suggests that irrigation to grow two crops a year may have also been part of the motivation for these projects (Harris 1977: 91).

Robert Carneiro's general explanation of cultural evolution through population growth, environmental circumscription, and warfare (see chapter 8) may have also some validity. While not environmentally circumscribed by different ecological zones, the Maya may have been forced to cluster around sources of drinking water, since there are few natural water courses in the lowlands. The porous limestone base of the lowlands drains off rainwater quickly, and there is evidence that as Mayan populations grew, increasing effort had to be made to dig reservoirs and canals. Whether this led to cultural com-

plexity through concentration of power in the hands of the administrators who organized these constructions (R. E. Adams 1977: 122–23),
or whether the Maya ever reached real periods of stress because of
water shortages will be difficult to determine until we have a much
clearer idea of the extent of Mayan irrigation systems and rural population densities. And these kinds of information will require expensive,
time-consuming, and difficult archaeological surveys.

We must also reserve judgment on the importance of warfare
among the Maya: few walled settlements have been found, although
some are moated, and there is little evidence of mass burials or concentrations of military goods.

In short, no "prime-mover" correlates well with the rise of Mayan
civilization, and we find ourselves falling back on the "synthetic" position: probably many factors, such as trade and warfare, played important roles in the process, and to label one as a prime mover seems at
best simplistic. We might, however, stress the following points. The
Mayan envronment was relatively undifferentiated in terms of natural
resources, but the swidden agricultural system was very productive.
This system used to be considered a primitive form of agriculture that
could support only sparse populations, but under conditions of primitive technology it is extremely well adapted and productive. It has also
been recently demonstrated (Matheny 1976) that the Maya did intensify this system to some degree by building terraces and irrigated
walled fields that were probably cropped at least annually.

Given this setting, under what conditions would it have been advantageous to organize into larger political and social units? Perhaps
the answer lies in the necessity of local exchange to meet the threat of
drought, disease, or disturbance. Rainfall is quite variable within the
Mayan area, and many other things can adversely affect each community's agricultural system. Because the communities were all so similar
in the crops they grew and their techniques for growing them, a major
drought, such as happens in this area every eight to ten years, could result in the starvation of many people in hundreds of hamlets. But this
could be in large part mitigated if many villages established exchange
networks that spread the risks. Each year earthquakes, droughts, disease, floods, warfare, and all the other calamities might wipe out some
sectors of the subsistence system, but if a village belonged to an organization that included many hamlets, it could get help or give help depending on its fortunes. Because of the inability to intensify drastically

agricultural production in any one area, cities were, of course, out of the question. Similarly, population-control regulators were very important, hence the monumental construction projects in this most unlikely of places.

Whatever is at the root of the Mayan cultural evolution, the collapse of this culture poses equally interesting questions. Warfare seems to have increased toward the end of the Mayan period, and we might ask why it became more prevalent then and why the Maya were unable to fight off its effects at this time, after so many centuries of successful dealings among themselves and with their neighbors. No appreciable land shortages or overpopulation seem to have occurred, nor is there much evidence of foreign military pressures on these people.

Another factor often cited as responsible for the downfall of the Maya is environmental collapse because of overexploitation. It is suggested that population growth and the requirements of trade forced the Maya to shorten their fallowing regime so much that the land was exhausted beyond its ability to recover. As production fell, populations also declined, and eventually total collapse resulted. There are insufficient data to test this idea, however, and even if we could demonstrate overexploitation, we would then have to explain why the Maya lost their centuries-old ability to monitor their population-to-resources balance in this way.

Still another factor considered as a cause of the Mayan collapse is disease. Analysis of bones from Mayan sites indicates widespread malnutrition and disease at the end of the Classic period, and some have taken this to mean that epidemics might have caused the Mayan collapse. This idea has a certain plausibility, because many epidemic diseases require relatively high population densities before they can spread, and the Mayan population densities were at a peak just before the collapse. But disease is not a satisfactory explanation by itself. Why, for instance, did not similar diseases strike the very dense cultures living elsewhere in Mesoamerica, including some that also lived in the humid tropical lowlands? Also, the industrial revolution in nineteenth-century Europe was marked by great malnutrition and disease, yet was a period of cultural "advance."

We have previously argued that the evolution of Mayan society could probably be tied to the necessity of spreading the "risk" of life in this area by integrating many different settlements under a centralized authority. But by the same token, such an integrated system might

eventually have encountered a series of catastrophes and internal problems spaced so closely together and in such a sequence that their effects
could not be successfully fought off. Earthquakes, disease, warfare,
drought, crop disease—all these have certain unavoidable periodicities,
and unfavorable conjunctions must necessarily arise if the system is
sufficiently long-lived. Also, it is important to recognize that the Maya
were not the only powerful political system in Mesoamerica at this
time. George Cowgill, in fact, has suggested an explanation of the
Mayan decline based on their competitive posture in relation to these
other systems.

> I suggest that in Late Classic times there was a general economic de-
> velopment of a number of regional [Mayan] centers, perhaps at least
> in part because of the *weakening* of highland states such as Teotihua-
> cán and Monte Albán.
>   . . . Eventually the major Maya centers may have begun to compete
> for effective mastery of the whole southern lowlands. This postulated
> "heating up" of military conflict, for which there is support in Late
> Classic art and inscriptions . . . , seems to me the spur . . . which
> might have driven the Maya to encourage population growth and in-
> tensify production beyond prudent limits. If so, the outcome of the
> competition was not an eventual winner . . . but disaster for all.
> (1976: 15–16)

The Mayan Achievement

Mayan civilization was one of great artistic and organizational
brilliance, and we cannot end our discussion of it without briefly noting some of its more spectacular accomplishments.

MAYAN ARCHITECTURE   Given the social and economic benefits that accrue from public-works projects, it is not at all surprising that the
Maya should build temples, pyramids, and platforms. They apparently
had no metal, winches, hoists, or wheeled carts, and they never developed the barrel-vault or arch constructions that allowed Old World
civilizations to build multistoried temples and palaces. Thus, the only
things they could build to any height were the basic geometric forms,
of which the pyramid is the most easily accomplished. And despite the
various hoaxes now current about the power of pyramids to sharpen

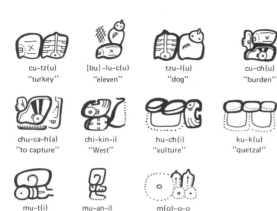

cu-tz(u)
"turkey"

[bu] -lu-c(u)
"eleven"

tzu-l(u)
"dog"

cu-ch(u)
"burden"

chu-ca-h(a)
"to capture"

chi-kin-il
"West"

hu-ch(i)
"vulture"

ku-k(u)
"quetzal"

mu-t(i)
"omen"

mu-an-il
"Muan" (month)

m(o)-o-o
"macaw"

14.20
Some standard Mayan glyphs and the phonetic values assigned to them by Y. V. Knorosov. The Mayan writing system has not yet been completely deciphered.

razor blades, preserve fruit, and heighten the pleasure of sexual activities, the coincidence of pyramids in many ancient civilizations seems largely accountable in terms of these basic facts of construction capabilities—especially for the Maya, whose homeland rested on a gigantic layer of limestone, which when wet could easily be cut with flint tools, and which dried to a considerable hardness in the hot Mesoamerican sun.

MAYAN WRITING   Based on the work of a sixteenth-century Spanish bishop, Brother Landa, Mayan writing (Figure 14.20) was at first thought to be alphabetic. But scholars quickly realized that Mayan writing was to be read in double columns, from left to right and from top to bottom, and by the turn of the last century Mayan glyphs had been identified for the "zero" and "twenty" signs, the cardinal points of the compass, the basic colors, Venus, the months of the year, and the "Long Count," the system of reckoning by which the Maya figured how many years had elapsed since the beginning of their time.

Landa published a Mayan "alphabet" of twenty-nine different symbols, and scholars attempted to crack the presumed alphabetic code of the ancient Mayan inscriptions on this basis. Little progress was made, however, and scholars began to suspect the script was like early Egyptian hieroglyphics. Beginning in 1952, a Russian authority on Egyptian hieroglyphics, Yuri Knorosov, wrote a series of papers in which he claimed that phonetic and semantic elements were mixed in Mayan script, as they are in Chinese, and that Mayan could be read as a syllabic system. Knorosov has since shown that he can make plausible readings of some Mayan inscriptions, but most of the language remains untranslated. At least some of the inscriptions are probably histories of specific royal leaders and their reigns, and decipherment might provide some greater insight into the cycles of Mayan culture history.

Unfortunately, only three Mayan "books" survive; the Dresden, Madrid, and Paris Codices. These are long strips of bark paper, which were covered with a layer of plaster and folded like screens. There are also of course many stone inscriptions in the same writing system.

THE MAYAN CALENDAR   The Maya actually had two calendars. One was the familiar solar calendar in which a year equaled 365 days, but whereas we intercalate an extra day every four years to compensate for the year being actually 364.25 days long, the Maya blithely ignored this and let the seasons creep around the calendar. And in contrast with our system of twelve months of from 28 to 31 days, the Maya had eighteen named months of 20 days each, with 5 days, which were considered highly unlucky, added to the end.

The second calendar involved a 260-day year, composed of the intermeshing of the sequence of numbers from one to thirteen with 20 named days (Figure 14.21). These two calendars ran parallel, and thus every particularly day in the 260-day calendar also had a position in the

14.21
One of the calendars in the Mayan calendrical system.

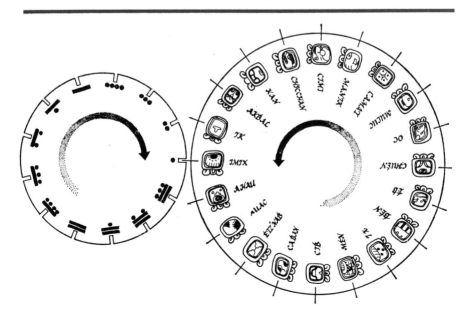

14.22
These warrior statues at Tula reflect the militarism of Toltec culture.

solar calendar. The calendars' permutations are such that each named day would not reappear in the same position for 18,980 days, or fifty-two of our solar years.

Every day on the Mayan calendar had its omens, and activities were rigorously scheduled by their astrological significance. In fact, with the possible exception of some southern Californians, few people have been as obsessed with astrology as the Maya. For reasons not altogether clear, the Maya believed that the world was created in 3113 B.C., and would be destroyed on December 24, A.D. 2011.

Post Classic Mesoamerica (ca. A.D. 900 to 1519)

At about A.D. 900, when Mayan political power in the lowlands was beginning to wane, much of highland Puebla, Mexico, and Hildago was apportioned among several competing power centers. One of these,

Cholula, in Puebla, stands along a route connecting the Valley of Mexico with the lowlands to the east, and the city's importance may have derived from defensive and commercial functions attendant on this route. After A.D. 900 a massive pyramid, covering sixteen hectares and rising to a height of fifty-five meters, was constructed at Cholula, along with many other buildings, most of which are still completely unexcavated. For a period after A.D. 900 Cholula seemed able to influence events in the Valley of Mexico. After A.D. 950 population densities in large areas of the Valley of Mexico declined, possibly as a result of conflict between Cholula and the city of Tula, located at the extreme northern end of the Valley of Mexico (Parsons 1974: 107).

14.23
Estimated population changes in a large part of the Valley of Mexico. Note the rapid increase in density after the collapse of Tula.

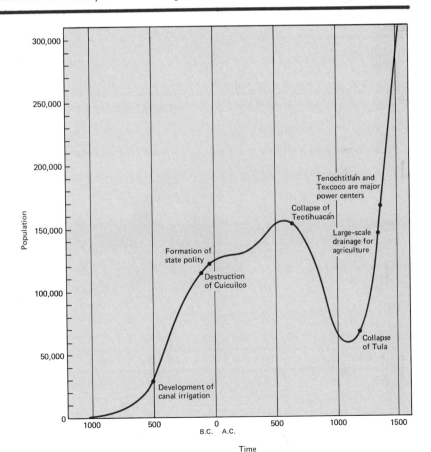

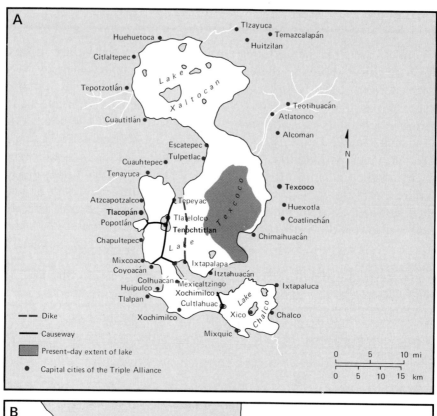

14.24
Major Aztec settlements in the Valley of Mexico (A) and the extent of the Aztec Empire (B). The various "domains" were originally largely independent political and cultural entities that eventually coalesced into the Aztec state.

At about A.D. 968 Tula apparently became the capital of the *Toltecs,* who established a military empire centered at Tula, Tollanzinco, Tenanco, and other towns north and west of the Valley of Mexico, and may soon have come into conflict with the power centers at Cholula and elsewhere in the Valleys of Mexico and Puebla. Eventually, through military and other means the Toltecs were able to dominate for a few centuries most of these rivals.

Excavations at Tula revealed the remains of an impressive city with an estimated population of 40,000 to 50,000, large temples and pyramids, magnificent sculpture and murals, and evidence of extensive craft specialization. The Toltecs established trade and military outposts in many areas of northern and western Mexico and exported metal, gemstones, and other commodities as far north as Arizona and New Mexico. To the south, the Toltecs established administrative control over Chichen Itza and perhaps other towns in the Mayan lowlands where the collapse of the Mayan civilization was delayed for a century or two (R. E. Adams 1977: 240).

Oral histories and art styles mark the Toltecs as an extremely militaristic people, who flourished on an intensive irrigation agricultural economy exploited by a well-structured taxation system. Eventually, however, perhaps because climatic changes seriously afflicted their agriculture (Weaver 1972: 214), Toltec power weakened, and, under the onslaught of invading Chichimec, a group from the North, the Toltecs broke up into many smaller, competitive groups. Tula itself was almost entirely destroyed by invaders at about A.D. 1156.

THE AZTECS

One of the last tribes to invade central Mexico from the North and West was the *Aztecs,* who formed the last and greatest aboriginal Mesoamerican state. Aztec histories and legends, as recorded by the Spanish, tell of their arrival in the Valley of Mexico as rag-tag foragers and primitive agriculturalists who at first were forced by the established residents of the valley to live in the swamps around the lake, subsisting on flies, snakes, and vermin. According to legend, rival political groups in the valley enlisted the Aztecs in their campaigns but avoided other contacts with them because of the Aztecs' predilections for human sacrifice and other barbarisms. At war with various groups, the Aztecs were forced to take refuge on islands in the lake where, according to legend, they built their first city, Tenochtitlán. In time Tenochtitlán grew to become a massive complex of pyramids, courts, and other buildings, now largely buried beneath the streets of Mexico City.

As allies of the Tepanec kingdom of Atzcapotzalco, the Aztecs conquered many of the surrounding cities, and at about A.D. 1427 they turned on their erstwhile allies and through savage warfare brought most of central Mexico under their control. Military expeditions conquered peoples all the way to the Guatemalan border, and garrison towns were established from the Pacific coast to the Gulf of Mexico.

Although the Aztecs are usually associated with militarism, they also created an impressive civil and commercial administration. Between about A.D. 1300 and 1520 they drained large areas of the Valley of Mexico, transforming them into productive agricultural plots. The Aztec economic system was made highly efficient by intense local specialization in one or more forms of agriculture or craft and commodity production, coupled with voluminous redistribution of products through a hierarchically arranged market system. Many commodities, including salt, reeds, fish, stone, cloth, various crops, ceramics, gold, and wood were exchanged among hundreds of communities. In fact, the improbable location of Tenochtitlán—on an island in the middle of the lake—is probably best understood in terms of its central role in these redistributive networks (Parsons 1974: 107). In 1519 Tenochtitlán is estimated to have had about 200,000 to 300,000 inhabitants, five times the population of London at that time (Coe 1962: 161), and there were many other large cities within the Aztec domain. Many cities had broad avenues, causeways, temples, pyramids, and other large buildings, often interspersed with gardens, courtyards, and large markets.

It is estimated that between 1 and 2 million people (Parsons 1974) lived in the Valley of Mexico in late Aztec times. In the southern areas of the valley's lake system, maize, beans, squash, tomatoes, and other crops were grown on *chinampas* (Figure 14.25) long rectangular plots of ground created out of the lake bed by piling up layers of aquatic weeds, mud, human feces, garbage, and other materials. Cyprus trees were planted along these *chinampas* to anchor the soil, the fertility of which was renewed annually with manure and garbage. If crops were transplanted and carefully tended, as many as seven per year could be grown, and ten to eighteen people could be supported on a single hectare of *chinampa* (R. E. Adams 1977: 28). The lake also provided many

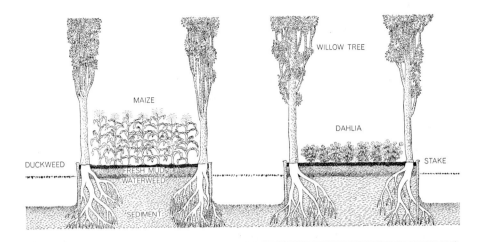

WILLOW TREE

MAIZE

DAHLIA

DUCKWEED

STAKE

FRESH MUD
WATERWEED

SEDIMENT

14.25
The spectacular increase in population densities in the Valley of Mexico was supported in part by the construction of *chinampas,* formed by piling mud and compost in long strips. With frequent manuring, chinampas could produce two or three lush crops a year.

fish, waterfowl, and salamanders, all of which were eaten in great quantities. Other food came from the hundreds of agricultural villages scattered throughout the valley (Figure 14.26). The central Aztec government demanded and received many diverse goods from towns and villages all over Mexico.

The Aztecs were organized into a highly stratified class system headed by a god-king. Beneath the king were the nobles, the *pilli,* all of whom belonged to the royal house, while the great mass of the populace were commoners, *macehuales,* and were organized in large clans, called *calpulli.* The *calpulli* were the basic units of Aztec society. Each was composed of several lineages, totaling several hundred people, one of whom was designated the *calpule,* or leader. Members of a *calpulli* usually lived in the same village or ward, fought together as a unit if drafted for war, held and worked land in common, paid taxes as a unit, and worshiped at the shrine maintained by the *calpulli.* The leaders of the *calpulli* were the direct link between the imperial government and the people.

The *calpulli* differed from one another in social rank. There was some social mobility for individuals—usually by virtue of extraordinary service to the state in warfare, trade, or religion. At the bottom of the social scale were slaves, who worked the fields, performed other menial tasks, and were sacrificed in enormous numbers to various gods.

The Aztecs believed that the present world was just one in a succession of creations by the gods and that constant effort was required to forestall the extinction of the sun and the utter disappearance of humanity. Human blood was an essential part of the ritual (Figure 14.27) whereby the end of the world was postponed, and each time a human heart was ripped from a sacrificed person, another small step was taken toward prolonging the daily rebirth of the sun (Soustelle 1961: 97). At times long lines of sacrificial victims snaked down the steps of the major pyramid mounds, on the top of which priests were kept busy cutting out each person's heart. After the heart and blood had been offered to the gods, the body was thrown down the steps of the pyramid and subsequently flayed and then, perhaps, eaten. Other victims were pitted in gladiatorial contests, or beheaded, drowned, or cast into fires. The Spanish conquistadores may have exaggerated the numbers of people sacrificed, but it seems inescapable that the Aztecs annually killed many tens of thousands and perhaps hundreds of thousands of people. This slaughter was not only accepted by the common people, but it seems to have been widely supported. All war captives knew their fate, and it was an act of honor to accept a sacrificial death. Young men were selected each year to lead a life of luxury surrounded by complaisant young women and feasting on the best of food, realizing full well that at the end of the year they would be sacrificed. And throughout the land parents turned over infants and children to government officials for use in annual sacrificial rites.

Many of the sacrificial victims, as well as soldiers who died in battle, those people struck by lightning, mothers who died in childbirth, and other special people were thought to spend eternity in various paradises, cosseted with the pleasures of this world. Less distinguished folk were thought to spend eternity in a drab and uncomfortable underworld, reached only after some years of wandering in an icy and hostile "purgatory."

With its emphasis on death, blood, and cosmic cataclysm, it is little wonder that Aztec theology struck the Spanish as somewhat heterodox. Even anthropologists, renowned for their cultural relativism, are impressed with the violence of Aztec religion. But, as we have seen elsewhere in this book, human sacrifice is an old and recurrent theme in the evolution of complex cultures; in Mesopotamia, China, North America, and most other places warfare and slaughter can be found which equaled that of the Aztecs in forms, if not in intensity.

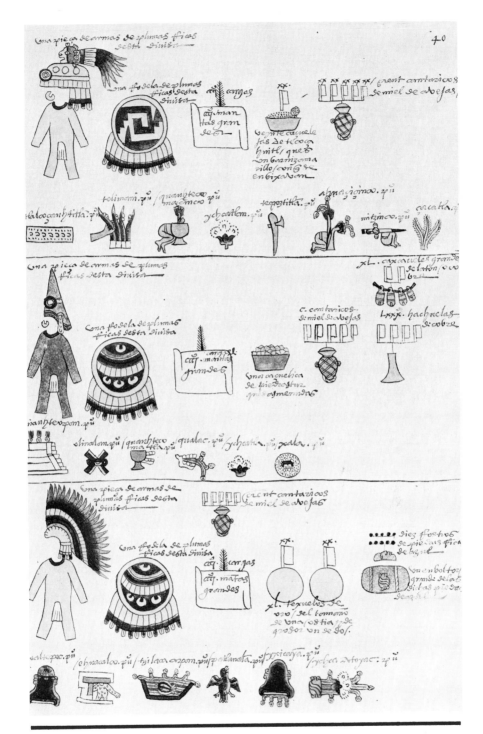

14.26
A Mexican tribute list for towns in Guerrero (from the Codex Mendoza). Each
year the people paid tribute in mantles, uniforms, shields, gourds, sage, amaranth,
and jade.

14.27
Aztec ritual. The priest was dressed (A) in the skin of a sacrificed person. Another person (B) was given a shield, mirror, and other ritual paraphernalia and played the part of the god Tezcatlipoca. In (C) and (D) the victim is sacrificed and eaten. From the Codex Florentino.

Why did so many ancient people consider it necessary to kill each other, and why did the Aztecs outstrip most previous cultures in this regard? Shelburne Cook (1946) calculates that warfare and human sacrifice together elevated the annual death rate by about 25 percent, and he interprets these as methods of population regulation. But the Aztecs could just as easily have controlled their birth rate by abortion or infanticide—particularly if they selectively killed young girls: it is a well known demographic fact that the key to fertility control is women, since even the massive slaughter of males (such as in the recent World Wars) has only a minor and short-term effect on population growth rates.

Michael Harner (1976) has argued that the key to Aztec sacrifice is the contribution the cannibalism of sacrificial victims made to the Aztec diet. Mesoamerica lacks any large domesticated animals that could have been effectively integrated with Aztec agricultural strategies, and this animal protein and fat deficiency may have been compensated for by cannibalism. There is little doubt that the Aztecs engaged in cannibalism, since several sixteenth-century Europeans described it as it happened, but we have insufficient evidence with which to evaluate Harner's thesis.

Despite their death cults, the Aztecs in everyday life were a colorful, and in some ways, engaging people. The Spanish remarked on their love of flowers and natural beauty, and their poetry contains many references to the joys of the natural world. Human beauty was esteemed and even the lower classes were concerned with personal appearances. The Spanish were amazed to find that Aztecs bathed their entire bodies most days—an obsession with personal cleanliness that would have struck even most eighteenth- and nineteenth-century Europeans as bizarre.

Dress for men and women was often a loincloth and a woven cloak, and brightly colored cotton fabrics were used for ornamentation. In the countryside women often went about naked to the waist, but middle- and upper-class urban women wore decorated blouses (Soustelle 1961: 135).

The diet of the Aztecs centered upon maize, beans, squash, and tomatoes, although the wealthier people could eat various fruits, nuts, meats, and other exotic foods. The relatively unvaried diet was sometimes alleviated with peyote and other natural stimulants and hallucinogens, and tobacco and *pulque,* an alcoholic cactus-derived drink, were also used.

THE SPANISH CONQUEST

The melancholy history of the conquest of Mesoamerica by Spanish adventurers in the early sixteenth century was recorded in detail by the Spanish themselves. In 1519 Hernán Cortez left Cuba with a sizable force of ships, men, armaments, and horses, and sailed to the coast of Veracruz. With the advantage of horses, cannons, war dogs, and an extraordinary esprit de corps, Cortez and his men were able to march directly into the Aztec capital at Tenochtitlán, where they were at first welcomed by the Aztec king, Moctezuma, who was under the delusion that the Spanish were gods returning to their ancestral homeland. He could hardly have been more wrong. Within a short time the Spanish had kidnapped and jailed him and were forming alliances with local non-Aztec peoples, who were only too happy to help the Spanish displace the Aztecs. Moctezuma and many of his people were eventually killed in a fierce battle at Tenochtitlán, after which Aztec resistance stiffened; but within a few years the Spanish had captured most of the Aztec heartland and Tenochtitlán. In 1524 they hanged the last Aztec king, and thereafter Spanish domination of Mexico was rapid.

Bibliography

Adams, R. E. W. 1977. *Prehistoric Mesoamerica*. Boston: Little, Brown.

Armillas, Pedro. 1971. "Gardens on Swamps." *Science*. 174: 653–61.

Blanton, Richard E. 1972. "Prehistoric Adaptation in the Ixtapalapa Region, Mexico." *Science*. 175: 1317–26.

————. 1976. "The Origins of Monte Alban." In *Cultural Change and Continuity*. ed., C. E. Cleland. New York: Academic Press.

Bray, Warwick. 1973. "The City State in Central Mexico at the Time of the Spanish Conquest." *Journal of Latin American Studies*. 4: 161.

————. 1976. "From Foraging to Farming in Early Mexico." In *Hunters, Gatherers and First Farmers Beyond Europe: An Archaeological Survey*. ed., J. V. S. Megaw. Leicester, England: Leicester University Press.

Brush, C. F. 1969. "A Contribution to the Archaeology of Coastal Guerrero, Mexico." Unpublished doctoral dissertation, Columbia University, New York.

Bullard, W. R., Jr. 1960. "Maya Settlement Pattern in Northeastern Peten, Guatemala." *American Antiquity.* 25: 355.

Coe, Michael D. 1962. *Mexico.* New York: Praeger.

_____. 1963. "Olmec and Chavín: A Rejoinder to Lanning." *American Antiquity.* 29(1): 101–4.

_____. 1965a. *The Jaguar's Children: Pre-Classic Central Mexico.* New York: Museum of Primitive Art.

_____. 1965b. "The Olmec Style and Its Distribution." *Handbook of Middle American Indians.* 3: 739–75.

_____. 1966. *The Maya.* New York: Praeger.

_____. 1968. "San Lorenzo and the Olmec Civilization." In *Dumbarton Oaks Conference on the Olmec,* ed. Elizabeth P. Benson. Dumbarton Oaks, Washington, D.C.

_____. 1970. "The Archaeological Sequence at San Lorenzo Tenochtitlan, Veracruz, Mexico." *Contributions of the University of California Archaeological Research Facility,* no. 8, pp. 21–34.

Cook, Shelburne. 1946. "Human Sacrifice and Warfare as Factors in the Demography of Precolonial Mexico." *Human Biology.* 18: 81–102.

Covarrubias, Miguel. 1946. "El arte 'Olmeca' o de La Venta." *Cuadernos Americanos.* 5: 153–79.

_____. 1957. *Indian Art of Mexico and Central America.* New York: Knopf.

Cowgill, George. 1974. "Quantitative Studies of Urbanization at Teotihuacan." In *Mesoamerican Archaeology: New Approaches,* ed. Norman Hammond. Austin: University of Texas Press.

_____. 1976. Public Lecture, Seattle.

Cowgill, Ursula. 1962. "An Agricultural Study of the Southern Maya Lowlands." *American Anthropologist.* 64: 273–86.

Culbert, T. Patrick. 1973. *The Classic Maya Collapse.* Albuquerque: University of New Mexico Press.

Drennan, Robert D. 1976. "Religion and Social Evolution in Formative Mesoamerica." In *The Early Mesoamerican Village,* ed. K. V. Flannery. New York: Academic Press.

Drucker, Phillip. 1959. *La Venta, Tabasco: A Study of Olmec Ceramics and Art.* Smithsonian Institution, Bureau of American Ethnology, Bulletin no. 170. Washington, D.C.

Earle, Timothy. 1976. "A Nearest-Neighbor Analysis of Two Formative Settlement Systems." In *The Early Mesoamerican Village,* ed. K. V. Flannery. New York: Academic Press.

Ferdon, E. M. 1959. "Agricultural Potential and the Development of Cultures." *Southwestern Journal of Anthropology.* 15: 1–19.

Flannery, Kent V. 1968. "The Olmec and the Valley of Oaxaca: A Model for Inter-

Regional Interaction in Formative Times." In *Dumbarton Oaks Conference on the Olmec,* ed. Elizabeth P. Benson. Dumbarton Oaks, Washington, D.C.

———. 1976a. "The Early Mesoamerican House." In *The Early Mesoamerican Village,* ed. K. V. Flannery. New York: Academic Press.

———. 1976b. "Evolution of Complex Settlement Systems." In *The Early Mesoamerican Village,* ed. K. V. Flannery. New York: Academic Press.

———. 1976c. "Linear Stream Patterns and Riverside Settlement Rules." In *The Early Mesoamerican Village,* ed. K. V. Flannery. New York: Academic Press.

———. 1976d. "Contextual Analysis of Ritual Paraphernalia from Formative Oaxaca." In *The Early Mesoamerican Village,* ed. K. V. Flannery. New York: Academic Press.

Flannery, Kent V. and Marcus C. Winter. 1976. "Analyzing Household Activities." In *The Early Mesoamerican Village,* ed. K. V. Flannery. New York: Academic Press.

Fry, Robert and Scott Cox. 1974. "The Structure of Ceramic Exchange at Tikal, Guatemala." *World Archaeology.* 6(2): 209–25.

Grennes-Ravits, Ronald and G. Coleman. 1976. "The Quintessential Role of Olmec in the Central Highlands of Mexico." *American Antiquity.* 41: 196–205.

Grove, David C. 1968. "The Pre-Classic Olmec in Central Mexico: Site Distribution and Inferences." In *Dumbarton Oaks Conference on the Olmec,* ed. Elizabeth P. Benson. Dumbarton Oaks, Washington, D.C.

Grove, D. C., Kenneth C. Hirth, David E. Buge, and Ann M. Cyphers. 1976. "Settlement and Cultural Development at Chalcatzingo." *Science.* 192: 1203–10.

Harner, Michael. 1977. "The Ecological Basis for Aztec Sacrifice." *American Ethnologist.* 4(1): 117–35.

Harris, Marvin. 1977. *Cannibals and Kings: The Origins of Cultures.* New York: Random House.

Haviland, W. A. 1967. "Stature at Tikal, Guatemala: Implications for Ancient Maya Demography and Social Organization." *American Antiquity.* 32: 316.

Heizer, Robert. 1968. "New Observations on La Venta." In *Dumbarton Oaks Conference on the Olmec,* ed. Elizabeth P. Benson. Dumbarton Oaks, Washington, D.C.

Lees, Susan H. 1973. *Sociopolitical Aspects of Canal Irrigation in the Valley of Oaxaca.* Memoir of the Museum of Anthropology, University of Michigan, no. 6. Ann Arbor.

MacNeish, Richard S. 1962. *Second Annual Report of the Tehuacan Archaeological-Botanical Project.* Andover, Mass.: R. S. Peabody Foundation for Archaeology.

———. 1964. "Ancient Mesoamerican Civilization." *Science.* 143(3606): 531–37.

Marcus, Joyce. 1973. "Territorial Organization of the Lowland Classic Maya." *Science.* 180: 911–16.

————. 1974. "The Iconography of Power Among the Classic Maya." *World Archaeology.* 6(1): 83–94.

————. 1976a. "The Size of the Early Mesoamerican Village." In *The Early Mesoamerican Village,* ed. K. V. Flannery. New York: Academic Press.

————. 1976b. "The Origins of Mesoamerican Writing." *Annual Review of Anthropology.* 5: 35–68.

————. 1976c. "The Iconography of Militarism at Monte Alban and Neighboring Sites in the Valley of Oaxaca." In *The Origins of Religious Art and Iconography in Preclassic Mesoamerica.* ed., H. B. Nicholson. Latin American Center, U.C.L.A.

Matheny, Ray T. 1976. "Maya Lowland Hydraulic Systems." *Science.* 193: 639–46.

Meggers, Betty J. 1954. "Environmental Limitation in the Development of Culture." *American Anthropologist.* 56(5).

Millon, René. 1974. "The Study of Urbanism at Teotihuacan, Mexico." In *Mesoamerican Archaeology: New Approaches,* ed. N. Hammond. Austin: University of Texas Press.

Palerm, A. and E. Wolf. 1957. "Ecological Potential and Cultural Development in Mesoamerica." In *Studies in Human Ecology. Social Science Monographs* 3: 1–38.

Parsons, Jeffrey R. 1968. "Teotihuacan, Mexico, and Its Impact on Regional Demography." *Science.* 162: 872–77.

————. 1971. *Prehistoric Settlement Patterns in the Texcoco Region, Mexico.* Memoir of the Museum of Anthropology, University of Michigan, no. 3. Ann Arbor.

————. 1974. "The Development of a Prehistoric Complex Society: A Regional Perspective from the Valley of Mexico." *Journal of Field Archaeology.* 1: 81–108.

Pelzer, Karl J. 1945. *Pioneer Settlement in the Asiatic Tropics.* American Geographical Society, Special Publications, no. 29. New York.

Pires-Ferreira, Jane W. 1975. *Formative Mesoamerican Exchange Networks with Special Reference to the Valley of Oaxaca.* Memoirs of the Museum of Anthropology, University of Michigan, no. 7. Ann Arbor.

Porter, Muriel Noé. 1953. *Tlatilco and the Pre-Classic Cultures of the New World.* Viking Fund Publications in Anthropology, no. 19. New York.

Puleston, Dennis E., and Olga S. Puleston. 1971. "An Ecological Approach to the Origins of Maya Civilization." *Archaeology.* 24(4): 330–36.

Pyne, Nanette M. 1976. "The Fire-Serpent and Were-Jaguar in Formative Oaxaca: A Contingency Table Analysis." In *The Early Mesoamerican Village,* ed. K. V. Flannery. New York: Academic Press.

Rathje, William L. 1971. "The Origin and Development of Lowland Classic Maya Civilization." *American Antiquity.* 36: 275–85.

————. 1973. "Classic Maya Development and Denouement: A Research Design." In *The Classic Maya Collapse,* ed. T. P. Culbert. Albuquerque: University of New Mexico Press.

Sahagún, Fray Bernardino de. 1976. *A History of Ancient Mexico.* Translated by Fanny R. Bandelier from the Spanish version of Carlos Maria de Bustamante. Glorieta, New Mexico: Rio Grande Press.

Sahlins, M. 1968. "Notes on the Original Affluent Society." In *Man the Hunter,* eds. R. B. Lee and I. DeVore. Chicago: Aldine.

Sanders, William T. 1965. *Cultural Ecology of the Teotihuacan Valley.* Department of Sociology and Anthropology, Pennsylvania State University.

————. 1973. "The Cultural Ecology of the Lowland Maya: A Re-Evaluation." In *The Classic Maya Collapse,* ed. T. P. Culbert. Albuquerque: University of New Mexico Press.

Sanders, William T. and Barbara Price. 1968. *Mesoamerica: The Evolution of a Civilization.* New York: Random House.

Siemens, Alfred H. and Dennis E. Puleston. 1972. "Ridged Fields and Associated Features in Southern Campeche: New Perspectives on the Lowland Maya." *American Antiquity.* 37(2): 228–39.

Sisson, E. B. 1970. "Settlement Patterns and Land Use in the Northwestern Chontalpa, Tabasco, Mexico: A Progress Report." *Ceramica de Cultura Maya.* 6: 41–54.

Soustelle, J. 1961. *Daily Life of the Aztecs,* trans. P. O'Brian. Stanford: Stanford University Press.

Tolstoy, Paul and A. Guínette. 1965. "Le Placement de Tlatilco dans de Cadre du Pré-Classique du Basin de Mexico." *Journal de la Société des Americanistes* (Paris). 54(1): 47–91.

Tolstoy, Paul and Louise Paradis. 1970. "Early and Middle Preclassic Culture in the Basin of Mexico." *Science.* 167(3917): 344–51.

Turner, B. L. II. 1974. "Prehistoric Intensive Agriculture in the Maya Lowlands." *Science.* 185: 118–24.

Wauchope, Robert, ed. 1965. *Handbook of Middle American Indians.* vol. 3. Austin: University of Texas Press.

Weaver, Muriel Porter. 1972. *The Aztecs, Maya, and Their Predecessors.* New York: Seminar Press.

Whalen, Michael E. 1974. "Community Development and Integration During the Formative Period in the Valley of Oaxaca, Mexico." Paper read at the Annual Meeting of the American Anthropological Association, Mexico City.

————. 1976. "Zoning Within an Early Formative Community in the Valley of Oaxaca." In *The Early Mesoamerican Village,* ed. K. V. Flannery. New York: Academic Press.

Winter, Marcus. 1972. "Tierras Largas: A Formative Community in the Valley of Oaxaca, Mexico." Unpublished doctoral thesis, University of Arizona.

————. 1976. "The Archaeological Household Cluster in the Valley of Oaxaca." In *The Early Mesoamerican Village,* ed. K. V. Flannery. New York: Academic Press.

Wolf, Eric. 1959. *Sons of the Shaking Earth.* Chicago: University of Chicago Press.

Wolf, Eric and A. Palerm. 1955. "Irrigation in the Old Acolhua Domain, Mexico." *Southwestern Journal of Anthropology.* 11: 265–81.

15

The Origins of
Cultural Complexity in Peru

In Peru the first "states" grew out of a maritime
economy not susceptible to control by corporate
authority. Like civilization in general, continued
development of corporate authority rested on the
furthering of institutions which allowed a few to
organize and many to labor. Fishing was a dead-
end for the emerging state, but farming and irrigation agriculture were the avenues to totalitar-
ian control.

M. Moseley 1975

The pattern of cultural evolution in ancient Peru was similar to that
in Mesoamerica. In both areas between 2000 B.C. and the arrival of
Europeans in the 16th century A.D., people developed intensive farming systems, built massive pyramids and temples, aggregated into towns,
established powerful armies, and organized themselves in complex hierarchical patterns of wealth, power, and prestige.

But there were also some significant differences that make the evolution of cultural complexity in Peru a unique and interesting case. In
Mesoamerica the first large sedentary communities appeared in most
areas only after maize and many other domesticated plants were incorporated into agricultural economies; but some archaeologists believe
that quite large and perhaps complex Peruvian communities were es-

tablished in coastal areas many centuries before domesticated plants or agriculture were of much importance. Even after most Peruvians came to rely on agriculture, in many areas they lived in dispersed towns and villages, in contrast to the vast urban centers of Mesoamerica, such as Teotihuacan and Tenochtitlan. And while the Peruvians never developed a writing system of any sort, they were able to establish a political system of a size, complexity, and coherence unmatched by anything in Mesoamerica or elsewhere in the New World. In trying to explain Peruvian prehistory, then, we must account both for its conformation to the general pattern of cultural evolution we have documented in other areas of the world and also for these unique characteristics.

The Ecological Setting

Like all the other areas where complex societies developed independently, Peru is a mosaic of highly varied physical environments. The Andes rise so sharply from the Pacific that only a thin strip of land, less than about sixty kilometers at its widest point, separates the mountains from the sea. And because the Andes shield the coast from the rain-bearing air currents crossing the continent from the Atlantic, most of this coastal strip is one of the world's driest deserts, where rain falls only once or twice every five years. In a few places winter fogs along the coast keep skies overcast and, in most years, provide enough moisture through condensation to support vegetation zones known as *lomas,* where grass and shrubs support a relatively rich fauna of birds, snails, lizards, and a few deer (Lanning 1967: 10). But most of the coastal strip is utterly dry, and when the wind blows, dunes can quickly cover houses and choke irrigation canals.

This desert is habitable only because of the fifty or so small rivers that flow down from the mountains, transverse the plain, and empty into the sea. Some contain water during only part of the year, but the larger, permanent ones support forests and shrubs and their attendant wildlife, and there are areas where the rivers keep the water table sufficiently high that cultivation is possible without irrigation. In some valleys, rivers have created broad alluvial plains that have high agricultural potential. Near the mouths of the rivers, fish, freshwater shrimp, and other resources can be particularly rich. Human life along the coast is tied directly to these rivers and streams because they provide

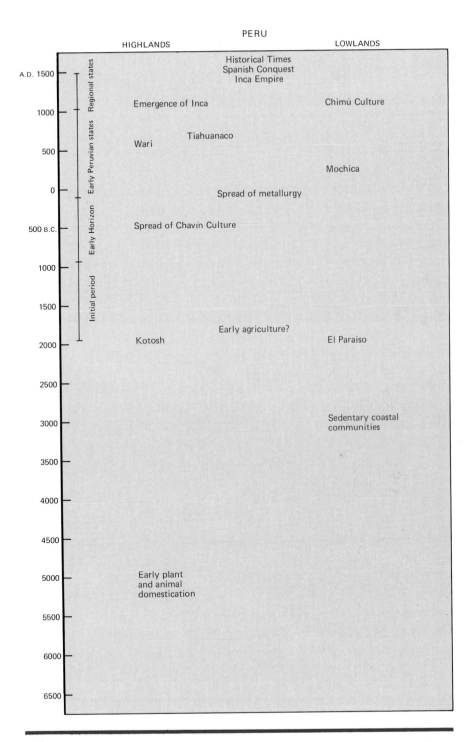

PERU

HIGHLANDS   LOWLANDS

Regional states | Early Peruvian states | Early Horizon | Initial period

A.D. 1500 —
                        Historical Times
                        Spanish Conquest
                        Inca Empire

1000 —   Emergence of Inca   Chimú Culture

                        Tiahuanaco
500 —   Wari

                                                Mochica

0 —   Spread of metallurgy

500 B.C. — Spread of Chavín Culture

1000 —

1500 —

                    Early agriculture?
2000 —   Kotosh   El Paraiso

2500 —

3000 —   Sedentary coastal
                                                communities

3500 —

4000 —

4500 —

5000 —   Early plant
            and animal
            domestication

5500 —

6000 —

6500 —

15.1
The cultural chronology of Highland and Lowland Peru.

15.2
Two views of Peru: sheep grazing on the puna at an elevation of about 4000 meters and an intermontane valley near Huarascán.

the only drinking water. At many places along the coast are extraordinarily rich concentrations of fish, birds, birds' eggs, sea mammals, mollusks, crustaceans, and several species of kelp and other plant foods.

These rich marine resources are produced by a fascinating interplay of wind and ocean currents, where winds drive water north along the coast while the earth's rotation from east to west pushes the water westward, creating an upwelling of water from the ocean floor. Carried with these deep waters are tremendous concentrations of phosphates and other nutrients that support countless billions of microscopic plants, and these form the basis of a complex food chain comprising anchovies and other small fish that eat the plants; larger fish, birds, and sea mammals that eat the anchovies; and, ultimately, people, who exploit many links in the chain.

Occasionally, shifts in wind and water change water temperatures and the plants die, cutting off the base of the food chain, and when this happens rotting plant and animal life fills the air with clouds of hydrogen sulfide that can blacken ships and houses (Idyll 1973). Several years may pass before the fertility of the sea is restored. The frequency in prehistory of *el niño,* as this disturbance is called, is unknown, but it has occurred with moderate impact four times since the last major disruption in 1925; and, assuming approximately the same conditions in ancient times, *el niño* may have been a limiting factor on human population densities in coastal Peru. The first several centuries of life on the coast were based chiefly on marine resources, and coastal populations would have had to adjust population size to these cyclical resource shortages; they may also have had a strong incentive to broaden their resource base by either growing or importing products to balance out periodic shortages.

In the mountains (Figure 15.2) human occupation has focused on small valleys, large basins, and high grassy plateaus (called *punas*). Hunters and gatherers here were succeeded after 1800 B.C. by agriculturalists who subsisted on potatoes, maize, quinoa, and other crops, and who in later periods, made tremendous investments in irrigation canals and terracing slopes to extend agricultural lands. For much of Peruvian prehistory these *punas* were inhabited to 4,500 meters and higher by hunters and gatherers, who were later replaced by llama and alpaca herders.

The eastern slopes of the Andes, the *montaña,* are wet and heavily forested, and the combination of steep slopes and intense rain apparently limited exploitation by prehistoric peoples, for only a few important archaeological sites have been found here. East of the Andes is the Amazon Basin, a tropical rainforest whose rubber, feathers, and other products were occasionally brought into early Peruvian economic systems, but which was never significantly colonized or controlled by either highland or coastal societies. Some archaeologists, however (e.g., Lathrap 1968), believe the origins of Andean civilization can be traced to groups living in the tropical forests and, later, moving into the highlands and coast.

In neither the highlands nor the coastal regions of Peru is the vegetative cover so thick that plowing is essential for agriculture. Significantly, most early complex cultures around the world developed in areas where intensive agriculture could be pursued without the turning under of native vegetation, and this was particularly important in ancient Peru because the country lacked a domesticable draught animal. Finally, there are few accessible sources of iron ore in Peru, and this may have been an important factor in later technological developments.

The Archaeological Record

EARLY HUNTERS AND GATHERERS (? TO 2500 B.C.)

A few Peruvian sites have been dated to 15,000 to 20,000 years ago, but the earliest cultures for which we have substantial archaeological evidence appeared about 7500 B.C. Most sites of this age are in highland caves and rock shelters, and the abundance of projectile points, scrapers, knife blades, and animal bones at these sites reflects an intensive exploitation of deer and guanaco (an animal related to the camel). Domesticated species of beans from Guitarrero Cave in the mountains of northern Peru have been dated to about 7500 B.C., but there is no evidence of cultivation or sedentary life at this time. Many groups probably followed a *transhumant* way of life, moving up and down the mountains to exploit various resources as they came in season. Alpacas and llamas require constant tending and frequent moves to new pasturages. The "thin" air, intense cold, blizzards, and thick fogs of the highlands make movement difficult, and over millennia of adapting to these conditions the Peruvians developed cardiovascular systems that permit them to follow annual rounds that would kill most non-Peruvians.

Except for an occasional small hunting camp, there is limited evidence of humans in the coastal areas before about 3200 B.C. (sea-level changes may have been considerable here), but shortly after this some groups worked out a subsistence system based on the seasonal exploitation of the *lomas,* supplemented by coastal resources. In winter, when condensed ground fog supported patches of vegetation, these hunters and gatherers walked the *lomas,* collecting wild seeds, wild potatoes, snails, birds, and a few deer, and occasionally augmenting their winter diet with shellfish and fish from coastal and riverine sources. The extent of *lomas* vegetation is quite variable from year to year, and it almost disappears during summer, and thus few groups probably keyed their subsistence to these vegetation zones. The fish, invertebrates, birds, and plant foods of the littoral were probably the major food sources for the earliest coastal populations.

EARLY SEDENTARY COMMUNITIES (2500 TO 1800 B.C.)

By about 2500 B.C. many small sedentary communities had appeared along the Peruvian coast (Figure 15.3), most of them concentrating on littoral and riverine resources, but perhaps also subsisting on squash, beans, and other cultivated crops.

There are few published detailed analyses of food remains from these early coastal settlements, and the possibilities of sampling error make it difficult to reconstruct with any accuracy human subsistence strategies during this period. The diet seems to have been based mainly on marine resources, with wild or domestic plants of only secondary importance (M. Parsons 1970: 297), but there was great variability from site to site. At Huaca Prieta de Chicama, for example, the people were probably growing two varieties of domesticated squash and several species of domesticated beans, and they were also collecting several species of wild plants, but there is no evidence of maize cultivation. There are no land mammal bones at the site, and few sea mammal remains, and littoral collecting activities apparently concentrated on mussels, clams, crabs, sea urchins, and birds—while fish, surprisingly, do not appear in these sites (ibid.: 298). At Chilca, the primary meat

Distribution of some early (5000 to 1300 B.C.) Peruvian sites.

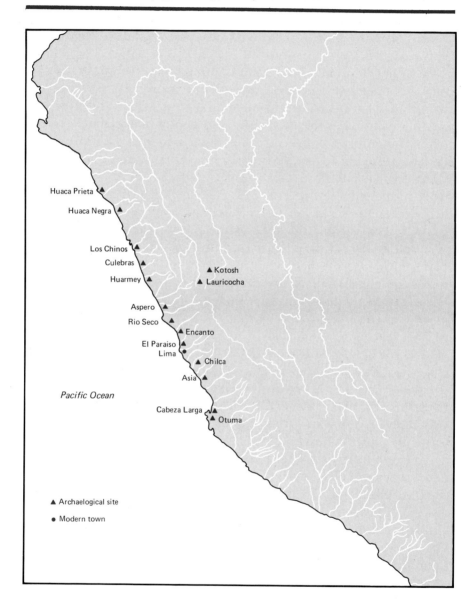

Huaca Prieta

Huaca Negra

Los Chinos

Culebras

Huarmey

Aspero

Rio Seco

Encanto

El Paraiso

Lima

Asia

Cabeza Larga

Otuma

Kotosh

Lauricocha

Chilca

Pacific Ocean

▲ Archaelogical site

● Modern town

source appears to have been sea lions, but mussels, other invertebrates, and a variety of collected plants were also important. At other sites the remains of sharks, rays, cormorants, gulls, pelicans, and other animals attest to the importance of the resources of the coastal shallows, as does the presence of fish hooks, nets, and lines. No boats have been found at any of these sites, but the kinds of fish and invertebrates usually eaten along the coast are easily taken with simple nets (ibid.: 292–93).

Nor does it appear that these coastal populations were doing much hunting, as few land mammal remains have been recovered at any of the sites. Guinea pigs, and perhaps dogs, however, may well have been raised and eaten in quantity.

By about 2000 B.C. at least a hundred communities dotted the Peruvian coastline, many of them on river deltas, bays, or right on the ocean beach. These communities varied greatly in size, shape, and adaptation. At Huaca Prieta de Chicama a complex of small houses was built using beach cobbles, whalebone, and wooden beams, and around the residences were large middens where the remains of shellfish and other food, as well as artifacts, were discarded. Baskets, reed mats, pounded bark cloth, fish nets, cotton goods, sinkers, scrapers, slings, bone needles, and gourd floats have been recovered (M. Parsons 1970: 297). Most of the other communities along the Peruvian coast at this time also seem to have been quite simple foraging-based communities, and few of them had more than several hundred inhabitants. At Chilca the burials of thirty adults and twenty-two children and adolescents were excavated, and only minor differences in grave goods or positioning of the corpses were found. Some people were interned with spindles and spindlewhorls, others with fish hooks and lines, still others with cotton and weaving tools or a pointed stick and spatula kit that may have been used in shellfish gathering (ibid.: 298–99).

Shortly after 2000 B.C. at least some communities began building monumental architecture, the most impressive of which is at El Paraiso (also known as Chuquitanta), on the banks of the Rio Chillon, about 2 kilometers inland from the sea (Figure 15.4). This site is dominated by a large "temple" complex consisting of a central large structure flanked by two protruding wings, the whole complex enclosing a large patio (Lanning 1967: 71). There are eight or nine distinct structural units at the site, each composed of a series of masonry room complexes. The two largest complexes are built on artificial mounds more than 250 meters in length and 50 meters in width, rising to a height of over

5 meters. These complexes are made up of rectangular rooms of various dimensions interconnected by doors and corridors (Moseley 1975: 26), and it has been estimated that there are over 50 hectares of such constructions at this site (Engl 1969). One complex of rooms, over 450 meters long, is among the largest buildings ever constructed in ancient Peru (Lanning 1967: 71).

The significance of El Paraiso is difficult to assess. Most of the occupational refuse at the site has been destroyed by centuries of plowing. Moseley concludes that El Paraiso's inhabitants subsisted principally on generalized foraging for shellfish, fish, sea mammals, and wild plants, and on animal products (1975: 24–27). Others (e.g., J. Parsons 1977) suspect these people may have cultivated some legumes, squash, and other crops. The paucity of residential remains at the site suggests it may have been mainly a ceremonial center (Moseley [1975] estimates its population at 1,500 to 3,000 people), but it is difficult to determine how much of the site was occupied at a single time or how long it took to build the whole complex.

As in Mexico, Mesopotamia, Egypt, and elsewhere, these monumental constructions may have been linked to agricultural redistribution. We might speculate that a central religious focus like El Paraiso would have helped groups organize together to meet cyclical resource

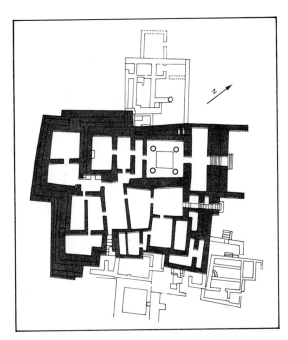

15.4
Photograph (left) and plan of El Paraiso, an early ceremonial center on the Peruvian coast.

shortages. In some senses the Peruvian coast is a "redundant" environment like that of the Mayan lowlands, and monumental architecture in both places may have served similar functions.

Despite the size of El Paraiso, there is no evidence of complex social stratification, such as great differences in cemetery wealth, luxury residences, or highly specialized arts and crafts.

Very little is known about developments in the Peruvian highlands between 2500 and 1800 B.C., when El Paraiso and other communities were flourishing along the coasts. Plant and animal remains do not preserve well in the wet highlands, and many areas most likely to have been farmed during this period may now be buried under thick layers of alluvial soil (Lanning 1967: 73). We do know, however, that between about 5500 and 4000 B.C. people at Ayacucho and elsewhere in the highlands may have been subsisting on several species of domestic plants and animals, including llamas, guinea pigs, gourds, squash, quinoa, amaranths, and chili peppers (Flannery 1973; Kaplan, Lynch, and Smith 1973). Domestic maize is found on the coast by about 2000 B.C. and, if this plant were brought into Peru from Mesoamerica by way of the Peruvian highlands, we would expect future research to locate maize remains in the Peruvian highlands in contexts dating to long before 2000 B.C. Even in areas too high for maize cultivation, squash, gourds, peppers, amaranths, and other plants were being domesticated and perhaps grown by 5000 B.C., and additional food was provided by hunting, llamas, and even domestic guinea pigs and dogs.

THE INITIAL PERIOD (1800 TO 900 B.C.)

Between 1800 and 900 B.C. Peruvian systems of settlement and subsistence changed drastically. Maize—possibly indigenous, but more likely an import from the north via the Peruvian highlands—was brought into intensive cultivation along the coast. In the highlands, where maize does not do well, tubers, quinoa, and other crops were the primary foods. Excavations at sites dating to shortly after 1800 B.C. show that along the coast people were probably eating fewer fish, shellfish, and other littoral, foraged foods, and increasing their consumption of maize, manioc, sweet potatoes, beans, peanuts, and other crops—although sampling biases in the archaeological record again make reconstructions of diets somewhat speculative. The discovery of manioc and peanuts here is interesting because these plants are native to the Amazon Basin, and their presence on the coast may indicate that Peruvian societies had established some minimal contacts with inland areas, but it is just as likely that these crops were introduced by slow village-to-village exchange (Lanning 1967: 89). The domestication of the llama around 1800 B.C. provided meat and wool, as well as important transport power—something totally absent in Mesoamerica. The increased importance of containers in agricultural societies is reflected in the first wide-scale distribution of pottery in Peru shortly after 1800 B.C., and there seems little need to explain early Peruvian ceramics—as some have—in terms of contacts with Japanese fishermen or other sources.

These various subsistence and technological changes were paralleled by fundamental changes in the distribution of settlements, as many of the fishing communities along the coast were slowly abandoned, and some of these people and their descendants may have moved inland to take up agriculture. There is as yet no direct evidence of irrigation systems in these areas until after about 400 B.C., but the distribution of settlements in the inland valleys and the botanical remains found at these sites suggest that simple irrigation canals were being constructed from about 1800 to 1200 B.C. to grow maize, squash, legumes, beans, sweet and white potatoes, and peanuts (Moseley 1975:

105). In particularly rich littoral environments large communities still supported themselves primarily through fishing, collecting, and minor agriculture—although in only a few areas along the coast is it possible to combine fishing and farming effectively (ibid.: 106).

The transition to inland settlement and an agricultural economy required major social and technological changes. Littoral resources could be exploited by many small independent groups with a very simple technology, and their availability in time and space was not subject to human manipulation (Moseley 1975: 106). Inland agricultural systems, however, required a technology for irrigation, ground preparation, harvesting, and storage, as well as organized, coordinated labor groups.

Pyramids were still being built close to the shore, but the largest constructions were now inland. At Cerro Sechin, for example, sometime before about 1000 B.C. a platform mound was built that stands over 30 meters high and is 550 by 400 meters at the base, making it one of the largest buildings of its type anywhere in Peru (ibid.: 107). It is difficult to determine how much of this was built in the early periods, however, and some of it may date to later periods.

Sedentary coastal communities were probably able to evolve agricultural economies quite readily, because they no doubt developed coordinated labor groups and a limited agricultural technology (for cotton and gourd crops) while still mainly collectors and fisherfolk. Previously, however, their population-to-resources balances may have been keyed to marine and littoral resources, and one would expect that it would take some time for these community systems to re-regulate their population densities and growth rates according to the productivity of the new agricultural economy—accounting, in part, perhaps, for the monumental architecture here.

Developments in the Peruvian highlands during this *Initial period* (1800 to 900 B.C.) are not nearly as well known as those in coastal areas. At Kotosh, a site at about the 1,800-meter-level on the eastern slopes of the Andes, a large temple complex may have been begun before 1800 B.C. The earliest structure was built on a stone-faced platform some 8 meters high, but little of the actual building has been excavated. It appears that the whole complex was substantially rebuilt at least five times during the Initial period (Lanning 1967: 92).

Little is known about the people who built these edifices, but the earliest of these "temples" may even have been erected by nonagriculturalists (Lumbreras 1974: 47). Most of the later constructions appear

Chavín-style artifacts have been found at many places within the area noted here.

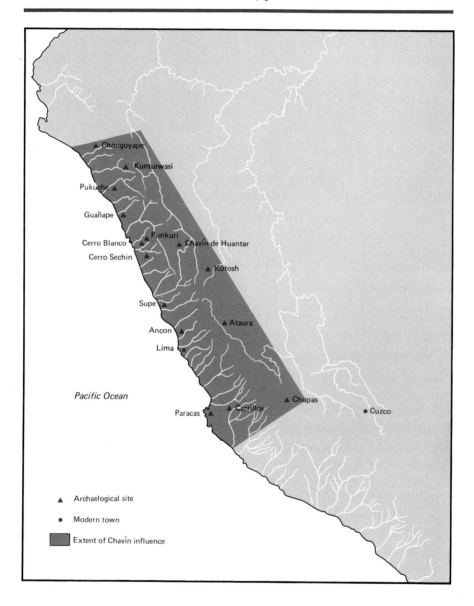

Chongoyape ▲

Kunturwasi ▲

Pukuche ▲

Guañape ▲

Cerro Blanco ▲   Punkuri ▲   ▲ Chavín de Huantar

Cerro Sechin ▲

▲ Kotosh

Supe ▲

▲ Ataura

Ancon ▲

Lima ●

Pacific Ocean

▲ Chupas   ● Cuzco

Paracas ▲   ▲ Cerrillos

▲   Archaelogical site

●   Modern town

■   Extent of Chavín influence

to have been the work of maize farmers who relied heavily on domesticated animals (ibid.: 54), but the paucity of habitation refuse near these massive stone constructions has led some to suspect that they may have been largely ceremonial, perhaps acting as focal points of trade and social exchange between widely spaced agricultural groups (Lanning 1967: 92). At least one other temple complex has been discovered in the highlands, and it is possible that the early appearance and spread of these complexes were in response to the staggering number of things that can go wrong for agriculturalists in these highlands. Highly localized hailstorms can wipe out a village's crops in minutes, earthquakes often send mud slides smashing through villages and farms, crop diseases now as in antiquity are endemic to the highlands, and these and other natural and human disasters in these highlands may have encouraged a centralized redistribution system—operated through temples—in order to spread the risks among many independent village communities.

THE EARLY HORIZON (900 TO 200 B.C.)

After about 900 B.C. people living at Chavín de Huantar (Figure 15.5) and other sites in the highlands of northern Peru began to use many of the same stylistic elements in their pottery, architecture, and other artifacts, and over succeeding centuries tens of thousands of people, from Ica in the South to Ecuador in the North, were participating in the *Chavín Horizon,* as this complex of stylistic elements was called. Chavín art is dominated by animal and human representations, with particular attention given to combinations of forms of people, jaguars, and snakes (Figure 15.6).

Some have argued that the spread of the Chavín art style reflects the religious—and perhaps even social and economic—organization of a large area of northern Peru, but this appears unlikely. The spread of these styles occurs at about the same time in some areas as apparent increases in product exchange, activity specialization, population densities, and investments in monumental buildings, but the general tenor of the Chavín diffusion is reminiscent of the initial spread of Olmec art in Mesoamerica—a relatively simple extension of aesthetic and perhaps religious traditions, in the absence of political hierarchies or economic elites (for a review see Benson 1971).

Chavín de Huantar, the site after which the art style is named, boasts a ceremonial complex composed of two low platform mounds, a massive terraced platform (called the *Castillo*), and a sunken court, forty-eight meters on a side and paved with stone. The Castillo is honeycombed with galleries and compartments at different levels. Interior support is provided by skillfully combined adobe walls and cut-stone beams, and many interior rooms appear to have been plastered and decorated with painted designs. Some of the galleries apparently served as repositories for offerings, since hundreds of finely crafted ceramic pots were found there, as well as masses of llama, guinea pig, and fish bones and seashells that had been imported over long distances (Lumbreras 1974: 62).

The ancient residential area at Chavín underlies a modern village, making it difficult to estimate its area—although it was probably at least fifty hectares (Sanders and Marino 1970: 70). Until additional excavations are conducted, we cannot analyze occupational specialization or mortuary and residential variability here during this period.

Goldsmithing was developed into a high art in the Chavín era, as craftsmen cut, embossed, annealed, cast, and welded gold into ear spools, nose ornaments, plaques, crowns, and face coverings for corpses. Copper and silver were also extensively used for making ornaments, and weaving became a fine art.

The central religious symbols of Chavín, the anthropomorphic feline, the cayman (relative of the crocodile), and bird motifs, were widely distributed over the northern highlands and the northern and central coasts, as were the ceramic and architectural styles associated with this cultural horizon (Sanders and Marino 1970: 71). A temple at La Copa has many characteristic Chavín motifs, as do coastal centers in the Nepena and Casma valleys.

Some have argued that the Chavín culture was among the first chiefdoms in Peru, meaning that it was organized around ranked lineages, with some groups having greater access to wealth and prestige (Sanders and Marino 1970: 73), but the evidence is uncertain. Some aspects of the Chavín culture may have been imported from Mesoamerica, perhaps from the Olmec, because some of the ceramics from Tlatilco, outside Mexico City, are said to be so similar to Chavín examples that it is hard to distinguish them; and there are other parallels, such as feline aesthetic motifs and the practice of cranial deformation.

It is very difficult, however, to imagine an Olmec group being able to influence developments in Peru to this degree, for by the time the Olmec first appeared in Mesoamerica, much of Peru was already inhabited by farmers living in sedentary nucleated communities. It would seem highly unlikely that an Olmec missionary or military group, arriving by sea (if they had boats) or land (if they could possibly march through the jungles and mountains of Central America), could abruptly walk into such an established cultural area as Peru and radically change it politically and religiously. Such things have happened,

15.6
Stone relief of the feline god, a standard Chavín motif.

15.7
Textile from the Paracas culture. First millennium B.C.

but generally in cases where one cultural group has a vastly superior technology and military apparatus.

Lanning makes the important point that, although the spread of the Chavín styles was accompanied by the spread of agricultural villages into areas not previously exploited, as well as by the multiplication of villages in other areas, these same patterns of growth were also taking place outside the Chavín sphere of influence (1967: 106).

In some important ways the Chavín phenomenon is reminiscent of the initial stages of cultural evolution in other areas, like ancient Southwest Asia, where the sudden appearance of regional pottery styles was also followed by the spread of a temple complex (the Ubaid culture), culminating in very rapid increases in cultural complexity. And when we also consider the Olmec, Harappan, and Lungshan cultures, we see these developments as a worldwide pattern. Religious traditions offer a superbly effective way to get people to act in coordinated ways, because the expenses of large buildings and the "furs and feathers" of office are cheap, compared to their power in directing the population toward specific economic and political goals. Llama herders from the mountains, maize farmers from the valleys, fishermen, artisans, and other specialists may have derived from the Chavín cult the kinds of administration and political support and integration that set the stage for the evolution of state societies.

EARLY PERUVIAN STATES (200 B.C. TO A.D. 1000)

In the first millennium A.D., Peruvian societies were transformed from relatively simple agricultural communities, perhaps organized along tribal lines, to highly stratified, populous, militaristic cultures that we can legitimately term *states*. Within this period the population of Peru rose from a few hundred thousand to approximately 4 or 5 million (Lanning 1967: 114–15), large cities appeared in scores of places, armies conquered thousands of square kilometers, irrigation systems were greatly extended, and the ceramic, architectural, metallurgical, and textile (Figure 15.7) arts reached such heights that archaeologists have traditionally referred to this period as the *Classic*.

The story of this transformation begins with the widespread disappearance of Chavín artistic styles at about 200 B.C., followed quickly by the emergence of as many as fifteen different areas of Peru as centers of regional development (Lumbreras 1974: 94). Ceremonial centers can be found in many places in the southern Peruvian highlands at this time, as well as in the Nazca Valley and other coastal regions. Less work has been done on the residential areas of these centers than on the monumental architecture, but it now appears that some of these were sizable towns, such as Tambo Viejo in the Acarí Valley (Nazca area), which contains hundreds of rectangular rooms, most of which seem to have been residences. Populations along the northern coast in the Mochica area were distributed in at least two different settlement sizes: villages, made up of complexes of about a hundred conjoined rooms, located along dry washes and hillsides in the upper ends of the valleys; and larger collections of thousands of conjoined rooms located on the broad alluvial plain (Sanders and Marino 1970: 74). Also numerous along the northern coast were great fortresses, comprising terraced adobe platforms with room complexes and defensive peripheral walls (ibid.: 74).

Along both the northern and southern coasts the agricultural system was still based on maize, beans, squash, potatoes, manioc, fish, and guinea pigs, and large fields were devoted to cotton cultivation. Llamas were kept for wool and transport. Maize could not be grown in higher elevations, but quinoa, oca, and other plant foods provided good substitutes, and in the Titicaca Basin lacustrine resources were intensively exploited.

The complexity of Classic period agriculture is well illustrated by the irrigation system of the Mochica state, where mud canals were built high in the hills, diverting water through kilometers of canals that snaked along the mountainside, down to the valleys. Because the Mochica worked only with mud, the construction of these canal systems had to be done with great precision; for if the water flowed too slowly, silt would accumulate so rapidly as to make the canal a vast waste of effort, or, if it flowed too fast, the whole system could be eroded. Cleaning the wind-blown sand from these systems probably required the annual orchestration of thousands of laborers.

Regional economies in these early states included many skillfully integrated elements (Schaedel 1971). The presence of huge drying racks in some coastal communities, as well as fish remains in many in-

15.8
By turning over patinated stones, the Nazca used color contrasts to form enormous designs on the floor of the Nazca Valley (ca. A.D. 500). Despite suggestions about the use of these markings as signs to visitors from outer space, these were probably calendrical or religious symbols.

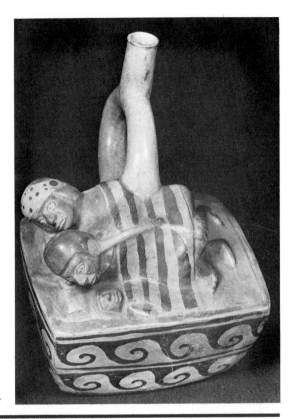

15.9
Mochican pottery celebrated
every variety of sexual activity.

land communities, indicate that fishing was probably highly organized (Lanning 1967: 120). The integration of llama and alpaca herding into the economy also required many specialists, from the herders to the weavers who turned out beautiful tapestries from llama wool. Products moved over trade routes extending north and south of Peru, and even onto offshore islands.

We know an enormous amount about the life in Peru during this period (200 B.C. to A.D. 1000) because the people recorded their activities in great detail in ceramics, sculpture, paintings, and tapestries. Pottery vessels depict people hunting deer with spears and clubs, fishermen putting to sea in small canoes, blowgun hunters taking aim at birds, weavers working under the direction of a foreman, and many people engaging in war, human sacrifice, and violence. People are also shown being carried on sedan chairs, seated on thrones, receiving tribute, and presiding at executions.

But most famous of all the aesthetic expressions of this period are the frank depictions—usually in pottery—of sexual practices (Figure 15.9). While every conceivable sexual variation is amply illustrated, the vast majority involve acts currently and widely considered "perverse" (although most of these are executed with great style and wit). Pots representing sexual themes in the most explicit terms may have been used in ordinary daily life, and to drink or pour from many of them is to perform, symbolically, at least, acts still widely banned.

If the sexual practices depicted in pottery are in any way a reflection of the actual proclivities of the people—and reports of the Spanish and the Inca suggest this was the case (but see Donnan 1976)—then the Mochica and their contemporaries may have devised a very efficient system of birth control. For although there are relatively few depictions of homosexuality (most involving lesbian relationships), procreative acts of sexual intercourse are much less celebrated than nonprocreative acts in this pottery.

Another central element of life in these early Peruvian states was warfare. Every well-surveyed coastal valley has been found to have fortresses and fortified settlements dating to this period, and weapons are common in these sites, particularly along the southern coast. Artistic representations focus on warriors, battle scenes, and mutilations, and trophy heads and mummified corpses showing signs of violence are frequently found in cemeteries (Lanning 1967: 121). The correlation between these signs of warfare and the increasing population densities and cultural complexity of this period has led some to infer a cause-and-effect relationship. We have already noted Carneiro's hypothesis that the early Peruvian state formed out of wars of conquest brought on by the insatiable appetites of a relentlessly expanding population, but there is little evidence for this theory.

Wari and Tiahuanaco

Between A.D. 600 and 800 the many rival "states" of Classic Peru gave way to several larger competing political systems, one centered at Wari in the Manteco Basin, another at Tiahuanaco, at the southern end of Lake Titicaca, and a third in the Moche-Chimú area (Figure 15.10). In these and perhaps other areas, wars of conquest brought large territories under centralized, hierarchically organized governments and lessened regional isolation (Lanning 1967: 127).

As examples of these large states, let us consider Wari and Tiahuanaco. Wari existed as a political system for only a century or two,

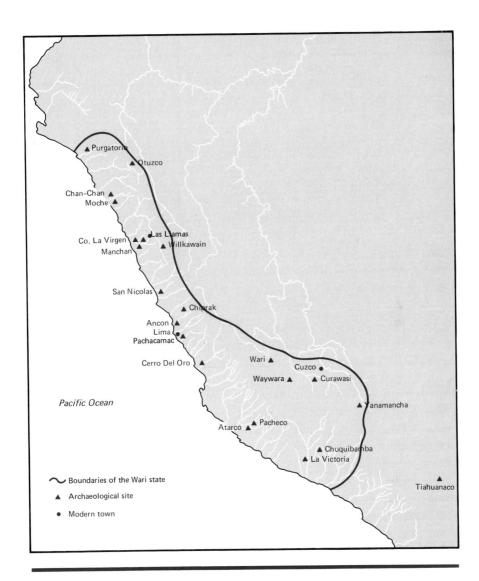

15.10
Boundary of the Wari state and location of some of the principal sites.

but at its high point it carried out political and economic activities over most of the coast and highlands between Cajamarca in the north and Sicuani in the south. The evidence for the Wari "empire" comes mainly from the distribution of specific art styles and religious symbols (particularly the Feline God and several forms of ceramic vessel decoration) over a wide area of the central highlands. Significantly, these motifs show up most frequently in the burials of individuals whose associated mortuary goods appear to reflect particularly high status. Also,

15.11
The fabled city of Chan-chan, composed of burial platforms, public buildings, shops, and residential quarters.

while these styles were spreading, there may have been some reorganization of settlement patterns. Within a century, the entire population of the valley, most of whom had formerly lived in small towns and villages, was concentrated around the city of Wari, which had expanded to the impressive size of roughly ten square kilometers, making it one of the largest residential sites in the ancient New World (Sanders and Marino 1970: 79).

If Wari were an expansionist state, it is probably significant that some of ancient Peru's major roadways may have been constructed during this period (Lumbreras 1974: 162), for such roads would have been very important in facilitating the exchange of goods and services over an area as large as that apparently administered from Wari.

By about A.D. 600 the population of Tiahuanaco may have reached nearly 20,000, most of whom were clustered around the monumental buildings at the southern end of Lake Titicaca. The economic and political influence of Tiahuanaco apparently extended over much of the Bolivian highlands, the southern highlands, and the far southern coast of Peru, and there were colonies in northern Chile and northwestern Argentina as well (Sanders and Marino 1970: 79). Subsistence at Tiahuanaco was based on potatoes, quinoa, fish and plants from the lake, and the herding of llamas and alpacas.

Very little is known about the extent and character of the Tiahuanaco culture. What we see archaeologically is the relatively sudden and widespread distribution of stylistic elements from Tiahuanaco itself, but we have no way of knowing whether this resulted from conquest, economic interchange, or religious movements.

REGIONAL STATES (A.D. 1000 TO 1476)

With the collapse of the Wari and Tiahuanaco political systems between A.D. 800 and A.D. 1000, at least seven different "kingdoms" became power centers in Peru, the best known and most developed of which was the *Chimú* state centered in the Moche Valley on the northern coast. A capital of the Chimú political system was the beautiful city of Chan-chan (Figure 15.11), a planned settlement covering nearly eight square kilometers—one of the largest pre-Columbian cities in the New World. It was divided into ten rectangular sectors, each containing houses, terraces, reservoirs, parks, roads, and public buildings (Lumbreras 1974: 183; Moseley 1975). Brilliantly carved friezes decorated many walls.

Nearly every valley under Chimú control possessed at least one large urban center, and each center was surrounded by a hierarchy of smaller settlements. Goldworking and silverworking (Figure 15.12) ceramics, weaving, and sculpture were all highly developed crafts. Chimú society seems to have been rigidly stratified according to wealth and prestige (Lumbreras 1974: 187), and extension of political and economic control appears to have been based on a highly efficient and very active army (Keatinge 1974: 79).

Perhaps the most significant development in Peru during this period (A.D. 1000 to 1476) was the multiplication of urban centers. Much of southern Peru remained largely rural, but in the northern half of the country some of the greatest cities of the preconquest period were built, including Chan-chan, Pacatnamú, Farfán, and Apurlé (Lanning 1967: 151).

15.12
Gold earplugs, with mosaic of turquoise, lapis lazuli, shell, and pearls.

THE IMPERIAL TRANSFORMATION (A.D. 1476 TO 1525)

The largest and most highly integrated political system ever to appear in the New World evolved in Peru within the space of only eighty-seven years. Centered in the Cuzco Valley, the *Inca* Empire (more properly known as the *empire of Tawantinsuyu*) eventually stretched from Colombia to central Chile and from the Pacific to the eastern jungles, tying together under the administration of a single royal lineage many diverse regional economic and political systems. At its height, as many as 6 million people may have been living under Inca rule in one of the most intricately ordered societies of all time.

Native and Spanish accounts say that the Inca began their rise to power out of the dissolution of the many small competing Peruvian states of the thirteenth and fourteenth centuries A.D. The people of Cuzco were attacked by a rival state at about A.D. 1435 (Lumbreras 1974: 217) and managed to prevail, and for the next several decades succeeding monarchs at Cuzco added new provinces to the empire by conquest, treaty, and simple annexation. The oral histories of the Inca—cross-checked and recorded by the Spanish—speak of brilliant military campaigns in which Inca kings smashed the rival power of Chan-chan in the 1460s, put down large-scale revolts in the 1470s, and extended the empire to its limits in the 1480s (Lanning 1967: 159–60).

The economic basis of the Inca Empire (Figure 15.13) was a highly integrated system of fishing, herding, and farming. In the highlands the Inca greatly extended agricultural productivity by terracing slopes (Figure 15.14) using natural fertilizers, and improving and centralizing the irrigation systems. Rivers were channeled through stone-lined canals, and lowland irrigation systems, which had existed for thousands of years, were greatly extended and brought under a centralized authority (Lanning 1967: 161). Llamas and alpacas were raised for wool, while dogs, muscovy ducks, and guinea pigs provided

15.13
The Inca (Tawantinsuyu) Empire, showing some of the principal roads and towns. Almost every settlement was connected to the two major north-south roads.

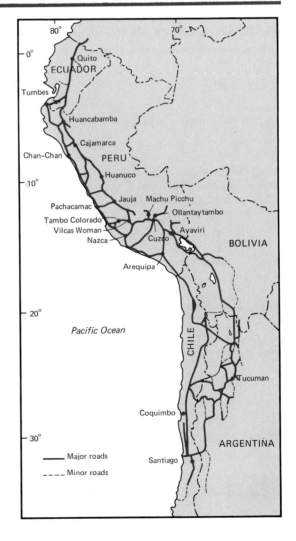

most of the meat. But the staple foods were maize, beans, potatoes, quinoa, oca, and peppers.

The food storage methods used by the Inca were very important in establishing imperial food reserves. Potatoes were alternately dried and frozen to produce a black, pulpy product called *chuño,* meat was turned into jerky, and grain was brewed into *chica,* a nutritious beer.

The people of the empire were complexly organized according to a decimal system in which there were administrators for every unit of taxpayer from 10 to 10,000 (Lanning 1967: 166). Most people were members of large kin groups, called *ayllu,* in which descent was reckoned through the male line and marriages were between members of the same *ayllu.* The *ayllu* were usually economically self-sufficient units, and were bound together by complex patterns of reciprocal obligations, such as requiring members to work each other's lands when one was absent and to support widows and the infirm (Bushnell 1963: 131). The populace was divided into twelve age groups, each with its own duties, and a labor tax was exacted from each. Farmers worked a

15.14
With the evolution of states in Peru, agriculture was intensified through construction of irrigation canals and terracing, such as these fields near Pisac.

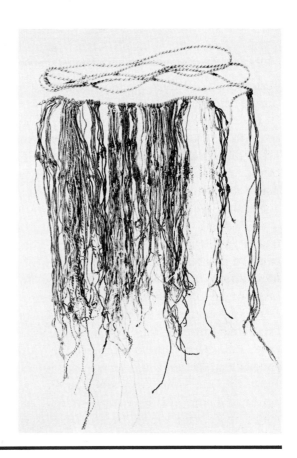

15.15
A *quipu,* a set of knotted
strings used for keeping accounts.

certain amount of time on state-owned plots, while craftsmen and specialists, such as runners, weavers, and goldsmiths, contributed according to their particular talents.

Records of taxes, transactions, and census figures were kept with
the aid of the *quipu,* a set of strings tied into knots at different levels
(Figure 15.15) according to a decimal notation system that could be
used by a special hereditary class of accountants to memorize the information (Lanning 1967: 166–67). A writing system of the type used
in early Mesopotamia would no doubt have conveyed more religious
and philosophical information, but looked at in terms of simple information storage and retrieval, the *quipu* appears to have been an adequate substitute for writing, particularly in view of the enormous Inca
bureaucracy.

Trade in foodstuffs appears to have been largely local (Lanning
1967: 167), but gold, fabrics, and other luxury goods were collected
from over the empire for distribution among the elites. Women, too,
were treated as commodities. Government agents visited each village

periodically and took the most beautiful girls of about age ten back to provincial capitals where most of them were taught spinning, weaving, and cooking, and were apportioned out as wives for the emperor and the nobles. Occasionally, particularly favored females would be sacrificed (ibid.: 133–34). Finely woven fabrics were also an important part of the Inca economic system. The finest fabrics were given to the emperor as much appreciated gifts, and cloths were used as currency and as elements in religious sacrifices (ibid.).

The Inca Empire was possible only because they developed a system of roads and transport of extraordinary efficiency. Most villages were largely self-sufficient, but the flow of goods and information and, most importantly, the armies required to create the empire were dependent on the road system, comprising an overall network of about 16,000 kilometers of paved roads (von Hagen 1952). Road beds were excavated through hillsides, swamps were crossed by drained causeways, walls were built to protect the roadway in the windy uplands, and wide rivers and ravines were crossed by suspension bridges made of woven vines hung from stone towers. All along the road were storehouses and administrative outposts, and runners stationed about a kilometer apart were reputed to carry messages over distances as great as 2,400 kilometers in just five days. Movement of goods along the coast was accomplished by large balsa-wood rafts equipped with sails and oars.

Although they were master builders, the Inca stressed the rural, village way of life, and it is doubtful that they ever constructed major urban settlements (Lanning 1967: 163). Typical Inca residential units were rectangular walled houses of stone or adobe, subdivided into smaller units. Most of the public constructions were not for urban dwellers, but in the form of palaces, temples, granaries, fortresses, barracks, and highway stations (ibid.). The skill used in these constructions is amazing, considering the limited technology. They cut stones into huge blocks by simple chipping and abrading with harder stones and then fitted them together (without the use of mortar) so precisely that, as the cliché goes, a knifeblade cannot be inserted between them (Figure 15.16).

The capital city of Cuzco was an orderly arrangement of houses, monumental buildings, and streets, well provided with a municipal water and drainage system. The great temple of Qori Kancha here had exterior walls measuring sixty-eight by fifty-nine meters, and a semicircular annex that rose to a height of more than thirty-four meters (Lumbreras 1974). A gold frieze about a meter wide ran along the exterior wall and the entrance way was heavily sheathed in gold plate. Many other structures at the capital were lavishly decorated with gold and silver (ibid.: 218–19).

The comparatively great internal security of the empire made it unnecessary to defend most settlements, except with occasional hilltop forts. The heart of the Inca army was the common foot soldier armed with club, mace, battle axe, or lance. Slings, bolas, and spear throwers were used prior to the main attack, but it was brutal hand-to-hand combat that usually decided the issue. One successful tactical innovation apparently introduced by the Inca was the practice of holding back a large body of troops who were thrown in at a critical juncture— a simple tactic similar in a way to Napoleon's fantastically successful use of reserves. There was apparently no standing army, but the superb administrative hierarchy made it possible to field large numbers of troops on very short notice.

15.16
Impressive Inca stonework at Pisac.

The Inca Achievement

The Inca achievement was essentially the result of refinements of administrative skills and mechanisms for the production, storage, and retrieval of information. In technology and subsistence they were not significantly advanced beyond their predecessors, but by devising an efficient transport system, and by organizing, monopolizing, and taxing economic productivity down to the last village, they were able to consolidate and integrate their territory on a scale not matched by any other pre-Columbian New World culture.

In the Inca Empire, as in Mesopotamia, we see a situation in which there appears to have been a breakdown in the factors limiting the size of competing states. With these competitive relationships broken down, Inca growth could continue virtually unchecked, the only restraints being those mandated by the limits of the administrative and communications systems.

THE EUROPEAN CONQUEST

The history of the Spanish conquest of Peru is yet another installment in the all-too-familiar story of colonial exploitation and violence (Prescott 1908). After sporadic, occasionally hostile contacts between 1527 and 1531, the Spanish under Francisco Pizarro set out toward the provincial capital at Cajamarca, the residence of the Atahualpa, the Inca king. Their trek took them through the heart of Inca military strength, and why they were never intercepted and massacred remains a mystery. Internecine warfare between rival claimants to the Inca throne at this time was probably a factor. In any case, the Peruvians soon had cause to regret their diffidence. Pizzaro and his men entered the city on 15 November 1532, and found it to be a massive, fortified center, but surprisingly, nearly deserted. After establishing himself in a fortress with a couple of cannons and his few score soldiers, Pizarro elected to wait until the Inca king made an effort to visit him. Eventually the emperor came, borne on a litter and preceded by thousands of soldiers, attendants, and subjects. The first Spaniard to approach the king was the chaplain, who, as part of Pizarro's contract with the king of Spain and the Pope, was charged with spreading the Christian faith. Throughout the trip to Cajamarca the chaplain and the Spanish had talked to the natives about Christianity—without too much success in converting them, apparently—yet the chaplain immediately began to harangue the king, through an interpreter, about the creation of the world, the fall of Adam and Eve, the Virgin Birth, the establishment of the papacy, and other dogma of the Christian faith, culminating with the announcement that the Pope had given Peru to the Spanish through his majesty, King Charles of Spain.

Not surprisingly, the Inca king took exception to parts of the chaplain's speech, particularly the legality of Peru being ceded to the Spanish, and he very understandably wanted to know how the Pope could give away something that was not his, and how it had happened that the god of the Christians had died, since the Inca deity, the Sun, was immortal and never in danger of falling into the hands of his enemies (Engl 1969: 119).

When the Atahualpa asked how the chaplain knew all these things, he was handed a breviary. The king, unable to open the clasp at first, finally broke it, looked briefly and no doubt uncomprehendingly inside, and then threw it away. At this point the Spanish attacked, and then the inexplicable happened: instead of killing the Spanish, the Inca fled, dropping their weapons and killing themselves in their panicked flight, and the Spanish were able to dispatch hundreds and capture the king with little trouble. They remained fortressed in Cajamarca for some months, detaining the king, who tried to win his release by offering to fill a room (supposed to have been 6.5 by 4.5 meters) with gold and by helping the Spanish in other ways. The Spanish meanwhile took masses of gold and silver in raids, most of it in the form of exquisitely wrought figures, which in most cases they melted into ingots.

Rumors of insurrections in the countryside convinced the Spanish to execute the Inca king, and they did so, considering themselves enlightened for giving him the option of being garroted rather than being burned at the stake—a reward to the king for allowing himself to be baptized. With the Atahualpa's death and the ensuing factionalism among rival claimants to the throne, as well as the devastation brought on by introduced diseases and the horror wrought on the populace through warfare and the destruction of the irrigation system, the population of Peru is thought to have dropped from over 6 million to less than 2 million within a few decades of the conquest.

The Origins of Complex Cultures in Peru: Conclusions

Not surprisingly, the evolution of cultural complexity in Peru is not explainable in terms of any single factor. As in other early complex societies, agriculture was the basis for later stages of evolutionary development, but some elements of cultural complexity may have been well developed before agriculture became a primary part of the subsistence strategy. Here too, then, the potential for food production was more important than whether the basis of food production was agriculture or intensive foraging.

Nor does large-scale irrigation seem to be the key. Such systems probably appeared in Peru—as in most other early complex societies— long after the appearance of the major elements of cultural complexity. On the other hand, we are not yet able to assess rigorously the role of irrigation in early Peru, and there is evidence that complex irrigation systems were in operation here long *before* full-fledged states and empires appeared (Service 1975: 196).

Population pressure and warfare, at least as proposed by Robert Carneiro (1970), also seem to be, at the very best, incomplete explanations. Carneiro argues that Peruvian cultural evolution resulted from human population growth within environmentally circumscribed valleys along the Peruvian coast. With their agricultural and marine resources, he suggests, these populations grew rapidly; but because these valleys are boxed in by the sea, the oceans, and adjoining deserts, the inhabitants had no way of coping with population growth except by intensification of agricultural productivity, and, later, when maximum productivity had been reached, by warfare. State-level societies then evolved because administrators were needed to tax and manage conquered territories, and a class society would presumably emerge as prisoners became slaves and war leaders became an elite class (ibid. 1970).

We have already reviewed extensively the idea that human population growth causes cultural evolution, and it was suggested that human population growth is usually the *result*, not the cause of these developments. In addition, warfare is somewhat suspect as a force in early Peruvian developments because there is no evidence of sustained warfare until well after the appearance of such things as monumental buildings, the coordination of regional economies, craft specialization, and the rise of great religious traditions. How, then, are we to account for Peruvian complex societies?

Obviously, the rich maritime and agricultural resources were essential ingredients in this development. In only a few areas of the world is it possible to produce and gather enough food to run complex cultures on the basis of primitive technologies, and Peru is one of these. We should not be too surprised that Peruvian developments were based initially on marine resources rather than agriculture, since there is nothing *necessary* about agriculture in this role; all that is required is a very high level of productivity, and coastal Peru clearly possessed that potential.

An important "negative" element in the evolution of Peruvian cultures appears to have been the fact that, unlike ancient China, Mesopotamia, or the Indus Valley, Peru was geographically isolated from other highly complex political systems. Evolving Old World civilizations soon came into contact with one another, and their political, economic, and social interchanges appear to have transformed each of them to some degree. But, except for Mesoamerica—which was very distant and cut off by ocean and jungle—Peru evolved alone.

The absence of a domesticable draught animal also was a limit on Peruvian development. Llamas compensated for this to a degree, but they cannot compare with the transport abilities of horses, mules, or oxen. It is difficult to judge the effects the presence of a domesticable draught animal in Peru would have had, but it may be significant that almost all agricultural areas of Peru today are plowed.

Nor is it easy to weigh the effect on Peruvian developments of the lack of accessible iron ore and the tardy development of bronze metallurgy. In the Old World ironworking seems to have been intimately associated with the expansion of great empires, and, had it been available, it might also have changed the character of later Peruvian developments. We still do not know the sources of Peruvian copper ores used in the production of bronze, but the spread of bronze weapons and implements throughout Peru and adjacent areas during the Inca period may have been as much of a stimulus to trade and agricultural technology as it was in the Old World.

Thus, in summary of Peruvian prehistory we see that cultural developments there paralleled those in other centers of independent complex society formation in most important details, including the initial spread of a religious cult, the importance of a highly productive economy, the widespread occurrence of monumental architecture, and the gradual emergence of highly stratified, integrated state and imperial political systems. The contrasting features of Peruvian developments, relative to various other early complex cultures, include a lesser degree of urbanism, the absence of a writing system, and, perhaps a somewhat greater degree of governmental control of everyday life, but these aspects do not seem as significant as the evident similarities. Like other early complex cultures, Peruvian developments do not appear to be interpretable in terms of simple "prime-mover" models of cultural evolution.

Bibliography

Benson, Elizabeth J., ed. 1971. *Dumbarton Oaks Conference on Chavin*. Dumbarton Oaks Research Library and Collection, Trustees for Harvard University. Washington, D.C.

Benson, Elizabeth P. 1972. *The Mochica: A Culture of Peru*. New York: Praeger.

Browman, David L. 1974. "Pastoral Nomadism in the Andes." *Current Anthropology*. 15(2): 188–96.

———. 1975. "Trade Patterns in the Central Highlands of Peru in the First Millennium B.C." *World Archaeology*. 6(3): 322–30.

Bushnell, G. H. S. 1963. *Peru*. Rev. ed. New York: Praeger.

Carneiro, Robert. 1970. "A Theory of the Origin of the State." *Science*. 169: 733–38.

Cohen, Mark N. 1976. "Population Pressure and the Origins of Agriculture: An Archaeological Example from the Coast of Peru." In *Advances in Andean Archaeology*. Chicago: Aldine.

Collier, D. 1961. "Agriculture and Civilization on the Coast of Peru." In *The Evolution of Horticultural Systems in Native South America: Causes and Consequences,* ed. J. Wilbert. Caracas: Sociedad de Ciencias Naturales La Salle.

Donnan, Christopher B. 1973. *Moche Occupation of the Santa Valley, Peru*. University of California Publication in Anthropology, no. 8. Berkeley.

———. 1976. *Moche Art and Iconography*. U.C.L.A. Latin American Center Publications. University of California, Los Angeles.

Engel, Frederick. 1957. "Early Sites on the Peruvian Coast." *Southwestern Journal of Anthropology*. 13: 54–68.

Engl, Lieselotti and Theo. 1969. *Twilight of Ancient Peru*, trans. Alisa Jaffe. New York: McGraw-Hill.

Flannery, Kent V. 1973. "The Origins of Agriculture." *Annual Review of Anthropology*. 2: 271–310.

Ford, J. A. 1969. "A Comparison of Formative Cultures in the Americas: Diffusion or the Psychic Unity of Man." *Smithsonian Contributions to Anthropology*, vol. 2. Washington, D.C.: Smithsonian Institution Press.

Gross, Daniel R. 1975. "Protein Capture and Cultural Development in the Amazon Basin." *American Anthropologist*. 77(3): 526–49.

Idyll, C. P. 1973. "The Anchovy Crisis." *Scientific American*. 228(6): 22–29.

Kaplan, L., T. Lynch, and E. E. Smith, Jr. 1973. "Early Cultivated Beans (*Phaseolus vulgaris*) from an Intermontane Peruvian Valley." *Science*. 179: 76–77.

Keatinge, Richard W. 1974. "Chimú Rural Administration Centers in the Moche Valley, Peru." *World Archaeology*. 6(1): 66–82.

Lanning, Edward P. 1967. *Peru Before the Incas*. Englewood Cliffs, N.J.: Prentice-Hall.

Lathrap, Donald W. 1968. "Relationships Between Mesoamerica and the Andean Areas." In *Handbook of Middle American Indians*, vol. 4. Austin: University of Texas Press.

Lumbreras, Luis G. 1974. *The Peoples and Cultures of Ancient Peru*, trans. Betty J. Meggers. Washington, D.C.: Smithsonian Institution Press.

Lynch, T. F. 1971. "Preceramic Transhumance in the Callejón de Huaylas, Peru." *American Antiquity*. 36: 139–48.

MacNeish, Richard S., A. Nelken-Turner, and A. Garcia Cook. 1970. *Second Annual Report of the Ayacucho Archaeological Botanical Project*. Andover, Mass.: Peabody Foundation.

MacNeish, Richard S., Thomas C. Patterson, and David L. Browman. 1975. *The Central Peruvian Prehistoric Interaction Sphere*. Andover, Mass.: Peabody Foundation.

Menzel, Dorothy. 1959. "The Inca Occupation of the South Coast of Peru." *Southwestern Journal of Anthropology*. 15(2): 125–42.

Mitchell, William P. 1973. "A Preliminary Report on Irrigation and Community in the Central Peruvian Highlands." Paper presented at 72nd Annual Meeting of the American Anthropological Association, New Orleans.

Morris, C. and D. E. Thompson. 1970. "Huanaco Viejo: An Inca Administrative Centre." *American Antiquity*. 35: 344–62.

Moseley, Michael E. 1972. "Subsistence and Demography: An Example of Interaction from Prehistoric Peru." *Southwestern Journal of Anthropology*. 28(1): 25–49.

———. 1975. *The Maritime Foundations of Andean Civilization*. Menlo Park, Calif.: Cummings Publishing Company.

Murra, John. 1958. "On Inca Political Structure." In *Systems of Political Control and Bureaucracy in Human Society*, ed. V. F. Ray. Seattle: University of Washington Press.

———. 1965. "Herds and Herders in the Inca State." In *Man, Culture and Animals*. Washington, D.C.: American Association for the Advancement of Science.

Murra, John and Craig Morris. 1976. "Dynastic Oral Tradition, Administrative Records, and Archaeology in the Andes." *World Archaeology*. 7(3): 269–79.

Parsons, James J. and William M. Denevan. 1967. "Pre-Columbian Ridged Fields." *Scientific American.* 217: 92–100.

Parsons, Jeffrey. 1968. "An Estimate of Size and Population for Middle Horizon Tiahuanaco, Bolivia." *American Antiquity.* 33(2): 243–45.

———. 1977. Personal communication with author.

Parsons, Jeffrey and Norbert Psuty. 1975. "Sunken Fields and Prehispanic Subsistence on the Peruvian Coast." *American Antiquity.* 40: 259–82.

Parsons, Mary. 1970. "Preceramic Subsistence on the Peruvian Coast." *American Antiquity.* 35: 292–303.

Patterson, Thomas C. 1966. "Early Cultural Remains on the Central Coast of Peru." *Nawpa Pacha.* 4: 145–55.

———. 1971a. "Chavín: An Interpretation of Its Spread and Influence." In *Dumbarton Oaks Conference on Chavin,* ed. E. Benson. Dumbarton Oaks, Washington, D.C.

———. 1971b. "Central Peru: Its Population and Economy." *Archaeology.* 24(4): 316–21.

Patterson, Thomas C. and Edward P. Lanning. 1964. "Changing Settlement Patterns on the Central Peruvian Coast." *Nawpa Pacha.* 2: 113–23.

Patterson, Thomas C. and M. E. Moseley. 1968. "Late Preceramic and Early Ceramic Cultures of the Central Coast of Peru." *Nawpa Pacha.* 6: 115–33.

Pickersgill, B. 1969. "The Archaeological Record of Chile Peppers (*Capsicum spp.*) and the Sequence of Plant Domestication in Peru." *American Antiquity.* 34: 54–61.

Pickersgill, B. and A. Bunting. 1969. "Cultivated Plants and the Kon-Tiki Theory." *Nature.* 222: 225–27.

Prescott, W. H. 1908. *History of the Conquest of Peru.* London and New York: Everyman's Library.

Rowe, J. H. 1946. "Inca Culture at the Time of the Spanish Conquest." *Bureau of American Ethnology Bulletin,* no. 143. 2: 183–331. Smithsonian Institution, Washington, D.C.

———. 1967. "Form and Meaning in Chavín Art." In *Peruvian Archaeology: Selected Readings.* Palo Alto: Peek Publishers.

Rowe, J. H., D. Collier, and G. Willey. 1950. "Reconnaissance Notes on the Site of Huari, near Ayacucho, Peru." *American Antiquity.* 16: 120–37.

Rowe, J. H. and D. Menzel, eds. 1961. *Peruvian Archaeology.* Berkeley: University of California Press.

Sanders, William T. and Joseph Marino. 1970. *New World Prehistory.* Englewood Cliffs, N.J.: Prentice-Hall.

Schaedel, R. P. 1971. "The City and the Origin of the State in America." Paper read at the 38th International Congress of Americanists, Buenos Aires.

Service, E. 1975. *Origins of the State and Civilization.* New York: W. W. Norton.

Thompson, Donald. 1968. "The Archaeological Evaluation of Ethnohistoric Evidences on Inca Culture." In *Anthropological Archeology in the Americas*, ed. B. J. Meggers. Anthropological Society of Washington. Washington, D.C.

Towle, Margaret A. 1961. *The Ethnobotany of Pre-Columbian Peru*. Chicago: Aldine.

Von Hagen, Victor W. 1952. "America's Oldest Roads." *Scientific American*. 187: 17–21.

―――. 1965. *The Desert Kingdoms of Peru*. London: Weidenfeld and Nicolson.

Willey, Gordon R. 1962. "The Early Great Art Styles and the Rise of Pre-Columbian Civilizations." *American Anthropologist*. 64: 1–14.

Wing, Elizabeth S. 1973. "Utilization of Animal Resources in the Andes." Report NSF GS 3021. Florida State Museum, Gainsville, Florida.

―――. 1973. "Animal Domestication in the Andes." Paper presented at the XII International Congress of Prehistoric and Protohistoric Sciences, Chicago.

16

Patterns of Cultural Change in Prehistoric North America

As Europeans invaded the interior of North America in the sixteenth and seventeenth centuries, they frequently encountered what they assumed were the relics of ancient high civilizations: thousands of large earthen mounds, some nearly as large as the greatest Egyptian pyramids, dotted every major river valley of the East, and in the Southwest the colonists stumbled upon large, neatly planned adobe towns that had obviously once been inhabited by thousands.

With an ethnocentrism characteristic of the age, the Europeans assumed that these impressive works had been constructed by the Celts, the Romans, or perhaps the Vikings; but they simply could not accept the possibility that the builders had been ancestors of the poor and "degenerate" Native Americans they saw about them. Some of the colonists even blamed the Indians for massacring what the Europeans be-

16.1
A Works Progress Administration (WPA)-sponsored archaeological excavation in Louisiana in the early 1930s. Many such projects were conducted at this time in various states.

lieved to be an ancient "superior" American race—the ultimate in adding insult to injury, given the Indians' eventual fate.

The truth, of course, is that these mounds and abandoned settlements had indeed been built by Native Americans many centuries before the Europeans arrived, and we now know that these ancient Americans had begun to travel much the same road to cultural complexity as had the people of Mesoamerica, Peru, and the Old World.

Prehistoric North American cultures are often dismissed as relatively unimportant because they were "contact cultures," meaning that their development was influenced by contact with the complex cultures of ancient Mesoamerica; and maize and other domesticated plants, as well as some aesthetic and religious elements, were indeed introduced into North America from the South. It is also true that, according to some criteria, aboriginal American cultures never reached the level of complexity attained in Mesoamerica, Mesopotamia, or in the other "independent" and ancient centers of cultural evolution: Cahokia, the largest prehistoric North America settlement, in East St. Louis, Illinois, of all places, probably had a maximum population of about 40,000, far fewer than the hundreds of thousands of people at Teotihuacán; the irrigation and agricultural systems of North America are dwarfed by those of Peru; and nowhere in North America were there written languages or imperially administered political and economic systems. Perhaps most significantly, no settlement in North America was composed of groups specializing in many diverse but interdependent economic and social activities—almost everyone was either a farmer or a forager.

But the native North Americans did develop some aspects of cultural complexity, and they did so largely independently. Moreover, the ecological and cultural reasons North American cultures did not exactly parallel those of Mexico or Peru provide some insights into the general evolution of culture.

Intensive archaeological research in North America has been in progress for many decades, and we should know more about developments there than virtually anywhere else in the world, given the high ratio of archaeologists per square kilometer. But, unfortunately, American archaeologists too have yielded to the temptation of giving most of their time and effort to rich tombs and large towns. And with the curious prevalent mentality that placidly accepts the conversion of vast ancient Native American cultural resources into parking lots and hamburger stands, the archaeological record of North America is disappearing at such a rapid rate that we shall never know many things about the prehistory of the continent.

The old, sometimes pejorative myths about Indians are now giving way in some circles to new ones stressing the social harmony, ecological purity, and superior metaphysics of ancient Native Americans. As with all cultures, there is much to admire about ancient North Americans, but the evidence suggests that most of the Indians of the last 1,500 years were very much like people in other evolving societies in the ancient world: harried, small-time farmers, worrying about this year's drought and next year's deluge, shifting their crops from year to year as they exhausted the soil and timber of one place after another, and as enmeshed in slavery, exploitation, and warfare as any ancient Chinese, Egyptian, or European.

The Ecological Setting

By about 5000 B.C. the huge glacial ice sheets that once covered much of eastern North America had retreated into Canada, and the distribution of plant and animal species in this region was roughly similar to that of the recent past. Ecologically, the North American East is extremely varied, including tropical swamps, deciduous and coniferous forests, grasslands, lush river valleys, coastal estuaries, and many subtle gradations between these various environmental zones (Figure 16.2).

Most of eastern North America is much farther from the equator than all the other areas where early complex societies developed independently, with the exception of North China; this is significant because northern latitudes have less solar radiation and fewer frost-free days, and thus lower absolute agricultural potential than tropical environments, *assuming a primitive agricultural technology*. Also, nowhere in eastern North America are there extensive, well-watered plains where vegetative cover was sufficiently thin that large-scale agriculture was possible without extensive land clearing and weeding, although in some coastal and riverine environments, plants and animals were sufficiently diverse and accessible that sedentary communities could be established on essentially a hunting and gathering economy.

Archaic Cultures of Eastern North America

The Archaic period (between about 8000 and about 2000 B.C.) is often described as one of cultural stasis in eastern North America, for it was less eventful here than in other areas of the world. With the gradual establishment of essentially modern distributions of plant and animal species after 8000 B.C., North American cultures assumed many different forms, as local environments evoked varying adaptations.

In the early part of this period, hunting was the primary food source in most areas, with fishing, nut collecting, and plant exploitation gaining importance only slowly (Ford 1974: 392). Many groups lived a highly mobile life, following carefully scheduled seasonal rounds and exploiting hundreds of plant and animal species as each became available with the changing seasons. Archaic hunters and gatherers in the lower Ohio Valley, for example, established fall camps in the uplands to harvest hickory nuts, and then moved back to the river bottoms in later fall and winter to hunt deer and migratory fowl. In spring they fished the backwater sloughs and ponds, then collected mussels and snails during the summer when they also harvested sunflower

16.2
Archaeological culture areas of North America.

seeds, pigweed, marsh elder, grapes, strawberries, and other plant foods (Fowler 1971: 393). And as with all hunters and gatherers, population densities were low and quite stable, although the size of social groups fluctuated with the seasons, with larger groups coming together when food was plentiful but dispersing into microbands of several families during the leaner seasons. Procurement areas were large, and cultural complexity quite low.

Some groups living in coastal zones did not make these seasonal treks, because their resources were concentrated for them by the juxta-position of the littoral and terrestrial environments, and it was prob-ably in these areas that the first sedentary communities appeared.

Copper, shell, exotic flint, and other commodities were traded hand to hand, but in low and highly variable volumes.

Beginning about 4000 B.C., however, population densities were apparently on the rise, and several important ecological changes were underway. Nut collecting and hunting remained important food sources, but people were broadening their diets to include increasing quantities of fruits, the seeds of various annual plants (e.g., goosefoot and sunflowers), fish, and other plant and animal species.

New subsistence technologies and strategies were being incorpo-rated into the hunting and gathering systems in order of their "cost" in terms of the required investments of time and energy. Fishing, for example, was largely ignored in the immediate post-Pleistocene era, even though the rivers of eastern North America contained such rich supplies of fish and other aquatic animal life that large sedentary com-munities were supported on these resources in later millennia. Since the mixed conifer and hardwood forests of the East contain few edible plants or animals during much of the year, fishing, when it finally be-came of widespread significance shortly before 3500 B.C., opened large woodland areas to human habitation.

ARCHAIC ADAPTATIONS AND PLANT DOMESTICATION

The richness of the eastern woodlands, with their large game, abundant rivers and streams, nuts, fruits, and other foods, and the intricate and skillful exploitation strategies of Native Americans in these areas com-bined to produce a balanced, flexible way of life of such "efficiency," to use Joseph Caldwell's (1971) term, that this way of life was not easily altered by the introduction of maize, beans, and other Mesoamerican domesticates.

Robert Dunnell (1967) has devised a classification of Archaic settlement and subsistence systems that provides a useful framework within which to view the evolution of agriculture in eastern North America. He distinguishes between *specialized* subsistence strategies, such as maize agriculture or caribou hunting, in which primary reliance is placed on just a few plant and animal species, and *generalized* subsistence systems, in which a much more diverse range of plant and animals species is utilized. Specialized systems tend to be more unstable because marked reductions in the one or two species on which these societies depend have severe consequences, whereas generalized systems can withstand the loss, say, of this year's nut crop or a poor wildfowl hunting season because they have many alternative food sources. Specialized systems, especially specialized agricultural systems, often are associated with relatively high population densities.

Another important distinction is between *sedentary* and *nonsedentary* settlement systems. In sedentary systems, of course, people reside in the same place all year long, while in nonsedentary ones the population relocates during the course of the year in response to cyclical environmental factors, such as the resources available during different seasons. Cross-cutting this distinction is another, the difference between *nucleated* and *dispersed* settlement systems. In nucleated settlements all or nearly all of the economic activities of a group are carried out by people who live in the same domestic unit, whether that be a village or a hunting and gathering band, whereas in dispersed settlements the full range of economic activities supporting a given population is carried out by people who live in separate places.

When we examine the archaeological record in eastern North America from the end of the Pleistocene to the arrival of the Europeans in the sixteenth century, we can see that after the long stasis of the Early and Middle Archaic, the overall trend was toward increasing numbers of sedentary communities that specialized first in hunting and intensive plant collecting and later in maize and bean agriculture. Throughout this period, however, the Archaic patterns of subsistence and settlement persisted in many areas.

Ceramic vessels, often associated with the agricultural way of life, appeared at several places in the American Southeast after 2500 B.C.

(Bullen 1971), but there is no necessary connection between their use and agriculture. Some have speculated that the techniques for making ceramic vessels were introduced into North America from Mexico, but it is more likely that pottery was independently invented in eastern North America at least once, and probably several times, as containers became increasingly important in plant collection and preparation. Few ancient peoples were unaware of the basic procedures of working with clay, but they would have had few incentives to make ceramic vessels as long as they were highly mobile hunters and gatherers and had access to gourds for the few rudimentary containers they might need.

Because plant remains preserve poorly in the North American East, we do not know in great detail how and when domesticated plants and agriculture were incorporated into cultural systems here. Domestication is typically a byproduct of systematic collection, and thus many native plants were undoubtedly being domesticated as, century after century, post-Pleistocene hunters and gatherers made their seasonal rounds. The sunflower (*Helianthus*), perhaps the most important North American domesticate, in its wild form was a much smaller plant with smaller seeds than are characteristic of modern varieties, but by 300 B.C. average seed size was increasing—presumably as part of the domestication process. Goosefoot (*Chenopodium*), marsh elder (*Iva*), sumpweed (*Aster*), and canary grass (*Phalaris*) were also probably being domesticated at the same time (Yarnell 1965).

The collection and domestication of these various plant species seem always and everywhere to have been much less important than hunting, fishing, and nut gathering, and there is little evidence that agriculture was being practiced at this time. That is, little energy was invested in modifying the environments of sunflowers and these other plants through hoeing, watering, or weeding. Melvin Fowler notes that most of the native plants apparently domesticated in the East are species that prefer open, disturbed areas, such as would have been provided by the refuse piles that must have become increasingly available as hunters and gatherers cluttered the landscape with snail and clam shells, fish bones, and other debris (1971).

Squash, pumpkin, and domesticated gourds were probably introduced into eastern North America from the Southwest at about 1000 B.C. (Ford 1974), but they do not appear to have been important foods —although gourds may have been widely grown and used as containers. There is no evidence of maize during this period.

16.3
The Poverty Point site in northern Louisiana includes an enormous octagonal
arrangement of concentric earth works (some of which have been washed away by
an arm of the Mississippi River). The site may have served as a redistributive
center for hunters and gatherers in this area.

Between 5000 B.C. and about 1500 B.C., while the domestication
of sunflowers and a few other plants was in progress, there were other
important cultural changes. At the Poverty Point site in Louisiana, vast
earthworks (Figure 16.3) were constructed sometime between 1300 and
200 B.C. by people who seem to have been living in large, planned villages. The Poverty Point people buried some of their dead under elaborate conical burial mounds, and they also engaged in a range of arts
and crafts that bespeak some degree of occupational specialization.
Skilled stoneworkers made vessels out of steatite and sandstone, tubular
pipes out of clay and stone, and axes, adzes, saws, weights, and other
implements of hard stones. The economic basis of the Poverty Point
cultures may have included some limited agriculture (Webb 1968), but
no substantial evidence of this exists; perhaps the larger Poverty Point
centers were redistribution centers for surrounding communities of
people still following the Archaic foraging-collecting way of life.

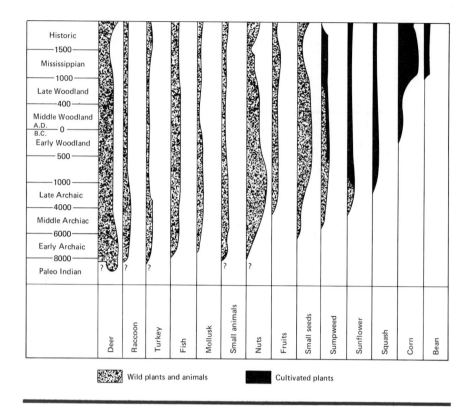

16.4
Estimated subsistence changes in the prehistoric Middle West. The stippled areas represent wild plants and animals, and the solid areas represent domesticates. The thickness of the areas reflects the relative importance of a resource.

The first and second millennia B.C. were a time of significant change in many areas of North America. Burial cults, comprising large earthen mounds, intentionally broken ornaments and tools buried with infants, and significant variations in mortuary wealth are found at Archaic sites from Newfoundland (Tuck 1971) to the lower Ohio Valley (Dragoo 1963). Dunnell (personal communication 1977) suggests that the increased ceremonialism and burial cults were the focus of re-distributive networks, as Late Archaic peoples gradually evolved settlement patterns in which several dispersed sedentary groups exploited local environments, but came together at certain times and locations to exchange products. In many areas of the North American East, particularly in relatively less-productive environments, such redistributional economies would have been more efficient—that is, supported more people with less energy output—than the ancient seasonal hunting and gathering rounds.

Much remains to be learned about Archaic developments in general, but the appearance of increased population densities, sedentary communities, mortuary ceremonialism, public architecture, and improved technologies indicates that some aspects of increasing cultural complexity were already present long before the appearance of agricultural economies.

Agriculture and the Woodland Period (800 B.C. to A.D. 800)

Between about 800 B.C. and A.D. 800, population densities in many parts of eastern North America increased sharply, maize agriculture became the basic subsistence strategy (Figure 16.4), gigantic earthworks were constructed, interregional trade expanded, and large nucleated settlements appeared. This era of change, usually referred to as the *Early Woodland period,* is associated with two major cultural traditions, the *Adena,* centered in the Ohio River Valley, and the *Hopewell,* centered in southern Ohio (Figure 16.5). These cultures are roughly contemporary, although the Hopewell was considerably larger and more elaborate; both are defined on the basis of certain styles of pottery, engraved stone tablets, textiles, and worked bone and copper.

Our picture of Adena and Hopewell life is somewhat distorted because research has focused on larger settlements and rich tombs, and although there is much to be learned from these sources, they tell us comparatively little about general subsistence and settlement.

The construction of Hopewell and Adena ceremonial mounds began with the clearing of a large area and the deposition of a thick layer of clean sand; then a large open or enclosed wood structure was erected; individual burials were made within the structure and the graves covered over with small mounds of earth; and finally, the wooden enclosure was burned to the ground, and the resulting ash layer covered over with layers of earth and stone. Human remains were sometimes cremated and only the ashes interred, while at other times successive burials were made, with each new group of corpses covered over with a deep blanket of earth.

Grave goods are not particularly profuse in Adena mounds, but Hopewell tombs often contain finely worked copper, pipestone, mica, obsidian, meteoric iron, shell, tortoise shell, shark and alligator teeth,

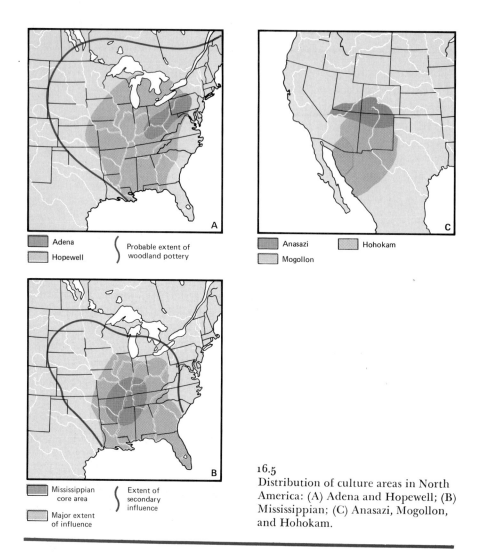

Adena
Hopewell
} Probable extent of woodland pottery

Anasazi   Hohokam
Mogollon

Mississippian core area
Major extent of influence
} Extent of secondary influence

16.5
Distribution of culture areas in North America: (A) Adena and Hopewell; (B) Mississippian; (C) Anasazi, Mogollon, and Hohokam.

bear teeth, ceramics, and other commodities; there is also evidence of the ultimate grave good—sacrificed humans. Adena and Hopewell settlements and mounds increased in size and number in the centuries before about A.D. 400, and major earthworks were often built near the burial mounds.

These burials appear to have been excellent reflectors of the dead person's rank and status within the community. Joseph Tainter (1973) carried out a statistical analysis of more than 500 Hopewell burials and concluded that there were six discrete levels of status within the Hopewell community, corresponding to six different forms of burial, ranging from simple holes in the ground to massive mounds in which the corpse was accompanied by the finest goods. In some Adena and Hopewell mounds infants and juveniles were found buried with great ceremony and rich goods, indicating no doubt the inheritance of rank and prestige and the control of the society's resources by a limited number of its people.

A centralized administration seems to be evident in the later Hopewell buildings and earthworks, many of which were precisely planned and relatively expensive to construct. One of the many puzzling things about these mound complexes is that in many areas they do not seem to have any associated residential zones. Some archaeologists assumed that any society capable of building such impressive works must certainly have been composed of sedentary agriculturalists, but early Adena and Hopewell peoples for the most part probably hunted and gathered essentially the same plant and animal species as did their ancestors, with deer, ducks, small mammals, fish, snails, mussels, pigweed, lambsquarter, sunflowers, and nuts providing much of their nutrition. Outside the Adena and Hopewell spheres of influence, the Archaic subsistence and settlement systems appear to have remained essentially unchanged (Dragoo 1976: 18–19).

Although domesticated maize was found at very few Hopewell and Adena sites, many later developments of this period, such as the in-

16.6
Beads made from freshwater pearls. From a burial in the American Middle West.

16.7
Great Serpent Mound, an Adena construction near Cincinnati.

creased mortuary complexity and the increasing size and number of
settlements and mounds, may have been directly tied to the incorporation of maize agriculture into subsistence systems. Settlements were
largely confined to broad alluvial valleys having the minimum 120
frost-free days a year necessary for maize to mature. Maize agriculture,
conducted on a swidden system, probably was begun in these zones late
in the first millennium B.C. (Farnsworth 1973; Prufer 1965; Struever
1964).

The earliest widespread occurrence of maize in the North American East was shortly after 300 B.C., but it remained only a minor part
of the subsistence base until about A.D. 300. Maize is very sensitive to
frost and length of daylight, and a substantial amount of time and cultivation was probably required to produce varieties that could mature
in the shorter days of northern areas. So adaptable is the plant, however, that it was a staple as far north as Ontario, Canada, by the time
the Europeans arrived in the sixteenth century. Primitive strains of
maize had such small cobs when first introduced from Mexico that con-

siderable selective breeding was required before it was worthwhile to do all the work of clearing land, weeding, and harvesting necessary for successful maize agriculture here. Nor was the Adena-Hopewell heartland so impoverished that hunters and gatherers were desperately trying to improve their subsistence base. Estimates of resources around the Hopewell settlement at Scoville, in the lower Illinois Valley, indicate that "within a half-hour's walk . . . there would annually be from 182,000 to 426,000 bushels of nuts and 48,000 to 484,000 bushels of acorns, 100 to 840 deer, 10,000 to 20,000 squirrels, and 200 turkeys. Not computed were seeds, fruits, smaller animals, fish, mussels, and migratory birds (6 million mallards were estimated to be in the Illinois River Valley in 1955)" (Jennings 1974: 232). Given these abundant environments, it is not surprising that maize agriculture apparently appeared first in poorer, more marginal environments and displaced hunting and gathering in the lushest environments only much later (Dunnell 1977).

The importation and circulation of copper from northern Michigan, shell from the Gulf Coast, and other exotic commodities suggest considerable contact between many of the settlements in this Hopewell interaction sphere. Within this sphere artifact styles and subsistence systems were very similar, but there is no evidence of state-level political centralization. Most of the Hopewell and Adena communities were small sedentary groups of hunters and gatherers who built the burial mounds and ceremonial complexes for reasons that perhaps had to do with redistribution and population control. Whereas Archaic hunters and gatherers met their needs by following seasonal rounds and exploiting a diversity of resources, Hopewell communities accomplished the same thing by exchanging products among themselves.

Comparatively little is known about daily life for the mass of the Hopewell or Adena peoples. The few houses excavated seem to be rectangular or ovoid constructions supported on posts and covered with bark or mats (Jennings 1974: 232). Most people apparently lived in small hamlets composed of a few such houses and associated pits and refuse piles. Some craft specialization is evident in the finely knapped flint and stone and in other sophisticated artifacts, and most of these communities were probably organized around a "big-man" and his favored lineage. The group in charge of redistribution could apparently call on a greater share of luxury items and even command the sacrifice of other people at their deaths.

THE HOPEWELL "COLLAPSE"

Shortly after A.D. 400, burial mounds and earthworks appear to have lost their importance in Hopewell and Adena communities, and the extensive trade networks that formerly had kept in circulation large quantities of exotic items seem to have broken down. Small burial mounds were built over the next several centuries, but the general trend was toward a "reordering of priorities" (Dragoo 1976: 22).

With Hopewell as with the Olmec, the Harappan cities, and many other "collapses" of ancient societies, archaeologists have often viewed these developments as the result of climate changes, warfare, disease, or a combination of these and other factors (Ford 1974). It may also be that the Hopewellian "decline" was an expression of the declining importance of the population control and redistribution functions of these ceremonial centers subsequent to the widespread adoption of maize agriculture, with its greater productivity.

Whatever the reasons behind these changes, the agricultural way of life *was* appearing over much of the North American East after A.D. 400, and as it spread, population densities increased and communities everywhere became stable and sedentary. Without plows or an advanced technology the most productive agricultural strategy was to burn off the vegetation on rich, well-drained alluvial plains, plant maize and a few other crops, do some minor weeding and cultivation during the growing season, and then harvest and store the maize. After one or two seasons a given plot of land became unproductive, and the areas of cultivation—and perhaps the whole village—would have to be shifted elsewhere.

Perhaps because of competition for land, there seems to have been a marked increase in interregional hostilities shortly after A.D. 700, and by about A.D. 800 many settlements were surrounded by defensive stockades (Dragoo 1976: 20).

Mississippian Cultures (A.D. 700 to A.D. 1650)

From about A.D. 600 to about A.D. 1650, the agricultural way of life spread over much of eastern North America, accompanied by a marked increase in the level of cultural complexity. Many societies of this pe-

16.8
A 1930s photograph of stone "blanks" (stone worked but not fashioned into tools)
from a Mississippian site. Massive "offerings" of such artifacts were frequently
enclosed in burial mounds in eastern North America.

riod are collectively referred to as the *Mississippian* culture, whose
most common artifacts are types of shell-tempered pottery, tiny triangular arrowheads, and truncated pyramid mounds, but even these do not
appear in all communities identified as Mississippian (Jennings 1974:
248). Collectively, Mississippian communities represent the high point
of cultural evolution in aboriginal North America, particularly in
terms of geographical extent of influence, ceremonialism, public works,
technology, population density, and social stratification (ibid.: 246).

Artifacts and mounds of the Mississippian type first appeared in
the lower Mississippi Valley, but they soon spread into the Tennessee
River drainage and by A.D. 800 to 900 occurred over much of the Ohio
and Missouri river valleys (see Figure 16.5) (Dragoo 1976: 20). Between A.D. 900 and A.D. 1600, large towns with impressive ceremonial
centers were built from Florida to northern Illinois, and from Ohio to
eastern Oklahoma, but the heartland of this culture was in the central
Mississippi Valley.

The largest Mississippian complex is Cahokia, in East St. Louis,
Illinois, where the central pyramid is over 30 meters high, 200 by 330
meters at the base, and covers an area of more than 6.5 hectares (Figure
16.9) (Fowler 1969). The 30,000 to 40,000 people estimated to have

16.9

A large central mound at Cahokia, a major Mississippian settlement in East Saint Louis, Illinois. Photograph was taken several decades ago, before the site was greatly damaged by looters and construction projects.

lived in the environs of Cahokia at about A.D. 1200 were distributed in four large towns, five smaller towns, and about forty-three villages (Pfeiffer 1977: 425), and no doubt people living within a large area around the settlement had some contact with Cahokia (Porter 1969). Some elite groups were permanent residents of Cahokia and other ceremonial centers, but the vast majority of the people apparently still lived in hamlets some distance from the centers, practiced maize agriculture supplemented by other crops, and did considerable hunting and gathering.

Cahokia is an impressive site, but it was probably not the urban-state center some have considered it. The extensive rebuilding of residential areas and the incremental nature of the mound construction, together with Cahokia's estimated trade and market functions, are consistent with a developed chiefdom (Ford 1974: 404).

Garbage from most Mississippian sites reflects a diverse food base, including bear, elk, deer, small mammals, waterfowl, shellfish, snails, turtles, berries, seeds, and nuts. The addition of beans to the agricultural system sometime around A.D. 900 probably greatly strengthened the role of agriculture in the economy (Ritchie 1969: 276), since beans provide a cheap, reliable source of protein. Fishing and waterfowl hunting still contributed greatly to the diet, however (Jennings 1974: 256).

Mississippian village residences were usually rectangular or ovoid wattle-and-daub structures, supported by internal wooden beams, with floors of packed earth (Jennings 1974: 256). The highest Mississippian population densities were in the rich river bottoms where it was possible to combine maize and bean farming with waterfowl exploitation (Smith 1974). In some areas the river annually renewed the fertility of the soil through alluviation, and permanent field agriculture was possible.

Our view of Mississippian life comes from both archaeological and ethnological sources, as Mississippian communities were still extant when the Europeans arrived in the sixteenth century. These colonists described intensely stratified societies where the elites were able to draw almost without limit on the resources of the communities. At Cahokia, for example, one adult male was buried with 20,000 shell beads, 800 arrowheads, sheets of mica and copper, and more than 50 young women who had been ritually strangled and arranged in neat rows (Pfeiffer 1977: 429). There are many other mortuary indications of social stratification, and a fairly complex administrative hierarchy must have existed to organize the monumental construction projects and the circulation of copper, chert, mica, shell, obsidian, and agricultural commodities.

Ethnographic accounts of Mississippian communities as they existed in the sixteenth and seventeenth centuries—long after the culmination of Mississippian culture—describe an intensely class-conscious society in which nobles and warriors alternately exploited and abused the *stinkards,* or commoners and slaves who made up most of the societies. The upper classes were slavishly obeyed and respected. They frequently married the lower classes, but the aristocrat could divorce or kill the lower-ranking spouse, given even minor cause.

THE SOUTHERN CULT

Many late Mississippian and later period mounds and burials contain ornaments, pottery, and other artifacts decorated with motifs almost identical to some Mesoamerican motifs, including plumed serpents, eagles, jaguars, and warriors carrying trophy heads, as well as the fifty-two-year calendar round. These motifs are found most frequently at the larger settlements and appear to have crossed regional cultural boundaries. Collectively, they are taken as evidence of a southern (Mesoamerican) religious cult (Willey 1966: 305). Opinions differ on their significance in terms of contacts with Mesoamerica, some considering them evidence of quite direct and sustained contacts, others seeing them as minor borrowings with little more than an accidental connection to Mesoamerican cultures. The southern cult, as well as the Adena and Hopewell mortuary ceremonialism, likely achieved importance in North America only after cultural complexity in the North had reached a stage where these elements "made sense" in terms of northern societies.

THE MISSISSIPPIAN COLLAPSE

After A.D. 1000 Mississippian "colonists" began to emigrate from the cultural heartland, and some groups may have founded quasimilitary enclaves in Alabama, Missouri, and elsewhere. Conceivably, these daughter communities were sent with the express purpose of extending Mississippian influence over other cultural groups, but an essentially Archaic way of life persisted in many outlying areas for centuries after European contact.

In contrast to most other ancient cultures, there is little question about the immediate cause of the decline of Mississippian culture. The Indians had no natural immunities to measles, smallpox, and cholera, and the densely settled Mississippian areas provided an ideal medium for the rapid spread of these highly contagious diseases (Stewart 1973). Within a few decades of European contact in the sixteenth century, the once highly integrated and proud Mississippian people, and other cultures as well, were a much reduced and poverty-stricken group, living amid thousands of abandoned settlements and eroding mounds attesting to their former greatness.

In summary of cultural developments in the North American East, we see that, point for point, peoples in this area followed the familiar script of cultural evolution. From a hunting and gathering base, specialized hunting and minor plant exploitation gradually gave way to an intricate "broad-spectrum" hunting-foraging economy, in which

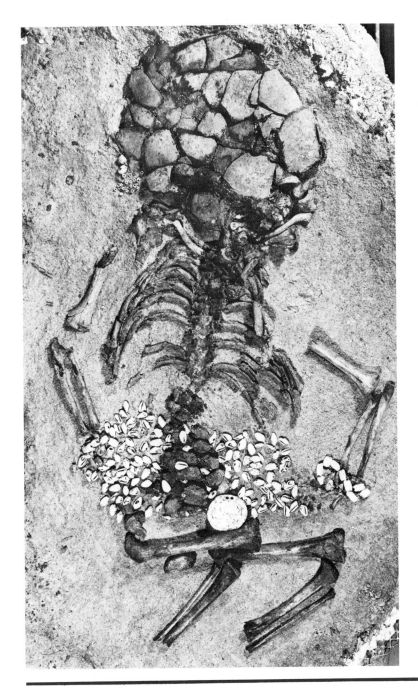

16.10
For many thousands of years eastern North American peoples used beads and shells to decorate corpses, as in this seventeenth-century A.D. child burial in North Carolina.

fishing, nut collecting, shellfishing, and other activities were added to
the subsistence repertoire according to what was probably a largely un-
cognized but very precise "cost-benefit" analysis; then, after centuries
of manipulation and selection, maize-based agriculture displaced less-
productive economies in many areas, with consequent increasing population densities and the establishment of large sedentary communities.
Once food production reached certain levels, the familiar harbingers
of increasing cultural complexity, such as the spread of religious and
stylistic traditions, monumental architecture, mortuary cults, and increasingly diverse and interdependent arts and crafts, also appeared.
Social and religious hierarchies emerged as "efficient" ways to make the
decisions necessary for the perpetuation of these increasingly complex
economies, and the institutionalization of prestige and privilege may
have arisen as an effective way of reducing competition between these
populations and of maximizing administrative efficiency by providing
training to members of favored lineages.

In these essentials, then, there is little to differentiate the sequence
of cultural evolution in North America from that in Mesoamerica, except that, given the available domesticates and technology, most of eastern North America had less agricultural potential than Mesoamerica,
causing these northern cultures to stabilize at a much lower level of
complexity. Had the Europeans not invaded and introduced their diseases, true state-level societies might well have evolved from the remnants of the Mississippian climax, but only if food production could
have been increased drastically through technological, agricultural, or
administrative innovations.

Prehistoric Agriculturalists in Southwestern North America

In our survey of early complex societies, the peoples of southwestern
North America must serve in a sense as negative examples, for although
they adopted maize-based agriculture, aggregated into large towns, and
evolved some occupational and administrative specialization, they never
produced class-structured, hierarchically organized, economically differentiated societies. Nor is there any mystery about this lack of development: southwestern cultures reached the threshold of cultural com-

16.11
A sixteenth-century painting by Jacques le Moyne of the burial of a Florida Indian chief. Arrows have been driven into the ground around the grave and the chief's houses (left rear) are being ceremonially burned.

plexity, but stalled there because their physical environment lacked the agricultural or economic productivity to support further development, given the available technology.

THE ECOLOGICAL SETTING

The dramatic mountains, crystal skies, and spaciousness of the Southwest make it an attractive place to live—if one has access to a municipal water system and a modern market and transport system. But from the perspective of a hunter and gatherer or subsistence farmer, the majority of the Southwest is a dry and barren land, with few rivers or streams, no verdant hardwood forests, and an extreme climate of searing summers and bitterly cold winters.

Analysis of tree rings and other botanical evidence suggests that over most of the last 10,000 years the Southwest has usually been at least as hot and dry as it is today. Two periods, however, seem to have been considerably more arid: between 5000 and 3000 B.C. and for

16.12

A typical adobe village in the southwestern United States. The photograph was taken in the 1930s, but the construction methods and village type illustrated go back many centuries.

about twenty-five years near the end of the thirteenth century A.D. These droughts may have reduced population densities and forced changes in subsistence practices, but the evidence is uncertain (Rice 1975).

EARLY AGRICULTURALISTS

Southwestern agricultural cultures, like those of Mesoamerica, evolved from the settlement and subsistence systems of hunters and gatherers who worked the deserts of North America (Willey 1966: 181). Hunters and gatherers probably moved into the Southwest during the moister Pleistocene periods, perhaps 20,000 or more years ago, and at first they may have relied principally on hunting. The increasing aridity of the post-Pleistocene period brought a growing dependence on seed and plant collecting and small mammal hunting, and by about 5000 B.C. the efficient *Cochise* desert foraging cultures (later known to some as the *Picosa* cultures [C. Irwin-Williams 1968]) were established over much of the Southwest. These people typically worked from base camps near permanent springs and in rock shelters, but they moved with the seasons as various resources became available at different elevations in the foothills and mountains.

Domesticated maize appeared in the Southwest by about 3500 B.C. but had little economic importance at first and was apparently not cultivated until about 3,000 years later, when three distinctive and largely contemporary cultural traditions evolved from the Picosa base: the *Hohokam,* which was restricted to a relatively small area; the more extensive *Anasazi* Pueblo; and the *Mogollon,* or western Pueblo (Jennings 1974: 283) (see Figure 16.5).

THE HOHOKAM

The Hohokam peoples, who flourished in the Salt and Gila river valleys (Arizona) between about 300 B.C. and A.D. 1200, apparently represent the confluence of Archaic hunting and gathering traditions and direct stimulation from Mesoamerican cultures. Some archaeologists (Emil Haury 1976) have concluded that late Hohokam house construction, ceramics, turquoise mosaic ornaments and other artifacts are so similar to Mesoamerican examples that they can only be the result of an immigration of Mexican people who transplanted their way of life directly to the Hohokam area, where previously there had been only hunters and gatherers (Jennings 1974: 285). It is possible, however, that Hohokam developments were made by native Archaic peoples themselves, who grafted imported agricultural and technological ideas onto their own ways of life.

One of the most interesting aspects of the Hohokam is their agricultural system. Their homeland is set in some of the driest deserts of North America, where summer temperatures have impressed even archaeological veterans of the Near East. Beginning at about 300 B.C. the Hohokam cut channels off the Salt and Gila rivers to run water to their garden plots of maize and other crops. Modern buildings have erased much of the Hohokam irrigation system, but two canals near Phoenix were over 16 kilometers long, several meters wide, and about 60 centimeters deep when first constructed. Tightly woven grass mats were probably used as gates to open and close canal segments, and earthen dams on the rivers in some places diverted water through canals for more than fifty kilometers across the desert floor, with many small branches serving individual fields.

In the recent past, southwestern Indian irrigation systems, as well as comparable agricultural systems elsewhere in the world, have been operated by a few thousand people in relatively simple tribal organizations in which no coercion, permanent authorities, or police agencies were necessary, and this might well have been the case among the Hohokam.

Although the largest irrigation systems were apparently built sometime after A.D. 800, by about A.D. 300 there were already indications of minor increases in the complexity of Hohokam cultures. Some low platform mounds, about 29 meters long, 23 meters wide, and 3 meters high, were built at about this time at the Snaketown site, and in subsequent centuries the people of Snaketown and several nearby communities built large sunken ball courts like those found in many areas of Mesoamerica. The Hohokam ball courts were east-west oriented oval depressions about 60 meters long, with 4.5- to 6-meter-high sloping earth embankments on a side (Washburn 1975: 124). Early Spanish observers of the ball game in Mesoamerica report that the objective was to try to knock a rubber ball (two of which have been found in the Southwest) through a goal using knees, elbows, or torso, and that losing players were sometimes executed. The southwestern ball courts were probably not stops on the northern road trips of the Mexican major leagues, but they do indicate very close southern affinities, as do the platform mounds. And between A.D. 900 and 1200, many other Mesoamerican elements were imported, including cotton textiles, certain ceramic motifs, pyrite mirrors, effigy vessels, cast copper bells, ear plugs, etched shell ornaments, and even parrots and macaws—probably imported from the South and kept and prized for their feathers (ibid.: 124).

Generally, however, there is little evidence in either subsistence practices, settlements, or mortuary ceremonies of evolving rank and wealth differences. Most of the Hohokam lived in small square pit houses roofed with clay and grass domes supported by a wooden pole framework. Early dwellings appear large enough for several families, but single-family residences became more popular in later periods.

Hohokam settlement patterns are not well known. There are few indications of a master plan in village layouts or of economic specialization of villages. Nor is there any suggestion that the villages were situated on the basis of defensive considerations (Willey 1966: 220–23). Every village probably repeated all the economic activities of every other village, except that some favored locations allowed a greater reliance on maize, beans, squash and other crops. Nonetheless, many atlatl dart points and arrowheads have been found at each Hohokam site, and botanical remains indicate that almost every community supplemented its diet with wild mustard, amaranths, chenopods, cactus fruits, mesquite, screwbeans, and other wild products (Washburn 1975: 124).

Between A.D. 1200 and 1400, people of the *Salado* cultures, who had been living to the north of the Hohokam, arrived in the Hohokam area and took up irrigated maize agriculture. The Hohokam and the Salado lived in close proximity for several centuries, each maintaining its distinctive artifactual and architectural styles until about A.D. 1400, when the area was nearly abandoned. Many Hohokam elements still survive in contemporary Papago Indian cultures.

THE ANASAZI

Like the Mogollon and Hohokam, the Anasazi may have developed out of Picosa desert foraging cultures, and their earliest prepottery representatives are widely known as the *Basketmaker* cultures. By the last century B.C., they were living in many sedentary settlements located on old river terraces and mesa tops or in river valleys in the high plateau country of the central Southwest. The earliest houses were circular structures of wattle-and-daub set on log bases, or semisubterranean houses whose walls were founded on cobblestone (Washburn 1975: 110). These early Anasazi did not use pottery, and although they ate maize, beans, and squash, they invested little labor in cultivating these crops, relying instead on wild foods, such as roots, bulbs, grass seeds, nuts, acorns, berries, cactus fruits, sunflowers, deer, rabbits, antelopes, and wild sheep.

After about A.D. 400 the Anasazi adopted the use of pottery and began building large pit houses, most of which were dug 30 to 180 centimeters into the ground, were circular or rectangular, from 3 to 7.5 meters in diameter, and were covered by log and mud roofs supported on center posts (Washburn 1975: 110). Interior walls were plastered with mud or faced with stone, access was through a descending passageway, and fireplaces and benches were standard furnishings. At some sites large ceremonial pit houses, or *kivas,* were built. After about A.D. 700 above-ground masonry houses were erected in some Anasazi communities, but the pit house and kiva combination continued to be the basic village type until the end of the thirteenth century A.D. (Jennings 1974: 302).

The evidence is not complete, but defensive considerations, greater exploitation of more productive strains of maize (Dickson 1975), and climatic changes beginning about A.D. 700 may have spurred the Anasazi into constructing the "cliff cities" for which they are world famous. Pollen and geological studies suggest that summer rainfall, in the form of torrential storms, increased after A.D. 700, while winter rainfall decreased, and the resulting changes in water tables and stream flows may have forced the Anasazi to congregate around larger, permanently flowing rivers (Washburn 1975: 114, but see Rice 1975). Hillsides were terraced to control erosion, and diversion canals and dams were constructed to control and store as much of the vital summer rainwater as possible. On Chapin Mesa, in the Mesa Verde area, for example, the older agricultural fields were extended by an elaborate check-dam system that added 8 or 12 hectares of cultivable land (Washburn 1975: 114). In some areas erosion forced frequent settlement relocations, and some communities met the changing agricultural conditions by scattering into small family groups; but the prevailing response was to aggregate into large towns along the major rivers. By about 1100 A.D. prosperous enclaves were established at Mesa Verde, Chaco Canyon, Canyon de Chelly, and elsewhere, and in some ways these communities represent the high point of southwestern culture. There were twelve large towns along Chaco Canyon, of which Pueblo Bonito was the largest, with over 800 rooms and perhaps 1,200 people (Figure 16.13).

By about A.D. 1150 most of the known cliff cities (Figure 16.14) in the Four Corners area had been established, all of very similar construction. Settlements grew by simple accretion; more rooms were added as needed. The remote location of the cliff towns may have had to do with defensive considerations, although defense against what enemy we do not know.

As beautiful as many late Anasazi settlements were, they do not appear to have been the work of a highly complex society. The buildings, while superbly adapted to their environment, are quite crudely constructed. There may have been minor occupational specialization in ceramic manufacture, weaving, and turquoise carving, but most if not all the people were subsistence farmers. Nor is any evidence of differential rank expressed in domestic architecture or in grave goods. Even the irrigation system, while intricate and efficient, was probably administered through simple kinship systems.

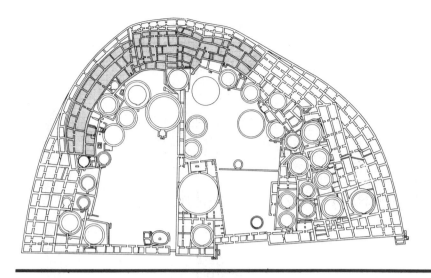

16.13
Floor plan and reconstruction of Pueblo Bonito, as it may have appeared at about
A.D. 1050.

16.14
Cliff Palace, Mesa Verde, Colorado, one of the most impressive cliff dwellings.

Shortly before 1300 B.C. many once prosperous Anasazi communities began to be abandoned, and in a short time the culture had disintegrated. People still lived in the Four Corners and adjacent areas, but at markedly reduced densities. The usual line-up of villains has been considered for the Anasazi collapse, including invaders from the North and West, drought, and changes in precipitation patterns, but once again none of these has been conclusively demonstrated to be the cause. When the Spanish arrived in the sixteenth century, they found the descendants of the Anasazi living along the Rio Grande in two- to three-storied apartment complexes in small villages, each of which was a largely autonomous political and economic unit (Washburn 1975: 118).

THE MOGOLLON

The Mogollon cultures, which also developed out of the Archaic desert foraging cultures of the last several millennia B.C., were concentrated in the mountains of east central Arizona and west central New Mexico. Sedentary villages and ceramics of the Mogollon type first appear at about 300 B.C. and over the succeeding centuries the basic housing unit changed from a crude pole-and-brush structure set over a shallow depression to a sturdy, deeply excavated pit house. By about A.D. 300 villages of about fifteen pit houses each were scattered along ridges, bluffs, and terraces, and nearly all the inhabitants of these settlements were subsisting on the maize-beans-squash complex, supplemented by many wild plants and game. Mogollon burials of this period were often simple inhumations in house floors accompanied by a few pottery vessels, turquoise ornaments, and stone tools (Washburn 1975: 119).

After about A.D. 1000 the Mogollon peoples apparently were heavily influenced by Anasazi groups, and the Swarts ruins, Mimbres Valley, New Mexico, may be an example of this. River boulders set in adobe were used to construct a large warren of conjoined rectangular rooms, access to which was apparently only through the roof, since there were no exterior doors. Inside walls were plastered with mud, and doorways led from one room to another. Storage bins, shelves, fireplaces, and benches constituted the essential furnishings (Willey 1966: 192). Corpses were frequently interred in the floors of abandoned rooms, in occupied rooms, or within the village compound; most burials were very simple, implying negligible social and economic differentiation.

The Mogollon built no pyramids, ball courts, or major irrigation systems, but they did produce an extraordinarily beautiful array of ceramics, particularly the "mimbres" ceramic forms. Much prized by collectors, these vessels are decorated with vivid figures of frogs, insects, fish, deer, and other animal life painted against black backgrounds.

The fusion of Mogollon and Anasazi cultural traditions continued through the twelfth and thirteenth centuries, and it was in this period that dramatic changes in settlement patterns occurred. Large areas in the uplands and in smaller valleys were almost totally abandoned, and settlements instead were concentrated in the major river valleys and on the larger plateaus. The small isolated hamlet-type settlement gave way in most areas to dense clusters of hamlets and to fully integrated villages that were as much as ten times the size of earlier settlements (Rice 1975: 281).

These settlement pattern changes have frequently been explained as responses to an increasingly arid environment (Schoenwetter 1962), but in a recent reexamination G. Rice (1975) argues that climatic changes were minor and that the most important factor here was increased use of a more productive strain of maize, followed by predictable population shifts and increases.

There is possible evidence of social ranking at the late Mogollon-Anasazi site of Grasshopper Pueblo (A.D. 1275 to 1400), where a few individuals were buried with particularly rich concentrations of grave goods, but mortuary variation here is no more pronounced than in many Paleolithic cultures, and little else about the society suggests any significant complexity.

In summary, the early agricultural societies of the Southwest demonstrate the obvious point that the evolution of cultural complexity is directly and indispensably tied to a certain minimum level of productivity. The peoples of the Southwest had no bias against cultural complexity, nor did they lack a domesticated plant, exposure to the "idea" of cultural complexity, or an efficient industrial and agricultural technology. They did, however, lack voluminous and stable water supplies adjacent to large, fertile fields. So did the peoples of the Valley of Mexico, of course, but the Southwest has little of the ecological complexity and generous summer rainfalls that supported cultural evolution in the Valley of Mexico.

Bibliography

Braun, D. P. 1974. "Explanatory Models for the Evolution of Coastal Adaptation in Prehistoric Eastern New England." *American Antiquity.* 39: 582–96.

Broyles, B. J. 1971. "Second Preliminary Report: The St. Albans Site, Kanawha County, West Virginia." West Virginia Geological and Economic Survey Report, Archaeological Investigation 3.

Bullen, Ripley P. 1971. "The Beginnings of Pottery in Eastern United States as Seen from Florida." *Eastern States Archaeological Federation Bulletin.* 30: 10–11.

Caldwell, Joseph. 1971. "Eastern North America." In *Prehistoric Agriculture,* ed. S. Struever. Garden City, N.Y.: Natural History Press.

Cleland, C. E. 1966. *The Prehistoric Animal Ecology and Ethnozoology of the Upper Great Lakes Region.* Museum of Anthropology, Anthropological Papers, University of Michigan, no. 29.

DeJarnette, D. L. 1967. "Alabama Pebble Tools: the Lively Complex." *Eastern States Archaeological Federation. Bulletin,* no. 26.

Dickson, D. B. 1975. "Settlement Pattern Stability and Change in the Middle Northern Rio Grande Region, New Mexico: A Test of Some Hypotheses." *American Antiquity.* 40(2): 159–71.

Dragoo, D. W. 1963. "Mounds for the Dead." *Annals of Carnegie Museum.* 37: 1–315.

———. 1976. "Some Aspects of Eastern North American Prehistory: A Review." *American Antiquity.* 41(1): 3–27.

Dunnell, R. C. 1967. "The Prehistory of Fishtrap, Kentucky: Archaeological Interpretation in Marginal Areas." Unpublished doctoral dissertation. Yale University.

———. 1977. Personal communication with author.

Farnsworth, K. B. 1973. "An Archaeological Survey of the Macoupin Valley." Illinois State Museum, Reports of Investigations, no. 26. Springfield.

Ford, R. I. 1974. "Northeastern Archeology: Past and Future Directions." In *Annual Review of Anthropology.* 3: 385–414.

Fowler, M. L. 1969. "Explorations into Cahokia Archaeology." *Illinois Archaeological Survey.* Bulletin 7.

———. 1971. "Agriculture and Village Settlement in the North American East: The Central Mississippi Valley Area, a Case History." In *Prehistoric Agriculture,* ed. S. Struever. Garden City, N.Y.: Natural History Press.

———. 1975. "A Pre-Columbian Urban Center on the Mississippi." *Scientific American.* August.

Gorenstein, Shirley, R. G. Farbis, J. M. Campbell, L. S. Cordell, D. K. Washburn, H. T. Irwin, and P. Tolstoy, eds., 1975. *North America.* New York: St. Martin's Press.

Griffin, J. B. 1967. "Eastern North American Archaeology: A Summary." *Science.* 156: 175–91.

Haury, Emil W. 1976. *The Hohokam: Desert Farmers and Craftsmen.* Tucson: University of Arizona Press.

Hill, James N. 1966. "A Prehistoric Community in Eastern Arizona." *Southwestern Journal of Anthropology.* 22(1): 9–30.

———. 1970. *Broken K Pueblo: Prehistoric Social Organization in the American Southwest.* Tucson: University of Arizona Press.

Houart, Gail L. 1971. "Koster: A Stratified Archaic Site in the Illinois Valley." Illinois State Museum, Reports of Investigations, no. 22. Springfield.

Irwin-Williams, C. 1968. "The Reconstruction of Archaic Culture History in the Southwestern United States." In *Archaic Prehistory in the Western United States,* ed. C. Irwin-Williams. Eastern New Mexico University Contributions in Anthropology. Portales.

Jennings, J. D. 1974. *Prehistory of North America.* 2nd ed. New York: McGraw-Hill.

Longacre, William A. 1975. "Population Dynamics at the Grasshopper Pueblo, Arizona." In *Population Studies in Archaeology and Biological Anthropology: A Symposium,* ed. A. C. Swedlund. *American Antiquity.* 40(2): 71–74. Memoir 30.

O'Brien, P. J. 1972. "Urbanism, Cahokia and Middle Mississippian." *Archaeology.* 25: 188–97.

Pfeiffer, John E. 1977. *The Emergence of Society.* New York: McGraw-Hill.

Porter, J. W. 1969. "The Mitchell Site and Prehistoric Exchange Systems at Cahokia: A.D. 1000± 300." *Illinois Archaeological Survey.* Bulletin 7.

Prufer, Olaf H. 1964. "The Hopewell Cult." *Scientific American.* December. 211: 90–102.

———. 1965. "The McGraw Site: A Study in Hopewellian Dynamics." Cleveland Museum of Natural History Scientific Publications. N.S., 4(1).

Rice, G. E. 1975. "A Systematic Explanation of a Change in Mogollon Settlement Patterns." Unpublished doctoral dissertation, University of Washington.

Ritchie, W. A. 1969. *The Archaeology of New York State.* 2nd ed. Garden City, N.Y.: Natural History Press.

Sayles, E. B. and E. Anteus. 1941. *The Cochise Culture.* Medallion Papers, no. 29. Gila Pueblo, Globe, Arizona.

Schoenwetter, J. 1962. "Pollen Analysis of Eighteen Archaeological Sites in Arizona and New Mexico." In *Prehistory of Eastern Arizona,* eds. P. S. Martin et al. *Fieldiana: Anthropology.* 53: 168–209.

Smith, Bruce. 1974. "Middle Mississippi Exploitation of Animal Populations: A Predictive Model." *American Antiquity.* 39(2): 274–91.

Stewart, T. D. 1973. *The People of America.* New York: Scribner's.

Struever, S. 1964. "The Hopewell Interaction Sphere in Riverine-Western Great

Lakes Culture History." In *Hopewellian Studies,* eds. J. R. Caldwell and R. L. Hall. Illinois State Museum Scientific Papers. 12: 85–106.

Struever, S. and Gail L. Houart. 1972. "Analysis of the Hopewell Interaction Sphere." In *Social Exchange and Interaction.* Museum of Anthropology, Anthropological Papers, no. 46, University of Michigan. Ann Arbor.

Struever, S. and K. D. Vickery. 1973. "The Beginnings of Cultivation in the Midwest-Riverine Area of the United States." *American Anthropologist.* 75: 1197–1220.

Tuck, J. A. 1971. "An Archaic Cemetery at Port au Choix, Newfoundland." *American Antiquity.* 36: 343–58.

Tainter, Joseph. 1975. "Social Inference and Mortuary Practices: An Experiment in Numerical Classification." *World Archaeology.* 7(1): 1–15.

Vogel, J. C. and N. J. Van Der Merwe. 1977. "Isotopic Evidence for Early Maize Cultivation in New York State." *American Antiquity.* 42(2): 238–42.

Washburn, D. K. 1975. "The American Southwest." In eds. S. Gorenstein et al. *North America.* New York: St. Martin's Press.

Willey, G. R. 1966. *An Introduction to American Archaeology. Volume 1: North and Middle American.* Englewood Cliffs, N.J.: Prentice-Hall.

Yarnell, R. A. 1965. "Early Woodland Plant Remains and the Question of Cultivation." *The Florida Archaeologist.* 18(2): 78–81.

Epilogue:
Prehistory in Perspective

What's past is prologue.

Shakespeare

In the preceding chapters we have reviewed at length the archaeological record of our first 3 million years, noting in the process many diverse attempts to explain in general and specific terms what happened in the past. We now come to the more difficult problem of attempting to gain some general perspective on this great mass of data and hypotheses, and of considering in broader terms the implications of our knowledge of prehistory.

At the most general level, our review of the archaeological record began with the problem of whether or not there was a general theory or model of culture and history that makes understandable the great complexity of the past. We wanted to see if the thousands of societies whose remains we have examined, from Olduvai Gorge to classical Greece, could be linked together and explained by reference to a body of cultural principles or laws. Is materialist determinism, free will, or some other concept the key to understanding the past?

These are, of course, the classic questions of the ages, and there is no pretense that they have been resolved here. Indeed, rather than demonstrating the power and accuracy of any specific models of culture and history, we have simply explored the limitations and potentials of some of the more obvious theoretical approaches, and we have encountered more explanations and hypotheses that do not "work" than those that do.

One of the earliest casualties revealed by our archaeological review is the nineteenth-century view of mechanical cultural evolutionism, with its belief in the gradual improvement of people and their societies through generation after generation as we "progressed" from rude, murderous savagery to the better, brighter world of industry, liberalism, and democracy. The Victorian proponents of evolutionism, who number among their ranks some of the most brilliant and creative scholars of history, have been maligned unmercifully for so long that it may seem unnecessary here to recite the well-known list of their sins. But even today many people, including anthropologists, tend to see the world and history in these same mechanical, evolutionist terms, with the strong implication that prehistory and history describe a "progressive" trajectory, leading to ourselves. Our review of the archaeological records reveals, however, that instead of a smooth rising curve of social, technological, and moral evolution, our past has been a series of fitful cycles, where social forms and technologies have reached their limits of growth and then failed, to be replaced by new social forms and technologies, more complex in some ways than their predecessors, but neither permanent nor "better" in any evident moral or philosophical sense. Clearly, there is nothing in the archaeological record to indicate that we are on a straight path to an earthly paradise. Today, two thirds of the world's population are "involuntary vegetarians" (M. Harris 1977: x) whose diet, morbidity and mortality rates, and general standard of living compare poorly with those of most Pleistocene hunting and gathering bands; and even in the most industrialized countries the vast majority labors longer for sustenance than did many of the people of prehistory. Moreover, the misery, poverty, wars, and assorted atrocities of the past several decades make the idea of mankind's moral evolution so laughable as to require no discussion.

But this lack of "progress" in the Victorian sense should not be taken as an indictment of the general cultural evolutionary model, for the archaeological record also demonstrates that, despite repeated reversals and long plateaus, the past 3 million years have witnessed a gradual increase in the complexity of cultures, as measured in terms of ability to divert energy to human use and in the size, differentiation, and interdependence of social, political, and economic systems. Moreover, cultural evolution has been patterned: domestication, agriculture, cultural complexity, and many specific cultural developments appeared independently but in very similar ways in various times and places.

Unfortunately, no general theory of culture has been able to provide a convincing framework within which these cultural parallels and transformations can be compellingly and precisely explained, and for this reason no general theory of culture has won universal acceptance. Most archaeologists employ an evolutionary perspective: they assume that cultural innovations are constantly arising in human societies, and that some of these innovations confer an adaptive advantage and are fixed within cultural systems and perpetuated until they too are outmoded and replaced. Most archaeologists also adopt a rather vague "vulgar" materialist determinism in the sense that they try to understand cultural forms and dynamics as expressions of technological, environmental, and economic variables. Thus, such things as the social egalitarianism of hunters and gatherers in the Pleistocene and the rigid social stratification of emerging states are generally understood as reactions to their respective economic bases. Nonetheless, even some of the most ardent materialists (e.g., M. Harris 1977) stress the importance of free will, religion, and ideology in "determining" the operations of societies, and no one argues that evolutionary cultural materialism is a complete, explanatory theory of culture.

Even among those archaeologists who retain the hope of making archaeology a formal, scientific, predictive discipline there is a growing trend away from the somewhat naive, almost "pseudo-scientism" of recent decades. Most scholars are no longer searching for mechanical cause and effect relationships in which specific changes in independent variables can be shown to result uniformly in predictable changes in dependent cultural variables, à la the classical view of the laws of thermodynamics. Instead, and in concert with contemporary perspectives in the natural sciences, archaeologists interested in explaining the past in general terms are more concerned with formulating statements of probability, such that, under specified conditions, estimates can be made about the likelihood that similar variables will give rise to similar consequences. And in this context there is growing question about the productivity and appropriateness of the so-called "positivist" model of science, in which one tries to establish absolute laws by deducing and testing hypotheses from the propositions subsumed under these general laws (e.g., L. Johnson 1972; Morgan 1973; Salmon 1975).

Our inability to explain major cultural transformations by constructing equations involving population growth, warfare, or some other limited set of factors has led some scholars to attempt to redefine the basic terms and objectives of analyzing the past. We have considered in this context several attempts to use general systems theory, noting that despite the elegant descriptions provided for some cultural changes through systems-theory analyses, fundamental questions remain about the ultimate utility of this approach as a way of explaining culture change. Some recent systems-theory analyses of archaeological data have involved game theory, mathematical modeling, and other complex procedures, and only many more years of additional research will reveal the extent to which we can explain the past from this perspective.

In addition to stimulating interest in general systems theory, the problems of explaining the development of human characteristics and institutions have resulted in renewed attempts to understand these matters from a biological perspective. The emerging discipline of sociobiology, for example, includes among its proponents those who argue that much of what we are or have been culturally is deeply embedded in the chemistry of our chromosomes, that war, greed, competition, egotism, innovation, and a long list of other human behaviors can be partially suppressed by the weight of cultural institutions, but that they persist in our physiology as potent behavioral determinates.

There is a certain attractiveness to this idea. It reduces some cultural problems to the biochemical and genetic level—a level of analysis that modern science has shown to be very productive, and it also seems to make clear why human societies have inevitably been associated with war, conflict, and social inequity: because 3 million years of evolution have shaped us that way. And thus, except for some recent Frankensteinian research with the mechanics of heredity, the sociobiological approach would seem to some extent to place fundamental changes in some human social patterns beyond the reach of human initiative.

The sociobiological perspective may well make highly significant contributions to the solution of anthropological problems (Alexander 1977), but it is unlikely that the causes and effects of the origins of culture, the evolution of agricultural economies, the rise of complex societies, or the other major problems of prehistory will be "resolved" by this approach. If there is a single major lesson of world prehistory, it would seem to be that cultures are marvelously adaptable, that, given compelling cultural reasons, people can use cultural forms to make cooperation or competition, murder or altruism, egalitarianism or privilege, or any other behaviors into vices or virtues, as the circumstances dictate.

Archaeologists are still searching for a general theory and model of culture, and they disagree sharply about how this goal might best be achieved. To a large extent, however, the great majority of archaeological fieldwork has been devoted not to the larger theoretical questions about *why* cultures change, but rather to the specific ways in which particular cultural forms have appeared and changed, and in these terms archaeology has made great progress. There is no need to review in detail the archaeological information we have considered in earlier chapters about early hominid taxonomy, Paleolithic technologies, the origins of domestication and agriculture, the rise of cultural complexity, and the many other prehistoric transformations that only a century ago were not even recognized, let alone understood. True, we have identified no "prime movers," factors whose effects are so potent that they can be used to explain much of the cultural developments of past and future societies, but we have identified many patterns and parallels. Cross-cutting cultural developments all over the world are the same essential expressions of religion, warfare, population growth, emerging social stratification, and evolving economic productivity.

It has proved rather difficult, however, to identify the main causal mechanisms in cultural evolution. We have seen, for example, that human population growth has been linked to almost every cultural transformation, from initial tool use to the appearance of industrial empires, and it is indeed true that the increasing rate of technological innovation and general cultural change is closely correlated with increasing worldwide population numbers. This relationship may even be said to be an explanatory one in the sense that the rate of technological change must be linked simply to the number of minds available to solve problems and produce innovations. But this is clearly an incomplete explanation of our past. The archaeological record time and time again discloses that the relationship between population growth and cultural change is neither consistent nor direct, and it remains for archaeologists to demonstrate the causal connections between the world's increasing population size and the specific, crucial transformations of prehistory and history.

All of the other "prime movers" have similar limitations. The recurrent nature of human interspecies violence, for example, from the casual cannibalism of early *Homo erectus* to World War II, clearly suggests that conflict is an evolutionary mechanism of considerable power; conflict must *do* something for societies, or it would be difficult to explain its depressing ubiquitousness in human affairs. But here too, the actual mechanisms whereby conflict interacted with other variables in most past societies to produce cultural change is unknown.

LESSONS OF PREHISTORY?

It would be gratifying if we could extract from our review of world prehistory some important predictions about the future of mankind, but archaeology is still very far from being a formal, predictive science, if indeed it will ever be one. This is especially true when we consider the long-range future, particularly now that mankind has instruments with which to terminate all human life on this planet. But even should we survive for millions of generations, the virtuosity of culture as an adaptive device makes extrapolations into the future an act of either ignorance or embarrassing temerity. What anthropologist, given the opportunity to stroll through Olduvai Gorge some Sunday morning 2 million years ago, could on the basis of that experience have predicted the gaudy technology and kaleidoscopic social and political forms of twentieth-century civilization?

Nonetheless, no student of world prehistory can overlook the persistent, powerful trends that tie the present, and perhaps the future, to the past. The evolution of technologies for energy capture, for example, seems to have been so basic to competitive success that we might expect that these technologies will continue to be important determinants of sociocultural and ideological forms. One obvious implication of this is that it might be naive to expect Egypt, Japan, Italy, and other energy-dependent countries to refrain from using nuclear energy because of the slight attendant risk of nuclear disaster. The matter of "evolutionary potential" would also seem to have some applicability to the future, even though the world is much different now from what it was during most of the last 9,000 years, when agricultural potential was the major ingredient in evolutionary success. Throughout prehistory the evolutionary advantage frequently shifted to "marginal" groups, less complexly organized cultures located on the peripheries of the richer established cultures. In the contemporary world, where fossil fuel and raw materials are of great import, the advantage may already have shifted from the West to Russia and China, and may soon also move to Near Eastern and African nations.

Any number of future developments could of course change these expectations dramatically. Should a simple, inexpensive technology for using solar energy be developed, there may well be a general leveling of wealth and power among nations, particularly if what are now the world's poorer countries curb their rates of population growth.

Another apparent lesson of prehistory has to do with the uses of religion. I shall let those with more confidence in their omniscience than myself pronounce on the ultimate nature of human religiosity; it is always sobering to recollect that neither the study of world prehistory nor any other art or science has much to offer in the way of a reason why we are out here, on a small planet in an incomprehensibly infinite universe, and to all evidence very much alone. Nonetheless, taken solely on the level of its effects on other aspects of culture, religion appears to operate principally as a highly adaptable, thermodynamically efficient mechanism of social control. We have seen in the archaeological and historical record an irrefutable demonstration that there is no act so repellent, be it sacrificing thousands of one's own countrymen or incinerating hundreds of thousands of one's "enemies," that it cannot be made not only acceptable, but entirely virtuous within the context of religious systems. The exploitation of the many by the few to build massive "worthless" pyramids and public buildings, the complete catalogue of sexual "perversions," the avoidance of certain kinds of food— all have been incorporated into state religions with no more difficulty than Christian faith, hope, or charity.

Nor should the apparent decline of formal theistic religions in the modern world be interpreted as a sign of religion's demise as an important cultural mechanism. One need only look at contemporary Communist countries, where avowedly secular, atheistic cultures have replaced traditional religions with ideologies no different in their essentials from Catholicism or Buddhism. For the future, there appears no reason to suspect that belief systems will be any less important, although clearly their contents will vary. The competitive advantage, as always, will lie with cultures that evolve belief systems that motivate people in specific, "efficient" directions, as is well illustrated in centuries past by the link between capitalism and Calvinism, and irrigation agriculture and the Sumerian pantheon.

The lessons of the archaeological record concerning the origins and significance of social and economic inequalities are not as clear as they might seem at first glance. There is the inescapable fact that there has never been an economically differentiated, complex society, even the supposedly "classless" Communistic societies, that was not also stratified into groups having differential access to wealth, power, and prestige. One need not be an orthodox Marxist or determinist to recognize that throughout prehistory and history the modes of production and the general ecological circumstances of cultures have played a major role in determining the stratification of societies into classes of varying wealth, power, and prestige; but it remains to be demonstrated that cultural complexity is inextricably linked to social stratification. It would appear that in the past the complexity of managing an economy based on agriculture and, later, agriculture in combination with fossil fuels, could work effectively only through administrative and social hierarchies and class-structured societies. But if in future centuries population densities are stabilized and perhaps reduced, if control of energy and food sources is decentralized and the production of material wealth made highly automated, it would seem at least possible that human societies will someday approximate the "social justice" of the late Pleistocene.

There are those who argue that social class and social competition, like warfare, are "hard-wired" into our physiology, but the archaeological record would seem to indicate that the distribution of power, prestige, and wealth can be modified by changes in the economic and technological basis of a given society.

Perhaps the archaeological record's bleakest implication concerning our future has to do with that ambiguous concept of "the quality of life." We have already noted that today most of the world's people have a diet and standard of living in many ways inferior to that of Pleistocene hunters and gatherers, and although medical technology, solar power, and contraceptives may change this by bringing the Western industrial standard of living to all parts of the world, this is by no means a certainty. Even given sufficient energy and rapid industrialization, fundamental questions remain about the short-term prospects for the quality of life on this planet. In the wealthiest countries today the abundance of luxury goods seems to convey a sense of ease and fulfillment, but modern economies work only because the vast majority of the population are coerced or are willing to spend most of their lives at hard labor, often with competitive pressures that produce unbalanced, unfulfilled lives. And it is not only the poorer, laboring class whose quality of life is questionable. It has been observed that a citizen of Athens in the fifth century B.C. would consider today's professionals—physicians, politicians, professors, and football players alike—to be in the main incomplete, undeveloped people, whose "success" has required them to devote so much of their lives to their specialty that they are grotesquely incompetent at the oratorical, conversational, athletic, philosophical, agricultural, and aesthetic skills that the Greeks would insist upon as necessary components of a "whole" person.

The past often takes on a rosy, romantic coloring from the perspective of the complexities and frustrations of the present, and we cannot ignore the illiteracy, warfare, and gross social exploitation that appear to be the very warp and woof of every ancient complex society, including ancient Athens; but one need not have brilliant insight to recognize that modern social and economic systems, whether they be capitalistic or socialistic, do not provide appropriate environments for the balanced, liberal, personal development of the majority. Even more chilling is the excellent possibility that "the quality of life," as measured in these terms, will continue to decline for at least the short-term future, as industrialization and multinational economies engulf the world. Gloomy predictions of this sort have a way of showing up in succeeding centuries as quaint quotations demonstrating the curious myopia of past generations, and I devoutly hope it will be so in this case. But despite the many advantages of modern technology, the long-term trend seems inexorably in the direction of greater specialization and compartmentalization of people, with consequent increasing alienation and frustration.

The Future of Archaeology

The archaeological record is disappearing at such a rapid rate that the future of *field* archaeology on the problems of prehistory is very much in doubt, as the worldwide wave of industrialism, the major destroyer of archaeological materials, seems destined to expand at ever-increasing speed.

Dismal as the loss of the archaeological record is, it may be that the major progress in archaeology in the next several generations will come not so much from the discovery of new bones and stones, but rather from a reconsideration of theoretical and methodological approaches and a reanalysis of existing data. We have recounted in this book the prospects of systems theory, simulation modeling, hypothesis testing, and other current analytical approaches, and these and more traditional perspectives are likely to increase considerably our knowledge about many specific problems, such as the origins of agriculture, the taxonomy of early humans, and the causes of urbanism. Does this mean that the general problem of the origins of cultural complexity will some day be as precisely solved as the formulae for making plastics? Probably not. These are very different kinds of questions with different criteria for solution. Yet, the history of science is replete with examples in which a seemingly impossible problem was not only solved but made routine; the general problems of prehistory we have discussed here may well fall into this category, to be solved in succeeding centuries in terms and with techniques which we now only dimly perceive. After all, people of only a few centuries ago no doubt would be astounded not only by our science and lush technology, but also by our knowledge of prehistory and the dynamics of culture.

Bibliography

Alexander, R. D. 1977. "Review of *The Use and Abuse of Biology: An Anthropological Critique of Sociobiology* by M. D. Sahlins." *American Anthropologist.* 79(4): 917–20.

Harris, M. 1977. *Cannibals and Kings.* New York: Random House.

Johnson, L. 1972. "Problems in 'Avant-Garde' Archaeology." *American Anthropologist.* 74: 366–77.

Kitto, H. D. F. 1951. *The Greeks.* Baltimore: Penguin.

Morgan, C. G. 1973. "Archaeology and Explanation." *World Archaeology.* 4: 259–76.

Salmon, M. H. 1975. "Confirmation and Explanation in Archaeology." *American Antiquity.* 4: 459–64.

Credits

Chapter 1

Chapter opener, French Cultural Service, New York.

1.1 Engraving by Theodor de Bry from *Americae*, 1592. Rare Book Division, The New York Public Library.

1.2 American Museum of Natural History.

1.3 The Bancroft Library, Univ. of California.

1.4 Hirmer Fotoarchiv, Munich.

1.5 George Eastman House, Rochester.

1.6 American Museum of Natural History.

1.8 Sir William Hamilton, *Campi Phlgraei* (1765), Illus. by Peter Fabris from Vol. 1, American Museum of Natural History; photo courtesy of Kay Zakariasen and David Hanson.

1.9 Danish National Museum, Copenhagen.

1.10 Radio Times Hulton Picture Library.

1.11 American Museum of Natural History.

1.12 From J. Steward, "Cultural Causality and Law: A Trial Formulation of the Development of Early Civilizations." *American Anthropologist*, 51:9, 1949, Chart II. Reproduced by permission of the Amer. Anthropological Assc.

Chapter 2

Chapter opener, Danish National Museum.

2.1 Frank Hole.

2.2 Danish National Museum.

2.3 The Oriental Institute, Univ. of Chicago.

2.4 From M. J. Aitken, "Magnetic Prospecting," in R. Berger, ed., *Scientific Methods in Medieval Archaeology* (Univ. of California Press, 1970), Fig. 2. Reproduced by permission of the Univ. of California Press.

2.5 Popperfoto, London.

2.6 From F. Hole, K. V. Flannery, and J. Neely, *Prehistory and Human Ecology of the Deh Luran Plain*, Mem. of the Museum of Anthropology, No. 1 (Univ. of Michigan, 1969), Fig. 15. Reproduced by permission of Museum of Anthropology–Publications.

2.7 From W. J. Judge, J. I. Ebert, and R. K. Hitchcock, "Sampling in Regional Archaeological Survey," in J. W. Mueller, ed., *Sampling in Archaeology* (Univ. of Arizona Press, copyright 1975), Fig. 6.4. Reproduced by permission of the Univ. of Arizona Press.

2.8 From J. D. Jennings, *Prehistory of North America* (McGraw-Hill, 1974), Fig. 1.4. © 1968, 1974 by McGraw-Hill, Inc., all rights reserved. Reproduced by permission of McGraw-Hill Book Co.

2.9 After M. S. Tite, *Methods of Physical Examination in Archaeology* (Seminar Press, 1972), Fig. 30. Copyright © by Academic Press, Inc. Reproduced by permission of Academic Press, Inc.

2.10 From J. W. Michaels, *Dating Methods in Archaeology* (Seminar Press, 1973), Fig. 1. © Academic Press, Inc. Reproduced by permission of J. W. Michaels and Academic Press, Inc.

2.11 From J. Deetz, *Invitation to Archaeology* (Doubleday, 1967), Fig. 4. © 1967 by James Deetz. Reproduced by permission of Doubleday & Co., Inc.

Chapter 3

Chapter opener, Geodetic Institute, Copenhagen.

3.1 After K. W. Butzer, 1971.

3.2 Bradford Washburn.

3.3 From F. P. Shepard, "Sea Level Changes in the Past 6000 Years: Possible Archaeological Significance," *Science*, v. 143, pp. 574–76, Figs. 1, 2, 7 February 1964. Copyright © 1964 by the Amer. Assc. for the Advancement of Science. Reproduced by permission of the AAAS and F. P. Shepard.

3.4 From *The National Atlas of the U.S.A.*, U.S. Geological Survey, 1970.

3.5 After Flint (1971) and Fagan (1977).

Chapter 4

Chapter opener, Geza Teleki.

4.1 American Museum of Natural History.

4.2 From G. Findlay, *Dr. Robert Broom, Paleontologist and Physician, 1866–1951* (A. A. Balkema, Cape Town). Reproduced by permission of A. A. Balkema.

4.3 After Jerison, 1976.

4.4 San Diego Zoological Society.

4.5 After Simons, 1977.

4.6 From J. B. Birdsell, *Human Evolution: An Introduction to the New Physical Anthropology*, 2nd ed. (Rand McNally, 1975), Fig. 6.7. Reproduced by permission of J. B. Birdsell.

4.7 From B. Fagan, *People of the Earth*, 3rd ed. (Little, Brown, 1980), Fig. 4.1. © 1980 by Brian M. Fagan. © 1977, 1974 by Little, Brown & Co., Inc. Reprinted by permission of Little, Brown & Co.

4.8 After Howells, 1973.

4.9 R. F. Sison, © National Geographic Society.

4.10A From M. D. Leakey, *Olduvai Gorge Vol. 3* (Cambridge Univ. Press, 1971), Fig. 8. Reproduced by permission of Cambridge Univ. Press.

4.10B From B. Fagan, *People of the Earth*, 2nd ed. (Little, Brown, 1977), drawing p. 60. Reproduced by permission of Little, Brown & Co., Inc.

4.11 From *The Annual Review of Anthropology*, Vol. 1, © 1972 by Annual Reviews, Inc. Reproduced by permission of B. G. Campbell and *The Annual Review of Anthropology*.

4.12 From W. Howells, *Evolution of Genus Homo* (Benjamin/Cummings Pub. Co., copyright © 1973), p. 47. Reproduced by permission of Benjamin/Cummings Pub. Co.

4.13 Irven DeVore, Anthro Photo.

4.14 From J. E. Pfeiffer, *The Emergence of Man*, rev. & enl. 1972 (Harper & Row), Illus. p. 100. Reproduced by permission of Harper & Row, Publishers, Inc.

4.15 Geza Teleki.

4.16 From M. D. Leakey, *Olduvai Gorge Vol. 3* (Cambridge Univ. Press, 1971), Fig. 47. Reproduced by permission of Cambridge Univ. Press.

4.17 From J. D. Speth and D. D. Davis, "Seasonal Variability in Early Hominid Predation," *Science*, vol. 192, pp. 441–45, Fig. 1, 30 April 1976. Copyright © 1976 by the Amer. Assc. for the Advancement

of Science. Reproduced by permission of the AAAS.

4.18, 19, 20 From B. G. Campbell, *Humankind Emerging*, 2nd ed. Figs. 10.19, 14.12, 11.8. Copyright © 1979 by B. G. Campbell. Reproduced by permission of Little, Brown & Co.

4.21 Henry de Lumley, Centre national de la recherche scientifique, Marseille.

4.22 American Museum of Natural History.

4.23 Bob Campbell © National Geographic Society, Inc.

Chapter 5

Chapter opener, Henry de Lumley, Centre national de la recherche scientifique, Marseille.

5.1 From B. G. Campbell, *Humankind Emerging*, 2nd ed. (Little, Brown, 1979), Fig. 15.2. Copyright © 1979 by B. G. Campbell. Reproduced by permission of B. G. Campbell and Little, Brown & Co.

5.2 From W. Howells, *Mankind in the Making* (Doubleday & Co.), drawings by J. Cirulis. Copyright © 1959, 1967, by William Howells. Reproduced by permission of Doubleday & Co., Inc.

5.3 Henry de Lumley, Centre national de la recherche scientifique, Marseille.

5.4 From F. Bordes, *The Old Stone Age* (Weidenfeld & Nicolson, 1968), Fig. 16. Reproduced by permission of Weidenfeld & Nicolson.

5.5 After B. G. Campbell, 1976.

5.6 Zdenek Burian.

5.7 From F. Bordes, *The Old Stone Age* (Weidenfeld & Nicolson, 1968). Reproduced by permission of Weidenfeld & Nicolson.

5.8 From J. Bordaz, *Tools of the Old and New Stone Age* (Doubleday, 1970). Copyright © 1970 by J. Bordaz. Copyright © 1958, 1969 by the Amer. Museum of Natural History. Reprinted by permission of Doubleday & Co., Inc.

5.9 From F. Bordes, *The Old Stone Age* (Weidenfeld & Nicolson, 1968), Figs. 55, 66. Reproduced by permission of Weidenfeld & Nicolson.

5.11 After Binford, 1968.

5.12 British Museum.

5.13 From W. A. Fairservis, *The Threshold of Civilization*, drawings by Jan Fairservis (Chas. Scribner's Sons, 1975), pp. 82–83. Reproduced by permission of Jan Fairservis.

5.14 French Cultural Service, New York.

5.15 From A. Leroi-Gourhan, "The Evolution of Paleolithic Cave Art," *Scientific American*, Feb. 1968, p. 66. Copyright © 1968 by Scientific American, Inc. All rights reserved.

5.16 Austrian Institute, New York.

5.18 From H. M. Wobst, "Boundary Conditions for Paleolithic Social Systems: A Simulation Approach," *American Antiquity,* 39:159, 1974. Reproduced by permission of the Society for Amer. Archaeology.

Chapter 6

Chapter opener, American Museum of Natural History.
6.1 Philadelphia Museum of Art.
6.2 After Jennings, 1974.
6.3 From C. Dunbar and K. Waage, *Historical Geology,* 3rd ed. (Wiley, 1969). Reproduced by permission of John Wiley & Sons, Inc.
6.4 After Haynes, 1974.
6.5 From R. F. Flint, *Glacial and Quaternary Geology* (Wiley, 1971), Fig. 29.7 (modified from Martin and Guilday in P. S. Martin and H. E. Wright, Jr., eds., *Pleistocene Extinctions: The Search for a Cause* (Yale Univ. Press, 1967, p. 1). Reproduced by permission of John Wiley & Sons, Inc., and Yale Univ. Press.
6.6 From R. S. MacNeish, "Early Man in the Andes," *Scientific American,* April 1971, pp. 40–41. Copyright © 1971 by Scientific American, Inc. All rights reserved.
6.7 From J. J. Hester, *Introduction to Archaeology* (Holt, Rinehart and Winston, 1976). Compiled from A. Krieger, "Early Man in the New World," in J. D. Jennings and E. Norbeck, eds., *Prehistoric Man in the New World* (University of Chicago Press, 1964). Reproduced by permission of the Univ. of Chicago Press.
6.9 After Jennings, 1974.
6.10 Joe Ben Wheat, Univ. of Colorado Museum.
6.11 From M. Lively, "The Lively Complex: Announcing a Pebble Tool Industry in Alabama," *Jour. of Alabama Archaeology,* v. XI, 2, Dec. 1965, Fig. 1. Reproduced by permission of The Alabama Archaeological Society.
6.12 From Don W. Dragoo, "Some Aspects of Eastern North American Prehistory," *American Antiquity,* 41:6, 1976, Fig. 1. Reproduced by permission of the Society for Amer. Archaeology.
6.13 From W. T. Sanders and J. Marino, *New World Prehistory,* © 1970, p. 115. Reproduced by permission of Prentice-Hall, Inc., Englewood Cliffs, N.J.
6.14 From J. D. Jennings, *Prehistory of North America* (McGraw-Hill, 1974), Figs. 4.19, 20, 21. Reproduced by permission of McGraw-Hill Book Co. and J. D. Jennings.

Chapter 7

Chapter opener, State Antiquities Organization, Baghdad.

7.1 From K. P. Oakley, *Man the Tool-Maker* (Univ. of Chicago Press, © 1949, 1961 by the Trustees of the British Museum. All rights reserved), Fig. 39. Reproduced by permission of the Univ. of Chicago Press and the Trustees of the British Museum (Natural History).
7.5 From F. Hole et al., *Prehistory and Human Ecology of the Deh Luran Plain,* Mem. of the Mus. of Anthropology, No. 1 (Univ. of Michigan, 1969), Fig. 115. Reproduced by permission of Mus. of Anthropology Publications.
7.6A From J. Mellaart, *The Neolithic of the Near East* (Charles Scribner's Sons, 1975), Fig. 4. © 1975 Thames and Hudson Ltd., London. Reproduced by permission of Charles Scribner's Sons and Thames and Hudson Ltd.
7.6B From K. V. Flannery, "The Origins of the Village as a Settlement Type in Mesoamerica and the Near East . . ." in Ucko et al., eds., *Man, Settlement and Urbanism* (Duckworth, 1972), Fig. 5. Reproduced by permission of Duckworth & Co. Ltd.
7.7 British School of Archaeology in Jerusalem.
7.8 State Antiquities Organization, Baghdad.
7.9 From G. Clark and S. Piggott, *Prehistoric Societies* (Knopf, 1965). Reproduced by permission of Alfred A. Knopf, Inc.
7.10 After Fagan, 1977.
7.11 From R. S. MacNeish, "The Origins of New World Civilization," *Scientific American,* Nov. 1964, p. 35. Copyright © 1964 by Scientific American, Inc. All rights reserved.
7.12 R. S. Peabody Foundation for Archaeology.
7.13 From W. Bray, "From Predation to Production: The Nature of Agricultural Evolution in Mexico and Peru," in G. Sieveking, I. H. Longworth, and R. E. Wilson, eds., *Problems in Economic and Social Archaeology* (Duckworth, 1977). Reproduced by permission of Duckworth & Co. Ltd.
7.14 R. S. Peabody Foundation for Archaeology.
7.15 Field Museum of Natural History, Chicago.

Chapter 8

Chapter opener, Hirmer Fotoarchiv, Munich.
8.1 After Wright, 1977.

Chapter 9

Chapter opener, British School of Archaeology in Jerusalem.
9.3 Robert Wenke.

9.4 Frank Hole.

9.5 British School of Archaeology in Jerusalem.

9.6 From J. Mellaart, *The Neolithic of the Near East* (Charles Scribner's Sons, 1975), Fig. 46. © 1975 Thames and Hudson Ltd., London. Reproduced by permission of Charles Scribner's Sons and Thames and Hudson Ltd.

9.7 From J. Mellaart, *Çatal Hüyük* (McGraw-Hill, 1967), pp. 118, 120, 125. © 1967 Thames and Hudson Ltd. Reproduced by permission of J. Mellaart.

9.9, 9.10 From J. Mellaart, *The Neolithic of the Near East* (Charles Scribner's Sons, 1975), Figs. 97, 91, 93, 94. © 1975 Thames and Hudson Ltd., London. Reproduced by permission of Charles Scribner's Sons and Thames and Hudson Ltd.

9.11 Hirmer Fotoarchiv, Munich.

9.12 From J. Mellaart, *The Neolithic of the Near East* (Charles Scribner's Sons, 1975), Fig. 86. © Thames and Hudson Ltd. Reproduced by permission of Charles Scribner's Sons and Thames and Hudson Ltd.

9.14 From G. A. Johnson, "Locational Analysis and the Investigation of Uruk Local Exchange Systems," in G. A. Sabloff, ed., *Ancient Civilization and Trade* (Univ. of New Mexico Press, 1975), Fig. 31. Reproduced by permission of the School of American Research, Santa Fe.

9.15 From R. M. Adams, *Land Behind Baghdad* (Univ. of Chicago Press, 1965), Fig. 11. © 1965 by the Univ. of Chicago Press. All rights reserved. Reproduced by permission of the Univ. of Chicago Press.

9.16 British Museum.

9.17 After Kramer, 1957.

9.18 State Antiquities Organization, Baghdad.

9.19 From S. N. Kramer, "The Sumerians," *Scientific American*, Oct. 1957, p. 76. Copyright © 1957 by Scientific American, Inc. All rights reserved.

9.20 (top) Hirmer Fotoarchiv, Munich. (bottom) British Museum.

9.21 British Museum.

9.22 (top) Hirmer Fotoarchiv, Munich. (bottom) University Museum, Philadelphia.

9.23 The Oriental Institute, Univ. of Chicago.

9.25 (top) Hirmer Fotoarchiv, Munich. (bottom) British Museum.

9.26 From H. T. Wright and G. A. Johnson, "Population, Exchange, and Early State Formation in Southwestern Iran," *American Anthropologist*, 77:270, 1975. Reproduced by permission of the Amer. Anthropological Assc.

Chapter 10

Chapter opener, Hirmer Fotoarchiv, Munich.

10.4 From R. Higgins, *Minoan and Mycenean Art* (Oxford University Press, New York),

© 1967 Thames and Hudson Ltd. Reproduced by permission of Thames and Hudson Ltd.

10.5, 10.6 Hirmer Fotoarchiv, Munich.

10.7 British Museum.

10.8 After Evans.

10.9 From Sir Arthur Evans, *Place of Minos at Knossos*, Vol. III, 1921. Reproduced by permission of William & James, London.

10.10 From C. Renfrew, *The Emergence of Civilization* (Methuen, 1972), Fig. 14.2. Reproduced by permission of Methuen & Co. Ltd.

10.12 Aerofilms.

10.14 Peter A. Clayton.

10.15 From M. I. Artamonov, "Frozen Tombs of the Scythians," *Scientific American*, May 1965. Copyright © Scientific American, Inc. All rights reserved.

Chapter 11

Chapter opener, The Metropolitan Museum of Art, New York, The Rogers Fund.

11.3 Seattle Art Museum.

11.4 Hirmer Fotoarchiv, Munich.

11.5 TWA.

11.6 The Metropolitan Museum of Art, New York.

11.7 From A. Wolinski and C. M. Sheikholeslami, *The Culture of Ancient Egypt* (Univ. of Washington Continuing Education, 1978), Study Guide, p. 18.

11.8 The Metropolitan Museum of Art, New York, The Rogers Fund.

11.9 From Karl Butzer, *Early Hydraulic Civilization in Egypt* (Univ. of Chicago Press, 1976), Fig. 3. Reproduced by permission of the Univ. of Chicago Press and Karl Butzer.

11.10 From G. and B. Isaac, "Africa," in R. Stigler, ed., *Varieties of Cultures in the Old World* (St. Martin's Press, 1975), Map 1.1. Reproduced by permission.

11.11 Rhodesia National Tourist Board.

11.12 After Shinnie, 1965.

11.13 From M. Shinnie, *Ancient African Kingdoms* (St. Martin's Press, 1965), p. 84. Reproduced by permission of St. Martin's Press, Inc.

Chapter 12

Chapter opener, National Museum, New Delhi.

12.2 After Dales, 1966.

12.3 From Sir M. Wheeler, *Civilization of the Indus Valley and Beyond* (Thames and Hudson, 1966), Fig. 14.16. Reproduced by permission of Thames and Hudson Ltd.

12.4 University Museum, Philadelphia.

12.5 From Sir M. Wheeler, *Civilization of the Indus Valley and Beyond* (Thames and

Hudson, 1966), Fig. 14.8. Reproduced by permission of Thames and Hudson Ltd.
12.6 Josephine Powell.
12.7 Jan Fairservis.
12.8 National Museum, New Delhi.
12.9 University Museum, Philadelphia.

Chapter 13

Chapter opener, Freer Gallery of Art, Washington, D.C.
13.2 After Clark, 1977.
13.3 From W. Watson, *Ancient China* (New York Graphic Society, 1974), Fig. 12.
13.4 From P. Wheatley, *The Pivot of the Four Quarters* (Aldine, 1971), Fig. 1. Reproduced by permission of P. Wheatley.
13.5 Judith M. Triestman, courtesy Doubleday & Co.
13.6 From A. Toynbee, ed., *Half the World* (Thames and Hudson, 1973). Reproduced by permission of Thames and Hudson Ltd.
13.7 Freer Gallery of Art, Washington, D.C.
13.9 From P. Wheatley, "Archaeology and the Chinese City," in *World Archaeology* (Routledge & Kegan Paul Ltd), vol. 2, Oct. 1970, Fig. 16. Reproduced by permission of P. Wheatley.
13.10 Institute of Archaeology, Academia Sinica, Peking.

Chapter 14

Chapter opener, Jeffrey House.
14.3 American Museum of Natural History.
14.4 From K. V. Flannery and M. Winter, "Analyzing Household Activities," in K. V. Flannery, ed., *The Early Mesoamerican Village* (Academic Press, 1976), Fig. 2.17. Reproduced by permission of Academic Press, Inc.
14.6 From T. K. Earle, "A Nearest Neighbor Analysis of Two Formative Settlement Systems," in K. V. Flannery, ed., *The Early Mesoamerican Village* (Academic Press, 1976), Fig. 7.9. Reproduced by permission of T. K. Earle and Academic Press, Inc.
14.7 From M. D. Coe, *Mexico* (Thames and Hudson), Fig. 17. Reproduced by permission of M. D. Coe.
14.8 Library of Congress.
14.9 From J. W. Pires-Ferreira, "Obsidian Exchange in Formative Mesoamerica," in K. V. Flannery, ed., *The Early Mesoamerican Village* (Academic Press, 1976), Fig. 10.8. Reproduced by permission of Academic Press, Inc.
14.10 The Metropolitan Museum of Art, New York, Michael C. Rockefeller Mem. Coll. of Primitive Art.

14.11 After Coe, 1962.
14.12 Both photos, Jeffrey House.
14.13 Robert Drennan.
14.14 Mexican National Tourist Council.
14.17 Jeffrey House.
14.18 Peabody Museum, Harvard University.
14.19 From K. V. Flannery, ed., *The Early Mesoamerican Village* (Academic Press, 1976), Fig. 6.5. Reproduced by permission of Academic Press, Inc.
14.20, 14.21 From M. D. Coe, *The Maya* (Praeger, 1966), Figs. 48 and 8. Reproduced by permission of M. D. Coe.
14.22 American Institute of Archaeology.
14.23 From J. R. Parsons, "The Development of a Prehistoric Complex Society: A Regional Perspective from the Valley of Mexico," *Jour. of Field Archaeology*, 1, 1974. Reproduced by permission of Jour. of Field Archaeology, © Trustees of Boston University.
14.25 From M. D. Coe, "The Chinampas of Mexico," *Scientific American*, July 1964, p. 94. Copyright © Scientific American, Inc. All rights reserved.
14.26, 14.27 American Museum of Natural History.

Chapter 15

Chapter opener, Jeffrey House.
15.2 (top), © Ellan Young (bottom), Jeffrey House.
15.3 From L. G. Lumbreras, *The Peoples and Cultures of Ancient Peru* (Smithsonian Institution Press, © 1974), Fig. 40. Reproduced by permission of the Smithsonian Institution Press.
15.4 Michael E. Mosely.
15.5 From L. G. Lumbreras, *The Peoples and Cultures of Ancient Peru* (Smithsonian Institution Press, © 1974), Fig. 54. Reproduced by permission of the Smithsonian Institution Press.
15.6, 15.7 Ferdinand Anton.
15.8 Copyright Marilyn Bridges.
15.9 Linden-Museum, Stuttgart.
15.10 From L. G. Lumbreras, *The Peoples and Cultures of Ancient Peru* (Smithsonian Institution Press, © 1974), Fig. 162. Reproduced by permission of the Smithsonian Institution Press.
15.11 David Brill © National Geographic Society.
15.12 Museo Rafael Larco Herrera, Lima.
15.13 From L. G. Lumbreras, *The Peoples and Cultures of Ancient Peru* (Smithsonian Institution Press, © 1974), Fig. 218. Reproduced by permission of the Smithsonian Institution Press.
15.14 Jeffrey House.
15.15 National Museum of Natural History, Smithsonian Institution.
15.16 Jeffrey House.

Chapter 16

Chapter opener, Rare Book Division, New York Public Library.

16.1 George Quimby.

16.2 From G. R. Willey, *An Introduction to American Archaeology*, v. 1 © 1966, p. 6. Reproduced by permission of Prentice-Hall, Inc., Englewood Cliffs, N.J.

16.3 J. Bird, American Museum of Natural History.

16.4 From R. I. Ford, "Northeastern Archaeology: Past and Future Directions," *Annual Review of Anthropology*, 3, 1974. © 1974 by Annual Reviews, Inc. Reproduced by permission of Annual Reviews, Inc., and R. I. Ford.

16.5 From J. D. Jennings, *Prehistory of North America*, 2nd ed. (McGraw-Hill, 1974), Fig. 6.2. Reproduced by permission of McGraw-Hill Book Co.

16.6 George Quimby.

16.7 Ohio Historical Society.

16.8, 9, and 10 George Quimby.

16.11 Rare Book Division, New York Public Library.

16.12 George Quimby.

16.13 From J. D. Jennings, *Prehistory of North America*, 2nd ed. (McGraw-Hill, 1974). Reproduced by permission of McGraw-Hill Book Co.

16.14 National Park Service.

Epilogue opener, Greek National Tourist Office, N.Y.

Index